ANIMALS
ANIMALS

SNAKES

BY MARIA MUDD RUTH

BENCHMARK BOOKS

MARSHALL CAVENDISH
NEW YORK

Series Consultant:
James Doherty
General Curator
The Bronx Zoo, New York

With thanks to
Christina Castellano of
The Department of Herpetology
at the Wildlife Conservation Society, New York
for her expert reading of the manuscript.

Benchmark Books
Marshall Cavendish Corporation
99 White Plains Road
Tarrytown, NY 10591–9001
Website: www.marshallcavendish.com

Library of Congress Cataloging-in-Publication Data
Ruth, Maria Mudd
Snakes / by Maria Mudd Ruth.
p. cm. – (Animals, animals)
Includes bibliographical references (p.48) and index
ISBN 0-7614-1262-x
1. Snakes–Juvenile literature. [1. Snakes.] I. Title. II. Series.
QL666.O6 M837 2001   597.96–dc   00-052322

Cover Photo: Visuals Unlimited: Tom J. Ulrich

The photographs in this book are used by permission and through the courtesy of: *Animals Animals:* Michael Fogden, 13, 43; Paul Freed, 34; Breck P. Kent, 29; Joe McDonald, 11, 17, 41; John Nees, 4; James H. Robinson, 22; Zig Leszczynski: 15, 24, 28. *Corbis:* Hulton-Deutsch, 7; Jeffrey L. Rotman, 38. *Visuals Unlimited, Inc.:* Dale R. Jackson, 27; Joe McDonald, 31, 37; MaryAnn McDonald, 20; G and C Merker, 19; Tom Ulrich, 33.

Printed in Hong Kong

1 3 5 6 4 2

CONTENTS

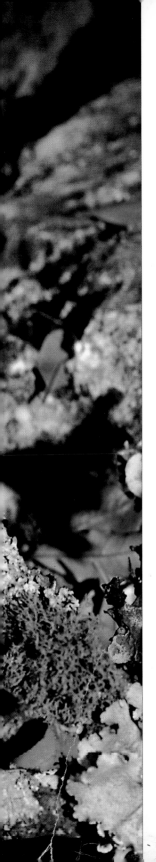

1

INTRODUCING SNAKES

Imagine you are at the zoo or in a pet store surrounded by glass cases containing dozens of snakes. What is your reaction? Maybe you are disgusted by the slithery creatures. Is it because they look "slimy?" Or, is it because they have no arms or legs, but can still move somehow? Is it because some of them are huge and might be poisonous? Or, do they seem sneaky and evil?

Maybe you are fascinated by snakes. You might wonder how they can be so flexible, why they flick their tongues

THIS BEAUTIFUL SNAKE IS A MEMBER OF THE PIT VIPER FAMILY. LIKE MOST SNAKES, ITS BODY IS SLENDER, VERY FLEXIBLE, AND COVERED IN OVERLAPPING SCALES THAT OFTEN CREATE DISTINCTIVE PATTERNS.

in and out, and how their scales can create such beautiful patterns.

Maybe you admire the power and strength of these animals—how they climb straight up trees using their trunk muscles and scales; how some snakes can overpower an animal much larger than themselves; or how dangerous their small fangs can be.

Or, perhaps the snakes make you a little nervous . . . even though you know the animals can't possibly escape their glass cases.

Chances are, you'll have more than one of these reactions. Maybe all of them. And you're not alone. Most people have mixed feelings about snakes. Throughout history and around the world, people have viewed snakes as powerful, scary, beautiful, fascinating, and dangerous. Ancient Greeks, for instance, associated snakes with healing power. Mesopotamians believed snakes were immortal because these creatures were "reborn" each time they shed their skins. The bible portrays the snake as a force of evil in the Garden of Eden. Many Native American cultures worshipped snakes for their power to protect against evil, bring rain, and ensure crop fertility. In Africa and Asia, snake

SNAKE CHARMING IS A TRADITIONAL KIND OF ENTERTAINMENT IN
MANY PARTS OF ASIA AND AFRICA. THIS WOMAN IS WORKING SLOWLY
AND CAREFULLY WITH A COBRA—A SNAKE THAT IS SHY AND NOT
AGGRESSIVE BUT WILL RAISE ITS BODY UP TO DEFEND ITSELF.

7

dances and snake-kissing rituals are performed to ensure bountiful crops. Snakes appear in many of today's jungle adventure movies and are seen as fearsome serpents that hunt and eat people (which they do not). Snakes have long been a part of our myths, folk tales, children's stories, paintings, sculptures, movies, dance, and music. But how much do we really know about snakes?

There are more than 2,300 different *species*, or kinds, of snakes. Snakes live on every continent of the globe except Antarctica. Snakes live in many different *habitats*, or places that have all the things they need to live and grow. Snakes live in deserts, rain forests, woodlands, mountains, oceans, along streams and lakes, in fields, and backyards. On land, snakes make their homes on the ground, in *burrows*, and in trees.

Snakes are often absent from islands, such as Iceland, Ireland, and New Zealand, which were formed before snakes had become established there.

Even though snakes live almost everywhere, they are not easy to find. This is because snakes stay hidden most of the time—beneath rocks, under logs, and among leaves. They hide to protect themselves from *predators*, or other animals that hunt them. Many snakes are *nocturnal*, that is, active at night, and are hard to see. *Diurnal* snakes, those that are active during the day, are also hard to find as their skin color and pattern *camouflages* them. This adds to the mystery of snakes and makes them difficult to observe and study in the wild. *Herpetologists*, or scientists who study snakes and other reptiles, have detailed information on only a few species of snakes. Their knowledge helps us learn about how snakes move, hunt, eat, hide, and grow. And it helps us understand just how fascinating snakes really are.

2
SNAKES OF THE WORLD

Snakes have been on the earth for more than 130 million years. Snakes are members of a class of animals called *reptiles*, which includes turtles, crocodiles, and lizards. Snakes are most closely related to lizards, but are different from lizards in three important ways. Unlike lizards, snakes do not have arms or legs: they use their muscles and scales to move across the ground or through the water; to hold onto their prey, they use their teeth or fangs. Snakes do not have ear openings on the outside of their bodies; they have no eardrums but can sense vibrations through the ground, as well as sounds in the air. And, no matter how long you stare at a snake, it will never blink. Snakes do not have eyelids. Clear scales cover their eyes and allow them to stay open all the time.

SNAKES' BODIES, HEADS, AND EVEN EYES ARE COVERED WITH OVER-LAPPING SCALES. THE SIZE, NUMBER, AND PATTERN OF THE SCALES IS DIFFERENT FOR EACH SPECIES.

Snakes have long, very flexible bodies. The spine of a large snake may have as many as 400 small bones or vertebrae. (The human back has just 32 or 33 vertebrae). These vertebrae allow snakes to curl, twist, and coil. Each vertebra forward of the tail is attached to a pair of ribs. As a snake swallows a large meal, its ribs spread open so the stomach can expand.

Snakes have unusual skin that stretches when they eat. People often think that snake skin is wet or slimy.

A snake's skeleton is made up of three main parts: the skull, vertebrae and ribs. The number of vertebrae in a snake's backbone ranges from about 150 to over 430, depending on the species.

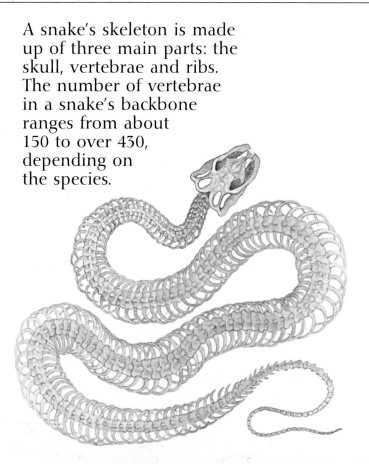

A snake's jaws are able to open wide enough to swallow prey larger than its own head.

In fact, it is covered with small, hard, dry scales that act like armor to help protect the snake from injury. The scales on the top or back of the snake may be smooth or have ridges. These scales range in color from beige and brown to brilliant yellows, reds, and greens. They are often arranged in beautiful patterns that help to identify the snake's species. The wide scales on its belly, called scutes, help the snake move along the ground with ease.

A SNAKE'S SCALES ARE NOT ALWAYS FLAT. THE EYELASH VIPER OF CENTRAL AMERICA HAS AN UNUSUAL CLUSTER OF SPINY SCALES OVER EACH EYE THAT RESEMBLE LASHES.

SNAKE LOCOMOTION

Snakes have four main ways of moving. Depending on the kind of snake and where it is trying to go, the snake will use one method or a combination. Snakes use their scales and muscles to glide smoothly over the ground, up a tree, or through the water.

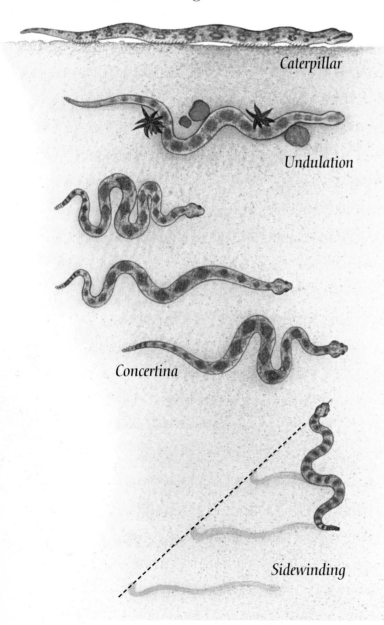

Caterpillar

Undulation

Concertina

Sidewinding

Caterpillar *(also called rectilinear)*: Snakes often use this method to climb trees. The snake keeps its body straight and uses its muscles to pull its belly scales forward. It then pushes the scales down and backward against the surface, moving forward like a caterpillar

Undulation: the snake's body forms a series of flowing S shapes along the ground.

Concertina: The snake moves the front part of its body forward and folds it slightly in a zigzag shape. Then the snake pulls its back end forward and folds it in a zigzag. This style is named after an accordion that moves and folds in much the same way.

Sidewinding: Used by snakes to move across shifting desert sands. The snake lifts the front of its body and moves it sideways in an arch. The front end comes to rest and the back end is lifted and moved sideways.

Snakes range in size from wormlike to positively gigantic. The Brahminy blind snake of Australia grows to just 6 inches (15 cm) long and could easily be mistaken for an earthworm. It has a blunt round head for burrowing and tiny spotlike eyes that barely

EVEN THE LARGEST AND MOST WELL-KNOWN SNAKES SUCH AS THIS ANACONDA ARE HARD TO LOCATE IN THE WILD. IT SPENDS MOST OF ITS TIME HIDDEN IN THE SWAMPS, STREAMS, AND RIVERS THROUGHOUT NORTHERN SOUTH AMERICA.

perceive light and dark. This small snake feeds on termites, ants, and ant larvae.

The world's largest snake is the legendary anaconda of South America. This powerful snake may grow to 33 feet (10 m) in length and weigh as much as 400 pounds (181 kg). Its diet includes birds, mammals—such as young pigs and full-grown deer—and caimans, which are members of the crocodile family.

Some of the most famous snakes in the world are the *venomous* snakes. These snakes use their hollow fangs to bite their prey and then inject them with a deadly poison called *venom*. The western diamondback rattlesnake of the American West and the black-necked spitting cobra of central Africa are two of the most feared venomous snakes.

Rattlesnakes, copperheads, coral, and cottonmouth snakes are the only venomous snakes in the United States whose venom can kill people. Such bites occur most often when a person disturbs a snake. If you see a snake, the best way to avoid getting bitten is to stop, then slowly back up so the snake can move away.

MOST SPECIES OF VENOMOUS SNAKES USE THEIR FANGS TO INJECT VENOM DIRECTLY INTO THEIR PREY OR PREDATORS. THE BLACK-NECKED SPITTING COBRA IS DIFFERENT. ITS FANGS PRODUCE TINY DROPLETS OF VENOM THAT SPRAY OUTWARD WHEN THE SNAKE COLLAPSES ITS LUNG AND BLOWS AIR OUT OF ITS MOUTH.

Many snakes have interesting habits. Yellow–bellied sea snakes spend their whole lives in the tropical waters of the Pacific and Indian oceans. With their flattened bodies and paddlelike tails they move swiftly underwater. They can stay submerged for an hour or more while they forage for small fish and eels. Eastern hognose snakes of the eastern United States often "play

17

dead" when confronted by a predator. Another U. S. resident, the eastern coral snake, will burrow headfirst into the ground and present its tail to the predator when pursued.

Garter snakes are among the most familiar snakes of North America. There are about fifty different species of garter snakes, including the common garter snake. This beautifully striped creature finds a home in gardens, vacant lots, woods, and farmland throughout most of the United States and southern Canada. In the spring and fall you may see them basking in the sun on a rock or log.

3
SNAKES ALIVE!

Snakes come into the world in two different ways. They hatch out of eggs or they are born live. Snake eggs are usually oval-shaped and covered with an almost rubbery shell. This shell allows water and oxygen to pass to the developing snake inside. Egg-laying snakes lay anywhere from one to one hundred eggs, though most lay between three and sixteen. The eastern hognose, the eastern coral snake, the Brahminy blind snake, and the black-necked spitting cobra all lay eggs, often in moist places

TWO BURMESE PYTHONS EMERGE FROM THEIR SOFT, CYLINDRICAL EGGS. THESE SNAKES MAY GROW TO NEARLY TWENTY FEET (6 M) IN LENGTH.

DURING INCUBATION, SNAKE EGGS SWELL AS THEY ABSORB WATER FROM RAIN OR THE WET GROUND. THESE EGGS, OF THE ROUGH GREEN SNAKE, WILL HAVE DOUBLED IN SIZE BY THE TIME THEY ARE READY TO HATCH.

such as rotting logs or piles of decaying vegetation. Most female snakes abandon their eggs after laying them. When the babies are ready to hatch, they cut through their shell with a small tooth called an "egg–tooth" and emerge into the world. Young snakes are not taught how to slither, hunt, or hide from predators.

They are on their own from the start and rely on *instinct* to survive.

Anacondas, yellow-bellied sea snakes, western diamondback rattlesnakes, and garter snakes are all born live. The size and number of baby snakes in each litter varies greatly from species to species. Large anacondas may deliver fifty baby snakes each measuring 3 feet (.9 m) long.

Snakes grow quickly and continue to grow throughout their entire lifetime. But their skin does not grow along with them. As the old skin dies and loosens, the snake rubs its face against rough objects. It continues rubbing and crawls forward out of its skin. It emerges with a bright and shiny skin and leaves its old skin behind–in one piece and turned completely inside out. Snakes may shed more often if their skin has been badly damaged, scraped, cut, or bitten.

Brahminy blind snakes are an all-female species that reproduces without males in a process similar to cloning.

SNAKES NEVER STOP
GROWING. THROUGHOUT
THEIR LIVES ALL SNAKES
SHED THEIR SKIN TO
ALLOW FOR GROWTH.
YOUNG SNAKES GROW
MORE QUICKLY THAN
ADULTS, SO THEY SHED
MORE OFTEN.

What do snakes do all day? A lot of their time is spent basking in the sun. Like other reptiles, snakes are cold-blooded. This does not mean that snake's blood is always cold. It means that their body temperature changes with that of the environment around them. When snakes are cold they move slowly, cannot feed, and are more likely to be caught by predators. So they lie in the sun and absorb heat from the sun as well as from the rock, log, or ground they are lying on. Yellow-bellied sea snakes warm up by basking on the surface of the water—often in large groups that can cover an area of over one square mile (1.6 sq km). Snakes can overheat, too. Like most animals, they cannot survive if their body temperature remains over 100° F (38°C) for a long period. Western diamondback rattlesnakes cool off in the shade or underground while anacondas may slip into deep water to escape the heat.

In some parts of the world, winter temperatures get too cold for snakes to warm up at all. So they hibernate, or become inactive or dormant. The eastern hognose snake simply burrows into loose soil during the winter. But in central Canada, red-sided garter snakes hibernate together—often by the thousands—in deep rocky pits in the ground. Scientists used to think the snakes huddled together just to stay warm, but now they think the snakes congregate so males and females can find each other more easily for mating.

Snakes spend a lot of time protecting themselves from predators. They will do almost anything to avoid getting into a fight since the beaks, claws, and teeth of predators can injure or kill them. When confronted, the hognose snake will first try to crawl away or burrow into the ground. If it cannot find a place to hide, the

WITHOUT FUR, FEATHERS, OR BODY FAT TO KEEP THEM WARM, SNAKES RELY ON THE SUN'S HEAT AND SUN-WARMED OBJECTS SUCH AS LOGS AND ROCKS TO RAISE THEIR BODY TEMPERATURE. LIKE MANY SNAKES, THIS BROWN WATER SNAKE MAY SPEND MANY HOURS A DAY BASKING IN THE SUN.

4

WHO'S FOR DINNER?

All snakes are *carnivores*, or meat eaters. Depending on the species of snake, "meat" includes everything from ants, termites, and worms to rodents, birds, small deer, and caimans. Some actively search for prey; others lie motionless and wait for their prey to come to them. All snakes are highly skilled hunters with specialized techniques for finding, capturing, and eating their prey.

Most snakes do not have an especially keen sense of sight. They do not have eardrums but are nevertheless very sensitive to sound vibrations

CAUGHT BY A CARNIVORE! USING ONLY ITS MOUTH AND KEEN SENSES, AN EASTERN RIBBON SNAKE CAPTURES A SMALL FROG CALLED A SPRING PEEPER.

passing through the ground. To "smell" their prey they rely on their nostrils and forked tongues. Common garter snakes, for instance, hunt during the day for frogs, toads, fish, and salamanders. As this snake moves through the grass, it flicks its tongue in and out. From the air or ground, the tongue picks up tiny scent particles left by a hopping toad. When the snake pulls its tongue in, it rubs these particles against two openings on the roof of its mouth. These openings lead to the *Jacobson's organ*, which is very sensitive to odors and sends messages about the odors to the snake's brain. As the snake nears the toad, and the scent becomes very strong, the garter snake quickly seizes the toad with its rows of backward curving teeth. The toad may struggle, but the snake slowly swallows the toad—head first and whole.

How can a garter snake swallow an animal bigger than its head? Snakes have upper and lower jaws that are loosely connected and can stretch wide apart.

Pit organs allow a snake to sense a change in temperature near its head of less than 1 degree F (0.5 ° C).

A WESTERN DIAMONDBACK RATTLESNAKE RELIES ON ITS FORKED TONGUE TO LEARN ABOUT ITS SURROUNDINGS AND LOCATE ITS PREY. THOUGH THEY LOOK SHARP, SNAKES DO NO USE THEIR TONGUES TO BITE OR INJURE THEIR PREY.

A WESTERN COTTONMOUTH OPENS ITS MOUTH WIDE, REVEALING THE SNAKE'S LOOSELY CONNECTED JAWS.

The Jacobson's organ is made up of two hollow sacs in the roof of a snake's mouth. The Jacobson's organ, together with the nostrils, give snakes a strong sense of smell.

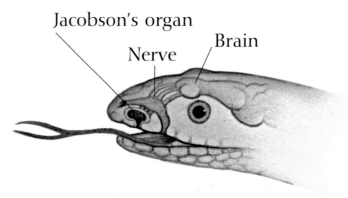

Jacobson's organ

Nerve

Brain

In addition, the left and right sides of each jaw can move forward and backward independently. When the garter snake seizes the toad, its jaws "crawl" forward—alternating left and right, upper and lower— over the prey. The snake's ribs, skin, and muscles stretch around the frog and move it toward the stomach and intestines. Snakes can digest everything except fur and feathers; bones can be completely digested within seventy-two hours.

Anacondas have a different hunting style. Because these snakes grow to be so large and heavy, they are slow on land and prefer to live in and near the water. Here, they can ambush their prey—amphibians, birds, and other animals that come to the water to feed or drink. Camouflaged by their green and black skin, anacondas lie motionless as the prey moves closer, unaware of the danger. The snake positions its head, then suddenly strikes at the prey, gripping it tightly in its jaws and looping its heavy body around it. Then the anaconda begins to constrict, or squeeze, the captured victim. Each time the animal exhales, the anaconda tightens its grip until the prey's heart can no longer pump blood and it dies. The anaconda then begins to swallow the kill.

The western diamondback rattlesnake uses a combination of hunting techniques. As this rattler forages across a rocky hillside, for example, it uses its tongue to locate the pathway used by a mouse. The rattler—well camouflaged by day and nearly invisible at night—positions itself beside the path and waits. Special heat-sensitive pits, called pit organs, on the rattler's face detect the body heat given off by the prey. The pits help aim its strike. When the mouse scurries along the path in front of the snake, the rattler strikes quickly, injecting venom through its fangs into the mouse's body. The snake lets go quickly to avoid being bitten by the mouse. The mouse staggers away, but soon collapses as the venom destroys its blood cells. The rattler then uses its forked tongue to smell its way to the mouse. As the rattler begins swallowing the mouse, it injects more venom into the mouse. Venom contains powerful digestive enzymes that eat away at the organs of the prey making it easier to digest.

IT MAY HAVE TAKEN DAYS OF WAITING IN JUST THE RIGHT SPOT BEFORE THIS RATTLESNAKE WAS ABLE TO SEIZE THIS MOUSE. THE SNAKE WILL DIGEST EVERY BIT OF THIS MOUSE, EXCEPT THE FUR.

5
SNAKES AND US

Despite our long history with snakes, they remain a mystery to us. We still have much to learn about where they live, how they behave, and why they are an important part of nature.

Less than 20 percent of all snakes are venomous–and only half of those can harm humans–and yet, these few snakes give the other 80 percent a bad reputation. Many harmless snakes are killed because people think they might be venomous. People have also over-hunted some species of snakes for food and to make shoes, handbags, and clothing from their beautifully patterned skins. Many species are collected by hunters who supply snakes to pet stores.

People also destroy the places where snakes live by clearing land for farms, houses, highways, and

FEAR OF SNAKES IS COMMON BUT NOT UNIVERSAL. THIS YOUNG WOMAN POSES WITH SEVERAL COBRAS SHE IS LEARNING TO CHARM FROM A MASTER SNAKE CHARMER IN INDIA.

industries. The San Francisco garter snake, for instance, once lived in wetland areas throughout California's San Francisco peninsula. This beautifully striped garter snake is harmless to humans and is very shy. Unfortunately for the snake, people wanted to live where the garter snake lived. Homes and highways were built, wetlands were drained and streams filled in or redirected, leaving the snakes with few places to survive. Today, the San Francisco garter snake lives in about thirty small pockets of wetland—all isolated from each other—south of the San Francisco Bay area. In 1967, these snakes were listed as an endangered species–one that would become extinct if they were not given special protection. Scientists hope to save this snake from extinction by conserving, or saving, certain wild areas where the snakes can live.

Why should we care about saving snakes? Snakes are important to people, especially farmers, because they hunt rats and mice that eat farmers' corn, wheat, and other grains. In addition to being farm pests, many rodents carry diseases that are trans–ferred to humans. When rodent–eating snakes are killed, the number of rodents increases, and so do the

THE SAN FRANCISCO GARTER SNAKE IS ONE OF AMERICA'S MOST BEAUTIFUL SNAKES AS WELL AS ONE OF ITS RAREST. IT IS AN ENDANGERED SPECIES THAT IS PROTECTED FROM BEING HUNTED, COLLECTED, OR HARMED.

chances of humans becoming infected with disease.

Snakes, especially small, young snakes, are an important food source in the animal kingdom. Hawks and owls, eagles and roadrunners, turtles and crocodiles, scorpions and fire ants, and other snakes all make meals of snakes. Every species, from the Brahminy blind snake to the mighty anaconda, is a potential meal. In their roles as predator and prey, snakes are important in the balance of nature. Though we may never feel the same way toward snakes as we do toward giant pandas or other "cuddly" animals, snakes deserve our respect and we must make an effort to learn about them and protect them.

carnivore: an animal or plant that eats meat

cold–blooded: having a body temperature that changes with the temperature of the animals surroundings. All reptiles are cold–blooded

diurnal: active during the day

enzyme: a molecule that speeds up chemical reactions in all living things.

habitat: the place that has all the living and nonliving things an organism needs to live and grow

herpetologist: a scientist who studies reptiles and amphibians

hibernate: to spend the winter in an inactive or dormant state, much like a deep sleep

instinct: a natural impulse; behavior that an animal is born knowing

mimic: to imitate

nocturnal: active during the night

predator: an animal that hunts and kills another animal

prey: an animal that is eaten by another animal

species: a group of animals that are all of the same kind and can produce offspring

venom: a chemical produced by the snake that is poisonous to other animals

BOOKS

Arnold, Caroline. *Snake.* New York: Morrow Junior Books, 1991.

Badger, David P. *Snakes.* Stillwater, MN: Voyageur Press, 1999.

Cannon, Janell. *Verdi.* San Diego, CA: Harcourt Brace, 1997.

Dewey, Jennifer Owings. *Rattlesnake Dance: True Tales, Mysteries, and Rattlesnake Ceremonies.* Honesdale, PA: Boyds Mill Press, 1997.

Ernst, Carl H. and George R. Zug. *Snakes in Question: the Smithsonian Answer Book.* Washington, DC: Smithsonian Institution Press, 1996.

Maestro, Betsy. *Take a Look at Snakes.* New York: Scholastic, 1992.

Markle, Sandra. *Outside and Inside Snakes.* New York: Macmillan Books for Young Readers, 1995.

Montgomery, Sy. *The Snake Scientist.* Boston: Houghton Mifflin, 1999.

WEBSITES

University of Michigan Museum of Zoology
http://animaldiversity.ummz.umich.edu

An Interactive Guide to Massachusetts Snakes
http://www.umass.edu/umext/nrec/snake_pit/index.html

ABOUT THE AUTHOR

Maria Mudd Ruth is the author of several natural history books for children, including *The Deserts of the Southwest, The Tundra, The Mississippi River,* and *The Pacific Coast* for the Ecosystems of North America series.

INDEX

48

Preface

PAYROLL ACCOUNTING AND TODAY'S BUSINESS ENVIRONMENT

Today's payroll accountant is a major player on a company's management team. Management's need for timely and accurate payroll cost data as a part of the total planning step has moved payroll from a disbursement and recording function to an integral part of the management process.

With constant changes in the legal environment, technology advancements in the administration of payroll functions and with tax withholding responsibilities, the payroll accounting occupation has become proactive. During this time when the need for accurate information is so critical, *Payroll Accounting* has established a record of being the most thorough book on the market. Each edition has been updated with the most current data available.

The 2003 edition of *Payroll Accounting* continues to provide the most user-friendly payroll accounting coverage in addition to adding significant resources that will aid instructors and student alike in their mastery of payroll accounting.

PAYROLL AND TECHNOLOGY

In this edition, we have incorporated technology to give instructor's full support for today's teaching options and students hands-on experience based on the practices of payroll specialists.

New! SELF-PACED, COMPUTER-BASED ADP TUTORIAL:

This FREE CD-ROM-based tutorial teaches learners to use *ADP PC/Payroll for Windows* to start a new payroll cycle, enter employee and pay information, transmit a payroll, and verify payroll with output reports. Upon completion of the tutorial, learners will receive a resume-quality certificate of accomplishment.

New! WEBTUTOR ON BLACKBOARD OR WEBCT:

These platform-based products give users access to study resources and interactive experiences beyond the classroom–the perfect way to reinforce and review concepts. Features include interactive quizzes, exciting payroll test-your-knowledge games, discussion threads, payroll calendars, chapter summaries, and more.

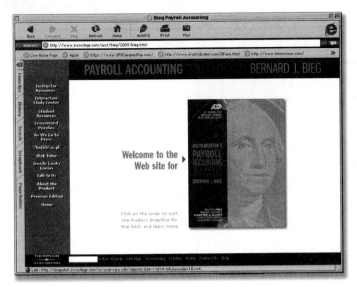

COMPLETE WEB SITE (http://bieg.swcollege.com):

This comprehensive and easy to use web site offers a complete Interactive Study Center containing Interactive Quizzes, E-Lectures, Excel spreadsheet templates, Payroll Crossword puzzle, and Internet Activities with payroll and tax accounting web links. Instructors enjoy easy access to the Solutions Manual, PowerPoint Presentations, and Transparency Masters.

COMPUTERIZED PAYROLL PROJECT–EXPANDED:

The text's comprehensive review problem has been expanded to include the integration of a SIMPLE Retirement plan. Learners can solve the updated payroll project with the forms provided, or with Klooster & Allen's Computerized Payroll Accounting Software.

MORE EXCEL TEMPLATES:

New Excel templates for selected end of chapter problems and the Continuing Payroll Problem provide students with additional practice. A printed Excel primer is located in the Appendix.

A Great Study Tool for the Payroll Certification Examination

The 2003 edition of *Payroll Accounting* continues to offer the course content and tutorials to help users prepare for the American Payroll Association's Fundamental Payroll Certification (FPC) designation exam:

REINFORCING ONLINE TUTORIALS

Learners can access Internet-based tutorials at the Bieg web site (http://bieg.swcollege.com)–a great way to get instant feedback and quickly master key concepts.

UP-TO-THE-MINUTE TAX LAW CHANGES.

Up-to-date knowledge is especially important for today's payroll specialists. This edition has been completely updated to reflect the tax law changes that affect payroll accounting. Users can find these changes listed on the "As We Go To Press" page in the text and on the web site.

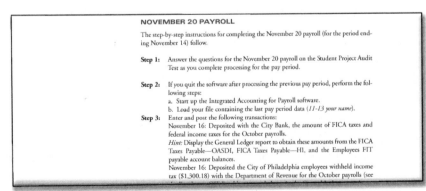

COMPREHENSIVE PAYROLL PROJECT:

Using the latest payroll software–available in Windows® format and packaged FREE with each text–users can review key concepts in a comprehensive review problem at the end of the book. New coverage on SIMPLE retirement plans has also been added to the project.

INTEGRATED PAYROLL LAW AND PRACTICE

Payroll laws are presented next to their respective practices–making it easy for learners to understand the *reasoning* behind confusing federal, state and local regulations.

Learning Objectives are enumerated at the beginning of each chapter and the numbers repeated next to the start of the applicable text coverage.

COVERAGE UNDER FUTA AND SUTA

LEARNING OBJECTIVE ① Other than a few significant exceptions as explained in this section, the coverage under FUTA is similar to that under FICA, as described in Chapter 3.

Employers—FUTA

The federal law levies a payroll tax on employers for the purpose of providing more uniform administration of the various state unemployment compensation laws. The federal law considers a person or a business an employer if *either* of the following two tests applies:

1. Pays wages of $1,500 or more during any calendar quarter in the current or preceding calendar year, or
2. Employs one or more persons, on at least some portion of one day, in each of 20 or more calendar weeks during the current or preceding taxable year.

Self-study quizzes appear throughout each chapter and test the understanding of major concepts.

Use of marginal icons ("On the Net," "News Alert," "IRS Connection," and "On the Job") helps integrate the real world applications of this facts-intensive area of study. "On the Net" icons allow optional integration of Internet research sites for learners, like the example that follows:

on the

Net

http://www.itsc.state.md.us/ directory/map.com This site provides an interactive map of unemployment-related state servers.

Payroll Accounting 2003   Unemployment Compensation Taxes   5-25

SELF-STUDY QUIZ 5-3. *The FUTA taxable wages of Davies Company during 2003 follows. List the amount and the due date of each deposit of FUTA taxes for the year.*

	Amount	Due Date
1st Quarter—$22,000	$_____	_____
2nd Quarter—$24,000	$_____	_____
3rd Quarter—$12,000	$_____	_____
4th Quarter—$10,000	$_____	_____

Penalties—FUTA

As indicated in Chapter 3, the Internal Revenue Code subjects employers to civil and criminal penalties for failing to file returns, pay the employment taxes when due, and make timely deposits. These penalties apply, generally, without regard to the type of tax or return involved. The last section of Chapter 3 presents all of the penalties.

The icons in each chapter highlight the most current forms, instructions, and wage and tax laws available.

New! Thorough End-of-Chapter materials include review questions, discussion questions, practical problems, and case problems. NEW matching exercises have been added for each chapter. Internet Activities have been increased.

MATCHING QUIZ

1. Biweekly	A. Remuneration paid twice a month
2. Commission	B. Exempt from some or all of the FLSA requirements
3. Tipped employee	C. Employee engages in interstate commerce or produces goods for such commerce
4. Common-law relationship	D. Remuneration paid every two weeks
5. Gross earnings	E. Employer has the right to control both what work will be done and how it will be done
6. Individual employee coverage	F. Engaged in a job in which tips of more than $30 a month are regularly received
7. EFTS	G. Payment to employee based on a stated percentage of revenue
8. Exempt employees	H. Regular earnings plus overtime earnings
9. Piece-rate system	I. Pay system based on an amount paid to the employee per units produced
10. Semimonthly	J. Electronic funds transfer system

The final payroll project can be completed manually (Chapter 7) or by using the computer (Appendix A). A Payroll CD, now in Windows, is free with the purchase of the text. Inspector CDs, which facilitate grading of the payroll project, are free to instructors. Additionally, the payroll project can be completed on Excel templates. An Excel Primer and instructions for the Glo-Brite Payroll Project are located in Appendix B.

CONTINUING PAYROLL PROBLEM

Refer to the partially completed payroll register that you worked on at the end of Chapter 4. You will now compute the employer's liability for unemployment taxes (FUTA and SUTA) for the pay of January 14. These computations will be used at the end of Chapter 6 in recording the payroll tax entries.

To compute the employer's liability for unemployment taxes, proceed as follows:

1. Enter each employee's gross earnings in the Taxable Earnings—FUTA and SUTA columns.
2. Total the Taxable Earnings—FUTA and SUTA columns.
3. At the bottom of your payroll register, compute the following for the total payroll:

a. Net FUTA tax. Since this is the first pay period of the year, none of the employees are near the $7,000 ceiling; therefore, each employee's gross earnings is subject to the FUTA tax.

b. SUTA tax. Since the Steimer Company is a new employer, Pennsylvania has assigned the company a contribution rate of 3.5% on the first $8,000 of each employee's earnings.

NOTE: Retain your partially completed payroll register for use at the end of Chapter 6.

Instructor Resources

SOLUTIONS MANUAL/TEST BANK (ISBN: 0-324-11875-9)

The Solutions Manual/Test Bank contains the Learning Objectives, Chapter Contents and the solutions to the End-of-Chapter material, including the Payroll Project. An Inspector CD-ROM contains the solutions to the Computerized Payroll Project (Appendix A) and the Excel spreadsheets. New to this addition, the Achievement Tests and Key are included in the Solutions Manual and are available for reprinting.

INSTRUCTOR'S RESOURCE CD-ROM (ISBN: 0-324-27138-7)

This complete instructor resource on CD-ROM contains the downloadable Solutions Manual, Test Bank, Achievement Test and Key, Excel Solutions, PowerPoint Presentation, and ExamView-Computerized Testing Software and PowerPoint Presentation.

WEB SITE

The Bieg web site provides the instructor password-protected access to the Solutions Manual, the Achievement Tests and Key, and the PowerPoint Presentations.

ACHIEVEMENT TEST (ISBN: 0-324-11879-1)

ACHIEVEMENT TEST KEY (ISBN: 0-324-11878-3)

Student Resources

WEBTUTOR ON WEBCT (0-324-18652-5) OR BLACKBOARD (0-324-18653-3)

This on-line study guide is available to students through the Bieg product site: http://bieg.swcollege.com. WebTutor is designed to provide students interactive instruction through the use of self-testing questions, learning objectives, interesting games, flash-cards, and tutorial assistance.

WEB SITE–http://bieg.swcollege.com

The Bieg web site also offers downloadable supplements, crossword puzzles, payroll and tax web links and more information about WebTutor.

Acknowledgements

My sincere appreciation is due to the many instructors and students who have contributed suggestions to make the textbook more interesting, understandable, and practical to those who pursue the study of payroll accounting.

As a result of their very helpful recommendations, the textbook will better satisfy the learning needs of students and the teaching needs of instructors. Prior reviewers of the textbook include:

Dawn Addington
Albuquerque Technical Vocational Institute

Denise Anderson
Portland Community College

Ken Arena
Martin Community College

Donna Atkins
Bee County College–Kingsville

Larry Bain
Weatherford College

Richard Barden
Southwestern Community College

Gregory Barnes
Clarion University of Pennsylvania

Jan Batman
Indian Hills Community College

Donna Bersch
Fox Valley Technical College–OshKosh

Joseph Bouchard
Yuba College

LeRoy Bowman
Ivy Technical State College

Walt Boyll
Central Community College

Virginia Bramblett
Athens Area Technical Institute

Madelyn Bruning
Pueblo Community College

J. Brusoe
Moraine Park Technical College

Dick Butenhoff
Waukesha County Technical College

Ed Butts
Grays Harbor College

James Byrne
Mt. San Antonio College

Leon Cabrera
Pueblo Community College

Linda Carey
Mid-State Technical College

Dorethia Carter
DeKalb Technical College

Lee Cartwright
Santa Fe Community College

Juanite Clobes
Gateway Technical College

Robert Close
El Dorado Center–Cosummes River College

Cheryl Collins
Golden West College

Don Craig
Del Mar College

Giles Dail
Edgecombe Community College

Lee Daugherty
Lorain County Community College

Laura Denton
Maysville Community College

Denise Dick
Louisiana Technical–HPL–Rod Brady Branch

CJ Dienethal
Riverside Community College

Howard Director
Nassau Community College

Marcia Eiser
Davis College

Acknowledgements

Zona Elkins
Blue Ridge Community College

Donna Elmore
Navarro College

Walter Erickson
St. Cloud Technical College

Martha Fife
James Sprunt Community College

Tanya Fontenot
Lamar Salter Technical College

Pat Gautier
Central Carolina Community College

Raymond Gonzalez
Los Angeles Trade Technical College

Aimee Goodwin
South Seattle Community College

Harry Gray
Ivy Technical State College–Indianapolis

Darwin Grimm
Iowa Lakes Community College

Dale Guimont
Anoka Technical College

Gary Guinn
Iowa Lakes Community College

Ken Haling
Gateway Technical College

Jillane Halverson
Winona Technical College

Juanita Hanson
North Iowa Area Community College

Sara Harris
Arapahoe Community College

Anita Harvey
Chippewa Valley Technical College

Ron Haugen
St. Cloud Technical College

Kay Hauser
Beaufort County Community College

Rebecca Helms
Ivy Technical State College

Brenda Hester
Volunteer State Community College

Bernie Hill
Spokane Falls Community College

Japan Holmes, Jr.
Savannah Technical Institute

Jerry Hoogers
Hennepin Technical College

Sharon Hoover
Scott Community College

Jay Horton
Greenville Technical College

Andy Howard
Lane Community College

Verne Ingram
Red Rocks Community College

Jane Ingrum
Columbus Technical Institute

Lynda Irby
Holmes Community College

Cynthia Jaksa
Rainy River Community College

JA Jensen
Southern Utah University

John Johnson
Seattle Central Community College

Betty Jolly
Caldwell Community College

Christine Kloezeman
Glendale Community College

Nick Kondyles
Baker College

Ronald Kremer
Wright State University

Leonard Krolak
Fergus Falls Community College

Roberta Kuhlman
Chaffey College

Denna Lacky
Flint River Technical Institute

Charlie LaClair
Cochise College

Jan Lange
*Minnesota West Community &
Technical College–Jackson Campus*

Ray Lewis
San Antonio College

Judy Lingo
Lane Community College

Rosemary Lint
Umpqua Community College

Bill Logan
Middle Georgia Technical Institute

J. Thomas Love
Walters State Community College

Judy Lyle
Lanier Technical Institute

Dorinda Lynn
Pensacola Junior College

Patricia Lynn
Pasadena City College

David Mack
Atlanta Area Technical College

Dennis Mackey
Gogebic Community College

Robert Maloney
University of Alaska–Anchorage

Wanda Metzgar
Boise State University

David Miller
Community College of San Francisco

Carol Moore
Northwest State Community College

Paul Morgan
*Mississippi Gulf Coast Community
College*

James Murray
Western Wisconsin Technical College

Lanny Nelms
Gwinnett Technical Institute

Al Nelson
Nicolet Area Technical College

Clara Nelson
Central Piedmont Community College

Robert Nieves
Fullerton City College

Joan Norton
Yakima Valley Community College

George Otto
Truman College

John Palafox
Ventura College

Keith Patterson
Ricks College

David Peterson
Madison Area Technical College

William Phipps
Vernon Regional Junior College

Jim Pratt
Utah Valley State College

Frank Praus
*University of North Dakota–Lake
Region*

Barbara Prince
Cabridge Community College

Jill Radcliffe
Ivy Technical State College

Al Rainford
Greenfield Community College

Alan Ransom
Cypress College

Tom Raotke
Mesabi Range Technical College

Sheris Red Feather
Oglala Lakota College

Pat Rittenbach
Blue Mountain Community College

Joe Rivkin
Harper College

Teresa Roberts
Wilson Technical Community College

Pam Sager
North Central Missouri College

Carol Schroeder
Fox Valley Technical College

Julie Scott
Carroll Technical Institute

William Serafin
*Community College of Alleghany
County–South Campus*

Al Setzer
Everett Community College

Carol Shipley
Northwest Technical College–Detroit Lakes

Robin Singleton
Louisiana Technical College

Lisa Sitkins
Baker College

Jon Smith
Vermillion Community College

Rene Smith
Horry-Georgetown Technical College

Jeffrey Soares
Abbie Business Institute

Albert Spencer
Kauai Community College

Lyle Stelter
Red Wing/Winona Technical College

Larry Swisher
Muskegon Community College

Roy Swisher
Lakeshore Technical College

Stella Tavares
Hawaii Community College

Ron Trontvet
Northland Community & Technical College

Phil Turner
Danville Area Community College

Richard Vernon
Community College of Aurora

Vicki Vorell
Cuyahoga Community College

Philip Waits
Harry Ayers State Technical College

Naomi Ward
Northwest Kansas Technical School

Alison Watkins
Valdosta Technical Institute

Carole Weber
Alexandria Technical College

Michael Welser
Feather River College

Geri Wendt
Chippewa Valley Technical College

Avalon White
Barton County Community College

Mary Ann Whitehurst
Griffin Technical Institute

Ed Winslow
Davidson Community College

Ray Wurzburger
New River Community College

Louis Yambor
Keiser College

Don Yount
Guilford Technical Community College

Joseph Zernick
Ivy Technical State College

In addition, the author would like to thank the following content-providers and author-contributors to the 2003 edition:

Tim Nygaard, *Madisonville Community College*, Madisonville, KY for writing the tutorials, quizzes, and discussion topics for WebTutor, authoring the Internet Activities in the text, and providing the Payroll Tax Internet links.

DeeDee Daughtry, *Johnston Community College*, Smithfield, NC for writing the QuizBowl feature in the WebTutor.

Bernie Hill, *Spokane Falls Community College*, Spokane, WA for preparing the Excel spreadsheet templates for the text problems and Continuing Payroll Problem, and for verifying the text and all elements of the WebTutor.

Peggy Hussey, for writing the Excel Primer and for preparing the Excel spreadsheet templates that accompany the Payroll Project.

Lisa Swallow, *University of Montana, College of Technology*, Missoula, MT for preparing the PowerPoint Lectures available on the web site.

Contents

The Need for Payroll and Personnel Records

As an employee, your favorite day of the week is PAYDAY.

However, your paycheck is the last step in a process that starts

with the application, the inter-

view, the hiring, the wage rates,

the withholding taxes, and the

payroll records.

What kind of information can be asked of job applicants? Is it

worthwhile to check references? Can credit reports be consid-

ered? The impact that various federal laws have on personnel and

payroll operations will be explored, and you will get a brief

look at topics that are covered in detail in subse-

quent chapters.

1

© Getty Images, Inc./Photodisc

AFTER STUDYING THIS CHAPTER, YOU SHOULD BE ABLE TO:

1. Identify the various laws that affect employers in their payroll operations.

2. Explain the recordkeeping requirements of these laws.

3. Explain the importance of a thorough recordkeeping system.

4. Describe the employment procedures generally followed in a Human Resources Department.

5. Recognize the various personnel records used by businesses and know the type of information shown on each form.

6. Describe the procedures employed in a typical payroll accounting system.

7. Identify the *payroll register* and the *employee's earnings record*.

LEARNING OBJECTIVES

Payroll professionals are responsible for issuing over four billion paychecks each year to over a hundred million people in the workforce of the United States. The processing of payrolls allows no margin for error. Employees, employers, and government agencies monitor the work performed by payroll professionals. A payroll accounting system is the only operation in a business that is almost completely governed by various federal, state, and local laws and regulations. Rules establish who is an employee, what is time worked, when overtime is to be paid, what deductions are made, when to pay an employee, and when taxes are paid. Lack of compliance with these laws and regulations can result in both fines and back-pay awards.

With each new year, payroll administrators must keep abreast of the changes in legislation that affect their firms' payroll recordkeeping. An understanding of the various laws affecting payroll operations helps you know the required payroll and personnel records and procedures. This chapter briefly examines the various laws that affect employers in their payroll operations and the payroll and personnel records that they use to meet the requirements of the laws. First, however, let's take a brief look at payroll accounting as a profession.

THE PAYROLL PROFESSION

With the increased responsibilities of payroll specialists, the profession has seen a significant increase in salary compensation. In a 2001 survey conducted for the American Payroll Association, the average salary of senior payroll managers rose to $73,555 while that of entry-level payroll clerks rose to $26,744.

Typically, an entry-level payroll clerk collects, reviews, approves, and records time records. Also, the clerk updates attendance records, including vacation, sick, and personal days. Once a payroll is processed, the clerk reviews the information to ensure the accuracy of each employee's paycheck. Subsequent job responsibilities will include entering the following information into the payroll system:

1. Time-worked data.
2. Pay rate changes.
3. Tax rate changes.
4. Employee authorized payroll deductions.
5. New employee information.
6. Marital and employee allowance changes.

Providing information to the Finance Department concerning the amounts to be paid for taxes, health insurance premiums, retirement plans, etc., may also be part of the evolving duties of the advancing payroll professional. One of the final stages involves the completion of payroll tax returns, employee information returns, federal and state census returns, and fringe benefit and welfare plan returns.

Payroll professionals must keep abreast of the changes in their field so that they can remain technically proficient. This need has spurred the development of an association of payroll practitioners—the American Payroll Association (APA). Membership in the association is open to anyone interested in or engaged in the support of payroll accounting. The APA offers professional training seminars and various publications to its members. In addition, each year the APA administers an examination for the payroll accountant and awards a certificate to those who pass the exam (Certified Payroll Professional). This testing and certification process has helped the payroll profession to gain recognition in the business community. The APA has also established guidelines for the conduct of the payroll professional. This "Code of Ethics," shown in Figure 1–1, sets the direction for the profession.[1]

One of a number of publications designed to provide current information to the practitioner is published by the Research Institute of America, Inc. This biweekly issue is entitled *Payroll Guide,* and it is a comprehensive review of changes in regulations affecting payroll reporting.[2]

---

1 For more information on the organization, write to: American Payroll Association, New York Educational Division, 30 E. 33rd Street, New York, NY 10016-5386; Tel: 212-686-2030.

2 *Payroll Guide* is published by the Research Institute of America Group, 90 Fifth Avenue, New York, NY 10011; Tel: 1-800-431-9025.

FIGURE 1-1

APA Code of Ethics

1. To be mindful of the personal aspect of the payroll relationship between employer and employee, and to ensure that harmony is maintained through constant concern for the Payroll Professional's fellow employees.
2. To strive for perfect accuracy and timeliness of all payroll activities.
3. To keep abreast of the state of the payroll art with regard to developments in payroll technologies.
4. To be current with legislative developments, actions on the part of regulatory bodies, and the like, in so far as they affect payroll.
5. To maintain the absolute confidentiality of the payroll, within the procedures of the employer.
6. To refrain from using Association activities for one's personal self-interest or financial gain.
7. To take as one's commitment the enhancement of one's professional abilities through the resources of the American Payroll Association.
8. To support one's fellow Payroll Professionals, both within and outside one's organization.

FAIR LABOR STANDARDS ACT

In the processing of payrolls, the first step is to determine gross pay. The Fair Labor Standards Act (FLSA) of 1938 affects this calculation. Commonly referred to as the Federal Wage and Hour Law, this law sets up minimum wage (currently $5.15 per hour) and overtime pay requirements. Other provisions of this law concern equal pay for equal work regardless of sex, restrictions upon the employment of child labor, public service contracts, and wage garnishment. These basic provisions apply to employers engaged in interstate commerce or in the production of goods and services for interstate commerce and to employees in certain enterprises which are so engaged, unless specifically exempted. The FLSA also imposes recordkeeping requirements on employers but prescribes no specific form of record. Figure 1–2 shows the basic requirements imposed on the employer concerning payroll and personnel records. Various components of the law have different informational requirements. The equal pay portion requires the identification of the sex of each employee in the payroll records. The child labor portion sets the date of birth requirement for only employees under 19.

All employers must keep records explaining the basis of wage differentials paid to employees of opposite sex for equal work performed in the same establishment. Such records include those relating to job evaluations, job descriptions, merit systems, seniority systems, and union contracts. The employer also must display a poster, available from the regional office of the Wage and Hour Division, that informs employees of their minimum wage, equal pay, overtime pay, and wage-collection rights, as well as child-labor restrictions. Chapter 2 presents a detailed discussion of this act and the standards established.

The payroll records must be available for inspection by the Department of Labor's Wage-Hour Division within 72 hours of the notice of audit.

STATE MINIMUM WAGE AND MAXIMUM HOURS LAWS

Most states have established minimum wage rates for covered employees, either by legislation or by administrative order of the legislature whereby minimum wage rates are fixed for specific industries. As noted earlier, the Fair Labor Standards Act, a federal law, also applies minimum wage and maximum hour provisions to employers. Where both federal and state regulations cover the same employee, the higher of the two rates prevails. For example, the minimum hourly wage in Alaska is $5.65, or 50¢ greater than the federal minimum wage. All workers covered by that state's legislation would receive the higher state rate.

Payroll managers must be familiar with the administrative orders of their particular state, since the wage orders not only set minimum wages but also contain provisions affecting pay

on the
Net
http://www.dol.gov/dol/esa/ public/minwage/america.htm This web site contains the minimum wage laws by state in map and text form.

FIGURE 1-2

Summary of Information Required by Major Federal Payroll Laws

	Item	Fair Labor Standards Act	Social Security	Income Tax Withholding	Unemployment Tax
EMPLOYEE DATA	Name	Yes	Yes	Yes	Yes
	Address	Yes	Yes	Yes	Yes
	Gender	Yes	....	....	....
	Date of birth	Yes	....	....	....
	Social Security Number	Yes	Yes	Yes	Yes
	Withholding allowances claimed	....	....	Yes	....
	Occupation	Yes	Yes	Yes	Yes
	Period employed	....	Yes	Yes	Yes
	State where services rendered	....	Yes	....	Yes
EMPLOYMENT DATA	Day and time of day when workweek begins	Yes	....	....	....
	Regular hourly rate of pay	Yes	....	....	....
	Basis of wage payments; e.g., $7.25 per hour; $58.00 per day	Yes	....	....	....
	Hours worked each day	Yes	....	....	....
	Hours worked each week	Yes	....	....	....
	Daily or weekly straight-time pay, exclusive of overtime pay	Yes	....	....	....
	Amount and nature of exempt pay	Yes	....	....	....
	Weekly overtime pay	Yes	....	....	....
	Total additions to or deductions from wages	Yes	....	....	....
	Total remuneration for payroll period	Yes	Yes	Yes	....
	Total remuneration for calendar year	....	Yes	....	Yes
	Date of payment	Yes	Yes	Yes	Yes
	Payroll period	Yes	Yes	Yes	Yes
TAX DATA	Employee's wages subject to tax for payroll period	....	Yes	Yes	....
	Employee's wages subject to tax for calendar year	....	Yes	....	Yes
	Taxable remuneration—if different from total remuneration, reason for difference	....	Yes	Yes	Yes
	Tax deductions from employee's wages	....	Yes	Yes	Yes
	Date tax collected if other than date of payment	....	Yes	Yes	....
	Tax paid by employer but not deducted from employee's wages	....	Yes	Yes	Yes
GEN'L	Specific form of records	No	No	No	No
	No. of years records must be kept	2–3	4	4	4

periods, pay for call-in time and waiting time, rest and meal periods, absences, meals and lodging, tips, uniforms, and other matters dealing with wages and hours. The state wage orders usually provide that the employer must keep records showing the wages paid, the hours worked, and such other information that will aid enforcement by state officials.

FEDERAL INSURANCE CONTRIBUTIONS ACT (FICA)

The Federal Insurance Contributions Act (FICA) is part of the social security program planned by the federal government to provide economic security for workers and their families. The act levies a tax on employers and employees in certain industries to be paid to the federal government and credited to the Federal Old-Age and Survivors' Trust Fund and the Federal Disability Insurance Trust Fund. The Old-Age, Survivors, and Disability Insurance (OASDI) tax levied on employees is a set percent of their gross wages, and it must be withheld from their pay. From these funds, the federal government makes payments to persons who are entitled to benefits under the Social Security Act.

FICA also provides a two-part health insurance program, commonly known as Medicare, for the aged and the disabled. The Hospital Insurance (HI) plan is financed by a separate tax on both employers and employees. A Supplementary Medical Insurance plan to cover medical services not covered under the basic program is voluntary and is financed by those who desire coverage, with a matching payment by the federal government. Social security benefits are also available to the self-employed person under the provisions of the Self-Employment Contributions Act (SECA). This act imposes a tax on the net earnings from self-employment derived by an individual from any trade or business carried on by that person.

Chapter 3 gives detailed information about FICA and exemptions from its coverage, and Appendix C briefly covers the benefits available. Although FICA does not recommend a specific form for records, Figure 1–2 shows the specific information needed and the period of time to be retained.

INCOME TAX WITHHOLDING LAWS

With the passage of the 16th Amendment in 1913, taxation of income became constitutional. Today, an *income tax* is levied on the earnings of most employees and is deducted from their gross pay. In some cases, this may involve three separate deductions from the employee's gross pay—a federal income tax, a state income tax, and a local (city) income or wage tax. All of the acts that levy these various income taxes provide for the collection of taxes at the source of the wages paid (payroll withholding).

Federal Income Tax Withholding Law

The collection of federal income taxes at the source of wages paid came into being with the enactment of the Current Tax Payment Act of 1943, commonly referred to as a withholding tax law. A percentage formula is used in an attempt to collect the approximate tax on wages or salaries by requiring the employer to withhold a specified amount from each wage or salary payment. These withholdings are then turned over to the federal government for the employee's tax account. Over the years, many changes have been made in the tax rates, exemptions, and allowable deductions. Chapter 4 covers the current requirements in detail. Employers must keep records showing the information referred to in Figure 1–2. However, the law does not prescribe any specific forms to be used for such recordkeeping.

State and Local Income Tax Withholding Laws

Most states impose *state* income taxes on individuals. The laws vary from state to state as to the amount to be withheld, exemptions from withholding, and the time for withholding reports to be filed. Employers may also be required by *local* income tax laws to deduct and withhold local income taxes on salaries or wages paid. Chapter 4 presents further discussion of the withholding of state and local income taxes.

on the

Net

http://www.payroll-taxes.com/
Payroll Tax Information Site. This site contains addresses, phone numbers, form numbers (with explanations), and filing dates for federal and state taxing authorities.

UNEMPLOYMENT TAX ACTS

Unemployment insurance taxes provide funds at the state level for compensating unemployed workers. Taxes levied by both the federal government (Federal Unemployment Tax Act) and the state government (State Unemployment Tax Acts) affect the employer.

Federal Unemployment Tax Act (FUTA)

Like the Federal Insurance Contributions Act, the Federal Unemployment Tax Act is incorporated in the Internal Revenue Code. If an employer employs one or more individuals in each of 20 or more weeks in occupations covered by FUTA or pays wages of $1,500 or more during any calendar quarter in the current or preceding calendar year, a federal unemployment insurance tax must be paid. The federal government uses the collected tax to pay state and federal administrative expenses of the unemployment program. Employers subject to FUTA receive credit against most of the FUTA tax when they contribute to their state unemployment compensation funds. Chapter 5 gives detailed information as to employers and employees who are subject to the requirements of the act. Employers subject to FUTA must keep permanent records that provide the information listed in Figure 1–2. FUTA prescribes no particular form for these records.

State Unemployment Tax Acts (SUTA)

All fifty states and the District of Columbia have enacted unemployment insurance laws. Each employer receives a credit against the FUTA tax because of the contribution (tax) to a state's unemployment compensation program. The taxes paid to the individual states by employers are used primarily for the payment of unemployment benefits.

The Social Security Act specifies certain standards that each state has to meet in passing an unemployment compensation law. These standards have resulted in a fairly high degree of uniformity in the requirements of state unemployment laws and in the records that must be kept by businesses. State laws do differ, however, making it necessary for employers to be familiar with the laws of the states in which they operate.

The state unemployment compensation laws require employers to keep payroll records similar to those required under the federal law. Penalties may be imposed for failure to keep the required records, for failure or delinquency in making the required returns, or for default or delinquency in paying the contributions. The required period for retaining records varies in different states, but in no case should the records be kept for a period of less than four years because of the federal requirement. Chapter 5 covers state unemployment compensation and tax acts.

FAIR EMPLOYMENT LAWS

Federal and state legislations have been enacted to enforce *fair employment practices.* Many of these laws deal with discrimination on the basis of age, race, color, religion, gender, or national origin.

Civil Rights Act of 1964

on the
JOB

The Supreme Court has ruled that this law does not protect U.S. citizens working abroad.

Title VII of the Civil Rights Act of 1964, entitled "Equal Employment Opportunity," provides for several fair employment practices. The act, as amended, forbids employers to discriminate in hiring, firing, promoting, compensating, or in any other condition of employment on the basis of race, color, religion, gender, or national origin. Guidelines, established by the Equal Employment Opportunity Commission (EEOC), also include physical characteristics in the definition of national origin discrimination. For example, unnecessary height or weight requirements could exclude some individuals on the basis of their national origin. The EEOC has also declared that sexual harassment violates the Civil Rights Act. Unwelcome sexual advances, requests for sexual favors, and other verbal or physical conduct of a sexual nature can constitute sexual harassment.

The EEOC prohibits unions from including or segregating their members on these bases, and employment agencies may not refer or refuse to refer applicants for employment on the basis of race, color, religion, gender, or national origin.

This act covers all employers who engage in an industry "affecting commerce" and who employ 15 or more workers for each working day in each of 20 or more weeks in the current or preceding calendar year. Employers specifically excluded from coverage of the fair employment practices include: the United States government (state and local governments are covered), a corporation wholly owned by the United States, Indian tribes, private membership clubs (other than labor unions) exempt from federal income tax, and religious societies in the employment of members of a particular religion to work on the societies' religious activities. Although the United States government is classified as an exempt employer, the act states that the policy of the United States government provides equal employment opportunities without discrimination and that the President should use his existing authority to implement this policy.

Title VII does not protect an employee from arbitrary treatment or dismissal. As long as the employer applies these policies in a nondiscriminatory manner, Title VII requirements have not been violated.

To accomplish the purpose of eliminating discrimination, the EEOC tries to obtain voluntary compliance with the law before filing a court action for an injunction. It can institute court proceedings for an injunction if it believes that any person or group of persons is not complying with the law. Where a state or local law forbids discriminatory practices, relief must first be sought under the state or local law before a complaint is filed with the Commission. More than half the states and some cities have laws that prohibit employers from discriminating on the basis of race, creed, color, or national origin. In most states, a special commission or the state Department of Labor administers the laws and may authorize cease and desist orders that are enforceable in the courts.

Executive Orders

Employers not subject to the Title VII coverage discussed above may come within the scope of the Civil Rights Act by reason of a contract or a subcontract involving federal funds. In a series of *executive orders,* the federal government has banned, in employment on government contracts, discrimination based on race, color, religion, gender, or national origin.

Age Discrimination in Employment Act (ADEA)

The Age Discrimination in Employment Act of 1967 (ADEA) prohibits employers, employment agencies, and labor unions from discriminating on the basis of age in their employment practices. The act covers only employers (who employ 20 or more workers), employment agencies, and labor unions engaged in an industry affecting interstate commerce. The act also covers federal, state, and local government employees, other than elected officials and certain aides not covered by civil service. The ADEA provides protection for virtually all workers over 40. A key exception involves executives who are 65 or over and who have held high policymaking positions during the two-year period before retirement. If such an employee is entitled to an annual retirement benefit from the employer of at least $44,000, the employee can be forcibly retired.

In order to prove compliance with the various fair employment laws, employers must keep accurate personnel and payroll records. All employment applications, along with notations as to their disposition and the reasons for the disposition, should be retained. All records pertaining to promotions, discharges, seniority plans, merit programs, incentive payment plans, etc., should also be retained.

Americans with Disabilities Act (ADA)

The Americans with Disabilities Act of 1990 (ADA) prohibits employers (with 15 or more employees), employment agencies, labor organizations, or joint labor-management committees from discriminating against qualified persons with disabilities because of their disability.

on the
Net
http://www.eeoc.gov/
EEOC Homepage. This page overviews guidelines and services of the Equal Employment Opportunity Commission (EEOC).

on the
JOB
Age discrimination charges filed with the Equal Employment Opportunity Commission jumped to over 17,000 in fiscal year ended September 30, 2001 (22 percent of all claims filed).

on the
JOB
The United States Department of Justice has stated that the ADA covers people with AIDS (Acquired Immune Deficiency Syndrome) and AIDS-related conditions.

The prohibition of disability-based discrimination applies to job application procedures, hiring, advancement, termination, compensation, job training, and other conditions of employment. In addition, reasonable accommodations, such as wheelchair-accessible restrooms and ramps for qualified disabled job applicants and workers, must be provided.

OTHER FEDERAL LAWS AFFECTING THE NEED FOR PAYROLL AND PERSONNEL RECORDS

Generally, the payroll and personnel records and reports that a business prepares and retains to meet the requirements of the laws already discussed provide sufficient information needed under the laws outlined in Figure 1–3 and discussed below.

Federal Personal Responsibility and Work Opportunity Reconciliation Act of 1996 (PRWORA)

News
A L E R T

Only half of the families with child support orders receive the full amount of their entitlement. In 4 out of 5 cases, court orders are ignored by "deadbeat parents."[3] Over 60 percent of child support payments are collected through payroll withholdings.

This act mandates that all states must establish new-hire reporting programs. Every employer is required to report the name, address, and social security number on each new employee and the employer's name, address, and federal employer identification number within 20 days of hire to the appropriate state agency. This information must then be forwarded by the state to the federal Office of Child Support Enforcement (OCSE) for entry into the National Directory of New Hires. Five states require the same information on independent contractors: California, Massachusetts, New Hampshire, New Jersey, and Iowa.

Employers with operations in more than one state may file one report with the state of their choice. That state is then to share the information with the other states.

The main reason for this requirement is to help in the enforcement of child support obligations. In addition, it will reduce fraud in the unemployment, workers' compensation, and public assistance programs. Failure to report this information will result in fines not to exceed $25.00 per new hire.

Employee Retirement Income Security Act of 1974 (ERISA)

This act covers employee pension and welfare plans established or maintained (1) by any employer engaged in commerce or in any industry or activity affecting commerce and (2) by any employee organization representing employees engaged in commerce or in any industry or activity affecting commerce. The legislation safeguards pension funds by regulating how the funds are to be raised and disbursed, who controls them, and what is to be done when funds are insufficient to pay promised benefits. The law *does not* require any employer to establish a pension plan; however, if there is an employer's pension plan, every employee is eligible after reaching age 21 or completing one year of service, whichever is later.

ERISA was primarily designed to ensure that workers covered by private pension plans receive benefits from those plans in accordance with their credited years of service with their employers. *Vesting* conveys to employees the right to share in a retirement fund if they are terminated before the normal retirement age. The vesting process is linked to the number of years needed for workers to earn an equity in their retirement plans and to become entitled to full or partial benefits at some future date if they leave the company before retirement. Once vested, a worker has the right to receive a pension at retirement age, based on years of covered service, even though the worker may not be working for the firm at that time. Currently, the law provides for full vesting of the employer's contributions in three years or gradually over six years (20 percent after two years and 20 percent a year for the next four years). The plan administrator must file an annual report (Form 5500) with the federal government by the end of the seventh month following the close of the plan year.

To protect against potential benefit losses because of a plan's termination, ERISA set up a government insurance program (The Pension Benefit Guaranty Corporation) to pay any benefits that could not be met with funds from the plan.

---

3 Sandy Becker, "The Challenges and Opportunities of New Hire Reporting," *PAYTECH*, January/February 1998, p. 28.

FIGURE 1 - 3

Federal Laws Affecting the Need for Payroll and Personnel Records

Law	Coverage	Contract Dollar Minimum	Major Provisions
Davis-Bacon Act (1931)	Laborers for contractors or subcontractors on federal government contracts for construction, alteration, or repair of public buildings or works.	$2,000	Minimum wage set by Secretary of Labor (weight is given to union wage scale prevailing in the project area).
Walsh-Healey Public Contracts Act (1936)	Laborers for contractors who furnish materials, supplies, articles, and equipment to any agency of the United States.	$10,000	Single minimum wage determined by Secretary of Labor for all covered employees in a given industry.
McNamara-O'Hara Service Contract Act (1965)	Service employees on contracts with the United States or the District of Columbia for the furnishing of services.	$2,500	Minimum wage set by Secretary of Labor based on minimum wage found to be prevailing in that locality.
Occupational Safety and Health Act (OSHA) (1970)	Any business involved in interstate commerce.	-0-	Sets specific occupational and health standards for employers; requires that records be kept of work-related deaths, illnesses, and injuries.
Vocational Rehabilitation Act (1973)	Companies with federal agency contracts.	$2,500	Must include in the contract an affirmative action clause requiring that the handicapped applicant or employee will be given appropriate consideration.
Vietnam Era Veterans' Readjustment Act (1974)	Government contractors with federal contracts or subcontracts.	$10,000	Requires contractors to take affirmative action to employ and advance in employment qualified veterans of the Vietnam era and disabled veterans.

Tax-Deferred Retirement Plans. Contributions to these plans are taken out of employees' wages before federal income taxes are withheld. This reduces the amount of earnings that are subject to federal income tax; however, these deductions are still taxable for social security. On retirement, the employees will receive their contributions back in the form of regular payments from their retirement plans. These payments are then subject to federal income tax.

- *401(k) Plan.* A standard tax-deferred retirement plan. A set percentage of an employee's wages is contributed on a pretax basis. Tax-sheltered contributions are limited to $12,000. Participants who are 50 and over can defer an additional $1,000 each year. Employers can limit the percentage of the employee's pay that can be contributed. This limit can be lower than the maximum set by law. Employees can add after-tax contributions to this total, and the employer can contribute to the employees' plan. Total annual contributions (employee and employer) to the plan cannot exceed the lesser of $40,000 or 25 percent of the employee's annual wages.

- *Simple Plans.* A small company plan for a company with up to 100 employees. The employer can offer a SIMPLE plan as part of a 401(k) plan. This plan allows employees to contribute a percentage of their pay toward retirement. The tax deferral limit is $8,000.
- *Section 403(b) Plan.* A plan for employees of tax-exempt organizations. Tax-sheltered contributions by the employees are limited to $12,000.
- *Section 457 Plan.* A plan for employees of state and local governments and of tax-exempt organizations other than churches. Tax-sheltered contributions by the employees are limited to the lesser of 100 percent of compensation or $12,000.

Individual Retirement Account (IRA). An *individual retirement account (IRA)* is a pension plan established and funded by an individual employee. The employee's contributions to an IRA may be made through the employer or a union or placed in an individual retirement savings account specified in the law. *Under certain conditions,* employees may put aside each year the lesser of $3,000 or 100 percent of their compensation without paying federal income taxes on their contributions. Qualified single-income couples can invest $3,000 into separate IRA accounts for each partner. Chapter 4 presents a more detailed discussion of IRA accounts.

Even though these contributions can be made through payroll deductions, the employer is not considered a pension plan sponsor and is not subject to ERISA as long as the following guidelines are met:

1. The employer makes no matching contributions.
2. Participation is not mandatory.
3. The employer does not endorse any IRA sponsors.

Disclosure Requirements. The reporting and disclosure requirements set forth by ERISA have tremendous implications for the recordkeeping requirements of employers. Informational reports must be filed with the U.S. Department of Labor, the IRS, and the government insurance program. In general, the reports consist of descriptions of the plans and the annual financial data. The plan descriptions include the eligibility requirements for participation and for benefits; provisions for nonforfitable pension benefits; circumstances that may result in disqualification, loss, or denial of benefits; and procedures for presenting claims. The annual reports include financial statements and schedules showing the current value of plan assets and liabilities, receipts and disbursements, and employer contributions; the assets held for investment purposes; insurance data; and an opinion of an independent qualified public accountant. Upon written request from the participants, the administrator must also furnish a statement, not more than once in a 12-month period, of the total benefits accrued, accrued benefits that are vested, if any, or the earliest date on which accrued benefits will become vested.

Immigration Reform and Control Act of 1986 (IRCA)

This act bars employers from hiring and retaining aliens unauthorized to work in the United States. It also requires all employers to verify employment eligibility for all individuals by examining the employee's verification documents and having the employee complete *Form I-9, Employment Eligibility Verification* (not illustrated). Form I-9 lists the documents that the employee must furnish to the employer. These documents identify the employee and, if an alien, verify authorization to work in the United States. Form I-9 must be completed within three business days of the date the employee starts to work. The form must be retained for three years after the date of hiring or for one year after the date the employment is terminated, whichever is longer. The Immigration and Naturalization

Service (INS) can levy fines if an audit uncovers recordkeeping violations. Civil penalties range from $100 to $1,000 for each violation.

Any person or entity found to have unlawfully employed an unauthorized alien is subject to civil fines ranging from $250 to $11,000. Criminal penalties are assessed where a pattern and practice of discrimination is found.

Family and Medical Leave Act of 1993 (FMLA)

This law requires employers that have 50 or more employees within a 75-mile radius to grant workers unpaid leave for a family or medical emergency. In cases of childbirth, adoption, or serious illness of the employee or the employee's child, spouse, or parent, the employer must offer the worker as many as 12 weeks of unpaid leave. During the leave, employers must continue health-care coverage, and they must also guarantee that the employee will return to the same job or to a comparable position. The employer can substitute an employee's earned paid leave for any part of the 12-week family leave.

Employers can exempt the following:

1. The highest-paid 10 percent of their workforce.
2. Those who have not worked at least one year and at least 1,250 hours in the previous 12 months for the company.

A survey by the Labor Department found that only 2 to 4 percent of eligible workers have taken time off under FMLA. Of these, more than half did so to attend to their own health needs.

OTHER STATE LAWS AFFECTING THE NEED FOR PAYROLL AND PERSONNEL RECORDS

States have enacted other laws which have a direct bearing on the payroll and personnel records that an employer must maintain and on the rights that must be extended to employees.

Workers' Compensation Laws

Workers' compensation insurance protects employees and their dependents against losses due to work-related injury, illness, or death. Most states have passed laws that require employers to provide workers' compensation insurance by one of the following plans:

1. Contribution to a state compensation insurance fund administered by an insurance department of the state.
2. Purchase of workers' compensation insurance from a private insurance company authorized by the state to issue this type of policy.
3. Establishment of a self-insurance plan, approved by the state, under which the company bears all risk itself.

Benefits are paid to cover medical bills and also to provide a percentage of the worker's regular wages during the time that the employee is unable to work.

The employer bears the cost of the workers' compensation insurance premiums, except in Montana, New Mexico, Oregon, and Washington, where both the employer and the employee contribute to the workers' compensation fund.

The insurance premiums are often based upon the total gross payroll of the business and may be stated in terms of an amount for each $100 of weekly wages paid to employees. The premium rates vary among types of jobs, and they vary in amount with the pay rate involved.

EXAMPLE

The rate for the office workers of the Volpe Parts Company is $0.30 per $100 of payroll, while the rate for machine-shop workers is $1.90 per $100 of payroll.

Because the premium rates vary according to the different degrees of danger in various classes of jobs, payroll records must indicate job classifications for rate purposes. If the employer has low accident experience, the rates may be reduced to a certain minimum.

State Disability Benefit Laws

California, Hawaii, New Jersey, New York, Rhode Island, and Puerto Rico have passed laws to provide *disability benefits* to employees absent from their jobs because of illness, accident, or disease *not arising out of their employment*. Chapter 5 presents further discussion of state disability benefit laws.

HUMAN RESOURCES AND PAYROLL ACCOUNTING SYSTEMS

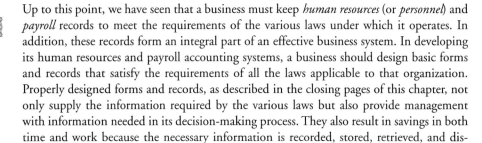

Up to this point, we have seen that a business must keep *human resources* (or *personnel*) and *payroll* records to meet the requirements of the various laws under which it operates. In addition, these records form an integral part of an effective business system. In developing its human resources and payroll accounting systems, a business should design basic forms and records that satisfy the requirements of all the laws applicable to that organization. Properly designed forms and records, as described in the closing pages of this chapter, not only supply the information required by the various laws but also provide management with information needed in its decision-making process. They also result in savings in both time and work because the necessary information is recorded, stored, retrieved, and distributed economically, efficiently, and quickly.

Before studying the employment process, it is important to examine the close relationship between the Payroll Department and the Human Resources Department. Some businesses consider payroll to be strictly an accounting function and, as such, place it under the direct control of the Chief Financial Officer. However, because of the need for quick interchange of information between the Payroll and the Human Resources Departments, the recent trend has been to place payroll under the control of the director of human resources. This movement toward centralization eliminates the duplication of many tasks, such as information reviews on both federal and state tax and census returns. With the required information in one department, the process of completing these forms is shortened. Further, questions from employees concerning sick pay, vacation pay, and other benefits can be answered from one source.

Individual computer programs have been developed for the combined needs of payroll and human resources. Information concerning such diverse activities as attendance, retirement benefits, health insurance coverages, and bonus pays is now available to designated employees in the Human Resources Department through a computer terminal.

HUMAN RESOURCES SYSTEM

In many medium-size and large companies, the **human resources system** embodies all those procedures and methods related to recruiting, selecting, orienting, training, and terminating personnel. Extensive recordkeeping procedures are required in order to:

1. Provide data for considering promotions and changes in the status and earnings of workers.
2. Provide the information required by various federal, state, and local laws.
3. Justify company actions if investigated by national or state labor relations boards.
4. Justify company actions in discussions with local unions or plant committees.

Before the Payroll Department can pay newly hired employees, the Human Resources Department must process those employees. Figure 1–4 charts the procedure that the Human Resources Department follows in this hiring process.

A number of companies that manufacture business forms have available standard personnel forms and records that may be successfully used if a business does not care to design its own special forms. In small companies, an application form or an employee history record may be the only document needed. Throughout the remainder of this chapter, several illustrations augment the discussion of the various human resources and payroll records. In the examples of these records, we shall follow Cheryl Crowson from her initial application for employment with the Palmero Maintenance Company to her entry onto the company's payroll records.

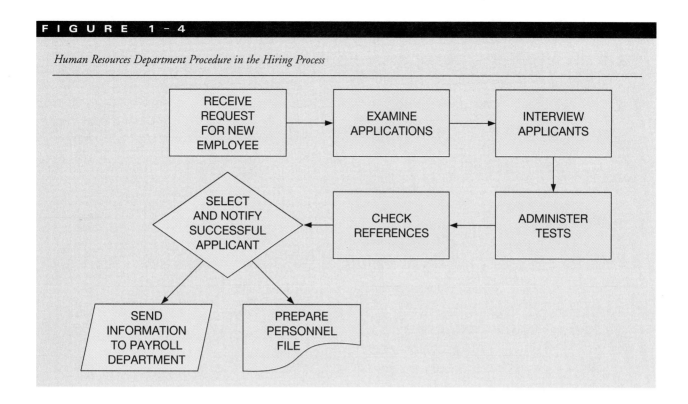

FIGURE 1-4

Human Resources Department Procedure in the Hiring Process

Requisition for Personnel

The *requisition for personnel* form notifies the Human Resources Department of the need for additional or replacement employees. The requisition for new employees can be initiated in a number of ways. Some companies send a memo to the Human Resources Department stating the title of the position to be filled, a brief description of the duties of the job, and the salary range. Other companies may use preprinted forms. A preprinted form should indicate the type and number of persons needed, the position to be filled, the rate of pay for the job, the salary range, the date the employee is needed, a summary of any special qualifications, and whether the position is permanent or temporary.

Application for Employment

Every business, regardless of size, should have an application form (similar to that in Figure 1–5) to be filled out by a person seeking employment. The *application form* gives the applicant an opportunity to provide complete information as to:

1. Personal information including the name, address, telephone number, and social security number of the applicant.
2. Educational background including a summary of the schools attended, whether the applicant graduated, and degrees conferred.
3. Employment and experience record.
4. Type of employment desired.
5. References.

The application form also provides information for the checking of references, serves as a guide to effective interviewing, and provides information for correlation with data obtained from employment tests. The form serves as a permanent record for the business.

Employers subject to fair employment laws must make certain that all aspects of the pre-hire inquiries are free of discrimination on the basis of race, color, religion, gender, national origin, or age. *Prehire inquiries* include questions asked in the employment interview and on application forms, resumes of experience or education required of an applicant, and

FIGURE 1-5

APPLICATION FOR EMPLOYMENT
An Affirmative Action/Equal Opportunity Employer

POSITION APPLIED FOR *Payroll Accounting Clerk*

This job application is valid only for the position you have listed above. If you wish to be considered for other positions, you will need to complete and/or submit a separate application for each position.

PERSONAL

Name   *Cheryl Crowson*

Address   *1630 West End Ave.*   *Huntington, WV 25703*
STREET   CITY   STATE   ZIP

Telephone   *(304) 555-2192*   *(304) 555-1618*
WORK   HOME   OTHER

Social Security Number   *199-00-6357*

Have you worked for Palmero Maintenance Company before? YES ☐ NO ☑
If Yes, when? _____

If hired, can you provide proof of identity and eligibility to work in the US? YES ☑ NO ☐

Have you been convicted of a felony? YES ☐ NO ☑ If Yes, describe. _____

EDUCATION

NAMES	ADDRESS	ACADEMIC MAJOR	NO. YEARS ATTENDED	DEGREE
HIGH SCHOOL *Centennial Senior*	*Stanford Road Huntington, WV*	*Business*	*4*	*Yes*
COLLEGE, JUNIOR COLLEGE OR UNIVERSITY *Huntington County Community*	*Swamp Road Huntington, WV*	*Business— Occupational*	*2*	*Associate*
TECHNICAL OR VOCATIONAL				

Other details of training: (Courses)   (Cert.)

FIGURE 1 - 5 *(Concluded)*

Application for Employment (page 2)

EMPLOYMENT HISTORY

List in sequence all employers, beginning with present/most recent employer, including military experience and apprenticeship. Explain any gaps in employment in comments section below. If additional space is needed, please attach sheet(s).

EMPLOYER / ADDRESS / JOB TITLE / SUPERVISOR / REASON FOR LEAVING	TELEPHONE	DATES EMPLOYED FROM	DATES EMPLOYED TO	Summarize the nature of the work performed and job responsibilities
Brennan Shipping Co.	(304) 555-1119	5/00	Present	Input time worked
ADDRESS 193 Mountain Blvd., Huntington, WV				information, checked
JOB TITLE Payroll Assistant		Hourly Rate/Salary $1,850	Per Month	payroll, distributed
IMMEDIATE SUPERVISOR Helen Young—Payroll Manager				
REASON FOR LEAVING Want to have more responsibility		Full-time ✔	Part-time	checks
MAY WE CONTACT FOR REFERENCE? ☒ YES ☐ NO ☐ LATER				

EMPLOYER / ADDRESS / JOB TITLE / SUPERVISOR / REASON FOR LEAVING	TELEPHONE	DATES EMPLOYED FROM	DATES EMPLOYED TO	Summarize the nature of the work performed and job responsibilities
AVS Drug	(304) 555-0101	9/98	5/00	Served as head cashier
ADDRESS Broad & Cherry Sts., Huntington, WV				and maintained inventory
JOB TITLE Clerk/Cashier		Hourly Rate/Salary $8.15	Per Hour	
IMMEDIATE SUPERVISOR John Stumley—Manager				
REASON FOR LEAVING Graduated college—Full-time position		Full-time	Part-time ✔	
MAY WE CONTACT FOR REFERENCE? ☒ YES ☐ NO ☐ LATER				

REFERENCES

Give names of persons we may contact to verify your qualifications for the position:

Edna White — Instructor — Teacher — Huntington County College
Name (Title) (Occupation) (Organization)

Swamp Road, Huntington, WV — Bus. No.: (304) 555-8000 — Home No.: (304) 555-2111
(Address)

Henry Stone — Controller — Finance — Brennan Shipping Co.
Name (Title) (Occupation) (Organization)

193 Mountain Blvd., Huntington, WV — Bus. No.: (304) 555-1119 — Home No.: (304) 555-8710
(Address)

I hereby certify that all statements made in this application (and accompanying resume, if any) are true and complete. I understand that any false or misleading statement on this application constitutes sufficient grounds for dismissal, if hired. I further certify that I may lawfully be employed in this country, and if employed will provide required documentation to verify identity and employment eligibility. In addition, in making this application for employment, I understand that the Company may investigate my employment and educational records. I hereby authorize my current and/or former employer(s) and school(s) to furnish the information requested by the Palmero Maintenance Company.

Signature of Applicant   Cheryl Crowson   Date   June 10, 20--

LEARNING OBJECTIVE 5

any kind of written testing. None of the federal civil rights laws specifically outlaw questions concerning the race, color, religion, gender, national origin, or age of an applicant. However, if the employer can offer no logical explanation for asking such questions, the EEOC and the Wage and Hour Administrator view such questions as discriminatory. Of course, prehire questions pertaining to religion, gender, national origin, or age are allowed when these factors are bona fide occupational qualifications for a job.

Asking an applicant's age or date of birth may tend to deter the older worker. Thus, if an application form calls for such information, a statement should appear on that form notifying the applicant that the ADEA prohibits discrimination on the basis of age with respect to individuals who are at least 40.

Reference Inquiry

Before employing an applicant, a company may check some of the references given on the application blank. Many businesses use a standard *reference inquiry form,* which is usually mailed to the person or company given as a reference. Other companies prefer a telephone reference check because they feel that a more frank opinion of the candidate is received over the telephone than in a letter. Some companies prefer not to check on personal references given by the job applicant, since these tend to be less objective than business references.

Today, any type of reference checking has taken on new meaning—expensive litigation. In most cases, respondents to these inquiries will verify dates of employment only, with no information on former employees' work habits. Because of this, many human resources departments give references only a cursory glance.

Some companies have made an "Employment Reference Release" part of the employment application. By signing the form, the applicant authorizes prior employers to release all information regarding employment with them, and the applicant releases the former employer from any legal liability for any damages that may result from the disclosure of this information.

The Fair Credit Reporting Act of 1968 subjects employers to certain disclosure obligations when they seek an *investigative consumer report* from a consumer reporting agency on a job applicant or in certain instances on present employees. An investigative consumer report usually contains information about the individual's character, general reputation, and mode of living. Generally, the employer must notify the applicant or the employee in writing that such a report is being sought. Also, the employer must notify the applicant or employee that he or she may request information from the employer about the nature and scope of the information sought. In the event employment is denied because of the consumer report information, the employer must inform the individual that this was the reason or part of the reason for denying employment. Also, the employer must furnish the applicant with the name and address of the consumer reporting agency that made the report.

Hiring Notice

After the successful applicant is notified of employment and the starting date, time, and to whom to report, a *hiring notice* is sent to the Payroll Department so that the new employee can be added properly to the payroll. A hiring notice such as that shown in Figure 1–6 usually gives the name, address, and telephone number of the new employee, the department in which employed, the starting date, the rate of pay, the number of withholding allowances claimed, and any other information pertaining to deductions that are to be made from the employee's wages.

Employee History Record

Although many businesses keep no personnel records other than the application blank, a need exists for a more detailed record such as the *employee history record,* which provides a continuous record of the relationship between the employer and the employee. The

FIGURE 1-6

Hiring Notice

HIRING NOTICE

NO. 220

SOCIAL SECURITY NO. 199-00-6357

DATE _____ June 28, 20--

NAME   Cheryl Crowson   CLOCK NO.   418

ADDRESS 1630 West End Ave., Huntington, WV ZIP   25703   PHONE NO.   555-1618

OCCUPATION   Payroll Clerk   DEPT. Accounting   GROUP NO.   --

STARTING DATE   July 1, 20--   TIME 8:00   A.M. / P.M.   RATE $24,000 yr.

MARRIED   SINGLE   x   BIRTH DATE 8/1/--

LAST EMPLOYMENT   Brennan Shipping Co.   LOCATION   Huntington, WV

DATE LEFT   June 30, 20--   REASON   Advancement

NO. OF WITHHOLDING ALLOWANCES   1

IN EMERGENCY NOTIFY   Robert Crowson   PHONE NO.   555-5136

EMPLOYEE'S SIGNATURE IN FULL   *Cheryl Crowson*

SUPERVISOR'S SIGNATURE   *Margaret T. Johnson*

EMPLOYMENT DEPARTMENT

ORIGINAL TO PAYROLL DEPT.
DUPLICATE RETAINED BY HUMAN RESOURCES DEPT.

---

employee history record, in addition to providing personal and other information usually found on an application blank, provides space to record the employee's progress, attendance, promotions, performance appraisals, and salary increases.

Change in Payroll Rate

The *change in payroll rate form* notifies the proper departments of a change in the employee's rate of remuneration. The change in rate may originate in the Human Resources Department or with the head of the department in which the employee works. In either event, the Payroll Department must be informed of the change for the employee so that the rate change is put into effect at the proper time and so that the records reflect the new rate. Figure 1–7 shows a form that may be used for this purpose.

PAYROLL ACCOUNTING SYSTEM

A *payroll accounting system* embodies all those procedures and methods related to the disbursement of pay to employees. A typical payroll accounting system includes the procedures shown in Figure 1–8 on page 1-21. The nature of the payroll records depends to a great extent on the size of the work force and the degree to which the recordkeeping is automated. This course describes and illustrates manual payroll accounting systems. Appendix A describes computerized payroll accounting systems, along with operating instructions for using the software available with this text. In most payroll systems—manual or automated—two basic records include the payroll register and the employee's earnings record.

IRS CONNECTION

In 2001, May 3 was the day on which the average American worker's income, since the beginning of the year, equaled the tax obligations to federal, state, and local governments. In other words, Americans spent 2 hours and 42 minutes of each working day laboring to pay taxes.

6 LEARNING OBJECTIVE

FIGURE 1-7

Change in Status Form

CHANGE OF STATUS

Please enter the following change(s) as of   January 1, 20--

Name Cheryl Crowson   Clock or Payroll No. 418   Soc. Sec. Number 199-00-6357

FROM

Job	Dept.	Shift	Rate
Payroll Clerk	Acct.	--	$24,000

TO

Job	Dept.	Shift	Rate
Accounting Clerk	Acct.	--	$25,000

REASON FOR CHANGE:

☐ Hired   ☐ Length of Serv. Increase
☐ Re-hired   ☐ Re-eval. of Existing Job
☒ Promotion   ☐ Resignation
☐ Demotion   ☐ Retirement
☐ Transfer   ☐ Layoff
☐ Merit Increase   ☐ Discharge
☐ Leave of Absence to _____
                                    Date

Other reason or explanation: _____
_____
_____

AUTHORIZED BY *Margaret T. Johnson* APPROVED BY *E. J. Dunn*

Prepare in triplicate: (1) Human Resources (2) Payroll (3) Employee's Department

---

LEARNING OBJECTIVE 7

Payroll Register

The *payroll register* is a multicolumn form used to assemble and summarize the data needed at the end of each payroll period. It provides a detailed listing of a company's complete payroll for that particular pay period. Thus, the payroll register lists all the employees who earned remuneration, the amount of remuneration, the deductions, and the net amount paid. The information provided in the payroll register is used primarily to meet the requirements of the Fair Labor Standards Act. However, the register also provides information for recording the payroll entries in the journal and for preparing reports required by other federal, state, and local laws. Figure 1–9 shows one form of payroll register. Another form, used in the Continuing Payroll Problem at the end of Chapters 2 through 6, is shown in the fold-out at the back of this book. Chapter 6 presents further discussion of the payroll register.

Employee's Earnings Record

In addition to the information contained in the payroll register, businesses must provide more complete information about the accumulated earnings of each employee. For that reason, it is necessary to keep a separate payroll record on each employee—the **employee's earnings record.** Each payday, after the information has been recorded in the payroll register, the information for each employee is transferred, or posted, to the employee's earnings record. The employee's earnings record provides the information needed to prepare periodic reports required by the withholding tax laws, the FICA tax law, and state unemployment or disability laws. Employers also use the employee's earnings record in preparing **Form W-2, Wage and Tax Statement.** This form shows the amount of wages paid each

F I G U R E   1 - 8

Procedures in a Payroll Accounting System

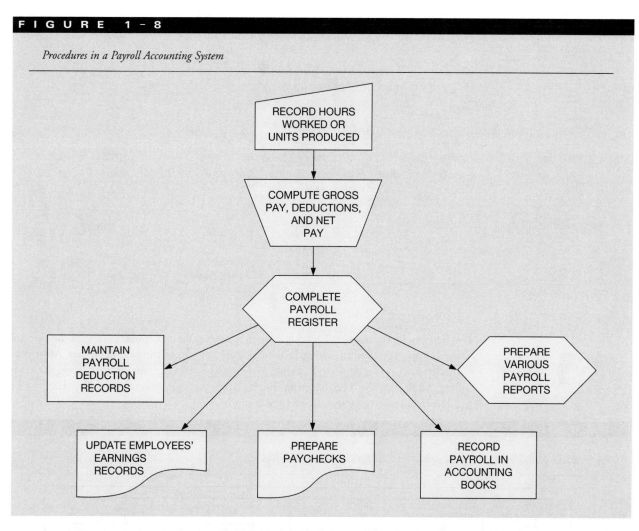

F I G U R E   1 - 9

Payroll Register

PAYROLL REGISTER

FOR WEEK ENDING   **January 19**   20 - -

No.	Name	Total Hours Worked	Regular Earnings			Overtime Earnings			Total Earnings	Deductions				Net Paid	
			Hrs.	Rate	Amount	Hrs.	Rate	Amount		OASDI Tax	HI Tax	Fed. Income Tax	State Income Tax	Check No.	Amount
1 403	*Springs, Carl A.*	40	40	7.75	310.00				310.00	19.22	4.50	34.00	9.05	504	243.23
2 409	*Wiegand, Sue T.*	42	40	7.20	288.00	2	10.80	21.60	309.60	19.20	4.49	12.00	7.30	505	266.61
3 412	*O'Neill, John B.*	38	38	9.10	345.80				345.80	21.44	5.01	16.00	8.91	506	294.44
4 413	*Bass, Marie S.*	44	40	8.80	352.00	4	13.20	52.80	404.80	25.10	5.87	47.00	12.75	507	314.08
5 418	*Crowson, Cheryl*	41	40	S	480.77	1	18.03	18.03	498.80	30.93	7.23	52.00	16.34	508	392.30
47	*Totals*				3,895.75			317.20	4,212.95	261.20	61.09	808.00	224.24		2,858.42

worker in the course of the trade or business of the employer. Figure 1–10 shows an example of the employee's earnings record. Chapter 6 presents a more detailed discussion of the preparation and use of the earnings record.

FIGURE 1-10

Employee's Earning Record

EMPLOYEE'S EARNINGS RECORD

Week	Week Ending	Total Hours Worked	Regular Earnings			Overtime Earnings			Total Earnings	Deductions				Net Paid		Cumulative Earnings
			Hrs.	Rate	Amount	Hrs.	Rate	Amount		OASDI Tax	HI Tax	Fed. Income Tax	State Income Tax	Check No.	Amount	
1	1/5	40	40	S	480.77				480.77	29.81	6.97	51.00	15.94	419	377.05	480.77
2	1/12	42	40	S	480.77	2	18.03	36.06	516.83	32.04	7.49	55.00	17.14	463	405.16	997.60
3	1/19	41	40	S	480.77	1	18.03	18.03	498.80	30.93	7.23	52.00	16.34	508	392.30	1,496.40

Sex	Department	Occupation	State Employed	S.S.No.	Name—Last First Middle	No. W/H Allow.
F M √	Accounting	Accounting Clerk (A)	West Virginia	199-00-6357	Crowson, Cheryl	1
						Marital Status S

Paycheck

When employees are paid by check, a check is written for each worker, using as the amount of net pay that figure appearing in the Net Paid column of the payroll register. Most paychecks, such as that depicted in Figure 1–11, carry a stub, or voucher, that shows the earnings and deductions. The following chapter covers paying workers in cash, by check, or by means of an electronic transfer of payroll funds.

FIGURE 1-11

Paycheck with Stub Showing Current and Year-to-Date Earnings and Deductions

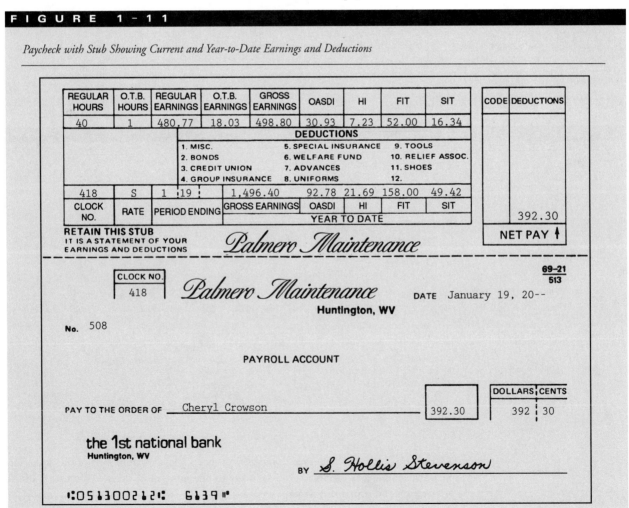

Payroll Accounting 2003 The Need for Payroll and Personnel Records 1-23

KEY TERMS

Application form *(p. 1-15)*
Change in payroll rate form *(p. 1-19)*
Disability benefits *(p. 1-14)*
Employee history record *(p. 1-18)*
Employee's earnings record *(p. 1-20)*
Executive orders *(p. 1-9)*
Fair employment practices *(p. 1-8)*
Form W-2, Wage and Tax Statement *(p. 1-20)*
401(k) plan *(p. 1-11)*
Hiring notice *(p. 1-18)*
Human resources system *(p. 1-14)*
Income tax *(p. 1-7)*

Individual retirement account (IRA) *(p. 1-12)*
Investigative consumer report *(p. 1-18)*
Payroll accounting system *(p. 1-19)*
Payroll register *(p. 1-20)*
Prehire inquiries *(p. 1-15)*
Reference inquiry form *(p. 1-18)*
Requisition for personnel *(p. 1-15)*
Section 403(b) plan *(p. 1-12)*
Section 457 plan *(p. 1-12)*
Simple plans *(p. 1-12)*
Unemployment insurance taxes *(p. 1-8)*
Vesting *(p. 1-10)*
Workers' compensation insurance *(p. 1-13)*

MATCHING QUIZ

_____ 1. Employee's earnings record

_____ 2. Payroll register

_____ 3. Executive orders

_____ 4. 401(k) plan

_____ 5. Individual retirement account

_____ 6. Unemployment insurance taxes

_____ 7. Vesting

_____ 8. Disability benefits

_____ 9. Income tax

_____ 10. Hiring notice

A. Method of deferring compensation on an elective, pre-tax basis

B. Record used in preparing employee's W-2

C. Protection against losses due to work-related injuries

D. Multicolumn form used to summarize data needed each paydate

E. Levy on earnings of most employees and deducted from their gross pay

F. Anti-discrimination orders for employers with contracts involving federal funds

G. Form sent to Payroll Department so that new employee is added to the payroll

H. Pension plan established by an individual employee

I. Levied by both the federal and state governments

J. Conveys to employees the right to share in a retirement fund

QUESTIONS FOR REVIEW

1. Under the FLSA, what information concerning employees' wages earned must be maintained by the employer?
2. Which act sets the minimum wage, and what is the current wage rate?
3. Who pays the social security taxes that are levied by the Federal Insurance Contributions Act?
4. How are the funds used which are provided by FUTA and SUTA?
5. What types of unfair employment practices are prohibited by the Civil Rights Act of 1964 as amended?
6. What is the purpose of the Age Discrimination in Employment Act (ADEA)?
7. Who is covered by the Walsh-Healey Public Contracts Act?
8. Explain the concept of vesting.
9. What is the maximum amount of tax-free contributions that an eligible employee can place in his or her IRA account each year?
10. What conditions must apply in order for an employer to be exempt from ERISA coverage for employee payroll deductions for individual retirement accounts (IRA)?
11. Under a salary reduction agreement (401-k plan), what is the taxability status (federal income and social security) for the amounts contributed by the employees?
12. What penalties are imposed for employing an unauthorized alien?
13. Under the Family and Medical Leave Act, what is the maximum number of weeks of unpaid leave that a covered employer is required to offer an employee whose spouse is seriously ill?
14. Summarize the procedure that may be followed by the Human Resources Department in hiring new employees.
15. What kinds of information are commonly provided by the jobseeker on the application for employment form?
16. What is the significance of the Civil Rights Act of 1964 and the Age Discrimination in Employment Act in the employer's use of prehire inquiries?
17. What obligations are imposed upon the employer by the Fair Credit Reporting Act of 1968?
18. What procedures are usually included in a typical payroll accounting system?
19. What two basic records are generated in most payroll accounting systems?
20. What uses are made of the information shown in the employee's earnings record?

QUESTIONS FOR DISCUSSION

1. What personnel records would you suggest for a small retailer with three employees?
2. What kind of problem can be encountered when requesting references from previous employers of job applicants?
3. In staffing their offices, some firms encourage in-house referrals (recommendations of their present employees). What are some possible objections to this practice as a means of obtaining job applicants? What advantages may be realized by the firm that uses in-house referrals?
4. The main office of a large bank has an annual turnover of 500 office workers. As an employment officer of this bank, discuss the sources you would use in obtaining replacement employees.
5. Among the questions asked on the application for employment form of Horner Company are the following:
   a. What is the name of your church and what religious holidays do you observe?
   b. What is the name of your birthplace?
   c. Are you a citizen of the United States?
   d. What foreign languages can you read, write, or speak fluently?
   In view of federal and state civil rights laws, do you believe that Horner Company is acting legally or illegally in asking each of the questions listed above?

CASE PROBLEM

C1. Paychecks Kept Coming.

Ken, a salaried employee, was terminated from his company in April of this year. Business had been slow since the beginning of the year, and each of the operating plants had laid off workers.

Ken's dismissal was processed through the Human Resources Department, but the information was not relayed to the corporate payroll office.

As had been the policy, checks for workers at remote sites were mailed to the employees. The mailing of Ken's checks continued for the next four weekly paydays. It wasn't until the monthly payroll reports were sent to Ken's supervisor that the error was detected.

Ken refused to return the four extra checks. What actions should the company take?[4]

Net activities

URLS are subject to change. Please visit the Bieg Payroll Accounting Web site: http://bieg.swcollege.com for updates.

1. The American Payroll Association uses the Computer Adaptive Technologies and Assessment Systems Inc. (CAT ASI) testing service for the Fundamental Payroll Certification (FPC) exam and the Certified Payroll Professional (CPP) exam.

   http://www.americanpayroll.org/
   http://www.asisvcs.com/

   Go to http://www.asisvcs.com and find the following information:
   a. What are the eligibility requirements for sitting for the Fundamental Payroll Certification (FPC) exam?
   b. What additional requirements are needed to sit for the Certified Payroll Professional (CPP) exam?
   c. What should a student study before taking the FPC exam?
   d. Where is the closest exam center for the Fundamental Payroll Certification (FPC) exam in your area?
   e. When must you register for the exam?

2. Go to http://www4.law.cornell.edu/uscode/ and type "sex age employment" in the search engine. Under what conditions may an employer pay different wages to employees of opposite sex?

3. Go to http://www.google.com/ and type "civil rights act of 1964" in the search engine. Find an appropriate link that assists you in answering the following questions:
   a. What does discrimination mean to you personally?
   b. What does discrimination mean according to the law?
   c. Discuss a circumstance where you or someone you know was discriminated against.

4. Go to a search engine and type in "illegal employment questions."

   http://www.google.com/
   http://www.ask.com/

   a. List five examples of illegal employment questions.
   b. Why do you think these questions are or are not legal to ask prospective employees?
   c. Have you ever been asked an illegal question when applying for employment? If so, did you answer it? Why or why not?

5. Why does a payroll system need security or controls? List three controls that you would want to have on your payroll system.

   http://www.umn.edu/ohr/payroll/internc.pdf

---

4 Reprinted with permission from *Payroll Guide Newsletter.* Volume 60, No. 21, Copyright © 2001 by Research Institute of America, 395 Hudson Street, New York, NY 10014. All rights reserved.

Who is an employee? What is considered time worked? What is

overtime, and how do we calculate it? Who is exempt? In this

Computing and Paying
Wages and Salaries

chapter we will discuss in detail

the law that affects the determi-

nation of gross pay.

So get out your calculators—we are ready to take the first

step in computing each employee's payroll check.

2

© Getty Images, Inc./Photodisc

AFTER STUDYING THIS CHAPTER, YOU SHOULD BE ABLE TO:

1. Explain the major provisions of the Fair Labor Standards Act.

2. Distinguish between the employees' *principal* activities and their *preliminary* and *postliminary* activities.

3. Describe the main types of records used to collect payroll data.

4. Perform the following computations:
   (a) Convert weekly wage rates to hourly wage rates.
   (b) Convert monthly and annual salary rates to hourly rates.
   (c) Compute regular earnings and overtime earnings to arrive at total gross earnings.
   (d) Compute overtime payments for pieceworkers using two different methods.
   (e) Compute earnings under incentive and commission plans.

5. Describe how wages are paid using (a) cash, (b) check, and (c) electronic transfer of funds.

LEARNING
OBJECTIVES

This chapter examines the major provisions of the Fair Labor Standards Act, how to determine hours worked by employees, commonly used methods to record time worked, the major methods of computing salaries and wages, and the methods of paying employees. Tracing its origin back to the 1930s, the Fair Labor Standards Act is the most encompassing of all the labor laws. However, it is also the one most violated.

THE FAIR LABOR STANDARDS ACT

The Fair Labor Standards Act (FLSA), commonly known as the Federal Wage and Hour Law, contains provisions and standards concerning minimum wages, equal pay for equal work regardless of sex, overtime pay, recordkeeping, and child labor. The Wage and Hour Division of the U.S. Department of Labor administers the act.

Coverage

The FLSA provides for two bases of coverage—enterprise coverage and individual employee coverage.

Enterprise Coverage.   *Enterprise coverage* includes all employees of an enterprise if:

1. At least two employees engage in interstate commerce or produce goods for interstate commerce. Interstate commerce refers to the trade, transportation, or communication among several states or between a state and any place outside that state. The law also covers employees if they handle, sell, or otherwise work on goods or materials that have been moved in or produced for interstate commerce, and
2. The business has annual gross sales of at least $500,000.

Coverage extends, *without regard to annual sales volume,* to those who operate:

1. A hospital.
2. A nursing home.
3. An institution for the mentally ill.
4. A school for mentally or physically handicapped or gifted children.
5. A preschool, elementary, or secondary school.
6. An institution of higher education.
7. A public agency.

The enterprise coverage under the FLSA does not apply to family establishments, often referred to as "mom and pop stores." Thus, if the only regular employees of an establishment include the owner, parent, spouse, child, or other immediate family members, the establishment is exempt from FLSA coverage.

Individual Employee Coverage.   Under *individual employee coverage,* the FLSA covers a worker if the employee either engages in interstate commerce or produces goods for such commerce. Coverage also includes employment in a fringe occupation closely related and directly essential to the production of goods for interstate commerce. Coverage depends on the activities of the individual employee and not on the work of fellow employees, the nature of the employer's business, or the character of the industry as a whole. Thus, even though a business does not meet the enterprise coverage test, it must pay FLSA wages to those workers eligible for individual coverage.

LEARNING OBJECTIVE

on the
JOB
A National Call Center has been established by the Department of Labor to answer employees' and employers' questions on a range of employment issues. The toll-free number is 1-866-4-USA-DOL.

on the
Net
http://www.dol.gov/dol/esa/
U.S. Department of Labor Employment Standards Administration homepage. This site contains various codes sections, such as affirmative action and workers' compensation. To find the most useful information, choose the ESA program that interests you, and then choose the "Statutory and Regulatory" option.

EXAMPLE

James Rineheart works for a small manufacturing firm that has an annual sales volume of $370,000. Although the firm does not meet the $500,000 volume-of-sales requirement for enterprise coverage, Rineheart is *individually* covered since he operates machinery used to produce goods for interstate commerce.

Employer

The FLSA defines an employer as "any person acting directly or indirectly in the interest of an employer" in relation to an employee. In order to protect employees, courts have defined "employers" in the broadest sense. Co-owners who control the day-to-day operations of the business are employers who are individually liable for violations of the law.

Employee

An individual is an *employee* if he or she performs services in a covered employment. As long as the common-law relationship of employer and employee exists and the employment is not exempt from the provisions of the law, both are covered and must observe its provisions. No differentiation is made between regular, temporary, substitute, or part-time workers.

A *common-law relationship* of employer and employee exists when the employer has the right to control both what work will be done and how it will be done. How the relationship is labeled is immaterial; it is the substance of the relationship that governs the worker's status.

To determine if a worker may be classified as an employee and if the employer has the right to control, the Internal Revenue Service uses a test based on behavioral control, financial control, and the relationship between the worker and the employer.

The three-prong "ABC test" defines an independent contractor as one who:

1. is free of direction and control in the performance of the work.
2. performs services outside the usual course of business of the company that has hired the contractor.
3. customarily engages in an independent occupation.

IRS CONNECTION

If you want the IRS to determine whether a worker is an employee, file **Form SS-8, Determination of Employee Work Status** for purposes of Federal Employment Taxes and Income Tax Withholding.

Employees of a Corporation.   Managers, superintendents, supervisors, department heads, and other executives of a corporation are considered employees under the FICA tax law. All officers, such as the president, vice president, secretary, and treasurer, are also employees of the corporation. Their salaries are taxable the same as the wages paid to other employees. A director of a corporation who performs no services other than attending and participating in meetings of the board of directors is not an employee.

Partnerships.   Partners generally are not employees of the partnership. In some cases, however, a partnership may operate as an association that may be classified as a corporation. In such situations, any partner who renders services similar to those of corporate officers would be an employee.

Statutory Nonemployees.   There are two categories of statutory nonemployees—direct sellers and licensed real estate agents. For federal tax purposes, they are considered to be self-employed as long as their earnings are based on the amount of sales and their services are performed under a written contract stating that they will not be treated as employees for federal tax purposes.

on the

J O B

Today nearly 25 percent of the workforce (35 million workers) is made up of temporary workers, consultants, and independent contractors.

Domestics.   Domestic workers also must be paid the minimum wage if:

1. They perform services in one or more homes for a total of more than 8 hours in any workweek, *or if*
2. They earn wages of at least $1,000 from an employer in a calendar year.

Domestic service consists of services of a household nature performed in or about a private home of the person who employs the domestic. Some typical domestics include cooks, butlers, maids, caretakers, gardeners, and chauffeurs. The term also includes a baby sitter employed on other than a casual basis, such as a person who sits for a child five days a week. If the domestics do not live in the household, they must be paid overtime compensation as well as the minimum wage. However, live-in domestics do not have to be paid overtime. A casual baby sitter (one employed on an irregular or intermittent basis) or a companion for the aged or infirm is not covered.

Wages

Wages include the remuneration or compensation paid employees. The terms wages and salaries are commonly used interchangeably. However, *wage* usually refers to remuneration paid on an hourly, weekly, or piecework basis. *Salary* usually refers to the remuneration paid on a monthly, *biweekly* (every two weeks), *semimonthly* (twice a month), or yearly basis.

The Minimum Wage

The FLSA of 1938 established a minimum wage of 25¢ per hour for a straight-time workweek of 44 hours. With the objective of improving the purchasing power of covered workers, succeeding amendments to the FLSA increased the minimum hourly rate and reduced the workweek. As of September 1, 1997, the minimum hourly wage was increased to its current rate of $5.15 and provides overtime pay for hours worked over 40 in a week.

There is also a provision for a training wage that allows employers to pay $4.25 per hour to newly hired employees under 20 years of age (opportunity wage). This only applies to the first 90 calendar days of employment.

Included in the regular rate of pay is all renumeration for employment paid to or on behalf of the employee. Some examples are:

1. Commission payments.
2. Earned bonuses.
3. Severance pay.
4. On-call pay.
5. Shift or weekend differentials.

The law also allows employers to credit the reasonable cost of housing, meals, and transportation to work that they provide towards payment of the minimum wage. To qualify, these facility credits must be furnished for the employer's benefit and must be accepted voluntarily by the employee.

Gifts paid to employees are not included in the employees' regular rate of pay as long as the amounts paid are not dependent on hours worked, production, or efficiency. Even the regular payment of a special-occasion bonus can still qualify as a gift payment. However, if the payment is so substantial that employees consider it part of the wages for which they work, the bonus is not considered a gift.

Paying Less Than the Minimum Wage

Under certain conditions, wages lower than the minimum wage may be paid to some employees.

1. Retail or service establishments and farms may employ full-time students at 85% of the minimum wage ($4.38 per hour).
2. Institutions of higher education may employ their own full-time students at 85% of the minimum wage.
3. Student-learners may be employed at 75% of the minimum wage if they are participating in a bona fide vocational training program conducted by an accredited school ($3.86 per hour).
4. Persons whose earning capacity is impaired by age, physical or mental deficiency, or injury may be employed at special minimum wage rates. However, a certificate authorizing employment at such rates must first be obtained.

on the JOB
The highest state minimum wage is $6.90 per hour, recognized by Washington.

on the JOB
Around 5 percent of the workers in the United States are paid the minimum wage rate.

SELF-STUDY QUIZ 2-1 *Indicate which of the following statements regarding the Fair Labor Standards Act are false.*

_____ 1. Under the FLSA, wages include sales commissions and bonuses paid for employee performance.

_____ **2.** Domestic workers must always be paid overtime compensation in addition to the minimum wage.

_____ **3.** A son working for his parents in a family-owned business is not covered under the FLSA.

_____ **4.** Individual employee coverage under the FLSA applies only if fellow employees are engaged in similar activities.

_____ **5.** A college may pay its own full-time students less than the minimum wage.

Note: Answers at back of book.

Paying a "Living Wage"

A growing number of cities have enacted local ordinances to require employers who do business with the government to pay a "living wage" to their low-wage workers. The movement, started by local advocates, grew out of the failure to keep the national minimum wage on pace with the needs of the working poor. Over 40 cities and counties have enacted such wage laws over the last five years.

E X A M P L E

Some of the cities that have instituted this living wage are Baltimore, Boston, and Los Angeles. Each city applies the law to different workers and applies different "living wage" rates.[1]

Tips

A *tip* (to insure promptness) is a gift or gratuity given by a customer in recognition of some service performed for him or her. A *tipped employee* is one who engages in an occupation in which tips of more than $30 a month are customarily and regularly received. Chapter 3 presents the rules for the reporting of tips by employees. An employer may consider, within prescribed limits, the tips received by a tipped employee as part of the employee's wages. In 1996, the Small Business Job Protection Act froze the minimum cash wage required for tipped employees at $2.13 per hour. Tips received by the employee are credited toward the remainder ($3.02) of the total minimum wage ($5.15 less $2.13). If tips received do not amount to at least $3.02 per hour, the employer must increase the hourly rate of pay so that the hourly wage plus the equivalent hourly rate of tips received equal, at a minimum, $5.15 per hour.

A L E R T

According to the Bureau of Labor Statistics, waiters and waitresses held the lowest-paid jobs. Including *reported* tips, the average yearly pay amounted to $13,430.

E X A M P L E

Bill Bixley, a waiter, earns a weekly wage of $90.00 for a 40-hour workweek and receives tips of $100.00 each week. Even though the hourly rate paid to Bixley ($90.00 ÷ 40 hours = $2.25) exceeds the minimum wage rate of $2.13, the employer must pay Bixley an extra $16.00 so that the tips received plus the wages paid equal the minimum wage of $5.15 per hour.

$5.15 × 40 =	$206.00
Weekly wage	(90.00)*
Tips received	(100.00)
Extra weekly pay	$ 16.00*

*90.00 + 16.00 = 106.00; 106.00 ÷ 40 hours = $2.65/hour

SELF-STUDY QUIZ 2–2. *Marion Yeld, a waitress, earns $85.20 a week for a 40-hour workweek. During one week, Yeld received tips of $90.*

1. What hourly rate is being paid to Yeld?

$_____

2. How much must the employer pay Yeld in addition to her $85.20 weekly wage?

$_____

---

1 "Minimum Wages, City by City," *The New York Times,* November 19, 1999, Section C, p. 1.

Workweek

The FLSA defines a *workweek* as a fixed and regularly recurring period of 168 hours—seven consecutive 24-hour periods. The individual employee's workweek is the statutory or contract number of hours to be worked regularly during that period. The workweek may begin on any day of the week and need not coincide with the calendar week. An employer may establish the same workweek for the business operations as a whole or assign different workweeks to individual workers or groups of workers.

An employer may change the day a workweek begins if intended to be a permanent change and not just to evade the overtime pay requirements of the FLSA. If, however, a union contract fixes the workweek, the employer's right to change the workweek depends upon the wording in the contract. Each workweek stands alone, and the overtime hours worked in one week may not be shifted to another workweek. Thus, each workweek is a separate unit for the purpose of computing overtime pay.

Overtime Hours and Overtime Pay. The FLSA requires overtime pay for all hours worked in excess of 40 in a workweek. The FLSA requires no overtime pay for daily hours worked in excess of any given number or for work on Saturdays, Sundays, holidays, or other special days. The law requires overtime pay to be one and one-half times the employee's regular hourly rate of pay, which must not be less than the statutory minimum.

With some restrictions, employees covered under FLSA can be required by their employers to work overtime. If they refuse, they can be fired under the law. There is also no limit on the overtime that can be required. However, in these cases, the state laws may be the governing force.

EXAMPLE

If an employee's regular rate of pay is $5.40 an hour, the overtime rate must be at least $5.40 × 1.5, or $8.10 an hour.

If an hourly-rate employee works in pay periods of two weeks or longer, the employer can elect to give the employee 1.5 hours off for every overtime hour. However, the time off must be in the same pay period as the overtime hours worked. In case of overtime hours for tipped employees, the tip credit that the employer takes ($5.15 − $2.13 = $3.02) remains the same for overtime hours. Therefore, for overtime hours, the tipped employee must be paid at one and one-half times the minimum wage rate ($5.15) less the tip credit ($3.02). This results in an overtime pay rate of $4.71 per hour ($7.73 − $3.02).

In cases where an employee works at different rates for different jobs during the same workweek, the employers can, at their option, calculate the overtime in one of two ways. (1) It may be calculated by taking the total earnings for both jobs, dividing by the total hours worked, then taking one-half of this rate, and multiplying by the overtime hours. (2) Or one could use an overtime rate based on the rate for the job performed after the 40th hour (the employee must have agreed to this in advance).

EXAMPLE

Robert Biester worked at two different pay rates during the past week. His main job paid $17.30/hour, while the extra job rate was $20.50. He worked the first 36 hours at Job "A" and 8 hours at Job "B."

Method (1)

Regular earnings	$622.80 (36 × $17.30)
Job B	$164.00 (8 × $20.50)
Overtime rate (1/2)	$ 8.94 ($786.80 ÷ 44 × 1/2)
Extra overtime pay	$ 35.76 (4 × $8.94)
Total pay	$822.56 ($622.80 + $164.00 + $35.76)

Method (2)

Job A .... $622.80 (36 × $17.30)
Job B .... $164.00 (8 × $20.50)
Overtime pay (Job B) .... $ 41.00 (4 × $10.25)
Total pay .... $827.80 ($622.80 + $164.00 + $41.00)

Exceptions to Overtime Hours and Overtime Pay Provisions. An exception to overtime hours and overtime pay applies to *hospital employees*. Hospitals may enter into an agreement with their employees under which a 14-day period, rather than a workweek, becomes the basis for computing overtime pay. Employees entering such an agreement must receive overtime pay at not less than one and one-half times their regular hourly rate for hours worked in excess of 8 hours in any workday or in excess of 80 hours in a 14-day period, whichever is the greater number of overtime hours. Although employers have the option of using the normal workweek or the 14-day period, they cannot change from one method to the other arbitrarily.

Pam Valenti, a lab technician, agreed that a 14-day period would be used to figure her overtime pay. Valenti works 12 hours in one day during the period and 8 hours in each of the 9 other days during the period, a total of 84 hours.

Valenti is entitled to 80 hours of straight-time pay and 4 hours of overtime pay for the 14-day period.

If Valenti worked only 7 hours in each of the 9 other days during the period, or a total of 75 hours, she would be entitled to 71 hours of straight-time pay and 4 hours of overtime pay for the 14-day period.

Employees in retail or service industries are exempt from the overtime provisions as long as their regular weekly rate of pay, including commissions, is at least one and one-half times the federal minimum wage rate and more than half of their pay over a monthly period comes from commissions. Minimum wage legislation also provides an exception for *employees receiving remedial education*. Under this law, employees who receive remedial education offered by their employers are permitted to work up to 10 hours overtime each week without receiving overtime compensation. The remedial training, which does not include training for a specific job, must be designed to provide reading and other basic skills at an eighth-grade level or below.

Compensatory Time Off. A state, a political subdivision of a state, or an interstate governmental agency may grant employees compensatory time off in lieu of overtime compensation. Employees working in public safety, emergency response, or seasonal activities may accumulate compensatory time off up to 480 hours. (The 480-hour limit represents 320 hours of overtime actually worked at the one and one-half overtime rate.) Employees may "bank" their hours and use them later as time off at time and one-half during the course of their employment.

Employees whose work does not include the preceding activities may bank 240 hours for compensatory time off. Upon reaching the 480- or 240-hour limit, an employee must receive either cash for additional hours of overtime worked or use some compensatory time before receiving further overtime compensation in the form of compensatory time off. Note that not all 480 or 240 hours have to be accrued before compensatory time off may be used. The FLSA also provides for the payment of cash for unused comp time when the employee terminates employment.

Support is growing for plans that would change the 40-hour workweek to a two-week, 80-hour schedule or a four-week, 160-hour schedule. These plans also propose allowing employees to exchange overtime pay for compensatory time off.

Equal Pay Act

The Equal Pay Act amended the FLSA to require that men and women performing equal work receive equal pay. The Equal Pay Law applies to any employer having workers subject to the minimum pay provisions of the Wage and Hour Law. The equal-pay requirements also apply to white-collar workers and outside salespersons, even though they are exempt from the minimum wage standards.

The Equal Pay Law prohibits an employer from discriminating by paying wages to employees of one sex at a lower rate than those paid the opposite sex for equal work on jobs that require equal skill, effort, and responsibility and that are performed under similar working conditions. However, wage differentials between sexes are allowable if based on a seniority system, a merit system, a payment plan that measures earnings by quantity or quality of production, or any factor other than sex. If an unlawful pay differential between men and women exists, the employer must raise the lower rate to equal the higher rate.

Exemptions from FLSA Requirements

Exempt employees (see Figure 2–1) are those workers exempt from some, or all, of the FLSA requirements such as minimum wages, equal pay, and overtime pay.

White-Collar Workers. The FLSA exempts some workers, such as executives, administrators, professional employees, and outside salespersons, from the minimum wage and overtime pay provisions if they satisfy certain tests.

Test of Exemption. To be eligible for this exemption, the employee must be paid on *a salary basis,* must be paid at least $250 per week, and must meet the "primary duty" requirements as listed in Figure 2–2. Employees paid by the hour are not exempt from the minimum wage and overtime pay requirements and thus do not qualify for the salary test even if their total weekly compensation exceeds the limits specified.

Highly Skilled Computer Professionals. Employees highly skilled in computer systems analysis, programming, or related work in software functions may be exempt from the minimum wage and overtime requirements. Some of the job titles in this exemption include:

- computer programmer
- systems analyst
- applications programmer
- applications systems analyst
- software engineer
- software specialist
- systems engineer

The exemption does not apply to workers who operate computers or manufacture, repair, or maintain computer hardware and related equipment. To be exempt from the overtime requirements, the computer professional must be paid:

1. On an hourly basis.
2. At a rate greater than $27.63 per hour.

A *salaried* computer professional may qualify for exemption as a *professional* and thus also be exempt from the overtime requirements, provided the employee:

1. Earns at least $170 a week.
2. Meets the other requirements of a professional as shown in Figure 2–2 on page 2-12.

Salary Basis. These white-collar employees must be paid their full salary in any week in which any work is performed without regard to the number of days or hours worked. However, deductions can be made from the salary if an exempt employee misses one or

FIGURE 2-1

Exemption Status of Workers Under FLSA

Employee Job Description	Minimum Wage Exemption	Equal Pay Exemption	Full Overtime Exemption
Agricultural employees.			X
Agricultural workers who are members of the employer's immediate family.	X	X	X
Air carrier employees if the carrier is subject to Title II of the Railway Labor Act.			X
Amusement or recreational establishment employees, provided the business has seasonal peaks.	X	X	X
Announcers, news editors, and chief engineers of radio or television stations in small communities.			X
Baby sitters (casual) and companions to ill or aged persons unable to care for themselves.	X	X	X
Drivers and drivers' helpers who make local deliveries and are paid on a trip-rate or similar basis following a plan approved by the government.			X
Executive, administrative, and professional employees including teachers and academic administrative personnel in schools.	X		X
Fruit and vegetable employees who are engaged in the local transportation of these items or of workers employed or to be employed in the harvesting of fruits or vegetables.			X
Household domestic service employees who reside in the household.			X
Motion picture theater employees.			X
Motor carrier employees if the carrier is subject to regulation by the Secretary of Transportation.			X
Newspaper employees if the newspaper is published on a weekly, semiweekly, or daily basis and if the circulation is less than 4,000 copies, with the major circulation in the county of publication or contiguous counties.	X	X	X
Railroad, express company, and water carrier employees if the companies are subject to Part I of the Interstate Commerce Act.			X
Salespersons for automobile, truck, or farm implement dealers; parts stock clerks or mechanics; salespersons for boat, trailer, or aircraft dealers.			X
Taxicab drivers.			X

more full days of work for personal reasons, other than sickness or accident. If the employee does not qualify for the employer's sick pay plan or has used up all available sick time, deductions can also be made for these full-day absences.

A proportionate share of an exempt employee's salary for the time actually worked is allowed only for the employee's first or last week of employment.

Partial-day absences cannot be deducted from the exempt employee's salary. However, the Wage and Hour Division has stated that the employer can require the employee to use any accumulated leave time to offset the time absent.

FIGURE   2 - 2

Indications of Exempt Status

Executive	Administrative	Professional	Outside Sales

1. Primary duty—managing
2. Regularly uses discretionary powers
3. Authority to hire, fire, promote
4. Supervises two or more employees
5. No more than 20% for nonexempt work
6. No educational requirement
	1. Primary duty—performs office work
	2. Regularly uses independent judgment
	3. Work done under general supervision
	4. Assists directly an executive
	5. No more than 20% for nonexempt work
	6. No educational requirement
		1. Primary duty—one of the following:
		  • Exercises creativity in doing one's job
		  • Imparts knowledge
		  • Works on intellectual level
		2. Regularly uses independent judgment
		3. No more than 20% for nonexempt work
		4. Specialized degree
			1. Primary duty—sales work away from employer's place of business
			2. No more than 20% for nonselling work
			3. Commissions comprise majority of compensation

on the
JOB

The Department of Labor prohibits occupational driving for minors except on an occasional or incidental basis. Permitted driving can only be done during daylight hours and in vehicles not exceeding 6,000 pounds. In New York state, 16- and 17-year-olds are prohibited from driving in Manhattan.

Child-Labor Restrictions

The FLSA prohibits a business from the interstate shipment of its goods or services if it employs child labor unlawfully. Under the FLSA, the Secretary of Labor issues regulations that restrict the employment of individuals under the age of 18. The restrictions divide child employment into nonfarm occupations and agricultural occupations.

Nonfarm Occupations.   The basic minimum age for most jobs is 16 years. This is the minimum age for work in manufacturing and processing jobs or in any other occupations except those declared by the Secretary of Labor as hazardous for minors under 18. The FLSA lists 17 occupations that are considered too dangerous. These include mining, forestry, excavation, roofing work, operation of certain power-driven tools, and most on-the-job driving.

Within certain limits 14- and 15-year-olds may be employed in retail, food service, and gasoline service establishments. For example, this age group may be employed in office and clerical work, including the operation of office machines; cashiering; selling; price marking and tagging by hand or by machine; errand and delivery work, kitchen work and other work involved in preparing and serving food and beverages; dispensing gasoline and oil; and car cleaning. The employment of minors between the ages of 14 and 16 cannot interfere with their schooling, health, and well-being. In addition, the following conditions must be met.

1. All work must be performed outside school hours.
2. There is a maximum 3-hour day and 18-hour week when school is in session (8 hours and 40 hours when not in session).
3. All work must be performed between 7 a.m. and 7 p.m. (9 p.m. during the summer).

Agricultural Occupations.   The employment of children under age 12 is generally prohibited in agricultural occupations, as described below.

1. During hours when school is in session.
2. Outside school hours on farms, including conglomerates, that used more than 500 man-days of labor in any quarter of the preceding calendar year.
3. Outside school hours on noncovered farms without parental consent.

However, children may work on farms owned or operated by their parents or guardians. Children 10 and 11 years old can work as hand harvest laborers outside school hours for up to eight weeks between June 1 and October 15, with a number of strict conditions on the employer. Children aged 12 and 13 may be employed only during hours when school is not in session provided there is parental consent or the employment is on a farm where the parents are employed. Children aged 14 and 15 may be employed, but only during hours when school is not in session. No child under the age of 16 may be employed in a hazardous farm occupation, such as operating large tractors, corn pickers, cotton pickers, grain combines, and feed grinders.

Certificate of Age. Employers cannot be charged with having violated the child-labor restrictions of the law if they have on file an officially executed *certificate of age* which shows that the minor has reached the stipulated minimum age. In most states a state employment or age certificate, issued by the Federal Wage and Hour Division or by a state agency, serves as proof of age. In some states a state or federal certificate of age, a state employment certificate, or a work permit may not be available. In such cases, the employer may rely on any one of the following documents as evidence of age for minor employees.

1. Birth certificate (or attested transcript thereof) or a signed statement of the recorded date and place of birth issued by a registrar of vital statistics or other officer charged with the duty of recording births.
2. Record of baptism (or attested transcript thereof) showing the date of birth of the minor.
3. Statement on the census records of the Bureau of Indian Affairs and signed by an administrative representative thereof showing the name, date, and place of the minor's birth.

The employer should maintain a copy of the document or indicate in the payroll records which document verified the minor's age.

Penalties

The U.S. government may bring civil or criminal actions against employers who violate the FLSA. Employers who willfully violate the wage and hour provisions of the law or the wage orders fixed by the Administrator of the Wage and Hour Division of the Department of Labor will be prosecuted and will be subject to a fine of not more than $10,000, or imprisonment for up to six months, or both. However, no person may be imprisoned for a first offense violation. If an imposed fine goes unpaid, however, the courts have the power to order imprisonment as an incident to the nonpayment. Violators of the child-labor provisions of the Act are subject to fines of $10,000 for each violation. Payroll managers should read the Fair Labor Standards Act and its amendments very carefully.

Areas Not Covered by the FLSA

The FLSA does not require employers to:

1. Pay extra wages for work on Saturdays, Sundays, or holidays.
2. Pay for holidays, vacations, or severance.
3. Limit the number of hours or work for persons 16 years of age or over.
4. Give days off on holidays.
5. Grant vacation time.

DETERMINING EMPLOYEE'S WORK TIME

To avoid paying for time not actually spent on the job and to eliminate payment for unnecessary overtime work, employers must know what types of employee activities count as working time under the law. Generally, the hours counted as working time include all the time that employees actually work or must be on duty. A distinction must be made between an employee's principal activities and the preliminary and postliminary activities.

2 LEARNING OBJECTIVE

Principal Activities

The *principal activities* of employees include those tasks employees must perform and include any work of consequence performed for the employer. Principal activities include those indispensable to the performance of productive work and those that are an integral part of a principal activity.

EXAMPLE

Ted Jambro is a lathe operator who oils and cleans his machines at the beginning of each workday and installs new cutting tools. These activities performed by Jambro are part of his principal activity.

The test of compensability with respect to principal activities requires that there be physical or mental exertion, controlled or required by the employer and performed for the employer's benefit.

Clothes-Changing Time and Wash-Up. Because of the nature of their work, some employees change clothes or wash on the employer's premises. Statutes or ordinances may require clothes changing or washing. Employees who spend time changing clothes or washing on the employer's premises regard this time as part of their principal activities. However, even where the nature of the job or the law requires clothes changing or wash-up, it may be excluded from time worked either expressly or by custom and practice under a collective bargaining contract.

Travel Time. The time spent by employees in traveling to and from work needs to be counted as time worked only if contract, custom, or practice so requires. In some situations, however, travel time between home and work counts as time worked. If an employee who regularly works at a fixed location is given a special one-day work assignment in another city, time worked includes the travel time.

EXAMPLE

Lisa Rubini receives an emergency call outside regular working hours and must travel a substantial distance to perform a job away from Rubini's usual work site for one of the employer's customers. The travel time counts as time worked.

When performed during the workday as part of an employee's principal activities, the travel time counts as time worked.

EXAMPLE

Reba Ferguson travels throughout the city to various job sites during regular working hours, 9 a.m. to 5 p.m., Mondays through Fridays. Such travel time counts as work time.

When Ferguson travels between workdays from one city to another, the travel time counts as working time when the hours correspond to regular working hours, even though the hours may occur on Saturday and Sunday.

For example, if Ferguson is sent on a trip requiring travel on Saturday and Sunday to be at a job the first thing Monday morning, the travel time on Saturday and Sunday between the hours of 9 a.m. and 5 p.m. counts as time worked, but travel time before 9 a.m. and after 5 p.m. does not count.

Idle Time. Readiness to serve can also be considered employment. If the time spent while idle was primarily for the benefit of the employer, this time must be compensated. However, if workers are required to carry a beeper, pager, or cell phone, this on-call time is not compensable, provided they can use this time for their own purposes.

Rest Periods and Coffee Breaks. The FLSA does not require that an employer give employees a rest period or a coffee break. However, the employer may grant such rest periods voluntarily; or the union contract or municipal or state legislation may require them. In these cases, the time spent on a rest period of 20 minutes or less counts as part of the hours worked. If longer than 20 minutes, the compensability for the time depends upon the employee's freedom during that time or upon the provisions of the union contract.

Seven states currently mandate rest periods for private-sector employees. The general rest period is 10 to 15 minutes in the middle of each 4-hour period.

Meal Periods. Bona fide meal periods (not including coffee breaks or snack times) during which the employee is completely relieved from duty are not considered working time. Lunch periods during which the employee must perform some duties while eating are not bona fide meal periods.

on the **JOB**
The seven states mandating paid rest breaks are California, Colorado, Kentucky, Minnesota, Nevada, Oregon, and Washington.

on the **JOB**
Roughly 20 percent of U.S. office workers eat lunch at their desks every day.

EXAMPLE

Virginia Sherr, an office worker, must eat at her desk and operate the switchboard at lunch time. Sherr must be paid for the lunch period.

Sleep Time. If required to be on duty for less than 24 hours, the employee is considered to be working even though the employee is sleeping or engaging in other personal activities. If over 24 hours, an agreement to exclude a sleeping period of not more than eight hours from time worked is binding.

Training Sessions. Generally, working time includes the time spent by employees in attending lectures and meetings for training purposes.

EXAMPLE

The working time spent by postal clerks in learning mail distribution practices and the operation of letter sorting machines counts as compensable time because it is (a) controlled and required by the employer, (b) for the primary benefit of the employer, and (c) an integral and indispensable part of the employees' principal work activities.

However, time spent in training sessions need not be counted as working time if ALL the following conditions are met.

1. Attendance by the employee is voluntary.
2. The employee does not produce any goods or perform any other productive work during the meeting or lecture.
3. The meeting or lecture takes place outside regular working hours.
4. The meeting or lecture is not directly related to the employee's work.

Preliminary and Postliminary Activities

Activities regarded as *preliminary* and *postliminary* need not be counted as time worked unless required by contract or custom. Some examples of activities regarded as preliminary and postliminary include: walking, riding, or traveling to or from the actual place where employees engage in their principal activities; checking in and out at the plant or office and waiting in line to do so; changing clothes for the convenience of the employee, washing up and showering unless directly related to the specific type of work the employee is hired to perform; and waiting in line to receive paychecks.

Absences

The FLSA does not require an employer to pay an employee for hours not worked because of illness. For employees on an hourly wage basis, the time card shows the exact hours worked; and the time off for absences does not count toward the 40 hours for overtime pay purposes even if the employee is paid for the absences. Employees on a salary basis are frequently paid for a certain number of days of excused absences after they have been employed by their company for a certain length of time.

Tardiness

Employers may handle tardiness in many ways. Frequently when an employee is late or leaves early, causing the time clock to print in red, the supervisor must O.K. the time card. Some companies require the employee to sign a special slip indicating the reason for being late or leaving early. Some companies keep time according to the decimal system whereby each hour is divided into units of tens (6 minutes times 10 periods in each hour). An employee who is late 1 through 6 minutes is penalized or "docked" one-tenth of an hour. One who is 7 through 12 minutes late is "docked" one-fifth of an hour, etc.

RECORDS USED FOR TIMEKEEPING

LEARNING OBJECTIVE 3

The FLSA requires employers subject to the law to keep certain time and pay records. For example, employers must keep records that indicate the hours each employee worked each workday and each workweek.

Even though the 40-hour, 5-day workweek is the most common work schedule, the schedules of American workers have been changing and becoming increasingly diverse. To improve declining productivity, to decrease job dissatisfaction, and to reduce absenteeism, many firms have adopted alternative work schedules, such as compressed workweeks, staggered work schedules, job sharing, and telecommuting.

How the employer chooses the methods of keeping time records depends on the size of the company and whether employees are paid on an hourly, weekly, biweekly, semimonthly, or monthly basis. Employees on a salary basis usually work a given number of hours each day, generally on a definite schedule. Employees on an hourly wage basis may work a varying number of hours with some "down time" and layoffs and some overtime work. All of this time must be recorded in some way.

Time Sheets

A *time sheet* provides the information required by law and the data used to compute the payroll. Many small businesses that must keep a record of time worked by each employee require each person to sign a *time sheet,* indicating the times of arrival and departure from work. These time reports are approved by the appropriate supervisor or department head at the end of the pay period. They are then forwarded to the Payroll Department for entry into the payroll system. Time sheets offer a simple method of accumulating employees' working times.

Time Cards

Under this timekeeping system, each employee receives a *time card* on which the time worked is recorded manually by the employee or automatically by a time clock. The time card is designed to fit various lengths of pay periods. Figure 2–3 shows one type of time card frequently used for a weekly pay period. The card provides space to record the hours worked, the rate of pay, deductions, and net pay. The Payroll Department inserts the handwritten figures to be used in computing total earnings, deductions, and net pay for the payroll period.

Some time clocks use the *continental system* of recording time, where each day consists of one 24-hour period, instead of two 12-hour periods. The time runs from 12 midnight to 12 midnight. Eight o'clock in the morning is recorded as 800; eight o'clock in the evening, as 2000.

The number of time-clock stations used by an employer depends on the number of hourly employees, the number of employee entrances, etc. Usually, each station has a centrally located time clock with an *In rack* on one side and an *Out rack* on the other. Before employees report for work on Monday morning, a card for each employee is placed in the rack. A clock number identifies each slot in the rack, and the cards are arranged chrono-

F I G U R E   2 - 3

Time Card

| No. **312** | Pay Ending _October 17, 20--_ |

NAME GARY A. SCHNEIDER   262-09-7471

	Hours	Rate	Amount		DEDUCTIONS	OASDI		32	66
Reg.	40	10.75	430 00			HI		7	64
O/T	6	16.13	96 78			FIT		81	00
						SIT		10	54
						Group Life Ins.		1	60
						Hospital Ins.		3	15
Total Earnings			526 78			U.S. Sav. Bonds		5	00
Less Deductions			141 59			Other			
NET PAY			385 19			Total		141	59

Days	MORNING IN	MORNING OUT	AFTERNOON IN	AFTERNOON OUT	OVERTIME IN	OVERTIME OUT	Daily Totals
1	M 7 59	M 12 03	M 1 00	M 5 05			8
2	TU 7 50	TU 12 04	TU 12 59	TU 5 07			8
3	W 7 51	W 12 01	W 12 50	W 5 04	W 5 29	W 7 35	10
4	TH 8 00	TH 12 02	TH 12 58	TH 5 03			8
5	FR 8 00	FR 12 05	FR 1 01	FR 5 06			8
6	SA 7 55	SA 12 04					4
7							

Signature _Gary A. Schneider_

logically by clock number. Each employee's card shows the clock number, name of employee, and a record of the hours worked. The payroll clerk collects the time cards at the end of the week and computes the total hours worked, including regular and overtime, during the week.

Computerized Time and Attendance Recording Systems

The main kinds of computerized time and attendance recording systems include:

1. *Card-generated systems*—employees use time cards similar to the traditional time cards illustrated earlier. Daily and weekly totals are calculated and printed on the time cards for data entry into the firm's computer system.
2. *Badge systems*—employees are issued plastic laminated badges containing punched holes or having magnetic strips or bar codes. The badges are used with electronic time clocks that collect and store data, which later become input to the computer system.
3. *Cardless and badgeless systems*—employees enter only their personal identification numbers (PIN) on a numerical or alphanumerical key pad. This system, like the badge system, uses time clocks to collect and store data for transmission to and processing by the firm's computer system.

4. *Personal computer-based systems*—employees swipe their identification cards across bar code readers connected to personal computers for easy recording of time worked.

For example, the Timekeeper, a self-contained, wall-mounted time clock, contains a computer system.[2] This time clock accepts time and attendance data from time cards and computes complex payroll and on-the-job information. Time-clock systems, such as the Timekeeper, eliminate most manual payroll processing operations. Employees receive their own time cards that show their daily attendance record, thus complying with federal, state, and union regulations. The Timekeeper also totals employee hours and rounds out employee time to fractions of an hour in accordance with the payroll practice of the firm.

The Timekeeper card, shown in Figure 2–4, is similar to the time card illustrated previously. The mark-sense field at the bottom of the card identifies each employee or supervisor and authorizes access to and use of the Timekeeper.

When an employee places the card in the time clock, the computer scans the card, optically verifies the employee's number, and locates the last print line on the card. The time of entry is then printed on the next line. Simultaneously, the computer stores the punch-in time in the system's memory. When an employee punches out, the Timekeeper again verifies the employee's identification number and computes and rounds off the daily and cumulative payroll hours. Next, the actual punch-out time and the computed cumulative hours are printed on the card and stored within the Timekeeper for transmission to a computer for payroll processing. Figure 2–5 on page 2-20 charts a computerized time and attendance recording system.

Next Generation

With more and more employees working outside the traditional office environment, the time clock has not been able to keep up with most companies' needs for time and attendance information. Many companies have been forced to acquire more automated systems.

Touch-Screen Technology.   In this system, data can be collected and processed instantaneously. The system requires employees to punch in and out on touch-screen personal computers (PCs), which are connected to the company's main computer server. These touch-screen kiosks are also used to provide information back to the employee regarding the organization.

Internet.   Some web-based time accounting systems now allow employees to "clock" in and out via the Internet. Employees use passwords to log on to a secured web site. This site can also be used by the employees to check their hours worked, vacation time accrued, and messages from the Human Resources Department. This can also be accomplished through the use of mobile and wireless data collection devices (cell phones and Personal Digital Assistants). Without ever visiting their office, employees can enter time and labor information.

Biometrics.   The need for greater security and precision has recently produced a more affordable alternative to companies that are searching for time and attendance systems. A biometric time system uses a time clock that reads an employee's unique fingerprint or handprint to validate the employee.[3] This technology is also available in other forms— voice recognition and iris scan. Figure 2–6 on page 2-21 illustrates a biometric time clock.

Fractional Parts of an Hour

The FLSA requires that employees be paid for *all* time worked, including fractional parts of an hour. An employer cannot use an arbitrary formula or an estimate as a substitute for determining precisely the compensable working time which is part of an employee's fixed or regular hours. The Wage and Hour Division allows employers to round off employees' worktime as shown on their time cards (to the nearest five, six, or fifteen minutes). The round-off process must be applied consistently so that over time employees are compensated for all time worked.

2 Information supplied by Kronos, Incorporated.
3 Eileen Gaughran, "Top 5 Time and Attendance Trends," *PAYTECH*, March/April 1999, pp. 24–25.

F I G U R E   2 - 4

Mark-Sense Time Card Used in the Timekeeper Computerized System

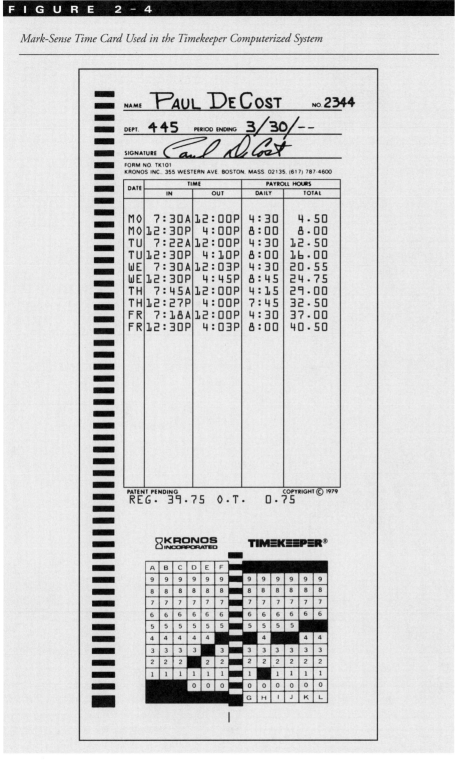

Source: Kronos, Inc.

Uncertain and indefinite working periods beyond the scheduled working hours cannot be practicably determined. Therefore, a few seconds or minutes may be disregarded. Some courts have allowed from 10 to 20 minutes to be ignored, while other courts have refused to apply the law to periods as small as 10 minutes. Generally, a few minutes of time spent by employees on the company premises for their own convenience before or after their workday are not included in the hours worked.

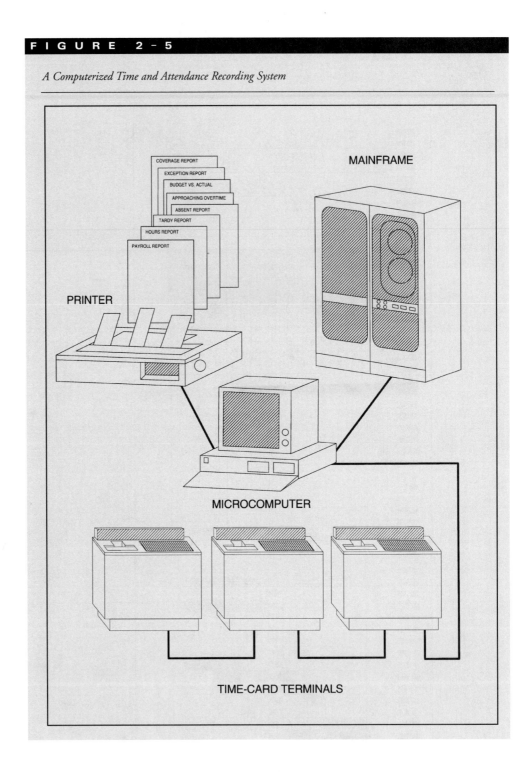

FIGURE 2-5

A Computerized Time and Attendance Recording System

METHODS OF COMPUTING WAGES AND SALARIES

LEARNING OBJECTIVE ④

Employees are usually paid for time worked at a time rate, such as hourly, weekly, biweekly, semimonthly, or monthly. The employee may also be paid at a piece rate, incentive rate, commission basis, or a combination of these rates.

Time Rate

To compute the wages of employees on an hourly basis, multiply the total regular hours worked by the regular hourly rate. If the employee works overtime, multiply the total overtime hours by the overtime rate. By adding the total regular earnings and the total over-

FIGURE 2-6

Biometric Time Clock

Source: Recognition Systems, Inc.

time earnings, we obtain the ***gross earnings.*** (In the examples that follow, if needed, rates have been rounded to two decimal places.)

Nick Sotakos works a 40-hour week at $6.20 an hour with overtime hours paid at 1½ times the regular rate.

Regular weekly earnings are.	$248.00 (40 × $6.20)
The overtime rate is	$9.30 ($6.20 × 1.5)
If Sotakos works 4 hours overtime, additional earnings for the 4 hours are	$37.20 (4 × $9.30)
Sotakos' weekly gross earnings are.	$285.20 ($248.00 + $37.20)
If paid only for time actually worked and he works only 36 hours during a week, Sotakos earns	$223.20 (36 × $6.20)

The employee's regular rate of pay includes *all payments* given for working a particular job. This does not include discretionary bonuses, gifts on special occasions, and contributions to certain welfare plans.

In the case of factory workers, many factories compute the actual time spent on a certain job so that amount can be charged to that job.

The Worker Economic Opportunity Act of 2001 excluded from employees' regular rate of pay the value of employer-provided rights to stock options, stock appreciation, and employee stock repurchase programs.

Sonla Butta spent 100 minutes on a certain job. The wages chargeable to that job at the regular hourly rate of $11.58 would be computed as follows:

$$\$11.58 \times \frac{100}{60} = \$19.30$$

Converting Weekly Wage Rates to Hourly Rates. When paying on a weekly basis, sometimes employers must convert the weekly wage rate to an hourly rate, especially to figure overtime earnings. To do this, divide the weekly wage rate by the number of hours in the regular workweek.

E X A M P L E

Joseph Gallo earns $412 a week for a workweek consisting of 40 hours. If Gallo worked 43 hours in a particular week, compute gross pay as follows:

$$\$412.00 \div 40 \text{ hours} = \$10.30 \text{ hourly wage rate}$$
$$\$10.30 \text{ hourly wage rate} \times 1.5 = \$15.45 \text{ overtime wage rate}$$
$$\text{Gross pay} = \$412 + (3 \text{ hours} \times \$15.45) = \$458.35$$

Converting Biweekly Wage Rates to Hourly Rates. If paying employees biweekly, divide the biweekly earnings by 2 to arrive at the weekly rate, and divide the weekly rate by the standard number of hours.

E X A M P L E

Patricia Mason earns $675 biweekly and works a standard 40-hour workweek. Compute Mason's hourly and overtime rates as follows:

$$\$675.00 \div 2 = \$337.50 \text{ regular weekly earnings}$$
$$\$337.50 \div 40 = \$8.44 \text{ regular hourly rate}$$
$$\$8.44 \times 1.5 = \$12.66 \text{ overtime hourly rate}$$

Converting Monthly Salary Rates to Hourly Rates. If workers paid on a monthly basis earn overtime pay for work beyond a 40-hour week, compute the hourly overtime rate by converting the monthly salary rate to an hourly rate.

E X A M P L E

Greg Pruit earns $2,600 per month and works a standard 40-hour week. During one week, Pruit earned 6 hours of overtime.

Step 1

Convert the monthly salary rate to a weekly rate by first annualizing the monthly salary. Then divide the annual salary by 52 weeks.

→ $2,600 monthly salary × 12 months = $31,200 annual salary
$31,200 annual salary ÷ 52 weeks = $600 weekly salary

Step 2

Divide the weekly rate by the standard number of hours in the workweek.

→ $600 weekly salary ÷ 40 hours = $15.00 hourly rate

Step 3

Compute the overtime rate by multiplying the hourly rate by 1.5.

→ $15.00 hourly rate × 1.5 = $22.50 overtime rate

Step 4

Compute the *gross pay* for the week by adding the overtime earnings to the regular weekly earnings.

Regular weekly earnings	$600.00
Overtime earnings (6 × 22.50)	135.00
Gross pay	$735.00

Converting Semimonthly Salary Rates to Hourly Rates. Semimonthly salary rates are converted the same as monthly rates except semimonthly earnings are multiplied by 24 instead of by 12 to compute the annual earnings.

EXAMPLE

Margaret Johnson earns $1,175 semimonthly.

Step 1

Annualize the salary. ➤ $1,175 × 24 = $28,200 annual rate

Step 2

Compute the weekly salary. ➤ $28,200 ÷ 52 = $542.31 weekly rate

Step 3

Compute the hourly rate. ➤ $542.31 ÷ 40 = $13.56 hourly rate

Step 4

Compute the overtime rate. ➤ $13.56 × 1.5 = $20.34 overtime rate

Numerous tables of decimal equivalents, such as the one shown in Figure 2–7, and other time-saving devices obtained in stationery and office supply firms help in computing wages at the hourly rate.

EXAMPLE

Weekly salary $550: $550 × 0.025 = $13.75 hourly rate; $550 × 0.0375 = $20.63 hourly overtime rate

Monthly salary $1,800: $1,800 × 0.00577 = $10.39 hourly rate; $1,800 × 0.00866 = $15.59 hourly overtime rate

Salaried with Fluctuating Workweek. Employers may pay employees who work fluctuating schedules a fixed salary, regardless of the number of hours worked. In such cases, overtime pay is found by dividing the normal salary by the total hours worked. An *extra half rate* is then paid for all hours worked over 40. However, some states prohibit or limit the use of this method of payment.

FIGURE 2-7

Table of Decimal Equivalents to Convert into Weekly, Hourly, and Hourly Overtime Salary Rates

To convert into:	Weekly Salary Rate	Hourly Salary Rate	Hourly Overtime Salary Rate
Multiply the: Weekly salary rate by	. . . .	0.025	0.0375
Semimonthly salary rate by	0.4615	0.01154	0.0173
Monthly salary rate by	0.2308	0.00577	0.00866
Yearly salary rate by	0.01923	0.00048	0.000721

EXAMPLE

Jeff MacCauley earns $739.20 a week with fluctuating workweek hours. If he worked 48 hours in one week, his gross pay would be calculated as follows:

$$\$739.20 \div 48 \text{ hours} = \$15.40 \text{ regular rate}$$
$$\$15.40 \times 0.5 = \$7.70 \text{ extra half pay rate}$$
$$8 \text{ hours O.T.} \times \$7.70 = \$61.60 \text{ extra pay}$$
$$\$739.20 + \$61.60 = \$800.80 \text{ weekly gross pay}$$

Fractional Cents. Practice in the treatment of fractions varies with different employers. In the case of union and other employment contracts, the method of computing regular and overtime hourly rates may be prescribed in the contracts.

SELF-STUDY QUIZ 2-3. *Compute the hourly and overtime rates for a standard 40-hour workweek for the following amounts:*

		Hourly Rate	Overtime Rate
1.	$525.00 weekly	_____	_____
2.	$892.00 biweekly	_____	_____
3.	$1,450.00 semimonthly	_____	_____
4.	$1,600.00 monthly	_____	_____

Piece Rate

Under the *piece-rate system,* the employer pays workers according to their output, such as an amount for each unit or piece produced. Thus, the wages increase as production increases. The employer keeps production records for each employee so that these records will be available when computing the wages earned by each employee. The Fair Labor Standards Act specifies that under a piece-rate system, the regular hourly rate of pay is computed as follows:

EXAMPLE

Peggy Zoe produced 12,500 items during a 40-hour workweek. Zoe is paid 0.030¢ per unit and receives a bonus 0.015¢ for each unit over 12,000 in a week. Zoe's weekly earnings are:

Step 1

Add the total weekly earnings from piece rates and all other sources, such as incentive bonuses. →

Regular earnings	12,500 × 0.030 = $375.00
Incentive earnings	500 × 0.015 = 7.50
Total weekly earnings	$382.50

Step 2

Divide the weekly earnings by total number of hours worked in the week for which such compensation was paid. →

$$\frac{\text{Total weekly earnings}}{\text{Total hours worked}} \quad \frac{\$382.50}{40} = \frac{\$9.56}{\text{per hour}}$$

The piece rate must at least equal the statutory minimum wage rate. In some instances, an employer may pay a worker an hourly rate for some hours and a piece rate for other hours during the week. In such cases, both the hourly rate and the piece-rate earnings must be at least the minimum rate.

Overtime Earnings for Pieceworkers—Method A. For overtime work, the pieceworker is entitled to be paid, in addition to piecework earnings for the entire period, a sum equal to one-half the regular hourly rate of pay multiplied by the number of hours worked in excess of 40 in the week.

Margo Adkins produced 3,073 pieces in a 44-hour workweek and is paid 14 ¾¢ for every unit produced.

Step 1

Compute the total regular weekly earnings. → 3,073 × 0.1475 = $453.27 regular weekly earnings

Step 2

Compute the regular hourly rate of pay. → $453.27 ÷ 44 hours = $10.30 regular hourly rate of pay

Step 3

Compute the overtime rate of pay and compute the overtime earnings. The regular earnings include the pay for the overtime hours at the regular rate. This is for the extra one-half time. →

0.5 × $10.30 = $5.15 overtime rate of pay
4 hours × $5.15 = $20.60 overtime earnings

Step 4

Compute the total regular and overtime earnings for the week. → $453.27 + $20.60 = $473.87 piecework and overtime earnings

Overtime Earnings for Pieceworkers—Method B. Another method of computing overtime payment for pieceworkers complies with the requirements of the FLSA. Before doing the work, piece-rate employees may agree with their employer, in advance of the work being done, to be paid at a rate not less than one and one-half times the piece rate for each piece produced during the overtime hours. No additional overtime pay will be due to the employees.

Assume that in the preceding example, Adkins earned overtime at a piece rate of one and one-half times the regular rate for all pieces produced during overtime hours. Of the total 3,073 pieces produced, 272 were produced in the 4 overtime hours. Adkins' total piecework and overtime earnings are as follows:

2,801 × 0.1475 = $413.15 piecework earnings
272 pieces × 0.2213 (0.1475 × 1.5) = $60.19 overtime earnings
$413.15 + $60.19 = $473.34 piecework and overtime earnings

SELF-STUDY QUIZ 2-4. *Bruce Eaton is paid 5¢ per unit under the piece-rate system. During one week, Eaton worked 46 hours and produced 5,520 units. Compute the following:*

1. The piecework earnings $_____
2. The regular hourly rate $_____
3. The overtime hourly rate $_____
4. The overtime earnings $_____
5. The total earnings $_____

Special Incentive Plans

Most wage systems involving special incentives are modifications of the piece-rate system described previously. Under many incentive plans, the company determines a standard for the quantity that an average worker can produce in a certain period of time. Workers failing to reach the standard earn a lower piece rate, while those who produce more than the standard receive a higher rate. With incentive plans, the computation of the payroll is usually more complicated than under the time-rate or piece-rate systems. Records of time worked as well as the production of each employee must be available in computing wages under most incentive plans.

EXAMPLE

Chu Wang, Inc., pays its blade polishers according to the following piece-rate incentive plan:

No. of Blades Polished Per 8-Hour Workday	Earnings Per Blade Polished
less than 1,850	0.0150
1,850 to 1,999	0.0165
2,000 (Daily Standard)	0.0180
2,001 to 2,100	0.0198
2,101 to 2,250	0.0217
over 2,250	0.0240

Commissions

The entire remuneration, or at least part of the remuneration, of certain employees may be on a commission basis. A *commission* is a stated percentage of revenue paid to an employee who transacts a piece of business or performs a service. Thus, a salesperson working in a certain territory may have a fixed salary each year plus a bonus for sales in excess of a certain amount.

EXAMPLE

Maria Fontana receives an annual $22,500 base salary for working a certain territory. A sales quota of $800,000 has been set for that territory for the current year. Fontana will receive a 6 percent commission on all sales in excess of $800,000. For the current year, the sales in the territory are $830,000. The bonus paid Fontana would be:

$1,800 (6% of $30,000)

Fontana's total earnings for the year would be:

$24,300 ($22,500 + $1,800)

There are numerous variations of the commission method of remuneration. Some businesses offer special premiums or bonuses for selling certain merchandise. For example, to help move merchandise in a ready-to-wear department, a department store will frequently pay a premium or a bonus to the salesperson who sells specific items of merchandise. Commissions are considered to be payments for hours worked and must be included in determining the regular hourly rate. This applies regardless of whether the commission is the sole source of the employee's compensation or is paid in addition to a salary or hourly rate. It does not matter whether the commission earnings are computed daily, weekly, monthly, or at some other interval. However, in the case of outside salespeople who are exempt from the FLSA, commissions paid to them do not have to meet the minimum wage criteria.

Profit-Sharing Plans

Many businesses have developed *profit-sharing plans* whereby the employer shares with the employees a portion of the profits of the business. Generally, profit-sharing plans include the following three types.

1. Cash payments based upon the earnings of a specified period.
2. Profits placed in a special fund or account to be drawn upon by employees at some future time. This plan may be in the form of a savings account, a pension fund, or an annuity.
3. Profits distributed to employees in the form of capital stock.

The payments made pursuant to a bona fide profit-sharing plan that meets the standards fixed by the Secretary of Labor's regulations are not deemed wages in determining the employee's regular rate of pay for overtime purposes.

Violations and Remedies

In a situation where an employer fails to pay an employee the minimum wage or the proper amount of overtime pay, the Wage and Hour Division will require the employer to pay enough backpay to satisfy the requirements of the law. In cases where the violations were willful, the FLSA provides for the payment of additional "liquidated damages" which will be equal to the amounts of the backpay and overtime awards. In cases of incorrect classification of an employee as exempt, the employee is entitled to retroactive overtime pay. The statute of limitations in these cases is two years unless the violation is willful. In that case, the government can go back three years.

METHODS OF PAYING WAGES AND SALARIES

The three main methods used in paying wages and salaries include (1) cash, (2) check, and (3) electronic transfer.

Paying Wages and Salaries in Cash

When a company pays wages and salaries in cash, a common procedure is used, as follows.

1. Compute the total wages earned, the deductions, and the net amount to be paid and record this information in the payroll register, as shown in Figure 1–9.
2. Prepare a supplementary payroll sheet showing the various denominations of bills and coins needed to pay the salary of each employee. The form in Figure 2–8 provides columns to list the names of the employees, the net amount to be paid, the denominations needed to pay each employee, the total amount needed to pay all employees, and the total number of each denomination needed to pay all employees.
3. Prepare a payroll slip by using the total amount of each denomination needed for the payroll.
4. Write a check for the total amount of the payroll and present it to the bank with the payroll slip to obtain the proper denominations.
5. Place the amount due to each employee in an envelope with a receipt showing the total earnings, the deductions, and the net amount paid. Distribute the prepared envelopes to the employees.

on the
JOB

In a survey conducted by KPMG Consulting, more than 72 percent of employers were found to have paid their employees on a biweekly basis.

Paying Wages and Salaries by Check

When paying wages and salaries by check, the employer prepares and signs the checks in the usual way. The check preparer should ensure the accuracy of the names of the payees and the net amounts of the checks. Employers must give employees a periodic statement showing the deductions that have been made from their wages for tax purposes. The employer may distribute these statements each payday or give them out monthly, quarterly, or annually. Also, employees receive a statement at the time they leave the employ of the company. Most employers who pay wages and salaries by check indicate on each check issued or on the check stub or earnings statement the various deductions made. (See Figure 2–9.)

Many businesses maintain a payroll account at their bank in addition to their regular checking account. In such a case, all checks to pay wages and salaries are issued against the payroll account rather than against the regular checking account. When the company maintains a separate payroll account, the usual procedure is as follows:

on the
JOB

The National Automated Clearing House Association estimated that employees spend an average of 8 to 24 hours per year depositing or cashing paychecks. In many cases, these transactions are made on company time.

Supplementary Payroll Sheet

		Bills					Coins				
Name of Employee	**Net Amount to Be Paid**	**$50**	**$20**	**$10**	**$5**	**$1**	**50¢**	**25¢**	**10¢**	**5¢**	**1¢**
Brandon, Paul C.	$ 268.62	5		1	1	3	1		1		2
Connor, Rose T.	271.40	5	1			1		1	1	1	
Day, Joseph R.	297.28	5	2		1	2		1			3
Gee, Margaret F.	704.92	14				4	1	1	1	1	2
Hawke, Sidney O.	271.64	5	1			1	1		1		4
Kirk, Evelyn A.	788.24	15	1	1	1	3			2		4
Lerro, Doris B.	268.12	5		1	1	3			1		2
Pesiri, Armand G.	878.80	17	1		1	3	1	1		1	
Topkis, Christine W.	284.65	5	1	1		4	1		1	1	
Vogel, John C.	724.10	14	1			4			1		
Total	$4,757.77	90	8	4	5	28	5	4	9	4	17

HENDRIX, INC. SUPPLEMENTARY PAYROLL SHEET — June 30, 20--

on the JOB

Studies have shown that the cost to produce one check is close to $1.30 (annual cost per employee: approximately $70).

1. Sets up a payroll account with a certain balance to be maintained at all times. A check against the regular checking account is issued and deposited in the payroll account. A small balance is desirable in the payroll account because it may be necessary to issue payroll checks before the regular payday. For example, if employees are leaving for vacation, they may receive their next payroll check before the regular payday.
2. Issues a check payable to Payroll, drawn on the regular checking account, equal to the total net pay, and deposited in the special payroll account at the bank.
3. Prepares individual checks, drawn against the special payroll account, and records the numbers of the payroll checks in the payroll register. Many companies having a large number of employees may use automatic means of signing the checks.

By maintaining a separate payroll account at the bank, the canceled payroll checks, accompanied by a statement of the payroll account balance, are returned separately from the canceled checks drawn upon the regular checking account, making it easier to reconcile both accounts. The payroll account balance as shown on the bank statement should always be equal to the sum of the total of the outstanding payroll checks and any maintained balance, less any service charge.

Earnings Statement (Check Stub) Showing Payroll Deductions

EMPLOYEE'S NAME	ARTHUR T. COCO					PENLAND EQUIPMENT COMPANY, SAN MATEO, FL 32088-2279			
PAY PERIOD ENDING	HOURS	RATE	GROSS EARNINGS	OASDI TAX	HI TAX	FED. WITH. TAX	STATE WITH. TAX	UNION DUES	NET EARNINGS PAID
5/16/	REG. T. 40 / O.T. 12	5.50 / 8.25	319.00	19.78	4.63	16.00		3.00	275.59

EMPLOYEE: THIS IS A STATEMENT OF YOUR EARNINGS AND DEDUCTIONS FOR PERIOD INDICATED. KEEP THIS FOR YOUR PERMANENT RECORD.

Paying Wages and Salaries by Electronic Transfer

Under an *electronic funds transfer system (EFTS)*, employers do not have to issue a paycheck to each worker, although the worker is given a stub showing the amounts deducted. Instead, the employer creates a computerized record for each employee. This record indicates:

1. The employee's bank.
2. The account number at the bank.
3. The net amount to be paid.

A day or two before payday the employer sends the information to the company's bank where the amounts due to any employees who also keep their accounts at that bank are removed and deposited to the appropriate accounts. That bank sends the remaining names to an automated clearinghouse which sorts out the other bank names and prepares a computer tape for each bank to receive funds electronically. For banks unable to receive entries in electronic form, the clearinghouse creates a printed statement showing the customers' names and the amounts for which their accounts are to be credited. The actual crediting of accounts and the settlement occur on payday.

Under a "paperless" deposit and bill-paying system, employers may deposit wages in bank accounts designated by the employees if the deposits are voluntarily authorized by the employees. Millions of written checks may be eliminated each month. After electronically transferring each employee's net pay directly into the worker's account, the employee can pay bills by authorizing the bank to automatically transfer funds from that account to the accounts of creditors such as the utility company and department stores.

Over 15 million American households do not have bank accounts; however, by using debit card-based accounts, the "unbanked" employees can opt for direct deposit of their paychecks. All transactions are completed electronically by using a Pay Card to make purchases at any point-of-sale terminal or to access cash at Automated Teller Machines (ATMs).[4]

Leading banks are now offering VISA Payroll Cards. These cards allow employers to deposit employees' pay directly into a prepaid card issued to the employee. The card is then used like any VISA debit or credit card and can also be used to access cash at certain automated teller machines (ATMs). Employees will then receive a monthly statement detailing their transactions.[5]

on the

JOB

One hundred percent of Canadian employees use direct deposit, while the rate in Germany is 95 percent, and the United States is only 46 percent.

Unclaimed Wages

Occasionally, a worker may terminate employment or be terminated and not claim the final wage payment. The payroll manager is then faced with the question of what to do with the worker's unclaimed wages. Even though a uniform law exists on the subject of unclaimed or abandoned property, varying practices occur in those states that provide for the disposition of unclaimed property, such as unclaimed wages. The uniform law, followed by most states, provides that the holder of any unclaimed property must file a report after a specified statutory period and then surrender the money to the state as abandoned property. The length of the statutory period varies widely from state to state. In other states, the holder of unclaimed property files a report with the state, and the state then files suit for possession of the property. Because of the different practices among states, payroll managers must be well acquainted with the laws of their own states in the event they are faced with the difficult problem of disposing of unclaimed wages.

---

4 "Pay Card Pays Off for Employees and Employers," *PAYTECH*, May/June 2000, p. 36.
5 "Card-Based Payroll Solutions," *PAYTECH*, April 2002, p. 22.

KEY TERMS

Biweekly *(p. 2-6)*
Commission *(p. 2-26)*
Common-law relationship *(p. 2-5)*
Continental system *(p. 2-16)*
Domestic service *(p. 2-5)*
Electronic funds transfer system (EFTS) *(p. 2-29)*
Employee *(p. 2-5)*
Enterprise coverage *(p. 2-4)*
Exempt employees *(p. 2-10)*
Gross earnings *(p. 2-21)*
Individual employee coverage *(p. 2-4)*
Piece-rate system *(p. 2-24)*

Principal activities *(p. 2-13)*
Profit-sharing plans *(p. 2-26)*
Salary *(p. 2-6)*
Semimonthly *(p. 2-6)*
Time card *(p. 2-16)*
Time sheet *(p. 2-16)*
Tip *(p. 2-7)*
Tipped employee *(p. 2-7)*
Wage *(p. 2-6)*
Wages *(p. 2-6)*
Workweek *(p. 2-8)*

MATCHING QUIZ

_____ 1. Biweekly

_____ 2. Commission

_____ 3. Tipped employee

_____ 4. Common-law relationship

_____ 5. Gross earnings

_____ 6. Individual employee coverage

_____ 7. EFTS

_____ 8. Exempt employees

_____ 9. Piece-rate system

_____ 10. Semimonthly

A. Remuneration paid twice a month

B. Exempt from some or all of the FLSA requirements

C. Employee engages in interstate commerce or produces goods for such commerce

D. Remuneration paid every two weeks

E. Employer has the right to control both what work will be done and how it will be done

F. Engaged in a job in which tips of more than $30 a month are regularly received

G. Payment to employee based on a stated percentage of revenue

H. Regular earnings plus overtime earnings

I. Pay system based on an amount paid to the employee per units produced

J. Electronic funds transfer system

QUESTIONS FOR REVIEW

1. Explain the two bases of coverage provided by the FLSA.
2. In determining the existence of an employer/employee relationship, the IRS groups the items of evidence into which three general categories?
3. What kinds of establishments may employ full-time students at 85 percent of the minimum wage?
4. Name some of the cities that have enacted the so-called "living wage" ordinances.
5. To what extent are tips considered wages under the FLSA?
6. Explain how a state employee working in the area of public safety may use compensatory time off in lieu of overtime compensation.

7. Under what conditions would an employee of a state receive cash for his or her compensatory time off?
8. The following employees are exempt from various requirements of the FLSA. Indicate from which requirement or requirements each of the following employees is exempt:
   a. Amusement park employee
   b. Taxicab driver
   c. Casual baby sitter
   d. Elementary school teacher
   e. Outside salesperson
9. What are the four types of exempt white-collar employees?

10. Do any of the four types of white-collar exemptions require the employee to have a specialized degree?

11. In order not to interfere with the schooling and well-being of minors between the ages of 14 and 16, employers of these minors must satisfy what three conditions?

12. In determining the working time of employees, how are the principal activities of employees defined?

13. Under what conditions is travel time counted as time worked?

14. A company grants its employees a 15-minute rest period twice each workday. Must the employees be paid for each rest period?

15. When is time spent by employees in attending lectures and meetings for training purposes not counted as working time?

16. How does a biometric time system identify an employee?

17. Explain how to calculate the overtime hourly rate for employees who are paid biweekly.

18. Explain the two methods that may be used to calculate overtime wages for a pieceworker.

19. In cases of willful failure to pay employees the minimum wage or the correct amount of overtime, the Wage and Hour Division will require the employer to take what kind of corrective action?

20. What is the uniform law on the subject of unclaimed or abandoned property?

QUESTIONS FOR DISCUSSION

1. At Struthers, Inc., factory employees work Monday through Friday at their regular hourly rates. On occasion they work on Saturdays, when they receive time and a half provided they worked 40 hours Monday through Friday.

   One week Sam Rico was absent Wednesday in order to attend a relative's funeral. Under the company's death-in-family policy, Rico's absence was paid. Therefore, during the workweek Rico worked 32 hours and was paid for 40. That same week Struthers scheduled overtime for Saturday, and Rico worked 8 hours. He expected to be paid for 12 hours. However, the payroll manager informed him that he was entitled to only 8 hours' pay on Saturday because he had worked only 40 hours during the entire week. Do you agree that Rico is entitled to overtime pay for Saturday's hours? Explain.

2. Along with many other companies, Gomez Printers observes the Friday after Thanksgiving as a paid holiday. The company requires each employee to make up Friday's lost hours in the following workweek by working extra hours without pay. Is Gomez Printers proceeding legally by requiring its employees to work extra hours without compensation to make up for the hours lost on the Friday holiday? Explain.

3. The Hudson Company needs time to calculate employees' overtime payments by the end of the pay period in which the overtime is worked. Can they pay the overtime payments with the following period's paycheck?

4. The Payroll Department of DuMont has a policy of waiting one full week before correcting any paycheck errors of $30 or less. However, any pay shortages that exceed $30 are made up the same day. Also, any amounts less than $30 are made up the same day when the particular circumstances of the employees indicate that it would place an undue hardship on them to wait until the next pay one week later.

   Denise Harris, an order checker in DuMont's Shipping Department, discovered an error of $28.34 in her weekly check. When Harris reported the error, a payroll clerk informed her that she would have to wait until the next week's paycheck to recover the amount, since the underpayment was less than $30.

   What is your reaction to DuMont's policy of providing for paycheck corrections? Assume that Harris protests the delay and in court argues that her earned wages should be paid on the date due. As the judge hearing the case, how would you decide?

5. In some companies, employees are permitted to pick up the payroll check of another employee as a favor. What is your reaction to this practice?

PRACTICAL PROBLEMS

Special forms required to solve the Practical Problems are provided along with the problems in each chapter.

NOTE: In this chapter and in all succeeding work throughout the course, *unless instructed otherwise,* calculate hourly rates and overtime rates as follows:

1. Carry the hourly rate and the overtime rate to 3 decimal places and then round off to 2 decimal places.
2. If the third decimal place is 5 or more, round to the next higher cent.
3. If the third decimal place is less than 5, simply drop the third decimal place.

Examples: $5.765 should be rounded to $5.77.
$5.764 should be rounded to $5.76.

Also, use the minimum hourly wage of $5.15 in solving these problems and all that follow.

2–1. LO 4.

The hours worked and the hourly wage rates for five employees of the Cooley Company for the week ended September 10 follow.

a. For each employee, compute the gross earnings.

b. Compute the total gross earnings for all employees.

Employee	Hours Worked	Regular Hourly Wage Rate	(a) Gross Earnings
Dempski, R.	38	$8.40	$ _____
Floyd, B.	40	6.25	_____
Iskin, J.	37	6.30	_____
Macintyre, H.	40	6.95	_____
Serock, P.	32½	6.15	_____
		(b) Total gross earnings.	$ _____

2–2. LO 4.

The wages and hours information for five employees of McNeese Enterprises for the week ended July 5 is given below. Employees work a standard 40-hour workweek and are paid time and one-half for all hours over 40 in each workweek.

a. For each employee, compute the regular earnings, overtime rate, overtime earnings, and total gross earnings.

b. Compute the total gross earnings for all employees.

(a)

Employee	Hours Worked	Regular Hourly Wage Rate	Regular Earnings	Overtime Rate	Overtime Earnings	Total Gross Earnings
Carman, T.	47	$ 9.45	$ _____	$ _____	$ _____	$ _____
Galasso, A.	42	11.90	_____	_____	_____	_____
Jones, B.	48	8.85	_____	_____	_____	_____
Rodna, G.	44	8.25	_____	_____	_____	_____
Wilmon, W.	45½	7.40	_____	_____	_____	_____
		(b) Total gross earnings				$ _____

Date _____   **Name** _____

2–3. LO 1.

Jack Parker, a white-collar exempt employee, started working for Castellano Company on Wednesday of this week. He worked 8 hours on Wednesday and 10 hours on both Thursday and Friday. His annual salary is $85,000, and he is paid weekly for a 5-day week. Determine his gross pay for his first partial week of work.

Gross pay . . . . $ _____

2–4. LO 1.

Bruce Cabot is a waiter at the Towne House, where he receives a weekly wage of $80 plus tips for a 40-hour workweek. Cabot's weekly tips usually range from $180 to $200.

a. Under the Fair Labor Standards Act, the minimum amount of wages that Cabot must receive for a 40-hour workweek is . . . . $ _____

b. Since they are in violation of the FLSA, the additional amount they should pay Cabot each week to meet the minimum wage requirement for a tipped employee is . . $ _____

2–5. LO 1.

Eleanor Wu, a full-time student at Southwestern University, is employed by Gifford's Dress Shop as a salesperson. Her hourly rate is $3.95. One week Wu worked 32¾ hours.

a. Wu's earnings for the week are . . . . $ _____

b. Is the hourly rate in violation of the FLSA? Explain.

_____

_____

c. If the hourly rate is in violation of the FLSA, the amount the dress shop should pay Wu is . . . . $ _____

2–6. LO 1.

Stephen Forte worked 47 hours during the week for Kyle Company at two different jobs. His pay rate was $9.90 for the first 30 hours, and his pay rate was $12.10 for the other 17 hours. Determine his gross pay for that week if there was no prior agreement on the method of compensating for the overtime.

Gross pay . . . . $ _____

2–7. LO 2.

John Porter is an hourly employee of the Motter Company located in New York City. This week Porter had to travel to the company's regional office in Albany. He left Sunday at noon and arrived in Albany at 3:00 p.m. During the week, he worked his normal 40 hours in the Albany office (Monday through Friday—9 a.m. to 5 p.m.). In addition, he attended the company's 4-hour work training session on Wednesday evening. Porter's hourly rate of pay is $14.80 per hour.

a. Porter's overtime earnings for the week are . . . . $ _____

b. Porter's total earnings for the week are . . . . $ _____

2–8. LO 4.

Peter Romez, a nonexempt employee, receives $415 for a regular 40-hour week and time and one-half for overtime. For a workweek of 46 hours, compute:

a. The regular earnings . . . . $ _____
b. The overtime earnings . . . . _____
c. The total earnings . . . . $ _____

2–9. LO 4.

Cal DiMangino earns $2,875 each month and works 40 hours each week. Compute:

a. The hourly rate . . . . $ _____

b. The overtime rate at time and
    one-half . . . . $ _____

2–10. LO 4.

Kathleen Otto, a medical secretary, earns $1,575 monthly for a 35-hour week. For overtime work, she receives extra pay at the regular hourly rate up to 40 hours and time and one-half beyond 40 hours in any week. During one semimonthly pay period, Otto worked 10 hours overtime. Only 2 hours of this overtime were beyond 40 hours in any one week. Compute:

a. The regular semimonthly earnings $ _____

b. The overtime earnings . . . .   _____

c. The total earnings . . . . $ _____

2–11. LO 4.

Bernice King is a salaried employee who works fluctuating work schedules. She is paid a fixed salary of $915 each week, with overtime (over 40 hours) paid at an extra half rate. This week, she worked 52 hours. Compute:

a. The overtime earnings . . . . $ _____

b. The total earnings . . . . $ _____

2–12. LO 3, 4.

The time card below shows the time worked one week by Henry Van Koski. The employer disregards any time before 8:00 a.m. or between 12:00 and 1:00 p.m. and after 5:00 p.m. Employees do not begin work until 8:00 a.m. or 1:00 p.m., and do not work beyond 5:00 p.m., unless they are asked to work overtime. Hours worked beyond the regular 8-hour day and on Saturday are paid at one and one-half times the regular rate. Hours worked on Sunday are paid double the regular rate. Fractions of the hour for time worked are based on full quarter-hour increments.

No.	72					
Name	Henry Van Koski				(a)	
Day	Morning		Afternoon		Overtime		Hours Worked
	In	Out	In	Out	In	Out	
M	7:50	12:00	12:50	5:01			
T	7:56	12:01	12:49	5:02	5:30	7:31	
W	7:59	12:02	12:58	5:03			
T	7:45	12:00	12:55	5:00	5:29	8:02	
F	8:01	12:01	1:00	5:01	6:00	7:30	
S	7:48	12:02					
S			2:00	6:03			
(b)	Total Hours Worked						
Remarks							

2–12. (Concluded)

Van Koski's regular wage rate is $10.78 per hour, and the regular workweek is 40 hours with five 8-hour days. Compute:

a. The hours worked each day. (Ignore the one-minute tardiness on Friday.) . . . . _____

b. The total hours worked. . . . . . . _____

c. The regular earnings . . . . $ _____

d. The overtime earnings . . . . _____

e. The total earnings . . . . $ _____

2–13. LO 3.

Under the decimal system of computing time worked at the Timmerman Company, production workers who are tardy are "docked" according to the schedule shown below.

Minutes Late in Ringing In	Fractional Hour Deducted
1 through 6	1/10
7 through 12	2/10
13 through 18	3/10
19 through 24	4/10
etc.	

The regular hours of work, Monday through Friday, are from 7:30 to 11:30 a.m. and from 12:30 to 4:30 p.m. During one week Henry Vanderhoff, who earns $12.15 an hour, reports in and checks out as shown below.

Employees are not paid for ringing in a few minutes before 7:30 and 12:30 nor for ringing out a few minutes after 11:30 and 4:30.

					(a)
DAY	**AM**		**PM**		**HRS WORKED**
	In	**Out**	**In**	**Out**	
M	7:28	11:31	12:29	4:31	
T	7:35	11:30	12:30	4:30	
W	7:50	11:33	12:27	4:32	
Th	7:27	11:31	12:50	4:33	
F	7:28	11:32	12:40	4:30	

Refer to the partial time card above and compute:

a. The hours worked each day. . . . _____

b. The total hours worked . . . . . . _____

c. The gross earnings for the week . . . . $ _____

2–14. LO 3, 4.

Potts, Inc., recently converted from a 5-day, 40-hour workweek to a 4-day, 40-hour workweek, with overtime continuing to be paid at one and one-half times the regular hourly rate for all hours worked beyond 40 in the week. In this company, time is recorded under the continental system, as shown on the time card at the right.

Sue Ellen Boggs is part of the Group B employees whose regular workweek is Tuesday through Friday. The working hours each day are 800 to 1200; 1230 to 430; and 600 to 800. The company disregards any time before 800, between 1200 and 1230, and between 430 and 600, and permits employees to ring in up to 10 minutes late before any deduction is made for tardiness. Deductions are made to the nearest 1/4 of an hour for workers who are more than 10 minutes late in ringing in.

Refer to the time card and compute:
a. The daily total hours. . . . . _____
b. The total hours for the week. . . . . . _____
c. The regular weekly earnings . . . . $_____
d. The overtime earnings (company rounds O/T rate to 3 decimal places) . . . . _____
e. The total weekly earnings . . . . $_____

No.	160				Hr. Rate	$8.45	
Name	Sue Ellen Boggs				O.T. Rate	$12.675	
Time	Mon	Tues	Wed	Thurs	Fri	Sat	
Evening — Out		802	801	805	800		
Evening — In		601	609	602	600		
Afternoon — Out		430	431	430	435		
Afternoon — In		1230	1231	1230	1238		
Morning — Out		1200	1202	1200	1203	1201	
Morning — In		755	750	813	759	800	Total for Week
Daily Totals	(a)						(b)

Remarks *13 minutes late Thursday – deduct ¼ hr.*

2–15. LO 4.

During the first week in November, Esther Coulter worked 45½ hours and produced 1,275 units under a piece-rate system. The regular piece rate is 28¢ a unit. Coulter is paid overtime according to the FLSA ruling for overtime work under a piece-rate system. Compute:

a. The piecework earnings . . . . $_____
b. The regular hourly rate . . . . $_____
   The overtime hourly rate . . . . $_____
c. The overtime earnings . . . . _____
d. The total earnings . . . . $_____

2–16. LO 4.

Refer to Problem 2–15. Assume that Coulter had agreed with her employer prior to the performance of the work that she would be paid one and one-half times the regular piece rate for all pieces produced during the overtime hours. Assume that her production totals for the week were: 1,075 pieces during regular hours and 200 pieces during overtime hours. Compute:

a. The piecework earnings . . . . . . $_____
b. The overtime earnings . . . . _____
c. The total earnings . . . . $_____

2–17. LO 4.

Joan Sullivan, a sales representative, earns an annual salary of $17,750 and receives a commission on that portion of her annual sales that exceeds $60,000. The commission is 8.5% on all sales up to $45,000 above the quota. Beyond that amount, she receives a commission of 10 percent. Her total sales for the past year were $228,000. Compute:

a. The regular annual salary . . . . . $ _____
b. The commission . . . . _____
c. The total annual earnings . . . . . $ _____

2–18. LO 4.

Joyce Sand is employed as a salesperson in the men's department of Lukens Fashions. In addition to her weekly base salary of $240, Sand is paid a commission of 1% on her total net sales for the week (total gross sales less any customer returns). During the past week, to promote the sale of its fine cashmere sweaters, Lukens agreed to pay Sand an additional PM (push money) of 2% of the total net sales of cashmere sweaters. Sand's weekly sales tally is given below.

Item	Gross Sales	Customer Returns
Regular sweaters	$400	$48
Cashmere sweaters	995	75
Ties	190	-0-
Dress shirts	445	39
Sports shirts	185	25

Compute Sand's total weekly earnings, showing her (a) weekly base salary, (b) commission, (c) PM, and (d) total weekly earnings.

a. Weekly base salary . . . . $ 240.00

    Weekly gross sales . . . . $ _____

       Less customer returns . . . .   _____

    Weekly net sales . . . . $ _____

b. Commission: $ _____ × 1% . . . .   _____

    Weekly gross sales of cashmere sweaters . . . . $ _____

       Less customer returns . . . .   _____

    Weekly net sales of cashmere sweaters . . . . $ _____

c. PM: $ _____ × 2% . . . .   _____

d. Total weekly earnings . . . . $ _____

2-19. LO 5.

Hendrix, Inc., pays its employees' weekly wages in cash. A supplementary payroll sheet that lists the employees' names and their earnings for a certain week is shown below. Complete the payroll sheet by calculating the total amount of payroll and indicating the least possible number of denominations that can be used in paying each employee. However, no employees are to be given bills in denominations greater than $20.

HENDRIX, INC.

Supplementary Payroll Sheet

For Period Ending August 15, 20—

Name of Employee	Net Amount Paid	Bills					Coins				
		$20	$10	$5	$1	50¢	25¢	10¢	5¢	1¢
Chad T. Biskis	$251.75									
Nicole A. Cibik	256.52									
Domingo M. Diaz	384.94									
Laura B. Elias	202.59									
Ari M. Fleischer	253.64									
Diane Y. Germano	296.50									
Arnold B. Herst	594.26									
Edward C. Kenner	399.89									
Kathleen J. Marfia	234.01									
Kimberly A. Picket	595.80									
Total										

Date _____   **Name** _____

CONTINUING PAYROLL PROBLEM

In the Continuing Payroll Problem, presented at the end of succeeding chapters, you will gain experience in computing wages and salaries and preparing a payroll register for the Steimer Company, Inc., a newly formed corporation. At the end of subsequent chapters, information will be presented so that the payroll register can be completed step by step as you proceed through the discussion material relating to that particular section of the payroll register.

The Steimer Company is a small manufacturing firm located in Pittsburgh, Pennsylvania. The company has a work force of both hourly and salaried employees. Each employee is paid for hours actually worked during each week, with the time worked being recorded in quarter-hour increments. The standard workweek consists of 40 hours, with all employees being paid time and one-half for any hours worked beyond the 40 regular hours.

Wages are paid every Friday, with one week's pay being held back by the company. Thus, the first payday for the Steimer Company is January 14 for the workweek ending January 7.

The information below will be used in preparing the payroll for the pay period ending January 7.

Time Card No.	Employee Name	Hourly Wage or Salary
11	Mary L. Lopenski	$ 6.50 per hour
12	Anthony P. Wren	6.25 per hour
13	Leroy A. Young	8.10 per hour
21	Lester D. Hayes	7.90 per hour
22	Meredith O. McGarry	5.75 per hour
31	Nancy B. Costello	315 per week
32	Gloria D. Hopstein	1,700 per month
33	Vernon U. Porth	2,350 per month
51	Marsha T. Stone	1,510 per month
99	Harold Y. Steimer	52,000 per year

Ms. Nancy B. Costello prepares the time clerk's report for each pay period. Her report for the first week of operations is given below.

TIME CLERK'S REPORT NO. 1									
For Period Ending January 7, 20--									

Time Card No.	Employee	Time Record						Time Worked	Time Lost
		M	T	W	T	F	S		
11	Mary L. Lopenski	8	8	8	8	8	—	40	
12	Anthony P. Wren	8	8	8	8	8	8	48	
13	Leroy A. Young	8	5½	8	8	8	—	37½	2½ hrs. tardy
21	Lester D. Hayes	10	10	8	8	10	—	46	
22	Meredith O. McGarry	8	8	8	8	8	—	40	
31	Nancy B. Costello	8	8	8	8	8	1¼	41¼	
32	Gloria D. Hopstein	8	8	8	8	8	—	40	
33	Vernon U. Porth	8	8	8	8	8	—	40	
51	Marsha T. Stone	8	8	8	8	8	4	44	
99	Harold Y. Steimer	8	8	8	8	8	—	40	

Using the payroll register for the Steimer Company, which is reproduced on a fold-out at the back of the book (PR-1), proceed as follows:

1. Enter each employee's time card number and name in the appropriate columns.
2. Record the regular hours and the overtime hours worked for each employee, using the time clerk's report as your reference.
3. Complete the Regular Earnings columns (Rate Per Hour and Amount) and the Overtime Earnings columns (Rate Per Hour and Amount) for each hourly employee. For salaried workers, complete the regular weekly earnings column and show the hourly overtime rate and earnings only if overtime was worked.
4. Record the Total Earnings for each employee by adding the Regular Earnings and the Overtime Earnings.

Note: Retain your partially completed payroll register for use at the end of Chapter 3.

CASE PROBLEM

C1. **Reducing the Cost of Compensated Leave Time. LO 1.**

For the past several weeks, Adele Delgado, payroll manager for the Petrillo Packing Company, has been studying the mounting costs of accrued vacations and sick leave. Most of her firm's employees are entitled to two weeks' vacation each year and the privilege of accruing their vacation time for future use. Also, the workers have a generous sick-leave plan that reimburses them while they are ill at home or in the hospital.

Scanning the employees' accrued vacation times on the computer printout, Delgado notes the line entry for John Mannick. Mannick recently retired and cashed in 14 weeks of accrued vacation—all paid at his current wage, which was much more than when he originally earned the vacations. And, of course, the firm's payroll taxes for the accrued vacation payout were significantly increased.

Delgado also knows that some workers feel short-changed if they do not use their sick leave each year. They realize that if the leave is not used, they lose it for that year. Probably, she thinks, this accounts for those who regularly become ill on Mondays or Fridays.

What solutions can you offer to limit the cost of and more effectively manage the firm's policies for compensated leave time?

Net activities

URLS are subject to change. Please visit the Bieg Payroll Accounting Web site: http://bieg.swcollege.com for updates.

1. Using a search engine, type "exempt work FLSA." Discuss the difference between exempt and non exempt work. Do you think the professor of your course is exempt or non exempt?

    http://www.google.com
    http://www.ask.com

2. Using a search engine, type in "living wage."
    a. Approximately how many places in the United States have ordinances requiring a "living wage"?
    b. What are the benefits of a living wage law?
    c. Who benefits from a living wage law?

    http://www.google.com
    http://www.ask.com

3. Using a search engine, search for three companies that offer on-line payroll services.
    a. How much do the companies charge for their services?
    b. How do they charge for their services? (i.e. do they charge by employee, per check, a flat fee?)

    c. Discuss the advantages and disadvantages of using such a service.

    http://www.google.com
    http://www.ask.com

4. Using a search engine, type in "biometric time system." Read several articles on biometric time systems. Next, read the article *Tracking Work Hours by Touch, Not a Punch* by Bonnie Rothman Morris at

    http://www.senseme.com/ scripts/articles/articles5.htm

    a. What are the advantages of a biometric time system?
    b. Does such a system violate or enhance privacy?

    http://www.google.com
    http://www.ask.com

5. Go to http://www.fms.treas.gov/eft/. What are the benefits of electronic funds transfers?

6. Go to http://www.toolkit.cch.com/text/P07_1310.asp. What are the procedures for making an electronic funds transfer?

In this chapter we study the first in a series of tax deductions that are withheld from an employee's gross wages.

Social Security Taxes

How do we determine taxable wages? What is FICA? How are self-employed people taxed? These questions will be answered.

The employer serves as a middleman for collecting taxes. What are his obligations? As collection agents for the government, we will learn the different requirements and procedures for depositing FICA and income taxes withheld from employees' wages. We'll also learn the penalties for failing to perform these duties.

3

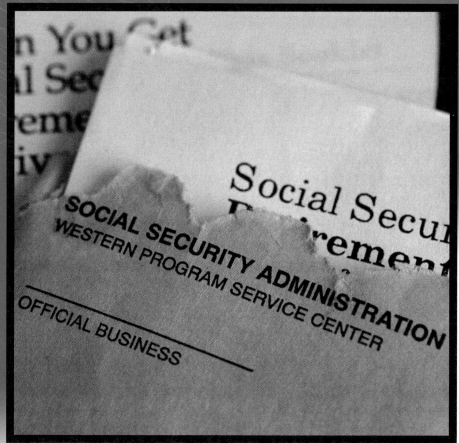

© Getty Images, Inc./Photodisc

AFTER STUDYING THIS CHAPTER, YOU SHOULD BE ABLE TO:

1. Identify, for social security purposes, those persons covered under the law and those services that make up employment.

2. Identify the types of compensation that are defined as wages.

3. Apply the current tax rates and wage base for FICA and SECA purposes.

4. Explain the importance of obtaining and correctly using the Employer's Identification Number and the Employee's Social Security Number.

5. Describe the different requirements and procedures for depositing FICA taxes and income taxes withheld from employees' wages.

6. Complete Form 941, Employer's Quarterly Federal Tax Return, and Form 8109, Federal Tax Deposit Coupon.

7. Recognize that, as collection agents for the government, employers may be subject to civil and criminal penalties if they fail to carry out their duties.

LEARNING OBJECTIVES

This chapter covers the government's old-age, survivors, and disability insurance benefits program (OASDI) and the retirees' health insurance program (HI). These programs are funded by Social Security and Medicare taxes imposed on employees and their employers. The taxes are calculated at a standard flat rate for every employee and employer. The statutes that provide the taxes include:

1. **Federal Insurance Contributions Act (FICA),** which imposes two taxes on employees and two taxes on employers. One of the taxes finances the federal old-age, survivors, and disability insurance program (OASDI). The other finances the hospital insurance (HI), or Medicare, program.
2. **Self-Employment Contributions Act (SECA),** which levies a tax upon the net earnings of the self-employed.

COVERAGE UNDER FICA

LEARNING OBJECTIVE 1

The retirement and disability parts of the social security program cover most workers in the United States. However, before an individual is considered to be "covered" for social security purposes, the following must be determined:

1. If the individual is an "employee," as defined by the common-law relationship of employer and employee.
2. If the service the individual renders is "employment," as defined by FICA tax law.
3. If the compensation the individual receives is "taxable wages," as defined by FICA tax law.

By identifying a "covered" employee and "covered" employment, it can then be determined who pays the tax and who will be entitled to benefits. Employees are *not* exempt from the FICA tax on the basis of income level or age.

Employee

As explained in Chapter 2, the test used by the IRS to determine a worker's classification is the Common-Law Test. Basically, if a business tells, or has a right to tell, a worker how, when, and where to work, then the worker is an employee.[1]

Occupations Specifically Covered by FICA. In addition to the Common-Law Test, FICA law also provides specific coverage for the following list of four occupations. Even though these workers are independent contractors under common law, they are treated by statute as employees. However, such persons are not covered by FICA if they have a substantial interest in the facilities used in connection with their jobs, or if the services consist of a single transaction.

1. Agent-drivers and commission-drivers who distribute food and beverage products, or handle laundry or dry cleaning.
2. Full-time life insurance salespersons.
3. Full-time traveling or city salespersons for one firm or person.
4. An individual who works at home on materials or goods that you supply and that must be returned to you or to a person you name, if you also furnish specifications for the work to be done.

Employees of the Federal Government. In general, *federal government employees* hired after 1983 are subject to full FICA coverage. For those covered by a retirement system and hired prior to 1984, only the Medicare (HI) portion applies. The following are exempt from both the OASDI and HI portions of the tax:

• Medical interns.
• Student nurses.
• Inmates of U.S. penal institutions.
• Those serving temporarily in case of fire, storm, earthquake, flood, or similar emergency.

---

1 *Payroll Manager's Letter,* Volume No. 13, July 7, 1998, p. 4.

Employees of State and Local Governments.   The following coverage levels apply:

- Work done after July 1, 1991, and *not covered* by a public retirement plan—full FICA coverage.
- Hired after March 31, 1986, and *covered* by a public retirement plan—HI coverage only.
- Hired prior to January 1, 1986, and *covered* by a public retirement plan—no FICA coverage.

Military Payments and Employer Supplemental Payments   OASDI/HI covers members of the uniformed services on active duty, with their contributions and benefits computed on their basic pay. Amounts paid in excess of their basic pay (such as for sea or foreign duty, hazardous duty, etc.) are not subject to FICA.

Some employers pay their workers the difference between the workers' salaries and the amounts they receive from the federal or state government while on duty with the armed forces or the state National Guard. If the worker is temporarily serving with the state National Guard, the payments are treated as wages and are subject to FICA.

Exempt Employees.   Employees of not-for-profit organizations are subject to FICA taxes. Some services, such as those performed by duly ordained ministers of churches, remain exempt from FICA taxes, but the individuals are then subject to self-employment tax on their net earnings. Ministers, certain members of religious orders, and Christian Science practitioners previously electing exemption from social security coverage may now be covered by filing a waiver form with the IRS. Once an election to be covered by social security is made, it is irrevocable.

Voluntary Coverage.   Coverage under FICA can be extended to certain classes of services that otherwise would be excluded. For example, service in the employ of a state or local government that began prior to April 1, 1986, is still exempt for the OASDI portion of the FICA tax. However, coverage can be extended to these employees by means of a voluntary agreement entered into by the state and Secretary of Health and Human Services. When a state elects voluntary coverage, it becomes responsible for the collection and payment of the FICA tax as if it were covered employment.

Household Employee

If a worker performs household services in or around your home subject to your will and control, as to both what must be done and how it will be done, that worker is your household employee. It does not matter whether you exercise this control as long as you have the legal right to control the method and result of the work.

However, in order for the household employee and the employer to be liable for the FICA taxes, the household employee must receive *$1,300 or more in cash wages* from any one employer in the year. Household employees do not include people (a) who work for you in your business, (b) who follow an independent trade, business, or profession in which they offer services to the general public, and (c) who are under the age of 18 unless their principal occupation is household employment.

Independent Contractor

The FICA tax law identifies ***independent contractors*** as persons who follow an independent trade, business, or profession where they offer their services to the public. The Small Business Administration estimates that nearly 5 million workers are independent contractors. The test in Figure 3–1 determines independent contractor status.

Employers do not pay or withhold payroll taxes on payments made to independent contractors. However, individual contractors are liable for social security taxes (self-employment taxes) on the net earnings of their businesses.

on the
JOB

Some examples of workers who *may* be household employees include:

- Baby sitters
- Caretakers
- Cooks
- Drivers
- Gardeners
- Governesses
- Housekeepers
- Maids

on the
JOB

Intentionally misclassifying an employee as an independent contractor may result in the employer being liable for 100 percent of the worker's FICA and federal income taxes, in addition to other penalties for failure to file returns and pay taxes.

FIGURE 3–1

Test for Independent Contractor Status

Workers *may* be classified as independent contractors if they:

1. Hire, supervise, and pay assistants.
2. Determine the sequence of their work.
3. Set their own hours of work.
4. Work for as many employers as they wish.
5. Are paid by the job.
6. Make their services available to the public.
7. Have an opportunity for profit or loss.
8. Furnish their own tools.
9. Have a substantial investment in their trade.
10. May be dismissed only under terms of contract.

If the IRS determines that an employer has misclassified a worker as an independent contractor, the employer faces substantial fines and penalties.

Employer

LEARNING OBJECTIVE 2

Every *person* is an *employer* if the person employs one or more individuals for the performances of services in the United States, unless such services or employment are specifically excepted by the law. The term "person," as defined in the law, means an individual, a trust or estate, a partnership, or a corporation.

The term *employment* means any service performed by employees for their employer, regardless of the citizenship or residence of either. FICA covers most types of employment, but there are specific exclusions. Some types of employment are wholly exempt from coverage, and others are exempt only if the cash wages received are less than a stipulated dollar amount, as shown in Figure 3–2.

If an employee's services performed during one-half or more of any period constitute covered employment, then all the employee's services for that pay period must be counted as covered employment, and vice versa. In these cases, a pay period cannot exceed 31 consecutive days.

SELF-STUDY QUIZ 3–1. *Which of the following are covered by FICA (indicate Yes or No)?*

_____ 1. Andrian Mitchell, a full-time life insurance salesperson.
_____ 2. John Sain, a federal government employee, hired in 1990.
_____ 3. Bonnie Stone, a real estate agent.
_____ 4. Stuart Schuck, who offers lawn care service to homeowners in the neighborhood.

Taxable Wages

The amount of wages paid by employers to their employees during the calendar year determines the amount of OASDI/HI taxes. The basis of payment may be hourly, daily, weekly, biweekly, semimonthly, monthly, annually, piece rate, or a percentage of profits. Wages include the following:

1. Actual money received by employees, whether called wages or salaries.
2. Cash value of meals and lodging provided for the convenience of the *employees*.
3. Bonuses and commissions paid by the employer with respect to employment.

Other common types of payments that are considered wages under FICA are listed in Figure 3–3 (on page 3–8).

FIGURE 3-2

Exempt Employment

Employment Type	Conditions of Exclusion
Agricultural services	Compensation of all farm workers is less than $2,500 in any calendar year, or compensation is less than $150 for each worker in a calendar year. Remuneration other than cash is not taxed.
Domestic service	Service performed in a local college club or a chapter of a college fraternity or sorority by a student who is *enrolled* and *regularly attending classes* at the school, college, or university.
Service performed by children under the age of 18, in parental business	This exclusion applies to children employed by a father or mother whose business is a sole proprietorship or a partnership. This exclusion does *not* apply to children under age 18 employed by a family-owned corporation.
Services performed by civilians for the U.S. government	Of any of its agencies if such agencies are specifically exempt from the employer portion of the FICA tax, or if such services are covered by a retirement system established by law.
Service performed by railroad workers	For employers covered by the Railroad Retirement Tax Act.
Services performed in the employment of foreign governments	Ambassadors, ministers, and other diplomatic officers and employees.
Services performed by an individual under the age of 18, as a newspaper distributor	Delivery or distribution of newspapers or shopping news, excluding delivery or distribution to a point for subsequent delivery or distribution.
Services performed by student nurses	In the employ of a hospital or a nurses' training school chartered or approved under state law, and the nurses are *enrolled* and *regularly attending classes* in that school. FICA only exempts the pay received by student nurses if the pay is nominal and their work is part-time and an integral part of the curriculum.
Services performed by students for their public or private school, college, or university	Working as "noncareer" employees while enrolled academically at least half-time (for undergraduates, at least six credit hours).

Tips. FICA considers cash tips of $20 or more in a calendar month to be taxable wages. Employees must report their tips in writing to their employers by the 10th of the month following the month in which the tips were received. Employers can require more frequent reporting. Rules for reporting tips by employees and employers are summarized below.

1. Employees can report tips on *Form 4070, Employee's Report of Tips to Employer,* shown in Figure 3–4 (see page 3-9).
2. Employees failing to report tips to their employers may be penalized 50 percent of the FICA tax due on the tips. The Tax Court may rule that the nonreporting of tip income constitutes fraud.

FIGURE 3-3

Other Types of Taxable Wages

Type of Wage	Conditions
Advance payments	For future work to be done by the individual receiving the advance where the employer considers the work satisfaction for the advance.
Back pay awards	Pay received in one period for employment in an earlier period, unless it is a settlement for failure to employ workers.
Bonuses	For services rendered by employees for an employer.
Cash and noncash prizes and awards	For outstanding work, exceeding sales quotas, contributing suggestions that increase productivity or efficiency.
Christmas gifts	Except gifts of nominal value (such as a turkey or a ham).
Commissions	On sales or insurance premiums paid as compensation for services performed.
Death benefits	Wage payments (not gratuity) to an employee's dependents after the employee's death. Payments made after the calendar year in which the employee died and employer-provided death-benefit plans are not taxed.
Dismissal pay	Payments by employer for involuntary separation of an employee from the employer's service.
Employees' federal income and social security taxes paid for by the employer	Payment of the employee portion of the FICA tax by the employer for domestics working in the employer's home and for agricultural laborers is an exception to this rule.
Fringe benefits—noncash	Personal use of company car, employer-provided vehicles for commuting, flights on employer-provided airplanes, and free or discounted flights on commercial airlines.
Guaranteed annual wage payments	Union contract agreements whereby an employer guarantees certain employees will either work during or be paid for each normal workweek in a calendar year.
Idle time or standby payments	Amounts paid workers who are at the beck and call of an employer but who are performing no work.
Insurance premiums paid by the employer for an employee's group-term life insurance coverage	Exceeding $50,000. For retired workers, their group-term life insurance that exceeds $50,000 is also subject to FICA.
Jury duty pay	The difference between the employee's regular wages and the amount received for jury duty, paid by employers.
Moving expense reimbursements	Unless the employee will be entitled to deduct these moving expenses in determining taxable income for federal income tax purposes.
Retroactive wage increases	
Sick pay—first six months	For sickness or accident disability. Payments under a state temporary disability law are also subject to FICA taxes.
Stock payments	The fair market value of stock transferred by employers to employees as remuneration for services.
Vacation pay	

3. Employers must collect the employee's FICA tax on the tips that each employee reports. The employer deducts the employee's FICA tax from the wages due the employee or from other funds the employee makes available.

4. Employers are also liable for their share of the FICA tax on any tips subject to the employee's FICA tax. However, businesses that provide food or beverages for consumption on their premises may take a business tax credit on the business income tax return. The credit is an amount equal to the employer's FICA tax paid on the tip income less the FICA tax paid on the excess of the federal minimum wage over the employee's actual hourly rate of pay.

5. Large food and beverage establishments (11 or more employees where tipping is customary) are required to allocate to their tipped employees the excess of 8% of the establishment's gross receipts over the tips actually reported by their employees. However, employers withhold FICA taxes only on the tips reported by employees, not from tips that are allocated. The amount of allocated tip income is shown separately on the employee's *Wage and Tax Statement (Form W-2)*, explained in Chapter 4.

6. Every large food or beverage establishment must report the amount of its receipts from food and beverage operations annually to the IRS and the amount of tips reported by its employees. [*Form 8027, Employer's Annual Information Return of Tip Income and Allocated Tips* (not illustrated)]

on the

JOB

Many restaurants now use software to help in tracking tips. Some programs add a "prompt" that freezes the computer screen as employees try to clock out if they have not entered their tips for the day.

Exempt Payments.   FICA tax only applies to types of compensation considered taxable under the law. Examples of compensation that the law excludes from the tax follow.

Meals and Lodging.   FICA exempts the value of meals or lodging furnished to employees for the *convenience of the employer*. The value of meals or lodging not meeting this test will be subject to FICA tax. The IRS places no specific value on meals or lodging furnished by employers to employees. Instead, the IRS relies on state valuations. Where a state has no law or regulation on the subject, fair value is defined as the reasonable prevailing value of the meals or lodging.

FIGURE 3-4

Form 4070, Employee's Report of Tips to Employer

Form **4070** (Rev. July 1999) Department of the Treasury Internal Revenue Service	**Employee's Report of Tips to Employer** ▶ For Paperwork Reduction Act Notice, see back of form.	OMB No. 1545-0065
Employee's name and address Morton O. Tanenbaum 1704 Elm St., San Diego, CA 92121-8837		Social security number 269 : 21 : 7220
Employer's name and address (include establishment name, if different) Holland House Inn 9 Fairway, San Diego, CA 92123-1369		1 Cash tips received $389.10
		2 Credit card tips received —
		3 Tips paid out —
Month or shorter period in which tips were received from July 1, 20___ , to July 31, 20___		4 Net tips (lines 1 + 2 - 3) $389.10
Signature *Morton O. Tanenbaum*		Date August 10, 20___

on the

Net

http://www.ssa.gov/SSA_Home.html
Social Security Online.
Maintained by the Social Security Administration, it contains general FICA information.

http://www.ssa.gov/employer_info/employer_guide.txt
"Employer's Guide to Filing Timely and Accurate W-2 Reports"

Sick Pay.   The *first six months of sick pay* an employee receives is considered wages and is subject to FICA tax. Payments made *after* the expiration of the six consecutive calendar months following the last month in which the employee worked for the employer are not taxed. The period off the job must be continuous for six months. Any return to work starts a new six-month period. FICA defines *sick pay* as any payment made to individuals due to personal injury or sickness that does not constitute wages. Sick pay payments must be part of a plan to which the employer is a party. Sick pay must not include amounts paid to individuals who are permanently disabled.

Sick pay payments may also be made by a third party, including insurance companies, trusts providing sick and accident benefits, and employers' associations funded to pay sickness and accident benefits. The third party is treated as a separate employer and must withhold and deposit the employees' FICA taxes. However, the third party may be relieved of the liability for the employer's share of the FICA taxes if the third party fulfills each of these requirements:

1. Withholds and deposits the employee portion of the FICA tax.
2. Notifies the employer of the amount of wages or compensation involved.

The liability for that share of the taxes then reverts back to the employer. For convenience, an employer may contract to have the third party deposit the employer portion of the tax as well as the employee portion.

Generally, payments made to employees or their dependents for medical or hospital expenses in connection with sickness or accident disability are not considered wages. However, these payments must be part of a plan established by the employer for all employees or for a particular class of employees.

Contributions to Deferred Compensation Plans.   Employee pretax contributions under a qualified cash or deferred compensation arrangement (*Tax-Deferred Retirement Plans*, as discussed in Chapter 1) are subject to FICA tax. However, the employers' matching contributions are tax-free.

Payments for Educational Assistance.   *Educational assistance* refers to the expenses that an employer pays for an employee's education, such as tuition, fees, and payments for books, supplies, and equipment. Also, educational assistance includes the cost of employer-provided courses of instruction (books, supplies, and equipment). Educational assistance excludes payment for tools or supplies that employees keep after they complete a course of instruction. Payments for job-related educational expenses are not subject to FICA taxes if the education maintains or improves skills required by the individual's employment. Payments for non-job-related educational expenses up to $5,250 are also exempt from FICA taxes.

SELF-STUDY QUIZ 3–2. *Which of the following are subject to FICA tax (indicate Yes or No)?*

_____ 1. A $15 gift certificate for a local grocery store given to employees as a Christmas gift.
_____ 2. Sales representatives using their company cars for personal use on weeknights and weekends.
_____ 3. Employer's contributions to a Simplified Employee Pension Plan for its employees.
_____ 4. A tuition reimbursement plan that pays tuition for employees successfully completing job-related courses.
_____ 5. Severance pay made to an employee discharged for theft.

Taxable Wage Base

The employer must consider the *taxable wage base* when computing the OASDI portion of the FICA tax. The law exempts wages that exceed this base during the calendar year ($89,700 estimated for 2003). Once the OASDI taxable wage base has been reached, all payments made to the employee during the remainder of the year are not taxable. The wage base applies to amounts *paid* employees in a calendar year and not to the time when the services were performed by the employees. The HI portion of the FICA tax does *not* have a ceiling; thus, employers compute this tax on the total wages and salaries paid during the year. Just as social security benefits increase each year based on changes in the Consumer Price Index, the taxable wage base is increased also.

IRS CONNECTION

The actual OASDI taxable wage base is not released until October of the prior year.

EXAMPLE

Renee Riley receives pay on January 3, 2003, for work done during the last week of December 2002. The wages would be taxed as income in the calendar year 2003, using 2003 tax rates.

Tax Rates.   The Social Security Act, as amended, imposes a separate tax on employers and employees for old-age, survivors, and disability insurance (OASDI) benefits and for hospital insurance (HI) benefits. The 2003 tax rates for both the employer and the employee portions of the tax follow:

	Rate	*Wage Base*
OASDI	6.20%	$89,700 (estimated)
HI	1.45%	None

IRS CONNECTION

Over 40 percent of U.S. workers pay more in payroll taxes than in income taxes.

Determining OASDI Tax:

If:

Cumulative Wages	+	Current Wage Payment	< OASDI Wage Base, then
$52,400	+	$3,000	= $55,400

Compute the OASDI tax on the entire wage payment. ($3,000 × 0.062 = $186.00)

If:

Cumulative Wages	+	Current Wage Payment	> OASDI Wage Base, then
$87,000	+	$3,000	= $90,000

Compute the OASDI tax on the part of the current wage payment that brings the cumulative wages up to OASDI taxable wage limit:

Cumulative Wages	+	Taxable Wages	= Cumulative Limit
$87,000	+	$2,700	= $89,700

on the
JOB

If you acquire substantially all of the business property of another employer, or a unit of that employer's business, you are considered a successor employer and can use the wages the prior employer paid to your new employees against the taxable wage base.

Employees' FICA (OASDI/HI) Taxes and Withholdings.   FICA requires employers to collect the OASDI/HI taxes from their employees and pay the taxes to the IRS at the same time they pay their own tax. The employer deducts the tax from the wages at the time of payment. The amount of each tax to be withheld is computed by applying to the employee's taxable wages the tax rate in effect at the time that the wages are received. In calculating the amounts of FICA taxes to withhold from employees' pays, the employer may disregard any fractional part of a cent, unless it is one-half cent or more, which must be rounded up one cent.

The liability for the tax extends to both the employee and the employer, but after the employer has collected the tax, the employee's liability ceases. The following examples illustrate the computation of the FICA taxes to be withheld.

EXAMPLE

1. Maria Schwant, employed by the Gobel Company, earned $460 during the week ended February 7, 2003. Prior to February 9, Schwant's cumulative gross earnings for the year were $2,765.70. FICA taxes to be withheld on $460 are computed as follows:

OASDI		*HI*	
Taxable Wages	$ 460	Taxable Wages	$ 460
Tax Rate	× 6.2%	Tax Rate	× 1.45%
OASDI Tax to Be Withheld	$ 28.52	HI Tax to Be Withheld	$ 6.67

2. Anne Fergo, a salaried employee of the Lafayette Advertising Agency, is paid every Friday. She earned $1,725 for this pay. Prior to the pay of November 21, 2003, she had earned $89,250. The FICA taxes to be withheld from Fergo's pay on November 21 are computed as follows:

OASDI		_HI_	
Taxable Wage Limit	$89,700	Taxable Wage Limit	NONE
Wages Paid to Date	89,250	Wages Paid to Date	$89,250
Taxable Wages This Pay	$ 450	Taxable Wages This Pay . .	$ 1,725
Tax Rate	× 6.2%	Tax Rate	× 1.45%
OASDI Tax to Be Withheld	$ 27.90	HI Tax to Be Withheld	$ 25.01

3. Marc Todd, president of Uni-Sight, Inc., is paid $3,700 semimonthly. Prior to his last pay on December 30, 2003, Todd had earned $95,100. The FICA taxes to be withheld from Todd's pay on December 30 are computed as follows:

OASDI		_HI_	
Taxable Wage Limit	$89,700	Taxable Wage Limit	NONE
Wages Paid to Date	95,100	Wages Paid to Date	$95,100
Taxable Wages This Pay	-0-	Taxable Wage This Pay . . .	$ 3,700
OASDI Tax to Be Withheld	-0-	Tax Rate	× 1.45%
		HI Tax to Be Withheld	$ 53.65

Sometimes an employee has paid FICA taxes on wages in excess of the taxable base because of having worked for more than one employer. If so, the employee is entitled to a refund for the overpayment. The amount of the overpayment is credited against the employee's federal income taxes for that year. Instructions are given on the _Individual Income Tax Return (Form 1040)_ that explain how the overpayment should be treated.

Employer's FICA (OASDI) Taxes. In addition to withholding the correct amount of FICA tax from the employees' taxable earnings, the employer must make contributions to the program. The employer's portion of the tax is based on the wages paid to the employees. The employer's taxes, however, are not computed on the wages paid each employee, but on the total taxable wages paid all employees. As with employee withholdings, once the OASDI taxable wage base is reached, the employer no longer contributes for that particular employee. The OASDI tax is 6.2 percent of each employee's wages paid, and the HI tax is 1.45 percent of each employee's wages paid.

EXAMPLE

The Bradford Company has 100 employees, each earning $375.25 a week.

OASDI

Amount of OASDI tax withheld from each employee's paycheck each week:	$23.27	(6.2% × $375.25)
Total tax withheld from the 100 employees' wages:	$2,327.00	($23.27 × 100)
Tax on employer:	$2,326.55	(6.2% × $37,525)

_HI_

Amount of HI tax withheld from each employee's paycheck each week:	$5.44	(1.45% × $375.25)
Total tax withheld from the 100 employees' wages is:	$544.00	($5.44 × 100)
Tax on employer:	$544.11	(1.45% × $37,525)

Successor Employer. Wages paid by the prior employer can be counted towards the annual OASDI wage base by a successor employer if all the following criteria are met:

1. The successor has acquired all the property used in the prior employer's business.

2. The affected employees were employed immediately before and continued working right after the transfer of the business.

3. Wages were paid by the prior employer during the calendar year of acquisition.

SELF-STUDY QUIZ 3–3. *McDuff's Fine Foods employs five people. For each person, compute the amount of OASDI and HI tax for the first week in January.*

Employee	Weekly Wage	OASDI	HI
Mary Britton	$ 225.00		
Bob Yold	300.00		
Martin Rold	175.00		
Maria Aldo	1,000.00		
Gil Hammerstien	2,200.00		

Compute the employer's portion of the FICA taxes, based on the payroll data above.

Will any of the employees exceed the taxable wage base during the year? If yes, on which payday will it occur?

A SELF-EMPLOYED PERSON

The Self-Employment Contributions Act (SECA) extended coverage under the social security system to the self-employed in 1951. Over the years, most self-employed persons have become covered by the law.

Self-Employment Income

SECA uses an individual's *self-employment income* as the basis for levying taxes and for determining the amount of income to credit toward OASDI insurance benefits or HI coverage. Self-employment income generally consists of the net earnings derived by individuals from a business or profession carried on as a sole proprietorship or as a partnership. Self-employed persons determine their net earnings by finding the sum of the following:

1. The **gross income** derived by an individual from any business or profession carried on, less allowable deductions attributable to such a business or profession, and

2. The **individual's distributive share** (whether or not distributed) of the ordinary net income or loss from any business or profession carried on by a partnership of which the individual is a member.

Usually the net business income of individuals, as shown in their income tax returns, makes up their net earnings from self-employment for the purpose of the Social Security Act. Earnings of less than $400 from self-employment are ignored. For computing the OASDI taxes, the maximum self-employment taxable income of any individual for 2003 is $89,700 (estimated). For the HI taxes, however, the total self-employment income is taxable. If the individual is also an employee of another company, the wages received can reduce the amount of self-employment income that is taxed for OASDI (wages + self-employment income > $89,700).

on the

Net

www.irs.ustreas.gov/prod/
forms_pubs/pubs/p15a02.htm

Lists **IRS criteria for determining employee versus independent contractor status.**

E X A M P L E

Beth Rolland receives wages of $90,000 from her job in 2003. She also earned $15,000 in self-employment income during the year. In computing her OASDI taxes, none of her self-employment income is considered, since her wages exceed the taxable wage base of $89,700. However, in computing her HI taxes, all of her earnings from self-employment are taxed.

If the wages received in 2003 amount to less than $89,700, any self-employment earnings amounting to $400 or more must be counted as self-employment income up to an aggregate amount of $89,700 for OASDI taxes.

EXAMPLE

George Talbot receives wages in 2003 amounting to $75,500. His net earnings from self-employment amount to $14,600. Talbot must count $14,200 of his earnings in determining taxable self-employment income for OASDI taxes.

FICA Taxable Wage Base	–	Wages Rec'd in 2003	=	Taxable Self-Employment Income
$89,700	–	$75,500	=	$14,200

Taxable Year. In computing the taxes on self-employment income, sole proprietors use the same taxable year as that used for income tax purposes. In the case of a partnership, the taxable year of the partners may not correspond with that of the partnership. In such instances, the partners are required to include in computing net earnings from self-employment their distributive share of the income or loss from the partnership for any taxable year ending with or within their taxable year.

Reporting Self-Employment Income. Sole proprietors report their self-employment income by transferring certain data from *Schedule C (Form 1040), Profit or Loss from Business* to *Schedule SE (Form 1040), Self-Employment Tax*. SECA requires self-employed persons to include SECA taxes in their quarterly payment of estimated income taxes. The taxpayer's estimated tax is the sum of the estimated income taxes and SECA taxes less any credits against the tax.

Self-Employment OASDI/HI Taxes. The self-employed tax rate for 2003 on the net earnings is 15.3%—12.4% for OASDI and 2.9% for HI.

SELF-STUDY QUIZ 3–4. *Lori Kinmark works as a jeweler for a local company. She earns $1,000 per week, plus a year-end bonus of $2,000. Kinmark also earns an additional net self-employment income of $28,000 per year.*

$ _____   **1.** Compute Kinmark's annual earnings from employment.

$ _____   **2.** Compute Kinmark's total earnings from job and from self-employment income.

$ _____   **3.** How much self-employment income should Kinmark include in computing taxable self-employment income for OASDI taxes?

$ _____   **4.** What are the total FICA taxes on her self-employment earnings?

APPLICATION FOR EMPLOYER IDENTIFICATION NUMBER (FORM SS-4)

Every employer of one or more persons must file an application for an identification number, *Form SS-4*, available from any IRS or social security office. Figure 3–5 shows a filled-in copy of Form SS-4. The employer should file this form early enough to allow for processing, preferably four to five weeks before the identification number (EIN) is needed. The employer files the application with the IRS service center where the federal tax returns are filed. If the employer has no legal residence, principal place of business, or principal office in any IRS district, the application should be sent to: Internal Revenue Service, Entity Control, Philadelphia, PA 19255-0005.

The employer must enter this EIN on all returns, forms, and correspondence sent to the District Director of Internal Revenue that relate to the taxes imposed under FICA. The employer uses the EIN in any correspondence with the Social Security Administration (SSA) and enters the number on forms issued by the SSA. Regardless of how many different business locations are operated, the employer receives only one EIN. The penalty for failing to supply the identification number is discussed later in this chapter. If the owner sells or otherwise transfers a business, the new owner must file an application for a new identification number.

---

on the

Net

http://www.irs.ustreas.gov/prod/ tax_edu/teletax/tc755.html
Information from the IRS on how to apply for an EIN.

http://www.irs.ustreas.gov/prod/ forms_pubs/forms.html

LEARNING OBJECTIVE **4**

IRS CONNECTION

Starting in 2002, employers could call the Social Security Administration (866-816-2065) to request an employer identification number for a new business. A pilot program is set to begin this year that will permit employers to get ID numbers via the Internet.

FIGURE 3-5

Form SS-4, Application for Employer Identification Number

Form **SS-4**	**Application for Employer Identification Number**	EIN
(Rev. February 1998) Department of the Treasury Internal Revenue Service	(For use by employers, corporations, partnerships, trusts, estates, churches, government agencies, certain individuals, and others. See instructions.) ▶ Keep a copy for your records.	OMB No. 1545-0003

Please type or print clearly.

1 Name of applicant (legal name) (see instructions)
Montana Mining, Inc.

2 Trade name of business (if different from name on line 1)

3 Executor, trustee, "care of" name
Care of Carla P. Ortiz

4a Mailing address (street address) (room, apt., or suite no.)
P.O. Box 447

5a Business address (if different from address on lines 4a and 4b)
1200 High Gap

4b City, state, and ZIP code
Butte, MT 59701-0210

5b City, state, and ZIP code
Butte, MT 59701-1200

6 County and state where principal business is located
Silver Bow, MT

7 Name of principal officer, general partner, grantor, owner, or trustor—SSN or ITIN may be required (see instructions) ▶ Grant X. Bilton, President 379-39-3280

8a Type of entity (Check only one box.) (see instructions)

Caution: If applicant is a limited liability company, see the instructions for line 8a.

☐ Sole proprietor (SSN) _____
☐ Partnership
☐ REMIC
☐ State/local government
☐ Church or church-controlled organization
☐ Other nonprofit organization (specify) ▶ _____
☐ Other (specify) ▶

☐ Personal service corp.
☐ National Guard
☐ Farmers' cooperative

☐ Estate (SSN of decedent) _____
☐ Plan administrator (SSN) _____
☒ Other corporation (specify) ▶ Extraction
☐ Trust
☐ Federal government/military
(enter GEN if applicable) _____

8b If a corporation, name the state or foreign country (if applicable) where incorporated

State: Montana

Foreign country:

9 Reason for applying (Check only one box.) (see instructions)
☒ Started new business (specify type) ▶ Mining
☐ Hired employees (Check the box and see line 12.)
☐ Created a pension plan (specify type) ▶

☐ Banking purpose (specify purpose) ▶ _____
☐ Changed type of organization (specify new type) ▶ _____
☐ Purchased going business
☐ Created a trust (specify type) ▶ _____
☐ Other (specify) ▶

10 Date business started or acquired (month, day, year) (see instructions)
July, 3, 20--

11 Closing month of accounting year (see instructions)
June

12 First date wages or annuities were paid or will be paid (month, day, year). Note: *If applicant is a withholding agent, enter date income will first be paid to nonresident alien. (month, day, year)* . . . . ▶ July 12, 20--

13 Highest number of employees expected in the next 12 months. Note: *If the applicant does not expect to have any employees during the period, enter -0-. (see instructions)* . . . . ▶

Nonagricultural	Agricultural	Household
450		

14 Principal activity (see instructions) ▶ Copper Extraction

15 Is the principal business activity manufacturing? . . . . ☐ Yes ☒ No
If "Yes," principal product and raw material used ▶

16 To whom are most of the products or services sold? Please check one box.
☐ Public (retail)   ☐ Other (specify) ▶   ☒ Business (wholesale)   ☐ N/A

17a Has the applicant ever applied for an employer identification number for this or any other business? . . . . ☐ Yes ☒ No
Note: *If "Yes," please complete lines 17b and 17c.*

17b If you checked "Yes" on line 17a, give applicant's legal name and trade name shown on prior application, if different from line 1 or 2 above.
Legal name ▶   Trade name ▶

17c Approximate date when and city and state where the application was filed. Enter previous employer identification number if known.
Approximate date when filed (mo., day, year) | City and state where filed | Previous EIN

Under penalties of perjury, I declare that I have examined this application, and to the best of my knowledge and belief, it is true, correct, and complete.

Business telephone number (include area code)
406-555-2400

Fax telephone number (include area code)

Name and title (Please type or print clearly.) ▶ Carla P. Ortiz, V.P., Finance

Signature ▶ *Carla P. Ortiz*   Date ▶ 7/3/--

Note: *Do not write below this line. For official use only.*

Please leave blank ▶	Geo.	Ind.	Class	Size	Reason for applying

For Paperwork Reduction Act Notice, see page 4.   Cat. No. 16055N   Form **SS-4** (Rev. 2-98)

on the

JOB

The employer must obtain each employee's SSN to enter on Form W-2 (discussed in Chapter 4). If the employer does not provide the correct name and SSN, he or she may owe a penalty.

If the employee's name is not correct as shown on the card, including a name change due to marriage or divorce, the employee should request a new card.

IRS CONNECTION

Employers may verify employees' social security numbers through the SSA's Enumeration Verification System (EVS). To verify up to five names and numbers, call 1-800-772-6270. For up to fifty, contact your local social security office. For more than fifty, preregistration is required. For information, call the EVS service at 410-965-7140.

EMPLOYEE'S APPLICATION FOR SOCIAL SECURITY CARD (FORM SS-5)

Under the Social Security Act, every employee and every self-employed person must have a social security number (SSN). The application for a SSN is available at any social security or IRS office. The *Application for a Social Security Card (Form SS-5)* can be filed with any field office of the SSA. Figure 3–6 shows a filled-in copy of Form SS-5.

The Social Security Act requires applicants for a social security card to furnish evidence of their age, identity, and U.S. citizenship or lawful alien status. Applicants may either apply by mailing the required documents and forms to their nearest social security office or apply in person. If they are age 18 or older and have never had a social security card, or are aliens whose immigration documents should not be sent through the mail, they must apply in person. After filing Form SS-5, the applicant will receive from the SSA a card showing the assigned social security number.

Upon receipt of their SSN, employees should inform their employers of the number assigned them. If employees change positions, they must notify the new employer of their SSN when they begin employment. If an employee changes his or her name by court order or by marriage, the individual should request a new social security card by completing Form SS-5. Employees may have their SSN changed at any time by applying to the SSA and showing good reasons for a change. Otherwise, only one number is assigned to an employee and the employee will continue to use that number regardless of the changes in positions or employers.

For aliens who must file U.S. tax returns but are not eligible to receive a social security number, the IRS has instituted *Form W-7, Application for IRS Individual Taxpayer Identification Number* (ITIN). An ITIN is intended for tax purposes only.

The Secretary of Health and Human Services is authorized to assure that SSNs are issued to or on behalf of children who are below school age at the request of their parents or guardians and to children of school age when they first enroll in school. Further, SSNs must be obtained for children age one or over who are claimed as dependents on federal income tax returns. Taxpayers must list on their tax returns the taxpayer identification numbers of any claimed dependents. The Secretary also ensures that SSNs are assigned to aliens when they are admitted to the United States under conditions that permit them to work.

Criminal penalties (of up to $5,000 or imprisonment of up to 5 years, or both) exist for persons involved in the following situations:

1. Knowingly and willfully using a SSN obtained with false information.
2. Using someone else's SSN.
3. Altering a social security card.
4. Buying or selling a card claimed to be issued by the Secretary.
5. Possessing a card or counterfeit card with the intent to sell or alter it.

Returns Required for Social Security Purposes

Employers covered under FICA are liable for their own FICA taxes and their employees' FICA and income taxes withheld from wages. Withholding of income taxes is discussed in Chapter 4. Every employer (except those employing agricultural workers) who is required to withhold income taxes from wages or who is liable for social security taxes must file:

1. A *quarterly* tax and information return. This return shows the total FICA wage paid and the total FICA taxes (employer and employee contributions) and federal income taxes withheld.
2. An *annual* return of withheld federal income taxes. This return covers *nonpayroll* items such as backup withholding, withholding on gambling winnings, pensions, annuities, IRAs, and military retirement.

Generally, an employer must either electronically transfer to the IRS or deposit in an authorized depository the income taxes and social security taxes withheld and the employer's FICA taxes.

FIGURE 3-6

Form SS-5, Application for a Social Security Card

SOCIAL SECURITY ADMINISTRATION
Application for a Social Security Card

Form Approved
OMB No. 0960-0066

INSTRUCTIONS
- Please read "How To Complete This Form" on page 2.
- Print or type using black or blue ink. DO NOT USE PENCIL.
- After you complete this form, take or mail it along with the required documents to your nearest Social Security office.
- If you are completing this form for someone else, answer the questions as they apply to that person. Then, sign your name in question 16.

1 NAME To Be Shown On Card
▶ Sandra   Mary   Carson
FIRST   FULL MIDDLE NAME   LAST

FULL NAME AT BIRTH IF OTHER THAN ABOVE
FIRST   FULL MIDDLE NAME   LAST

OTHER NAMES USED

2 MAILING ADDRESS Do Not Abbreviate
▶ 18 Dundee Avenue
STREET ADDRESS, APT. NO., PO BOX, RURAL ROUTE NO.
Sacramento   California   95814
CITY   STATE   ZIP CODE

3 CITIZENSHIP (Check One)
[X] U.S. Citizen [ ] Legal Alien Allowed To Work [ ] Legal Alien Not Allowed To Work [ ] Foreign Student Allowed Restricted Employment [ ] Conditionally Legalized Alien Allowed To Work [ ] Other (See Instructions On Page 2)

4 SEX [ ] Male [X] Female

5 RACE/ETHNIC DESCRIPTION (Check One Only—Voluntary)
[ ] Asian, Asian-American Or Pacific Islander [ ] Hispanic [X] Black (Not Hispanic) [ ] North American Indian Or Alaskan Native [ ] White (Not Hispanic)

6 DATE OF BIRTH 8 1 -- MONTH DAY YEAR

7 PLACE OF BIRTH (Do Not Abbreviate) Oakland California
CITY   STATE OR FOREIGN COUNTRY   FCI   Office Use Only

8 MOTHER'S MAIDEN NAME Ruth Ann Archer
FIRST   FULL MIDDLE NAME   LAST NAME AT HER BIRTH

9 FATHER'S NAME Roger Paul Carson
FIRST   FULL MIDDLE NAME   LAST

10 Has the person in item 1 ever applied for or received a Social Security number before?
[ ] Yes (If "yes", answer questions 11-13.) [X] No (If "no", go on to question 14.) [ ] Don't Know (If "don't know", go on to question 14.)

11 Enter the Social Security number previously assigned to the person listed in item 1.
□□□ - □□ - □□□□

12 Enter the name shown on the most recent Social Security card issued for the person listed in item 1.
FIRST   MIDDLE   LAST

13 Enter any different date of birth if used on an earlier application for a card.
MONTH DAY YEAR

14 TODAY'S DATE ▶ 1 12 -- MONTH DAY YEAR **15 DAYTIME PHONE NUMBER** ▶ (916) 555-4321 AREA CODE

DELIBERATELY FURNISHING (OR CAUSING TO BE FURNISHED) FALSE INFORMATION ON THIS APPLICATION IS A CRIME PUNISHABLE BY FINE OR IMPRISONMENT, OR BOTH.

16 YOUR SIGNATURE
▶ *Sandra M. Carson*

17 YOUR RELATIONSHIP TO THE PERSON IN ITEM 1 IS:
[X] Self [ ] Natural Or Adoptive Parent [ ] Legal Guardian [ ] Other (Specify)

DO NOT WRITE BELOW THIS LINE (FOR SSA USE ONLY)					
NPN		DOC	NTI	CAN	ITV
PBC	EVI	EVA	EVC	NWR	DNR	UNIT
EVIDENCE SUBMITTED				SIGNATURE AND TITLE OF EMPLOYEE(S) REVIEWING EVIDENCE AND/OR CONDUCTING INTERVIEW	

DATE

DCL   DATE

Form **SS-5** (5/88)

Any employer who fails to pay the withheld income taxes and FICA taxes, fails to make deposits and payments, or does not file the tax returns as required by law may be required to deposit such taxes in a special trust account for the U.S. government and file monthly tax returns. Figure 3–7 lists and briefly describes the major forms used to prepare FICA tax returns and deposits.

Deposit Requirements (Nonagricultural Workers)

LEARNING OBJECTIVE 5

The requirements for depositing FICA taxes and income taxes withheld from employees' wages vary according to the amount of such taxes reported during a *lookback period.* Depending on the total amount of taxes involved (federal income tax and FICA tax withheld from employees' earnings plus the employer's portion of the FICA tax), employers may have to pay their taxes several times a month or monthly. Some employers may not have to make any deposits but, instead, may pay their taxes at the time of filing their quarterly return, Form 941, discussed later in this chapter.

The amount of employment taxes that the employer reports on the quarterly returns for the four quarters in the lookback period determines if the employer is a monthly or a semiweekly depositor. A lookback period consists of four quarters beginning July 1 of the second preceding year and ending June 30 of the prior year. These four quarters are the employer's lookback period even if no taxes were reported for any of the quarters. Figure 3–8 shows the lookback period for 2003. Each November, the IRS notifies employers whether they will be a monthly or a semiweekly depositor for the next calendar year.

Monthly Depositors.   A *monthly depositor* is one who reported employment taxes of *$50,000* or *less* for the four quarters in the lookback period. Monthly depositors are required to deposit their taxes in an authorized financial institution by the 15th day of the following month. If a deposit is required to be made on a day that is not a banking day, the deposit is considered timely if it is made by the close of the next banking day.

A *new employer* becomes a monthly depositor until a lookback period that can be used to determine deposit frequency is established. However, if an unsatisfied deposit of $100,000 or more triggers the $100,000 One-Day Rule (discussed on page 3-20) at any time during the year, the new employer becomes a semiweekly depositor for the remainder of the current calendar year and the subsequent calendar year.

EXAMPLE

1. The Robart Company's deposit status for 2003 was determined by using the lookback period shown in Figure 3–8. During the two quarters of 2000, Robart reported employment taxes (FICA & Employees' Income Tax) of $16,000. For each of the two quarters in 2002, the company reported taxes of $10,000. Since the taxes reported by Robart during the lookback period do not exceed $50,000, the company is classed as a monthly depositor and follows the monthly rule for the current year, 2003.

2. Valencia, Inc., is a monthly depositor. For July taxes, Valencia must deposit the $11,000 on or before August 15, 2003.

Semiweekly Depositors.   A *semiweekly depositor* is one who reported employment taxes of more than $50,000 for the four quarters in the lookback period. Depending upon what day of the week the employer makes wage payments, deposits must be made as follows:

Payment Days	Deposit by
Wednesday, Thursday, and/or Friday	Following Wednesday
Saturday, Sunday, Monday, and/or Tuesday	Following Friday

FIGURE 3 - 7

Major Forms for Preparing FICA Tax Returns and Deposits

Form 941, Employer's Quarterly Federal Tax Return	Required of all covered employers, except employers of household and agricultural employees, who withhold income tax and social security taxes. (See Figure 3–11.)
Form 941c, Supporting Statement to Correct Information	Used to correct income and social security tax information previously reported on Forms 941, 941-M, 941-SS, 943, 945.
Form 941-V, Form 941 Payment Voucher	Filled in by employers with a total tax liability of less than $2,500 for the quarter who are making payment with Form 941.
Form 941-M, Employer's Monthly Federal Tax Return	Required of employers who have not complied with the requirements for filing returns or paying or depositing all taxes reported on quarterly returns. Notification to file Form 941-M is received from the District Director, and pread-dressed forms are mailed to the employer monthly.
Form 941-PR, Employer's Quarterly Federal Tax Return	Required of employers to report social security taxes for workers in Puerto Rico.
Form 941-SS, Employer's Quarterly Federal Tax Return	Required of employers to report social security taxes for workers in American Samoa, Guam, the Northern Mariana Islands, and the Virgin Islands.
Form 943, Employer's Annual Tax Return for Agricultural Employees	Used by employers of agricultural workers for reporting FICA and income taxes on wages paid.
Form 945, Annual Return of Withheld Federal Income Tax	Required of employers to report income tax withheld from nonpayroll payments.
Form 8109, Federal Tax Deposit Coupon	Completed at the time of depositing various types of taxes such as withheld income and FICA (Form 941), agricultural withheld income and FICA (Form 943), and federal unemployment (Form 940, as will be discussed in Chapter 5).

If a semiweekly deposit period spans two quarters, the liability that applies to one quarter is separate from the liability that applies to the other quarter. Even though the deposits are made on the same day, two separate deposits must be made.

FIGURE 3 - 8

Lookback Period for Calendar Year 2003

2001		2002	
July–Sept.	Oct.–Dec.	Jan.–Mar.	Apr.–June

EXAMPLE

1. The Meyer Company's deposit status for 2003 was determined by using the lookback period shown in Figure 3–8. In the two quarters of 2001, Meyer reported taxes of $35,000. The taxes reported in the two quarters of 2002 totaled $30,000. **Since the total taxes reported during the four quarters of the lookback period exceeded $50,000, Meyer is subject to the semiweekly rule for the current year, 2003.**

2. The employees of DeVeau, a semiweekly depositor, are paid every Monday. On October 6, 2003, DeVeau has accumulated taxes totaling $24,000. DeVeau is required to deposit the $24,000 on or before the following Friday, October 10.

3. Yeltz Inc., a semiweekly depositor, has accumulated taxes on Saturday, September 27, 2003, and on Tuesday, September 30, 2003. The company needs to make two separate deposits on Friday, October 3, even though they are part of the same semiweekly deposit period.

One-Day Rule.   If on any day during a deposit period, an employer has accumulated $100,000 or more in undeposited employment taxes, the taxes must be deposited by the close of the next banking day. When determining whether the $100,000 threshold is met, a monthly depositor takes into account only those taxes accumulated in the calendar month in which the day occurs. A semiweekly depositor takes into account only those taxes accumulated in the Wednesday-Friday or Saturday-Tuesday semiweekly periods in which the day occurs.

EXAMPLE

1. On Tuesday, January 7, 2003, Parker Company accumulated $105,000 in employment taxes for wages paid on that day. Regardless of Parker's deposit status, the firm is required to deposit the $105,000 by the next banking day, Wednesday, January 8. Note that if Parker was not subject to the semiweekly rule on January 7, 2003, the company would become subject to that rule as of January 8, 2003.

2. The Quincy Company is subject to the semiweekly rule. On Monday, February 3, 2003, Quincy accumulated $120,000 in employment taxes. The firm is required to deposit the $120,000 by the next banking day, Tuesday, February 4.

   On Tuesday, February 4, Quincy accumulates $30,000 more in employment taxes. Even though Quincy had a previous $120,000 deposit obligation that occurred earlier in the semiweekly period, Quincy now has an additional and separate deposit obligation that must be met by the following Friday, February 7.

Accumulated Employment Taxes Less Than $2,500 at the End of a Calendar Quarter.   If during a calendar quarter the accumulated employment taxes are less than $2,500, no deposits are required. The taxes may be paid to the IRS at the time of filing the quarterly return, Form 941, discussed later in this chapter. However, if the employer wishes, the taxes may be fully deposited by the end of the next month.

The Safe Harbor Rule (98 Percent Rule).   The amount deposited by an employer may be affected by the *safe harbor rule.* Under this rule, an employer satisfies the deposit obligations provided:

1. The amount of any shortfall (under deposit) does not exceed the greater of $100 or 2 percent of the amount of employment taxes required to be deposited.
2. The employer deposits the shortfall on or before the shortfall make-up date.

   A *shortfall* is the excess of the amount of employment taxes required to be deposited over the amount deposited on or before the last date prescribed for the deposit. The shortfall make-up rules follow:

1. *Monthly depositors:* The shortfall must be deposited or remitted by the quarterly return due date, in accordance with the applicable form and instruction.

2. *Semiweekly depositors and those subject to the $100,000 one-day rule:* The shortfall must be deposited on or before the first Wednesday or Friday, whichever is earlier, falling on or after the 15th day of the month following the month in which the deposit was required to be made.

> **E X A M P L E**
>
> **1.** On Friday, June 6, 2003, Rogers, Ltd., a semiweekly depositor, pays wages and accumulates employment taxes. Rogers makes a deposit on Wednesday, June 11, in the amount of $4,000. Later it was determined that Rogers was actually required to deposit $4,080 by Wednesday.
>
> Rogers has a shortfall of $80. The shortfall is less than the greater of $100 or 2 percent of the amount required to be deposited. Therefore, Rogers satisfies the safe harbor rule so long as the $80 shortfall is deposited by Wednesday, July 16.
>
> **2.** On Friday, October 24, 2003, Stacy Company, a semiweekly depositor, pays wages and accumulates employment taxes. Stacy makes a deposit of $30,000 but later finds that the amount of the deposit should have been $32,000.
>
> The $2,000 shortfall ($32,000 − $30,000) exceeds the greater of $100 or 2 percent of the amount required to be deposited (2% × $32,000 = $640). Thus, the safe harbor rule was not met. As a result, Stacy is subject to a failure-to-deposit penalty, as described later in this chapter.

Deposit Requirements for Employers of Agricultural Workers.   The deposit-making rules that apply to employers of agricultural laborers resemble those for employers of nonagricultural workers (Figure 3–9). However, there are exceptions, explained in the instructions accompanying *Form 943, Employer's Annual Tax Return for Agricultural Employees.*

Deposit Requirements for Employers of Household Employees.
Household or domestic employees are usually not subject to federal income tax withholding, but they may voluntarily request that federal income taxes be withheld from their wages. Even though federal income taxes are not withheld from their wages, they are subject to FICA taxes if each worker has been paid cash wages of $1,300 or more in a calendar year. Noncash items given to household employees are not subject to FICA tax.

F I G U R E   3 - 9

Summary of Deposit Rules for Nonagricultural Employers

Accumulated Unpaid Liability	Deposit Requirement
1. $50,000 or less in the lookback period	**1.** Monthly taxes must be deposited on or before the 15th of the following month.
2. More than $50,000 in the lookback period	**2.** (a) Payday on Wednesday, Thursday, and/or Friday—must be deposited on or before following Wednesday. (b) Payday on Saturday, Sunday, Monday, and/or Tuesday—must be deposited on or before following Friday.
3. $100,000 or more on any day	**3.** Must be deposited by the close of the next business day.
4. Less than $2,500 at end of calendar quarter	**4.** Must be paid by end of following month, either as a deposit or with the quarterly tax return (Form 941).

Employers who withhold and pay FICA taxes and federal income taxes for household services must report these taxes on *Form 1040, Federal Individual Income Tax Return.* However, if the employer is a sole proprietor and files *Form 941, Employer's Quarterly Federal Tax Return for Business Employees,* the taxes for the household employees must be included on Form 941.

Deposit Requirements for State and Local Government Employers.
Each state and local government employer must file its return on Form 941 with the IRS and deposit its FICA taxes through the federal deposit system. State and local government employers must make their tax deposits according to the same deposit schedule used by private employers.

Procedures for Making Deposits.
There are two methods of depositing employment taxes. The original paper-based system is being replaced over time by an electronic depositing system.

Electronic Deposits.
Many employers must now make their deposits via the Electronic Federal Tax Payment System (EFTPS). Any employer who makes more than $200,000 in aggregate deposits (not just employment tax deposits) in 2001 or was required to use EFTPS in 2002 must make electronic deposits in 2003.

This system is a communications network that facilitates the direct transfer of funds from the employer's bank to the Treasury Department. Generally, these transfers are transacted by touch-tone phone, personal computer, or online.

To use the online option, the employer must have Internet access. Enrollment in EFTPS-Online can be done at http://www.eftps.gov.

Once enrolled in the EFTPS program, an employer can switch between the phone, computer software, or online methods anytime. The linkage on all the methods is provided by the company's Employer Identification Number.

There are two electronic methods of deposit. The employer can instruct the Treasury Financial Agent for the area to withdraw funds from the employer's bank account and route them to the Treasury's account at the Federal Reserve Bank (ACH Debit Method). The employer could also instruct the bank to send each payment directly to the Treasury's account at the Federal Reserve Bank (ACH Credit Method).

To enroll, an employer must complete *Form 9779, EFTPS Business Enrollment Form.* Enrollment takes from three to six weeks, and a confirmation package will be sent by the IRS to the employer with a Personal Identification Number (PIN) and payment instructions.

Employers who are mandated to use this system will be assessed a 10 percent penalty on every tax deposit that is not made through EFTPS.

on the
JOB

If a deposit is required and the employer has not yet received the Employer Identification Number, the deposit must be mailed directly to the Internal Revenue Service with an explanation attached.

FTD Coupons.
Businesses not making deposits by EFTPS will use preprinted *Federal Tax Deposit Coupons, Form 8109,* to make payments at an authorized federal depository. Employers indicate on the coupon the type of tax being deposited. Figure 3–10 shows a sample coupon. The "TYPE OF TAX" section on the form is completed by darkening the 941 block.

Employers must make their deposits of taxes either at a Treasury Tax and Loan institution or by mailing it to Financial Agent, Federal Tax Deposit Processing, P.O. Box 970030, St. Louis, Missouri, 63917. They must make payment with an *immediate credit item.* An *immediate credit item* is a check or other instrument of payment for which the receiving bank gives immediate credit in accordance with its check-collection schedule. If a deposit is not made with an immediate credit item, the bank stamps the coupon to reflect the name of the bank and the date on which the proceeds of the accompanying payment instrument are collected. This date determines the timeliness of the payment.

The timeliness of deposits is determined by the date received by the institution. A deposit will be considered timely if the employer establishes that it was mailed at least two days before the due date. Deposits of $20,000 by an employer required to deposit tax more than once a month must be received by the due date to be timely.

FIGURE 3-10

Form 8109-B, Federal Tax Deposit Coupon, and a Portion of the Accompanying Instructions[2]

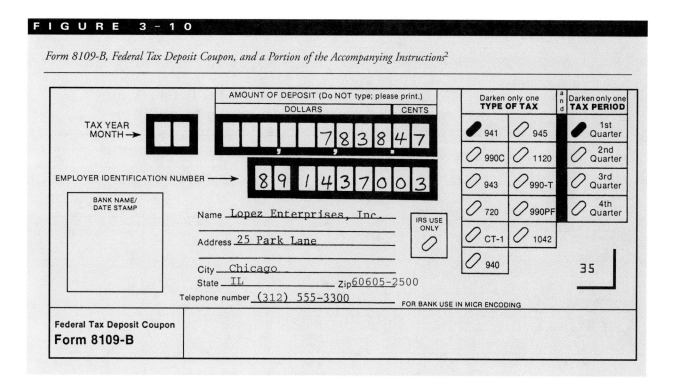

Each FTD coupon has a stub that the employer keeps as a record of payment. The canceled check, bank receipt, or money order is the employer's receipt. The FTD coupon itself is not returned to the employer but is used to credit the employer's tax account, identified by the employer's identification number entered on the coupon. The bank stamps the date and bank name on the coupon and forwards the tax deposit to the IRS for posting to the taxpayer's account. The IRS reconciles the tax deposits with the payments claimed by the employer on each quarterly return (Form 941). At this point, settlement of the employer's tax liability is made.

SELF-STUDY QUIZ 3–5.

_____ **1.** Braxton Industries, a semiweekly depositor, pays its employees every Friday. When should the company deposit the employment taxes for each weekly payday?

_____ **2.** What rule should Jackson Repair, a new company, follow in making its deposits for accumulated employment taxes?

_____ **3.** Quincy Motors (a semiweekly depositor) accumulates taxes of $105,000 on Monday and must deposit this amount on Tuesday, the next banking day. On Tuesday, the company accumulates additional taxes of $20,000. What deposit rule should Quincy follow for depositing the additional $20,000?

PREPARING FORM 941 (EMPLOYER'S QUARTERLY FEDERAL TAX RETURN)

Generally, the employer must make a quarterly return of FICA taxes and withheld income taxes for the three months of each calendar quarter, using *Form 941, Employer's Quarterly Federal Tax Return.* Figure 3–11 shows a completed copy of Form 941. Once the form has been filed, the employer receives preaddressed forms every three months. If the employer

6 LEARNING OBJECTIVE

---

2 Form 8109-B is used by employers if: (1) preprinted deposit coupons (Forms 8109) have not been received, or (2) the employer is a new entity and the initial supply of preprinted deposit coupons has not been received.

F I G U R E   3 - 1 1

Form 941, Employer's Quarterly Federal Tax Return

Form **941** (Rev. January 2002) Department of the Treasury Internal Revenue Service (99)	**Employer's Quarterly Federal Tax Return** ▶ See separate instructions revised January 2002 for information on completing this return. Please type or print.

Enter state code for state in which deposits were made **only** if different from state in address to the right ▶ (see page 2 of instructions).

Name (as distinguished from trade name)	Date quarter ended MAR 31, 20--	OMB No. 1545-0029
		T
Trade name, if any LOPEZ ENTERPRISES, INC.	Employer identification number 89-1437003	FF
		FD
Address (number and street) 25 PARK LANE	City, state, and ZIP code CHICAGO, IL 60605-2500	FP
		I
		T

If address is different from prior return, check here ▶

IRS Use

1 1 1 1 1 1 1 1 1 1   2   3 3 3 3 3 3 3   4 4 4   5 5 5
6   7   8 8 8 8 8 8   9 9 9 9 9   10 10 10 10 10 10 10 10 10

If you do not have to file returns in the future, check here ▶ ☐ and enter date final wages paid ▶
If you are a seasonal employer, see **Seasonal employers** on page 1 of the instructions and check here ▶ ☐

1	Number of employees in the pay period that includes March 12th . ▶	**1**	24

2	Total wages and tips, plus other compensation	**2**	7489592	
3	Total income tax withheld from wages, tips, and sick pay	**3**	12372	13
4	Adjustment of withheld income tax for preceding quarters of calendar year	**4**	-0-	
5	Adjusted total of income tax withheld (line 3 as adjusted by line 4—see instructions) . . .	**5**	12372	13

6	Taxable social security wages	**6a**	74895 92	× 12.4% (.124) =	**6b**	9287	09
	Taxable social security tips	**6c**	-0-	× 12.4% (.124) =	**6d**	-0-	
7	Taxable Medicare wages and tips . . .	**7a**	74895 92	× 2.9% (.029) =	**7b**	2171	98

8	Total social security and Medicare taxes (add lines 6b, 6d, and 7b). Check here if wages are not subject to social security and/or Medicare tax . . . . ▶ ☐	**8**	11459	07
9	Adjustment of social security and Medicare taxes (see instructions for required explanation) Sick Pay $ _____ ± Fractions of Cents $ __.41__ ± Other $ _____ =	**9**		41
10	Adjusted total of social security and Medicare taxes (line 8 as adjusted by line 9—see instructions)	**10**	11459	48
11	**Total taxes** (add lines 5 and 10)	**11**	23831	61
12	Advance earned income credit (EIC) payments made to employees	**12**	-0-	
13	Net taxes (subtract line 12 from line 11). **If $2,500 or more, this must equal line 17, column (d) below (or line D of Schedule B (Form 941))**	**13**	23831	61
14	Total deposits for quarter, including overpayment applied from a prior quarter	**14**	23831	61
15	**Balance due** (subtract line 14 from line 13). See instructions	**15**	-0-	

16 **Overpayment.** If line 14 is more than line 13, enter excess here ▶ $ _____
and check if to be: ☐ Applied to next return **or** ☐ Refunded.

- **All filers:** If line 13 is less than $2,500, you need not complete line 17 or Schedule B (Form 941).
- **Semiweekly schedule depositors:** Complete Schedule B (Form 941) and check here . . . . ▶ ☒
- **Monthly schedule depositors:** Complete line 17, columns (a) through (d), and check here. . . . . ▶ ☐

17	**Monthly Summary of Federal Tax Liability.** Do not complete if you were a semiweekly schedule depositor.		
(a) First month liability	**(b)** Second month liability	**(c)** Third month liability	**(d)** Total liability for quarter

Third Party Designee	Do you want to allow another person to discuss this return with the IRS (see separate instructions)? ☐ **Yes.** Complete the following. ☐ **No**

Designee's name ▶   Phone no. ▶ ( )   Personal identification number (PIN) ▶

Sign Here   Under penalties of perjury, I declare that I have examined this return, including accompanying schedules and statements, and to the best of my knowledge and belief, it is true, correct, and complete.

Signature ▶ *David S. Lopez*   Print Your Name and Title ▶ President   David S. Lopez   Date ▶ 4/30/--

For Privacy Act and Paperwork Reduction Act Notice, see back of Payment Voucher.   Cat. No. 17001Z   Form **941** (Rev. 1-2002)

has not received the form, the employer should request one from an IRS office in time to file the return when due.

All nonpayroll items (backup withholding and withholding from pensions, annuities, IRAs, military retirement and gambling winnings) have been removed from Form 941 and are reported on *Form 945, Annual Return of Withheld Federal Income Tax* (Chapter 4).

Completing the Return

Fill in the State Code box in the upper left corner as follows:

1. Use the Postal Service two-letter state abbreviation as the State Code.
2. If you made your deposits in a state other than that shown in the address on the form, enter the state code for that state.
3. Enter the code "MU" in the box if you deposit in more than one state.
4. If you deposit in the same state as shown in your address, don't make an entry in this box.
5. If it is the final Form 941 for a business, check the appropriate box and enter the date of the final wage payment. In case of a merger of two firms, the noncontinuing firm should file its final Form 941.
6. Seasonal employers who have no tax liability during certain quarters should check the seasonal employer box. These employers do not file a return for the quarters in which they did not pay any wages.
7. In addition, semiweekly and next-day depositors must complete Schedule B of *Form 941, Employer's Record of Federal Tax Liability,* instead of Form 941, line 17. The employer's tax liability is listed by each payday (see Figure 3–12).

To complete Form 941, lines 1–17, the employer obtains the information from various sources, such as those listed in Figure 3–13 (see page 3-27). Some additional information that must be considered in completing these lines are:

a. Line 1—complete only for the January–March quarterly return.
b. Line 4—do not use for adjustments that occurred in a prior year.
c. Line 6C—do not include allocated tips on this line.
d. Line 9—correct errors in taxes reported on earlier returns. Adjustments for a prior year also necessitate the filing of Form W-2C, Corrected Wage and Tax Statement, as explained in Chapter 4.

Signing Form 941

The form must be signed by the employer or other person who is required to withhold and pay the tax. If the employer is:

1. An *individual,* the return should be signed by that person.
2. A *corporation,* the return should be signed by its president, vice president, or other principal officer authorized to sign the return. Corporate officers or duly authorized agents may use facsimile signatures under certain conditions.
3. A *partnership* or *other unincorporated organization,* a responsible and duly authorized partner or officer having knowledge of the firm's affairs should sign the return.
4. A *trust* or *estate,* the return should be signed by the fiduciary of the trust or estate.
5. A *political body,* such as a state or territory, the return should be signed by the officer or employee having control of the wage payments or officer properly designated for that purpose.

In cases where the employer pays wages through an agent, authorization may be obtained for the agent to sign the appropriate tax returns.

Filing Form 941

The law requires employers to file Form 941 on or before the last day of the month following the close of the calendar quarter for which the return applies. If an employer makes timely tax deposits for the quarter, the employer may file Form 941 on or before the 10th day of the second month following the close of the calendar quarter.

on the

J O B

If an employer does not deposit social security, Medicare, and withheld income taxes on time, the IRS can require the employer to file monthly returns for these taxes on **Form 941-M, Employer's Monthly Federal Tax Return.**

CONNECTION

Internal Revenue Service forms and publications are available by calling 1-800-829-3676 or by accessing its Internet website at http://www.irs.ustreas.gov.

FIGURE 3-12

Employer's Record of Federal Tax Liability

SCHEDULE B (FORM 941)
(Rev. November 1998)
Department of the Treasury
Internal Revenue Service

5151

Employer's Record of Federal Tax Liability

▶ See Circular E for more information about employment tax returns.

▶ Attach to Form 941 or 941-SS.

OMB No. 1545-0029

Name as shown on Form 941 (or Form 941-SS)	Employer identification number	Date quarter ended
Lopez Enterprises	89-1437003	3/31/--

You must complete this schedule if you are required to deposit on a semiweekly schedule, or if your tax liability on any day is $100,000 or more. Show tax liability here, not deposits. (The IRS gets deposit data from FTD coupons or EFTPS.)

A. Daily Tax Liability—First Month of Quarter

1		8		15		22		29	
2		9		16		23		30	
3		10		17		24		31	
4		11		18		25			
5		12	4019 12	19		26	3819 35		
6		13		20		27			
7		14		21		28			

A   Total tax liability for first month of quarter . . . . ▶ **A**   7838 47

B. Daily Tax Liability—Second Month of Quarter

1		8		15		22		29	
2		9	4026 82	16		23	3913 96	30	
3		10		17		24		31	
4		11		18		25			
5		12		19		26			
6		13		20		27			
7		14		21		28			

B   Total tax liability for second month of quarter . . . . ▶ **B**   7940 78

C. Daily Tax Liability—Third Month of Quarter

1		8	4107 19	15		22	3945 17	29	
2		9		16		23		30	
3		10		17		24		31	
4		11		18		25			
5		12		19		26			
6		13		20		27			
7		14		21		28			

C   Total tax liability for third month of quarter . . . . ▶ **C**   8052 36

D   Total for quarter (add lines **A**, **B**, and **C**). This should equal line 13 of Form 941 (or line 10 of Form 941-SS) ▶ **D**   23831 61

For Paperwork Reduction Act Notice, see page 2.   Cat. No. 11967Q   **Schedule B (Form 941) (Rev. 11-98)**

F I G U R E   3 - 1 3

Sources of Information for Completing Form 941

Line Number	Source of Information
1	Payroll register.
2	General ledger accounts for wages and salaries; Forms 4070, or employees' written statements reporting cash tips.
3	General ledger accounts.
4	Forms 941 previously filed and general ledger accounts—to determine amount of errors made in income tax withheld from wages paid in earlier quarters of the calendar year.
5	Add lines 4 and 3 if additional income tax withheld is being reported; subtract line 4 from line 3 if the amount of income tax withheld is being reduced.
6a	Payroll register; include any social security taxes (OASDI) paid for employees, sick pay, and taxable fringe benefits subject to OASDI. Do not include any tips. Do not report any employees' wages that exceed $89,700, the taxable wage base for 2003.
6c	Forms 4070, or employees' written statements to report cash tips. Enter all tips reported until tips and wages for each employee reach $89,700. Report this information even if you are unable to withhold the employee OASDI tax. Do not include allocated tips, which should be reported on Form 8027.
7a	Payroll register; Forms 4070, or employees' written statements to report cash tips. Report amounts paid to certain federal, state, and local government employees who are subject only to the HI portion of the FICA tax.
8	Add lines 6b, 6d, and 7b.
9	Forms 941 previously filed. Correct errors in social security taxes reported on earlier return or correct errors in credits for overpayments of penalty or interest paid on tax for an earlier quarter. If you report both an underpayment and an overpayment, show only the difference.
	Use Form 941c to explain any amount on line 9, other than adjustments for fractions of cents or third-party sick pay. Or, you may attach a statement that shows the nature of error(s) being corrected.
	Use form W-2c, Statement of Corrected Income and Tax Amounts, to adjust an employee's social security, wages, tips, or tax withheld for a prior year. Also, complete Form W-3c, Transmittal of Corrected Income and Tax Statements.
	To adjust for the tax on tips: Include the total uncollected employee social security tax for lines 6d and 7b.
	To adjust for the tax on third-party sick pay: Deduct the social security tax on third-party sick pay for which you are not responsible. Enter the amount of the adjustment in the space for "Sick Pay."
	To adjust for fractions of cents: If there is a difference between the total tax on line 8 and the total deducted from your employees' wages or tips plus the employer's tax on those wages or tips (general ledger accounts) because of fractions of cents added or dropped in collecting the tax, report the difference. Enter this difference in the space for "Fractions of Cents."
10	Add line 9 to line 8 if you are reporting additional taxes for an earlier quarter. Subtract line 9 from line 8 if you are deducting the amount of taxes reported for an earlier quarter or claiming credit for overpayments of penalty or interest paid on tax for an earlier quarter.
11	Record total taxes by adding lines 5 and 10.
12	If applicable, show the amount of any advance earned income credit (EIC) payments made (discussed in Chapter 4). The amount of the advance EIC payments does not change the amount deducted and withheld from employees' pay for income tax and employee FICA taxes. Advance EIC payments that you make are treated as made from the amounts withheld as income tax and employee FICA taxes and your FICA tax contributions.
13	Determine net taxes by subtracting line 12 from line 11.
14	General ledger accounts, previous Form 941; record the total deposits for the quarter, including any overpayment applied from previous quarter.
15	Compute balance due by subtracting line 14 from line 13. Pay the balance due IRS.
16	Compute overpayment by subtracting line 13 from line 14 and indicate if amount is to be applied to the next return or refunded.
17	General ledger accounts; to be completed only by monthly depositors.

Payments can be made with Form 941 only if either the net taxes for the quarter (line 13) are less than $2,500 or the payment serves as a deposit for a monthly depositor in accordance with the accuracy of deposits rule (can be more than $2,500). In both cases, a Form 941-V (Payment Voucher) must be filed with Form 941.

EXAMPLE

1. An employer files a return by April 30 for the calendar quarter ending March 31.
2. An employer makes timely deposits for the quarter ending March 31. The form can be filed on or before May 10.
3. The Pruit Company was not required to make any deposits for FICA taxes during the quarter ending March 31. The company makes its deposit for the first quarter taxes on April 25 for taxes due. Pruit can still file Form 941 on or before May 10 for the first quarter return.

If the last day for filing a quarterly return falls on Saturday, Sunday, or a legal holiday, the employer may file the return on the next business day. If the return is filed by mailing, the employer should mail the return in sufficient time for it to reach the IRS Center no later than the next business day under ordinary handling of the mail.

Individual employers file quarterly returns with the IRS Center of the region in which the employer's principal place of business or office or agency is located. The return may still be filed at the local office of the district director of the IRS if the taxpayer hand delivers the return.

Electronic Filing of Form 941

Using an electronic data interchange format, employers can now file Form 941 electronically using a personal computer, modem, and specialized tax preparation software. This option is available to any business taxpayer who can meet the program's requirements. Currently, it is a two-step process:

1. Electronic submission of the Form 941 data.
2. Mailing of a paper signature document *(Form 4996, Electronic/Magnetic Media Filing Transmittal for Wage and Withholding Tax Returns).*

Interested filers must submit a letter of application to the IRS center in Memphis at least 15 days prior to the beginning of the tax quarter. The taxpayer must also make a test transmission at least 20 days prior to the due date of the first electronically filed Form 941.

TeleFile

With the success of a pilot program launched in the Southeast by the IRS, a Form 941 TeleFile pilot program has been expanded to include certain invited employers from across the country. The system works through an 800-number that connects the user to a voice processing system that prompts the employer to make entries using the telephone keypad. A business can use the Form 941 TeleFile if it is a monthly depositor and has been sent the 941 TeleFile package by the IRS.

FAILURE-TO-COMPLY PENALTIES

Employers act as collection agents for the government by collecting employment taxes and paying them to the appropriate government agency. Employers who fail to carry out their duties as collection agents are subject to civil and criminal penalties. The penalties may be additions to the tax, interest charges, and fines and imprisonment. Penalties also apply to federal income taxes (Chapter 4) and federal unemployment taxes (Chapter 5) and are imposed on employers who fail to do the following:

1. File employment tax returns.
2. Fully pay taxes when due.
3. Make timely deposits.

on the
JOB

You can correct errors on prior period Forms 941 by making an adjustment on the current Form 941 being filed. For example, if an error was made in reporting social security taxes in the 3rd quarter of 2002 and discovered in the 1st quarter of 2003, the error may be adjusted when filing Form 941 for the first quarter of 2003.

Prior period adjustments require supporting information. File **Form 941c, Supporting Statement to Correct Information,** with Form 941. Do not file Form 941c separately.

LEARNING OBJECTIVE **7**

4. Furnish wage and tax statements.
5. File or provide information returns.
6. Supply identification numbers.

The penalty depends on the degree of willfulness present in the employer's conduct. Persons other than the employer who have the duty or responsibility for collecting, accounting for, and paying any taxes may also be assessed penalties. Passing bad checks in payment of any employment tax also carries a penalty.

Once Form 941 is received, it usually takes the IRS about five weeks to notify an employer of any tax delinquencies.

Failure to File Employment Tax Returns

If an employer fails to file an employment tax return on the date prescribed for filing, a certain percentage of the amount of tax required to be reported will be added to the tax. Employers may avoid this addition if they show to the satisfaction of the IRS that failure to file was due to reasonable cause and not willful conduct.

Additions to the Tax	5 percent combined penalty of the net amount of tax that should have been reported less any amounts timely paid; an additional 5% for each additional month or fraction of a month during which failure continues, not to exceed 25 percent.
	15 percent per month, not to exceed 75 percent, for fraudulent failure to file.
Criminal Penalties	Not more than $25,000 ($100,000 for corporations), imprisonment of not more than 1 year, or both.
	Not more than $100,000, imprisonment of no more than three years, or both for willfully signing a return not true and correct as to every material statement.

E X A M P L E

Ned Fromton, an employer, files his employment tax return 20 days after the due date of the return. The amount of tax that was unpaid is $6,000. Fromton's penalty is:

Failure to file (5% × $6,000) = $300   Note—any fraction of a month counts as a whole month.

Failure to Fully Pay Employment Taxes

Employers who fail to pay the amount as shown on a return by the due date are faced with the following civil and criminal penalties.

Additions to the Tax	0.5 percent of the amount shown as tax on a return per month or fraction of a month, not to exceed 25 percent. The amount on which the penalty is calculated can be reduced by payments made on or before the beginning of the month. If both penalties to file a return and to fully pay the tax apply in the same month, the failure to file penalty is reduced by the amount of the failure to pay fully penalty. There is also a separate 0.5 percent per month penalty for failing to pay a tax amount due that was not shown on the return within 21 days of the notice and demand from the IRS. The penalty is based on the amount in the IRS notice. In addition, any taxes due will bear interest at the rate of 6 percent per year. Large corporate underpayments ($100,000) will carry the rate of 8 percent.[3]

3 The IRS sets the interest rate each calendar quarter, based on the short-term Treasury bill rate for the first month in each calendar quarter, plus 3 percentage points, and applies it for the following calendar quarter. The rate stated is for the second quarter of 2002.

Additions to the Tax	20 percent of the underpayment for negligence (failure to make a reasonable attempt to comply) or intentional disregard (careless, reckless, or intentional disregard of the law) of the payment rules.
	75 percent of the underpayment if underpayment is due to fraud with the intent to evade the tax.
The 100% Penalty	100 percent of the tax due for willfully failing to collect, account for, or pay over employment taxes or willfully attempting to evade or defeat the taxes.
Tax Levies	Levy on and seize any property and property rights held by the employer at the time of levy for failure of the employer to pay any taxes, 10 days after notice and demand for payment.
Criminal Penalties	Not more than $10,000, imprisonment of no more than five years, or both, for willful failure to pay the tax. These penalties are in addition to the 75 percent fraud penalty.

EXAMPLE

The Yeld Company failed to pay their employment taxes of $5,000 for March (due April 15) until May 20. The failure to pay penalty assessed against the Yeld Company is:

Failure to Pay Tax ($5,000 × 1%)	=	$50.00
Interest on Taxes Due ($5,000 × 0.08 × 35/365)	=	38.36
Total Penalty		$88.36

Note—In addition, a penalty for failure to make a timely deposit will also be assessed.

Failure to Make Timely Deposits

Penalties may apply if employers do not make required deposits on time in an authorized government depository.

Deposits made 1 to 5 days late	2 percent of the undeposited taxes
Deposits made 6 to 15 days late	5 percent of the undeposited taxes
Deposits made 16 or more days late	10 percent of the undeposited taxes
Deposits made at unauthorized financial institutions or directly to IRS	10 percent of the undeposited taxes
Deposits subject to electronic deposit requirements but not deposited by EFTPS	10 percent of the tax deposit required
Amounts unpaid more than 10 days after IRS notice	15 percent of the undeposited taxes

EXAMPLE

Greerson Inc. must make a deposit of $1,800 on June 15. The deposit was made 12 days late. The penalty assessed against Greerson is:

Failure to make timely deposit ($1,800 × 5%) = $90

Failure to Furnish Payee Statements

If employers willfully fail to furnish their employees with properly executed wage and tax statements, or willfully furnish false or fraudulent statements (employee's copy of W-2 or recipient's Form 1099—discussed in Chapter 4), the civil penalty is $50 for each statement.

Maximum Penalty	$100,000 in any calendar year.
Intentional Disregard	$100 per statement or, if greater, 10 percent of the amount required to be shown on the statement. No limit on the maximum penalty for the calendar year.
Criminal Penalties	$1,000 fine, imprisonment for not more than one year, or both, for each offense.

Failure to Furnish Information Returns

Employers who fail to timely file their information returns with the government (any 1099 series or Forms W-2) are subject to $50 for each failure. These penalties also apply to failures to include all required information on the forms, to supply only correct information, to file magnetically if required, and to report correct taxpayer identification numbers.

Correction within 30 days	$15 per failure, maximum fine $75,000.
Correction after 30 days, before August 1	$30 per failure, maximum fine $150,000.
Not filed correctly by August 1	$50 per return, maximum fine $250,000.
Intentional Disregard	$100 per statement or, if greater, 10 percent of the amount to be shown on the statement. No limit on the maximum penalty for the calendar year.

Bad Checks

Checks or money orders not tendered in good faith	2 percent of the amount. If the check is less than $750, penalty is $15 or the amount of the check, whichever is less.

KEY TERMS

Educational assistance *(p. 3-10)*   Lookback period *(p. 3-18)*   Semiweekly depositor *(p. 3-18)*
Employer *(p. 3-6)*   Monthly depositor *(p. 3-18)*   Shortfall *(p. 3-20)*
Employment *(p. 3-6)*   Person *(p. 3-6)*   Sick pay *(p. 3-10)*
Immediate credit item *(p. 3-22)*   Safe harbor rule *(p. 3-20)*   Taxable wage base *(p. 3-10)*
Independent contractors *(p. 3-5)*   Self-employment income *(p. 3-13)*

MATCHING QUIZ

_____ 1. Employer's FICA tax rates

_____ 2. Form SS-4

_____ 3. Semiweekly depositor

_____ 4. Taxable for FICA

_____ 5. Nontaxable for FICA

_____ 6. Self-employed's FICA tax rates

_____ 7. Form 941

_____ 8. Monthly Depositor

_____ 9. Taxable wage base

_____ 10. Form SS-5

A. Cash value of meals provided for employees' convenience

B. By the 15th day of the following month

C. Employer's Quarterly Federal Tax Return

D. Application for Employer Identification Number

E. 6.2% and 1.45%

F. Employee's application for Social Security Card

G. Applies only to the OASDI portion of the FICA tax

H. More than $50,000 in employment taxes in the lookback period

I. 12.4 percent and 2.9 percent

J. Employer's matching contributions into employees' deferred compensation arrangements

QUESTIONS FOR REVIEW

1. For social security purposes, what conditions must an individual meet to be classified as a "covered" employee?
2. Under what conditions does a common-law relationship exist between an employee and an employer?
3. Summarize the test conditions under which a worker is classified as an independent contractor.
4. For social security purposes, what conditions must an individual meet to be classified as a "covered" employer?
5. What are an employer's responsibilities for FICA taxes on:
   a. Tips reported by employees?
   b. Wages paid tipped employees?
6. What is the FICA tax liability status of pretax contributions to a qualified deferred compensation arrangement?
7. What conditions exclude sick pay from the definition of wages for FICA tax purposes?
8. John Luis receives wages from 3 employers during 2003. Is he entitled to a refund on the OASDI taxes paid on wages in excess of limit? If so, how can he receive a refund?
9. What are the self-employment tax rates for 2003? Explain how the tax is computed.
10. How does an employer file an application for an employer identification number?
11. Summarize the deposit rules for nonagricultural employees.
12. Which employers must deposit their employment taxes electronically?
13. How are the electronic tax deposits transferred from the employer's account to the IRS?
14. How often must an employer file Form 941?
15. List the penalties imposed on the employer for the following:
   a. Filing Form 941 late.
   b. Seven days late making a deposit.
   c. Issuing a bad check to the IRS.

QUESTIONS FOR DISCUSSION

1. In order to improve the cash flow of the company, Ned Nash decided to postpone depositing all employment taxes a few months ago. He told his sales manager, "I'll pay up before the IRS catches up with me." What risks does Nash face by not upholding his responsibility for the collection and payment of employment taxes?
2. On Wednesday, June 15, Lapoint Company had employment taxes of $25,000 that were required to be deposited on or before Wednesday, June 22. The deposit was mailed and postmarked Wednesday, June 22, and delivered on Thursday, June 23. What deposit rules is Lapoint following? Was the deposit made in a timely manner?
3. During a recent strike at the Ultima Hotel, union members were paid strike benefits by their union. Don Volmer, a union representative, participates in negotiations with the hotel.
   a. Are the strike benefits paid to union members taxable under FICA?
   b. Are the payments Volmer receives for his services as a union negotiator subject to FICA taxes?
4. When employees of the County Bank are summoned to serve on jury duty, the firm pays its workers the difference between their regular wages and the amount received for jury duty. One such employee has been receiving $365 per week. She just completed a five-day week of jury duty, for which she was paid $65 ($9 per day plus 20 cents per mile from her house to the courthouse, a 20-mile round trip). How much of the employee's earnings are subject to FICA tax?

PRACTICAL PROBLEMS

3–1. LO 3.

The biweekly taxable wages for the employees of Stork Foods follow. Compute the FICA taxes for each employee and the employer's FICA taxes.

Employee No.	Employee Name	Biweekly Taxable Wages	FICA Taxes OASDI	HI
711	Burke, Mark	$479.68	$ _____	$ _____
512	Celeo, Mary	495.00	_____	_____
624	Filmore, Juanita	385.25	_____	_____
325	Harrison, Bob	397.25	_____	_____
422	Lang, Will	785.00	_____	_____
210	Pagat, Mel	775.50	_____	_____
111	Troy, Sheila	495.25	_____	_____
		Totals	$ _____	$ _____

Employer's OASDI $ _____ $ _____
                   Total Taxable   Employer's OASDI
                      Wages   Tax

Employer's HI Tax $ _____ $ _____
                   Total Taxable   Employer's HI
                      Wages   Tax

3–2. LO 3.

During 2003, Sharon Gilmore, president of Perkins Company, was paid a semimonthly salary of $6,800. Compute the amount of FICA taxes that should be withheld from her:

	OASDI	HI
a. 9th paycheck	$ _____	$ _____
b. 14th paycheck	$ _____	$ _____
c. 24th paycheck	$ _____	$ _____

3–3. LO 3.

Artis Norton began working as a part-time waiter on June 1, 2003, at Sporthouse Restaurant. The cash tips of $160 that he received during June were reported on Form 4070, which he submitted to his employer on July 1. During July, he was paid wages of $525 by the restaurant. Compute:

	OASDI	HI
a. The amount of FICA taxes that the employer should withhold from Norton's wages during July.	$ _____	$ _____
b. The amount of the employer's FICA taxes on Norton's wages and tips during July.	$ _____	$ _____

3–4. LO 2.

Ken Gorman is a maitre d' at Carmel Dinner Club. On February 6, his gross pay was $800 (3 days working, 1 paid vacation day, and 1 paid sick day). He also reported to his employer tips of $900 for the previous month (applicable taxes to be deducted out of this pay). Ken belongs to the company's 401(k) plan and has 5 percent of his gross pay ($800) deducted each week (salary reduction). Carmel Dinner Club also provides a matching contribution ($40) into the plan for Ken. This week's pay would have a:

a. Deduction for OASDI tax $ _____

b. Deduction for HI tax $ _____

3–5. LO 3.

The annual salaries paid each of the officers of Groton, Inc., follow. The officers are paid semimonthly on the 15th and the last day of the month. Compute the FICA taxes to be withheld from each officer's pay on (a) September 30 and (b) December 31.

September 30

Name and Title	Annual Salary	OASDI Taxable Earnings	OASDI Tax	HI Taxable Earnings	HI Tax
Lerner, Jake, President	$120,000				
Oldman, Clara, VP Finance	91,200				
Burke, Sarah, VP Sales	69,600				
Aneson, Max, VP Mfg.	54,000				
White, Beth, VP Personnel	51,600				
Jackson, Bart, VP Secretary	49,200				

December 31

Name and Title	Annual Salary	OASDI Taxable Earnings	OASDI Tax	HI Taxable Earnings	HI Tax
Lerner, Jake, President	$120,000				
Oldman, Clara, VP Finance	91,200				
Burke, Sarah, VP Sales	69,600				
Aneson, Max, VP Mfg.	54,000				
White, Beth, VP Personnel	51,600				
Jackson, Bart, VP Secretary	49,200				

3–6. LO 3.

Audrey Martin and Beth James are partners in the Country Gift Shop, which employs the individuals listed below. Paychecks are distributed every Friday to all employees. Based on the information given, compute the amounts listed below.

Name and Position	Salary	OASDI Taxable Earnings	OASDI Tax	HI Taxable Earnings	HI Tax
Zena Vertin, Office	$ 535 per week				
Nicole Norge, Sales	1,980 per month				
Bob Mert, Delivery	485 per week				
Audrey Martin, Partner	650 per week				
Beth James, Partner	650 per week				
Totals		$	$	$	$

Employer's OASDI Tax $ _____
Employer's HI Tax $ _____

3-34

3–7. LO 3.

The Volpe Corporation has only five employees who are all paid $625 per week. Compute the total FICA taxes that the employer would withhold from the five employees each week and the amount the company would pay as their own liability for the employer's share of the FICA taxes on the weekly wages of the five employees:

Employees' total OASDI .... $ _____
Employees' total HI .... $ _____
Employer's total OASDI .... $ _____
Employer's total HI .... $ _____

3–8. LO 3.

Hugh Crandal was paid a salary of $58,200 during 2003 by the Pope Company. In addition, during the year Crandal started his own business as a public accountant and reported a net business income of $38,000 on his income tax return for 2003. Compute the following:

a. The amount of FICA taxes that was withheld from his earnings during 2003 by the Pope Company.

OASDI $ _____
HI $ _____

b. Crandal's self-employment taxes on the income derived from the public accounting business for 2003.

OASDI $ _____
HI $ _____

3–9. LO 3.

The Tyler Spa Company pays its salaried employees monthly on the last day of each month. The annual salary payroll for 2003 follows. Compute the following for the payroll of December 31.

Employee	Annual Salary	OASDI Taxable Wages	OASDI Tax	HI Tax
Darton, Carla	$22,150			
Drake, Neville	18,900			
Ferrins, Margaret	24,000			
Guild, Ben	91,680			
Hart, Nora	20,900			
Kyle, Jacob	19,500			
Lorenzo, Maria	18,540			
Quinn, Susan	56,900			
Roper, Hugh	17,850			
Washington, Ted	51,200			
Totals		$	$	$

Employer's OASDI Tax _____

Employer's HI Tax _____

3–10. LO 3.

The monthly and hourly wage schedule for the employees of Quirk, Inc., follows. No employees are due overtime pay. Compute the following for the last monthly pay of the year:

a. The total wages of each part-time employee for December 2003.
b. The OASDI and HI taxable wages for each employee.
c. The FICA taxes withheld from each employee's wages for December.
d. Totals of columns.
e. The employer's FICA taxes for the month.

Employees	Total Monthly Payroll	OASDI Taxable Wages	HI Taxable Wages	OASDI Tax	HI Tax
Full-Time Office:					
Adaiar, Gene	$1,400.00				
Crup, Jason	1,300.00				
Essex, Joan	1,975.00				
Garza, Irma	1,985.00				
Leason, Mel	1,900.00				
Pruit, Marne	7,000.00				
Rubble, Deanne	2,400.00				
Simpson, Dick	3,985.00				
Truap, Ann	5,000.00				
Wilson, Trudy	1,500.00				

	Hours Worked	Hourly Rate	Total Part-Time Wages				
Part-Time Office:							
Kyle, Judy	170	$5.25					
Laird, Sharon	170	5.35					
Maxwell, Sara	140	6.10					
Nelson, Donna	145	5.20					
Scott, Kim	162	5.65					
Totals							

Employer's FICA taxes   OASDI $ _____   HI $ _____

3–11. LO 6.

Stan Barker opened Quik-Stop Market on January 2, 2003. The business is subject to FICA taxes. At the end of the first quarter of 2003, Barker must file Form 941, Employer's Quarterly Federal Tax Return. Using Form 941, reproduced on the next page, prepare, sign, and date the return on the basis of the information shown below.

Employer's address: **234 Oak, Austin, TX 78711-0234**
Employer's ID number: **61-1325874**

Each employee is paid semimonthly on the 15th and last day of each month. Shown below is the payroll information for the first quarter of 2003. All pay periods were the same.

PAYROLL INFORMATION FOR JANUARY–MARCH

Employee	SSN	Quarterly Wage	OASDI Tax	HI Tax	Federal Income Tax	Total Deductions	Net Pay
Albert Greer	384-10-7233	$ 3,480	$ 215.76	$ 50.46	$ 264	$ 530.22	$ 2,949.78
Patty Dilts	345-90-8451	3,510	217.62	50.88	528	796.50	2,713.50
Jerod Hughs	528-09-3668	7,740	479.88	112.26	1,212	1,804.14	5,935.86
Denise Eaton	766-43-6527	3,900	241.80	56.58	552	850.38	3,049.62
Totals		$18,630	$1,155.06	$270.18	$2,556	$3,981.24	$14,648.76

Employer's FICA taxes $1,155.06 $270.12
For the Quarter OASDI HI

The total taxes per payday are:
Employees' FICA Tax—OASDI	$192.51
Employer's FICA Tax—OASDI	192.51
Employees' FICA Tax—HI	45.03
Employer's FICA Tax—HI	45.02
Employees' FIT Tax	426.00
Total	$901.07

None of the employees reported tips during the quarter. No advance earned income credit (EIC) payments were made to the workers.

Note: Lines 6b and 7b of Form 941, tax on total taxable wages, are computed by multiplying by the combined tax rate for both employer and employee. Small differences due to rounding may occur between this total and the total taxes withheld from employees each pay period and the amount of the employer's taxes calculated each pay period. This difference is reported on line 9 as a deduction or an addition as "Fractions of Cents."

Form 941
(Rev. January 2002)
Department of the Treasury
Internal Revenue Service (99)

Employer's Quarterly Federal Tax Return

▶ See separate instructions revised January 2002 for information on completing this return.

Please type or print.

Enter state code for state in which deposits were made **only** if different from state in address to the right ▶ ☐

Name (as distinguished from trade name)	Date quarter ended **MAR 31, 2003**
Trade name, if any **QUIK-STOP MARKET**	Employer identification number **61-1325874**
Address (number and street) **234 OAK**	City, state, and ZIP code **AUSTIN, TX 78711-0234**

OMB No. 1545-0029

T	
FF	
FD	
FP	
I	
T	

If address is different from prior return, check here ▶ ☐

IRS Use

```
1 1 1 1 1 1 1 1 1 1    2    3 3 3 3 3 3 3    4 4 4    5 5 5
6   7   8 8 8 8 8 8 8   9 9 9 9   10 10 10 10 10 10 10 10 10 10
```

If you do not have to file returns in the future, check here ▶ ☐   and enter date final wages paid ▶

If you are a seasonal employer, see **Seasonal employers** on page 1 of the instructions and check here ▶ ☐

1	Number of employees in the pay period that includes March 12th . ▶	**1**
2	Total wages and tips, plus other compensation	**2**
3	Total income tax withheld from wages, tips, and sick pay	**3**
4	Adjustment of withheld income tax for preceding quarters of calendar year	**4**
5	Adjusted total of income tax withheld (line 3 as adjusted by line 4—see instructions) . .	**5**
6	Taxable social security wages **6a**	× 12.4% (.124) = **6b**
	Taxable social security tips **6c**	× 12.4% (.124) = **6d**
7	Taxable Medicare wages and tips . . . **7a**	× 2.9% (.029) = **7b**
8	Total social security and Medicare taxes (add lines 6b, 6d, and 7b). Check here if wages are not subject to social security and/or Medicare tax . . . . ▶ ☐	**8**
9	Adjustment of social security and Medicare taxes (see instructions for required explanation) Sick Pay $ _____ ± Fractions of Cents $ _____ ± Other $ _____ =	**9**
10	Adjusted total of social security and Medicare taxes (line 8 as adjusted by line 9—see instructions)	**10**
11	**Total taxes** (add lines 5 and 10)	**11**
12	Advance earned income credit (EIC) payments made to employees	**12**
13	Net taxes (subtract line 12 from line 11). **If $2,500 or more, this must equal line 17, column (d) below (or line D of Schedule B (Form 941))**	**13**
14	Total deposits for quarter, including overpayment applied from a prior quarter	**14**
15	**Balance due** (subtract line 14 from line 13). See instructions	**15**
16	**Overpayment.** If line 14 is more than line 13, enter excess here ▶ $ _____ and check if to be: ☐ Applied to next return **or** ☐ Refunded.	

● **All filers:** If line 13 is less than $2,500, you need not complete line 17 or Schedule B (Form 941).
● **Semiweekly schedule depositors:** Complete Schedule B (Form 941) and check here . . . . ▶ ☐
● **Monthly schedule depositors:** Complete line 17, columns (a) through (d), and check here. . . . . ▶ ☐

17	**Monthly Summary of Federal Tax Liability.** Do not complete if you were a semiweekly schedule depositor.		
(a) First month liability	**(b)** Second month liability	**(c)** Third month liability	**(d)** Total liability for quarter

Third Party Designee

Do you want to allow another person to discuss this return with the IRS (see separate instructions)? ☐ **Yes.** Complete the following.   ☐ **No**

Designee's name ▶	˙Phone no. ▶ ( )	Personal identification number (PIN) ▶ ☐☐☐☐☐

Sign Here

Under penalties of perjury, I declare that I have examined this return, including accompanying schedules and statements, and to the best of my knowledge and belief, it is true, correct, and complete.

Signature ▶   Print Your Name and Title ▶   Date ▶

For Privacy Act and Paperwork Reduction Act Notice, see back of Payment Voucher.   Cat. No. 17001Z   Form **941** (Rev. 1-2002)

3–12. LO 6.

During the fourth calendar quarter of 2003, the Bayview Inn, owned by Diane R. Peters, employed the persons listed below. Also given are the employees' salaries or wages and the amount of tips reported to the owner. The tips were reported by the 10th of each month. The Federal Income Tax and FICA tax to be withheld from the tips were estimated by the owner and withheld equally over the 13 weekly pay periods. The employer's portion of FICA tax on the tips was estimated as the same amount.

Employee	Salary or Wage	Quarter's Wages	Quarter's Tips	Quarter's OASDI	Quarter's HI	Quarter's FIT
Grant Frazier	$25,000/year	$ 6,250.01		$ 387.53	$ 90.61	$ 845.00
Joseph LaVanga	18,000/year	4,499.95		278.98	65.26	546.00
Susanne Ayers	250/week	3,250.00	$ 2,240.90	340.47	79.56	520.00
Howard Cohen	225/week	2,925.00	2,493.10	335.92	78.52	611.00
Lee Soong	250/week	3,250.00	2,640.30	365.17	85.41	650.00
Mary Yee	250/week	3,250.00	2,704.00	369.20	86.32	663.00
Helen Woods	325/week	4,225.00		261.95	61.23	429.00
Koo Shin	325/week	4,225.00		261.95	61.23	533.00
Aaron Abalis	400/week	5,200.00		322.40	75.40	689.00
David Harad	170/week	2,210.00		137.02	32.11	234.00
		$39,284.96	$10,078.30	$3,060.59	$715.65	$5,720.00

Employees are paid weekly on Friday. The following paydays occurred during this quarter:

October	November	December
4 weekly paydays	4 weekly paydays	5 weekly paydays

Taxes withheld for the 13 paydays in the fourth quarter follow:

	Federal Income Tax	Weekly Employees' and Employer's FICA Taxes Withheld		Weekly Employees' and Employer's FICA Taxes on Tips	
		OASDI	HI	OASDI	HI
	$440 per week	$187.36	$43.83	$48.07	$11.24
		187.36	43.82	48.07	11.24

Based on the information given, complete Form 941 on the following page.

Form **941**
(Rev. January 2002)
Department of the Treasury
Internal Revenue Service (99)

Employer's Quarterly Federal Tax Return
▶ See separate instructions revised January 2002 for information on completing this return.
Please type or print.

OMB No. 1545-0029

Enter state code for state in which deposits were made **only** if different from state in address to the right ▶ ⬚
(see page 2 of instructions).

Name (as distinguished from trade name)

Date quarter ended
DEC 31, 2003

Trade name, if any
BAYVIEW INN
Address (number and street)
404 UNION AVE.

Employer identification number
65-4263607
City, state, and ZIP code
MEMPHIS, TN
38112-1404

| T |
| FF |
| FD |
| FP |
| I |
| T |

If address is different from prior return, check here ▶ ⬚

IRS Use

```
1 1 1 1 1 1 1 1 1    2    3 3 3 3 3 3 3    4 4 4    5 5 5
6    7    8 8 8 8 8 8 8    9 9 9 9    10 10 10 10 10 10 10 10 10
```

If you do not have to file returns in the future, check here ▶ ⬚ and enter date final wages paid ▶
If you are a seasonal employer, see **Seasonal employers** on page 1 of the instructions and check here ▶ ⬚

1 Number of employees in the pay period that includes March 12th . ▶ | 1 |
2 Total wages and tips, plus other compensation . . . . | 2 |
3 Total income tax withheld from wages, tips, and sick pay . . . . | 3 |
4 Adjustment of withheld income tax for preceding quarters of calendar year . . . . . | 4 |
5 Adjusted total of income tax withheld (line 3 as adjusted by line 4—see instructions) . | 5 |
6 Taxable social security wages . . . . . | 6a | | × 12.4% (.124) = | 6b |
   Taxable social security tips . . . . . . | 6c | | × 12.4% (.124) = | 6d |
7 Taxable Medicare wages and tips . . . | 7a | | × 2.9% (.029) = | 7b |
8 Total social security and Medicare taxes (add lines 6b, 6d, and 7b). Check here if wages are not subject to social security and/or Medicare tax . . . . ▶ ⬚ | 8 |
9 Adjustment of social security and Medicare taxes (see instructions for required explanation)
   Sick Pay $ _____ ± Fractions of Cents $ _____ ± Other $ _____ = | 9 |
10 Adjusted total of social security and Medicare taxes (line 8 as adjusted by line 9—see instructions) . . . . | 10 |
11 **Total taxes** (add lines 5 and 10) . . . . | 11 |
12 Advance earned income credit (EIC) payments made to employees . . . . | 12 |
13 Net taxes (subtract line 12 from line 11). **If $2,500 or more, this must equal line 17, column (d) below (or line D of Schedule B (Form 941))** . . . . | 13 |
14 Total deposits for quarter, including overpayment applied from a prior quarter . . . . . | 14 |
15 **Balance due** (subtract line 14 from line 13). See instructions . . . . | 15 |
16 **Overpayment.** If line 14 is more than line 13, enter excess here ▶ $ _____
    and check if to be: ⬚ Applied to next return **or** ⬚ Refunded.

- **All filers:** If line 13 is less than $2,500, you need not complete line 17 or Schedule B (Form 941).
- **Semiweekly schedule depositors:** Complete Schedule B (Form 941) and check here . . . . ▶ ⬚
- **Monthly schedule depositors:** Complete line 17, columns (a) through (d), and check here. . . . . . . ▶ ⬚

17	**Monthly Summary of Federal Tax Liability.** Do not complete if you were a semiweekly schedule depositor.		
(a) First month liability	**(b)** Second month liability	**(c)** Third month liability	**(d)** Total liability for quarter

Third Party Designee

Do you want to allow another person to discuss this return with the IRS (see separate instructions)?   ⬚ **Yes.** Complete the following.   ⬚ **No**

Designee's name ▶
Phone no. ▶ (   )
Personal identification number (PIN) ▶ ☐☐☐☐☐

Sign Here

Under penalties of perjury, I declare that I have examined this return, including accompanying schedules and statements, and to the best of my knowledge and belief, it is true, correct, and complete.

Signature ▶
Print Your Name and Title ▶
Date ▶

For Privacy Act and Paperwork Reduction Act Notice, see back of Payment Voucher.   Cat. No. 17001Z   Form **941** (Rev. 1-2002)

3–13. LO 5, 6.

The taxable wages and withheld taxes for the Stafford Company (EIN 25-7901462), semiweekly depositor, for the first quarter of 2003 follow.

Semimonthly Paydays	Gross and Taxable Wages	FICA Withheld OASDI	FICA Withheld HI	Federal Income Tax Withheld
1/15	$ 24,500	$1,519.00	$ 355.25	$ 3,185.00
1/31	23,985	1,487.07	347.78	3,090.00
2/15	25,190	1,561.78	365.26	3,410.00
2/28	25,530	1,582.86	370.19	3,497.00
3/15	24,950	1,546.90	361.78	3,385.00
3/29	25,100	1,556.20	363.95	3,400.00
	$149,255	$9,253.81	$2,164.21	$19,967.00

a. Complete Schedule B of Form 941 on page 3-42 for the first quarter for the Stafford Company.

b. List the due dates of each deposit in the first quarter.

Paydays	Deposit Due Dates
January 15	_____
January 31	_____
February 14	_____
February 28	_____
March 14	_____
March 31	_____

Employer's Record of Federal Tax Liability

5151

► See Circular E for more information about employment tax returns.

► Attach to Form 941 or 941-SS.

OMB No. 1545-0029

Name as shown on Form 941 (or Form 941-SS)	Employer identification number	Date quarter ended

You must complete this schedule if you are required to deposit on a semiweekly schedule, or if your tax liability on any day is $100,000 or more. Show tax liability here, not deposits. (The IRS gets deposit data from FTD coupons or EFTPS.)

A. Daily Tax Liability—First Month of Quarter

1		8		15		22		29	
2		9		16		23		30	
3		10		17		24		31	
4		11		18		25			
5		12		19		26			
6		13		20		27			
7		14		21		28			

A Total tax liability for first month of quarter . . . . ► | **A** |

B. Daily Tax Liability—Second Month of Quarter

1		8		15		22		29	
2		9		16		23		30	
3		10		17		24		31	
4		11		18		25			
5		12		19		26			
6		13		20		27			
7		14		21		28			

B Total tax liability for second month of quarter . . . . ► | **B** |

C. Daily Tax Liability—Third Month of Quarter

1		8		15		22		29	
2		9		16		23		30	
3		10		17		24		31	
4		11		18		25			
5		12		19		26			
6		13		20		27			
7		14		21		28			

C Total tax liability for third month of quarter . . . . ► | **C** |

D Total for quarter (add lines **A, B,** and **C**). This should equal line 13 of Form 941 (or line 10 of Form 941-SS) ► | **D** |

3–14. LO 6, 7.

The Trainer Company is a monthly depositor whose tax liability for March 2003 is $2,505.

1. Complete the Federal Tax Deposit Coupon for the March taxes.

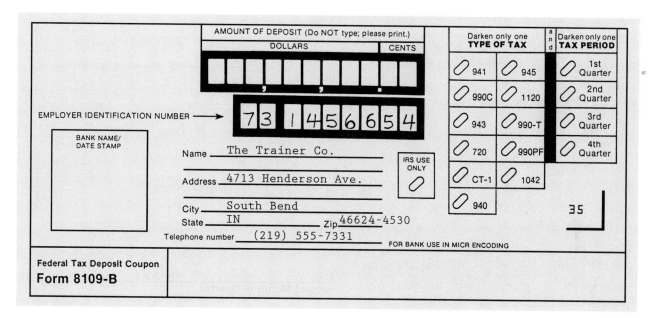

2. What is the due date for the deposit of these taxes? _____

3. Assume that no deposit was made until May 2. Compute the following penalties:

    a. Penalty for failure to make timely deposit. $_____

    b. Penalty for failure to fully pay tax. $_____

    c. Interest on taxes due and unpaid. $_____

    d. Total penalty imposed. $_____

3–15. LO 3.

At the Payne Die Company, office workers are employed for a 40-hour workweek on either an annual or a monthly salary basis.

    Given on the form on the following page are the current annual and monthly salary rates for five office workers for the week ended December 12, 2003 (50th payday of the year). In addition, with this pay, these employees are paid their sliding-scale annual bonuses. The bonuses are listed on the register.

For each worker compute:

1. Regular earnings for the weekly payroll ended December 12, 2003.

2. Overtime earning (if applicable).

3. Total regular, overtime earnings, and bonus.

4. FICA taxable wages for this pay period.

5. FICA taxes to be withheld for this pay period.

3–15. (Concluded on page 3-45)

PAYNE DIE COMPANY

Employee	Salary	Hours Worked	Annual Bonus	Regular Earnings	Overtime Earnings	Total Earnings
Lentz, R.	97,240 /yr.	40	$30,000	_____	_____	_____
Steyer, C.	91,000 /yr.	40	25,000	_____	_____	_____
Long, S.	6,240 /mo.	40	20,000	_____	_____	_____
Richey, S.	4,680 /mo.	40	15,000	_____	_____	_____
Taveau, G.	2, 900 /mo.	48	8,000	_____	_____	_____
			Totals	_____	_____	_____

Employer's FICA taxes for week ended December 12, 2003: $ _____ $ _____
                                                           OASDI   HI
                                                                           (left side)

CONTINUING PAYROLL PROBLEM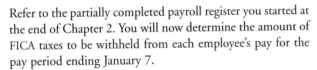

Refer to the partially completed payroll register you started at the end of Chapter 2. You will now determine the amount of FICA taxes to be withheld from each employee's pay for the pay period ending January 7.

1. In the Taxable Earnings columns, record the amount of each employee's weekly earnings that is subject to FICA taxes.

2. Using the amount recorded in step (1), compute the taxes for each employee and record in the appropriate column.

Note: Keep your partially completed payroll register for use at the end of Chapter 4.

CASE PROBLEMS

C1. Auditing Form 941. LO 5, 6.

Your assistant has just completed a rough draft of Form 941, shown on page 3-47, for the quarter ending March 31, 20—. As the supervisor and authorized signer, you are auditing the form before it is mailed to ensure its accuracy.

Four of the company's general ledger accounts are shown on the following pages. Employees are paid on the 15th and last day of each month. The company is a semiweekly depositor. Indicate any changes that should be made on the form before it is signed, dated, and mailed.

PAYNE DIE COMPANY (Concluded)

Cumulative Earnings as of Last Pay Period	FICA Taxable Wages This Pay Period		FICA Taxes to Be Withheld		Employee
	OASDI	HI	OASDI	HI	
$91,630.00	_____	_____	_____	_____	Lentz, R.
85,750.00	_____	_____	_____	_____	Steyer, C.
70,560.00	_____	_____	_____	_____	Long, S.
52,920.00	_____	_____	_____	_____	Richey, S.
34,890.00	_____	_____	_____	_____	Taveau, G.

(right side)

<u>C1.</u>   **Continued**

FICA TAXES PAYABLE—OASDI   Account No. 214

Date		Debit	Credit	Balance Debit	Balance Credit
20—					
Jan.	15		773.96		773.96
	15		773.94		1,547.90
	19	1,547.90			—
	31		843.78		843.78
	31		843.78		1,687.56
Feb.	2	1,687.56			—
	15		833.74		833.74
	15		833.72		1,667.46
	22	1,667.46			—
	28		803.79		803.79
	28		803.79		1,607.58
Mar.	3	1,607.58			—
	15		786.72		786.72
	15		786.73		1,573.45
	20	1,573.45			—
	31		787.88		787.88
	31		787.87		1,575.75
Apr.	5	1,575.75			—

FICA TAXES PAYABLE—HI   Account No. 215

Date		Debit	Credit	Balance Debit	Balance Credit
20—					
Jan.	15		181.01		181.01
	15		181.01		362.02
	19	362.02			—
	31		197.34		197.34
	31		197.32		394.66
Feb.	2	394.66			—
	15		194.98		194.98
	15		194.98		389.96
	22	389.96			—
	28		187.98		187.98
	28		187.98		375.96
Mar.	3	375.96			—
	15		184.01		184.01
	15		183.99		368.00
	20	368.00			—
	31		184.26		184.26
	31		184.24		368.50
Apr.	5	368.50			—

EMPLOYEES FEDERAL INCOME TAX PAYABLE   Account No. 216

Date		Debit	Credit	Balance Debit	Balance Credit
20—					
Jan.	15		1,980.00		1,980.00
	19	1,980.00			—
	31		2,217.00		2,217.00
Feb.	2	2,217.00			—
	15		2,016.00		2,016.00
	22	2,016.00			—
	28		2,007.00		2,007.00
Mar.	3	2,007.00			—
	15		1,970.00		1,970.00
	20	1,970.00			—
	31		1,887.00		1,887.00
Apr.	5	1,887.00			—

WAGES AND SALARIES   Account No. 511

Date		Debit	Credit	Balance Debit	Balance Credit
20—					
Jan.	15	12,483.16		12,483.16	
	31	13,609.40		26,092.56	
Feb.	15	13,447.13		39,539.69	
	28	12,964.43		52,504.12	
Mar.	15	12,689.02		65,193.14	
	31	12,707.69		77,900.83	

Form **941**
(Rev. January 2002)
Department of the Treasury
Internal Revenue Service (99)

Employer's Quarterly Federal Tax Return

▶ See separate instructions revised January 2002 for information on completing this return.

Please type or print.

Enter state code for state in which deposits were made **only** if different from state in address to the right ▶ ⬚ (see page 2 of instructions).

Name (as distinguished from trade name)

Trade name, if any
COASTAL COMPANY

Address (number and street)
77 CASTRO

Date quarter ended
MAR 31, 2003

Employer identification number
77-2267142

City, state, and ZIP code
**SAN FRANCISCO, CA
94117-6903**

OMB No. 1545-0029

| T |
| FF |
| FD |
| FP |
| I |
| T |

If address is different from prior return, check here ▶ ⬚

IRS Use

1 1 1 1 1 1 1 1 1   2   3 3 3 3 3 3   4 4 4   5 5 5
6   7   8 8 8 8 8 8 8   9 9 9 9 9   10 10 10 10 10 10 10 10 10 10

If you do not have to file returns in the future, check here ▶ ⬚ and enter date final wages paid ▶

If you are a seasonal employer, see **Seasonal employers** on page 1 of the instructions and check here ▶

1	Number of employees in the pay period that includes March 12th . ▶ **1**	17		
2	Total wages and tips, plus other compensation	**2**	77900	38
3	Total income tax withheld from wages, tips, and sick pay	**3**	12077	00
4	Adjustment of withheld income tax for preceding quarters of calendar year . . .	**4**	-0-	
5	Adjusted total of income tax withheld (line 3 as adjusted by line 4—see instructions) . . .	**5**	12077	00

6	Taxable social security wages	**6a**	77900 38	× 12.4% (.124) =	**6b**	9659	65
	Taxable social security tips	**6c**	-0-	× 12.4% (.124) =	**6d**	-0-	
7	Taxable Medicare wages and tips . . .	**7a**	77900 38	× 2.9% (.029) =	**7b**	2259	11

8	Total social security and Medicare taxes (add lines 6b, 6d, and 7b). Check here if wages are not subject to social security and/or Medicare tax . . . . ▶ ⬚	**8**	11918	76
9	Adjustment of social security and Medicare taxes (see instructions for required explanation) Sick Pay $ _____ ± Fractions of Cents $ ____.04____ ± Other $ _____ =	**9**		04
10	Adjusted total of social security and Medicare taxes (line 8 as adjusted by line 9—see instructions)	**10**	11918	80
11	**Total taxes** (add lines 5 and 10)	**11**	23995	80
12	Advance earned income credit (EIC) payments made to employees . . .	**12**	-0-	
13	Net taxes (subtract line 12 from line 11). **If $2,500 or more, this must equal line 17, column (d) below (or line D of Schedule B (Form 941))**	**13**	23995	80
14	Total deposits for quarter, including overpayment applied from a prior quarter	**14**	23997	80
15	**Balance due** (subtract line 14 from line 13). See instructions	**15**	18	00
16	**Overpayment.** If line 14 is more than line 13, enter excess here ▶ $ _____ and check if to be: ⬚ Applied to next return **or** ⬚ Refunded.			

- **All filers:** If line 13 is less than $2,500, you need not complete line 17 or Schedule B (Form 941).
- **Semiweekly schedule depositors:** Complete Schedule B (Form 941) and check here . . . . ▶ ⬚
- **Monthly schedule depositors:** Complete line 17, columns (a) through (d), and check here. . . . . ▶ ⬚

17	**Monthly Summary of Federal Tax Liability.** Do not complete if you were a semiweekly schedule depositor.		
(a) First month liability	**(b)** Second month liability	**(c)** Third month liability	**(d)** Total liability for quarter
8189.14	8063.96	7742.70	23995.80

Third Party Designee	Do you want to allow another person to discuss this return with the IRS (see separate instructions)? ⬚ **Yes.** Complete the following. ⬚ **No**
	Designee's name ▶ Phone no. ▶ ( ) Personal identification number (PIN) ▶ ⬚⬚⬚⬚⬚

Sign Here

Under penalties of perjury, I declare that I have examined this return, including accompanying schedules and statements, and to the best of my knowledge and belief, it is true, correct, and complete.

Signature ▶   Print Your Name and Title ▶   Date ▶

For Privacy Act and Paperwork Reduction Act Notice, see back of Payment Voucher.   Cat. No. 17001Z   Form **941** (Rev. 1-2002)

C2.   Household Employee? LO 1.

Nelson operates a placement service for companionsitting for the elderly. He placed Martha Jackson with Mrs. Mock, an elderly woman who needed a person to assist with her personal needs, household care, and companionship. Jackson is paid directly from Mrs. Mock. Jackson had to pay a placement fee of $50 to Nelson. Is Jackson an employee of Nelson or a household employee of Mrs. Mock? Explain.

Net activities

URLS are subject to change. Please visit the Bieg Payroll Accounting Web site: http://bieg.swcollege.com for updates.

1. Go to http://www.electronicaccountant.com/ PracticalAccountant/index.cfm/txFuse/dspShellContent/ fuseAction/DISPLAY/numContentID/6310/ numTaxonomyID/179.htm

   Il Ristorante Della Patata, a popular local eatery, has recently hired you to do its payroll. Unfortunately, your predecessor left you with no formal method of maintaining employee tip records. You are to meet with your staff this Friday and provide them with information and and a recommendation for tip reporting procedures. Prepare a short presentation on the methods that can be used and your recommendation as to which method should be used.

2. Go to a search engine and type "safeguard your social security number." Discuss the following questions:
   a. Why is it important to safeguard your social security number?
   b. What can you do to safeguard your social security number?

   c. Discuss what you would do if your identity were stolen.

   http://www.google.com
   http://www.ask.com

3. Go to http://www.eftps.gov/.
   a. How long does it take a taxpayer to enroll in the Electronic Federal Tax Payment System (EFTPS)?
   b. What are the advantages of EFTPS?

4. Go to http://www.irs.gov/businesses/display/0,,il%3D2& genericId%3D10063,00.html.
   a. Who can use the TeleFile system?
   b. Why would a business want to use the TeleFile system?

5. Go to http://www.ssa.gov/pubs/10022.html. Discuss the following questions.
   a. How is self-employment income treated differently from income when you work for an employer.
   b. How do you report self-employment income?

Income Tax Withholding

After reading this chapter, we finally understand all those boxes and how they were calculated on the W-2 form that we received at year's end. What are taxable fringe benefits? How do we withhold on tips? What are pre-tax deductions? How do you fill out a W-4 form?

After studying forms W-2, W-2c, W-3, W-4, W-5, 941, 1099-MISC, etc., we realize why the Internal Revenue Service needs over 100,000 employees.

4

© Getty Images, Inc./Photodisc

AFTER STUDYING THIS CHAPTER, YOU SHOULD BE ABLE TO:

1. Explain coverage under the federal income tax withholding law by determining: (a) the employer-employee relationship, (b) the kinds of payments defined as wages, and (c) the kinds of employment excluded under the law.

2. Explain the types of withholding allowances that may be claimed by employees for income tax withholding purposes.

3. Explain the purpose of Form W-4 and list the proper procedures for using the information contained on the form.

4. Compute the amount of federal income tax to be withheld using: (a) the percentage method and (b) the wage-bracket method.

5. Compute the amount of federal income tax to be withheld using alternative methods such as quarterly averaging and annualizing of wages.

6. Compute the withholding of federal income taxes on supplementary wage payments.

7. Explain how employees may receive Advance Earned Income Credit and how the employer computes the amount of the advance.

8. Complete Form W-2 and become familiar with other wage and tax statements.

9. Review completion of *Form 941, Employer's Quarterly Federal Tax Return.*

10. Describe the major types of information returns.

11. Explain the impact of state and local income taxes on the payroll accounting process.

At the beginning of World War II, the income tax became the principal source of revenue to finance government operations. The Ruml plan put the collection of this tax on a pay-as-you-go basis. This chapter describes the employer's responsibility for withholding income taxes from employees' wages and paying these taxes to the federal government. In addition, many employers must also comply with state, city, and county income tax withholding laws. Employers must be aware of these laws to avoid possible penalties.

COVERAGE UNDER FEDERAL INCOME TAX WITHHOLDING LAWS

LEARNING OBJECTIVE 1

Before an individual withholds any tax under the tax law, the following conditions must exist:

1. There must be, or have been, an employer-employee relationship.
2. The payments received by the employee must be defined as wages under the law.
3. The employment must not be exempted by the law.

Employer-Employee Relationship

As discussed in Chapter 3, establishing the correct relationship between the employer and employee is a very important factor in complying with the Social Security Tax Law. This also applies to the Federal Income Tax Withholding Law.

Employers can be sole proprietorships, partners, corporations, not-for-profit corporations, and federal and state governments. No distinctions are made between classes or grades of employees—from executives to entry-level personnel. Neither partners nor directors of a corporation are considered employees unless they perform services other than participation in board meetings.

Taxable Wages

For withholding purposes, the term *wages* includes the total compensation paid to employees for services. Employers withhold federal income taxes on the *gross amount* of wages before deductions such as state and local taxes, insurance premiums, savings bonds, profit-sharing contributions, and union dues. Examples of employee compensation subject to withholding include:

- Wages and salaries
- Vacation allowances
- Supplemental payments
- Bonuses and commissions
- Fringe benefits
- Tips
- Cash awards

Employees may receive compensation in ways other than their regular wage payments. Figure 4–1 shows some special types of payments that are also subject to federal income tax withholding.

Fringe Benefits

Unless the law says otherwise, fringe benefits are subject to federal income tax withholding. In general, the taxable portion is the amount by which the fair market value of the benefits exceed what the employee paid, plus any amount the law excludes. Fringe benefits include employer-provided items such as:

- Cars
- Free or discounted flights
- Discounts on property or services
- Vacations
- Memberships in social or country clubs
- Tickets for entertainment and sporting events

IRS CONNECTION

Since the Income Tax Reform Act of 1986, it has been estimated that the Internal Revenue Code has been amended some 4,000 times. The original Income Tax Code of 1914 contained 14 pages of law, and the forms consisted of four pages, including the instructions to complete the forms. There were 4,000 employees of the IRS in 1914. Today there are 9,400 pages of laws, 4,000 pages of IRS forms, and 115,000 employees.

FIGURE 4-1

Taxable Payments to Employees

Disabled Worker's Wages	Withhold for wages paid after the year in which the worker became entitled to disability insurance under the Social Security Act.
Meals and Lodging	Unless furnished for the employer's convenience and on the employer's premises, as a condition of employment. Cash allowances for meals and lodging are taxable. If more than half of the meals provided to employees on the employer's premises are for the convenience of the employer, then these meals are treated as for the employer's convenience.
Moving Expenses	Nonqualified reimbursed and employer-paid expenses are subject to withholding. Nonqualified expenses include cost of sale of old residence, purchase of new residence, house hunting, temporary living expenses, and meals.
Partially Exempt Employment	If the employee spends half or more time in a pay period performing services subject to employment taxes, all pay in that pay period is taxable.
Payments to Nonresident Aliens	Subject to withholding (unless excepted by regulations).
Sick Pay	Subject to withholding whether paid by the employer or third party (to the extent of the employer's contribution into the plan).
Supplemental Unemployment Compensation	To the extent they are includible in an employee's gross income It does not include separation due to disciplinary problems or age.
Travel and Business Expenses (non-accountable plans)	If (1) the employee is not required to or does not substantiate lexpenses with receipts or (2) the employee receives travel advances and does not or is not required to return any unused amount of the advance.

Withholding on Fringe Benefits.   Determination of the value of the fringe benefit must be made by January 31 of the following year. For withholding and depositing purposes, reasonable estimates may be used before that date. The employer may add the value of fringe benefits to regular wages for a payroll period and figure withholding taxes on the total or may withhold the tax on the value of the benefits at the flat 27 percent supplemental wage rate.

The employer may choose not to withhold income tax on the value of an employee's personal use of a vehicle. The employer must, however, withhold social security, Medicare, or railroad retirement taxes on the use of the vehicle. The employer may make a reasonable estimate of the value of the fringe benefits on the dates the employer chooses for the purpose of making deposits. In general, the employer must figure the value of fringe benefits no later than January 31 of the next year.

Flexible Reporting.   With noncash fringe benefits, the employer has the option of treating the benefits as being paid on any basis (paying monthly, at year-end, etc.). As long as the benefits are treated as paid by December 31, the employer can choose any option.

Due to a *special period rule,* employers can even use October 31 as the cutoff date for valuing the noncash fringe benefit. This rule allows employers to treat noncash fringe benefits of November and December as being provided in the following year and, therefore, taxed in the next year.

If this special rule is applied to a particular benefit, it must apply to all employees who receive this benefit. Also, if applied, the employer must notify the employees of this special rule treatment prior to giving them their W-2 forms.

EXAMPLE

Employers may treat the value of a single fringe benefit as paid on one or more dates in the same calendar year even if the employee receives the entire benefit at one time.

A one-time receipt of a $1,000 fringe benefit in 2003 can be treated as four payments of $250, each in a different pay period of 2003.

Nontaxable Fringe Benefits

Fringe benefits that are nontaxable include:

- Services provided at no additional cost
- Qualified employee discounts
- Working condition fringes
- Minimal value fringes
- Qualified transportation fringes
- Use of on-premises athletic facilities
- Reduced tuition for education

Services the employer provides at no additional cost, qualified employee discounts, meals at employer-run eating establishments, and reduced tuition provided to officers, owners, or highly paid employees are excluded from their income only if the benefits are given to employees on a nondiscriminatory basis.

Traveling Expenses

Accountable Plan.   Employee expense reimbursement amounts paid under an accountable plan are not subject to income tax withholding. An accountable plan requires the employer's reimbursement or allowance arrangement to meet all three of the following rules:

1. Business connected.
2. Adequate accounting within a reasonable time period.
3. Employee return of excess of substantiated amounts.

Nonaccountable Plan.   A nonaccountable plan is an arrangement that does not meet all of the requirements above. All amounts paid under this plan are considered wages and are subject to income tax withholding.

Taxable Tips

As reported in Chapter 3, employees must report cash tips to the employer by the 10th of the month following the month they receive the tips. This report includes tips paid by the employer for charge customers and tips the employee receives directly from the customers. Tips of less than $20 in a month and noncash tips need not be reported.

Withholding from Tips.   The employer collects income tax, as well as social security taxes, on reported tips. The following procedures apply to withholding income tax on reported tips:

1. The employer collects the tax from the employee's wages, or from other funds the employee makes available.
2. When tips are reported in connection with employment where the employee also receives a regular wage, compute the withholding tax on the aggregate—treat tips as a

on the
JOB

If you need to determine if a certain type of payment or individual is subject to income tax withholding, check **Circular E, Employer's Tax Guide.** Special classes of employment and payments are listed, along with their treatment under employment tax laws.

supplemental wage payment.

3. If the withholding tax exceeds the amount of wages paid to the employee, the employee must pay the uncollected portion of the taxes directly to the IRS when filing the annual income tax return (Form 1040).

4. The employer is not required to audit or verify the accuracy of the tip income reported.

Allocated Tips. Large food and beverage establishments that have customary tipping and normally had more than 10 employees on a typical business day in the preceding year may be required to allocate tips among employees if:

> *The total tips reported by the employees during any payroll period are less than 8 percent of the establishment's gross receipts for that period.*

The amount of allocated tips to employees equals:

> *The difference between tips reported and 8 percent of gross receipts, other than carry-out sales and sales with at least a 10 percent service charge added.*

The tip allocation may be made using one of three methods: hours worked, gross receipts, good faith agreement. Federal income taxes are to be withheld only on the tips reported to the employer; no taxes are withheld on the tips that are merely allocated.

Payments Exempt from Withholding

The law excludes certain payments and payments to certain individuals from federal income tax withholding, as shown in Figure 4–2.

SELF-STUDY QUIZ 4–1. *Check any item of employee compensation not subject to withholding:*

_____ **a.** Company-provided lunches at the plant to reduce tardiness by keeping employees on the premises.

_____ **b.** Year-end bonuses to managers and supervisors.

_____ **c.** Work-out room for employee use during lunch hours.

_____ **d.** Travel advances to salespersons for overnight sales calls out of town.

_____ **e.** Employer-paid sick pay.

_____ **f.** Memberships in the local country club for department managers.

_____ **g.** Meals provided by a local restaurant for its employees.

Pretax Salary Reductions

An employee can authorize an employer to deduct certain withholdings from his or her pay on a pretax basis. These withholdings are taken from the gross pay and, therefore, reduce the amount of pay that is subject to federal income tax.

Cafeteria Plans. Some employers offer their employees a choice between cash (pay) or qualified (nontaxable) benefits. Employees can select various levels of health, accident, and life insurance coverage or choose to contribute to cash or deferred plans. The salary reductions are used to pay for the desired benefit, and these pretax contributions are not included in taxable wages for FIT. Contributions are also exempt from FICA taxes, except for those made to cash or deferred arrangements and life insurance coverage in excess of $50,000.

Deferred Arrangements. Many deferred arrangements are usually set up as retirement plans. The most common of these is the ***defined contribution plan*** that provides future benefits based solely on the amount paid by each employee and employer into the account, plus investment gains. These plans are tax-deferred savings or stock accounts held in trust for employees. The most popular types of retirement accounts are the 401(k) and IRAs (see page 4-22).

F I G U R E   4 - 2

Exempt Payments

Type of Payment or Individual	Conditions
Advances	For travel and other business expenses reasonably expected to be incurred.
Accident and Health Insurance Payments	Exempt except 2% shareholder-employees of S corporations.
De Minimus Fringe Benefits	Benefits of so little value as to make accounting for the benefit unreasonable and administratively impractical.
Deceased Person's Wages	Paid to the person's beneficiary or estate.
Dependent Care Assistance	To the extent it is reasonable to believe the amounts will be excludable from gross income. Up to $5,000 can be excluded from an employee's gross income without being subject to social security, medicare, or income tax withholding.
Domestic Service	Private home, local college club, or local chapter of college fraternity or sorority.
Educational Assistance	If education maintains or improves employee's skills required by the job. For the non-job-related educational assistance, up to $5,250 per year of employer-provided assistance for undergraduate and graduate education is tax-free.
Employee Business Expense Reimbursements	Accountable plans for amounts not exceeding specified government rates for mileage, lodging, meals, and incidental expenses.
Employee-Safety and Length-of-Service Awards	If merchandise costs $400 or less. Rises to $1,600 for a written nondiscriminatory plan.
Employer-Provided Parking	Up to $180 per month.
Foreign Service by U.S. Citizens	As employees for affiliates of American employers if entitled to exclusion under section 911 or required by law of foreign country to withhold income tax on such payment.
Group-Term Life Insurance Costs	The employer's cost of group-term life insurance less than $50,000.
Individuals Under 18	For delivery or distribution of newspapers, shopping news and vendors of newspapers and magazines where payment is the difference between the purchase and sales price.
Long-Term Care Insurance Premiums	Employer-paid premiums for long-term care insurance up to a limit.
Ministers of Churches, Members of Religious Orders	Performing services for the order agency of the supervising church, or associated institution.
Moving Expense Reimbursements	For qualified expenses, if the employee is entitled to a deduction for these expenses on the individual's federal income tax return.
Public Officials	For fees only, not salaries.
Retirement and Pension Plans	• Employer contributions to a qualified plan. • Employer contributions to IRA accounts under a SEP [see section 402(g) for salary reduction limitation]. • Employer contributions to section 403(b) annuity contract [see section 402(g) for limitation]. • Elective contributions and deferrals to plans containing a qualified cash or deferred compensation arrangement, such as 401(k).
Sickness or Injury Payments	Payments made under worker's compensation law or contract of insurance.

Daniel Rowland, an employee for the Harden School, belongs to a tax-deferred retirement plan to which he contributes 3 percent of his pay which is matched by the school. His biweekly pay is $2,500. Because of the deferral (3% × $2,500 = $75), $2,425 is subject to federal income tax withholding.

WITHHOLDING ALLOWANCES

The law entitles employees to exempt a portion of their earnings from withholding by claiming a personal allowance and allowances for their dependents if they furnish their employers with a claim for the allowances. Employees may also claim special allowances and allowances for itemized deductions and tax credits. However, employees cannot claim the same withholding allowances with more than one employer at the same time.

Personal Allowances

Employees can claim a *personal allowance* for themselves and each qualified dependent, provided they are not claimed on another person's tax return. In 2002, the amount of the personal allowance was $3,000, and this was treated as a deduction in computing taxable income. A married employee may also claim one personal allowance for his or her spouse if the spouse is not claimed as a dependent on another person's tax return.

Allowances for Dependents

Employees may claim one allowance for each dependent (other than a spouse) who will be claimed on their federal income tax returns. To qualify as a dependent, the person must meet specific requirements that are listed in the instructions accompanying the individual's federal income tax return.

Additional Withholding Allowance

Employees can also reduce the amount of withholding by claiming a *special withholding allowance,* whether or not they plan to itemize deductions on their tax return. An additional withholding allowance can be claimed by a person under any one of the following situations:

1. Single person who has only one job.
2. Married person who has only one job with nonworking spouse.
3. Person's wages from a second job or the spouse's wages (or both) equal $1,000 or less.

This allowance is only used to compute the employee's income tax withholding. The employee *cannot claim* this allowance on his or her income tax return.

Other Withholding Allowances

Withholding allowances reduce the overwithholding of income taxes on employees' wages. In addition to the allowances already discussed, employees may be entitled to withholding allowances based on estimated tax credits, such as child care, and itemized deductions for medical expenses, mortgage interest, and charitable contributions. Employees take these credits when filing their federal income tax returns. The number of withholding allowances is determined on the worksheet that accompanies *Form W-4, Employee's Withholding Allowance Certificate,* and is then reported on that form.

With the tax credits for children and higher education costs, many employees are eligible for reduced withholding.

Form W-4 (Employee's Withholding Allowance Certificate)

The employer uses the information from *Form W-4, Employee's Withholding Allowance Certificate,* to compute the amount of income tax to withhold from employees' wages. The employer must have Form W-4 on file for each employee. This form contains the withholding allowance certificate (shown in Figure 4–3), detailed instructions, and worksheets for employees to use in completing the certificate.

FIGURE 4-3

W-4 Employee's Withholding Allowance Certificate

Form **W-4**	**Employee's Withholding Allowance Certificate**	OMB No. 1545-0010
Department of the Treasury Internal Revenue Service	For Privacy Act and Paperwork Reduction Act Notice, see page 2.	2002

1 Type or print your first name and middle initial **Albert J.** | Last name **Cox** | 2 Your social security number **542 13 6921**

Home address (number and street or rural route) **421 Eastmont**

3 ☒ Single ☐ Married ☐ Married, but withhold at higher Single rate.
Note: *If married, but legally separated, or spouse is a nonresident alien, check the Single box.*

City or town, state, and ZIP code **Richland, WA 99352**

4 If your last name differs from that on your social security card, check here. **You must call 1-800-772-1213 for a new card** . . . ☐

5 Total number of allowances you are claiming (from line **H** above **OR** from the applicable worksheet on page 2) **5 | 4**

6 Additional amount, if any, you want withheld from each paycheck . . . . **6 | $ 0**

7 I claim exemption from withholding for 2001, and I certify that I meet **BOTH** of the following conditions for exemption:
Last year I had a right to a refund of **ALL** Federal income tax withheld because I had **NO** tax liability **AND**
This year I expect a refund of **ALL** Federal income tax withheld because I expect to have **NO** tax liability.
If you meet both conditions, write "EXEMPT" here . . . . **7 |**

Under penalties of perjury, I certify that I am entitled to the number of withholding allowances claimed on this certificate, or I am entitled to claim exempt status.

Employee's signature (Form is not valid unless you sign it) **Albert J. Cox** | **Date** *January 2* 2002

8 Employer's name and address (Employer: Complete lines 8 and 10 only if sending to the IRS.) | 9 Office code (optional) | 10 Employer identification number

Cat. No. 10220Q

---

on the JOB

Nonresident aliens must fill out Form W-4 with single status and one allowance and request an additional amount withheld (for a weekly pay, $7.60).

on the JOB

Employers may establish systems that allow employees to file and make changes to their W-4s by means of a computer network or voice response technology. However, these employers must also make the paper W-4 option available.

Completing Form W-4. The employee completes Form W-4 when he or she begins work for an employer. Employers must retain the withholding certificate as a supporting record of the withholding allowances used in deducting income taxes from the employees' salaries and wages. Once filed, the certificate remains in effect until an amended certificate takes effect. Withholding certificates should be retained as long as they are in effect and for four years thereafter. If the employee does not complete the W-4, the employer withholds taxes as if the employee is single, with no withholding allowances.

Since the employers are required to get each employee's social security number on Form W-4, they can request to see the employee's social security card, and they can photocopy the card for their files.

Withholding Allowances. The number of withholding allowances claimed on Form W-4 may differ from the number of exemptions claimed on the employee's tax return. The process of determining the correct number of withholding allowances begins with the number of personal exemptions the employee expects to claim on his or her tax return. The employee then increases or decreases this number based on the employee's desire for a higher paycheck or a higher tax refund. The worksheets provided with Form W-4 enable the employee to determine the exact number of allowances to enter on the certificate.

Changing Form W-4. If the status of an employee changes with respect to the number of withholding allowances or marital status, the employee files an amended W-4. If there is a *decrease* in the number of allowances, the employee must furnish the employer with a new certificate within 10 days. If the employee has an *increase* in the number of allowances, the employee does not have to file a new certificate. The employer makes the certificate effective no later than the start of the first payroll period ending on or after the 30th day from the date the replacement Form W-4 is received. The employer may not repay or reimburse the employee for income taxes overwithheld before the effective date of the new certificate, but may reimburse the employee after that date if the employer failed to implement the new certificate.

Exemption from Income Tax Withholding.   Employees may claim exemption from income tax withholding if they had no income tax liability last year and expect none in the current year. The exemption is valid for one year and must be claimed on a new Form W-4 filed by February 15 of each year. If a new certificate is not filed, taxes are withheld at the single rate with zero withholding allowances.

EXAMPLE

Single persons who made less than $7,700 in 2002 owed no federal income tax. Married couples filing jointly with combined wages up to $13,850 incurred no tax liability.

Employees may not claim exemption from withholding if (1) another person claims the employee as a dependent on their tax return *and* (2) income exceeds $750 and includes more than $250 of unearned income (interest, dividends).

Additional and Voluntary Withholding Agreements.   In some instances, employees want additional federal income taxes withheld from their wages, such as a person with two or more jobs, or a married couple where both work. The simplest way to increase the amount of tax withheld is to reduce the number of withholding allowances claimed.

If an employee receives payments not classified as wages, or an employer-employee relationship does not exist, individuals can voluntarily request that the employer or the one making the payments withhold federal income taxes from their payments. These individuals need only furnish a Form W-4. Requests for additional and voluntary withholding become effective when the employer accepts them and begins to withhold tax. The agreements remain in effect until the specified termination date or until the termination is mutually agreed upon. Either party may terminate an agreement prior to a specified date or mutual agreement by furnishing the other party with a signed, written notice of termination.

EXAMPLE

Individuals who may wish to request additional withholding or a voluntary agreement to withhold include:

- Clergy
- Two wage-earner married couples
- Domestic workers in a private home
- Individuals receiving interest and dividends
- Individuals receiving self-employment income

Sending Forms W-4 to the IRS.   To curb the practice of filing false Forms W-4 by claiming unreasonable numbers of allowances or total exemption from withholding, the IRS requires employers to submit a copy of each form on which:

1. An employee claims 11 or more withholding allowances, or
2. An employee, usually earning more than $200 a week at the time the certificate was filed, claims to be exempt from withholding.

Figure 4–4 outlines the procedures to follow in submitting Forms W-4 to the IRS.

Withholding on Nonresident Aliens.   To avoid underwithholding, nonresident aliens (who cannot claim the standard exemption and are limited to one allowance when filing their personal U.S. income tax returns) should (1) not claim exemption from income tax

IRS CONNECTION

Employees who claim more allowances than they are entitled to can be hit with a $500 penalty.

FIGURE 4-4

Procedures for Submitting Forms W-4

- Send Forms W-4 that meet the prescribed conditions each quarter with Form 941, unless you file Form 941 on magnetic media. In such cases, complete boxes 8 and 10 on any Forms W-4 you send.
- Send copies of any written statements from employees in support of the claims made on the form, even if the Forms W-4 are not in effect at the end of the quarter.
- In certain cases, the IRS may notify you in writing that you must submit specified forms more frequently to your district director separate from Form 941.
- Unless notified, base withholding on the Forms W-4 that you send to the IRS.
- If notified by the IRS, base withholding on the number of allowances shown in the IRS notice. The employee will also receive a similar notice.
- If the employee later files a new Form W-4, follow it only if exempt status is not claimed or the number of withholding allowances does not exceed the IRS notice.
- If the employee later files a new Form W-4 that does not follow the IRS notice, disregard it and continue to withhold based on the IRS notice.
- If the employee prepares a new Form W-4, explaining any difference with the IRS notice, and submits it to you, send the Form W-4 and explanation to the IRS office shown in the notice. Continue to withhold according to the IRS notice until notified.

withholding; (2) request withholding as single, regardless of actual status; and (3) claim only one allowance. Residents of Canada, Mexico, Japan, or Korea may claim more than one allowance.

Other Withholdings

Federal income taxes are also withheld from other kinds of payments made to current and former employees, as described below.

Withholding for Pension or Annuity Payments.   Generally, the withholding of federal income taxes applies to payments made from pension, profit-sharing, stock bonus, annuity, and certain deferred compensation plans and individual retirement arrangements. You treat the payments from any of these sources as wages for the purpose of withholding. Unless the recipients of pension or annuity payments elect *not* to have federal income taxes withheld from such payments, the taxes will be withheld. Payers must withhold on monthly pension and annuity payments exceeding $1,225 ($14,700 a year), unless the payees elect otherwise. If the recipients do not instruct the payers to the contrary, the payers are required to withhold income taxes as if the recipients were *married and claiming three withholding allowances.*

By completing Form W-4P or a substitute form furnished by the payer, an employee can elect to have no income tax withheld from the payments received. The form may also be used to change the amount of tax that would ordinarily be withheld by the payers. Once completed, Form W-4P remains in effect until the recipient changes or revokes the certificate. The payer must notify the recipients each year of their right to elect to have no taxes withheld or to revoke their election.

Withholding from Sick Pay.   *Form W-4S, Request for Federal Income Tax Withholding from Sick Pay,* must be filed with the payer of sick pay if the employee wants federal income taxes to be withheld from the payments. Form W-4S is filed only if the payer is a third party, such as an insurance company. The form should not be filed with the worker's employer, who makes such payments, since employers already must withhold income taxes from sick pay.

Withholding on Government Payments. Form W-4V can be used to request federal income tax withholding on government payments (such as social security benefits or unemployment compensation). This request is voluntary. The individual can choose to have 7%, 10%, 15%, or 27% withheld from each payment.

Invalid Forms

Any unauthorized change or addition to Form W-4 makes it invalid. If an employee indicates in any way that his or her Form W-4 is not correct, the Form W-4 becomes invalid. A request should be made to the employee for another Form W-4. If not provided, the employer should withhold taxes as if the employee were single, claiming no allowances, unless the employee had an earlier W-4 that was valid. In this case, the employer should use the prior W-4 to determine the tax withholding.

Employee Penalties

Employees who willfully file false information statements (Form W-4) are, in addition to any other penalty, subject to fines of up to $1,000 or imprisonment for up to one year or both.

Employees claiming excess deductions are subject to a $500 civil penalty for each offense.

SELF-STUDY QUIZ 4–2

1. Grace Kyle submitted a new Form W-4 claiming one additional withholding allowance. Kyle also requested to be reimbursed for the overwithholding prior to the change. How should the payroll manager respond to Kyle?
2. Bob Bradley is upset because his paycheck on February 28, 2003, has federal income tax withheld, even though he filed a W-4 in 2002 claiming exemption from withholding. What should the payroll manager say to Bradley?
3. Greg Volmer, married with a nonemployed spouse, has three dependent children. How many allowances can Volmer claim on his W-4?

FEDERAL INCOME TAX WITHHOLDING

After the employer learns from Form W-4 the number of withholding allowances for an employee, the employer selects a withholding method. Employers usually choose either the *percentage method* or the *wage-bracket method.* Both distinguish between married and unmarried persons, and both methods provide the full benefit of the allowances claimed by the employee on Form W-4.

Both methods take into account a *standard deduction,* an amount of money used to reduce an individual's adjusted gross income in arriving at the taxable income. For 2002, the following standard deductions apply:

Joint return filers and surviving spouses	$7,850
Married persons filing separately	3,925
Head of household filers	6,900
Single filers	4,700

These amounts are increased for single and married individuals or surviving spouses age 65 or older or blind.

Each year, the standard deductions are adjusted for inflation. The adjustment also applies to the additional standard deductions available to elderly or blind persons.

The choice of methods is usually based on the number of employees and the payroll accounting system used. The employer can change from one method to another at any time, and different methods may be used for different groups of employees.

LEARNING OBJECTIVE

CONNECTION

In fiscal year 2000, the IRS collected $1,137 trillion in individual income taxes, and 67 percent of this amount was collected through payroll withholdings.

Percentage Method

To compute the tax using the percentage method, follow these steps:

Step 1

Determine the amount of gross wages earned. If the wage ends in a fractional dollar amount, you may round the gross pay to the nearest dollar.

→ Nick Volente, single, claims two allowances and earns $802.63 semimonthly.

Round Gross Wages to $803.00

Step 2

Multiply the number of allowances claimed by the amount of one allowance for the appropriate payroll period, as shown in the Table of Allowance Values in Figure 4–5.

→ Table of Allowance Values for semimonthly payroll period shows $125.00.

Multiply $125.00 × 2 = $250.00

Step 3

Subtract the amount for the number of allowances claimed from the employee's gross pay to find the excess of wages over allowances claimed.

→
Gross pay	$803.00
Less: Allowances	250.00
Excess wages	$553.00

Step 4

Determine the withholding tax on the excess of wages over allowances claimed by referring to the appropriate Percentage Method Withholding Table.

→ Compute tax from Tax Table 3(a), page T–3.

15% of ($553 − $356) + $24.60 = $54.15

SELF-STUDY QUIZ 4–3. *Gina Swant, married and claiming 3 allowances, receives a salary of $1,100.25 each week. Compute the amount to withhold for federal income tax using the percentage method and Figure 4–5. Show the results of each step, as described for figuring withholding using the percentage method.*

Step 1 Result _____   Step 2 Result _____

Step 3 Result _____   Step 4 Result _____

Wage-Bracket Method

The IRS provides statutory wage-bracket tables for weekly, biweekly, semimonthly, monthly, and daily or miscellaneous pay periods. Copies may be obtained from the District Director of Internal Revenue. Tax Table B at the end of the textbook provides tables for weekly, biweekly, semimonthly, monthly, and daily pay periods for single and married persons effective January 1, 2002.

FIGURE 4 - 5

Table of Allowance Values for 2002

Weekly	57.69	Biweekly	115.38	Semimonthly	125.00	Monthly	250.00
Quarterly	750.00	Semiannual	1500.00	Annual	3,000.00	Daily/Misc.	11.54

To use the wage-bracket method, follow these steps:

Step 1

Select the withholding table that applies to the employee's marital status and pay period. → Rebecca Northwood is married and claims 3 allowances. She is paid weekly at a rate of $810.

Step 2

Locate the wage bracket (the first two columns of the table) in which the employee's gross wages fall. → Locate the appropriate wage bracket (see Figure 4–6):

At least $810 but less than $820

Step 3

Follow the line for the wage bracket across to the right to the column showing the appropriate number of allowances. Withhold this amount of tax. → Move across the line to the column showing 3 allowances.

The tax to withhold is $66.

FIGURE 4 - 6

Married Persons—Weekly Payroll Period

If the wages are–		And the number of withholding allowances claimed is—										
At least	But less than	0	1	2	3	4	5	6	7	8	9	10
		The amount of income tax to be withheld is—										
$750	$760	$83	$74	$66	$57	$48	$40	$31	$23	$17	$11	$5
760	770	85	76	67	59	50	41	33	24	18	12	6
770	780	86	77	69	60	51	43	34	26	19	13	7
780	790	88	79	70	62	53	44	36	27	20	14	8
790	800	89	80	72	63	54	46	37	29	21	15	9
800	810	91	82	73	65	56	47	39	30	22	16	10
810	820	92	83	75	66	57	49	40	32	23	17	11
820	830	94	85	76	68	59	50	42	33	24	18	12
830	840	95	86	78	69	60	52	43	35	26	19	13
840	850	97	88	79	71	62	53	45	36	27	20	14

SELF-STUDY QUIZ 4–4. *Quirk Motors uses the wage-bracket method to withhold from the semimonthly earnings of its employees. For each employee, compute the amount to be withheld from their earnings for the payroll period ending March 14.*

Employee	Marital Status	No. of Allowances	Salary	Federal Income Tax Withheld
Kyle Lamb	S	1	$1,100	_____
Zed Nurin	S	0	850	_____
Carol Hogan	M	4	975	_____
Marla Vick	M	2	3,000	_____
Al Marks	S	3	1,200	_____

OTHER METHODS OF WITHHOLDING

 LEARNING OBJECTIVE 5

In addition to the two principal methods of withholding previously described, employers may use other methods such as *quarterly averaging* and *annualizing wages.*

EXAMPLE

QUARTERLY AVERAGING. Turner, Inc., estimates that Carl Moyer will be paid $6,000 during the second quarter of the year. Moyer is married, claims five withholding allowances, and is paid semimonthly.

Step 1—Divide the estimated quarterly wages by 6 (the number of semimonthly pay periods in the quarter).

$$\$6,000 \div 6 = \$1,000$$

Step 2—Find the amount of federal income tax to withhold from each semimonthly payment.

MARRIED Persons—SEMIMONTHLY Payroll Period
Wages at least $1,000 but not more than $1,020 for 5 allowances = $12

The withholding is based on the average payment instead of the actual payment.

EXAMPLE

ANNUALIZING WAGES. Marc Field, married with 3 allowances, receives $1,050 semimonthly. Under the annualizing method, do the following:

Step 1—Multiply the semimonthly wage by 24 pay periods to compute his annual wage.

$$\$1,050 \times 24 = \$25,200$$

Step 2—Subtract withholding allowances of $9,000 (3 × $3,000).

$$\$25,200 - 9,000 = \$16,200$$

Step 3—Use Tax Table 7(b) and apply the Percentage Method to the taxable wages.

$16,200 × 10% of the excess over $6,450. ($16,200 − $6,450) × 0.10 = $975.00.

$975.00 ÷ 24 semimonthly payroll = $40.63 per paycheck

SUPPLEMENTAL WAGE PAYMENTS

 LEARNING OBJECTIVE 6

Supplemental wage payments include items such as vacation pay, bonuses, commissions, and dismissal pay. Since these types of payments may be paid at a different time than the regular payroll and not related to a particular payroll, the employer must decide whether to lump the regular wages and supplemental wages together or withhold from the supplemental wages separately. The IRS has issued rules that indicate which method the employer should use.

Vacation Pay

Vacation pay is subject to withholding as though it were a regular payment made for the payroll period or periods occurring during the vacation. If the vacation pay is for a time longer than your usual payroll period, spread it over the pay period(s) for which you pay it. If an employee is paid weekly and is paid for two weeks of vacation, treat each vacation week separately and calculate the tax on each vacation week using the weekly tax tables or wage brackets.

When vacation pay is in lieu of taking vacation time, treat it as a regular supplemental wage payment and calculate the tax on the total as a single payment. A lump-sum vacation payment on termination of employment is also treated as a supplemental wage payment.

Supplemental Wages Paid with Regular Wages

If the employer pays supplemental wages with regular wages but does not specify the amount of each type of wage, the employer withholds as if the total were a single payment for a regular payroll period.

EXAMPLE

Ashley Watson, married with 3 allowances, earns a monthly salary of $1,800. She also receives a bonus on sales that exceed her quota for the year. For this year, her bonus amounts to $4,600. Watson's employer pays her the regular salary and the bonus together on her December paycheck. The withholding for the December pay is computed on the total amount of $6,400 ($1,800 + $4,600). After deducting the allowances, using the percentage Tax Table 4(b), the amount to withhold is $879.28.

However, if the employer indicates specifically the amount of each payment, the employer may withhold at a flat 27 percent rate on the supplemental wages, if the tax is withheld on the employee's regular wages at the appropriate rate.

EXAMPLE

If you indicate separately on Watson's paycheck stub the amount of each payment, the amount of federal income tax to be withheld is computed as follows:

		Taxes Withheld	
Regular monthly earnings	$1,800	$ 53.00	(from wage-bracket tax tables*)
Annual bonus	4,600	1,242.00	(4,600 × 27%)
Totals	$6,400	$1,295.00	

*The percentage table could also be used.

Supplemental Wages Paid Separately from Regular Wages

If the supplemental wages are paid separately, the income tax withholding method depends on whether or not you withhold income tax from the employee's regular wages. If you withhold income tax from the employee's regular wages, you can use either of the following methods for supplemental wages.

Method A.   Add the supplemental wages and regular wages for the most recent payroll period. Then, figure the income tax as if the total were a single payment. Subtract the tax already withheld from the regular wage. Withhold the remaining tax from the supplemental wage.

EXAMPLE

Brian Early, married with 2 allowances, is paid $985 semimonthly. The tax to be withheld under the wage-bracket method on each semimonthly pay is $47. Early is paid his regular wage on June 15. On June 18, he receives a bonus of $500. The tax on the bonus is computed as follows:

Regular wage payment	$ 985
Bonus	500
Total	$1,485

Tax on total from the wage-bracket table in Tax Table B	$121
Less: Tax already withheld on $985	47
Tax to be withheld from $500 bonus	$ 74

If you did not withhold income tax from the employee's regular wage payment, use Method A.

Method B.   Withhold a flat 27 percent on the supplemental pay.

EXAMPLE

The tax withheld on Brian Early's June 18 bonus of $500 is computed as follows:

Bonus	$500
Tax rate	× 27%
Tax withheld on bonus	$135

If a supplemental payment is paid in a year where no regular wages are paid, the payment is treated as a regular wage payment, and withholding is determined by the rules that apply to a miscellaneous payroll period.

SELF-STUDY QUIZ 4–5. *Milton Stewart, married with 2 allowances, received his regular semimonthly wage of $1,450 on June 15. On June 20, he received a semiannual bonus of $500. Compute the amount of federal income tax to be withheld on the bonus using each method for computing supplemental wage payments. The employer uses the wage-bracket tables.*

Method A _____
Method B _____

Gross-Up Supplementals

In order to give an employee the intended amount of a supplemental payment, the employer will need to gross up the payment so that after the appropriate payroll taxes are withheld, the net amount left is equal to the original intended payment.

A special "*gross-up*" formula can be applied in this situation:

$$\text{Grossed-Up Amount} = \frac{\text{Intended payment}}{1 - \text{applicable tax rates (FICA, 27\% Federal Income Tax rate, and state tax rate)}}$$

EXAMPLE

Grossing-up. Cotter Company wants to award a $4,000 bonus to Donna D'Amico. In addition, they want the net bonus payment to equal $4,000. Assuming D'Amico is still under the OASDI/FICA limit, the calculation would be:

A. $$\frac{4,000}{1 - 0.27 \text{ (supplemental W/H rate)} - 0.062 \text{ (OASDI)} - 0.0145 \text{ (HI)}}$$

B. $\dfrac{4,000}{0.6535} = \$6{,}120.89$ grossed-up bonus

If state or local taxes apply, they must also be included in the formula.

ADVANCE EARNED INCOME CREDIT

The *earned income credit (EIC)* reduces federal income taxes and is intended to offset living expenses for an eligible employee (see Figure 4–7) who has a qualifying child and for the low-income taxpayers who have no qualifying children. The credit can be claimed at the time of filing their individual income tax returns, and they receive a lump-sum tax refund. For 2002, the refund, as calculated at the time of filing Form 1040, could be as much as $2,506 if the employee had one qualifying child; with two or more qualifying children, $4,140. However, to get these payments in advance with his or her paycheck, the employee must give the employer a properly completed *Form W-5, Earned Income Credit Advance Payment Certificate*. The employer must make advance EIC payments to employees who complete and sign Form W-5. For 2002, the maximum *advance* payment (up to 60% of the credit available) was $1,503. Employees will receive the balance of the credit when they file their federal income tax returns.

Form W-5

Eligible employees who want to receive advance EIC payments must file Form W-5 with their employer. On this form, the employee shows the following:

- Expected eligibility for the credit in 2002.
- If they have a qualifying child.
- If they are married.
- If married, whether their spouse has a certificate in effect with any other employer.
- If another W-5 is on file with another current employer.

An employee can have only one certificate in effect with a current employer. If the employee is married and the employee's spouse works, each spouse files a separate Form W-5. This form remains in effect until the end of the calendar year or until the employee revokes the certificate or files another one. A new certificate must be filed by December 31 in order to continue receiving payment in the new year. Figure 4–8 shows an example of a filled-in Form W-5.

Employee's Change of Status

If circumstances change after an employee has submitted a signed Form W-5 that make the employee ineligible for the credit, he or she must revoke the certificate within 10 days after learning of the change. The employee then gives the employer a new Form W-5 stating that he or she is no longer eligible for advance EIC payments. If the employee's situation changes because his or her spouse files a Form W-5, the employee must file a new certificate showing that his or her spouse has a certificate in effect with an employer.

LEARNING OBJECTIVE

on the

JOB

This complex credit, established in 1975, has supplied more than $25 billion to low-income workers.

A L E R T

In studies conducted by the U.S. General Accounting Office, the earned-income credit was not claimed by 25 percent (4.3 million) of eligible households.

on the

JOB

For 2002, taxpayers with no qualifying children and incomes between $6,150 and $11,060 ($7,150 and $12,060 if married filing jointly) can receive a maximum EIC of $376 (with their tax return filing).

IRS CONNECTION

An employee receiving advance earned income credit payments in the paycheck, who finds out that he or she is ineligible, must pay back the advance payments when filing the federal income tax return (Form 1040).

FIGURE 4–7

Employees Eligible for Advance EIC

Only eligible employees can receive advance EIC payments. The eligibility requirements are summarized below.

1. Employee must have a qualifying child, as defined on Form W-5;
2. Employee's expected 2002 earned income and adjusted gross income must each be less than $29,201 (30,201 if filing jointly); and
3. Expect to be able to claim the EIC for 2002.

FIGURE 4 - 8

Earned Income Credit Advance Payment Certificate

Form **W-5**	**Earned Income Credit Advance Payment Certificate**

► Use the current year's certificate only.
► Give this certificate to your employer.
► This certificate expires on December 31, 2002.

OMB No. 1545-1342

20**02**

Department of the Treasury
Internal Revenue Service

Print or type your full name	Your social security number
Mary Sue Graser	269 11 0001

Note: *If you get advance payments of the earned income credit for 2002, you **must** file a 2002 Federal income tax return. To get advance payments, you **must** have a qualifying child and your filing status must be any status **except** married filing a separate return.*

1   I expect to have a qualifying child and be able to claim the earned income credit for 2002, I do not have
     another Form W-5 in effect with any other current employer, and I choose to get advance EIC payments .   ☒ Yes ☐ No
2   Check the box that shows your expected filing status for 2002:
     ☒ Single, head of household, or qualifying widow(er)   ☐ Married filing jointly
3   If you are married, does your spouse have a Form W-5 in effect for 2002 with any employer? . . . . .   ☐ Yes ☐ No

Under penalties of perjury, I declare that the information I have furnished above is, to the best of my knowledge, true, correct, and complete.

Signature ► *Mary Sue Graser*   Date ► *1/24/02*

Cat. No. 10227P

Employer Responsibilities

Employers must notify employees who have no income tax withheld that they may be eligible for EIC payments. The employer may use any of the following methods to notify employees.

1. The IRS Form W-2, which has the required statement about the EIC on the back of Copy C.
2. A substitute Form W-2 with the same EIC statement on the back of the employee's copy.
3. Notice 797, Possible Federal Refund Due to the Earned Income Credit (EIC).
4. Your written statement with the same wording as Notice 797.

Computing the Advance EIC

Employers must include the advance EIC payment with wages paid to their eligible employees who have filed Form W-5. In determining the advance payment, the employer considers the following factors:

1. Wages and reported tips for the pay period.
2. Whether the employee is married or single.
3. Whether a married employee's spouse has a Form W-5 in effect with an employer.

To figure the amount of the advance payment, the employer uses either the *Tables for Percentage Method of Advance EIC Payments* or *Tables for Wage-Bracket Method of Advance EIC Payments.* There are separate tables for employees whose spouses have a certificate in effect, without spouses filing certificate, or single/head of household.

EXAMPLE

Renee Riley is paid $150 per week. She has filed Form W-5 showing that she is married and that her husband has given his employer Form W-5. Using the "Married With Both Spouses Filing Certificate" in Figure 4–9, the advance EIC payment is $13.

Paying the Advance EIC

The advance EIC payments do not affect the amount of income taxes or FICA taxes withheld from employees' wages. Since the EIC payments are not compensation for services rendered, they are not subject to payroll taxes. Generally, the employer pays the amount of

FIGURE 4-9

MARRIED with Both Spouses Filing Certificate—Weekly Payroll Period

MARRIED With Both Spouses Filing Certificate

Wages At least	But less than	Payment to be made	Wages At least	But less than	Payment to be made	Wages At least	But less than	Payment to be made	Wages At least	But less than	Payment to be made	Wages At least	But less than	Payment to be made	Wages At least	But less than	Payment to be made	Wages At least	But less than	Payment to be made
$0	$5	$0	$30	$35	$6	$60	$65	$12	$165	$175	$11	$225	$235	$5	$285	---	$0
5	10	1	35	40	7	65	70	13	175	185	10	235	245	4			
10	15	2	40	45	8	70	135	14	185	195	9	245	255	3			
15	20	3	45	50	9	135	145	14	195	205	8	255	265	2			
20	25	4	50	55	10	145	155	13	205	215	7	265	275	1			
25	30	5	55	60	11	155	165	12	215	225	6	275	285	1			

the advance EIC payment from withheld income taxes and FICA taxes. It is possible that for a payroll period the advance EIC payments may be more than the withheld income taxes and the FICA taxes. In such cases, the employer can:

1. Reduce each advance EIC payment proportionately, or
2. Elect to make full payment of the advance EIC amount and treat such full amounts as an advance payment of the company's employment payroll taxes.

The amount of the advance EIC payments does not change the amount that employers must withhold from their employees' wages for income taxes and FICA. Advance EIC payments made by the employer are treated as having been made from amounts withheld as income tax, employee FICA taxes, and from the employer's FICA taxes. The amount of advance EIC payments is considered to have been paid over to the IRS on the day the wages are paid to employees.

E X A M P L E

Nolan Inc., has 10 employees who are each entitled to advance EIC payments of $12. The total advance payments made by Nolan for the payroll period amount to $120. The total income tax withheld for the payroll period is $110. The total FICA taxes for employees and employer are $128.

Nolan is considered to have made a deposit of $120 from the advance EIC payments on the day the wages are paid. The $120 is treated as if the company has paid the total $110 in income tax withholding and $10 of the employee FICA taxes to the IRS. The company must deposit only $118 of the remaining FICA taxes.

Employer's Returns and Records

The employer takes into account the amount of the advance EIC payments when completing Form 941. The amount of the advance EIC payments is subtracted from the total amount of income taxes and FICA taxes in order to determine the net taxes due for the quarter. All records of advance EIC payments should be retained four years and be available for review by the IRS. These records include:

1. Copies of employees' Forms W-5.
2. Amounts and dates of all wage payments and advance EIC payments.
3. Dates of each employee's employment.
4. Dates and amounts of tax deposits made.
5. Copies of returns filed.

SELF-STUDY QUIZ 4–6.

1. During one week, Georgia Brewer earned $175. She and her spouse have both filed Form W-5. Using the information presented in Figure 4–9, compute the amount of advance EIC payment Brewer is entitled to receive.

   $_____

2. On a certain payday, the Gregory Company made advance EIC payments to its employees that amounted to more than the federal income taxes withheld. Does the company have to make a tax deposit for this payday? Explain.

TAX-DEFERRED RETIREMENT ACCOUNTS

As covered in Chapter 1, these types of accounts allow employees to contribute amounts from their wages into retirement accounts. These contributions reduce the amount of the employees' wages that are subject to federal income tax. These tax-deferred plans set limits on the amounts that employees can contribute tax free and also provide for additional contributions to be made into the accounts by the employers. The following information applies to 2003:

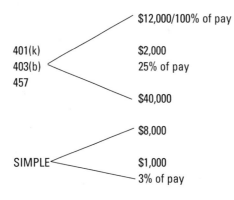

	$12,000/100% of pay	lesser is maximum employee deferred contribution
401(k) 403(b) 457	$2,000	extra deferred if age 50 or over maximum
	25% of pay	contribution of employer
	$40,000	maximum total combined contribution
	$8,000	maximum employee deferred contribution
SIMPLE	$1,000	extra deferred if age 50 or over
	3% of pay	employer must match employee's contribution up to this maximum

Individual Retirement Accounts

Beyond the various payroll-related tax deferred accounts, individuals can set up their own retirement accounts. Under certain conditions, an employee may put aside each year the lesser of $3,000 or 100% of their compensation without paying federal income taxes on their contributions. Eligible employees may make an additional $3,000 contribution on behalf of a nonworking or low-earning spouse provided the combined compensation is at least equal to the total combined IRA contribution. For individuals age 50 or older, the limit is increased by $500 in 2002. To be eligible for such deductible (tax-free) contributions, either of the following two conditions must be met:

1. The individual does not belong to a company-funded retirement plan.
2. The individual has adjusted gross income less than $40,000. (In the case of a married employee, the combined adjusted gross income must be less than $60,000.)

If the employee belongs to another qualified plan, partial tax-free deductions are allowed if:

1. The employee is single or head of household and has adjusted gross income less than $44,000.
2. The employee is married, filing a joint return, and has adjusted gross income less than $64,000.
3. The employee is married, filing separately, and has adjusted gross income less than $10,000.

If an employee's spouse belongs to a company-funded retirement plan, the employee is not considered an active participant in the plan. However, the non-active spouse's tax-free IRA deduction ($3,000) will begin to phase out between $150,000 to $160,000 of their total adjusted gross income.

Roth IRA

Another type of IRA allows taxpayers and their spouses to make annual *nondeductible* contributions of up to $3,000. The amount that may be contributed is reduced by the amount contributed into other IRAs. Allowable contributions are phased out for those with adjusted gross income of between $95,000 to $110,000 for single taxpayers and $150,000 to $160,000 for joint taxpayers.

The advantage of this type of IRA is that distributions made out of the fund at retirement are tax-free.

WAGE AND TAX STATEMENTS

Employers must furnish *wage and tax statements* to employees informing them of the wages paid during the calendar year and the amount of taxes withheld from those wages. The employer sends copies of these statements to the federal government and, in many cases, to state, city, and local governments.

8 LEARNING OBJECTIVE

Form W-2

Form W-2, Wage and Tax Statement, shown in Figure 4–10, is prepared if any of the following items apply to an employee during the calendar year:

1. Income tax or social security taxes were withheld.
2. Income tax would have been withheld if the employee had not claimed more than one withholding allowance or had not claimed exemption from withholding on Form W-4.

on the

JOB

On Form W-2, enter name exactly as shown on employee's social security card. Do not include titles (Mr., Mrs., Dr., etc.), suffixes (RN, MD, CPA, etc.), or Jr. or Sr.

FIGURE 4-10

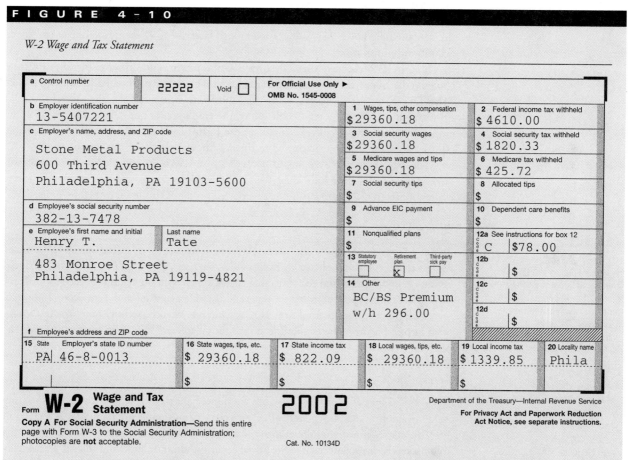

W-2 Wage and Tax Statement

Do Not Cut, Fold, or Staple Forms on This Page — Do Not Cut, Fold, or Staple Forms on This Page

3. Any amount was paid for services, if the employer is in a trade or business. The cash value of any noncash payments made should be included.
4. Any advance EIC payments were made.

on the
Net

For access to all federal tax forms, see the **IRS Digital Daily** forms download page:

http://www.irs.ustreas.gov/prod/forms_pubs/forms.html

IRS CONNECTION

Time extensions for filing W-2s can be requested by sending Form 8809 (Request for Extension of Time to File Information Returns) to the IRS by February 28. An additional 30-day extension can be requested by submitting another Form 8809 before the end of the initial extension period.

Figure 4–11 summarizes the instructions for completing each of the boxes on Form W-2. If an entry does not apply to the firm or employee, leave the box blank. Employers must give employees Form W-2 on or before January 31 following the close of the calendar year. When employees leave the service of the employer, you may give them Form W-2 any time after employment ends. If employees ask for Form W-2, the employer should give it to them within 30 days of their request or the final wage payment, whichever is later. In instances where terminated workers may be rehired at some time before the year ends, the employer may delay furnishing the form until January 31 following the close of the calendar year. Employers distribute Form W-2 copies as follows:

Copy A—To the Social Security Administration *by the end of February* following the year for which Form W-2 is applicable.
Copy 1—To the state, city, or local tax department.
Copy B—To employees for filing with their federal income tax return.
Copy C—To employees for their personal records.
Copy 2— To employees for filing with their state, city, or local income tax returns.
Copy D—Retained by the employer.

If 250 or more Forms W-2 are being filed, reporting must be done on magnetic media in lieu of the W-3. These forms can also be filed electronically with the IRS with an extended deadline of March 31.

Employers that are going out of business must send W-2 forms to the employees by the date the final Form 941 is due. One month later, the W-2 forms are due at the Social Security Administration.

If Form W-2 has been lost or destroyed, employers are authorized to furnish substitute copies to the employee. The substitute form should be clearly marked **REISSUED STATEMENT**. Do not send Copy A of the substitute statement to the Social Security Administration. If, after a reasonable effort, the employer cannot deliver a Form W-2, the employer retains the employee's copies of the form for a four-year period. A "reasonable effort" means the forms were mailed to the last known address of the employee.

The IRS allows employers to put W-2s on a secure Web site and provide employees with passwords to access their individual W-2s. The employees must agree to receive the information in electronic form, and it must be posted on the Web site on or before January 31.

Form W-2c

To correct errors in previously filed Forms W-2, employers file *Form W-2c, Statement of Corrected Income and Tax Amounts,* shown in Figure 4–12 (see page 4-27). File Copy A with the Social Security Administration and the remaining copies as noted on the bottom of each form. Form W-3c should accompany all corrected wage and tax statements unless the correction is for only one employee or to correct employees' names, addresses, or social security numbers. In the case of an incorrect address, the employer can mail the "incorrect" W-2 in an envelope bearing the corrected address.

on the
J O B

The Social Security Administration reports that 10 percent of all W-2s received have an incorrect name/social security number combination.

Form W-3

Form W-3, Transmittal of Wage and Tax Statements, must be filed with the Social Security Administration by employers and other payers as a transmittal for Forms W-2. On Form W-3, the employer indicates the number of documents being transmitted. Form W-3 and the accompanying documents enable the Social Security Administration and the IRS to compare the totals to the amounts for the income tax withholdings, social security wages, social security tips, Medicare wages and tips, and the advanced earned income credits, as reported on the employer's 941s for the year. The IRS will require explanations of any differences and corrections to any errors. Figure 4–13 (see page 4-28) shows a completed Form W-3. The employer

FIGURE 4-11

How to Complete Form W-2

Box A—Control number: For the employer to identify the individual Forms W-2. Up to 7 digits may be used to assign the number, which the employer uses when writing the Social Security Administration about the form. The employer does not have to use this box.

Void: Put an X in this box when an error has been made. Amounts shown on void forms should not be included in your subtotal Form W-2.

Box B—Employer's identification number (EIN): Enter the number assigned to you by the IRS. Do not use a prior owner's EIN. If you do not have an EIN when filing Forms W-2, enter "Applied For." You can get an EIN by filing Form SS-4.

Box C—Employer's name, address, and ZIP code: This entry should be the same as shown on your Form 941 or 943.

Box D—Employee's social security number: An employee who does not have an SSN should apply for one by completing Form SS-5.

Box E—Employee's name: The name should be entered exactly as shown on the employee's social security card.

Box F— Employee's address and ZIP code: This box is combined with Box E on all copies except Copy A, to allow you to mail employee's copies in a window envelope or as a self-mailer.

Box 1—Wages, tips, other compensation: Record, before any payroll deductions, the total of (1) wages, prizes, and awards paid; (2) noncash payments (including certain fringe benefits); (3) tips reported by employee to employer (not allocated tips); (4) certain employee business expense reimbursements; (5) cost of accident and health insurance premiums paid on behalf of 2% or more shareholder employees by an S corporation; (6) taxable benefits made from a Section 125 (cafeteria plan); and (7) all other compensation including certain scholarships and fellowship grants and payments for moving expenses. Other compensation is an amount you pay your employee from which federal income tax is not withheld. You may show other compensation on a separate Form W-2.

Box 2—Federal income tax withheld: Record the amount of federal income tax withheld from the employee's wages for the year.

Box 3—Social security wages: Enter the total wages paid (before payroll deductions) subject to employee social security (OASDI) tax. Do not include social security tips and allocated tips. Generally, noncash payments are considered wages. Include employee business expenses reported in Box 1. Include employer contributions to qualified cash or deferred compensation plans and to retirement arrangements described in Box 12 (Codes D, E, F, and G), even though the deferrals are not includible in Box 1 as wages, tips, and other compensation. Include any employee OASDI and HI taxes and employee state unemployment compensation taxes you paid for your employee rather than deducting it from wages. Report in this box the cost of group-term life insurance coverage over $50,000 that is taxable to former employees. Report the cost of accident and health insurance premiums paid on behalf of 2% or more shareholder-employees by an S corporation only if the exclusion under Section 312(a)(2)(B) is not satisfied. Do not enter more than the maximum OASDI taxable wage base for the year.

Box 4—Social security tax withheld: Record the total social security (OASDI) tax (not your share) withheld or paid by you for the employee. Include only taxes withheld for the year's wages.

Box 5—Medicare wages and tips: Enter the Medicare (HI) wages and tips. Be sure to enter tips the employee reported even if you did not have enough employee funds to collect the HI tax for those tips. Report in this box the cost of group-term life insurance coverage over $50,000 that is taxable to former employees.

Box 6—Medicare tax withheld: Enter the total employee Medicare (HI) tax (not your share) withheld or paid by you for your employee. Include only taxes withheld for the year's wages.

Box 7—Social security tips: Record the amount the employee reported even if you did not have enough employee funds to collect the social security (OASDI) tax for the tips. The total of Boxes 3 and 7 should not be more than the maximum OASDI wage base for the year. But report all tips in Box 1 along with wages and other compensation.

Box 8—Allocated tips: If you are a large food or beverage establishment, record the amount of tips allocated to the employee. Do not include this amount in Boxes 1, 3, 5, or 7.

Box 9—Advance EIC payment: Record the total amount paid to the employee as advance earned income credit payments.

Box 10—Dependent care benefits: Record the total amount of dependent care benefits paid or incurred by you for your employee. This total should include any amount in excess of the exclusion ($5,000).

Box 11—Nonqualified plans: Enter the amount from a Nonqualified deferred compensation plan or Section 457 plan that was distributed or became taxable because the substantial risk of forfeiture lapsed. Include this amount in Box 11 only if it is also includible in Boxes 1, 3, and 5. Report distributions to beneficiaries of deceased employees on Form 1099-R.

FIGURE 4-11

Concluded

Box 12—Complete and code this box for all applicable items listed below in the Reference Guide. Additional information about any coded item may be found in the IRS's Instructions for Form W-2. Do not enter more than four codes in this box. If you are reporting more than four items, use a separate Form W-2 or a substitute Form W-2 to report the additional items.

Use a capital letter when entering each code and enter the dollar amount on the same line. Use decimal points.

Box 13: Mark the boxes that apply.

Statutory employee: Mark this box for statutory employees whose earnings are subject to social security (OASDI) and Medicare (HI) taxes but not subject to federal income tax withholding.

Retirement plan: Mark this box if the employee was an active participant (for any part of the year) in a retirement plan such as 401(k) and SEP.

Third-party sick plan: Mark this box only if you are a third-party, sick-pay payer filing a Form W-2 for an insured's employee.

Box 14—Other: Use this box for any other information you want to give your employee. Label each item. Examples are union dues, health insurance premiums deducted, moving expenses paid, nontaxable income, or educational assistance payments.

Boxes 15 through 20—State or local income tax information: You do not have to complete these boxes, but you may want to if you use copies of this form for your state and local returns. The ID number is assigned by each individual state. The state and local information boxes can be used to report wages and taxes on two states and two localities. Keep each state's and locality's information separated by the dotted line.

Reference Guide for Box 12 Codes

A—Uncollected social security (OASDI) tax on tips
B—Uncollected Medicare (HI) tax on tips
C—Group-term life insurance over $50,000
D—Elective deferrals to a Section 401(k) cash or deferred arrangement
E—Elective deferrals to a Section 403(b) salary reduction agreement
F—Elective deferrals to a Section 408(k)(6) salary reduction SEP
G—Elective and nonelective deferrals to a Section 457(b) deferred compensation plan (state and local government and tax-exempt employers)
H—Elective deferrals to a Section 501(c)(18)(D) tax-exempt organization plan
J—Nontaxable sick pay
K—20% excise tax on excess golden parachute payments
L—Substantiated employee business expense (federal rate)
M—Uncollected social security (OASDI) tax on group-term life insurance coverage
N—Uncollected Medicare (HI) tax on group-term life insurance coverage
P—Excludable reimbursed moving expenses
Q—Military employee basic housing, subsistence and combat zone pay
R—Employer contributions to medical savings account
S—Employee salary reduction contributions to a 408(p) SIMPLE retirement plan
T—Employer-provided qualified adoption benefits
V—Exercise of nonstatutory stock options

files all Forms W-3 with one W-3. Forms W-3 and the related documents are filed with the Social Security Administration by the end of February each year. Form W-3 is mailed to employers during the fourth quarter.

The information shown on Form W-3 is matched against the employer's Forms 941 for the year. If the totals do not match, the IRS notifies the employer of the discrepancy, and the employer is required to provide additional information.

Penalties

The following penalties are imposed for late or incorrect filing of W-2s:

1. If filed correctly within 30 days after the due date, $15 per return ($75,000 maximum penalty/$25,000 for small businesses).

FIGURE 4-12

Form W-2c, Statement of Corrected Income and Tax Amounts

a Tax year/Form corrected 2002 / W-2	44444	Void ☐	For Official Use Only ▶ OMB No. 1545-0008	

b Employee's name, address, and ZIP code Henry T. Tate 483 Monroe Street Philadelphia, PA 19119-4821	☐ Corrected name (if checked, also complete box h)	c Employer's name, address, and ZIP code Stone Metal Products 600 Third Avenue Bensalem, PA 19040-5001

d Employee's correct SSN 382-13-7478	Complete boxes g and/or h (below) only if incorrect on last form filed.	e Employer's Federal EIN 13-5407221	f Employer's state ID number 46-8-0013
g Employee's **incorrect** SSN	h Employee's name (as **incorrectly** shown on previous form)		Note: Only complete money fields that are being corrected (except MQGE).

Previously reported	**Correct information**	**Previously reported**	**Correct information**
1 Wages, tips, other compensation	1 Wages, tips, other compensation	2 Federal income tax withheld 4610.00	2 Federal income tax withheld 4160.00
3 Social security wages	3 Social security wages	4 Social security tax withheld	4 Social security tax withheld
5 Medicare wages and tips	5 Medicare wages and tips	6 Medicare tax withheld	6 Medicare tax withheld
7 Social security tips	7 Social security tips	8 Allocated tips	8 Allocated tips
		13 Statutory employee ☐ Retirement plan ☐ Third-party sick pay ☐	13 Statutory employee ☐ Retirement plan ☐ Third-party sick pay ☐

For Privacy Act and Paperwork Reduction Act Notice, see separate instructions.

Form **W-2c** (Rev. 12-2001)   **Corrected Wage and Tax Statement**   Cat. No. 61437D

Copy A For Social Security Administration

Department of the Treasury Internal Revenue Service

Do Not Cut, Fold, or Staple Forms on This Page   Do Not Cut, Fold, or Staple Forms on This Page

---

2. If filed between 30 days after the due date and August 1, $30 per return ($150,000 maximum penalty/$50,000 for small businesses).

3. After August 1, $50 per return ($250,000 maximum penalty/$100,000 for small businesses).

4. Penalties of $100 per return for intentional disregard of the requirements for filing, providing payee statements, and reporting incorrect information (no maximum penalty).

5. Filing W-2s with mismatched names and social security numbers, $50 per form.

Form W-3c

The *Transmittal of Corrected Income and Tax Statements, Form W-3c,* is used to accompany copies of Form W-2c, sent to the Social Security Administration. This form can also be used to correct a previously filed Form W-3.

Privately Printed Forms

Employers may use their own forms by obtaining specifications for the private printing of Forms W-2 from any IRS center or district office. To the extent that the privately printed forms meet the specifications, the employer may use them without prior approval of the IRS.

FIGURE 4-13

Form W-3, Transmittal of Wage and Tax Statements

DO NOT STAPLE OR FOLD

a Control number	33333 — For Official Use Only ▶ OMB No. 1545-0008

b Kind of Payer: 941 [X], Military [ ], 943 [ ], CT-1 [ ], Hshld. emp. [ ], Medicare govt. emp. [ ], Third-party sick pay [ ]

1 Wages, tips, other compensation $ 2620736.40
2 Federal income tax withheld $ 330317.19
3 Social security wages $ 2066400.00
4 Social security tax withheld $ 128116.80

c Total number of Forms W-2: 132　**d** Establishment number

5 Medicare wages and tips $ 2620736.40
6 Medicare tax withheld $ 38000.68

e Employer identification number: 88-1936281

7 Social security tips $
8 Allocated tips $

f Employer's name
Grove Electronics
33 Vista Road
Vallejo, CA 94590-0033

9 Advance EIC payments $ 778.00
10 Dependent care benefits $
11 Nonqualified plans $
12 Deferred compensation $ 319530.00
13 For third-party sick pay use only
14 Income tax withheld by payer of third-party sick pay $

g Employer's address and ZIP code
h Other EIN used this year

15 State / Employer's state ID number
16 State wages, tips, etc. $
17 State income tax $
18 Local wages, tips, etc. $
19 Local income tax $

Contact person
Telephone number (415) 555-3200
For Official Use Only

E-mail address
Fax number ( )

Under penalties of perjury, I declare that I have examined this return and accompanying documents, and, to the best of my knowledge and belief, they are true, correct, and complete.

Signature ▶ *Carl W. Tolan*　Title ▶ President　Date 2/28/03

Form **W-3** Transmittal of Wage and Tax Statements　**2002**　Department of the Treasury Internal Revenue Service

SELF-STUDY QUIZ 4–7.

1. The Marquat Company deducts union dues from its employees' paychecks each month during the year and sends them to the local union office. How should the company report this deduction on the employees' Forms W-2?

2. Gringle's terminated 10 of its employees on July 15. The company informed each employee that it may rehire them again during its peak season in September. When should the company furnish each employee with a W-2 statement?

3. While preparing her 2003 personal income tax return, Connie Becker, an employee of Trident Mills, discovered that she had lost her Form W-2. What procedures should the company follow to prepare a new Form W-2 for Becker?

RETURNS EMPLOYERS MUST COMPLETE

LEARNING OBJECTIVE 9

Employers must file returns reporting the amount of wages paid and the amount of taxes withheld at designated times, beginning with the first quarter in which taxable wages are paid. Rules that require different returns for different types of employees further complicate the accounting tasks and payroll procedures. Figure 4–14 briefly summarizes the major returns completed by employers.

The most recent information with regard to withholding, deposit, and payment and reporting of federal income taxes, FICA taxes, and FUTA taxes is available in *Circular E, Employer's Tax Guide.* This circular is sent to employers prior to the start of the new year and is also available at district offices of the IRS.

FIGURE 4-14

Major Returns Filed by Employers

Form 941, Employer's Quarterly Federal Tax Return	For reporting federal income taxes withheld during the calendar quarter and the employer and employee portions of the FICA taxes. Form 941 is illustrated in Chapter 3.
Form 941-M, Employer's Monthly Federal Tax Return	For reporting federal income taxes withheld and FICA taxes on a monthly basis. The IRS may require monthly returns and payments of taxes from employers who have not complied with the requirements for filing returns or the paying or depositing of taxes reported on quarterly returns. You are not required to file this return unless notified by the IRS.
Form 942, Employer's Quarterly Tax Return for Household Employees	For reporting federal income taxes withheld as a result of voluntary withholding agreements between employers and their domestic employees. Form 942 is also completed by employers who are liable for FICA taxes on wages paid to domestic workers.
Form 943, Employer's Annual Tax Return for Agricultural Employees	For reporting the withholding of federal income taxes and FICA taxes on wages paid to agricultural workers. Form 943 is used for agricultural employees even though the employer may employ nonagricultural workers.
Form 945, Annual Return of Withheld Federal Income Tax	Used to report tax liability for nonpayroll items such as backup withholding and withholding on gambling winnings, pensions, and annuities, and deposits made for the year. ***Backup withholding*** occurs when an individual receives taxable interest, dividends, and certain other payments and fails to furnish the payer with the correct taxpayer identification numbers. Payers are then required to withhold 30 percent of those payments. Backup withholding does not apply to wages, pensions, annuities, or IRAs.

INFORMATION RETURNS

The IRS requires employers to file *information returns* to report compensation paid to certain individuals who are not employees. These returns allow the IRS to determine if taxpayers are reporting their true income. Figure 4–15 briefly summarizes the major information returns required by the IRS. The employer sends copies of the returns to the payee by the end of January. These forms can be sent to the contractors electronically as long as they agree in advance to this method of delivery.

To transmit each type of Form 1099 to the IRS, the employer uses *Form 1096, Annual Summary and Transmittal of U.S. Information Returns.* Employers use a separate Form 1096 to transmit each type of information return. For example, one Form 1096 is used to transmit all Forms 1099-MISC (see Figure 4–16 on page 4-31), and another Form 1096 is used to transmit all Forms 1099-INT. The employer files Form 1096 and all accompanying forms to the IRS on or before the last day of February of the year following the payment. For returns filed electronically, the due date is March 31. Penalties previously listed for late submission of Forms W-2 also apply to the Form 1099 series (see page 4-30).

INDEPENDENT CONTRACTOR PAYMENTS

Payments made to independent contractors (individuals or partnerships) of at least $600 must be reported on Form 1099-Miscellaneous Income. This does not apply to contractors who are incorporated unless the payments are medical or health-care related. Since payments to these independent contractors are not generated by payroll departments, the accounts payable departments usually complete the appropriate 1099 Forms.

10 LEARNING OBJECTIVE

IRS CONNECTION

The federal government estimates a $20 billion shortfall each year because they cannot match unfiled 1099s to personal income tax returns.

Verification of taxpayers' identification numbers via the Internet can be done through access to the Internal Revenue Service.

FIGURE   4 - 1 5

Major Information Returns

Form 1099-DIV, Dividends and Distributions	For reporting dividends totaling $10 or more to any person; foreign tax withheld and paid on dividends and other distributions on stock for a person; distributions made by corporations and regulated investment companies (including money market funds) as part of liquidation.
Form 1099-G, Certain Government Payments	For reporting unemployment compensation payments, state and local income tax refunds of $10 or more, taxable grants, income tax refunds, and agricultural subsidy payments.
Form 1099-INT, Interest Income	For reporting payments of (a) interest of $10 or more paid or credited on earnings from savings and loans, credit unions, bank deposits, corporate bonds, etc.; (b) interest of $600 or more from other sources; (c) forfeited interest due on premature withdrawals of time deposits; (d) foreign tax eligible for the recipient's foreign tax credit withheld and paid on interest; (e) payments of any interest on bearer certificates of deposit.
Form 1099-MISC, Miscellaneous Income (See Figure 4–16)	For reporting miscellaneous income, such as rents, royalties, commissions, fees, prizes, and awards of at least $600 paid to nonemployees, and any backup withholding. Gross royalty payments of $10 or more must also be reported on this form. Life insurance companies may use either 1099-MISC or Form W-2 to report payments to full-time life insurance sales agents.
Form 1099-PATR, Taxable Distributions Received From Cooperatives	For cooperatives to report patronage dividends paid and other distributions made that total $10 or more during the year.
Form 1099-R, Distributions From Pensions, Annuities, Retirement or Profit-Sharing Plans, IRAs, Insurance Contracts, etc.	For reporting all distributions from pensions, annuities, profit-sharing and retirement plans, and individual retirement arrangements made by employees' trusts or funds; federal, state or local government retirement system; life insurance companies.
Form 5498, Individual Retirement Arrangement Information Form 8027, Employer's Annual Information Return of Tip Income and Allocated Tips	For reporting contributions received from each person to an IRA or simplified employee pension plan (SEP) and qualified deductible voluntary employee contributions to a plan maintained by the employer.

BACKUP WITHHOLDING

Independent contractors must provide taxpayer identification numbers to their employers (orally, in writing, or on Form W-9). If this is not done and the company anticipates paying the contractor $600 or more, the company must withhold federal income taxes of 30 percent of the payments made. This withholding must continue until the number is reported. Failure to withhold will result in the payer being held liable by the IRS for the 30 percent withholding.

on the

Net

For electronic filing of tax return and payment options, go to:
Electronic Filing for Businesses:
http://www.irs.ustreas.gov/
prod/elec_svs/eftps.html

MAGNETIC FILING FORM W-2 AND INFORMATION RETURNS

If employers file 250 or more Forms W-2 or other information returns (for each type of information return), they must use magnetic media or electronic filing instead of paper forms. Filing Forms W-2 does not require approval of the medium by the Social Security Administration. However, the employers must use *Form 6559, Transmitter Report and Summary of Magnetic Media,* to identify themselves when submitting magnetic media files.

FIGURE 4-16

Form 1099-MISC, Miscellaneous Income

9595	☐ VOID	☐ CORRECTED		

PAYER'S name, street address, city, state, ZIP code, and telephone no.	**1** Rents $	OMB No. 1545-0115	**Miscellaneous Income**
Worldwide Publishing Co. 40 Fifth Avenue New York, NY 10011-4000 (212) 555-2000	**2** Royalties $ 34,970.65	2002 Form **1099-MISC**	

PAYER'S Federal identification number 75-4013736	RECIPIENT'S identification number 461-91-4821	**3** Other income $	**4** Federal income tax withheld $	**Copy A**
		5 Fishing boat proceeds	**6** Medical and health care payments $	**For Internal Revenue Service Center** File with Form 1096.

RECIPIENT'S name Laurie T. Musberger	**7** Nonemployee compensation $	**8** Substitute payments in lieu of dividends or interest $	**For Privacy Act and Paperwork Reduction Act Notice, see the 2001 General Instructions for Forms 1099, 1098, 5498, and W-2G.**
Street address (including apt. no.) 1043 Maple Drive	**9** Payer made direct sales of $5,000 or more of consumer products to a buyer (recipient) for resale ► ☐	**10** Crop insurance proceeds $	
City, state, and ZIP code Chicago, IL 60615-3443	**11**	**12**	
Account number (optional)	2nd TIN not. ☐	**13** Excess golden parachute payments $	**14** Gross proceeds paid to an attorney $	

15	**16** State tax withheld $ $	**17** State/Payer's state no. 85-33378	**18** State income $ $

Form **1099-MISC**   Cat. No. 14425J   Department of the Treasury - Internal Revenue Service

---

For other information returns, the employer obtains prior approval of the medium. The employer must complete *Form 4419, Application for Filing Information Returns Magnetically/Electronically,* and file it with the IRS. If employers can prove that filing Forms W-2 or other information returns magnetically would be an undue hardship, they may request a waiver by submitting *Form 8508, Request for Waiver From Filing Information Returns on Magnetic Media,* to the IRS 45 days prior to the due date of the return.

WITHHOLDING STATE INCOME TAX

In addition to federal income taxes, many states also have income tax withholding requirements. The situation is further complicated if an employer has employees in several states. This requires employers to know how much tax to withhold, what types of employees and payments are exempt, and how to pay the tax. Employers must also be informed about each state's regulations regarding:

1. The required frequency of making wage payments.
2. The acceptable media of payment.
3. The maximum interval between the end of a pay period and the payday for that period.
4. The time limits for making final wage payments to employees who are discharged, laid off, quit, or go on strike.

11 LEARNING OBJECTIVE

on the

JOB

Only nine states do not have a state income tax—Alaska, Florida, Nevada, New Hampshire, South Dakota, Tennessee, Texas, Washington, and Wyoming.

5. How often to inform employees of the deductions made from their wages.
6. The maximum amount of unpaid wages to pay the surviving spouse or family of a deceased worker.

Wage-bracket tables and percentage method formulas are used in many states to determine the amount of state income taxes to withhold from their employees' wages. Each state also determines for state income tax purposes the taxability status of the various fringe benefits discussed in this chapter. Even though most states do not tax deductons made for cafeteria plans and 401(k) accounts, some states do not allow for the tax sheltering of these deductions from employees' wages. Once again, it is the employer's responsibility to know the laws of the states in which they conduct business.

Most states having income tax laws require employers to withhold tax from both nonresidents and residents, unless a *reciprocal agreement* exists with one or more states to the contrary. For example, a reciprocal agreement may exist between two states where both states grant an exemption to nonresidents who work in each of those states.

State Income Tax Returns and Reports

Payroll managers should be familiar with four main types of state income tax returns or reports:

1. **Periodic withholding returns** on which you report the wages paid and the state tax withheld during the reporting period. Figure 4–17 shows the *Employer Deposit Statement of Income Tax Withheld* used by employers in Pennsylvania. Depending on the amount of state income taxes withheld for each quarterly period, employers may be required to pay the taxes semimonthly, monthly, or quarterly. Some states require employers to deposit their withheld income taxes through electronic funds transfer (EFT).

2. **Reconciliation returns** that compare the total amount of state tax paid as shown on the periodic returns with the amounts of state tax declared to have been withheld from employees' wages. Figure 4–18 shows *The Employer Quarterly Reconciliation Return of Income Tax Withheld* for use by employers in Pennsylvania. Employers who have computer systems may submit their information on magnetic media.

FIGURE 4-17

Form PA-501R, Pennsylvania Employer Deposit Statement of Income Tax Withheld

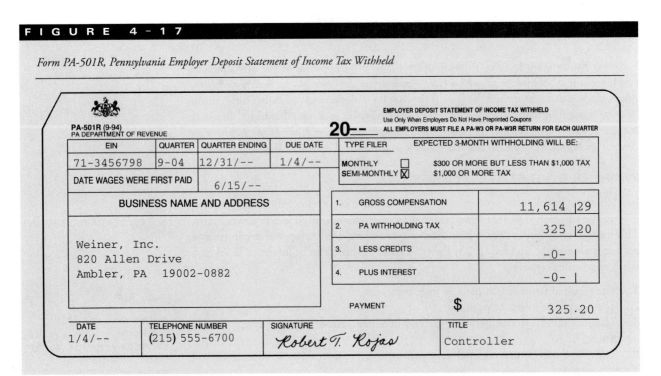

FIGURE 4-18

Form PA-W3R, Pennsylvania Employer Quarterly Reconciliation Return of Income Tax Withheld

PA-W3R PA DEPARTMENT OF REVENUE		**20--**		**EMPLOYER QUARTERLY RECONCILIATION RETURN OF INCOME TAX WITHHELD** For Use ONLY When Employers Do Not Have Preprinted Coupons

EIN	QUARTER	QUARTER ENDING	DUE DATE	BUSINESS NAME AND ADDRESS
71-3456798	9-04	12/31/--	1/31/--	Weiner, Inc. 820 Allen Drive Ambler, PA 19002-0882

RECORD OF PA WITHHOLDING TAX BY PERIOD

PERIOD	SEMI-MONTHLY AMOUNTS WITHHELD	PERIOD	MONTHLY AMOUNTS WITHHELD
1ST HALF OF MONTH ►	331.34	1ST MONTH ►	
2ND HALF OF MONTH ►	310.17	2ND MONTH ►	
1ST HALF OF MONTH ►	325.39	3RD MONTH ►	
2ND HALF OF MONTH ►	365.74		
1ST HALF OF MONTH ►	304.51		
2ND HALF OF MONTH ►	325.20		
TOTAL (ENTER TOTAL ON LINE 2)	1,962.35	TOTAL (ENTER TOTAL ON LINE 2)	

QUARTERLY FILERS COMPLETE LINES 1-5 ONLY.

1. TOTAL COMPENSATION SUBJECT TO PA TAX		70,083.81
2. TOTAL PA WITHHOLDING TAX (FROM LEFT) ►		1,962.35
3. TOTAL DEPOSITS FOR QUARTER (INCLUDING VERIFIED OVERPAYMENTS)		1,962.35
4. OVERPAYMENT (IF LINE 3 IS GREATER THAN LINE 2)		-0-
5. TAX DUE/PAYMENT (IF LINE 2 IS GREATER THAN LINE 3) ►		-0-

Under penalties of perjury, I declare that I have examined this return and to the best of my knowledge and belief, it is true, correct and complete.

Date	Telephone Number	Signature	Title
1/31/--	(215) 555-6700	*Robert T. Rojas*	Controller

3. **Annual statements** to employees showing the amount of wages paid during the year and the state tax withheld from those wages.

4. **Information returns** used to report payments to individuals that are not subject to withholding and/or are not reported on the annual employee wage and tax statements. See Figure 4–15 for a listing of the major information returns.

Since the requirements for transmitting returns and reports vary from state to state, employers should become familiar with the tax regulations of the state in which their business is located and of the state or states in which their employees reside. Because federal regulations require filing of information returns on magnetic media, many states permit employers to submit wage information on magnetic disk or tape. Also, many states take part in the Combined Federal/State Filing Program, which enables employers to file information returns with the federal government and authorize release of the information to the applicable state. To participate in this program, employers must first obtain permission from the IRS.

Withholding Local Income Taxes

In addition to state income tax laws, many cities and counties have passed local income tax legislation requiring employers to deduct and withhold income taxes or license fees on salaries or wages paid. In Alabama, several cities have license fee ordinances that require the withholding of the fees from employees' wages. Certain employees in Denver, Colorado, are subject to the withholding of the Denver Occupational Privilege Tax from their compensation. In Kentucky, a number of cities and counties impose a license fee (payroll tax).

Figure 4–19 shows the coupon that must be completed by employers in Philadelphia. All must withhold the city income tax from compensation paid their employees. Depending upon the amount of taxes withheld, employers may be required to make deposits weekly, monthly, or quarterly. For any late payments of the tax, the city imposes a penalty on the underpayment. Employers must file annual reconciliation returns by the end of February, reporting the amount of taxes deducted during the preceding calendar year.

F I G U R E   4 - 1 9

Philadelphia Wage Tax Coupon

Monthly Wage Tax

1. TAX DUE PER WORKSHEET, *Line 8*	
1,088	50

WEINER, INC.
820 ALLEN DRIVE
AMBLER, PA 19002-0882

Account #: 3256301   From: 12/1

Tax Type: 01   To: 12/31

Period/Yr: 4/02   Due Date: 1/15

2. INTEREST AND PENALTY	
-0-	

Signature: *Robert T. Rojas*
I hereby certify that I have examined this return
and that it is correct to the best of my knowledge.

Phone #: (215) 555-6700

Philadelphia Revenue Department
P.O. Box 8040
Philadelphia, PA 19101-8040

3. TOTAL DUE (LINE 1 & 2)	
1,088	50

Make checks payable to:
CITY OF PHILADELPHIA

33301043097000000006100044000000000000000000000000009297801000000000002

KEY TERMS

Annualizing wages *(p. 4-16)*

Backup withholding *(p. 4-29)*

Defined contribution plan *(p. 4-7)*

Earned income credit (EIC) *(p. 4-19)*

Gross-up supplementals *(p. 4-18)*

Information returns *(p. 4-29)*

Percentage method *(p. 4-13)*

Personal allowance *(p. 4-9)*

Quarterly averaging *(p. 4-16)*

Reciprocal agreement *(p. 4-32)*

Special withholding allowance *(p. 4-9)*

Standard deduction *(p. 4-13)*

Supplemental wage payments *(p. 4-16)*

Wage and tax statements *(p. 4-23)*

Wage-bracket method *(p. 4-13)*

Wages *(p. 4-4)*

MATCHING QUIZ

_____ 1. Personal allowance

_____ 2. Taxable tips

_____ 3. Backup withholding

_____ 4. Form W-5

_____ 5. Roth IRA

_____ 6. Standard deduction

_____ 7. Pretax salary reductions

_____ 8. Form 1096

_____ 9. Nontaxable fringe benefits

_____ 10. Flexible reporting

A.   Earned income credit advance payment certificate

B.   Annual nondeductible contributions of up to $3,000

C.   Annual summary and transmittal of U.S. information returns

D.   Allows employers to use any basis as the time period for payment of noncash fringe benefits

E. $3,000 deduction in computing taxable income

F.   Withholdings from gross pay that reduce the amount of pay subject to federal income tax

G.   Qualified employee discounts

H.   Amount of money used to reduce an individual's adjusted gross income to taxable income

I.   Withhold federal income taxes of 30 percent of payments made

J. $20 or more in a month

QUESTIONS FOR REVIEW

NOTE: Use Tax Tables A and B at the back of this textbook and the tax regulations presented in this chapter to answer all questions and solve all problems.

1. How is the amount of a fringe benefit that is taxable to an employee determined?
2. To what extent are cash tips treated as remuneration subject to federal income tax withholding?
3. For each of the following kinds of wage payments, indicate whether or not the wages are exempt from the withholding of federal income taxes:
   a. Three weeks' vacation pay.
   b. Weekly advance to a sales representative for traveling expenses to be incurred.
   c. Weekly wages paid the housekeeper in a college fraternity.
   d. Monthly salary received by Rev. Cole Carpenter.
   e. Payments under a worker's compensation law for sickness or injury.
4. What is a personal allowance? What was the amount of a personal allowance for 2002?
5. On July 15, William Mitchell amended his Form W-4 to increase the number of withholding allowances from four to seven. Mitchell asked for a refund of the amount of overwithheld income taxes from January 1 to July 15 when the number of allowances was only four. Should Mitchell be reimbursed for the income taxes overwithheld before the effective date of the amended Form W-4?
6. Under what conditions may employees be exempt from the withholding of federal income taxes during 2003? How do such employees indicate their no-tax-liability status?
7. Under what conditions must employers submit copies of Form W-4 to the IRS?
8. Commencing in June, Slade Exon is eligible to receive monthly payments from a pension fund. What procedure should Exon follow if he does not wish to have federal income taxes withheld from his periodic pension payments?

9. Rhonda Gramm is single, and her wages are paid weekly. Under the percentage method, what is the amount of Gramm's one weekly withholding allowance? Howard Heinz, married, claims two withholding allowances, and his wages are paid semimonthly. What is the total amount of his semimonthly withholding allowance?
10. What are the penalties imposed on employees for filing false information on Form W-4?
11. The Baucus Company has just completed the processing of its year-end payroll and distributed all the weekly paychecks. The payroll department is now computing the amount of the annual bonus to be given each worker. What methods may be used by the company in determining the amount of federal income taxes to be withheld from the annual bonus payments?
12. From what source do employers obtain the funds needed to make advance EIC payments to their eligible employees?
13. Orrin D'Amato, single, participates in his firm's pension retirement plan. This year his adjusted gross income will be about $60,000. How much of his compensation may D'Amato contribute to an IRA this year without paying federal income taxes on the contribution?
14. For what purpose do employers complete Form W-3?
15. Why must some employers file Form 1096?
16. What is the penalty for filing W-2s with mismatched names and social security numbers?
17. What formula is used to "gross-up" supplemental payments in order to cover the taxes on the supplemental payments?
18. What is the maximum contribution that an employer can make to an employee's SIMPLE account?
19. What is the maximum amount that an employee can shelter into a 401(k) plan?
20. How is the *special period rule* for the reporting of fringe benefits applied?

QUESTIONS FOR DISCUSSION

1. Alex Oberstar, a cook in the Lagomarsino Company cafeteria, is furnished two meals each day during his eight-hour shift. Oberstar's duties require him to have his meals on the company's premises. Should the cash value of Oberstar's meals be included as part of his taxable wages? Explain.
2. The Solomon Company ordinarily pays its employees on a weekly basis. Recently, one of the employees, Bernard Nagle, was sent from the home office on a three-week trip. Nagle has now returned to the office,

and you are preparing a single check covering his three-week services. Should you withhold federal income taxes on the total gross earnings for the three-week period or should you compute the federal income taxes as if Nagle were receiving three separate weekly wage payments?
3. Investigate your state's income tax withholding law (or that of some other state assigned by your instructor), and find the answers to the following questions:
   a. Who must withhold the tax?

b. How are covered employers and covered employees defined?

c. Are there any reciprocal agreements the state has entered into? If so, describe them.

d. How is the withholding rate determined?

e. What payments are subject to withholding?

f. What payments are not subject to withholding?

g. Are there any employee withholding exemptions?

h. What methods of withholding are permitted?

i. Describe each of the returns required by the state.

j. What kinds of information must be retained by employers in their withholding tax records?

k. What penalties are imposed for failure to comply with the withholding law?

l. Are any employers required to deposit their withheld income taxes through electronic funds transfer (EFT)? If so, what requirements does the state impose?

4. Janice Sikorski, one of your firm's workers, has just come into the payroll department and says to you: "I am thinking of amending my Form W-4 so that an addi-tional $10 is withheld each week. That way I will get a fat refund next year. What do you think of my idea?" How would you reply to Sikorski?

5. Anita Leland, a waitress in the Atlantis Casino, reported tips of $467 to her employer last year. Two months after she filed her federal income tax return, Leland received a letter from the IRS informing her that she had earned $5,260 in tips rather than the $467 reported and that she owed the government $1,872.94 in back taxes.

a. How is the IRS able to determine the amount of tips received by a waitress in a casino?

b. If the IRS is correct in its determination of the tips received, is Atlantis subject to a penalty for not hav-ing withheld payroll taxes on all the tips Leland received during the year?

6. John Engles, an ex-employee, is entitled to a taxable fringe benefit during the first part of this year. Because he wasn't paid any wages this year, can his employer report the taxable fringe benefit on Form 1099?

PRACTICAL PROBLEMS

4–1. LO 4.

Joseph English is a waiter at the Delphi Lounge. In his first weekly pay in March, he earned $120.00 for the 40 hours he worked. In addition, he reports his tips for February to his employer ($450.00), and the employer withholds the appropriate taxes for the tips from this first pay in March.

Calculate his net take-home pay assuming the employer withheld federal income tax (wage-bracket, married, 2 allowances), social security taxes, and state income tax (2%).

4–2. LO 4.

Use the percentage method to compute the federal income taxes to withhold from the wages or salaries of each employee.

Employee No.	Employee Name	Marital Status	No. of Withholding Allowances	Gross Wage or Salary	Amount to Be Withheld
1	Amoroso, A.	M	4	$1,610 weekly	_____
2	Finley, R.	S	0	$825 biweekly	_____
3	Gluck, E.	S	5	$9,630 quarterly	_____
4	Quinn, S.	M	8	$925 semimonthly	_____
5	Treave, Y.	M	3	$1,975 monthly	_____

4–3. LO 4.

Use (a) the percentage method and (b) the wage-bracket method to compute the federal income taxes to withhold from the wages or salaries of each employee.

Employee	Marital Status	No. of Withholding Allowances	Gross Wage or Salary	Percentage Method	Wage-Bracket Method
Astin, N.	S	2	$475 weekly	_____	_____
Copeland, S.	S	1	$960 weekly	_____	_____
Jensen, R.	M	6	$1,775 biweekly	_____	_____
Schaffer, H.	M	4	$1,480 semimonthly	_____	_____
Yelm, T.	M	9	$5,380 monthly	_____	_____

4–4. LO 4.

Eaton Enterprises uses the wage-bracket method to determine federal income tax withholding on its employees.

Compute the amount to withhold from the wages paid each employee.

Employee	Marital Status	No. of Withholding Allowances	Payroll Period W=Weekly S=Semimonthly M=Monthly D=Daily	Wage	Amount to Be Withheld
Hal Bower	M	1	W	$1,350	_____
Ruth Cramden	S	1	W	$590	_____
Gil Jones	S	3	W	$675	_____
Teresa Kern	M	6	M	$4,090	_____
Ruby Long	M	2	M	$2,730	_____
Katie Luis	M	8	S	$955	_____
Susan Martin	S	1	D	$96	_____
Jim Singer	S	4	S	$2,610	_____
Martin Torres	M	4	M	$3,215	_____

4–5. LO 4.

The names of the employees of the Western Music Shop are listed on the following payroll register. Employees are paid weekly. The marital status and the number of allowances claimed are shown on the payroll register, along with each employee's weekly salary. Complete the payroll register for the payroll period ending December 13, the 50th weekly payday. The state income tax rate is 2% of total earnings, the city income tax rate is 1.5% of the total gross earnings, and the wage-bracket method is used for federal income taxes.

LAMBRIGHT MUSIC SHOP

PAYROLL REGISTER

FOR PERIOD ENDING   20

EMPLOYEE NAME	MARITAL STATUS	NO. OF W/H ALLOW.	TOTAL EARNINGS	DEDUCTIONS					
				(a) FICA		(b) FIT	(c) SIT	(d) CIT	(e) NET PAY
				OASDI	HI				
Bennet, Marvin	M	3	1 8 0 0 00						
Green, Robert	S	1	2 8 5 00						
Herd, Ben	M	0	1 5 5 00						
Larson, Beverly	S	3	3 2 4 25						
Maston, Roberta	S	1	3 7 5 00						
Nash, Tim	S	2	5 5 8 50						
Stelt, Harold	S	1	4 7 0 50						
Zelder, Nadine	M	3	3 8 0 00						
Totals									

Compute the employer's FICA taxes for the pay period ending December 12.

OASDI Taxes		HI Taxes	
OASDI taxable earnings	$_____	HI taxable earnings	$_____
OASDI taxes	$_____	HI taxes	$_____

4-6

The Damerly Company (a California employer) wants to give a holiday bonus check of $250 to each employee. Since it wants the check amount to be $250, it will need to gross up the amount of the bonus. Calculate the withholding taxes and the gross amount of the bonus to be made to John Rolen if his cumulative earnings for the year are $46,910. Besides being subject to social security taxes and federal income tax, a 6 percent California income tax must be withheld on supplemental payments.

4-38

4–7. LO 4, 6. ✖

The names of the employees of Cox Security Systems and their regular salaries are shown in the following payroll register. Note that Hill and Van Dyne are paid monthly on the last pay day, while all others are paid weekly.

In addition to the regular salaries, the company pays an annual bonus based on the amount of earnings for the year. For the current year, the bonus amounts to 8% of the annual salary paid to each employee. The bonus is to be paid along with the regular salaries on December 26, but the amount of the bonus and the amount of the regular salary will be shown separately on each employee's earnings statement. Assume that all employees received their regular salary during the entire year.

Prepare the payroll for the pay period ending December 26, showing the following for each employee:

Use the wage-bracket method to withhold federal income tax from the regular salaries.

Withhold a flat 27 percent on the annual bonus.

Total salaries and bonuses are subject to a 2 percent state income tax and a 1 percent city income tax.

FOR PERIOD ENDING _____ 20___

EMPLOYEE NAME	MARITAL STATUS	NO. OF W/H ALLOW.	EARNINGS			DEDUCTIONS					
			REGULAR	(a) SUPPL.	(b) TOTAL	(c) FICA OASDI	HI	(d) FIT	(e) SIT	(f) CIT	(e) NET PAY
Hill, J. Harvey	M	5	5 5 0 0 00 (M)*								
Van Dyne, Joyce S.	M	2	2 8 5 0 00 (M)*								
Abbott, Leslie N.	S	1	5 2 0 00								
Bunger, Russel L.	M	4	4 6 5 00								
Noblet, Thomas D.	M	2	3 8 0 00								
Short, Frank C.	S	1	3 5 0 00								
Toban, Harriette O.	M	2	5 7 5 00								
Wyeth, Amy R.	S	0	4 2 5 00								
Totals											

Compute the employer's FICA taxes for the pay period ending December 26.

OASDI Taxes
  OASDI taxable earnings $_____

  OASDI taxes $_____

HI Taxes
  HI taxable earnings $_____

  HI taxes $_____

(M)* indicates monthly pay.

4-8. LO 4, 6.

During the quarter ending December 31 of the current year, Cox Security Systems had 13 weekly paydays and three monthly paydays.

Using the data given in Problem 4–7, complete the following form to show:

a. Total earnings paid during the quarter, including both the regular and the supplemental earnings.

b. Total amount of FICA taxes withheld during the quarter.

c. Total amount of federal income taxes withheld during the quarter.

d. Total amount of state income taxes withheld during the quarter.

e. Total amount of city income taxes withheld during the quarter.

f. Total net amount paid each employee during the quarter.

EMPLOYEE NAME	(a) TOTAL EARNINGS	(b) FICA OASDI	(b) FICA HI	DEDUCTIONS (c) FIT	(d) SIT	(e) CIT	(f) NET PAY
Hill, J. Harvey							
Van Dyne, Joyce S.							
Abbott, Leslie N.							
Bunger, Russel L.							
Noblet, Thomas D.							
Short, Frank C.							
Toban, Harriette O.							
Wyeth, Amy R.							
Totals							

4–9. LO 4, 7. ✖

The employees of Evergreen Garden Center are paid weekly. The names of five employees of the company are given on the following payroll register. The payroll register also shows the marital status and number of withholding allowances claimed and the total weekly earnings for each worker. Assume that each employee is paid the same weekly wage on each payday in 2003. Also shown below is the wage-bracket table for Advance Earned Income Credit (EIC) Payments for a weekly payroll period. Each employee listed on the payroll register has completed a Form W-5 indicating that the worker is not married. Complete the payroll register for the weekly period ending November 21, 2003. The state income tax rate is 1.5 percent on total earnings.

EMPLOYEE NAME	MARITAL STATUS	NO. OF W/H ALLOW.	TOTAL EARNINGS	(a) FICA OASDI	(a) FICA HI	(b) FIT	(c) SIT	(d) ADVANCE EIC PAYMENT	(e) NET PAY
Allen, R.	S	4	2 2 9 00						
Dilts, Y.	S	1	4 1 2 00						
Martin, E.	S	2	2 1 5 00						
Roselli, T.	S	3	3 7 6 00						
Whitman, Q.	S	1	1 2 5 00						
Totals									

WEEKLY Payroll Period

SINGLE or HEAD OF HOUSEHOLD

Wages At least	But less than	Payment to be made	Wages At least	But less than	Payment to be made	Wages At least	But less than	Payment to be made	Wages At least	But less than	Payment to be made	Wages At least	But less than	Payment to be made	Wages At least	But less than	Payment to be made
$0	$5	$0	$50	$55	$10	$100	$105	$20	$270	$280	$27	$370	$380	$17	$470	$480	$8
5	10	1	55	60	11	105	110	21	280	290	26	380	390	16	480	490	7
10	15	2	60	65	12	110	115	22	290	300	25	390	400	15	490	500	6
15	20	3	65	70	13	115	120	23	300	310	24	400	410	15	500	510	5
20	25	4	70	75	14	120	125	24	310	320	23	410	420	14	510	520	4
25	30	5	75	80	15	125	130	26	320	330	22	420	430	13	520	530	3
30	35	6	80	85	16	130	135	27	330	340	21	430	440	12	530	540	2
35	40	7	85	90	17	135	140	28	340	350	20	440	450	11	540	550	1
40	45	8	90	95	18	140	260	29	350	360	19	450	460	10	550	- - -	0
45	50	9	95	100	19	260	270	28	360	370	18	460	470	9			

4–10. LO 4.

Joe Kohlhepp (age 48) is employed by King Company and is paid a salary of $42,640. He has just decided to join the company's Simple Retirement Account (IRA form) and has a few questions. Answer the following for Joe:

a. What is the maximum that he can contribute into this retirement fund? $_____

b. What would be the company's contribution? $_____

c. What would be his weekly take-home pay with the retirement contribution deducted (married, 2 allowances, wage-bracket method, and a 2.3 percent state income tax)? $_____

d. What would be his weekly take-home pay without the retirement contribution deduction? $_____

4–11. LO 9.

During the fourth quarter of 2003, there were seven biweekly paydays on Friday (October 3, 17, 31; November 14, 28; December 12, 26) for Emerald City Repair. Using the forms supplied below and on pages 4-43–4-46, complete the following for the fourth quarter:

a. Federal Tax Deposit Coupons (monthly depositor), Forms 8109. The employer's phone number is (501) 555-7331. Federal Deposit Liability Each Pay $401.28

b. Employer's Quarterly Federal Tax Return, Form 941. The form is signed by you.

c. Employer's Report of State Income Tax Withheld for the quarter, due on or before February 2, 2004.

Quarterly Payroll Data

Total Earnings	OASDI	HI	FIT	SIT	EIC Payments
$18,725.00	$1,160.95	$271.53	$1,701.00	$1,310.75	$1,757.00

Employer's OASDI	$1,160.95
Employer's HI	$271.53

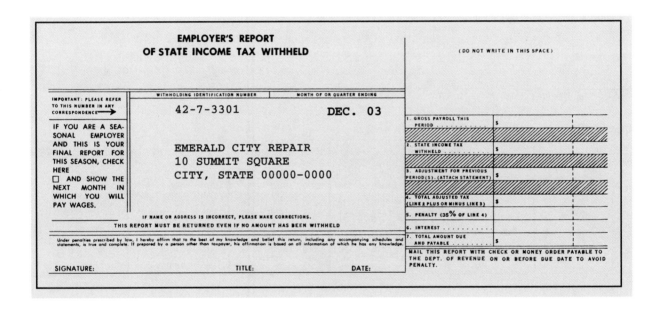

4–11. (continued)

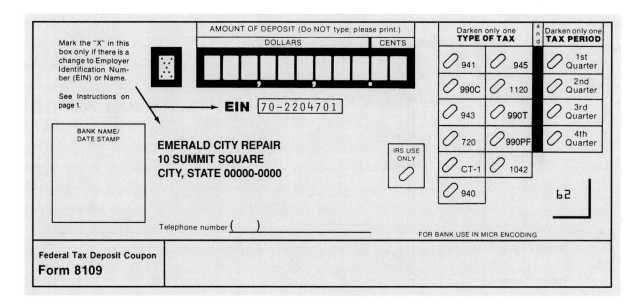

To be deposited on or before _____

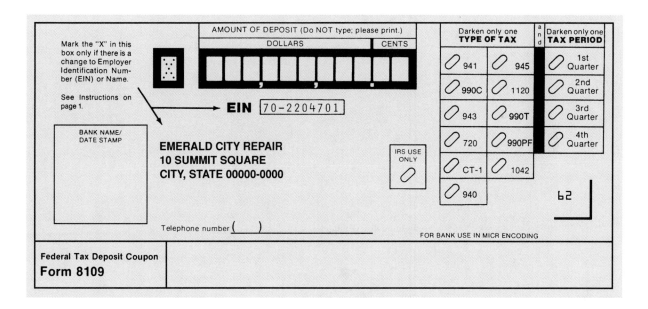

To be deposited on or before _____

4–11. (continued)

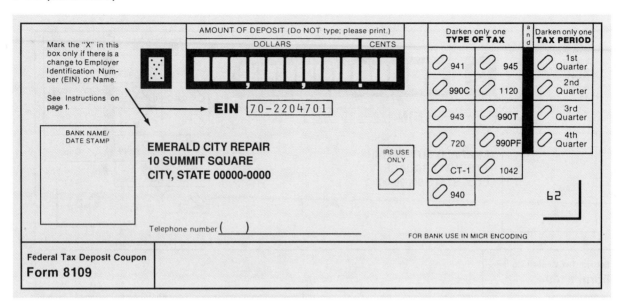

To be deposited on or before _____

Date _____ Name _____

4–11. (concluded)

Form 941
(Rev. January 2002)
Department of the Treasury
Internal Revenue Service (99)

Employer's Quarterly Federal Tax Return
▶ See separate instructions revised January 2002 for information on completing this return.
Please type or print.

Enter state code for state in which deposits were made **only** if different from state in address to the right ▶ (see page 2 of instructions).

Name (as distinguished from trade name)

Trade name, if any
EMERALD CITY REPAIR
Address (number and street)
10 SUMMIT SQUARE

Date quarter ended
DEC. 31, 2003
Employer identification number
70-2204701
City, state, and ZIP code
CITY, STATE
00000-0000

OMB No. 1545-0029

T	
FF	
FD	
FP	
I	
T	

If address is different from prior return, check here ▶

IRS Use

1 1 1 1 1 1 1 1 1 1 2   3 3 3 3 3 3 3   4 4 4   5 5 5
6   7   8 8 8 8 8 8 8   9 9 9 9   10 10 10 10 10 10 10 10 10 10

If you do not have to file returns in the future, check here ▶ ☐ and enter date final wages paid ▶
If you are a seasonal employer, see **Seasonal employers** on page 1 of the instructions and check here ▶ ☐

1	Number of employees in the pay period that includes March 12th . ▶	1
2	Total wages and tips, plus other compensation	2
3	Total income tax withheld from wages, tips, and sick pay	3
4	Adjustment of withheld income tax for preceding quarters of calendar year	4
5	Adjusted total of income tax withheld (line 3 as adjusted by line 4—see instructions) . .	5
6	Taxable social security wages . . . . . **6a** _____ × 12.4% (.124) =	**6b**
	Taxable social security tips . . . . . . **6c** _____ × 12.4% (.124) =	**6d**
7	Taxable Medicare wages and tips . . . **7a** _____ × 2.9% (.029) =	**7b**
8	Total social security and Medicare taxes (add lines 6b, 6d, and 7b). Check here if wages are not subject to social security and/or Medicare tax . . . . ▶ ☐	8
9	Adjustment of social security and Medicare taxes (see instructions for required explanation) Sick Pay $_____ ± Fractions of Cents $_____ ± Other $_____ =	9
10	Adjusted total of social security and Medicare taxes (line 8 as adjusted by line 9—see instructions)	10
11	**Total taxes** (add lines 5 and 10)	11
12	Advance earned income credit (EIC) payments made to employees . . .	12
13	Net taxes (subtract line 12 from line 11). **If $2,500 or more, this must equal line 17, column (d) below (or line D of Schedule B (Form 941))**	13
14	Total deposits for quarter, including overpayment applied from a prior quarter	14
15	**Balance due** (subtract line 14 from line 13). See instructions	15

16 **Overpayment.** If line 14 is more than line 13, enter excess here ▶ $ _____
and check if to be: ☐ Applied to next return **or** ☐ Refunded.

● **All filers:** If line 13 is less than $2,500, you need not complete line 17 or Schedule B (Form 941).
● **Semiweekly schedule depositors:** Complete Schedule B (Form 941) and check here . . . . ▶ ☐
● **Monthly schedule depositors:** Complete line 17, columns (a) through (d), and check here. . . . . . . ▶ ☐

17 **Monthly Summary of Federal Tax Liability.** Do not complete if you were a semiweekly schedule depositor.

(a) First month liability	(b) Second month liability	(c) Third month liability	(d) Total liability for quarter

Third Party Designee
Do you want to allow another person to discuss this return with the IRS (see separate instructions)? ☐ **Yes.** Complete the following. ☐ **No**
Designee's name ▶ _____ Phone no. ▶ ( ) Personal identification number (PIN) ▶ ☐☐☐☐☐

Sign Here
Under penalties of perjury, I declare that I have examined this return, including accompanying schedules and statements, and to the best of my knowledge and belief, it is true, correct, and complete.
Signature ▶ _____ Print Your Name and Title ▶ _____ Date ▶ _____

For Privacy Act and Paperwork Reduction Act Notice, see back of Payment Voucher.   Cat. No. 17001Z   Form **941** (Rev. 1-2002)

4–12. LO 4, 8.

During the first week of 2004, the Payroll Department of the Figley Corporation is preparing the Forms W-2 for distribution to its employees along with their payroll checks on January 2. In this problem, you will complete six of the forms in order to gain some experience in recording the different kinds of information required.

Assume each employee earned the same weekly salary for each of the 52 paydays in 2003.

Using the following information obtained from the personnel and payroll records of the firm, complete Copy A of the six Forms W-2 reproduced on the following pages. Also complete Form W-3. The form is to be signed by the President, Harold W. Rasul, and is prepared by Roberta P. Kurtz.

Company Information:

Address: 4800 River Road
          Philadelphia, PA 19113-5548
Telephone number:(215) 373-0017
Fax number (215) 373-0010

State identification number: 46-3-1066
Federal identification number: 13-7490972

Income Tax Information:

The wage-bracket method is used to determine federal income tax withholding. Calculate the annual federal income tax withheld by using the weekly wage-bracket table and multiply the answer by 52. The other taxes withheld are shown below.

Employee Data	Payroll Data	Annual Taxes Withheld	
Patricia A. Grimes	Single, 1 allowance	1,337.96	Social security tax withheld
54 Gradison Place	$415 per week	313.04	Medicare tax withheld
Philadelphia, PA 19113-4054	SS#: 376-72-4310	604.24	State income tax withheld
	Deduction for 401(k) plan: $50/week	979.16	Local income tax withheld
Roberta P. Kurtz	Married, 1 allowance	1,563.64	Social security tax withheld
56 Andrews Court, Apt. 7	$485 per week	365.56	Medicare tax withheld
Philadelphia, PA 19103-3356	SS#: 272-33-8804	706.16	State income tax withheld
	Dependent care payment: $950 $70/week—401(k)	1,144.52	Local income tax withheld
David P. Markle	Single, 0 allowances	1,176.06	Social security tax withheld
770 Camac Street	$365 per week	275.08	Medicare tax withheld
Philadelphia, PA 19101-3770	SS#: 178-92-3316	531.44	State income tax withheld
	Union dues withheld: $102	861.64	Local income tax withheld
Harold W. Rasul	Married, 7 allowances	4,368.69	Social security tax withheld
338 North Side Avenue	$1,350	1,021.96	Medicare tax withheld
Philadelphia, PA 19130-6638	SS#: 269-01-6839	1,965.60	State income tax withheld
	Cost of group-term life insurance exceeding $50,000: $262.75	3,186.04	Local income tax withheld
	No income tax withheld on insurance cost, but FICA taxes are withheld. $100/week—401(k)		
Christine A. Shoemaker	Married, 2 allowances	1,031.68	Social security tax withheld
4900 Gladwynne Terrace	$320 per week	241.28	Medicare tax withheld
Philadelphia, PA 19127-0049	SS#: 368-14-5771	465.92	State income tax withheld
	Advance EIC payments: $16 per week Union dues withheld: $102	755.04	Local income tax withheld
Angelo Zickar	Single, 1 allowance	1,257.36	Social security tax withheld
480-A Hopkinson Tower	$390 per week	294.32	Medicare tax withheld
Philadelphia, PA 19101-3301	SS#: 337-99-8703	567.84	State income tax withheld
	Educational assistance payments (job-required): $675 $50/week—401(k)	920.40	Local income tax withheld

4–12. (continued)

a Control number	22222	Void ☐	For Official Use Only ▶ OMB No. 1545-0008		

b Employer identification number	1 Wages, tips, other compensation $	2 Federal income tax withheld $

c Employer's name, address, and ZIP code	3 Social security wages $	4 Social security tax withheld $
	5 Medicare wages and tips $	6 Medicare tax withheld $
	7 Social security tips $	8 Allocated tips $

d Employee's social security number	9 Advance EIC payment $	10 Dependent care benefits $

e Employee's first name and initial Last name	11 Nonqualified plans $	12a See instructions for box 12 $
13 Statutory employee ☐ Retirement plan ☐ Third-party sick pay ☐	12b $
14 Other	12c $
	12d $

f Employee's address and ZIP code

15 State Employer's state ID number	16 State wages, tips, etc. $	17 State income tax $	18 Local wages, tips, etc. $	19 Local income tax $	20 Locality name
	$	$	$	$	

Form **W-2** Wage and Tax Statement

2003

Department of the Treasury—Internal Revenue Service

Copy A For Social Security Administration—Send this entire page with Form W-3 to the Social Security Administration; photocopies are **not** acceptable.

Cat. No. 10134D

For Privacy Act and Paperwork Reduction Act Notice, see separate instructions.

Do Not Cut, Fold, or Staple Forms on This Page — Do Not Cut, Fold, or Staple Forms on This Page

---

a Control number	22222	Void ☐	For Official Use Only ▶ OMB No. 1545-0008		

b Employer identification number	1 Wages, tips, other compensation $	2 Federal income tax withheld $

c Employer's name, address, and ZIP code	3 Social security wages $	4 Social security tax withheld $
	5 Medicare wages and tips $	6 Medicare tax withheld $
	7 Social security tips $	8 Allocated tips $

d Employee's social security number	9 Advance EIC payment $	10 Dependent care benefits $

e Employee's first name and initial Last name	11 Nonqualified plans $	12a See instructions for box 12 $
13 Statutory employee ☐ Retirement plan ☐ Third-party sick pay ☐	12b $
14 Other	12c $
	12d $

f Employee's address and ZIP code

15 State Employer's state ID number	16 State wages, tips, etc. $	17 State income tax $	18 Local wages, tips, etc. $	19 Local income tax $	20 Locality name
	$	$	$	$	

Form **W-2** Wage and Tax Statement

2003

Department of the Treasury—Internal Revenue Service

Copy A For Social Security Administration—Send this entire page with Form W-3 to the Social Security Administration; photocopies are **not** acceptable.

Cat. No. 10134D

For Privacy Act and Paperwork Reduction Act Notice, see separate instructions.

Do Not Cut, Fold, or Staple Forms on This Page — Do Not Cut, Fold, or Staple Forms on This Page

4–12. (continued)

a Control number	22222	Void ☐	For Official Use Only ▶ OMB No. 1545-0008	

		1 Wages, tips, other compensation $	2 Federal income tax withheld $
b Employer identification number			
c Employer's name, address, and ZIP code		3 Social security wages $	4 Social security tax withheld $
		5 Medicare wages and tips $	6 Medicare tax withheld $
		7 Social security tips $	8 Allocated tips $
d Employee's social security number		9 Advance EIC payment $	10 Dependent care benefits $
e Employee's first name and initial Last name		11 Nonqualified plans $	12a See instructions for box 12 $
		13 Statutory employee ☐ Retirement plan ☐ Third-party sick pay ☐	12b $
		14 Other	12c $
			12d $
f Employee's address and ZIP code			

15 State Employer's state ID number	16 State wages, tips, etc. $	17 State income tax $	18 Local wages, tips, etc. $	19 Local income tax $	20 Locality name
	$	$	$	$	

Form **W-2** Wage and Tax Statement

2003

Department of the Treasury—Internal Revenue Service

Copy A For Social Security Administration—Send this entire page with Form W-3 to the Social Security Administration; photocopies are **not** acceptable.

Cat. No. 10134D

For Privacy Act and Paperwork Reduction Act Notice, see separate instructions.

Do Not Cut, Fold, or Staple Forms on This Page — Do Not Cut, Fold, or Staple Forms on This Page

a Control number	22222	Void ☐	For Official Use Only ▶ OMB No. 1545-0008	

		1 Wages, tips, other compensation $	2 Federal income tax withheld $
b Employer identification number			
c Employer's name, address, and ZIP code		3 Social security wages $	4 Social security tax withheld $
		5 Medicare wages and tips $	6 Medicare tax withheld $
		7 Social security tips $	8 Allocated tips $
d Employee's social security number		9 Advance EIC payment $	10 Dependent care benefits $
e Employee's first name and initial Last name		11 Nonqualified plans $	12a See instructions for box 12 $
		13 Statutory employee ☐ Retirement plan ☐ Third-party sick pay ☐	12b $
		14 Other	12c $
			12d $
f Employee's address and ZIP code			

15 State Employer's state ID number	16 State wages, tips, etc. $	17 State income tax $	18 Local wages, tips, etc. $	19 Local income tax $	20 Locality name
	$	$	$	$	

Form **W-2** Wage and Tax Statement

2003

Department of the Treasury—Internal Revenue Service

Copy A For Social Security Administration—Send this entire page with Form W-3 to the Social Security Administration; photocopies are **not** acceptable.

Cat. No. 10134D

For Privacy Act and Paperwork Reduction Act Notice, see separate instructions.

Do Not Cut, Fold, or Staple Forms on This Page — Do Not Cut, Fold, or Staple Forms on This Page

4–12. (continued)

a Control number	22222	Void ☐	For Official Use Only ▶ OMB No. 1545-0008		

b Employer identification number	1 Wages, tips, other compensation $	2 Federal income tax withheld $
c Employer's name, address, and ZIP code	3 Social security wages $	4 Social security tax withheld $
	5 Medicare wages and tips $	6 Medicare tax withheld $
	7 Social security tips $	8 Allocated tips $
d Employee's social security number	9 Advance EIC payment $	10 Dependent care benefits $
e Employee's first name and initial Last name	11 Nonqualified plans $	12a See instructions for box 12 Code $
	13 Statutory employee ☐ Retirement plan ☐ Third-party sick pay ☐	12b Code $
	14 Other	12c Code $
		12d Code $
f Employee's address and ZIP code		

15 State Employer's state ID number	16 State wages, tips, etc. $	17 State income tax $	18 Local wages, tips, etc. $	19 Local income tax $	20 Locality name
	$	$	$	$	

Form **W-2** **Wage and Tax Statement**   **2003**   Department of the Treasury—Internal Revenue Service

Copy A For **Social Security Administration**—Send this entire page with Form W-3 to the Social Security Administration; photocopies are **not** acceptable.

For Privacy Act and Paperwork Reduction Act Notice, see separate instructions.

Cat. No. 10134D

Do Not Cut, Fold, or Staple Forms on This Page — Do Not Cut, Fold, or Staple Forms on This Page

---

a Control number	22222	Void ☐	For Official Use Only ▶ OMB No. 1545-0008		

b Employer identification number	1 Wages, tips, other compensation $	2 Federal income tax withheld $
c Employer's name, address, and ZIP code	3 Social security wages $	4 Social security tax withheld $
	5 Medicare wages and tips $	6 Medicare tax withheld $
	7 Social security tips $	8 Allocated tips $
d Employee's social security number	9 Advance EIC payment $	10 Dependent care benefits $
e Employee's first name and initial Last name	11 Nonqualified plans $	12a See instructions for box 12 Code $
	13 Statutory employee ☐ Retirement plan ☐ Third-party sick pay ☐	12b Code $
	14 Other	12c Code $
		12d Code $
f Employee's address and ZIP code		

15 State Employer's state ID number	16 State wages, tips, etc. $	17 State income tax $	18 Local wages, tips, etc. $	19 Local income tax $	20 Locality name
	$	$	$	$	

Form **W-2** **Wage and Tax Statement**   **2003**   Department of the Treasury—Internal Revenue Service

Copy A For **Social Security Administration**—Send this entire page with Form W-3 to the Social Security Administration; photocopies are **not** acceptable.

For Privacy Act and Paperwork Reduction Act Notice, see separate instructions.

Cat. No. 10134D

Do Not Cut, Fold, or Staple Forms on This Page — Do Not Cut, Fold, or Staple Forms on This Page

4–12. (concluded)

DO NOT STAPLE OR FOLD

a Control number	33333	For Official Use Only ▶ OMB No. 1545-0008		

| b Kind of Payer ▶ | 941 ☐ Military ☐ 943 ☐ | Hshld. emp. ☐ Medicare govt. emp. ☐ Third-party sick pay ☐ | **1** Wages, tips, other compensation $ | **2** Federal income tax withheld $ |
| | CT-1 ☐ | | **3** Social security wages $ | **4** Social security tax withheld $ |

c Total number of Forms W-2	d Establishment number	**5** Medicare wages and tips $	**6** Medicare tax withheld $

e Employer identification number	**7** Social security tips $	**8** Allocated tips $

f Employer's name	**9** Advance EIC payments $	**10** Dependent care benefits $

	11 Nonqualified plans $	**12** Deferred compensation $

	13 For third-party sick pay use only

	14 Income tax withheld by payer of third-party sick pay $

g Employer's address and ZIP code	

h Other EIN used this year	

15 State Employer's state ID number	**16** State wages, tips, etc. $	**17** State income tax $
	18 Local wages, tips, etc. $	**19** Local income tax $

Contact person	Telephone number ( )	For Official Use Only
E-mail address	Fax number ( )	

Under penalties of perjury, I declare that I have examined this return and accompanying documents, and, to the best of my knowledge and belief, they are true, correct, and complete.

Signature ▶ _____   Title ▶ _____   Date ▶ _____

Form **W-3** Transmittal of Wage and Tax Statements   **20 --**   Department of the Treasury
Internal Revenue Service

Send this entire page with the entire Copy A page of Form(s) W-2 to the Social Security Administration. Photocopies are not acceptable.

Do not send any payment (cash, checks, money orders, etc.) with Forms W-2 and W-3.

CONTINUING PAYROLL PROBLEM

Refer to the partially completed payroll register which you worked on at the end of Chapter 3. You will now determine the amount of income tax to withhold for each employee, proceeding as follows:

1. In the appropriate columns of your payroll register, record the marital status and number of withholding allowances claimed for each employee, using the information provided.
2. Record the payroll deductions for the SIMPLE plan that the employer has established for participating employees.

All of the employees are participatng and their weekly contributions are listed below. The tax deferral on these deductions applies only to the federal income tax.

3. Record the amount of federal income taxes, using the wage-bracket method.
4. Record the state income taxes on the gross weekly earnings for each employee. The rate is 2.8 percent for the state of Pennsylvania.
5. Record the city income taxes on the gross weekly earnings of each employee. The rate is 1 percent for the city of Pittsburgh residents.

Time Card No.	Marital Status	No. of Allowances	SIMPLE Deductions
11	S	1	$20
12	S	0	50
13	M	2	40
21	M	4	50
22	S	2	20
31	M	3	40
32	M	6	50
33	S	1	60
51	M	5	30
99	M	7	80

CASE PROBLEMS

C1. **Answering Employees' Questions About Wage Reporting.**

During the past week, one of your newly employed payroll associates dropped into your office to ask several questions regarding wage reporting for federal income and social security tax purposes. If you were the payroll supervisor, how would you answer each of the following questions raised by your associate?

1. I just noticed that the social security number is wrong on three of the employees' W-2 forms. How do I go about correcting the forms? Will the employees be penalized for filing incorrect forms?

2. Eileen Huang informed me today that we had withheld too much Medicare tax from her pay last year. She is right! What forms do I use to make the correction?

3. You asked me last week to locate one of our former employees, Warren Bucks. I can't seem to track him down. What should I do with his Form W-2?

4. Is it okay to use titles like "M.D." and "Esq." when I keyboard data in the W-2 forms?

C2. **Classified as an Employee and Independent Contractor.**

The Yeager Company pays John Kerr a salary as an employee and also fees for work he does as an independent contractor. Does this violate IRS rules?

Net activities

1. The IRS has an automatic withholding calculator:

    http://www.irs.gov/businesses/display/
    0,,i1%3D2&genericId%3D14807,00.html

    Here are some things that are needed to calculate appropriate withholding for you:

    - Have your most recent pay stubs handy.
    - Have your most recent income tax return handy.
    - Fill in all information that applies to your situation.
    - Estimate values, if necessary, remembering that the results can only be as accurate as the input you provide.

    (a) Why would you want to increase or decrease the number of your withholding allowances?

    Using the calculator:

    (b) What would you have to do to increase the amount of your tax refund at the end of the year?

    (c) What would you have to do to increase the amount of your paycheck during the year?

2. Do you qualify for the Advance Earned Income Credit?

    http://www.irs.gov/individuals/display/
    0,,i1%3D1%26genericId%3D13712,00.html#1

    (a) What are the requirements for receiving the Advance Earned Income Credit?

    (b) How does an employee receive their Advance Earned Income Credit if qualified?

3. Go to:

    http://www.eftps.gov/.

    (a) How long does it take a taxpayer to enroll in the Electronic Federal Tax Payment System (EFTPS)?

    (b) What are the advantages of the EFTPS?

4. Go to:

    http://www.irs.gov/businesses/display/
    0,,i1%3D2&genericId%3D10063,00.html.

    (a) Who can use the TeleFile system?

    (b) Why would a business want to use the TeleFile system?

5. Go to:

    http://www.ssa.gov/pubs/10022.html.

    (a) How is self-employment income treated differently than income when you work for an employer?

    (b) How do you report self-employment income?

What happens if the paycheck STOPS???

Who qualifies for unemployment compensation? What factors

Unemployment Compensation Taxes

determine the amount that the employer pays? How and when is it paid? What employees are protected?

Chapter 5 explains how the Federal Unemployment Tax Act is implemented. It describes the factors that determine eligibility for state unemployment compensation benefits.

5

© Getty Images, Inc./Photodisc

AFTER STUDYING THIS CHAPTER, YOU SHOULD BE ABLE TO:

1. Describe the basic requirements for an individual to be classified as an employer or an employee under the Federal Unemployment Tax Act.

2. Describe the factors considered in determining the coverage of interstate employees.

3. Identify generally what is defined as taxable wages by the Federal Unemployment Tax Act.

4. Compute the federal unemployment tax and the credit against this tax.

5. Describe how an experience-rating system is used in determining employers' contributions to state unemployment compensation funds.

6. Complete the reports required by the Federal Unemployment Tax Act.

7. Describe the types of information reports under the various state unemployment compensation laws.

8. Describe the factors that determine eligibility for unemployment compensation benefits.

LEARNING OBJECTIVES

The Social Security Act of 1935 ordered every state to set up an unemployment compensation program in order to provide payments to workers during periods of temporary unemployment. Payroll taxes at both the federal and state levels fund this unemployment insurance program. The Federal Unemployment Tax Act (FUTA) imposes a tax on employers based on wages paid for covered employment. It is *not* collected or deducted from employees' wages. The funds collected by the federal government as a result of this tax pay the cost of administering both the federal and the state unemployment insurance programs. The FUTA tax is *not* used for the payment of weekly benefits to unemployed workers. Such benefits are paid by the states in accordance with each state's unemployment tax law (SUTA). These unemployment benefits are paid out of each state's trust fund, which is financed by state unemployment taxes. Because all states conform to standards specified in FUTA, considerable uniformity exists in the provisions of the state unemployment compensation laws. However, many variations in eligibility requirements, rates of contributions, benefits paid, and duration of benefits exist. All the states, Puerto Rico, the Virgin Islands, and the District of Columbia have enacted unemployment compensation laws that have been approved by the Social Security Administration.

You can realize the extent of the federal-state unemployment insurance program in terms of the people involved by the fact that in July 2002 the number of unemployed persons was 8.3 million out of a civilian labor force of about 142.4 million. At that time, the jobless rate was 5.9%. *Unemployed persons* include young people seeking positions for the first time, seasonal workers unemployed a part of each year, and workers who lost their jobs through various causes and cannot find other suitable employment.

COVERAGE UNDER FUTA AND SUTA

LEARNING OBJECTIVE 1

Other than a few significant exceptions as explained in this section, the coverage under FUTA is similar to that under FICA, as described in Chapter 3.

Employers—FUTA

The federal law levies a payroll tax on employers for the purpose of providing more uniform administration of the various state unemployment compensation laws. The federal law considers a person or a business an employer if *either* of the following two tests applies:

1. Pays wages of $1,500 or more during any calendar quarter in the current or preceding calendar year, or

2. Employs one or more persons, on at least some portion of one day, in each of 20 or more calendar weeks during the current or preceding taxable year.

A number of points serve to clarify the meaning of the two alternative tests: (a) a calendar week is defined as seven successive days beginning with Sunday; (b) the 20 weeks need not be consecutive; (c) the employees need not be the same employees; (d) regular, part-time, and temporary workers are considered employees; (e) in determining the employer's status, employees include individuals on vacation or sick leave; and (f) members of a partnership are not considered to be employees. As soon as an employer meets either test, the employer becomes liable for the FUTA tax for the entire calendar year.

EXAMPLE

In the Vemor Company, the 20th week of having one or more employees does not occur until November of 2003. The company becomes liable for FUTA tax on all taxable wages paid beginning with January 1, 2003.

Other covered employers are:

1. Agricultural employers who in the present or previous year paid $20,000 or more to farm workers in any calendar quarter and/or employed 10 or more farm workers during some part of a day during any 20 different weeks.

2. A household employer who during the present or previous year paid $1,000 or more during any quarter for household services in a private home, college club, or local fraternity or sorority club.

Once attained, the employer status continues until the employer fails to meet the test for coverage during a year. In this case, liability under FUTA would end as of January 1 of the next year.

Generally, the nature of the business organization has no relevance in determining employer status. Thus, the employer may be an individual, corporation, partnership, company, association, trust, or estate. There may be instances where it is difficult to determine which of two entities is the employer for purposes of FUTA. As under FICA, the question is answered by determining which entity has the ultimate right to direct and control the employees' activities. It is not necessary that the employer actually direct or control the manner in which the services are performed; it is sufficient if the employer has the right to do so. Other factors characteristic of an employer include the right to discharge and the furnishing of tools and a place to work.

Employers—SUTA

In general, employers specifically excluded under the federal law are also excluded under the state laws. However, as a result of variations found in state unemployment compensation laws, not all employers covered by the unemployment compensation laws of one or more states are covered by FUTA. For example, the services performed by some charitable organizations may be covered by a state's unemployment compensation act, but these same services may be exempt from FUTA coverage.

Employees—FUTA

Every individual is considered an employee if the relationship between the worker and the person for whom the services are performed is the legal common-law relationship of employer and employee. This individual would then be counted in determining whether the employer is subject to FUTA. Chapters 3 and 4 cover the nature of this common-law relationship.

For the purpose of the FUTA tax, the term "employee" also means any of the following who perform service for remuneration:

1. An agent-driver or a commission-driver who distributes food or beverages (other than milk) or laundry or dry-cleaning services for the principal.
2. A traveling or a city salesperson engaged in full-time soliciting and transmitting to the principal orders for merchandise for resale or supplies for use in business operations.

If a person in one of these categories has a substantial investment in facilities used to perform the services (not including transportation facilities), the individual is an independent contractor and not a covered employee. Also, individuals are not covered if their services are a single transaction that is not part of a continuing relationship with the persons for whom they are performed.

The work performed by the employee for the employer includes any services of whatever nature performed within the United States, regardless of the citizenship or residence of either. FUTA coverage also includes service of any nature performed outside the United States by a citizen of the United States for an American employer. The major exception is that service performed in Canada or in any other adjoining country with which the United States has an agreement relating to unemployment does not constitute covered employment.

An employee may perform both included and excluded employment for the same employer during a pay period. In such a case, the services that predominate in the pay period determine the employee's status with that employer for the period. FUTA wholly exempts some services from coverage. Among those *excluded* from coverage in 2003 are:

1. Casual laborers, unless cash remuneration paid for such service is $50 or more in a calendar quarter and the person to whom it is paid is regularly employed by the one for whom the services were performed during that period.

on the

Net

http://www.itsc.state.md.us/ directory/directory/map.html
This site provides an interactive **map of unemployment-related state servers.**

2. Directors of corporations, unless they perform services for the corporation other than those required by attending and participating in meetings of the board of directors.

3. Foreign students and exchange visitors who are carrying out the purposes for which they are admitted into the United States, such as studying, teaching, or conducting research. If employed for other purposes, they would not be excluded.

4. Government employees of international organizations, such as the United Nations.

5. Independent contractors, such as physicians, lawyers, dentists, veterinarians, contractors, subcontractors, public stenographers, auctioneers, and others who follow an independent trade, business, or profession in which they offer their services to the public.

6. Individuals under 18 years of age who deliver or distribute newspapers or shopping news (other than delivery or distribution to any point for subsequent delivery and distribution) and retail vendors of any age who sell and distribute newspapers and magazines to the ultimate consumer.

7. Insurance agents or solicitors paid solely on a commission basis.

8. Members of partnerships.

9. Service performed by an individual for a son, daughter, or spouse, or by a child under the age of 21 for a parent.

10. Services performed by a student who is enrolled and regularly attending classes at a school, college, or university, if service is performed for that school, college, or university.

11. Services performed by employees or employee representatives for employers covered by either the Railroad Retirement Tax Act or the Railroad Unemployment Insurance Act.

12. Services performed by individuals in fishing and related activities if the vessel is less than ten net tons.

13. Services performed in the employ of a religious, educational, or charitable organization that is exempt from federal income tax. This exemption includes service in church-sponsored elementary and secondary schools.

14. Services performed in the employ of foreign, federal, state, or local governments and certain of their instrumentalities. However, taxes imposed by FUTA apply to these federal instrumentalities: federal reserve banks, federal loan banks, and federal credit unions.

15. Students enrolled full-time in a work-study or internship program, for work that is an integral part of the student's academic program.

16. Student nurses and hospital interns.

Employees—SUTA

The definition of "employee" as established by FUTA applies to a majority of the states, although minor variations exist in the state laws. One variation involves firms that employ persons who work in more than one state. In these cases, the employer must determine which state covers the workers for unemployment compensation purposes.

LEARNING OBJECTIVE 2

Coverage of Interstate Employees.   An *interstate employee* is an individual who works in more than one state. To prevent duplicate contributions on the services of interstate employees, all states have adopted a uniform four-part definition of employment to determine which state will cover such employees. This definition covers the entire services of an interstate worker in one state only—that state in which the worker will most likely look for a job if he or she becomes unemployed. Several factors that must be considered in determining coverage of interstate employees, in their order of application, include:

1. Place where the work is *localized.*
2. Location of *base of operations.*
3. Location of place from which operations are *directed or controlled.*
4. Location of employee's residence.

Place Where the Work Is Localized.   Under this main criterion of coverage adopted by the states, if all the work is performed within one state, it is clearly "localized" in that state and constitutes "employment" under the law of that state. In some cases, however, part of the person's work may be performed outside the state. In such instances, the entire work may be treated as localized within the state if the services performed in other states are temporary or transitory in nature.

E X A M P L E

Carson Thomson is a sales representative whose regular sales territory lies within Arizona. Thomson is covered by the laws of Arizona, with respect to his total employment, even though he makes frequent trips to the firm's showrooms in Los Angeles to attend sales meetings and to look over new lines of goods.

Location of Base of Operations. Often a worker may perform services continually in two or more states. In such situations, the employment in one state is not incidental to the employment in the other state. Thus, the test of localization does not apply, and the base of operations test must be considered. Under this test, the employee's services may be covered by the laws of a single state even though the services are not localized within that state. The base of operation is the place of a more or less permanent nature from which the employee starts work and to which the employee customarily returns. It could be a particular place where his or her (a) instructions are received, (b) business records are maintained, (c) supplies are sent, or (d) office is maintained (may be in the employee's home).

E X A M P L E

Mitch Goldman travels through four southern states for the Irwin Company, which is headquartered in Georgia. His work is equally divided among the four states. When working in Georgia, he reports to the main office for instructions. The location of his base of operations is clearly Georgia, and his services are subject to the Georgia laws.

Location of Place From Which Operations Are Directed or Controlled. Often an employee's services are not localized in any state. Or, it may be impossible to determine any base of operations. If the place of control can be fixed in a particular state in which some service is performed, that will be the state in which the individual is covered.

E X A M P L E

Joyce Mendes is a sales representative whose sales territory is so widespread that she does not retain any fixed business address or office. She receives all orders or instructions by mail or wire wherever she may happen to be. Clearly the work is not localized in any state, and no fixed base of operations exists. However, the services performed by Mendes may still come under the provisions of a single state law—the law of that state in which is located the place of direction or control, provided that some of Mendes's work is also performed in that state.

Location of Employee's Residence. If an employee's coverage cannot be determined by any of the three tests described, a final test, that of the employee's residence, is used. Thus, the worker's service is covered in its entirety in the state in which the employee lives, provided some of the service is performed in that state.

E X A M P L E

Robert Donald is employed by the Prang Company of Illinois. He lives in Iowa, and his work territory includes Iowa, Minnesota, and Wisconsin. Since neither the base of operations nor the place from which his work is directed is in a state in which he works, he is covered in his state of residence (Iowa).

Reciprocal Arrangements and Transfers of Employment. If coverage of interstate employees cannot be determined using these factors, states may enter into arrangements under which the employer may elect coverage of the employee in one state.

on the
JOB

The only states that do not participate in reciprocal arrangements are Alaska, Kentucky, Mississippi, New Jersey, and New York, plus Puerto Rico.

These agreements, known as *reciprocal arrangements,* provide unemployment insurance coverage and payment of benefits to interstate workers. The most widely accepted type of interstate coverage arrangement is the Interstate Reciprocal Coverage Arrangement. Under this arrangement, an employer can elect to cover all of the services of a worker in any one state in which (a) the employee performs any work, (b) the employee maintains a residence, or (c) the employer maintains the place of business.

EXAMPLE

Morris Davidson is a salesperson for the Tannenbaum Company. His sales territory includes parts of Connecticut and Massachusetts, and his services can be considered localized in both states. Under the Interstate Reciprocal Coverage Arrangement, the company elects to cover Davidson under the law of Massachusetts.

Once the employer chooses the state in which all the services of the interstate workers are to be covered and the employee consents to the coverage, this state approves the election of coverage. Then, the appropriate agencies of the other states in which services are performed are notified so that they can agree to the coverage in the state of election. Since they are usually done on a case-by-case basis, new arrangements must be agreed upon for each employee.

Another aspect of reciprocal arrangements concerns the transfer of an employee from one state to another during the same calendar year. An employer can include, for purposes of determining the taxable wage base in the second state, wages paid an employee with respect to employment covered by the unemployment compensation law of the previous state.

EXAMPLE

The Karlson Company has paid wages of $4,000 to an employee in State A. During the year, the employee is transferred to State B, which has a $7,000 taxable salary limitation for its state unemployment tax. The company has a credit of $4,000 against this $7,000 limit. Thus, the company has to pay State B's unemployment tax on only the next $3,000 of wages earned by that worker in State B during the remainder of the calendar year.

Coverage of Americans Working Overseas.   As mentioned before, coverage extends to U.S. citizens working abroad for American employers. The state of the employer's principal place of business would provide the coverage. If the principal place of business cannot be determined, the state of incorporation or the state of residence of the individual owner would be the state of coverage.

Wages—FUTA

LEARNING OBJECTIVE 3

Generally, *wages* means all remuneration for employment, including the cash value of all remuneration paid in any medium other than cash, with certain exceptions.

During 2003, taxable wages include only the first $7,000 of remuneration paid by an employer to an employee with respect to employment during any calendar year. The basis upon which the remuneration is paid is immaterial. It may be paid on a piece-work basis or it may be a percentage of profits; it may be paid hourly, daily, weekly, biweekly, semi-monthly, monthly, or annually. Some of the more common types of payments made to employees and the taxability status of these payments include the following:

Taxable Wages for Unemployment Purposes

1. Advance payment for work to be done in the future.
2. Bonuses as remuneration for services.
3. Cash and noncash prizes and awards for doing outstanding work, for exceeding sales quotas, or for contributing suggestions that increase productivity or efficiency.
4. Christmas gifts, excluding noncash gifts of nominal value.

on the

JOB

Wages paid by a previous employer can be counted by the successor in figuring the wage limit if both are covered employers in the year that the acquisition took place.

5. Commissions as compensation for covered employment.
6. Contributions by an employer to a supplemental unemployment individual-account plan, to which the employee has a fully vested and nonforfeitable right.
7. Dismissal payments.
8. Employer contributions to cash or deferred arrangements to the extent that the contributions are not included in the employee's gross income.
9. Idle time and standby payments.
10. Payment by the employer of the employee's FICA tax or the employee's share of any state unemployment compensation tax without deduction from the employee's wages.
11. Payments representing compensation for services by an employee paid to the dependents after an employee's death. Payments in the nature of a gratuity rather than compensation for services are nontaxable. Any payments made by an employer to an employee's estate or to the employee's survivors after the calendar year in which the employee died are excluded from the definition of wages and thus may not be taxed.
12. Payments to employees or their dependents on account of sickness or accident disability. These payments are *not* taxable after the expiration of six months following the last calendar month in which the employee worked. Payments for work missed due to pregnancy are not classified as taxable wages during the first six months of absence.
13. Payments under a guaranteed annual wage plan.
14. Retroactive wage increases.
15. Tips, including charged tips, reported by the employee to the employer.
16. Transfer of stock by an employer to the employees as remuneration for services. (The fair market value of the stock at the time of payment is the taxable base.)
17. Vacation pay.

Nontaxable Wages for Unemployment Purposes

1. Advances or reimbursement of ordinary and necessary business expenses incurred in the business of the employer.
2. Allowances made to an individual by a prospective employer for expenses incurred in connection with interviews for possible employment.
3. Bonuses under a supplemental compensation plan paid upon retirement, death, or disability of an employee.
4. Caddy fees.
5. Commissions paid to insurance agents and solicitors who are paid solely by commission. Such persons are classified as independent contractors, not employees.
6. Courtesy discounts to employees and their families.
7. Educational assistance payments to workers.
8. Payments made by an employer under a plan established by the employer for health, accident, or life insurance, or retirement benefits on behalf of the employees or their dependents.
9. Reimbursement of an employee's moving expenses if, at the time of payment, it is reasonable to believe that the employee will be entitled to a deduction for those expenses at the time of filing his or her federal income tax return.
10. Retirement pay.
11. Strike benefits paid by a union to its members.
12. Value of meals and lodging furnished employees for the convenience of the employer.
13. Workers' compensation payments.

Wages—SUTA

The definition of taxable wages is fairly uniform under the various state unemployment compensation laws. However, some variations exist among the states as to the status of particular kinds of payments. For example, about one-sixth of the states have ruled that Christmas bonuses or gifts are "wages" when substantial, contractual, or based on a percentage of the employee's wages or length of service. New Hampshire, however, does not include gifts or gratuities of $25 or less as wages, unless paid under a contract related to past or future employment. A further variation in defining taxable wages among the states arises in the treatment of *dismissal payments*. Generally, such payments are considered wages whether or not the employer must legally make the payments. However, in some states, dismissal payments do not constitute wages unless the employer must legally make them. Puerto Rico does not consider any type of dismissal payment to be wages. In Puerto Rico, tips are also not considered taxable wages.

UNEMPLOYMENT COMPENSATION TAXES AND CREDITS

The base of the unemployment compensation tax is wages *paid* rather than *wages payable*. Thus, an employer is liable for the unemployment compensation tax in the year in which wages are paid employees, not necessarily in the year in which the services are rendered. Thus, if an employee performs services in 2002 but is not paid for them until 2003, the employer is liable for the tax in 2003, and the 2003 tax rates apply. Wages are considered paid when actually paid or when *constructively paid*. Wages are considered constructively paid when credited to the account of, or set apart for, an employee so that they may be drawn upon at any time, even though they are not actually possessed by the employee.

Tax Rate—FUTA

News
A L E R T

The gross FUTA tax rate of 6.2% will remain in effect through 2007.

Under FUTA, all employers, as defined earlier, are subject to a tax with respect to having individuals in their employ. For 2003, the employer's tax rate is 6.2% of the first $7,000 wages paid each employee during the calendar year. Thus, an employer is liable for the FUTA tax on wages paid each employee until the employee's wages reach the $7,000 level. If an employee has more than one employer during the current year, the taxable wage base applies separately to each of those employers, unless one employer has transferred the business to the second.

E X A M P L E

Assume that in 2003, an employer had charged the wages account for $63,910. Of this amount, $720 will not be paid until the first payday in 2004. Further, the wages actually paid to employees in 2003 in excess of $7,000 each amounted to $19,840. The gross FUTA tax imposed on the employer is computed as follows:

Total amount charged to wages during 2003		$63,910.00
Less:		
Wages not to be paid until 2004	$ 720	
Wages paid in excess of $7,000 limit	19,840	20,560.00
Total taxable wages		$43,350.00
Rate of tax		× 6.2%
Amount of gross FUTA tax		$ 2,687.70

LEARNING OBJECTIVE 4

Credits Against FUTA Tax.　The actual FUTA tax paid is usually only 0.8%, since employers are entitled to a credit against their FUTA tax liability for contributions made under approved state unemployment compensation laws. The maximum credit permitted is 5.4% (90% of 6%). Thus, in the preceding example where the *gross* FUTA tax rate is 6.2%, the *net* FUTA rate would be 0.8% if the full 5.4% credit applied. Even if employers pay a SUTA rate of less than 5.4%, they still get the full credit against the FUTA tax.

The net FUTA tax may be computed in two ways:

E X A M P L E

1. Total taxable earnings (above example)	$43,350.00
Net rate of tax (6.2% − 5.4%)	× 0.8%
Amount of net FUTA tax	$ 346.80

2. Amount of gross FUTA tax (6.2%) .... $ 2,687.70
   Total taxable wages $43,350
   Credit against tax .... × 5.4%
   Total credit 2,340.90
   Amount of net FUTA tax .... $ 346.80

To obtain the maximum credit of 5.4% against the federal tax, the employer must make the state contributions on or before the due date for filing the annual return under FUTA (see page 5-20)—January 31. If the employer is late in paying the state contributions, the credit is limited to 90% of the amount of the deposit that would have been allowed as a credit if the late contributions had been paid on time.

EXAMPLE

The Sutcliffe Company had taxable wages totaling $87,500 in 2003. During the year, the company was late in paying some of its state contributions. The penalty for tardiness is shown in the following calculation of the firm's net FUTA tax for 2003:

Amount of gross FUTA tax ($87,500 × 6.2%) .... $ 5,425.00
State taxable wages................................ $87,500
Sutcliffe's SUTA tax rate .... × 5.4%
Sutcliffe's SUTA tax .... $ 4,725

Breakdown of Sutcliffe's SUTA tax payments:
Before 1/31/03—$3,000 × 100% credit .... (3,000.00)
After 1/31/03—$1,725 × 90% credit .... (1,552.50)
Amount of net FUTA tax .... $ 872.50

If the company had made timely payments of its state contributions, the amount of its net FUTA tax would have been reduced to $700, for a savings of $172.50, as follows:

Amount of gross FUTA tax ($87,500 × 6.2%) .... $ 5,425.00
Total taxable wages $87,500
Credit against tax .... × 5.4%
Total credit 4,725.00
Amount of net FUTA tax ($87,500 × 0.8%) .... $ 700.00
                             − $700.00 = $172.50, savings

Experience Rating. In some cases, employers may pay contributions into their state unemployment fund at a rate lower than 5.4%. The method by which the employer contributions may be adjusted because of a favorable employment record is referred to as *experience rating* or *merit rating*. Thus, an employer's favorable experience rate (employment record) qualifies the employer for a SUTA rate lower than 5.4%. As noted before, FUTA provides for a credit equal to the employer's SUTA rate plus an additional credit so that the *full 5.4% credit* still applies. In this way, employers who have steady employment histories and therefore lower SUTA tax rates, are not penalized when the FUTA tax is paid.

SELF-STUDY QUIZ 5–1. *Garo Company pays taxable wages (FUTA and SUTA) of $188,000 during 2003. Garo Company has a state unemployment tax rate of 4.1% for 2002 because of its past employment record. Compute Garo Company's 2003 FUTA and SUTA taxes.*
$_____ FUTA
$_____ SUTA

If an employer receives an additional credit against the FUTA tax because the state experience rate is less than 5.4%, the additional credit is not subject to the 90% FUTA credit limitation for late SUTA payments. The credit reduction applies only to actual SUTA tax payments made after January 31, 2004.

EXAMPLE

Rudder Company has a $70,000 federal and state taxable payroll and has earned a reduced state tax rate of 4%. If their state tax payments are not timely, the FUTA tax calculation is as follows:

Basic FUTA tax ($70,000 × 0.062)		$4,340
Less 90% credit for state taxes ($70,000 × 0.04 × 90%)	$2,520	
Less additional credit for state tax if rate were 5.4%		
[$70,000 × (0.054 − 0.04)]	980	
Total credit		3,500
Net FUTA tax		$ 840

If Rudder Company had made its SUTA payments before the due date of Form 940, the credit for the payments (4%) and the additional credit (1.4%) would have provided a total credit of $3,780 and a FUTA tax savings of $280.

Where contributions are paid into more than one state unemployment compensation fund, the credit against the federal tax is still limited to 5.4%.

EXAMPLE

The contribution rate of Domski Supply in Kansas is 5.5% and in Missouri, 2%. The credit against the gross FUTA tax on the wages paid is 5.4% in each state.

The unemployment compensation laws of certain states set the taxable wage base at a figure higher than the first $7,000 paid to each employee. For example, in Arkansas, the wage base for 2002 was the first $9,000. In such states, the total contributions that the employer must pay into the state fund may exceed 5.4% of the taxable wages as established by FUTA (first $7,000 of each employee's earnings). However, the maximum credit that can be claimed against the gross FUTA tax for the state contributions is 5.4% of the first $7,000 of each individual employee's earnings.

Title XII Advances. States that experience financial difficulties and are unable to pay their unemployment compensation benefits may borrow funds from the federal government under Title XII of the Social Security Act. The states use these funds, called *Title XII advances,* to pay their regular unemployment benefits. Under the repayment provisions established by the federal government, if a state defaults in its payments, the credit against the gross FUTA tax is reduced by 0.3% beginning the *second taxable year after the advance.* This penalty increases by an additional 0.3% for each succeeding year in which there is a balance due the federal government. Thus, employers in those states have their gross FUTA tax rate increased by 0.3% the second year after the advance, then by 0.6%. The credit reduction is capped if certain solvency requirements are met by the state. The credit reduction applicable to employers in the affected states is limited to either 0.6% of wages paid or the percentage credit reduction in effect in the state for the preceding taxable year if greater than 0.6%. The determination of the credit reduction is made on or before November 10 of each year.

Tax Rates—SUTA

Figure 5–1 presents a summary of each state's 2002 unemployment compensation laws, including the tax rates and the wage limitations. The tax rate applied to each employer within a particular state yields the funds used by that state in paying benefits to its unemployed workers. Currently, all states have enacted *pooled-fund laws* as a basis for their unemployment insurance systems. By means of pooled funds, the cost of unemployment benefits is spread among all the employers in a particular state.

Employer Contributions. Every state has its own unemployment compensation law with varying tax rates and taxable wage bases. To minimize the impact of unemployment insurance taxes on newly covered employers, each state sets an initial contributions

on the

JOB

The last state to declare its employers ineligible for the full credit against FUTA taxes was Michigan in 1992.

FIGURE 5-1

Summary of State Unemployment Compensation Laws (2002)
Warning: The Provisions of the state laws are subject to change at any time.

State	Size of Firm (One employee in specified time and/or size of payroll[1])	Contributions (On first $7,000 unless otherwise indicated)		Benefits (Excluding dependency allowances)			
		Employer Min.-Max.	Employee	Waiting Period (weeks)	Max. per Week	Min. per Week	Max. Duration (weeks)
ALABAMA	20 weeks	0.6%–6.2% on first $8,000		none	$190	$45	26
ALASKA	any time	1.0%–5.4% on first $26,000	0.50% on first $26,000	1	248	44	26
ARIZONA	20 weeks	0.05%–5.4%*		1	205	40	26
ARKANSAS	10 days	0.5%–6.4% on first $9,000*		1	333	60	26
CALIFORNIA	over $100 in any calendar quarter	0.7%–5.4%*	0.9% on first $46,327 (disability ins.)	1	230	40	26
COLORADO	any time	0.0%–5.4% * on first $10,000		1	390	25	26
CONNECTICUT	20 weeks	0.5%–5.4% on first $15,000		none	397	15	26
DELAWARE	20 weeks	0.3%–8.2% on first $8,500		none	315	20	26
DISTRICT OF COLUMBIA	any time	1.6%–7.0% on first $9,000		1	309	50	26
FLORIDA	20 weeks	0.1%–5.4%		1	275	34	26
GEORGIA	20 weeks	0.025%–5.4% on first $8,500		none	284	39	26
HAWAII	any time	0.0%–5.4% on first $29,300	0.5% of maximum weekly wages of $682.59, not to exceed $3.45 per week (disability ins.)	1	395	5	26
IDAHO	20 weeks or $300 in any calendar quarter	0.2%–5.4% on first $27,600		1	315	51	26
ILLINOIS	20 weeks	0.6%–6.8% on first $9,000		1	315	51	26
INDIANA	20 weeks	0.2%–5.4%		1	312	50	26
IOWA	20 weeks	0.0%–7.5% on first $18,600		none	283	42	26
KANSAS	20 weeks	0.04%–7.4% on first $8,000*		1	333	83	26
KENTUCKY	20 weeks	0.0%–9.0% on first $8,000*		none	341	39	26

1 This is $1,500 in any calendar quarter in current or preceding calendar year unless otherwise specified.
*Allow voluntary contributions

(continued on next page)

FIGURE 5 - 1 *(Continued)*

Summary of State Unemployment Compensation Laws (2002)
Warning: The Provisions of the state laws are subject to change at any time.

State	Size of Firm (One employee in specified time and/or size of payroll[1])	Contributions (On first $7,000 unless otherwise indicated)		Benefits (Excluding dependency allowances)			
		Employer Min.-Max.	Employee	Waiting Period (weeks)	Max. per Week	Min. per Week	Max. Duration (weeks)
LOUISIANA	20 weeks	0.15%–6.2%		1	$258	$10	26
MAINE	20 weeks	1.71%–5.4% on first $12,000*		1	272	12	26
MARYLAND	any time	0.3%–7.5% on first $8,500		none	280	25	26
MASSACHUSETTS	13 weeks	1.325%–7.225% on first $10,800		1	512	21	30
MICHIGAN	20 weeks or $1,000 in calendar year	0.1%–8.1% on first $9,500*		none	300	59	26
MINNESOTA	20 weeks	0.17%–9.07% on first $21,000*		1	427	38	26
MISSISSIPPI	20 weeks	0.7%–5.4%		1	200	30	26
MISSOURI	20 weeks	0.0%–6.0%*		1	250	45	26
MONTANA	over $1,000 in current or preceding year	0.1%–6.4% on first $18,900		1	286	68	26
NEBRASKA	20 weeks	0.05%–5.4%*		1	252	36	26
NEVADA	$225 in any quarter	0.25%–5.4% on first $20,900		none	301	11	26
NEW HAMPSHIRE	20 weeks	0.05%–6.5% on first $8,000		none	331	32	26
NEW JERSEY	$1,000 in any year	0.3%–5.4% on first $23,500*	0.925% (0.5% for disability ins.; 0.425% for unempl. comp.)	1	475	69	26
NEW MEXICO	20 weeks or $450 in any quarter	0.05%–5.4% on first $15,900*		1	267	50	26
NEW YORK	$300 in any quarter	0.9%–8.1% on first $8,500*	0.5% of weekly wages, not to exceed 60¢ per week (disability ins.)	1	405	40	26
NORTH CAROLINA	20 weeks	0.00%–5.7% on first $15,500*		1	375	15	26
NORTH DAKOTA	20 weeks	0.49%–10.09% on first $17,400*		1	290	43	26
OHIO	20 weeks	0.1%–6.5% on first $9,000*		1	303	83	26
OKLAHOMA	20 weeks	0.0%–5.4% on first $10,500		1	291	16	26

1 This is $1,500 in any calendar quarter in current or preceding calendar year unless otherwise specified.
*Allow voluntary contributions

(continued on next page)

FIGURE 5 – 1   (Concluded)

Summary of State Unemployment Compensation Laws (2002)
Warning: The Provisions of the state laws are subject to change at any time.

State	Size of Firm (One employee in specified time and/or size of payroll[1])	Contributions (On first $7,000 unless otherwise indicated)		Benefits (Excluding dependency allowances)			
		Employer Min.-Max.	Employee	Waiting Period (weeks)	Max. per Week	Min. per Week	Max. Duration (weeks)
OREGON	18 weeks or $225 in any quarter	0.9%–5.4% on first $25,000		1	$400	$93	26
PENNSYLVANIA	any time	1.479%–9.0712% on first $8,000*		1	430	35	26
PUERTO RICO	any time	1.4%–5.4%		1	133	7	26
RHODE ISLAND	any time	1.66%–9.76% on first $12,000	0.3% on first $9,000 (disability ins.)	1	415	52	26
SOUTH CAROLINA	20 weeks	0.54%–5.4%	1.5% on first $44,000 (disability ins.)	1	268	20	26
SOUTH DAKOTA	20 weeks	0.0%–7.7%*		1	234	28	26
TENNESSEE	20 weeks	0.0%–10.0%		1	255	30	26
TEXAS	20 weeks	0.3%–6.54% on first $9,000		1	294	56	26
UTAH	$140 in calendar quarter in current or preceding calendar year	0.1%–8.1% on first $22,000		1	355	22	26
VERMONT	20 weeks	0.4%–5.4% on first $8,000		1	312	39	26
VIRGIN ISLANDS	any time	0.1%–6.0% on first $15,900		1	312	34	26
VIRGINIA	20 weeks	0.00%–5.4% on first $8,000		1	232	50	26
WASHINGTON	any time	0.47%–5.4% on first $28,500		1	496	106	30
WEST VIRGINIA	20 weeks	1.5%–8.5% on first $8,000*		1	338	24	28
WISCONSIN	20 weeks	0.0%–9.75% on first $10,500*		none	313	46	26
WYOMING	$500 in current or preceding calendar year	0.15%–6.1% on first $14,700		1	283	22	26

1 This is $1,500 in any calendar quarter in current or preceding calendar year unless otherwise specified.
*Allow voluntary contributions

rate for new employers that will apply for a specific period of time. During this period of time, the new employer's employment record can be developed and an experience rating can later be established. A state may assign a contributions rate of not less than 1% to newly covered employers on some "reasonable basis" other than employment experience. Once the new employer has accumulated the experience required under the provisions of the state law, a new rate will be assigned. For example, New York applies 4.0% to new employers.

Employee Contributions.   Some states, as shown in Figure 5–1, impose a contributions requirement on employees in addition to the contributions made by the employer.

EXAMPLE

1. Fay Nannen earns $320 during the first week of February while working for Dango, Inc. Since the company is located in New Jersey, Nannen would have $2.96 deducted from her pay (0.925% of $320). This 0.925% tax would be deducted on the first $23,500 paid to her during the year. (In New Jersey, 0.5% of the employees' contributions is for the disability benefit plan and 0.425% for the unemployment insurance fund.)
2. John Garrison works in Puerto Rico and earns $450 each week. He would contribute $1.35 (0.3% of $450) of each pay to a disability fund. This 0.3% deduction would continue until his cumulative pay for the year reached $9,000.

SELF-STUDY QUIZ 5–2. *Moss Company paid wages of $6,000 to John Castellano in Arizona. During the year, Castellano transferred to the company's office in Colorado, and he received $26,000 for the rest of the year. The company's unemployment tax rate for Colorado is 2.9%. What would the Moss Company pay to Colorado for unemployment taxes on John's wages?*

$ _____

LEARNING OBJECTIVE 5

Experience Rating.   As indicated earlier, the concept of experience rating is based upon the payment of state unemployment taxes according to the employer's stability of employment. As an employer experiences a lower employee turnover, generally the state unemployment tax rate will lower.

In all states, some type of experience-rating plan provides for a reduction in the employer's tax contributions based on the employer's experience with the risk of unemployment. Of the several formulas used to determine the contribution rates, the most commonly used is the *reserve-ratio formula:*

$$\text{Reserve Ratio} = \frac{\text{Contributions less Benefits Paid}}{\text{Average Payroll}}$$

The amount of the unemployment compensation contributions (taxes paid), the benefits paid by the state, and the employer's payroll are entered by the state on each employer's record. The benefits paid are subtracted from the contributions, and the balance of the employer's account is divided by the average payroll for a stated period of time to determine the reserve ratio. Under this plan, the balance carried forward each year equals the difference between the employer's total contributions and the total benefits paid to former employees by the state. The contribution rates are then established according to a schedule under which the higher the reserve ratio, the lower the tax rate.

Employers who have built up a balance in their reserve account (contributions paid in less benefits charged) are sometimes referred to as *positive-balance employers.* The larger the positive balance in a company's reserve account, the lower its tax rate will be. Employers whose reserve accounts have been charged for more benefits paid out than contributions paid in are referred to as *negative-balance employers,* and their high tax rates reflect this fact.

Computing the Contribution Rate.   In an experience-rating system, the rate of contributions for employers is based on the employment experience of the employer. The rate is determined by computing the total of the reserve built up by employer contributions over a certain period of time and by computing the ratio of the amount in the reserve account to the employer's average annual payroll as determined under the state's formula.

EXAMPLE

The Parson Company is an employer located in a state with an unemployment compensation law containing merit-rating provisions for employers who meet certain requirements. Below is a summary of the total wages for the years 1999 to 2002, inclusive. For the purpose of the illustration, assume that the total wages and taxable wages are the same amount.

Quarter	1999	2000	2001	2002
1st	$11,000	$10,000	$ 8,500	$10,500
2nd	10,000	9,000	9,500	11,000
3rd	10,000	9,500	10,000	11,000
4th	10,500	9,750	9,500	9,500
Total	$41,500	$38,250	$37,500	$42,000

The State Unemployment Compensation Commission maintains a separate account for each employer. The account is credited with contributions paid into the unemployment compensation fund by the employer and is charged with unemployment benefits paid from the fund.

For 2003, the state law set up the following contribution rate schedule for employers:

Reserve Ratio	Rate
Negative reserve balance	6.7%
0% to less than 8%	5.9%
8% to less than 10%	5.0%
10% to less than 12%	4.1%
12% to less than 15%	3.2%
15% and over	2.5%

The state law under discussion defines: *average annual payroll*—average of last three years, *annual payroll*—wages paid from October 1 to September 30 each year.

The following computations show the state contributions made by the Parson Company for the calendar years 1999 to 2002, inclusive, the federal tax imposed under FUTA, and the method of arriving at the contribution rate for the calendar year 2003:

1999

Taxable wages	$41,500
Rate (SUTA)	× 2.7%
State contributions	$1,120.50
Federal tax: 0.8% of $41,500	332.00
Total unemployment tax	$1,452.50

2000

Taxable wages	$38,250
Rate (SUTA)	× 2.7%
State contributions	$1,032.75
Federal tax: 0.8% of $38,250	306.00
Total unemployment tax	$1,338.75

2001

Taxable wages	$37,500
Rate (SUTA)	× 3.4%
State contributions	$1,275.00
Federal tax: 0.8% of $37,500	300.00
Total unemployment tax	$1,575.00

2002

Taxable wages	$42,000
Rate (SUTA)	× 3.7%
State contributions	$1,554.00
Federal tax: 0.8% of $42,000	336.00
Total unemployment tax	$1,890.00

Remember that the average annual payroll is the average of the last three annual payrolls, with each annual payroll period running from October 1 to September 30.

Assume that the Parson Company paid state contributions of $960 in 1997 and $1,010 in 1998 and that $1,850 was charged to the employer's account for unemployment compensation benefits during 2001 and 2002. The contribution rate for 2003 is computed as follows:

Computation of rate for 2003:

Annual payroll period ending 9/30/00	$ 39,000
Annual payroll period ending 9/30/01	37,750
Annual payroll period ending 9/30/02	42,000
Total of last 3 annual payroll periods	$118,750
Average annual payroll:	

$118,750 divided by 3 = $39,583

Contributions for 1997	$ 960.00
Contributions for 1998	1,010.00
Contributions for 1999	1,120.50
Contributions for 2000	1,032.75
Contributions for 2001	1,275.00
Contributions for 2002 (first nine months)	1,202.50
Total contributions	$6,600.75
Less amount of benefits paid	1,850.00
Balance in reserve account 9/30/02	$4,750.75

$4,750.75, divided by average annual payroll, $39,583 = 12%

Since the reserve is 12% of the average annual payroll, the tax rate for 2003 is 3.2% (the ratio is between 12% and 15%).

Voluntary Contributions.   In some states (see Figure 5–1), employers may obtain reduced unemployment compensation rates by making *voluntary contributions* to the state fund. Employers deliberately make these contributions in addition to their regularly required payments of state unemployment taxes. The voluntary contributions increase the balance in the employer's reserve account so that a lower contribution rate may be assigned for the following year. Thus, the new lower tax rate will save the employer more in future state unemployment tax payments than the amount of the voluntary contribution itself.

E X A M P L E

To illustrate the tax saving that may be realized as a result of making voluntary contributions, consider the following case of the Werner Company, which is subject to the unemployment compensation law of a state that uses the reserve-ratio formula to determine experience ratings. The following contribution rate schedule applies for 2004:

Reserve Ratio	Rate
0% to less than 1%	6.2%
1% to less than 1.4%	5.6%
1.4% to less than 1.8%	5.0%
1.8% to less than 2.2%	4.4%
2.2% to less than 2.6%	3.8%
2.6% to less than 3.0%	3.2%
3.0% and over	2.6%

For the three 12-month periods ending on June 30, 2003, the company had an average annual taxable payroll of $330,000. This is the base that the state uses as the average payroll. As of June 30, 2003, the credits to the employer's account exceeded the benefits paid by $6,800. Thus, the 2004 reserve ratio is 2.06% ($6,800 ÷ $330,000), which would result in the assignment of a 4.4% tax rate, as shown in the preceding table. If the employer's 2004 total taxable payroll were $390,000, the SUTA contribution would amount to $17,160.

If the Werner Company makes a voluntary contribution into the state fund within the time period specified by the state law, the tax for 2004 will be less. For example, if the company contributes $460, the reserve ratio will be 2.2% ($7,260 ÷ $330,000). As a result, the tax rate will be reduced to 3.8%, with the following savings realized in 2004:

Tax Payment with No Voluntary Contribution (4.4% × $390,000) =		$17,160
Tax Payment with Voluntary Contribution	$ 460	
(3.8% × $390,000) =	14,820	15,280
Tax Savings		$ 1,880

An employer who desires to make a voluntary contribution usually must determine the amount of the contribution needed in order to obtain a lower contribution rate. In some states, the agencies provide worksheets that aid employers in determining the amount of voluntary contributions required. California and Ohio compute the voluntary contribution amount needed and include it in the rate notices sent to all employers. Instead, the state may give the employer credit against any future SUTA taxes due. As with the regular contributions, the state must receive the voluntary contributions by a certain date before they can be credited to the employer's account and be used in computing a new tax rate. In some states, the employer may have a certain number of days following the mailing of the tax rate notice to make the voluntary contributions. For instance, in Arizona, the voluntary contributions must be paid by January 31. In West Virginia, the contribution must be sent in within 30 days of the mailing of the rate notice.

News ALERT

If there are unpaid taxes and penalties due, states may apply the voluntary contributions to these amounts first.

UNEMPLOYMENT COMPENSATION REPORTS REQUIRED OF THE EMPLOYER

Employers liable for both the FUTA and the SUTA tax must file periodic reports with both the federal and the state governments. For FUTA tax reporting, employers file an annual return (either Form 940 or 940-EZ) and generally make quarterly tax payments. Also, employers covered by state unemployment compensation laws generally submit two major kinds of reports. One is a tax return, on which the employer reports the tax due the state. The other is a wage report, which reflects the amount of taxable wages paid to each of the employer's covered employees.

6 LEARNING OBJECTIVE

Annual FUTA Return—Form 940

Form 940, Employer's Annual Federal Unemployment (FUTA) Tax Return, is the prescribed form for making the return required of employers in reporting the tax imposed under FUTA. Figure 5–2 shows a filled-in copy of this form.

FIGURE 5-2

Form 940, Employer's Annual Federal Unemployment (FUTA) Tax Return (page 1)

Be sure to complete both sides of this form, and sign in the space provided on the back.

(continued on next page)

Completing the Return. Employers complete Questions A, B, and C. If the employer answers "NO" to any of the questions, Form 940 must be completed. The information needed to complete Form 940 may be obtained from the sources listed in Figure 5–3 (see page 5-22). If all of these questions are answered "YES," the employer can file the simplified annual tax return, Form 940-EZ, shown in Figure 5–4 (see page 5-23).

Payment of Balance Due. After computing the final net FUTA tax (Part II, Line 7), the employer compares the net tax with the total deposits for the year in order to determine the balance due. Depending on the amount of the liability, the employer either deposits the balance due, electronically transfers, or remits it directly to the IRS with Form 940.

Not Liable. If an employer who is not liable for FUTA tax receives a FORM 940, the employer should write "NOT LIABLE" on the face of the form, sign the return, and mail it to the IRS.

F I G U R E　5 - 2　*(concluded)*

Form 940, Employer's Annual Federal Unemployment (FUTA) Tax Return (page 2)

Form 940 (2003)　　　　　　　　　　　　　　　　　　　　　　　　　　　　　　Page **2**

Part II　**Tax Due or Refund**

1	Gross FUTA tax. Multiply the wages from Part I, line 5, by .062 . . . . **1**	3745 59
2	Maximum credit. Multiply the wages from Part I, line 5, by .054 . . **2**　　　3262 29	

3　Computation of tentative credit (**Note:** *All taxpayers must complete the applicable columns.*)

(a) Name of state	(b) State reporting number(s) as shown on employer's state contribution returns	(c) Taxable payroll (as defined in state act)	(d) State experience rate period From	To	(e) State experience rate	(f) Contributions if rate had been 5.4% (col. (c) x .054)	(g) Contributions payable at experience rate (col. (c) x col. (e))	(h) Additional credit (col. (f) minus col.(g)) If 0 or less, enter -0-.	(i) Contributions paid to state by 940 due date
PA	20747	40,000.00	1/1	12/31	2.4	2160.00	960.00	1200.00	960.00
IN	83-48032	7040.58	1/1	12/31	2.2	380.19	154.89	225.30	154.89
KY	7321	13372.22	1/1	12/31	2.0	722.10	267.44	454.66	267.44

3a	Totals . . . ▶　　60412.80		1879.96	1382.33
3b	**Total tentative credit** (add line 3a, columns (h) and (i) only　for late payments, also see the instructions for Part II, line 6) . . . . ▶　**3b**		3262	29
4				
5				
6	**Credit:** Enter the smaller of the amount from Part II, line 2 or line 3b; or the amount from the worksheet in the Part II, line 6 instructions **6**		3262	29
7	**Total FUTA tax** (subtract line 6 from line 1). If the result is over $100, also complete Part III . . **7**		483	30
8	Total FUTA tax deposited for the year, including any overpayment applied from a prior year . . **8**		483	30
9	**Balance due** (subtract line 8 from line 7). Pay to the **"United States Treasury."** If you owe more than $100, see **Depositing FUTA Tax** on page 3 of the separate instructions . . . . ▶　**9**		-0-	
10	**Overpayment** (subtract line 7 from line 8). Check if it is to be: ☐ **Applied to next return** or ☐ **Refunded** . . . . ▶　**10**			

Part III　**Record of Quarterly Federal Unemployment Tax Liability** (Do not include state liability.) **Complete only if** line 7 is over $100. See page 6 of the separate instructions.

Quarter	First (Jan. 1 Mar. 31)	Second (Apr. 1 June 30)	Third (July 1 Sept. 30)	Fourth (Oct. 1 Dec. 31)	Total for year
Liability for quarter	203.42	159.95	98.83	21.10	483.30

Third Party Designee　Do you want to allow another person to discuss this return with the IRS (see instructions page 4)? ☐ **Yes.** Complete the following. ☐ **No**

Designee's name ▶　　　　Phone no. ▶ (　　)　　　　Personal identification number (PIN) ▶ ☐☐☐☐☐

Under penalties of perjury, I declare that I have examined this return, including accompanying schedules and statements, and, to the best of my knowledge and belief, it is true, correct, and complete, and that no part of any payment made to a state unemployment fund claimed as a credit was, or is to be, deducted from the payments to employees.

Signature ▶　*J. D. Shannon*　　　Title (Owner, etc.) ▶　Owner　　　Date ▶　2/02/04

Signing Form 940.　Form 940 must be signed by:

1. The individual, if a sole proprietorship.

2. The president, vice president, or other principal officer, if a corporation.

3. A responsible and duly authorized member, if a partnership or other unincorporated organization.

4. A fiduciary, if a trust or estate.

Filing the Return.　The employer must file the annual return no later than January 31 following the close of the calendar year. If, however, the employer has made timely deposits that pay the FUTA tax liability in full, as discussed below, the company may delay the filing of Form 940 until February 10. The return must be filed on a calendar-year basis even though the company operates on a fiscal-year basis different from the calendar year. If January 31 falls on Saturday, Sunday, or a legal holiday, the return may be filed on the following business day. A mailed return bearing a postmark indicating it was mailed on or

on the

If only household employees are involved, the employer need not make deposits or file Form 940. Instead, the information is reported and the tax is paid with the employer's individual income tax return (Form 1040 with Schedule H attached).

FIGURE   5 - 3

Sources of Information for Completing Form 940

Line No.	Source of Information
A	State unemployment tax forms
B	General ledger account for SUTA Taxes Payable
C	State unemployment tax forms

Part I—Computation of Taxable Wages

1	General ledger account(s) for wages and salaries
2	Personnel records, time sheets, and employee earnings records
3	Employee earnings records
4	Follow directions for addition.
5	Follow directions for subtraction.

Part II—Tax Due or Refund

1 and 2	Follow directions for multiplication.
3	From the appropriate states' unemployment tax returns
6	Determine the smaller of Part II, line 2, or line 3b.
7	Follow the directions for subtraction.
8	General ledger account for FUTA Taxes Payable
9 and 10	Compare the net tax with the total deposits for the year.

Part III—Record of Quarterly Federal Unemployment Tax Liability

1	From the quarterly balances in the FUTA taxes payable account in the general ledger

before the due date will be considered to have been timely filed even though received after the due date.

Upon application of the employer, the district director or the director of a service center may grant a reasonable extension of time in which to file the return, but not for payment of the tax. However, no extension will be granted for a period of more than 90 days. Generally, the application for an extension must be written on or before the filing due date. The return must be filed with the IRS center for the district in which the employer's principal place of business or office or agency is located. The instructions for Form 940 list the addresses of the IRS centers.

Once an employer has filed Form 940, the IRS will send the employer a preaddressed Form 940 near the close of each subsequent calendar year.

Electronic Filing.   Under the 940 e-filing program, businesses can use a personal computer, modem, and specialized software to file Forms 940. They must submit their electronic forms through a third-party transmitter. Filers must first submit an electronic letter of application to the IRS through their transmitter.

Amending the Return.   When filing a corrected return, the employer must complete a new Form 940 for the year being amended. The "Amended Return" box on Form 940 should be checked, and the correct figures should be completed on the form. The return must be signed, and an explanation of the reasons for filing an amended return should be attached.

Final Return.   If a company has ceased doing business, a final Form 940 must be completed (check box on Form 940 to indicate a final return) and the balance of the tax paid. In addition, a statement giving the name and address of the person(s) in charge of the required payroll records must be included with Form 940.

FIGURE 5-4

Form 940-EZ, Employer's Annual Federal Unemployment (FUTA) Tax Return

Form **940-EZ**

Department of the Treasury
Internal Revenue Service   (99)

Employer's Annual Federal Unemployment (FUTA) Tax Return

OMB No. 1545-1110

20**03**

▶ See separate Instructions for Form 940-EZ for information on completing this form.

T	
FF	
FD	
FP	
I	
T	

You must complete this section. ▶

Name (as distinguished from trade name)

Trade name, if any
YANGO SUPPLY COMPANY

Address and ZIP code
13 M STREET
SALEM, OR 97311-9595

Calendar year
2003

Employer identification number
15 8590113

Answer the questions under **Who May Use Form 940-EZ** on page 2. If you cannot use Form 940-EZ, you must use Form 940.

A Enter the amount of contributions paid to your state unemployment fund. (see separate instructions) . . . ▶ $ ....12410|00...

B (1) Enter the name of the state where you have to pay contributions . . . . ▶ Oregon................

(2) Enter your state reporting number as shown on your state unemployment tax return ▶ 163-97557

If you will not have to file returns in the future, check here (see **Who Must File** in separate instructions), and complete and sign the return. ▶ ☐

If this is an Amended Return, check here . . . . ▶ ☐

Part I   **Taxable Wages and FUTA Tax**

1	Total payments (including payments shown on lines 2 and 3) during the calendar year for services of employees	**1**	478231	19
2	Exempt payments. (Explain all exempt payments, attaching additional sheets if necessary.) ▶	**2**		
3	Payments of more than $7,000 for services. Enter only amounts over the first $7,000 paid to each employee. **(see separate instructions)**	**3** 303231 19		
4	Add lines 2 and 3	**4**	303231	19
5	**Total taxable wages** (subtract line 4 from line 1) . . . . ▶	**5**	175000	00
6	**FUTA tax.** Multiply the wages on line 5 by .008 and enter here. **(If the result is over $100, also complete Part II.)**	**6**	1400	00
7	Total FUTA tax deposited for the year, including any overpayment applied from a prior year	**7**	1400	00
8	**Balance due** (subtract line 7 from line 6). Pay to the "United States Treasury." . . . . ▶	**8**	−0−	
	If you owe more than $100, see **Depositing FUTA tax** in separate instructions.			
9	Overpayment (subtract line 6 from line 7). Check if it is to be: ☐ Applied to next return or ☐ Refunded ▶	**9**		

Part II   **Record of Quarterly Federal Unemployment Tax Liability** (Do not include state liability.) **Complete only if line 6 is over $100.**

Quarter	First (Jan. 1 – Mar. 31)	Second (Apr. 1 – June 30)	Third (July 1 – Sept. 30)	Fourth (Oct. 1 – Dec. 31)	Total for year
Liability for quarter	719.90	360.18	319.92	−0−	1400.00

Third Party Designee

Do you want to allow another person to discuss this return with the IRS (see instructions page 4)? ☐ **Yes.** Complete the following. ☐ **No**

Designee's name ▶

Phone no. ▶ ( )

Personal identification number (PIN) ▶

Under penalties of perjury, I declare that I have examined this return, including accompanying schedules and statements, and, to the best of my knowledge and belief, it is true, correct, and complete, and that no part of any payment made to a state unemployment fund claimed as a credit was, or is to be, deducted from the payments to employees.

Signature ▶ *William H. Yango*   Title (Owner, etc.) ▶ President   Date ▶ 2/02/04

Annual FUTA Return—Form 940-EZ

Employers who have uncomplicated tax situations may use a streamlined Form 940. In order to use *Form 940-EZ, Employer's Annual Federal Unemployment (FUTA) Tax Return*, an employer must satisfy three simple tests:

1. Must have paid state unemployment taxes to only one state.
2. Must have made the state unemployment tax payments by the due date of Form 940-EZ (January 31).
3. All wages that were taxable for FUTA purposes were also taxable for state unemployment tax purposes.

Quarterly Deposit Form—FUTA

The employer computes the net FUTA tax on a quarterly basis during the month following the end of each calendar quarter by multiplying 0.8% by that part of the first $7,000 of each of the employee's annual wages that the employer paid during the quarter. If the employer's tax liability exceeds $100, the employer must deposit it with an authorized depository on or before the last day of the month following the end of the quarter. If the employer deposits social security (FICA) and withheld federal income taxes (FIT) electronically, the employer is required to deposit all federal depository tax liabilities (including FUTA) electronically. Chapter 3 enumerated the requirements for each employer.

A similar computation and deposit for each of the first three quarters of the year is made. Each quarterly deposit for the coupon-based deposit system is to be accompanied by a pre-inscribed *Federal Tax Deposit Coupon (Form 8109)*. Figure 5–5 shows a filled-in copy of this deposit form. If the tax liability for the first quarter is $100 or less, a deposit is not required; however, the employer must add the amount of the liability to the amount subject to deposit for the next quarter, in order to compare the total tax due with the $100 minimum for that quarter.

If the employer is required to deposit employment taxes electronically (see Chapter 3), the quarterly FUTA taxes must also be paid using the EFTPS.

EXAMPLE

As shown in Figure 5–2, the tax liability of the Shannon Heating Company for the 1st quarter of 2003 was $203.42; since the liability exceeded $100, a deposit was made on April 30, 2003. The tax liability for the 2nd quarter was $159.95, and a deposit was made on July 31, 2003. The tax liability for the 3rd quarter was $98.83, but since this amount was less than the $100 limit, no deposit was required. The tax liability for the 4th quarter was $21.10. Since the accumulated liability of $119.93 exceeded the $100 limit, a deposit of $119.93 was made on February 2, 2004, as shown on Form 8109 in Figure 5–5.

At the time of filing the annual return on Form 940, the employer pays the balance of tax owed for the prior year and not yet deposited. If the amount of tax reportable on Form 940 exceeds by more than $100 the sum of amounts deposited each quarter, the employer must deposit the total amount owed either electronically or by using Form 8109 on or before January 31 following the year for which Form 940 is filed. If the amount owed is $100 or less, the employer may remit it with the annual form. A voucher (Form 940-V), attached to the bottom of Form 940, should be filled in if payment accompanies the filing.

FIGURE 5-5

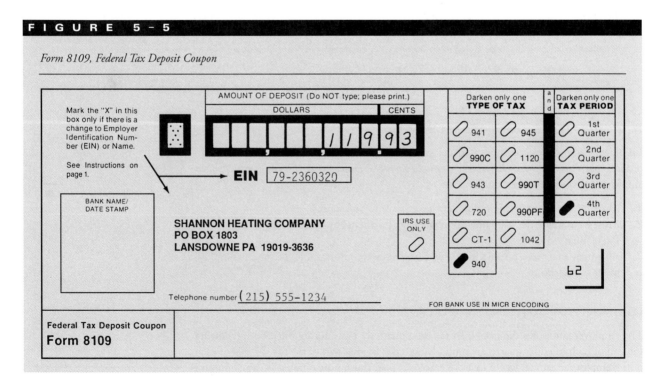

Form 8109, Federal Tax Deposit Coupon

SELF-STUDY QUIZ 5–3. *The FUTA taxable wages of Davies Company during 2003 follows. List the amount and the due date of each deposit of FUTA taxes for the year.*

	Amount	Due Date
1st Quarter—$22,000	$_____	_____
2nd Quarter—$24,000	$_____	_____
3rd Quarter—$12,000	$_____	_____
4th Quarter—$10,000	$_____	_____

Penalties—FUTA

As indicated in Chapter 3, the Internal Revenue Code subjects employers to civil and criminal penalties for failing to file returns, pay the employment taxes when due, and make timely deposits. These penalties apply, generally, without regard to the type of tax or return involved. The last section of Chapter 3 presents all of the penalties.

Information Reports—SUTA

A wide variation exists in the official forms that the states provide for filing the reports required under the unemployment compensation laws. Therefore, the employer must become familiar with the law and regulations of each state in which liability might be incurred.

    The reports required of the employers by the individual states determine: (1) the employer's liability for the contributions, (2) the amount of the contribution due on a quarterly basis, and (3) the amount of benefits to which employees will be entitled if they become unemployed. The most important of the required reports follow:

7 LEARNING OBJECTIVE

1. Status reports
2. Contribution reports
3. Wage information reports
4. Separation reports
5. Partial unemployment notices

Status Reports. Under the unemployment compensation laws of most states, new employers must register or file an initial statement or *status report.* This report determines the employer's liability for making contributions into the state unemployment compensation fund.

Contribution Reports. All employers liable for contributions under the unemployment compensation law of any state must submit a quarterly *contribution report* or tax return. This report provides a summary of the wages paid during the period and shows the computation of the tax or contribution. Usually, the report must be filed on or before the last day of the month following the close of the calendar quarter, and the tax or contribution must be paid at the same time. Figure 5–6 shows an illustration of a quarterly tax calculation report.

Wage Information Reports. In most states employers must make *wage information reports* concerning individual employees. Usually, employers file these reports with the quarterly contribution reports. Figure 5–7 on page 5-27 shows an example of a quarterly wage information report. On the report are listed all employee names, SSNs, taxable wages, taxable tips, and the employer's federal account number. In addition, the number of credit weeks earned by each employee during the quarter could be required. (A *credit week* is defined by the state's unemployment compensation law; for example, Pennsylvania defines

News ALERT

As part of a feasibility study, employers in Montana are filing just one form for both federal and state unemployment purposes. The form is filed with the state, which then electronically forwards the federal data to the IRS.

FIGURE 5-6

Pennsylvania Form, UC-2. Employer's Report for Unemployment Compensation

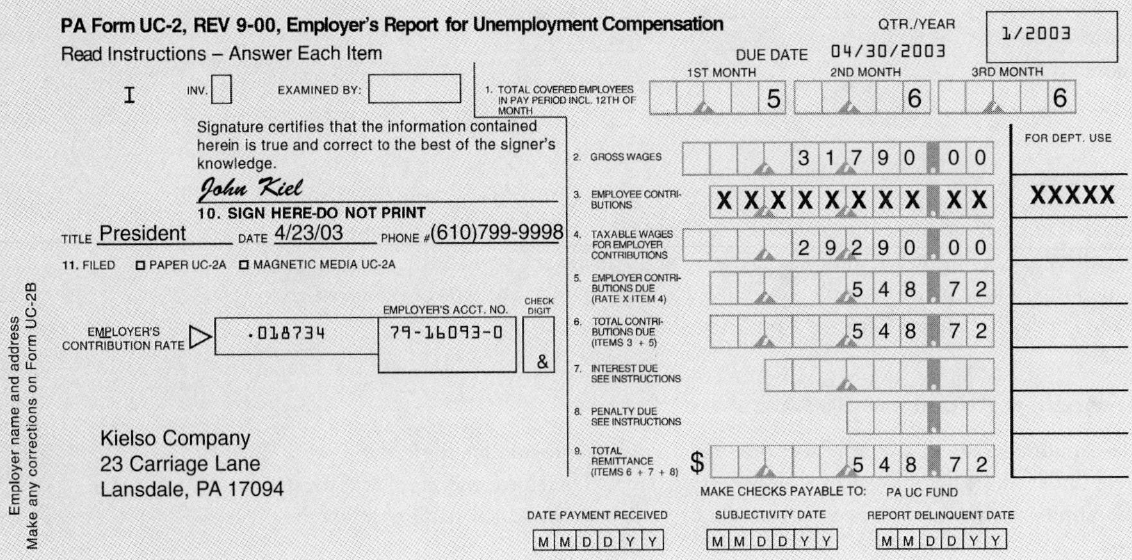
PA Form UC-2, REV 9-00, Employer's Report for Unemployment Compensation
Read Instructions – Answer Each Item

QTR./YEAR 1/2003
DUE DATE 04/30/2003

I INV. EXAMINED BY:

1. TOTAL COVERED EMPLOYEES IN PAY PERIOD INCL. 12TH OF MONTH — 1ST MONTH 5; 2ND MONTH 6; 3RD MONTH 6

Signature certifies that the information contained herein is true and correct to the best of the signer's knowledge.

John Kiel
10. SIGN HERE-DO NOT PRINT

TITLE President DATE 4/23/03 PHONE #(610)799-9998

11. FILED ☐ PAPER UC-2A ☐ MAGNETIC MEDIA UC-2A

		FOR DEPT. USE
2. GROSS WAGES	31790 00	
3. EMPLOYEE CONTRIBUTIONS	XXXXXXXX XX	XXXXX
4. TAXABLE WAGES FOR EMPLOYER CONTRIBUTIONS	29290 00	
5. EMPLOYER CONTRIBUTIONS DUE (RATE X ITEM 4)	548 72	
6. TOTAL CONTRIBUTIONS DUE (ITEMS 3 + 5)	548 72	
7. INTEREST DUE SEE INSTRUCTIONS		
8. PENALTY DUE SEE INSTRUCTIONS		
9. TOTAL REMITTANCE (ITEMS 6 + 7 + 8)	$ 548 72	

EMPLOYER'S CONTRIBUTION RATE ▷ .018734
EMPLOYER'S ACCT. NO. 79-16093-0
CHECK DIGIT &

MAKE CHECKS PAYABLE TO: PA UC FUND

Employer name and address
Make any corrections on Form UC-2B

Kielso Company
23 Carriage Lane
Lansdale, PA 17094

DATE PAYMENT RECEIVED M M D D Y Y
SUBJECTIVITY DATE M M D D Y Y
REPORT DELINQUENT DATE M M D D Y Y

a credit week as any calendar week in the quarter during which the person earned remuneration of not less than $50.)

Most states permit the use of the same magnetic tape for reporting state wage information that is used for federal social security reporting purposes. The payroll manager should contact the state agency to determine whether federal-state combined magnetic tape reporting is acceptable.

Separation Reports. Whenever a worker becomes separated from employment, a ***separation report,*** providing a wage and employment record of the separated employee and the reason for leaving, might be required. Usually, a copy of the report is given to the worker in order that the individual may be informed of any entitlement to unemployment insurance benefits.

Partial Unemployment Notices. Most states require employers to give ***partial unemployment notices*** to those workers who become "partially unemployed," so that they are informed of their potential eligibility for partial unemployment benefits. ***Partial unemployment*** refers to employment by the individual's regular employer but on a reduced scale because of lack of work. In most states, the notice must be given to the worker immediately after a week of partial employment has been completed. After that, the employer ordinarily furnishes the worker with some kind of low-earnings report during each week of partial employment so that the worker will be assured of the receipt of supplemental or partial benefits.

on the JOB

State unemployment insurance records must be preserved by employers for a certain number of years based on each state's requirements. The minimum periods range from a low in Mississippi of three years to a high in Tennessee of seven years.

Penalties—SUTA

All states have some form of penalty for failure to pay, for the late payment of contributions, and also for failure to file reports. Some states impose a 10% penalty if the failure to pay the tax is due to negligence, and in a few states, a 50% penalty is imposed if the fail-

FIGURE 5-7

Pennsylvania Form, UC-2A. Employer's Report for Unemployment Compensation

PA Form UC-2A, Rev 6-2000, Employer's Quarterly Report of Wages Paid to Each Employee

See instructions on separate sheet. Information MUST be typewritten or printed in BLACK ink. Do NOT use commas (,) or dollar signs ($). If typed, disregard vertical bars and type a consecutive string of characters. If hand printed, print in CAPS and within the boxes as below:

SAMPLE Typed: `1 2 3 4 5 6 . 0 0`   **SAMPLE Handwritten:** `1 2 3 4 5 6 . 0 0`   **SAMPLE Filled-in:** → ●

Employer name (make corrections on Form UC-2B)	Employer PA UC account no.	Check digit	Quarter and year Q/YYYY	Quarter ending date MM/DD/YYYY
Kielso Company	79-16093-0	&	1/2003	03/31/2003

1. Name and telephone number of preparer

Nancy Heller
(215) 557-1212

2. Total number of pages in this report: **1**

3. Total number of employees listed in item 8 on all pages of Form UC-2A: **7**

4. Plant number (if approved)

5. Gross wages, MUST agree with item 2 on UC-2 and the sum of item 11 on all pages of Form UC-2A

`3 1 7 9 0 . 0 0`

6. Fill in this circle if you would like the Department to preprint your employees names & SSNs on Form UC-2A next quarter → ●

7. Employee's social security number	8. Employee's name FI MI LAST	9. Gross wages paid this qtr Example: ***123456.00	10. Credit weeks
1 1 1 0 9 8 2 7 1	J L CARROLL	6 3 0 0 . 0 0	1 3
0 9 5 1 9 1 9 1 8	C H LONG	1 9 0 0 . 0 0	5
2 1 2 1 6 3 7 9 0	H M DORSEY	2 9 9 0 . 0 0	1 3
0 9 1 7 8 6 5 1 0	M F ERNST	2 1 0 0 . 0 0	1 3
1 0 9 0 5 0 0 9 3	J B KIEL	1 0 5 0 0 . 0 0	1 3
1 7 0 9 1 9 0 0 8	A W PINKETT	4 1 0 0 . 0 0	1 3
0 8 9 8 7 1 7 9 2	L B GOLIC	3 9 0 0 . 0 0	1 3

List any additional employees on continuation sheets in the required format (see instructions).

▲ Batch #   For Dept. Use Only

11. Total gross wages for this page: → `3 1 7 9 0 . 0 0` ▲

12. Page 1 of 1

ure to pay is due to fraud. Many states also deny experience rates to employers who are delinquent in filing reports or paying contributions. In some states, employers who have been delinquent in paying their contributions may be required to pay the contributions monthly rather than quarterly.

UNEMPLOYMENT COMPENSATION BENEFITS

Unemployment compensation benefits, payments made to workers temporarily unemployed, are provided primarily under the unemployment compensation law of each state. Each state specifies the qualifications to be met by the unemployed worker in order to be eligible for benefits, the amount of the benefits to be paid each individual, and the duration of the period for which benefits will be paid.

As discussed in Chapter 4, payers of unemployment compensation benefits must send copies of Form 1099-G to the Internal Revenue Service and to the person receiving the benefits. This form is used only when the total benefits paid are $10 or more. These benefits are includable in the recipient's gross income for federal income tax purposes.

Employee Benefits—SUTA

There is no uniform rate of unemployment benefits payable by all states. The amount of the benefits that an unemployed worker is entitled to receive usually is about 50% of the regular weekly wages subject to minimum and maximum amounts specified by the state's law. Maximum weekly benefits vary widely among states, from 50% to 70% of average weekly wages. Figure 5–1 shows the minimum and maximum amounts of benefits (excluding dependency allowances) provided under the laws of each state. The maximum amount of benefits allowed under the various state laws ranges from 26 to 30 times the individual's weekly benefit amount.

Dependency Allowances. The state unemployment compensation laws often provide for payment of a *dependency allowance,* which is an additional weekly benefit to unemployed workers with dependents. For example, Connecticut provides for a weekly dependency allowance of $10 each for the claimant's nonworking spouse and each child and stepchild (but for no more than five dependents). However, the total dependency allowance cannot exceed 50% of the benefit otherwise payable to the claimant. In those states that provide dependency allowances, the allowances are sometimes made only to workers with dependent children of a stipulated age.

LEARNING OBJECTIVE

Eligibility for Benefits. The unemployment compensation laws of all the states require that a claimant meet certain conditions before becoming eligible to receive benefits. An analysis of the required qualifications in most states reveals that the claimant must:

1. File a claim for benefits.
2. Be able to work.
3. Be available for work.
4. Be actively seeking work or making a reasonable effort to obtain work.
5. Have earned a certain amount of wages or worked a certain number of weeks in covered employment.
6. Have registered at the local state employment office.
7. Have served the required waiting period.
8. Not be disqualified under any of the other provisions of the law.

on the
JOB

Companies can take the following steps to prevent undeserving employees from collecting benefits:
• Complete separation reports
• Written evidence
• Clearly stated terms of employment
• Copies of company's employee policies
• Use probationary periods
• Require written resignations
• Report to state all supplemental payments to ex-employees

Disqualification of Benefits. Certain disqualifications are set up in the state laws to conserve the funds and to ensure the intended purpose of *unemployment insurance,* which is to compensate for involuntary unemployment. While wide variation occurs in the state laws, some of the more common reasons for disqualification include the following:

1. Discharge for misconduct.
2. Voluntarily leaving work without good cause.
3. Unemployment due to a labor dispute.[2]
4. Leaving work to attend school.
5. Commitment to a penal institution.
6. False or fraudulent representation to obtain benefits.
7. Refusal of suitable employment.
8. Receipt of certain kinds of remuneration.

Most state laws provide that an unemployed individual shall not be entitled to unemployment compensation benefits during any week in which the person receives remuneration from other sources, such as workers' compensation for temporary partial disability, old-age benefits under the Social Security Act, vacation allowances, dismissal wages, earnings from self-employment, or unemployment compensation benefits from another state. In some cases, however, if such remuneration is less than the benefits due the individual, the person shall receive the amount of the benefits less such remuneration.

In cases of conflict over the reasons for the worker's separation from employment, the burden of proving that the separation was not voluntary rests with the claimant. If it is found that the claimant quit, proof must be submitted that the claimant did so for reasons that are considered necessitous and compelling under the law.

Tracking Recipients. New hire reports are now being used by some states to reduce unemployment insurance taxes. These reports are matched with unemployment claims to identify people who continue to accept unemployment insurance benefits after they have become reemployed.

Benefits for the Unemployed as a Result of a Major Disaster. The Disaster Relief Act provides unemployment benefits to persons who become unemployed as a result of a major disaster. The benefits will be available so long as the individual's unemployment caused by a major disaster continues or until the individual is reemployed in a suitable position. In no event, however, will the benefits be paid for longer than one year after the disaster has been declared.

Benefits for Federal Employees. The Federal Employee Unemployment Compensation program of the Social Security Act provides unemployment insurance for federal civilian employees. If a federal civilian worker becomes unemployed, eligibility for benefits is determined under the unemployment law of the state in which the person last worked in federal civilian employment. If eligible, the person is entitled to unemployment benefits in the amounts and under the conditions provided by the state unemployment insurance law.

Benefits for Ex-Service Personnel. The Federal Unemployment Compensation for Ex-Servicemen program of the Social Security Act provides unemployment compensation benefits for ex-service personnel. The benefits are determined by the unemployment insurance law of the state in which the person first files a claim that establishes a benefit year as the most recent separation from active military service.

Disability Benefits. Five states—California, Hawaii, New Jersey, New York, and Rhode Island—and Puerto Rico provide for the payment of *disability benefits* to workers who suffer wage losses through unemployment due to nonoccupational disease or injury. The programs in these states have developed in response to the need for protecting workers not eligible for either workers' compensation or unemployment insurance benefits. The programs are not health insurance as such, for benefits are paid only to offset the wage loss of an employee who becomes sick or suffers an accident not connected with work.

on the
JOB
In the matching process, the state of Illinois found more than 38,000 improper benefit payments totaling $3.3 million over a 16-month period.

---

2 Most states provide benefits to strikers who have been replaced by nonstriking employees, and many states allow strikers to collect benefits in cases where their employers continue to operate.

Payments of disability benefits under the state laws are, for the most part, financed by employee contributions. In Hawaii, New Jersey, New York, and Puerto Rico, however, employers are required to contribute. In California, New Jersey, and Puerto Rico, the benefits are provided under a state-administered plan, but employers may substitute their own plans if they so wish. However, such "private" or "voluntary" plans must provide benefits at least as favorable as those payable under the state plan.

Supplemental Unemployment Benefits (SUB).   Many union contracts provide for the private supplementation of state unemployment compensation benefits to provide payments to employees during periods of layoff. In nearly all of the states that have investigated the *Supplemental Unemployment Benefits (SUB)* plan benefits in relation to state unemployment compensation benefits, it has been ruled that workers who receive SUB may also simultaneously be paid unemployment compensation benefits. A SUB plan is usually one of two types: (a) the *pooled-fund plan* or (b) the *individual-account plan.*

Pooled-Fund Plan.

This plan, also known as the "auto" or "Ford-type" plan, is the most common type of SUB plan. Under this plan, employers contribute to a general fund a certain number of cents for each hour worked by employees currently on the job. Employees usually have a right to benefits from the fund only upon layoff and only after meeting stipulated eligibility requirements.

Individual-Account Plan.

Under this plan, found mainly in the plate glass industry, contributions are paid to separate trusts for each employee, and the employee has a vested and nonforfeitable right to the amount in the fund. Workers are entitled to the fund upon layoff and have a right to the fund when their employment is terminated. In the event the worker dies, the designated beneficiary receives the content of the trust.

Work Sharing Program.

The Department of Labor allows states to establish programs that provide unemployment benefits to workers whose hours have been reduced. Under this work sharing plan, the employer can reduce employees' workweek instead of laying off people. All employees would then be eligible for a proportionate share of their unemployment benefits.

Currently, seventeen states allow for working sharing programs. In each of these states, the employer must first submit a plan to the state for approval.

Summary of Source and Duration of Benefits

Figure 5–8 shows how the federal-state unemployment insurance system operates in a state in which the basic duration of benefits is 26 weeks. In addition to the basic 26 weeks, in times of high unemployment, legislation has been enacted that extends the federal-state benefits program.

on the
JOB

In Europe, jobless benefits are commonly paid to employees of companies that reduce the hours of all employees rather than lay off individual employees.

FIGURE   5 - 8

Sources and Duration of Benefits

Weeks of Unemployment	Source of Benefits	Starting Point	Life of Program
1st to 26th	Regular state program (funded entirely from state unemployment accounts)	Operates continuously	Permanent
27th to 52nd	Federal program—Job Creation and Worker Assistance	In states where unemployment tops 4%	12/31/02

KEY TERMS

Constructively paid *(p. 5-10)*
Contribution report *(p. 5-25)*
Dependency allowance *(p. 5-28)*
Disability benefits *(p. 5-29)*
Dismissal payments *(p. 5-10)*
Experience rating *(p. 5-11)*
Individual-account plan *(p. 5-30)*
Interstate employee *(p. 5-6)*
Merit rating *(p. 5-11)*
Negative-balance employers *(p. 5-16)*
Partial unemployment *(p. 5-26)*
Partial unemployment notices *(p. 5-26)*
Pooled-fund laws *(p. 5-12)*

Pooled-fund plan *(p. 5-30)*
Positive-balance employers *(p. 5-16)*
Reciprocal arrangements *(p. 5-8)*
Reserve-ratio formula *(p. 5-16)*
Separation report *(p. 5-26)*
Status report *(p. 5-25)*
Supplemental Unemployment Benefits (SUB) *(p. 5-30)*
Title XII advances *(p. 5-12)*
Unemployment compensation benefits *(p. 5-28)*
Unemployment insurance *(p. 5-28)*
Voluntary contributions *(p. 5-18)*
Wage information reports *(p. 5-25)*

MATCHING QUIZ

_____ 1. Reciprocal arrangements

_____ 2. Title XII advances

_____ 3. Negative-balance employers

_____ 4. Form 940-EZ

_____ 5. Disability benefits

_____ 6. Merit rating

_____ 7. Form 8109

_____ 8. Job Creation and Worker Assistance Act

_____ 9. Wage information reports

_____10. Voluntary contributions

A. Extra state unemployment contributions in addition to employers' regular SUTA tax payments

B. Favorable employment records results in a lower SUTA tax

C. Federal tax deposit coupon

D. Employer's annual FUTA Tax return

E. Provided for additional 26 weeks of unemployment benefits

F. Provide unemployment insurance coverage and payment of benefits to interstate workers

G. Borrowings from federal government to pay unemployment compensation benefits

H. Employers whose reserve account has been charged with more benefits paid out than contributions made

I. Payments made to workers who lose wages due to nonoccupational injury

J. Quarterly reports submitted to the state listing employees, SSN's, and taxable wages.

QUESTIONS FOR REVIEW

1. How are the employer's contributions to FUTA used by the federal government?
2. What two alternative tests are applied to a business in order to judge whether it is an "employer" and, therefore, subject to the FUTA tax?
3. To what extent does FUTA coverage extend to services that a citizen of the United States performs for an American employer outside the United States?
4. Charlie Carlson is a full-time student at Wenonah College and works part-time in the school's maintenance

department. Must the college pay a FUTA tax on Charlie's earnings?
5. Under the Interstate Reciprocal Coverage Arrangement, the services of a worker can be covered in the state of the election of the employer as long as one of three factors exists. What are those three conditions?
6. Which of the following types of payments are taxable under FUTA?
   a. Commissions as compensation for covered employment.

b. Christmas gifts of nominal value.

c. Courtesy discounts to employees.

d. Reimbursement of ordinary and necessary business expenses.

e. Dismissal payments.

7. What is an employer required to do in order to obtain the maximum credit of 5.4% against the FUTA tax?

8. An employer, because of a favorable experience rating, is permitted to pay a state contribution at a reduced rate of 1.5%. What percentage of taxable wages must be paid in the aggregate to the federal and state governments?

9. What are two situations in which an employer could be liable for a net FUTA tax greater than 0.8%?

10. What is the purpose of Title XII advances?

11. How is the SUTA tax rate determined for a new employer?

12. In 2002:
   a. Which state had the widest range of SUTA tax rates for employers?
   b. Which state paid the highest weekly maximum benefit (excluding dependency allowances) to qualified unemployed workers?

   c. Which state had the highest taxable wage base for the SUTA tax?

13. a. For an employer who is subject to FUTA, what are the basic forms that must be filed with the federal government?
   b. When must these forms be filed?
   c. How are taxable wages computed on the annual return?

14. What special steps must be taken when completing Form 940 for a company that has ceased operations during the year?

15. Which employers can file Form 940-EZ?

16. When does an employer have to pay the FUTA taxes?

17. What is a separation report?

18. What is covered by California's disability benefit plan?

19. What percentage of an employee's weekly wage is paid to the employee as an unemployment benefit?

20. How often do employers file wage and contribution reports with their states?

QUESTIONS FOR DISCUSSION

1. Can the owner of a small business receive unemployment compensation? Explain.

2. What arguments could be made for raising the upper limits of the SUTA tax rates?

3. Check the unemployment compensation law of your state and determine the answers to the following questions:
   a. How do nonprofit organizations, subject to coverage, make payments to the unemployment compensation fund?
   b. Can part-time teachers collect unemployment compensation between school terms?
   c. Can professional athletes receive unemployment compensation?
   d. Are aliens covered by the unemployment compensation law?
   e. How do employers protest or appeal benefit determinations and charges against their accounts?
   f. Briefly describe how a person's weekly benefit rate and maximum benefit amount are determined.
   g. Can an unemployed worker collect additional benefits if he or she has dependents? If so, how much is paid for each dependent?
   h. Does the state provide payment of partial benefits?
   i. Are benefits payable to a female during pregnancy?
   j. Can employers make voluntary contributions to their state unemployment reserve accounts?

   k. For what reasons may an unemployed worker be disqualified from receiving unemployment benefits?
   l. What steps are taken by the state unemployment agency to prevent the improper payment of claims?

4. As a way of curbing the unemployment rate, California has instituted a "shared-work compensation" program. Under this program, a company faced with a layoff of its workers may place its entire work force on a four-day workweek during the period of hardship. During this period of reduced workweeks, the employees collect partial unemployment benefits. When business rebounds, the firm returns to its normal five-day workweek, and the unemployment compensation benefits cease. Participation in the program must be approved by both the employer and the unions. If, however, the firm is not unionized, management has the discretion of putting the plan into effect.
   a. What are the benefits of such a shared-work compensation program to (1) the employer and (2) the employees?
   b. What disadvantages do you see in the operation of a shared-work compensation program, especially from the viewpoint of organized labor?

PRACTICAL PROBLEMS

5–1. LO 4, 5.

During the year, Nanchez Company has a SUTA tax rate of 5.9%. The taxable payroll for the year for FUTA and SUTA is $67,000. Compute:

a. Net FUTA tax . . . . $ _____
b. Net SUTA tax . . . .   _____
c. Total unemployment taxes . . $ _____

5–2. LO 4, 5.

Parrett Company's payroll for the year is $737,910. Of this amount, $472,120 is for wages paid in excess of $7,000 to each individual employee. The SUTA rate in Parrett Company's state is 2.9% on the first $7,000 of each employee's earnings. Compute:

a. Net FUTA tax . . . . $ _____
b. Net SUTA tax . . . .   _____
c. Total unemployment taxes . . $ _____

5–3. LO 4, 5.

Garrison Shops had a SUTA tax rate of 3.7%. The state's taxable limit was $8,000 of each employee's earnings. For the year, Garrison Shops had FUTA taxable wages of $67,900 and SUTA taxable wages of $83,900. Compute:

a. Net FUTA tax . . . . $ _____
b. Net SUTA tax . . . . $ _____

5–4. LO 4, 5.

Due to its experience rating, Ianelli, Inc., is required to pay unemployment taxes on its payroll as follows:

1. Under SUTA for Illinois on taxable payroll of $18,000, the contribution rate is 4%.
2. Under SUTA for Indiana on taxable payroll of $24,000, the contribution rate is 2.65%.
3. Under SUTA for Ohio on taxable payroll of $79,000, the contribution rate is 2.9%.
4. Under FUTA, the taxable payroll is $103,500.

Compute:

a. SUTA taxes paid to Illinois . . $ _____
b. SUTA taxes paid to Indiana . $ _____
c. SUTA taxes paid to Ohio . . . $ _____
d. FUTA taxes paid . . . . $ _____

5–5. LO 1, 4.

The Brooks Company began its operations in August of the current year. During August and September, the company paid wages of $6,950. For the last quarter of the year, the taxable wages paid amounted to $12,910. None of the employees were paid more than $7,000 this year.

a. Is The Brooks Company liable for FUTA tax this year? Explain.
b. If so, what is the amount of the *gross* FUTA tax before any credit is granted for the SUTA tax? . . . . $ _____

5–6. LO 1, 3, 4, 5.

In September 2003, Haley Paint Corporation began operations in a state that requires new employers of one or more individuals to pay a state unemployment tax of 3.5% of the first $7,000 of wages paid each employee.

An analysis of the company's payroll for the year shows total wages paid of $177,610. The salaries of the president and the vice president of the company were $20,000 and $15,000, respectively, for the four-month period, but there were no other employees who received wages in excess of $7,000 for the four months. Included in the total wages were $900 paid to a director who only attended director meetings during the year, and $6,300 paid to the factory superintendent.

Besides the total wages of $177,610, a payment of $2,430 was made to O'Hara Accounting Company for an audit they performed on the company's books in December 2003. Compute:

a. Net FUTA tax . . . . $_____
b. SUTA tax . . . . $_____

5–7. LO 2, 3, 4, 5.

In April of the current year, Korn Steel Company transferred Harry Marsh from its factory in Tennessee to its plant in South Carolina. The company's SUTA tax rates based on its experience ratings are 3.2% in Tennessee and 3.8% in South Carolina. Both states base the tax on the first $7,000 of each employee's earnings. This year, Korn Steel Company paid Harry Marsh wages of $9,900; $2,800 were paid in Tennessee and the remainder in South Carolina. Compute:

a. Amount of SUTA tax the company must pay to Tennessee on Marsh's wages . . $_____
b. Amount of SUTA tax the company must pay to South Carolina on Marsh's wages . . . . $_____
c. Amount of the net FUTA tax on Marsh's wages . . . . $_____

5–8. LO 3, 4.

The partnership of Edward and Farnam paid the following wages during this year:

M. Edward (partner)	$21,000
S. Farnam (partner)	19,000
N. Pearson (supervisor)	12,500
T. Grunhart (factory worker)	9,700
R. Rice (factory worker).	9,200
D. Brown (factory worker).	7,900
S. Koenig (bookkeeper)	10,900
C. Chang (maintenance)	4,500

In addition, the partnership owed $200 to Chang for work he performed during December. However, payment for this work will not be made until January of the following year. The state unemployment tax rate for the company is 2.15% on the first $9,000 of each employee's earnings. Compute:

a. Net FUTA tax for the partnership for this year . . . . $_____
b. SUTA tax for this year . . . . . . $_____

5–9. LO 4, 5.

Demigold Company paid wages of $170,900 this year. Of this amount, $114,000 was taxable for net FUTA and SUTA purposes. The state's contribution tax rate is 3.1% for the Demigold Company. Due to cash flow problems, the company did not make any SUTA payments until after the Form 940 filing date. Compute:

a. Amount of credit the company would receive against the FUTA tax for its SUTA contributions .... $ _____

b. Amount that the Demigold Company would pay to the federal government for its FUTA tax .... $ _____

c. Amount that the company lost because of its late payments .... $ _____

5–10. LO 4, 5.

During 2003, the Jordan Company was subject to the Alaska state unemployment tax of 4.2%. The company's taxable earnings for FUTA were $86,700 and for SUTA, $171,000. Compute:

a. SUTA tax that the Jordan Company would pay to the state of Alaska .... $ _____

b. Net FUTA tax for 2003 ..... $ _____

c. Amount of employees' unemployment tax for 2003 (use the employee's tax rate shown in Figure 5–1 on p. 5-13) .... $ _____

5–11. LO 5.

The following unemployment tax rate schedule is in effect for the calendar year 2003 in State A, which uses the reserve-ratio formula in determining employer contributions:

Reserve Ratio	Contributions Rate
0.0% or more, but less than 1%	6.7%
1.0% or more, but less than 1.2%	6.4%
1.2% or more, but less than 1.4%	6.1%
1.4% or more, but less than 1.6%	5.8%
1.6% or more, but less than 1.8%	5.5%
1.8% or more, but less than 2.0%	5.2%
2.0% or more, but less than 2.2%	4.9%
2.2% or more, but less than 2.4%	4.6%
2.4% or more, but less than 2.6%	4.3%
2.6% or more, but less than 2.8%	4.0%
2.8% or more, but less than 3.0%	3.7%
3.0% or more, but less than 3.2%	3.4%
3.2% or more	3.1%

Grant Company, which is located in State A, had an average annual payroll of $850,000 for the three 12-month periods ending on June 30, 2002 (the computation date for the tax year 2003). As of June 30, 2002, the total contributions that had been made to Grant Company's reserve account, in excess of the benefits charged, amounted to $17,440. Compute:

a. Grant Company's reserve ratio for 2002 .... _____ %

b. 2003 contributions rate for the company .... _____ %

c. Smallest contribution that the company can make in order to reduce its tax rate if State A permits voluntary contributions .... $ _____

d. Tax savings realized by the company, taking into consideration the voluntary contribution made in "c" if the taxable payroll in 2003 is $980,000 .... $ _____

5–12. LO 5.

As of June 30, 2002 (the computation date for the 2003 tax rate), Zimfer Company had a negative balance of $867 in its unemployment reserve account in State A. The company's average payroll over the last three 12-month periods amounted to $360,000. The unemployment compensation law of State A provides that the tax rate of an employer who has a negative balance on the computation date shall be 7.2% during the following calendar year. Using the tax rate schedule presented in Problem 5–11, compute:

a. The smallest voluntary contribution that Zimfer Company should make in order to effect a change in its tax rate . . . . $_____

b. The amount of the tax savings as a result of the voluntary contribution if Zimfer Company's taxable payroll for 2003 is $420,000 . . $_____

5–13. LO 3, 4, 5.

Marlene Grady and Pauline Monroe are partners engaged in operating The MGM Doll Shop, which has employed the following persons since the beginning of the year:

V. Hoffman (general office worker)	$1,700 per month
A. Drugan (saleswoman)	$15,000 per year
G. Beiter (stock clerk)	$180 per week
S. Egan (deliveryman)	$220 per week
B. Lin (cleaning and maintenance, part-time)	$160 per week

Grady and Monroe are each paid a weekly salary allowance of $950.

The doll shop is located in a state that requires unemployment compensation contributions of employers of one or more individuals. The company is subject to state contributions at a rate of 3.1% for wages not in excess of $8,100. Compute each of the following amounts based upon the 41st weekly payroll period for the week ending October 10, 2003:

a. Amount of FICA taxes (OASDI and HI) to be withheld from the earnings of each person. (Refer to Chapter 3.)

	OASDI	HI
M. Grady	$_____	$_____
P. Monroe	_____	_____
V. Hoffman	_____	_____
A. Drugan	_____	_____
G. Beiter	_____	_____
S. Egan	_____	_____
B. Lin	_____	_____

b. Amount of the employer's FICA taxes for the weekly payroll . . . . .   _____

c. Amount of state unemployment contributions for the weekly payroll . . . . $_____

d. Amount of the net FUTA tax on the payroll . . . . $_____

e. Total amount of the employer's payroll taxes for the weekly payroll . . . . $_____

5–14. LO 5.

Glavine Steel Company is located in State H, which enables employers to reduce their contribution rates under the experience-rating system. From 1989 to 1998, inclusive, the company's total contributions to state unemployment compensation amounted to $14,695. For the calendar years 1999 to 2002, inclusive, the contribution rate for employers was 2.7%.

The contributions of each employer are credited to an account maintained by the State Unemployment Compensation Commission. This account is credited with contributions paid into the account by the employer and is charged with unemployment benefits that are paid from the account. Starting January 1, 2003, the contributions rate for all employers in State H will be based on the following tax-rate schedule:

Reserve Ratio	Contributions Rate
Contributions falling below benefits paid	7.0%
0.0% to 7.9%	5.5%
8.0% to 9.9%	4.5%
10.0% to 11.9%	3.5%
12.0% to 14.9%	2.5%
15.0% or more	1.5%

The annual payroll for calculation purposes is the total wages payable during a 12-month period ending with the last day of the third quarter of any calendar year. The average annual payroll is the average of the last three annual payrolls. The SUTA tax rate for the year is computed using the information available (benefits received and taxes paid) as of September 30 of the preceding year.

The schedule below shows the total payroll and the taxable payroll for the calendar years 1999 to 2002.

Calendar Year	1999		2000		2001		2002	
	Total Payroll	Taxable Payroll	Total Payroll	Taxable Payroll	Total Payroll	Taxable Payroll	Total Payroll	Taxable Payroll
First Quarter	$12,000	$12,000	$11,000	$11,000	$13,000	$13,000	$10,000	$10,000
Second Quarter . . .	11,750	11,750	11,500	11,400	12,750	12,700	9,300	9,300
Third Quarter	12,500	12,250	12,750	12,400	12,200	12,000	9,350	9,350
Fourth Quarter . . .	13,000	12,500	12,500	12,200	14,000	13,750	—	—

Unemployment benefits became payable to the company's qualified unemployed workers on January 1, 1990. Between that time and September 30, 2002, total benefits amounting to $15,100.90 were charged against the employer's account. Compute:

a. Contributions rate for 2003 . . . _____ %

b. Rate for 2003 if $2,000 additional benefits had been charged by mistake to the account of the Glavine Steel Company by the State Unemployment Compensation Commission . . . . _____ %

5–15. LO 6.

As the accountant for Monroe Trucking Company, you are preparing the company's annual return, Form 940. Use the following information to complete Form 940 on pages 5-39 and 5-40.

The net FUTA tax liability for each quarter of 2003 was as follows: 1st, $97; 2nd, $87; 3rd, $69.70; and 4th, $59.50. Since the net FUTA tax liability did not exceed $100 until the end of the 2nd quarter, the company was not required to make its first deposit of FUTA taxes until July 31, 2003. The second deposit was not required until January 31, 2004. Assume that the federal tax deposit coupons (Form 8109) were completed and the deposits were made on these dates.

a. State F's reporting number: 73902.
b. Monroe Trucking Company has one employee who performs all of his duties in another state—State P. The employer's identification number for this state is 7-115180.
c. Total payments made to employees during calendar year 2003:

State F	$53,450
State P	9,100
Total	$62,550

d. Payments made to employees in excess of $7,000: $23,400.
e. Amount contributed to unemployment compensation fund of State F under merit rating, 1.8% of $32,150, or $578.70, for calendar year 2003. For State P, the contribution was 3.6% of $7,000 (the taxable salary limit), or $252.
f. Form is to be signed by Elmer P. Lear, Vice President.

5–15 (Continued).

Form **940**	**Employer's Annual Federal Unemployment (FUTA) Tax Return**	OMB No. 1545-0028

Department of the Treasury
Internal Revenue Service   (99)

► **See separate Instructions for Form 940 for information on completing this form.**

2003

		T	
		FF	
	Calendar year	FD	
	2003	FP	
		I	
		T	

You must complete this section. ►

Name (as distinguished from trade name)

Trade name, if any
MONROE TRUCKING COMPANY

Address and ZIP code
423 BRISTOL PIKE
NEWTON, STATE F 18940-4523

Employer identification number
54 0663793

A Are you required to pay unemployment contributions to only one state? (If No, skip questions B and C.) ☐ Yes ☐ No

B Did you pay all state unemployment contributions by February 2, 2004? ((1) If you deposited your total FUTA tax when due, check Yes if you paid all state unemployment contributions by February 10, 2003. (2) If a 0% experience rate is granted, check Yes. (3) If No, skip question C.) . . . . ☐ Yes ☐ No

C Were all wages that were taxable for FUTA tax also taxable for your state s unemployment tax? . . . . . ☐ Yes ☐ No

If you answered No to any of these questions, you must file Form 940. If you answered Yes to all the questions, you may file Form 940-EZ, which is a simplified version of Form 940. (Successor employers see **Special credit for successor employers** on page 3 of the instructions.) You can get Form 940-EZ by calling 1-800-TAX-FORM (1-800-829-3676) or from the IRS Web Site at **www.irs.gov.**

If you will not have to file returns in the future, check here (see **Who Must File** in separate instructions), **and complete and sign the return** . . . . ► ☐
If this is an Amended Return, check here . . . . ► ☐

Part I	**Computation of Taxable Wages**

1 Total payments (including payments shown on lines 2 and 3) during the calendar year for services of employees **1**

2 Exempt payments. (Explain all exempt payments, attaching additional sheets if necessary.) ► _____ _____ **2**

3 Payments of more than $7,000 for services. Enter only amounts over the first $7,000 paid to each employee. (See separate instructions.) Do not include any exempt payments from line 2. The $7,000 amount is the Federal wage base. Your state wage base may be different. **Do not use your state wage limitation.** **3**

4 Add lines 2 and 3 . . . . **4**

5 **Total taxable wages** (subtract line 4 from line 1) . . . . ► **5**

Be sure to complete both sides of this form, and sign in the space provided on the back.

5–16 (Continued).

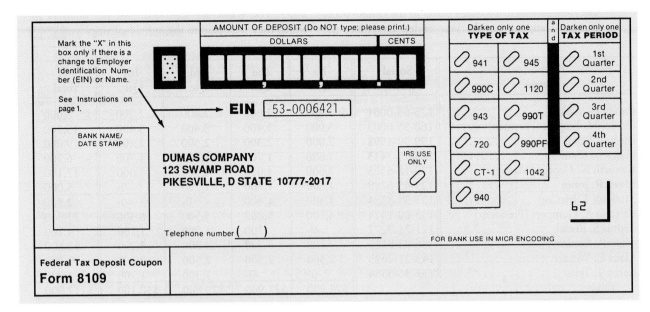

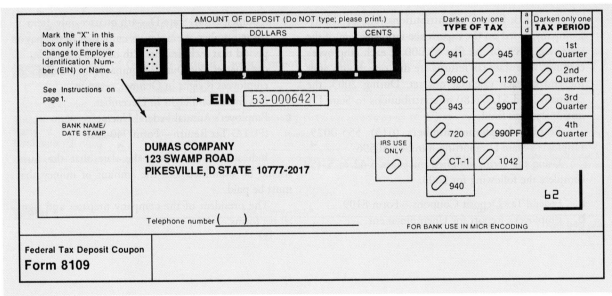

5–16 (Continued).

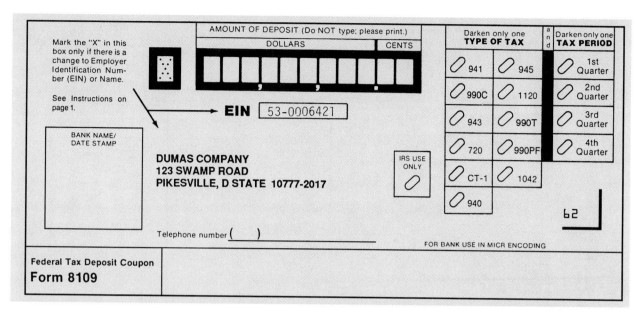

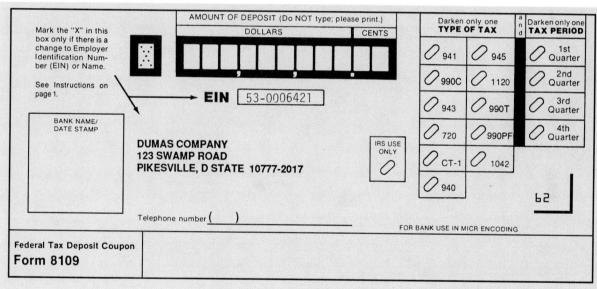

5–16 (Continued).

PA Form UC-2, Rev 6-2000, Employer s Report for Unemployment Compensation QTR./YEAR 4/2003

Read Instructions Answer Each Item DUE DATE 02/02/2004

DETACH HERE

INV. ☐ EXAMINED BY:

Signature certifies that the information contained herein is true and correct to the best of the signer's knowledge.

10. SIGN HERE-DO NOT PRINT

TITLE ______ DATE ______ PHONE # ______

11. FILED ☐ PAPER UC-2A ☐ MAGNETIC MEDIA UC-2A

EMPLOYER S CONTRIBUTION RATE	EMPLOYER S ACCT. NO.	CHECK DIGIT
2.8%	80596	&

Employer name and address
Make any corrections on Form UC-2B

Dumas Company
123 Swamp Road
Pikesville, D State 10777-2017

	1ST MONTH	2ND MONTH	3RD MONTH	FOR DEPT. USE
1. TOTAL COVERED EMPLOYEES IN PAY PERIOD INCL. 12TH OF MONTH				
2. GROSS WAGES				
3. EMPLOYEE CONTRIBUTIONS	XXXXXXXX XX			XXXXX
4. TAXABLE WAGES FOR EMPLOYER CONTRIBUTIONS				
5. EMPLOYER CONTRIBUTIONS DUE (RATE X ITEM 4)				
6. TOTAL CONTRIBUTIONS DUE (ITEMS 3 + 5)				
7. INTEREST DUE SEE INSTRUCTIONS				
8. PENALTY DUE SEE INSTRUCTIONS				
9. TOTAL REMITTANCE (ITEMS 6 + 7 + 8)	$.			

DETACH HERE

MAKES CHECKS PAYABLE TO:"PA UC FUND

DATE PAYMENT RECEIVED SUBJECTIVITY DATE REPORT DELINQUENT DATE

PA Form UC-2A, Rev 6-2000, Employer s for Unemployment Compensation

See instructions on separate sheet. Information MUST be typewritten or printed in BLACK ink. Do NOT use commas (,) or dollar signs ($). If typed, disregard vertical bars and type a consecutive string of characters. If hand printed, print in CAPS and within the boxes as below:

SAMPLE Typed: 1 2 3 4 5 6 . 0 0 **SAMPLE Handwritten:** 1 2 3 4 5 6 . 0 0 **SAMPLE Filled-in:** → ●

Employer name (make corrections on Form UC-2B)	Employer PA UC account no.	Check digit	Quarter and year Q/YYYY	Quarter ending date MM/DD/YYYY
		&	4/2003	12/31/2003

1. Name and telephone number of preparer

2. Total number of pages in this report

3. Total number of employees listed in item 8 on all pages of Form UC-2A

4. Plant number (if approved)

5. Gross wages, MUST agree with item 2 on UC-2 and the sum of item 11 on all pages of Form UC-2A

6. Fill in this circle if you would like the Department to preprint your employees names & SSNs on Form UC-2A next quarter → ○

7. Employee s social security number	8. Employee s name FI	MI	LAST	9. Gross wages paid this qtr Example:"123456.00	10. Credit weeks
				.	
				.	
				.	
				.	
				.	
				.	
				.	
				.	
				.	
				.	

List any additional employees on continuation sheets in the required format (see instructions).

Batch # For Dept. Use Only

11. Total gross wages for this page: → .

12. Page ____ of ____

CONTINUING PAYROLL PROBLEM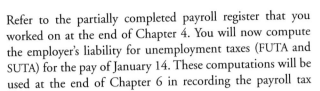

Refer to the partially completed payroll register that you worked on at the end of Chapter 4. You will now compute the employer's liability for unemployment taxes (FUTA and SUTA) for the pay of January 14. These computations will be used at the end of Chapter 6 in recording the payroll tax entries.

To compute the employer's liability for unemployment taxes, proceed as follows:

1. Enter each employee's gross earnings in the Taxable Earnings—FUTA and SUTA columns.
2. Total the Taxable Earnings—FUTA and SUTA columns.
3. At the bottom of your payroll register, compute the following for the total payroll:

a. Net FUTA tax. Since this is the first pay period of the year, none of the employees are near the $7,000 ceiling; therefore, each employee's gross earnings is subject to the FUTA tax.

b. SUTA tax. Since the Steimer Company is a new employer, Pennsylvania has assigned the company a contribution rate of 3.5% on the first $8,000 of each employee's earnings.

NOTE: Retain your partially completed payroll register for use at the end of Chapter 6.

CASE PROBLEM

C1.   Reducing a High Unemployment Tax Rate.
Over the past two years, Kermit Stone, the controller of Hilton Company, has been concerned that the company has been paying a large amount of money for state unemployment taxes. On reviewing the "unemployment file" with the head accountant, Deborah Murtha, he learns that the company's tax rate is near the top of the range of the state's experience-rating system.

After calling the local unemployment office, Stone realizes that the turnover of employees at Hilton Company has had an adverse effect on the company's tax rates. In addition, after consulting with Murtha, he discovers that the eligibility reports that come from the state unemployment office are just signed and sent back to the state without any review.

The eligibility reports are notices that an ex-employee has filed a claim for unemployment benefits. By signing these reports "blindly," the company, in effect, tells the state that the employee is eligible for the benefits. Any benefits paid are charged by the state against Hilton Company's account.

Stone is convinced that the rates the company is paying are too high, and he feels that part of the reason is the "blind" signing of the eligibility reports. Besides this, he wonders what other steps the company can take to lower its contributions rate and taxes.

Submit recommendations that might help Stone reduce the "unfair" burden that the unemployment compensation taxes are leveling on Hilton Company.

Net activities

URLS are subject to change. Please visit the Bieg Payroll Accounting Web site: http://bieg.swcollege.com for updates.

1. The Department of Labor has a section on Federal Unemployment:

    http://workforcesecurity.doleta.gov/unemploy/taxinfo.asp

    What is the maximum amount of Federal unemployment taxes an employer will pay per worker in a given year?

2. The Department of Labor provides a map with links to State Unemployment Departments:

    http://workforcesecurity.doleta.gov/map.asp

Using current information, choose the state you live in and one neighboring state.
a. Compare the rates between your state and the neighboring state. How do the rates differ?
b. How can an employer decrease its experience rating?

3. Take a look at the Railroad Retirement Tax Act:

    http://www.rrb.gov/opa/ib2/ib2_ret.html,

Then take a look at the current payroll tax withholding:

    http://www.rrb.gov/AandT/pl/pl0206.html.

Discussion:
a. How much is currently withheld from railroaders' checks?

5–16 (Concluded).

Form **940-EZ**	**Employer's Annual Federal Unemployment (FUTA) Tax Return**	OMB No. 1545-1110
Department of the Treasury Internal Revenue Service (99)	► See separate Instructions for Form 940-EZ for information on completing this form.	20**03**

	T	
	FF	
	FD	
	FP	
	I	
	T	

You must complete this section. ►

Name (as distinguished from trade name)

Trade name, if any

DUMAS COMPANY

Address and ZIP code
123 SWAMP ROAD
PIKESVILLE, D STATE 10777-2017

Calendar year
2003

Employer identification number
53 : 0006421

*Answer the questions under **Who May Use Form 940-EZ** on page 2. If you cannot use Form 940-EZ, you must use Form 940.*

A Enter the amount of contributions paid to your state unemployment fund. (see separate instructions) . . . ► $ _____

B (1) Enter the name of the state where you have to pay contributions . . . . ► _____

(2) Enter your state reporting number as shown on your state unemployment tax return ► _____

If you will not have to file returns in the future, check here (see **Who Must File** in separate instructions), **and complete and sign the return.** ► ☐

If this is an Amended Return, check here . . . . ► ☐

Part I   Taxable Wages and FUTA Tax

1	Total payments (including payments shown on lines 2 and 3) during the calendar year for services of employees	**1**	
2	Exempt payments. (Explain all exempt payments, attaching additional sheets if necessary.) ► _____	**2**	
3	Payments of more than $7,000 for services. Enter only amounts over the first $7,000 paid to each employee. **(see separate instructions)**	**3**	
4	Add lines 2 and 3	**4**	
5	**Total taxable wages** (subtract line 4 from line 1) . . . . ►	**5**	
6	**FUTA tax.** Multiply the wages on line 5 by .008 and enter here. **(If the result is over $100, also complete Part II.)**	**6**	
7	Total FUTA tax deposited for the year, including any overpayment applied from a prior year . . .	**7**	
8	**Balance due** (subtract line 7 from line 6). Pay to the **"United States Treasury."** . . . . . ►	**8**	
	If you owe more than $100, see **Depositing FUTA tax** in separate instructions.		
9	**Overpayment** (subtract line 6 from line 7). Check if it is to be: ☐ **Applied to next return** or ☐ **Refunded** ►	**9**	

Part II   Record of Quarterly Federal Unemployment Tax Liability (Do not include state liability.) **Complete only if line 6 is over $100.**

Quarter	First (Jan. 1 – Mar. 31)	Second (Apr. 1 – June 30)	Third (July 1 – Sept. 30)	Fourth (Oct. 1 – Dec. 31)	Total for year
Liability for quarter					

Third Party Designee

Do you want to allow another person to discuss this return with the IRS (see instructions page 4)? ☐ **Yes.** Complete the following. ☐ **No**

Designee's name ►

Phone no. ► (   )

Personal identification number (PIN) ►

Under penalties of perjury, I declare that I have examined this return, including accompanying schedules and statements, and, to the best of my knowledge and belief, it is true, correct, and complete, and that no part of any payment made to a state unemployment fund claimed as a credit was, or is to be, deducted from the payments to employees.

Signature ► _____   Title (Owner, etc.) ► _____   Date ► _____

For Privacy Act and Paperwork Reduction Act Notice, see separate instructions.   ▼ **DETACH HERE** ▼   Cat. No. 10983G   Form **940-EZ** (2001)

b. Can an employee enrolled in the Railroad Retirement Tax Act ever receive less than they would have under Social Security?

c. What are some of the differences between Social Security and the Railroad Retirement Tax Act?

4. Go to the California State Disability Insurance page:

http://www.edd.ca.gov/diind.htm.

a. What does the California Disability Insurance program cover?

b. How is the California Disability Insurance program funded?

c. Roger Orfield had a skiing accident, and the doctor told him he must not work for the next four weeks. Roger earns $3,000 per month.
   - How long must Roger wait before collecting Disability Insurance?
   - How much will Roger be able to collect?
   - What is the maximum length of time Roger could collect Disability Insurance if his doctor tells him he is unable to work?
   - Is his disability check taxable?

Now is the time to discuss the accounting part of payroll accounting. Remember those debits and credits? In this chapter

Analyzing and Journalizing Payroll Transactions

the costs of the payroll will be recorded in the journal and ledger of the company. The payments of various payroll-related liabilities will also be illustrated.

Get ready to prepare payroll registers, employees' earnings records, and then journalize and post payroll entries. Also, learn what adjustments must be made at the end of the fiscal period.

LEARNING OBJECTIVES

AFTER STUDYING THIS CHAPTER, YOU SHOULD BE ABLE TO:

1. Record payrolls in payroll registers and post to employees' earnings records.

2. Journalize the entries to record the payroll, payroll taxes, and payment of payroll-related liabilities.

3. Post to the various general ledger accounts that are used to accumulate information from the payroll entries.

4. Explain the payment and the recording of the payroll tax deposits.

5. Understand the need for end-of-period adjustments.

6. Identify the general ledger accounts used to record payroll transactions.

This chapter presents the procedures for recording the payroll in a payroll register and for transferring information from the payroll register to the employees' earnings records. Also, we shall analyze typical transactions pertaining to a company's payroll, record these transactions in the company's book of original entry, and post them to the proper ledger accounts.

THE PAYROLL REGISTER

LEARNING OBJECTIVE 1

As you have seen in Figure 1–9 and in completing the Continuing Payroll Problem, the payroll register gives detailed information about the payroll for each pay period. To summarize, the payroll register may provide the following types of information:

1. The title of the form.
2. The period covered by the payroll and the paydate.
3. Department or branch. Some large businesses with many departments or branches prepare a separate sheet in the payroll register for each department or branch on each payday. Other firms provide "distribution" columns such as "Sales Salaries," "Office Salaries," and "Plant Wages" for classifying the gross wages and salaries according to the nature of the wage and salary expense. The total of each distribution column shows the total amount for that department's wage expense.
4. A column to record the name of each employee. Many businesses provide a column to record an identifying number such as the time clock number for each employee.
5. Marital status and number of withholding allowances. This information determines the income tax deductions.
6. A record of time worked. Many companies show detailed information in the payroll register as to hours worked each day by each employee.
7. Some companies provide separate columns to show a total of regular hours worked and a total of overtime hours worked during the pay period. This information helps a business that schedules much overtime work.
8. The regular rate of pay and the amount earned at the regular rate.
9. A space to record the overtime rate and the total earnings at the overtime rate. Some companies prefer to show an Overtime Premium Earnings column in place of the Overtime Earnings column. With this approach, the regular earnings is equal to the

FIGURE 6-1

Payroll Register (left side)

FOR WEEK ENDING **January 17, 20--**   Payday January 17, 20 —

	NO.	NAME	MARITAL STATUS	NO. W/H ALLOW.	TIME RECORD M	T	W	T	F	S	REGULAR EARNINGS HOURS	RATE PER HOUR	AMOUNT		OVERTIME EARNINGS HOURS	RATE PER HOUR	AMOUNT		
1	10	Collins, Chris R.	M	2	8	8	8	8	8	4	40	15 20	6 0 8	00	4	22 80		9 1	20
2	12	Banks, Carolyn B.	M	4	8	8	8	8	10		40	17 10	6 8 4	00	2	25 65		5 1	30
3	13	Carson, Henry S.	S	1	8	8	8	8	8		40	16 30	6 5 2	00					
4	23	O'Brien, LuAnn T.	M	2	8	8	8	8	8	8	40	15 90	6 3 6	00	8	23 85		1 9 0	80
5	24	Rudolph, Beth M.	S	1	8	8	8	0	8		32	16 10	5 1 5	20					
36		Totals											224 9 7	20				22 6 5	50

regular hourly rate of pay multiplied by the total hours worked, and the overtime premium is equal to the extra one-half rate of pay multiplied by the overtime hours.

[e.g., Collins   ($15.20 × 44 hours) + ($7.60 × 4 hours)]

10. A column to record the total earnings.
11. Information about deductions from total earnings. A separate column may be provided for each type of deduction. The various deductions will be discussed later in this chapter.
12. A column to show the net amount paid (total earnings less deductions). When paying by check, a company usually provides a column for the number of each employee's check.
13. Some firms provide special columns in the payroll register to indicate that portion of the employee's wages taxable under the Federal Insurance Contributions Act (OASDI and HI) and other laws that require payment of taxes only on wages up to the taxable limits.

The partial payroll register shown in Figure 6–1 contains most of the information outlined above. This register is used to compute the pay for hourly workers for a weekly pay period. The layout of the section devoted to time or hours worked will vary, depending on the payroll period and the work schedules of each individual business. Although a few small businesses still prepare the payroll manually, most businesses use computers to process their payrolls. Therefore, the payroll registers and other payroll records will be computer generated.

Proving the Totals of the Payroll Register

As shown later in this chapter, the payroll register provides the information needed in preparing the *journal entries* to record (1) the wages earned, deductions from wages, and net amount paid each payday and (2) the employer's payroll taxes. Prior to making the journal entry to record the payroll, check the accuracy of the amounts entered in the payroll register by proving the totals of the money columns. Prove the partial payroll register shown in Figure 6–1 as follows:

on the

JOB

According to a survey done by the American Payroll Association, close to 20 percent of large employers outsource their payroll operations, while 44 percent have their tax filings done by contractors.

FIGURE 6 – 1

Payroll Register (right side)

DEPT. ACCOUNTING 10

TOTAL EARNINGS			DEDUCTIONS							NET PAID				TAXABLE EARNINGS						
		FICA		FED. INCOME TAX	STATE INCOME TAX	GROUP INS.	CHECK NO.	AMOUNT				FICA		FUTA & SUTA		
		OASDI	HI								OASDI	HI			
6 9 9 20	4 3 35	10 14	57 00	4 78	9 00	898	5 7 4 93	6 9 9 20	6 9 9 20	6 9 9 20	1
7 3 5 30	4 5 59	10 66	45 00	6 11	9 00	899	6 1 8 94	7 3 5 30	7 3 5 30	7 3 5 30	2
6 5 2 00	4 0 42	9 45	80 00	5 04	3 90	900	5 1 3 19	6 5 2 00	6 5 2 00	6 5 2 00	3
8 2 6 80	5 1 26	11 99	76 00	6 14	9 00	901	6 7 2 41	8 2 6 80	8 2 6 80	8 2 6 80	4
5 1 5 20	3 1 94	7 47	55 00	3 90	3 90	902	4 1 2 99	5 1 5 20	5 1 5 20	5 1 5 20	5
247 6 2 70	153 5 29	3 59 06	37 14 00	5 5 25	5 4 70		190 4 4 40	247 6 2 70	247 6 2 70	247 6 2 70	36

Proof:

Regular earnings	$22,497.20	
Overtime earnings	2,265.50	
Total earnings		$24,762.70
FICA tax withheld—OASDI	$ 1,535.29	
FICA tax withheld—HI	359.06	
Federal income taxes withheld	3,714.00	
State income taxes withheld	55.25	
Group insurance withheld	54.70	
Total deductions		$ 5,718.30
Total net pay		19,044.40
Total earnings		$24,762.70

In preparing the journal entry to record a payroll, you make an entry each payday to record the aggregate amount of wages earned, deductions made, and net payments to all employees, as determined from the Totals line of the payroll register. After making the journal entry, you must transfer, or post, the information from the journal to the appropriate general ledger accounts.

Some companies use a formal *payroll journal* instead of a payroll register to record each payroll. When you record the payroll in a payroll journal, you post directly from the payroll journal to the general ledger accounts.

In most companies having computer-driven payroll systems, the payroll programs are interfaced with the general ledger programs. In these systems, computers generate the payroll entries into a printed journal-entry format and post to the various general ledger accounts automatically from these entries.

Using the Information in the Payroll Register

In addition to serving as the source for preparing journal entries to record the payroll and the employer's payroll taxes, the payroll register provides information that meets some of the recordkeeping requirements of the various payroll acts. Also, the register provides data used in preparing periodic reports required by various laws.

Besides the information contained in the payroll register, businesses must provide information about the accumulated earnings of each employee. Therefore, companies keep a separate payroll record on each employee—the employee's earnings record. This record, introduced in Figure 1–10, is discussed in the following section.

THE EMPLOYEE'S EARNINGS RECORD

The employee's earnings record, a supplementary record, provides information for:

1. *Preparing the payroll register.* The earnings record contains the information needed to compute gross earnings and to determine the amount to withhold for income tax purposes.
2. *Preparing reports* required by state unemployment compensation or disability laws.
3. *Determining when the accumulated wages of an employee reach the cutoff level* for purposes of FICA (OASDI), FUTA, or SUTA. As shown in Figure 6–2, a special "Cumulative Earnings" column is provided so that the total amount of accumulated wages can be recorded each pay period. Thus, when the FICA (OASDI), FUTA, or SUTA cutoff has been reached, the record shows that the employee or the employer no longer has a liability for that particular tax during the rest of the calendar year. (In Figure 6–1, the FUTA and SUTA taxable wage cutoffs are the same [$7,000]. However, another separate column would be needed in the payroll register if there were a different cutoff for the SUTA tax.)

FIGURE 6-2

Employee's Earnings Record (page 1)

WEEK	20— WEEK ENDING	TOTAL WORKED DAYS	TOTAL WORKED HRS.	REGULAR EARNINGS HRS.	REGULAR EARNINGS RATE	REGULAR EARNINGS AMOUNT	OVERTIME EARNINGS HRS.	OVERTIME EARNINGS RATE	OVERTIME EARNINGS AMOUNT	FICA OASDI	FICA HI	FEDERAL INCOME TAX	STATE INCOME TAX	GROUP INSURANCE	NET PAID CK. NO.	NET PAID AMOUNT	CUMULATIVE EARNINGS	TIME LOST
1	1/3	5	44	40	15 20	6 0 8 00	4	22 80	9 1 20	4 3 35	1 0 14	5 7 00	4 78	9 00	510	5 7 4 93	6 9 9 20	
2	1/10	5	42	40	15 20	6 0 8 00	2	22 80	4 5 60	4 0 52	9 48	5 1 00	4 47	9 00	706	5 3 9 13	1 3 5 2 80	
3	1/17	6	44	40	15 20	6 0 8 00	4	22 80	9 1 20	4 3 35	1 0 14	5 7 00	4 78	9 00	898	5 7 4 93	2 0 5 2 00	
4																		
5																		
6																		
7																		
8																		
9																		
10																		
11																		
12																		
13																		
QUARTER TOTAL																		
1																		
2																		
13																		
QUARTER TOTAL																		
SEMIANNUAL TOTAL																		

DEPARTMENT	OCCUPATION	WORKS IN (STATE)	S.S. ACCOUNT NO.	NAME—LAST	FIRST	MIDDLE	NO. W/H ALLOW.
A-10	Adm. Ass't	XXX	204-43-1186	Collins	Chris	Ruth	2

SEX: F | M — X

MARITAL STATUS M

4. *Preparing payroll analyses* for governmental agencies and for internal management control. Information such as the department in which the employee works and the job title serves as the basis for such analyses.
5. *Settling employee grievances* regarding regular pay and overtime pay calculations and the withholding of amounts for income taxes and other purposes.
6. *Completing Forms W-2,* which show for each employee the annual gross earnings, income taxes withheld, wages subject to FICA taxes, and FICA taxes withheld.

A business keeps an employee's earnings record for each employee whose wages are recorded in the payroll register. Each payday, after the information has been recorded in the payroll register, the information for each employee is posted to the employee's earnings record. The columns are arranged so that the information can be transferred easily. The earnings record shown in Figure 6–2 is arranged for weekly pay periods. You will note that totals are provided for each quarter so that you can enter information easily on the quarterly tax returns. The bottom of page 1 of the earnings record shows a line for semiannual totals. The bottom of page 2 of the form, which is not illustrated, shows a line for annual totals, which you will need in preparing Form 940 or Form 940-EZ, W-2s, and other annual reports.

RECORDING THE GROSS PAYROLL AND WITHHOLDINGS

LEARNING OBJECTIVE 2

After you have recorded the payroll in the payroll register and posted to the employees' earnings records, you must enter the information in the employer's accounting system. An entry for the totals of each payroll period should be made in the general journal and posted to the general ledger. You can obtain the amounts needed for this entry from the Totals line at the bottom of the last payroll register sheet.

The following journal entry to record the payroll includes a debit to the appropriate expense account(s) for the gross payroll and credits to the various liability accounts for the withholdings from the pay and for the net amount to be paid employees:

	Debit	Credit
Salary Expense	XXX	
Liabilities (Withholdings)		XXX
Cash or Salaries Payable (Net Pay)		XXX
To record the payment of salaries and the liabilities for the employees' taxes withheld.		

Gross Payroll

You should record the total gross payroll (regular earnings and overtime earnings) as the debit portion of the payroll entry. The account has a title such as *Wages Expense* or *Salaries Expense.* In the case of a company with many departments or cost centers, the accounts would have titles such as *Wages Expense—Department A, Wages Expense—Maintenance,* and *Wages Expense—Residential Services.* These accounts show the total gross earnings that the employer incurs as an *expense* each payday.

FICA Taxes—Employee

The employer must withhold FICA taxes for each employee. Since the employer has withheld these taxes from the pay of the employees and now owes this amount to the IRS, the taxes withheld represent a *liability* of the employer. When recording the payroll, you should credit accounts entitled *FICA Taxes Payable—OASDI* and *FICA Taxes Payable—HI* for the amounts withheld.

Federal Income Taxes

Employers must withhold a percentage of their employees' wages for income tax purposes. Chapter 4 presented the methods of determining the amounts to be withheld from wages for income tax purposes. As with FICA taxes withheld, the employer also owes to the IRS the federal income taxes withheld from the employees' pay. You should keep a separate account in the general ledger for recording the employer's *liability* for the amount of federal income taxes withheld. A suitable title for this account, *Employees Federal Income Taxes Payable*, may be abbreviated to read *Employees FIT Payable*. The account is credited for the total amount of federal income taxes withheld each payday and is subsequently debited for the amounts paid to a depositary or to the IRS.

State and City Income Taxes

Employers may be required to withhold state and city income taxes in addition to the federal income taxes. You should keep a separate account in the general ledger for recording the employer's *liability* for the amount of each kind of income tax withheld. Account titles that may be used include *Employees State Income Taxes (SIT) Payable* and *Employees City Income Taxes (CIT) Payable*.

Employees' Contributions to State Funds

A few states require employees to contribute to state unemployment compensation or disability funds. In states requiring employee contributions, the employer deducts the amount of the contributions from the employees' wages at the time the wages are paid. The *liability* for employees' contributions may be recorded in the same account as the employer's SUTA contributions; namely, *SUTA Taxes Payable*. If employees make contributions to a disability benefit fund, this amount is usually reported separately to the state and should be recorded in a separate liability account such as *Employees Disability Contributions Payable*.

Advance Earned Income Credit

As discussed in Chapter 4, advance EIC payments can be paid to eligible employees in their paychecks. These payments are added to the employees' net pay, and the employer pays these advances out of the withheld taxes for social security (FICA) and federal income tax (FIT).

Since these advances increase the net pay, they increase the credit to cash in the payroll entry. These advances also reduce the employer's liability for the payment of FICA taxes and FIT taxes to the IRS. The tax liability accounts should be reduced by the total of these EIC payments to the employees. Therefore, the liability account (usually FIT Payable) should be reduced and the credit to that account in the payroll entry will be less than the amount actually withheld from the employees for that payday. If the total amount of the advances is greater than the total FIT withheld, the excess should reduce the amount of the credit to the FICA liability accounts (OASDI and HI) in the payroll entry.

E X A M P L E

The Evergreen Company's payroll data for the first pay in January is:

Total Earnings	$1,357.00
Deductions:	
OASDI	(84.13)
HI	(19.67)
FIT	(85.00)
SIT	(20.37)
Addition:	
EIC	59.00
Net pay	$1,206.83

The entry to record the payroll is:

Wages Expense	1,357.00	
FICA Taxes Payable—OASDI		84.13
FICA Taxes Payable—HI		19.67
FIT Taxes Payable		26.00 ($85.00 − $59.00)
SIT Taxes Payable		20.37
Cash		1,206.83

Net Pay

The total of the net amount paid to the employees each payday is credited to either the *cash* account or the *salaries payable* account.

SELF-STUDY QUIZ 6–1. *The totals from the payroll register of the Olt Company for the week of January 22 show:*

Gross earnings	$95,190.00
Withholdings:	
FICA taxes—OASDI	5,901.78
FICA taxes—HI	1,380.26
Federal income tax	14,270.00
State income tax	1,427.85
State unemployment tax—employee portion	951.90
Net pay	71,258.21

Journalize the entry to record the payroll of January 22.

RECORDING PAYROLL TAXES

In this section, we will analyze the journal entries that record the *employer's* payroll taxes, each of which has been discussed in preceding chapters:

1. *FICA*—taxes imposed under the Federal Insurance Contributions Act for old-age, survivors, and disability insurance (OASDI) and hospital insurance (HI) benefits.
2. *FUTA*—taxes imposed under the Federal Unemployment Tax Act.
3. *SUTA*—contributions to the unemployment compensation funds of one or more states.

The following accounts will be needed in the general ledger if the employer is subject to FICA taxes, FUTA taxes, and SUTA taxes:

1. *Payroll Taxes*—an expense account for the FICA, FUTA, and SUTA taxes on the employer.
2. *FICA Taxes Payable—OASDI*—a liability account for the tax withheld from employees' wages plus the employer's portion of the tax.
3. *FICA Taxes Payable—HI*—a liability account for the tax withheld from employees' wages plus the employer's portion of the tax.
4. *FUTA Taxes Payable*—a liability account for the accumulation of the employer's federal unemployment taxes payable to the federal government.
5. *SUTA Taxes Payable*—a liability account for the amount payable to state unemployment compensation fund(s).

The following journal entry to record the payroll taxes includes a debit to the tax expense account for the total of the employer's payroll taxes and a credit to the various tax liability accounts:

	Debit	Credit
Payroll Taxes	XXX	
Liabilities (Various Taxes).		XXX
To record the payroll taxes and liabilities of the employer.		

FICA Taxes—Employer

The law states specifically that deductions made from the wages of employees under FICA should be recorded immediately as liabilities on the books of the company. The law does not require that employers record their part of the FICA taxes at the time the *wages are paid*. However, in order to place the tax expense in the proper accounting period, the common practice is to record the employer's FICA tax liabilities each payday.

The taxes on the employer represent both business expenses and liabilities of the employer. The employer may deduct the employer's FICA contributions as a *business expense* in the calculation of the company's net income for federal income tax purposes (and the costs of all other payroll taxes).

SUTA Taxes

Under the state unemployment compensation laws, employers must pay contributions into one or more state unemployment compensation funds. When an employer must make contributions to the state unemployment compensation funds of more than one state, it may be advisable to keep a separate liability account for the contributions payable to each state.

FUTA Tax

An employer subject to the gross FUTA tax of 6.2% may be able to claim credit in paying the federal tax because of contributions made to state unemployment compensation funds. As discussed in Chapter 5, the maximum credit is 5.4%, even though the amount of state contributions is more or less than 5.4%. Thus, the net FUTA tax (6.2% − 5.4%) is 0.8%. Although you do not actually claim the credit against the FUTA tax until Form 940 or Form 940-EZ is filed with the Internal Revenue Service, you may record the FUTA tax at the net amount (0.8%) at the time you make the entry to record the employer's payroll taxes for each payroll period.

EXAMPLE

The employees of the Absicon Company earn wages during the year amounting to $26,400, all of which is subject to the gross FUTA tax of 6.2%. The company must make contributions to the unemployment compensation fund of the state in which the business is located at the rate of 2.8% of the wages paid each employee. Absicon computes the federal and state unemployment taxes as follows:

SUTA tax, 2.8% of $26,400 =		$739.20
Gross FUTA tax, 6.2% of $26,400 =	$1,636.80	
Less: Credit for SUTA tax, 5.4% of $26,400 =	−1,425.60	211.20 (net FUTA tax)
Total unemployment taxes		$950.40

More simply, the net FUTA tax is computed by multiplying the taxable wages, $26,400, by the net FUTA tax rate, 0.8%, yielding $211.20.

The FUTA tax, like the FICA taxes and the contributions to the state for unemployment compensation purposes, is a social security tax. Thus, the FUTA tax can be charged to the same expense account as the other payroll taxes on the employer, the payroll taxes account. However, since employers may be required to pay the net FUTA tax quarterly and to pay the FICA taxes more frequently, an employer should keep separate liability accounts for recording these two taxes.

SELF-STUDY QUIZ 6–2. *Olt Company's gross payroll for the week of January 22 was $95,190.00. This total pay was taxable for federal (0.8%) and state (3.15%) unemployment taxes.*

Journalize the entry to record Olt Company's payroll taxes for this pay.

Entries to Record Wages and Payroll Taxes

In the following illustrations of recording (or journalizing) wages and the payroll taxes imposed under both the federal and state laws, the employer is responsible for the following taxes:

 **LEARNING OBJECTIVE**

1. FICA tax—OASDI on employees: 6.2%.
2. FICA tax—HI on employees: 1.45%.
3. FIT withheld from employees.

4. FICA tax—OASDI on employers: 6.2%.

5. FICA tax—HI on employers: 1.45%.

6. Net FUTA tax: 0.8%.

7. SUTA tax: 2.4%.

The weekly payroll amounts to $3,200, and the entire amount is subject to all social security and unemployment taxes. You record this information in two separate journal entries. In the first entry, you record the wages expense of the employer and the liabilities for the FICA taxes and FIT withheld in a two-column general journal as follows:

	Debit	Credit
Wages Expense	3,200.00	
FICA Taxes Payable—OASDI		198.40
FICA Taxes Payable—HI		46.40
Employees FIT Payable		230.00
Cash		2,725.20

To record the payment of wages and the liability for the employees' FICA taxes and FIT withheld.

We can analyze this entry in T-accounts as follows:

WAGES EXPENSE		FICA TAXES PAYABLE—OASDI	
3,200.00			198.40[1]

This debit represents the employees' gross earnings for the pay period. This results in an increase in the operating expenses of the employer.

This credit results in an increase in a liability of the employer.

FICA TAXES PAYABLE—HI		EMPLOYEES FIT PAYABLE	
	46.40[2]		230.00[3]

This credit results in an increase in a liability of the employer.

This credit results in an increase in a liability of the employer.

CASH	
	2,725.20[4]

This credit results in a decrease in an asset.

---

1 The amount credited to FICA Taxes Payable—OASDI is computed as follows: 6.2% of $3,200 = $198.40, amount deducted from employees' wages

2 The amount credited to FICA Taxes Payable—HI is computed as follows: 1.45% of $3,200 = $46.40, amount deducted from employees' wages

3 The amount credited to Employees FIT Payable is obtained by using one of the withholding methods explained in Chapter 4.

4 The amount credited to Cash is computed as follows:

$3,200.00	gross wages earned
−474.80	employees' taxes withheld
$2,725.20	net amount paid employees

In the second entry, you record the employer's payroll taxes as follows:

	Debit	Credit
Payroll Taxes	347.20	
FICA Taxes Payable—OASDI		198.40
FICA Taxes Payable—HI		46.40
FUTA Taxes Payable		25.60
SUTA Taxes Payable		76.80

To record the payroll taxes and the employer's liability for the taxes.

Let's analyze this entry by means of T-accounts as shown below.

PAYROLL TAXES

347.20*

This debit results in an increase in the operating expenses.

FICA TAXES PAYABLE—OASDI

198.40

198.40

The second credit amount, representing the employer's OASDI tax, also increases the employer's liability. The amount is determined as shown in the computation of the payroll taxes.

FICA TAXES PAYABLE—HI

46.40

46.40

The second credit amount, representing the employer's HI tax, also increases the employer's liability. The amount is determined as shown in the computation of the payroll taxes.

FUTA TAXES PAYABLE

25.60

This credit results in an increase in a liability of the employer. The amount is determined as shown in the computation of the payroll taxes.

SUTA TAXES PAYABLE

76.80

This credit results in an increase in a liability of the employer. The amount is determined as shown in the computation of the payroll taxes.

*The amount debited to Payroll Taxes is computed as follows:

6.2% of $3,200 =	$198.40	employer's OASDI tax
1.45% of $3,200 =	46.40	employer's HI tax
0.8% of $3,200 =	25.60	employer's net FUTA tax
2.4% of $3,200 =	76.80	employer's SUTA tax
Total payroll taxes	$347.20	

In the preceding illustration, no contributions were required of employees for state unemployment compensation purposes. Assume that the employees had been required to make contributions of 1% to state unemployment compensation funds. The payroll entry would then appear as follows:

	Debit	Credit
Wages Expense	3,200.00	
FICA Taxes Payable—OASDI		198.40
FICA Taxes Payable—HI		46.40
Employees FIT Payable		230.00
SUTA Taxes Payable		32.00
Cash		2,693.20

To record the payment of wages and the liability for the employees' FICA, FIT, and SUTA taxes withheld.

In a small company with few employees, you can compute the hours worked, determine net pay, and prepare the paychecks or pay envelopes in a relatively short period of time. For such companies, a journal entry crediting the cash account for the total net pay is a logical, efficient procedure.

In larger companies, however, the calculation of hours worked, the determination of net pay, and the preparation of paychecks may extend over the greater part of a workday, or even longer. In such companies, because of the workload involved in meeting each payroll and especially when the paychecks must be mailed to far-flung branch offices, the paychecks may be prepared several days in advance of their actual distribution to the workers. Further, the preparation of the workers' paychecks may occur in one accounting period, although the actual payment is made in the following accounting period. Thus, to show an accurate picture of the firm's liability for the payroll, at the time of recording the payroll, the net pay is accrued and credited to a liability account such as Salaries Payable or Accrued Salaries Payable, instead of to the cash account. Later, when the paychecks are given to the workers, an entry is made to record the payment of the payroll.

	Debit	Credit
Salaries Payable	XXX	
Cash		XXX

To record the payment of wages for the pay period ended July 20, 20--.

RECORDING WORKERS' COMPENSATION INSURANCE EXPENSE

As indicated in Chapter 1, most states have passed laws that require employers to provide workers' compensation insurance to protect their employees against losses due to injury or death incurred during employment. The expense account, *Workers' Compensation Insurance Expense,* can be used to record the premiums paid by the company to provide this coverage. Usually, the employer estimates and pays the premium in advance. The insurance premium, often based upon the total gross payroll of the business, may be stated in terms of an amount for each $100 of weekly wages paid to employees. At the end of the year, all the payrolls are audited, and the company pays an additional premium or receives credit for an overpayment. Since the premium rate varies with the hazard involved in the work performed, your personnel and payroll records should provide for a careful classification of employees by kind or grade of work and a summary of labor costs according to the insurance premium classifications.

EXAMPLE

The McMahon Company has only two different grades of work—office clerical and machine shop. The premium rates for the year are $0.18 per $100 of payroll for the office clerical workers and $2.90 per $100 of payroll for the machine-shop workers. Based upon past experience and budgetary projections for the year, the company estimates its annual premium to be $8,900 and sends a check for that amount to the insurance carrier at the beginning of the year. The entry to record this transaction is as follows:

Workers' Compensation Insurance Expense	8,900.00	
Cash		8,900.00

The effect of this entry, when posted to the ledger accounts, increases the operating expenses of the company and decreases the assets.

At the end of the year, the payrolls for the year are audited and analyzed and the current rates are applied to determine the actual premium as follows:

Work Grade	Total Payroll	Rate per $100	Premium
Office clerical	$ 81,000	$0.18	$ 145.80
Machine shop	312,000	2.90	9,048.00
Total	$393,000		$9,193.80
Less: Estimated premium paid in January			8,900.00
Balance due			$ 293.80

Iowa has the highest payout of workers' compensation benefits— a maximum of $984 a week to temporarily disabled workers.

A check is written for the balance due the insurance company, and the following entry is made in the journal:

Workers' Compensation Insurance Expense	293.80	
Cash		293.80

RECORDING THE DEPOSIT OR PAYMENT OF PAYROLL TAXES

The journal entries required to record the deposit or payment of FICA taxes and income taxes withheld and the payment of FUTA and SUTA taxes are explained below.

4 LEARNING OBJECTIVE

Depositing FICA Taxes and Federal Income Taxes Withheld

As explained in Chapter 3, the requirements for depositing FICA taxes and federal income taxes withheld from employees' wages vary in relation to the total amount of such taxes.

On April 15, the ledger accounts FICA Taxes Payable—OASDI, FICA Taxes Payable—HI, and Employees FIT Payable of the Nannan Company appear as follows:

FICA TAXES PAYABLE—OASDI

	4/15	697.07
	4/15	697.07
		1,394.14

FICA TAXES PAYABLE—HI

	4/15	163.02
	4/15	163.02
		326.04

EMPLOYEES FIT PAYABLE

	4/15	1,601.19

The company must deposit or electronically transfer the FICA and the federal income taxes. The following journal entry records this transaction:

FICA Taxes Payable—OASDI	1,394.14	
FICA Taxes Payable—HI	326.04	
Employees FIT Payable	1,601.19	
Cash		3,321.37

When posted, the debits of \$1,394.14 and \$326.04 to FICA Taxes Payable—OASDI and FICA Taxes Payable—HI remove the liabilities for the employer's share, as well as the employees' share, of the FICA taxes imposed. The debit to Employees FIT Payable removes the liability for the total amount of federal income taxes withheld from the employees' wages during the period. The credit to Cash reduces the assets of the company.

Paying State or City Income Taxes

When the employer turns over to the state or city the amount of income taxes withheld from employees' wages, the appropriate journal entry would be recorded as follows:

	Debit	Credit
Employees SIT Payable	XXX	
or		
Employees CIT Payable	XXX	
Cash		XXX

Paying FUTA and SUTA Taxes

At the time of depositing the FUTA taxes that have accumulated during the preceding calendar quarter, an entry is made as follows:

	Debit	Credit
FUTA Taxes Payable	XXX	
Cash		XXX

The quarterly payment of state unemployment contributions is recorded as follows:

	Debit	Credit
SUTA Taxes Payable.	XXX	
Cash		XXX

RECORDING END-OF-PERIOD ADJUSTMENTS

LEARNING OBJECTIVE 5

In most cases, the end of the fiscal (accounting) period does not coincide with the end of the payroll period. Therefore, adjustments are commonly made to record the end-of-period wages and accrued vacation pay.

Wages

To record the adjustment for end-of-period wages, the wages for this last payroll period must be split between the fiscal period just ending (accrued wages) and the fiscal period just beginning. For instance, if the fiscal period ends on Wednesday (e.g., December 31) and payday takes place every Friday, the wages earned by the employees on Monday, Tuesday, and Wednesday are an expense of the fiscal period just ended. However, the wages earned on Thursday and Friday (payday) apply to the new fiscal period.

In order to record the wage expense properly for the fiscal period ended, an adjusting entry must be made on the last day of the fiscal period. However, since there is no actual wage payment, there is no need to credit any withholding accounts. The debit part of the entry would be based on the gross pay for the work days to be accrued. The credit part of the entry involves a single liability account for the total wage expense. In the case above, the wage expenses of Monday, Tuesday, and Wednesday would be recorded in the following *adjusting entry:*

	Debit	Credit
Wages Expense	XXX	
Wages Payable		XXX
To record wages incurred but unpaid as of the end of		
the fiscal period.		

Since the accumulation of payroll data (timesheets, registers, etc.) is such a time-consuming process, the amount of the adjustment could be based on a percentage of the previous period's payroll. For instance, if the accrual is for three workdays out of a five-workday week, 60% of the prior week's gross pay could be used as the amount of the adjustment.

In a situation where the employer holds back one week's pay (earnings for the current week are not paid until the following Friday), the adjusting entry for the example shown above would accrue eight days of expense (one full workweek plus Monday, Tuesday, and Wednesday).

Vacation Pay

Another adjustment required at the end of the accounting period concerns vacation pay. If a company has a vacation policy, the employees earn the right for paid future absences during the current period. Therefore, an expense account should be created for the amount of the vacation time earned by the employees and a liability should be accrued at the end of the current period. Whether making the adjustment each payday, each month, or each year, the expense must be recorded when the liability is created, which is in the period when the employees earn it.

EXAMPLE

The employees of Dansly Company are entitled to one day's vacation for each month worked. The average daily pay for each of the 50 employees is $130. The adjusting entry to record the vacation expense of $6,500 ($130 × 50) at the end of each month is:

Vacation Benefits Expense	6,500.00	
Vacation Benefits Payable		6,500.00

When employees eventually use their vacation time, the payment entry debits Vacation Benefits Payable, not Wages Expense, since the expense was previously recorded in the adjusting entry, as shown above. Another method that is used by most companies ignores the split between regular pay and vacation pay in the payroll entry. Instead, an adjusting entry is made at the end of each month for the expense and the liability to bring the balance in the liability account (Vacation Benefits Payable) either up to or down to the current total of unused vacation for the company with the offsetting debit or credit made to a vacation expense account.

Postretirement benefits such as health care and pensions also require adjusting entries of this type. These benefits must be reported as expenses during the employees' working years when they earn the entitlements.

RECORDING TRANSACTIONS PERTAINING TO OTHER PAYROLL DEDUCTIONS

Up to this point in our discussion of deductions made from wages and salaries, we have been limited to FICA taxes, state unemployment contributions, and income taxes. However, most companies have other deductions that must be taken into consideration when preparing the payroll. Regardless of the number or the types of deductions made from employees' wages, we must provide a systematic means of keeping a record of the total wages for each employee, the deductions for each purpose, and the net amount paid. It is impossible to say that a certain type of record is satisfactory for every organization or even for each company doing a certain kind of business. Each business organization has its own

on the

According to the World Tourism Organization, the average number of vacation days provided to workers is 42 in Italy, 37 in France, 28 in Britain, 26 in Canada, and 13 in the United States.

problems and peculiarities that will affect the type of record needed. It is important, therefore, that we keep all the records required by law, as well as those needed for other purposes.

Although you should have a separate column in the payroll register for each deduction, the payroll register may become too cumbersome if there are too many columns for deductions. Many businesses, therefore, use a payroll register with a separate column for each of the major deductions and lump all other deductions together in one column headed "Other Deductions." Some companies use only one column for deductions and place the entire total in that column. If this practice is followed, it is usually necessary to have a supplementary record of deductions showing a detailed breakdown of the total for each employee. This supplementary record serves as the basis for obtaining the figure for total deductions shown in the payroll register.

The deductions for FICA taxes, income taxes, disability benefits, and state unemployment benefits are required by law. Most other payroll deductions result from company policies, collective bargaining agreements, court orders, or employee authorizations. Some of the purposes for making deductions include:

1. Group insurance.
2. Health insurance.
3. Purchase of government bonds.
4. Union dues.
5. Garnishment of wages.
6. Child support.
7. Pension and retirement contributions.

Group Insurance

Many companies have a *group insurance* program for employees. Such programs usually permit employees to obtain life insurance at a much lower rate than would be possible if the employee purchased the insurance as an individual. Under some group insurance plans, the employer and the employee share the cost of the insurance premium. The employees' share may be deducted from their wages every payday, every month, or every quarter.

When recording a payroll which makes deductions from employees' wages for group insurance, the amount withheld from their wages is applied toward the payment of their share of the premium. The total amount withheld is credited to a *liability* account with a title such as *Group Insurance Premiums Collected* or *Group Insurance Payments Withheld.* This general ledger account serves the same purpose as the accounts used to record payroll taxes withheld from employees' wages. When the premiums are paid to the insurance company, the liability account will be debited.

Health Insurance

Many companies have developed their own health insurance plans for employees or are members of private insurance groups that provide coverage for employees of companies that are members of the group. If employees bear the cost or a portion of the cost of such insurance, the portion paid by the employees is usually deducted every payday from the wages of the employees. The amounts withheld from the employees' wages for health insurance are credited to a *liability* account such as *Health Insurance Premiums Collected.*

Employers often pay the premium for health insurance in advance to the insurance carrier. At the time of paying the premium, a prepaid expense account such as *Prepaid Health Insurance* is debited for the amount paid the carrier. This account is adjusted periodically through the health insurance or fringe benefit expense account and, if applicable, the employees' withholding account.

Purchase of Government Savings Bonds

Employees are encouraged to invest a certain amount of their wages in government savings bonds. Such plans or similar savings plans encourage employees to save a certain amount of each salary payment. The theory behind such deductions is that most employees will not miss a small amount that is set aside each payday, and over a period of time the deductions accumulate into a sizable amount.

Employees authorize their employer to make payroll deductions for the purchase of savings bonds by completing authorization forms that indicate the amount to be withheld and the frequency. The amounts withheld from the paychecks are set aside by the employer, acting in a trustee position, until a sufficient amount has been accumulated for the purchase of savings bonds for the employees. The minimum denomination for Series EE savings bonds for new participants in a payroll savings plan is $100. A $100 bond can be purchased as soon as the participant has accumulated the $50 purchase price in his or her withholding account.

EXAMPLE

Wayne Richards has authorized his employer to withhold $10 from his pay every two weeks toward the purchase of a Series EE U.S. savings bond, which has a maturity value of $100. At the time of preparing each biweekly payroll, the employer credits the liability account *U.S. Savings Bonds Deductions Payable* for $10. After the employer has recorded five similar entries, the balance of the liability account will be $50, the amount required for the purchase of one $100 Series EE U.S. savings bond. At this time, the employer purchases the bond, which is later delivered to the employee. The journal entry to record this transaction includes a debit of $50 to the liability account *U.S. Savings Bonds Deductions Payable* and a corresponding credit to the cash account.

Union Dues

In companies in which employees are members of unions that require employees to pay dues to the union, many employees pay their dues, assessments, and initiation fees through deductions from wages, known as a ***check-off system.*** Amounts withheld from union members' wages are credited to a *liability* account such as *Union Dues Payable.* Monthly, or as agreed upon by the union and the employer, the amounts withheld are turned over to the treasurer of the union. At this time, a journal entry is made in which the payment of union dues is recorded by debiting the liability account and crediting the cash account.

Garnishment of Wages

Garnishment refers to the legal or equitable procedure by which a portion of the wages of any person must be withheld for payment of a debt. Through the garnishment process, a creditor, with the aid of the courts, may require the employer to hold back a portion of the debtor's wages and pay that amount to the court or to the creditor. In some companies, the amounts to be held back are deducted each payday from the employee's wages.

The Consumer Credit Protection Act limits the amount of wages subject to garnishment, in general, to 25% of a worker's disposable earnings. ***Disposable earnings*** are the earnings remaining after withholding for income taxes and for other amounts required by law.

The provisions of the Consumer Credit Protection Act also prohibit an employer from discharging an employee simply because the employee's wages are subject to garnishment for one indebtedness. If another garnishment for a second indebtedness should arise, the worker could be discharged, provided a considerable amount of time had *not* elapsed between the two occasions of indebtedness. The payroll manager should also be aware that state garnishment laws that are more favorable to employees have priority over the federal law.

Child Support

The Family Support Act of 1988 requires the immediate withholding for child-support payments for all cases supported by a court order. The amount withheld is equal to the amount of the deliquency, subject to the limits prescribed in the federal garnishment law. Employers may withhold a fee, set by each state, for administrative costs. (In cases of support orders,

on the

JOB

Under the Family Support Act, all states must permit child-support garnishment from the beginning of the support payments. In the past, some states garnished wages for child support only after the parent had fallen behind in payments.

IRS CONNECTION

The IRS also collects support payments by withholding from income tax refunds due delinquent payers.

the limits on the amounts that can be taken from an employee's pay range from 50% to 65% of weekly disposable wages, depending on the employee's number of dependents.)

Federal Tax Levy

Federal tax levies are not restricted by the Consumer Credit Protection Act and take second priority after wages withheld for child support (if received prior to the tax levy). The only portions of wages that are exempt from a federal tax levy is the taxpayer's standard deduction and the personal exemptions allowed for the tax year divided by the number of pay periods in the year.

The IRS uses Form 668-W (not illustrated) to notify an employer of a tax levy. Copies of the form must then be forwarded to the employee for completion of a statement of filing status and exemptions. This information will then allow the employer to compute the actual levy. If the employee fails to return the signed statement within three working days to the employer, the exempt amount is based on married-filing-separately status with one personal exemption.

Pension and Retirement Contributions

Since in many instances social security benefits are inadequate for retired employees and their dependents, many firms provide pension and retirement plans that will supplement the government benefits. Although the benefit formulas and eligibility rules vary, the coverage is about the same for production workers, office employees, and managers. Many pension plans are financed solely by employer contributions, but other plans involve employee contributions. Once these contributions are deducted from the employees' pay, they become a liability for the employer and are recorded as such in the payroll entry. This would also apply to employee contributions into 401(k) plans.

Some employers also provide their employees with the opportunity to set up their own Individual Retirement Accounts (IRA) through a payroll deduction plan (see page 1-12). These voluntary contributions are deducted from the paychecks of the employees who set up their own retirement accounts. These deductions are recorded as a liability in the payroll entry. This liability account will be cleared as the employer pays the contributions to the financial institution that is in charge of each employee's retirement account.

SUMMARY OF ACCOUNTS USED IN RECORDING PAYROLL TRANSACTIONS

LEARNING OBJECTIVE 6

The following listing summarizes some of the general ledger accounts that may be used to record payroll transactions:

1. *Wages and Salaries*—an operating expense account in which the gross payroll is recorded.
2. *Payroll Taxes*—an operating expense account in which are recorded all payroll taxes on the employer under FICA, FUTA, and the various state unemployment compensation laws.
3. *Workers' Compensation Insurance Expense*—an operating expense account in which are recorded the premiums paid by the company to provide coverage for employees against employment-related injury or death.
4. *Vacation Benefits Expense*—an operating expense account in which are recorded the costs of the vacation time that has been earned by employees.
5. *FICA Taxes Payable—OASDI*—a current liability account in which are recorded deductions made from employees' wages and the employer's portion of the OASDI tax.
6. *FICA Taxes Payable—HI*—a current liability account in which are recorded deductions made from employees' wages and the employer's portion of the HI tax.
7. *FUTA Taxes Payable*—a current liability account in which are recorded the employer's federal unemployment taxes.
8. *SUTA Taxes Payable*—a current liability account in which are recorded the amounts due the states for the employer's unemployment compensation contributions. This account may also be credited for amounts deducted from employees' wages, if employees must contribute to state unemployment compensation funds.

9. *Employees FIT Payable*—a current liability account in which are recorded deductions made from employees' wages for federal income taxes.

10. *Employees SIT Payable*—a current liability account in which are recorded deductions made from employees' wages for state income taxes.

11. *Health Insurance Premiums Collected*—a current liability account in which are recorded deductions made from employees' wages for their share of the premiums paid for health insurance coverage.

12. *Union Dues Payable*—a current liability account in which are recorded the deductions made from union members' wages for their union dues, assessments, or initiation fees.

13. *Wages Payable*—a current liability account in which are recorded the wages that have been earned by employees but not yet paid to them.

14. *Vacation Benefits Payable*—a current liability account in which are recorded the costs of the vacation time that has been earned by employees but not yet used.

ILLUSTRATIVE CASE

The following illustrative case shows the accounting procedures used by Brookins Company in recording payroll transactions during the third quarter of its fiscal year. The fiscal year of the company ends on June 30, 20—. Brookins pays employees semimonthly on the 15th and the last day of the month. When the 15th or the last day of the month falls on Saturday or Sunday, employees are paid on the preceding Friday.

On January 1, 20—, the balances of the accounts used in recording payroll transactions follow. These account balances are shown in the general ledger on pages 6-26 through 6-28.

Acct. No.	Account Title	Account Balance
11	Cash	$85,000.00
20	FICA Taxes Payable—OASDI	734.29
21	FICA Taxes Payable—HI	171.73
22	FUTA Taxes Payable	122.00
23	SUTA Taxes Payable	40.50
25	Employees FIT Payable	1,472.00
26	Employees SIT Payable	474.42
28	Union Dues Payable	80.00
51	Wages and Salaries	46,500.00
55	Payroll Taxes	4,254.50

The first $89,700 in wages and salaries paid is subject to the OASDI tax on both the employer (6.2%) and the employees (6.2%). The total wages and salaries paid are subject to the HI tax on both the employer (1.45%) and the employees (1.45%). The employer is also subject to a net FUTA tax of 0.8%, based on the first $7,000 in earnings paid each employee during a calendar year, and a SUTA tax of 2.3%, based on the first $7,000 in earnings paid during a calendar year. The state does not require contributions of employees for unemployment compensation or disability insurance.

The wage-bracket method is used to determine the amount of federal income taxes to be withheld from the employees' earnings. The state income tax law requires that a graduated percentage of the gross earnings of each employee be withheld each payday. Under the check-off system, union dues are withheld each payday from the union workers who are employed in the plant. On or before the fourth of each month, the dues collected during the preceding month are turned over to the treasurer of the union.

In the following narrative of transactions, the January 14 (Friday) payroll transaction is explained in detail on page 6-20. All other transactions are stated briefly. Adjacent to the narrative are the journal entries to record the transactions. The ledger accounts showing the transactions posted are on pages 6-26 through 6-28.

Narrative of Transactions	Journal	P.R.	Debit	Page 15 Credit
	20—			
Jan. 4. Paid the treasurer of the union $80, representing the union dues withheld from the workers' earnings during the month of December.	Jan. 4 Union Dues Payable . . . . Cash . . . . To record payment of union dues withheld during December.	28 11	80.00	80.00
Jan. 14. Paid total wages and salaries of all employees, $3,890. All the earnings are taxable under FICA. In addition to the social security taxes, the company withheld $455 from the employees' earnings for federal income taxes, $85.58 for state income taxes, and $45 for union dues. (See the explanation of the January 14 payroll transaction given below.)	14 Wages and Salaries . . . . FICA Taxes Payable—OASDI . . . . . FICA Taxes Payable—HI . . . . Employees FIT Payable . . . . Employees SIT Payable . . . . Union Dues Payable . . . . Cash . . . . To record the payment of wages and the liabilities for the employees' taxes withheld.	51 20 21 25 26 28 11	3,890.00	241.18 56.41 455.00 85.58 45.00 3,006.83
Jan. 14. Recorded the employer's payroll taxes for the first pay in January. All the earnings are taxable under FICA, FUTA, and SUTA.	14 Payroll Taxes . . . . FICA Taxes Payable—OASDI . . . . . FICA Taxes Payable—HI . . . . FUTA Taxes Payable . . . . SUTA Taxes Payable . . . . To record the payroll taxes and liabilities of the employer.	55 20 21 22 23	418.18	241.18 56.41 31.12 89.47
Jan. 18. Electronically transferred to the IRS the FICA taxes and employees' federal income taxes withheld on the two December payrolls. At the end of December, the total liability for FICA taxes and federal income taxes withheld was $2,378.02. (January 17 is Martin Luther King, Jr.'s birthday, which is a bank holiday.)	18 FICA Taxes Payable—OASDI . . . . FICA Taxes Payable—HI . . . . Employees FIT Payable . . . . Cash . . . . To record deposit of FICA taxes and federal income taxes withheld for the 12/15 and 12/31 payrolls.	20 21 25 11	734.29 171.73 1,472.00	2,378.02
	18 Employees SIT Payable . . . . Cash . . . . To record payment of state income taxes withheld during 4th quarter.	26 11	474.42	474.42

Analysis of the January 14 payroll transaction follows:

1. Wages and Salaries is debited for $3,890, the total of the employees' gross earnings.
2. FICA Taxes Payable—OASDI is credited for $241.18, the amount withheld from the employees' earnings for OASDI taxes.
3. FICA Taxes Payable—HI is credited for $56.41, the amount withheld from the employees' earnings for HI taxes.
4. Employees FIT Payable is credited for $455, the amount withheld from employees' earnings for federal income tax purposes.
5. Employees SIT Payable is credited for $85.58, the amount withheld from employees' earnings for state income taxes.
6. Union Dues Payable is credited for $45, the amount withheld from union members' earnings.
7. Cash is credited for $3,006.83, the net amount paid the employees ($3,890 gross earnings – $241.18 OASDI – $56.41 HI – $455 FIT – $85.58 SIT – $45 union dues).

8. Payroll Taxes is debited for $418.18, the amount of taxes imposed on the employer under FICA, FUTA, and SUTA. The computation of the total payroll taxes is:

FICA—OASDI:	6.2% of $3,890 =	$241.18
FICA—HI:	1.45% of $3,890 =	56.41
FUTA:	0.8% of $3,890 =	31.12
SUTA:	2.3% of $3,890 =	89.47
Total payroll taxes		$418.18

9. FICA Taxes Payable—OASDI is credited for the amount of tax on the employer, which is 6.2% of $3,890, or $241.18.
10. FICA Taxes Payable—HI is credited for the amount of tax on the employer, which is 1.45% of $3,890, or $56.41.
11. FUTA Taxes Payable is credited for $31.12, the liability incurred because of the taxes imposed on the employer under FUTA.
12. SUTA Taxes Payable is credited for $89.47, the amount of the contributions payable to the state.

Narrative of Transactions	Journal		P.R.	Debit	Page 16 Credit

Jan. 31. Paid total wages and salaries, $4,100. All of this amount constitutes taxable earnings under FICA. Withheld $483 for federal income taxes, $90.20 for state income taxes, and $45 for union dues.	Jan. 31	Wages and Salaries . . . .
		FICA Taxes Payable—OASDI . . . . .
		FICA Taxes Payable—HI . . . .
		Employees FIT Payable . . . .
		Employees SIT Payable . . . .
		Union Dues Payable . . . .
		Cash . . . .
		    To record the payment of wages
		    and the liabilities for
		    the employees' taxes withheld.
			51
			20
			21
			25
			26
			28
			11
				4,100.00	
					254.20
					59.45
					483.00
					90.20
					45.00
					3,168.15

Jan. 31. Recorded the employer's payroll taxes for this payroll. All the earnings are taxable under FICA, FUTA, and SUTA.	31	Payroll Taxes . . . .
		FICA Taxes Payable—OASDI . . . . .
		FICA Taxes Payable—HI . . . .
		FUTA Taxes Payable . . . .
		SUTA Taxes Payable . . . .
		    To record the payroll taxes and
		    liabilities of the employer.
			55
			20
			21
			22
			23
				440.75	
					254.20
					59.45
					32.80
					94.30

Jan. 31. Electronically transferred $122 to remove the liability for FUTA taxes for the fourth quarter of the previous year.	31	FUTA Taxes Payable . . . .
		Cash . . . .
		    To record the deposit of
		    FUTA taxes for the fourth
		    quarter.
			22
			11
				122.00	
					122.00

Jan. 31. Filed the state unemployment contributions return for the quarter ending December 31, and paid $40.50 to the state unemployment compensation fund.	31	SUTA Taxes Payable . . . . Cash . . . . To record payment of contributions to state unemployment compensation fund for the fourth quarter.	23 11	40.50·	 40.50
Jan. 31. Filed the *Employer's Annual Federal Unemployment (FUTA) Tax Return, Form 940-EZ,* for the preceding calendar year. No journal entry is required since the liability for FUTA taxes was removed by the timely transfer on January 31, 20—. No taxes were paid at the time of filing the annual return.					
Jan. 31. Filed the quarterly return (Form 941) with the IRS Center for the period ended December 31. No journal entry is required since the liability for FICA taxes and employees' federal income taxes withheld was removed by the timely transfer on January 18, 20—. No taxes were paid or deposited at the time of filing Form 941.					

Feb. 4. Paid the treasurer of the union $90, representing the union dues withheld from the workers' earnings during the month of January.	Feb. 4	Union Dues Payable . . . .
		Cash . . . .
		    To record the payment of the
		    union dues withheld during
		    January.
			28
			11
				90.00	
					90.00

Narrative of Transactions	Journal			Page 17
		P.R.	Debit	Credit

		P.R.	Debit	Credit
Feb. 15. Paid total wages and salaries, $4,000. All of this amount is taxable under FICA. Withheld $470 for federal income taxes, $88 for state income taxes, and $45 for union dues.	Feb. 15　Wages and Salaries	51	4,000.00	
	FICA Taxes Payable—OASDI	20		248.00
	FICA Taxes Payable—HI	21		58.00
	Employees FIT Payable	25		470.00
	Employees SIT Payable	26		88.00
	Union Dues Payable	28		45.00
	Cash	11		3,091.00
	To record the payment of wages and the liabilities for the employees' taxes withheld.			
Feb. 15. Recorded the employer's payroll taxes. All the earnings are taxable under FICA, FUTA, and SUTA.	15　Payroll Taxes	55	430.00	
	FICA Taxes Payable—OASDI	20		248.00
	FICA Taxes Payable—HI	21		58.00
	FUTA Taxes Payable	22		32.00
	SUTA Taxes Payable	23		92.00
	To record the payroll taxes and liabilities of the employer.			
Feb. 15. Electronically transferred $2,160.48 to remove the liability for the FICA taxes and the employees' federal income taxes withheld on the January 14 and January 31 payrolls.	15　FICA Taxes Payable—OASDI	20	990.76	
	FICA Taxes Payable—HI	21	231.72	
	Employees FIT Payable	25	938.00	
	Cash	11		2,160.48
	To record the deposit of FICA taxes and federal income taxes withheld for the January 14 and January 31 payrolls.			
Feb. 28. Paid total wages and salaries, $4,250. All of this amount is taxable under FICA. Withheld $502 for federal income taxes, $93.50 for state income taxes, and $50 for union dues.	28　Wages and Salaries	51	4,250.00	
	FICA Taxes Payable—OASDI	20		263.50
	FICA Taxes Payable—HI	21		61.63
	Employees FIT Payable	25		502.00
	Employees SIT Payable	26		93.50
	Union Dues Payable	28		50.00
	Cash	11		3,279.37
	To record the payment of wages and the liabilities for the employees' taxes withheld.			
Feb. 28. Recorded the employer's payroll taxes. All the earnings are taxable under FICA, FUTA, and SUTA.	28　Payroll Taxes	55	456.88	
	FICA Taxes Payable—OASDI	20		263.50
	FICA Taxes Payable—HI	21		61.63
	FUTA Taxes Payable	22		34.00
	SUTA Taxes Payable	23		97.75
	To record the payroll taxes and liabilities of the employer.			
Mar. 4. Paid the treasurer of the union $95, representing the union dues withheld from the workers' earnings during the month of February.	Mar. 4　Union Dues Payable	28	95.00	
	Cash	11		95.00
	To record the payment of the union dues withheld during February.			

Narrative of Transactions	Journal	P.R.	Debit	Page 18 Credit
Mar. 15. Paid total wages and salaries, $4,300. All of this amount is taxable under FICA. Withheld $554 for federal income taxes, $94.60 for state income taxes, and $50 for union dues.	Mar. 15 Wages and Salaries	51	4,300.00	
	FICA Taxes Payable—OASDI	20		266.60
	FICA Taxes Payable—HI	21		62.35
	Employees FIT Payable	25		554.00
	Employees SIT Payable	26		94.60
	Union Dues Payable	28		50.00
	Cash	11		3,272.45
	To record the payment of wages and the liabilities for the employees' taxes withheld.			
Mar. 15. Recorded the employer's payroll taxes. All the earnings are taxable under FICA, FUTA, and SUTA.	15 Payroll Taxes	55	462.25	
	FICA Taxes Payable—OASDI	20		266.60
	FICA Taxes Payable—HI	21		62.35
	FUTA Taxes Payable	22		34.40
	SUTA Taxes Payable	23		98.90
	To record the payroll taxes and liabilities of the employer.			
Mar. 15. Electronically transferred $2,234.26 to remove the liability for FICA taxes and the employees' federal income taxes withheld on the February 15 and February 28 payrolls.	15 FICA Taxes Payable—OASDI	20	1,023.00	
	FICA Taxes Payable—HI	21	239.26	
	Employees FIT Payable	25	972.00	
	Cash	11		2,234.26
	To record the deposit of FICA taxes and federal income taxes withheld for the February 15 and February 28 payrolls.			
Mar. 31. Paid total wages and salaries, $4,320. All of this amount is taxable under FICA. Withheld $570 for federal income taxes, $95.04 for state income taxes, and $50 for union dues.	31 Wages and Salaries	51	4,320.00	
	FICA Taxes Payable—OASDI	20		267.84
	FICA Taxes Payable—HI	21		62.64
	Employees FIT Payable	25		570.00
	Employees SIT Payable	26		95.04
	Union Dues Payable	28		50.00
	Cash	11		3,274.48
	To record the payment of wages and the liabilities for the employees' taxes withheld.			
Mar. 31. Recorded the employer's payroll taxes. All of the earnings are taxable under FICA, FUTA, and SUTA.	31 Payroll Taxes	55	464.40	
	FICA Taxes Payable—OASDI	20		267.84
	FICA Taxes Payable—HI	21		62.64
	FUTA Taxes Payable	22		34.56
	SUTA Taxes Payable	23		99.36
	To record the payroll taxes and liabilities of the employer.			

EMPLOYEES SIT PAYABLE   26

Date	Item	P.R.	Dr.	Cr.	Balance Dr.	Balance Cr.
20—						
Jan. 1	Bal.	✓				474.42
14		J15		85.58		560.00
18		J15	474.42			85.58
31		J16		90.20		175.78
Feb. 15		J17		88.00		263.78
28		J17		93.50		357.28
Mar. 15		J18		94.60		451.88
31		J18		95.04		546.92

UNION DUES PAYABLE   28

Date	Item	P.R.	Dr.	Cr.	Balance Dr.	Balance Cr.
20—						
Jan. 1	Bal.	✓				80.00
4		J15	80.00			———
14		J15		45.00		45.00
31		J16		45.00		90.00
Feb. 4		J16	90.00			———
15		J17		45.00		45.00
28		J17		50.00		95.00
Mar. 4		J17	95.00			———
15		J18		50.00		50.00
31		J18		50.00		100.00

WAGES AND SALARIES   51

Date	Item	P.R.	Dr.	Cr.	Balance Dr.	Balance Cr.
20—						
Jan. 1	Bal.	✓			46,500.00	
14		J15	3,890.00		50,390.00	
31		J16	4,100.00		54,490.00	
Feb. 15		J17	4,000.00		58,490.00	
28		J17	4,250.00		62,740.00	
Mar. 15		J18	4,300.00		67,040.00	
31		J18	4,320.00		71,360.00	

PAYROLL TAXES   55

Date	Item	P.R.	Dr.	Cr.	Balance Dr.	Balance Cr.
20—						
Jan. 1	Bal.	✓			4,254.50	
14		J15	418.18		4,672.68	
31		J16	440.75		5,113.43	
Feb. 15		J17	430.00		5,543.43	
28		J17	456.88		6,000.31	
Mar. 15		J18	462.25		6,462.56	
31		J18	464.40		6,926.96	

KEY TERMS

Business expense *(p. 6-11)*
Check-off system *(p. 6-19)*
Disposable earnings *(p. 6-19)*
Garnishment *(p. 6-19)*

Group insurance *(p. 6-18)*
Journal entries *(p. 6-5)*
Payroll journal *(p. 6-6)*

MATCHING QUIZ

_____ 1. Employee's Earnings Record

_____ 2. Advance Earned Income Credit

_____ 3. Disposable earnings

_____ 4. Regular earnings plus overtime earnings

_____ 5. Payroll Taxes

_____ 6. Overtime premium earnings

_____ 7. Wages Payable

_____ 8. Payroll Journal

_____ 9. Form 668-W

_____ 10. Garnishment

A. Expense account for FICA, FUTA, SUTA taxes on the employer

B. Legal procedure by which a portion of wages of a person must be withheld for payment of a debt

C. Reduce employer's liability for the payment of FICA and FIT taxes to the IRS

D. Notifies employer of a tax levy

E. Used to complete Form W-2

F. Provides information needed in preparing the joournal entries for payroll

G. Debit portion of payroll entry

H. Earnings remaining after withholding for income taxes and for other amounts required by law

I. One half regular pay rate multiplied by overtime hours

J. Liability account for wages that have been earned by employees but not yet paid

QUESTIONS FOR REVIEW

1. What are the main kinds of information contained in a payroll register?
2. For what reason are "distribution" columns sometimes provided in the payroll register?
3. Explain the use of the "Cumulative" column in the employee's earnings record.
4. In Philadelphia, Pennsylvania, most workers are subject to three income taxes upon their earnings—federal, state, and city. Should an employer in Philadelphia record the liability for the withholding of all three income taxes in one liability account such as Income Taxes Payable?
5. What special accounts must usually be opened in the general ledger to record payroll tax entries?
6. Is it necessary for an employer who is subject to FICA and FUTA taxes to keep a separate expense account for the taxes under each act?
7. What is the effect of each of the following postings upon the assets, liabilities, and owner's equity of a company?
   a. A debit to Wages.
   b. A credit to FICA Taxes Payable—HI.
   c. A debit to SUTA Taxes Payable.
   d. A credit to Cash.
8. Why is it necessary to classify employees by kind of work performed when computing the cost of workers' compensation insurance?
9. What accounts are debited and credited when an employer records the electronic transfer of FICA taxes and federal income taxes that have been withheld?
10. How is the amount of accrual entry for the portion of a weekly payroll that is accrued at the end of an accounting period determined?
11. How will payroll deductions from employees' wages for their portion of 401(k) plans be recorded?
12. When are expenses of benefits such as vacation pay and retirement pay recorded? Explain.
13. What is meant by the *garnishment* of wages?
14. What portions of an employee's wages are exempt from a federal tax levy?
15. What payroll-related expenses does an employer incur because of its employees?

QUESTIONS FOR DISCUSSION

1. In what respect does an employee's earnings record resemble a ledger?
2. The Golic Corporation has undertaken a cost study of its operations. One area of concern to the company is the total cost of labor, particularly the cost of employee benefits. Prepare a list of the different kinds of costs that a company might incur as part of its "total package" salary cost.
3. Along with five payroll deductions required by law (FICA—OASDI and HI, Employees FIT, Employees SIT, and Employees CIT), five other deductions are typically made from the employees' earnings in The Cranston Company. What leeway does the company have as to the level of detail shown in the payroll register in recording these ten deductions?

PRACTICAL PROBLEMS

Omit the writing of explanations for the journal entries.

6–1. LO 2, 4.

a. Gail Winters, an employer, is subject to FICA taxes but exempt from FUTA and SUTA taxes. During the last quarter of the year, her employees earned monthly wages of $8,500, all of which is taxable. The amount of federal income taxes withheld each month is $1,040. Journalize the payment of wages, and record the payroll tax on November 30.

JOURNAL

	DATE	DESCRIPTION	POST. REF.	DEBIT	CREDIT	
1						1
2						2
3						3
4						4
5						5
6						6
7						7
8						8
9						9
10						10

b. Prior to posting the November 30 payroll transaction, the FICA Taxes Payable—OASDI, the FICA Taxes Payable—HI, and the Employees FIT Payable accounts had zero balances. Winters must pay the FICA taxes and income taxes withheld on the November 30 payroll. Journalize the electronic transfer of the payroll taxes on December 15.

JOURNAL

	DATE	DESCRIPTION	POST. REF.	DEBIT	CREDIT	
1						1
2						2
3						3
4						4
5						5
6						6

6–2. LO 2.

The employees of Morton Music Company earn total wages of $4,690 during January. The total amount is taxable under FICA, FUTA, and SUTA. The state contribution rate for the company is 3.6%. The amount withheld for federal income taxes is $685. Journalize the payment of the monthly wages, and record the payroll taxes.

JOURNAL

	DATE	DESCRIPTION	POST. REF.	DEBIT	CREDIT	
1						1
2						2
3						3
4						4
5						5
6						6
7						7
8						8
9						9
10						10
11						11
12						12
13						13
14						14

6–3. LO 2.

Tex, Inc., has a semimonthly payroll of $38,000 on September 15. The total payroll is taxable under FICA Taxes—HI; $32,850 is taxable under FICA Taxes—OASDI; and $9,300 is taxable under FUTA and SUTA. The state contribution rate for the company is 3.1%. The amount withheld for federal income taxes is $5,780. The amount withheld for state income taxes is $809.

a. Journalize the payment of the wages, and record the payroll taxes on September 15.

b. Assume that the employees of Tex, Inc., must also pay state contributions (disability insurance) of 1% on the taxable payroll of $29,300 and that the employees' contributions are to be deducted by the employer. Journalize the September 15 payment of wages, assuming that the state contributions of the employees are kept in a separate account.

JOURNAL

	DATE	DESCRIPTION	POST. REF.	DEBIT	CREDIT	
1						1
2						2
3						3
4						4
5						5
6						6
7						7
8						8
9						9
10						10
11						11
12						12
13						13
14						14
15						15
16						16
17						17
18						18
19						19
20						20
21						21
22						22
23						23
24						24
25						25
26						26
27						27

6-4. LO 2.

Kip Bowman is owner and sole employee of KB Corporation. He pays himself a salary of $1,500 each week.

Additional tax information includes:

FICA tax—OASDI	6.2% on first $89,700
FICA tax—HI	1.45% on total pay
Federal income tax	$232.00 per pay
State income tax	22% of the federal income tax withholding
Federal unemployment tax	0.8% on first $7,000
State unemployment tax	0.05% on first $14,000

Additional payroll deductions include:

401(k) plan	3% per pay
Child support garnishment	$100 per pay
Health insurance premium	$95 per pay

Record the payroll entry and payroll tax entry for the pay of the week ended June 4 (his year-to-date pay is $31,500).

JOURNAL

	DATE	DESCRIPTION	POST. REF.	DEBIT	CREDIT	
1						1
2						2
3						3
4						4
5						5
6						6
7						7
8						8
9						9
10						10
11						11
12						12
13						13
14						14
15						15
16						16
17						17
18						18
19						19
20						20

6–5. LO 2.

The employees of Pelter Company earn wages of $12,000 for the two weeks ending April 20. FIT taxes of $260 were withheld. The entire amount of wages is subject to the FICA taxes, but only $9,800 is taxable under the federal and state unemployment compensation laws. The state contribution rate of the employer is 2.9%. All employees are subject to state unemployment contributions of 0.5% on the April 20 taxable wages of $9,800, and the employees' contributions are to be deducted by the employer. Journalize the payment of the wages, and record the payroll taxes, assuming that the contributions of the employer and the employees are recorded in one account, SUTA Taxes Payable.

JOURNAL

	DATE	DESCRIPTION	POST. REF.	DEBIT	CREDIT	
1						1
2						2
3						3
4						4
5						5
6						6
7						7
8						8
9						9
10						10
11						11
12						12

6–6. LO 2.

The following information pertains to the payroll of Furphy Textile Company on June 1:

a. The total wages earned by employees are $2,180.

b. The state unemployment insurance contribution rate is 2.5%.

c. The entire amount of wages is taxable under FICA, FUTA, and SUTA.

d. The amount withheld from the employees' wages for federal income taxes is $309; for state income taxes, $43.10; and for group insurance, $16.80.

e. The amount of the advance earned income credit payments made to the employees is $131.

Journalize the payment of wages, and record the payroll taxes on June 1.

JOURNAL

	DATE	DESCRIPTION	POST. REF.	DEBIT	CREDIT	
1						1
2						2
3						3
4						4
5						5
6						6
7						7
8						8
9						9
10						10
11						11
12						12
13						13
14						14
15						15

6–7. LO 4.

On December 31, 2003, Reuter Company has a balance of $98.75 in the FUTA taxes payable account. This represents the employer's liability for the fourth quarter taxes.

Journalize the entry Reuter Company should make in January 2004 to record the last transfer (payment) of FUTA taxes for 2003.

JOURNAL

	DATE	DESCRIPTION	POST. REF.	DEBIT	CREDIT	
1						1
2						2
3						3
4						4
5						5
6						6

6–8. LO 5.

On December 31, 20--, Gorman Company needed to record its accrued wages for year-end. December 31 is a Tuesday, and Gorman Company must account for two days of wages.

The company operates on a five-day workweek, and the prior week's gross pay (December 27 payday) was $32,650, and the net pay was $21,330.

Journalize the adjusting entry to be made on December 31 for the accrued wages.

JOURNAL

	DATE	DESCRIPTION	POST. REF.	DEBIT	CREDIT	
1						1
2						2
3						3
4						4
5						5
6						6

6–9.

Kelsey Gunn is the only employee of the Arsenault Company. His pay rate is $23.00 per hour with an overtime rate of 1½ times for hours over 40 in a workweek.

For the week ending March 31, 20--, he worked 48 hours. Calculate his gross pay for the week using the overtime premium approach to calculate the overtime pay.

a. Regular pay _____
b. Overtime premium pay _____
c. Gross pay _____

Since the company holds back one week of pay, Gunn will not be paid until April 7, 20--. What adjusting entry would the company make in order to record Gunn's salary in the first quarter of this year?

d. _____

6–10. LO 2.

In Oregon, employers who are covered by the state workers' compensation law must withhold employee contributions from the wages of covered employees at the rate of 2.0¢ for each hour or part of an hour that the worker is employed. Every covered employer is assessed 2.0¢ per hour for each worker employed for each hour or part of an hour. The employer-employee contributions for workers' compensation are collected monthly, quarterly, or annually by the employer's insurance carrier, according to a schedule agreed upon by the employer and the carrier. The insurance carrier remits the contributions to the state's Workers' Compensation Department.

The Brunansky Company, a covered employer in Oregon, turns over the employer-employee workers' compensation contributions to its insurance carrier by the 15th

of each month for the preceding month. During the month of July, the number of full-time employee-hours worked by the company's employees was 24,190; the number of part-time employee-hours was 2,440.

a. The amount the company should have withheld from its full-time and part-time employees during the month of July for workers' compensation insurance is . . . . $ _____

b. The title you would give to the general ledger account to which the amount withheld from the employees' earnings would be credited is:

_____

c. Journalize the entry on July 31 to record the employer's liability for workers' compensation insurance for the month.

JOURNAL

	DATE		DESCRIPTION	POST. REF.	DEBIT	CREDIT	
1							1
2							2
3							3
4							4
5							5

d. Journalize the entry on August 15 to record payment to the insurance carrier of the amount withheld from the employees' earnings for workers' compensation insurance and the amount of the employer's liability.

JOURNAL

	DATE	DESCRIPTION	POST. REF.	DEBIT	CREDIT	
1						1
2						2
3						3
4						4
5						5

6–11. LO 1.

The form on page 6-39 shows the amounts that appear in the Earnings to Date column of the employees' earnings records for 10 workers in Unger Company. These amounts represent the cumulative earnings for each worker as of October 18, the company's last payday. The form also gives the gross amount of earnings to be paid each worker on the next payday, October 25.

In the state where Unger Company is located, the tax rates and bases are as follows:

Tax on Employees:
FICA—OASDI .... 6.2% on first $89,700
FICA—HI .... 1.45% on *total earnings*
SUTA .... 0.5% on first $8,000

Tax on Employer:
FICA—OASDI .... 6.2% on first $89,700
FICA—HI .... 1.45% on *total earnings*
FUTA .... 0.8% on first $7,000
SUTA .... 1.8% on first $8,000

In the appropriate columns of the form on page 6-39, do the following:

1. Compute the amount to be withheld from each employee's earnings on October 25 for (a) FICA—OASDI, (b) FICA—HI, and (c) SUTA, and determine the total employee taxes.

2. Record the portion of each employee's earnings that is taxable under FICA, FUTA, and SUTA, and calculate the total employer's payroll taxes on the October 25 payroll.

UNGER COMPANY

	Employee	Earnings to Date	Gross Earnings, Oct. 25	Taxes to Be Withheld From Employees' Earnings Under				Employer Taxes: Portion of Employees' Earnings Taxable Under			
				FICA				FICA			
				OASDI	HI	SUTA		OASDI	HI	FUTA	SUTA
1.	Weiser, Robert A.	$89,790	$790								
2.	Stankard, Laurie C.	14,950	295								
3.	Grow, Joan L.	4,060	240								
4.	Rowe, Paul C.	8,190	235								
5.	McNamara, Joyce M.	7,460	195								
6.	O'Connor, Roger T.	89,410	810								
7.	Carson, Ronald B.	8,905	280								
8.	Kenny, Ginni C.	4,325	175								
9.	Devery, Virginia S.	57,010	590								
10.	Wilson, Joe W.	3,615	205								
	Total employee taxes			$	$	$		$	$	$	$
				1.(a)	1.(b)	1.(c)					
	Total taxable earnings							$	$	$	$
	× Applicable tax rate										
	Totals							$	$	$	$
	Total payroll taxes			$							

2.

6-39

6–12. LO 2, 3, 4, 5 and 6.

In the Illustrative Case in this chapter, payroll transactions for Brookins Company were analyzed, journalized, and posted for the third quarter of the fiscal year. In this problem, you are to record the payroll transactions for the last quarter of the firm's fiscal year. The last quarter begins on April 1.

    Refer to the Illustrative Case on pages 6-21 to 6-28 and proceed as follows:

a. Analyze and journalize the transactions described in the following narrative. Use the two-column journal paper provided on pages 6-41 to 6-45. Omit the writing of explanations in the journal entries.

b. Post the journal entries to the general ledger accounts on pages 6-46 to 6-51.

Narrative of Transactions:

Apr. 1. Paid the treasurer of the union the amount of union dues withheld from workers' earnings during March.

15. Payroll: $6,105. All wages and salaries taxable. Withheld $565 for federal income taxes, $107.32 for state income taxes, and $50 for union dues.

15. Paid the treasurer of the state the amount of state income taxes withheld from workers' earnings during the first quarter.

15. Electronically transferred funds to remove the liability for FICA taxes and employees' federal income taxes withheld on the March payrolls.

29. Payroll: $5,850. All wages and salaries taxable. Withheld $509 for federal income taxes, $128.90 for state income taxes, and $55 for union dues.

29. Filed the *Employer's Quarterly Federal Tax Return (Form 941)* for the period ended March 31. No journal entry is required, since the FICA taxes and federal income taxes withheld have been timely paid.

29. Electronically transferred the FUTA taxes for the period ended March 31.

29. Filed the state contribution return for the quarter ended March 31 and paid the amount to the state unemployment compensation fund.

May 2. Paid the treasurer of the union the amount of union dues withheld from workers' earnings during April.

13. Payroll: $5,810. All wages and salaries taxable. Withheld $507 for federal income taxes, $125.05 for state income taxes, and $55 for union dues.

16. Electronically transferred funds to remove the liability for FICA taxes and federal income taxes withheld on the April payrolls.

31. Payroll: $6,060. All wages and salaries taxable. Withheld $533 for federal income taxes, $119.00 for state income taxes, and $50 for union dues.

June 3. Paid the treasurer of the union the amount of union dues withheld from workers' earnings during May.

15. Payroll: $6,380. All wages and salaries taxable, except only $5,000 is taxable under FUTA and SUTA. Withheld $549 for federal income taxes, $128.70 for state income taxes, and $50 for union dues.

15. Electronically transferred funds to remove the liability for FICA taxes and federal income taxes withheld on the May payrolls.

30. Payroll: $6,250. All wages and salaries taxable, except only $4,770 is taxable under FUTA and SUTA. Withheld $538 for federal income taxes, $127.60 for state income taxes, and $50 for union dues.

    c. Answer the following questions:

        1. The total amount of the liability for FICA taxes and federal income taxes withheld as of June 30 is . . . . $_____

        2. The total amount of the liability for state income taxes withheld as of June 30 is . . . . $_____

        3. The amount of FUTA taxes that must be paid to the federal government on or before August 1 (July 31 is a Sunday) is . . . . $_____

        4. The amount of contributions that must be paid into the state unemployment compensation fund on or before August 1 is . . . . $_____

        5. The total amount due the treasurer of the union is . . . . $_____

        6. The total amount of wages and salaries expense since the beginning of the fiscal year is . . . . $_____

        7. The total amount of payroll taxes expense since the beginning of the fiscal year is . . . . $_____

        8. Using the partial journal below, journalize the entry to record the vacation accrual at the end of the company's fiscal year. The amount of Brookins Company's vacation accrual for the fiscal year is $15,000.

JOURNAL

	DATE	DESCRIPTION	POST. REF.	DEBIT	CREDIT	
1						1
2						2
3						3
4						4
5						5
6						6

Date _____   Name _____

6–12 (Continued).

JOURNAL

	DATE		DESCRIPTION	POST. REF.	DEBIT	CREDIT	
1							1
2							2
3							3
4							4
5							5
6							6
7							7
8							8
9							9
10							10
11							11
12							12
13							13
14							14
15							15
16							16
17							17
18							18
19							19
20							20
21							21
22							22
23							23
24							24
25							25
26							26
27							27
28							28
29							29
30							30
31							31
32							32
33							33
34							34

6–12 (Continued).

JOURNAL

	DATE		DESCRIPTION	POST. REF.	DEBIT		CREDIT		
1									1
2									2
3									3
4									4
5									5
6									6
7									7
8									8
9									9
10									10
11									11
12									12
13									13
14									14
15									15
16									16
17									17
18									18
19									19
20									20
21									21
22									22
23									23
24									24
25									25
26									26
27									27
28									28
29									29
30									30
31									31
32									32
33									33
34									34

6–12 (Continued).

JOURNAL

	DATE	DESCRIPTION	POST. REF.	DEBIT	CREDIT	
1						1
2						2
3						3
4						4
5						5
6						6
7						7
8						8
9						9
10						10
11						11
12						12
13						13
14						14
15						15
16						16
17						17
18						18
19						19
20						20
21						21
22						22
23						23
24						24
25						25
26						26
27						27
28						28
29						29
30						30
31						31
32						32
33						33
34						34

6–12 (Continued).

JOURNAL

	DATE		DESCRIPTION	POST. REF.	DEBIT	CREDIT	
1							1
2							2
3							3
4							4
5							5
6							6
7							7
8							8
9							9
10							10
11							11
12							12
13							13
14							14
15							15
16							16
17							17
18							18
19							19
20							20
21							21
22							22
23							23
24							24
25							25
26							26
27							27
28							28
29							29
30							30
31							31
32							32
33							33
34							34

6–12 (Continued).

ACCOUNT				CASH				ACCOUNT NO. 11	

DATE		ITEM	POST. REF.	DEBIT	CREDIT	BALANCE	
						DEBIT	CREDIT
20— Apr.	1	*Balance*	✓			5 8 2 3 3 04	

6–12 (Continued).

FICA TAXES PAYABLE—OASDI ACCOUNT NO. 20

DATE		ITEM	POST. REF.	DEBIT	CREDIT	BALANCE	
						DEBIT	CREDIT
20—Apr.	1	Balance	✓				1 0 6 8 88

6–12 (Continued).

ACCOUNT			FICA TAXES PAYABLE—HI				ACCOUNT NO. 21	

DATE		ITEM	POST. REF.	DEBIT	CREDIT	BALANCE		
						DEBIT	CREDIT	
20— Apr.	1	Balance	✓				2 4 9 98	

6–12 (Continued).

FUTA TAXES PAYABLE ACCOUNT NO. 22

DATE		ITEM	POST. REF.	DEBIT	CREDIT	BALANCE	
						DEBIT	CREDIT
20— Apr.	1	Balance	✓				1 9 8 88

ACCOUNT **SUTA TAXES PAYABLE** ACCOUNT NO. 23

DATE		ITEM	POST. REF.	DEBIT	CREDIT	BALANCE	
						DEBIT	CREDIT
20— Apr.	1	Balance	✓				5 7 1 78

6–12 (Continued).

ACCOUNT   **EMPLOYEES FIT PAYABLE**   ACCOUNT NO. 25

DATE		ITEM	POST. REF.	DEBIT	CREDIT	BALANCE	
						DEBIT	CREDIT
20— Apr.	1	Balance	✓				1 1 2 4 00

ACCOUNT   **EMPLOYEES SIT PAYABLE**   ACCOUNT NO. 26

DATE		ITEM	POST. REF.	DEBIT	CREDIT	BALANCE	
						DEBIT	CREDIT
20— Apr.	1	Balance	✓				5 4 6 92

6–12 (Concluded).

ACCOUNT **UNION DUES PAYABLE** ACCOUNT NO. 28

DATE		ITEM	POST. REF.	DEBIT	CREDIT	BALANCE	
						DEBIT	CREDIT
20— Apr.	1	Balance	✓				1 0 0 00

ACCOUNT **WAGES AND SALARIES** ACCOUNT NO. 51

DATE		ITEM	POST. REF.	DEBIT	CREDIT	BALANCE	
						DEBIT	CREDIT
20— Apr.	1	Balance	✓			7 1 3 6 0 00	

ACCOUNT **PAYROLL TAXES** ACCOUNT NO. 55

DATE		ITEM	POST. REF.	DEBIT	CREDIT	BALANCE	
						DEBIT	CREDIT
20— Apr.	1	Balance	✓			6 9 2 6 96	

CONTINUING PAYROLL PROBLEM ✕

In this last phase of your work on the Continuing Payroll Problem, you will record the amounts withheld for group and health insurance and calculate the net pay for each employee. Refer to the partially completed payroll register upon which you were working at the end of Chapter 5, and proceed as follows:

1. In the appropriate column of the payroll register, record the amount to be withheld for group life insurance. Each employee contributes 85¢ each week toward the cost of group insurance coverage, with the exception of McGarry and Porth, who are not yet eligible for coverage under the company plan.

2. Record the amount to be withheld for health insurance. Each employee contributes $1.65 each week toward the cost of health insurance.

3. Record the net pay for each employee. The net pay for each employee is obtained by subtracting the total amount of all deductions from the total earnings.

4. Each worker is to be paid by check. Assign check numbers commencing with No. 313.

5. Foot all money columns of the payroll register, and prove the accuracy of the column totals.

6. On a separate sheet of paper:
   a. Prepare the journal entries as of January 12 to record the payroll and the payroll taxes for the week ending January 7. Credit Salaries Payable for the total net pay.

      Use the following tax rates and bases: employer's FICA—OASDI, 6.2% on the first $89,700; employer's FICA—HI, 1.45% on total earnings; FUTA, 0.8% on the first $7,000; and SUTA, 3.5% on the first $8,000.
   b. Prepare the journal entry to record the payment of the payroll on January 14, when the paychecks are distributed to all workers.

Your work on the Continuing Payroll Problem is now completed, and you may be asked to submit your payroll register to your instructor. The experience you have gained in working on each of the succeeding phases of the Continuing Payroll Problem will aid you in undertaking the payroll work involved in Chapter 7. In the Comprehensive Payroll Project, you will be responsible for all aspects of payroll operations for a company for an entire calendar quarter.

CASE PROBLEM

C1. **Budgeting for Additional Payroll Costs.**

Frank Flynn is the payroll manager for Powlus Supply Company. During the budgeting process, Sam Kinder, Director of Finance, asked Flynn to arrive at a set percentage that could be applied to each budgeted salary figure to cover the additional cost that will be incurred by Powlus Supply for each employee. After some discussion, it was determined that the best way to compute this percentage would be to base these additional costs of payroll on the average salary paid by the company.

Kinder wants this additional payroll cost percentage to cover payroll taxes (FICA, FUTA, and SUTA) and other payroll costs covered by the company (workers' compensation expense, health insurance costs, and vacation pay).

Flynn gathers the following information in order to complete the analysis:

Average annual salary	$24,000
FICA rates	6.2% and 1.45%
FUTA	0.8% on 1st $7,000
SUTA	3.3% on 1st $10,400
Workers' compensation costs	$0.97 per $100 of payroll
Health insurance costs	$75.15 per month
Vacation pay earned	2 weeks' pay earned each year to be used in following year.

Compute the percentage that can be used in the budget.

Net activities

1. Go to a search engine such as http://www.google.com/ or http://www.ask.com/. Type "payroll accounting systems."

   Discussion or group project:
   (a) Locate three vendors for payroll accounting systems, or accounting systems that include a payroll module.
   (b) What do the systems include? What are the features? Will they tie in to the general ledger? Will they file electronically?
   (c) Which payroll system would you recommend?

2. Go to the treasury department's Web site: http://www.publicdebt.treas.gov/mar/marfaqpr.htm and answer the following questions:

   Discuss
   (a) What procedures should an employer follow to buy U.S. Savings Bonds from their employee's withholdings?
   (b) Are U.S. Savings Bonds a good investment?

3. The Consumer Credit Protection Act governs garnishment of wages. Go to http://www.dol.gov/asp/programs/handbook/garnish.htm or http://www4.law.cornell.edu/uscode/15/1671.html.

   (a) What is the maximum amount that an employer is allowed to garnish from an employee?
   (b) Name several reasons why an employee's paycheck can be garnished.
   (c) You received a garnishment order for one of your employees. She is not paying her child support as the court ordered. You think this situation is terrible. Can you fire the employee?

4. Go to: http://www.afscme.org/wrkplace/cafe.htm then http://www.irs.gov/formspubs/display/0,,i1%3D50&genericId%3D79381,00.html.

   (a) What is a cafeteria plan?

   Now go to http://www.taxplanet.com/taxguide/job/flexiblespendingaccts/flexiblespendingaccts.html.

   (b) What is a Flexible Spending account?
   (c) Discuss: What is the difference between a cafeteria plan and a Flexible Spending account?

5. Go to http://www.401k.com/.

   (a) What is a 401(k)?
   (b) Why not just save for your retirement on your own?
   (c) What is the maximum amount an employee can contribute to a 401(k)?

Is there any real-world application for what we have learned in the first six chapters? Are we ready to take charge of the payroll

Payroll Project

processing operations? Do we know where to get the information needed to complete the payroll-related tax forms? When do we pay our employer's taxes without penalty? Have we learned the necessary journal entries and ledger postings?

It's time to begin our test—Chapter 7.

7

CHAPTER 7 CONSISTS OF A SIMULATION, OR PRACTICE SET, FOR PAYROLL ACCOUNTING. YOU WILL APPLY THE KNOWLEDGE ACQUIRED IN THIS COURSE TO PRACTICAL PAYROLL SITUATIONS. THIS SIMULATION IS A CULMINATION OF THE INFORMATION PRESENTED IN THE TEXTBOOK.

AFTER COMPLETING THE PROJECT, YOU SHOULD BE ABLE TO:

1. Prepare payroll registers.

2. Maintain employees' earnings records.

3. Journalize and post payroll and payroll tax entries.

4. Complete federal, state, and city tax deposit forms and journalize the transactions.

5. Prepare various quarter-end and year-end payroll tax forms.

6. Make the accrual entries for the payroll at the end of a year.

The Payroll Project will provide you with extended practice in keeping payroll records and accounting for payroll transactions. Your completion of this project involves an application of the information learned in the preceding chapters. The work provided resembles that prevailing in the office of every employer in the United States subject to the provisions of the federal wage and hour law, income tax withholding laws, the social security laws, and the unemployment compensation laws. Even though most payroll systems now employ computers, it is important that the practitioner understand the operations performed by the computer.

If your assignment involves the use of Appendix A (computerized option) to complete this project, it is suggested that you do at least one of the payrolls manually so that you gain a thorough understanding of the steps needed to be completed on a typical payday.

In this project, you are employed by the Glo-Brite Paint Company. As the payroll clerk in the Accounting Department, you have been in charge of the payroll records since the company first began operations on January 5 of the current year. The company employs about 800 individuals; but for the purpose of this project, payroll records will be kept for only a dozen or so employees. By understanding the principles of payroll accounting for a few employees, you should be able to keep similar records for several hundred employees.

For purposes of this project, you will assume that the payroll records, tax reports, and deposits have been completed and filed for the first three quarters of this year. Your work will involve the processing of the payrolls for the last quarter of the year and the completion of the last quarterly and annual tax reports and forms.

BOOKS OF ACCOUNT AND PAYROLL RECORDS

The books of account and payroll records that you will use in this project are described below.

Journal

You will use a two-column general journal to record all transactions affecting the accounts in the general ledger. This book of original entry serves as a posting medium for transactions affecting the payroll accounts.

General Ledger

A general ledger, used in keeping the payroll accounts, is ruled with balance-column ruling, which makes it possible to keep a continuous record of each account balance. Some of the ledger accounts will have beginning balances carried over from the first three quarters of the year.

The chart of accounts in Figure 7–1 has been used in opening the general ledger accounts (pages 7-35 to 7-42). The Glo-Brite Paint Company has other accounts in its general ledger, but those listed in the partial chart of accounts are the only accounts required in completing this project.

Payroll Register

The payroll register provides the information needed for journalizing each payroll and for posting to the employees' earnings records.

Employee's Earnings Record

The employee's earnings record provides a summary of each employee's earnings, deductions, and taxable wages. The information recorded in this record is posted from the payroll register.

From the personnel data given in Figure 7–2 (on page 7-6), an employee's earnings record has been maintained for each employee (pages 7-44 to 7-48). The first line of each

FIGURE 7-1

Partial Chart of Accounts

Account Title	Account No.
Cash	11
Payroll Cash	12
FICA Taxes Payable—OASDI	20.1
FICA Taxes Payable—HI	20.2
FUTA Taxes Payable	21
SUTA Taxes Payable	22
Employees FIT Payable	24
Employees SIT Payable	25
Employees CIT Payable	26
Group Insurance Premiums Collected	27
Union Dues Payable	28
Administrative Salaries	51
Office Salaries	52
Sales Salaries	53
Plant Wages	54
Payroll Taxes	56

of these records shows the employee's cumulative figures for the first three quarters of the year. Note that only one-half page has been used for each employee's earnings record.

GENERAL INFORMATION

The home office and the manufacturing plant of the Glo-Brite Paint Company are located at 2215 Salvador Street, Philadelphia, PA 19175-0682. The company's federal identification number is 31-0450660; the state identifying number, 146-3-3300; and the city identifying number, 501-6791855.

Regular Hours of Work

The workweek for all employees is 40 hours. The office is open from 8:00 a.m. to 5:00 p.m. each day, except weekends. Glo-Brite allows one hour for lunch, 12:00 p.m. to 1:00 p.m. The plant operates on a five-day workweek of eight hours per day, with normal working hours from 7:00 a.m. to 11:00 a.m. and 12:00 p.m. to 4:00 p.m.

Overtime

All employees except for the exempt administrative employees—the president (O'Neill), the sales manager (Ferguson), sales representative (Mann), and supervisor (Sokowski)—are paid *time and a half* for any overtime exceeding 40 hours a week. Workers in the plant (Bonno and Ryan) are paid *time and a half* for any hours worked over eight each workday and for work on Saturdays and *twice* the regular hourly rate of pay for work on Sundays or holidays.

Timekeeping

All office and plant employees, except the president, the sales manager, sales representatives, and supervisors, must ring in and out daily on a time clock. Also, those employees who

FIGURE 7-3

Glo-Brite Payroll Taxes

Payroll Taxes Levied Upon the Glo-Brite Paint Company and Its Employees

Federal Income Taxes (FIT)	Withheld from each employee's gross earnings in accordance with information given on Form W-4 and employee's earnings record. Wage-bracket method is used to determine FIT withholding.*
Pennsylvania State Income Taxes (SIT)	2.8 percent withheld from each employee's gross earnings during the fourth quarter.*
Philadelphia City Income Taxes (CIT)	4.5385 percent withheld from gross earnings of each employee.*
Pennsylvania State Unemployment Taxes (SUTA)	*Employer:* 3.5 percent on first $8,000 gross earnings paid each employee during the calendar year.
Federal Unemployment Taxes (FUTA)	Net tax rate of 0.8 percent on first $7,000 gross earnings paid each worker in the calendar year.
Federal Insurance Contributions Act (FICA)	*OASDI—Employer and Employee:* 6.2 percent on first $89,700 gross earnings paid each worker in the calendar year.
	HI—Employer and Employee: 1.45 percent on total gross earnings paid each worker in the calendar year.

*Tax withholdings for FIT, SIT, CIT, and SUTA are based on rates used in 2001. Rates for 2002 were not available at the time

FIGURE 7-4

Deposit Rules

Deposit Rules for the Glo-Brite Paint Company

Federal	The FICA taxes and FIT taxes must be deposited *on or before the 15th of the month following the month* in which the taxes were withheld. Since Glo-Brite is a new employer and has no tax liabilities during the lookback period, the company is subject to the monthly deposit rule.
Pennsylvania	Since the state income taxes withheld total $1,000 or more each quarter, the company must remit the withheld taxes semi-monthly. The taxes must be remitted within three banking days after the semimonthly periods ending *on the 15th and the last day of the month*.
Philadelphia	Since the city income taxes withheld are more than $350 but less than $16,000 each month, the company is subject to the monthly rule. The city income taxes withheld during the month must be remitted *by the 15th day of the following month*.

FIGURE 7-5

Glo-Brite Labor Cost Accounts

Personnel	Accounts to Be Charged
President (O'Neill)	Administrative Salaries
Executive Secretary (Ford) Programmer (Williams) Time Clerk (Russell) Student (Accounting Trainee)	Office Salaries
Sales Manager (Ferguson) Sales Representative (Mann)	Sales Salaries
Workers (Bonno and Ryan) Supervisor (Sokowski)	Plant Wages

Union Dues

Both workers in the plant (Bonno and Ryan) are union members. Under the check-off system, $8 is deducted *each payday* from the plant workers' earnings for union dues, assessments, and initiation fees. A notation to this effect has been made on each plant worker's earnings record. On or before the tenth of each month, the amounts withheld during the preceding month are turned over to the treasurer of the union.

Distribution of Labor Costs

Figure 7–5 shows how the salaries and wages are to be charged to the labor cost accounts.

NARRATIVE OF PAYROLL TRANSACTIONS

October 9, 20—

No. 1 The first payroll in October covered the two workweeks that ended on September 26 and October 3. This payroll transaction has been entered for you in the payroll register, the employees' earnings records, the general journal, and the general ledger. By reviewing the calculations of the wages and deductions in the payroll register and the posting of the information to the employees' earnings records, you can see the procedure to be followed each payday.

Wages and salaries are paid by issuing special payroll checks. When the bank on which they are drawn receives such checks, they will be charged against the payroll cash account.

Observe the following rules in computing earnings each pay period:

1. Do not make any deduction from an employee's earnings if the employee loses less than 15 minutes of time in any day. Time lost that exceeds 15 minutes is rounded to the nearest quarter-hour and deducted. If the time lost by an employee is not to be deducted, the time clerk will make a notation to that effect on the Time Clerk's Report.

2. In completing the time record columns of the payroll register for all workers, you should place an 8 in the day column for each full day worked (refer to page PR-2 at the end of the book). If an employee works less than a full day, show the actual hours for which the employee will be paid.

Time Clerk's Report No. 38 For the Week Ending September 26, 20—									
Employee	**Time Record**							**Time Worked**	**Time Lost**
	S	M	T	W	T	F	S		
Bonno, A. V.		8	8	8	8	8		40 hrs.	...
Ford, C. L.		8	8	8	8	8		40 hrs.	...
Russell, V. A.		8	8	8	8	8		40 hrs.	...
Ryan, N. A.		8	8	8	8	8		40 hrs.	...
Student		8	8	8	8	8		40 hrs.	...
Williams, R. V. ...		8	8	D	8	8		32 hrs.	8 hrs.*

*Time lost because of personal business; charged to personal leave; no deduction for this time lost.
D = lost full day

3. In the case of an employee who begins work during a pay period, compute the earnings by paying the employees their weekly rate for *any full week* worked. For any *partial week,* compute the earnings for that week by multiplying the hours worked by the hourly rate of pay.

4. If time lost is to be deducted from a salaried employee's pay, the employee's pay must be determined by multiplying the actual hours worked for that week by the hourly rate. If hours are missed but no pay is deducted, include those hours in the Time Record columns on the payroll register. The following schedule shows the weekly and hourly wage rates of the salaried employees:

Employee	Weekly Rate	Hourly Rate
Ferguson, James C.	$1,125.00	$28.13
Ford, Catherine L.	450.00	11.25
Mann, Dewey W.	675.00	16.88
O'Neill, Joseph T.	1,153.85	28.85
Russell, Virginia A.	345.00	8.63
Sokowski, Thomas J.	1,025.00	25.63
Student	270.00	6.75
Williams, Ruth V.	611.54	15.29

5. Plant workers (Bonno and Ryan), other than supervisors, are employed on an hourly basis. Compute the wages by multiplying the number of hours worked during the pay period by the employee's hourly rate.

6. The information needed and the sequence of steps that are completed for the payroll are presented in the following discussion.

The time clerk prepared Time Clerk's Reports Nos. 38 and 39 from the time cards used by the employees for these workweeks. Inasmuch as the president, sales manager, the sales representatives, and the supervisors do not ring in and out on the time clock, their records are not included in the time clerk's report, but their salaries must be included in the payroll.

Time Clerk's Report No. 39 For the Week Ending October 3, 20—									
Employee	**Time Record**							**Time Worked**	**Time Lost**
	S	M	T	W	T	F	S		
Bonno, A. V.		8	8	8	8	8		40 hrs.	...
Ford, C. L.		8	8	8	8	8		40 hrs.	...
Russell, V. A.		8	8	8	8	8		40 hrs.	...
Ryan, N. A.		8	8	8	8	8		40 hrs.	...
Student		8	8	8	8	8		40 hrs.	...
Williams, R. V.		8	8	8	8	8		40 hrs.	...

① The following schedule shows the hourly wage rates of the two hourly employees used in preparing the payroll register for the payday on October 9.

Employee	**Hourly Rate**
Bonno, Anthony V.	$17.65
Ryan, Norman A.	18.00

② The entry required for each employee is recorded in the payroll register. The names of all employees are listed in alphabetical order, including yours as "Student." The fold-out payroll register forms needed to complete this project are bound at the back of the book (pages PR-1, PR-3, and PR-4).

No deduction has been made for the time lost by Williams. Thus, the total number of hours (80) for which payment was made is recorded in the Regular Earnings Hours column of the payroll register. However, a notation of the time lost (D) was made in the Time Record column. When posting to Williams's earnings record, 80 hours is recorded in the Regular Earnings Hours column (no deduction for the time lost).

In computing the federal income taxes to be withheld, the wage-bracket tables in Tax Table B at the back of the book were used (pages T-7 to T-16).

Each payday, $8 was deducted from the earnings of the two plant workers, for union dues.

Payroll check numbers were assigned beginning with check No. 672.

In the Labor Cost Distribution columns at the extreme right of the payroll register, each employee's gross earnings were recorded in the column that identifies the department in which the employee regularly works. The totals of the Labor Cost Distribution columns provide the amounts to be charged to the appropriate salary and wage expense accounts and aid department managers and supervisors in comparing the actual labor costs with the budgeted amounts.

Once the net pay of each employee was computed, all the amount columns in the payroll register were footed, proved, and ruled.

③ An entry was made in the journal (page 7-26) transferring from the regular cash account to the payroll cash account the amount of the check issued to Payroll to cover the net amount of the payroll; next, the entry was posted.

④ Information from the payroll register was posted to the employees' earnings records (see pages 7-46 to 7-48).

Note that when posting the deductions for each employee, a column has been provided in the earnings record for recording each deduction for FICA (OASDI and

PAY POINTS

Use tax tables for biweekly payroll period.

HI), FIT, SIT, and CIT. All other deductions for each employee are to be totaled and recorded as one amount in the Other Deductions column. Subsidiary ledgers are maintained for Group Insurance Premiums Collected and Union Dues Withheld. Thus, any question about the amounts withheld from an employee's earnings may be answered by referring to the appropriate subsidiary ledger. In this project, your work will not involve any recording in or reference to the subsidiary ledgers.

⑤ The proper journal entry recorded salaries, wages, taxes, and the net amount of cash paid from the totals of the payroll register. The journal entry to record the payroll for the first pay in the fourth quarter appears below and in the general journal (page 7-26).

Administrative Salaries	2,307.69	
Office Salaries	3,353.08	
Sales Salaries	3,600.00	
Plant Wages	4,902.00	
FICA Taxes Payable—OASDI		878.09
FICA Taxes Payable—HI		205.37
Employees FIT Payable		1,22400
Employees SIT Payable		396.57
Employees CIT Payable		642.78
Union Dues Payable		16.00
Payroll Cash		10,799.96

The amounts charged the salary and wage expense accounts were obtained from the totals of the Labor Cost Distribution columns in the payroll register. As shown in the listing of the labor cost accounts, Figure 7–5, the salaries and wages were charged as follows:

Administrative Salaries

Joseph T. O'Neill (President)

Office Salaries

Catherine L. Ford (Executive Secretary)
Virginia A. Russell (Time Clerk)
Student (Accounting Trainee)
Ruth V. Williams (Programmer)

Sales Salaries

James C. Ferguson (Sales Manager)
Dewey W. Mann (Sales Representative)

Plant Wages

Anthony V. Bonno (Mixer Operator)
Norman A. Ryan (Electrician)
Thomas J. Sokowski (Supervisor)

FICA Taxes Payable—OASDI and FICA Taxes Payable—HI were credited for $878.09 and $205.37, respectively, the amounts deducted from employees' wages.

Employees FIT Payable, Employees SIT Payable, Employees CIT Payable, and Union Dues Payable were credited for the total amount withheld for each kind of deduction from employees' wages. In subsequent payroll transactions, Group Insurance Premiums Collected will be credited for the amounts withheld from employees' wages for this type of deduction. Finally, Payroll Cash was credited for the sum of the net amounts paid all employees.

⑥ The payroll taxes for this pay were then recorded in the general journal (page 7-26) as follows:

Payroll Taxes 1,231.49
   FICA Taxes Payable—OASDI 878.09
   FICA Taxes Payable—HI 205.36
   FUTA Taxes Payable 26.24
   SUTA Taxes Payable 121.80

Payroll Taxes was debited for the sum of the employer's FICA, FUTA, and SUTA taxes. The taxable earnings used in computing each of these payroll taxes were obtained from the appropriate column totals of the payroll register. Note that only part of Ford's wages are taxable for FUTA. The computation of the debit to Payroll Taxes was:

FICA—OASDI:	6.2% of $14,162.77 =	$ 878.09
FICA—HI:	1.45% of $14,162.77 =	205.36
FUTA:	0.8% of $3,280.00 =	26.24
SUTA:	3.5% of $3,480.00 =	121.80
Total Payroll Taxes		$1,231.49

FICA Taxes Payable—OASDI was credited for $878.09, the amount of the liability for the employer's portion of the tax. FICA Taxes Payable—HI was credited for $205.36, the amount of the liability for the employer's share of this tax. FUTA Taxes Payable was credited for the amount of the tax on the employer for federal unemployment purposes ($26.24). SUTA Taxes Payable was credited for the amount of the contribution required of the employer under the state unemployment compensation law. This same amount, $121.80, was charged as part of the debit to Payroll Taxes.

⑦ The journal entries were posted to the proper ledger accounts (pages 7-35 to 7-42).

October 15

This is the day on which the deposits of FICA and FIT taxes and the city of Philadelphia income taxes for the September payrolls are due. However, in order to concentrate on the fourth-quarter payrolls, we will assume that the deposits for the third quarter and the appropriate entries were already completed.

October 20

No. 2 On this date, the Glo-Brite Paint Company must deposit the Pennsylvania state income taxes withheld from the October 9 payroll.

The deposit rule states that if the employer expects the aggregate amount withheld each quarter to be $1,000 or more, the employer must pay the withheld tax semimonthly. The tax, along with the deposit statement (Form PA 501R), must be remitted within three banking days after the close of the semimonthly periods ending on the 15th and the last day of the month.

① Prepare the journal entry to record the deposit of the taxes, and post to the appropriate ledger accounts.

② Complete one of the Pennsylvania deposit statements (Form PA-501R) that appear on pages 7-52 to 7-54. The company's telephone number is (215) 555-9559.

PAY POINTS

On all tax and deposit forms requiring a signature, use Joseph O'Neill's name.

October 23

No. 3   Prepare the payroll for the last pay period of October from Time Clerk's Reports Nos. 40 and 41.

The proper procedure in recording the payroll follows:

① Complete the payroll register.

Inasmuch as only a portion of the payroll register sheet was used in recording the October 9 payroll, the October 23 payroll should be recorded on the same sheet to save space. On the first blank ruled line after the October 9 payroll, insert "Payday October 23—For Period Ending October 17, 20—." On the following lines, record the payroll information for the last pay date of October. When recording succeeding payrolls, continue to conserve space by recording two payrolls on each separate payroll register sheet.

The workers in the plant (Bonno and Ryan) are paid *time and a half* for any hours worked over eight each workday and for work on Saturdays and are paid *twice* the regular hourly rate for work on Sundays or holidays.

With this pay period, the *cumulative earnings* of several employees exceed the taxable income base set up by FUTA and SUTA. This factor must be considered in preparing the payroll register and in computing the employer's payroll taxes. Refer to each employee's earnings record to see the amount of cumulative earnings.

② Make the entry transferring from Cash to Payroll Cash the net amount of the total payroll, and post.

③ Post the required information from the payroll register to each employee's earnings record.

④ Record in the journal the salaries, wages, taxes withheld, group insurance premiums collected, union dues withheld, and net amount paid, and post to the proper ledger accounts.

The entry required to record the October 23 payroll is the same as that to record the October 9 payroll, except it is necessary to record the liability for the amount withheld from the employees' wages to pay their part of the group insurance premium. The amount withheld should be recorded as a credit to Group Insurance Premiums Collected.

⑤ Record in the journal the employer's payroll taxes and the liabilities created; post to the appropriate ledger accounts.

PAY POINTS

Plant Worker: time and a half—over 8 hours and Saturdays; double time—Sundays or holidays.

PAY POINTS

Be sure to deduct 30¢ premium for each $1,000 of group insurance carried by each employee.

Time Clerk's Report No. 40
For the Week Ending October 10, 20—

Employee	S	M	T	W	T	F	S	Time Worked	Time Lost
Bonno, A. V.		8	8	8	8	8	4	44 hrs.	. . .
Ford, C. L.		4	8	8	8	8		36 hrs.	4 hrs.*
Russell, V. A.		8	8	8	8	8		40 hrs.	. . .
Ryan, N. A.		8	8	8	8	8		40 hrs.	. . .
Student		8	8	8	8	8		40 hrs.	. . .
Williams, R. V.		8	8	8	8	8		40 hrs.	. . .

*Time lost on account of death of relative; charged against annual personal leave; no deduction for time lost.

Time Clerk's Report No. 41 For the Week Ending October 17, 20—								
Employee	Time Record						Time Worked	Time Lost
	S	M	T	W	T	F	S		

Employee	S	M	T	W	T	F	S	Time Worked	Time Lost
Bonno, A. V.		8	8	8	8	8		40 hrs.	. . .
Ford, C. L.		8	8	8	8	8		40 hrs.	. . .
Russell, V. A.		8	8	8	8	8		40 hrs.	. . .
Ryan, N. A.		8	8	8	8	8	8	48 hrs.	. . .
Student		8	8	8	8	8		40 hrs.	. . .
Williams, R. V. ...		8	8	8	8	8		40 hrs.	. . .

November 4

No. 4　Deposit with the state of Pennsylvania the amount of state income taxes withheld from the October 23 payroll.

No. 5　Virginia Russell completed a new Form W-4, changing the number of withholding allowances to 2. Change Russell's earnings record (her marital status has not changed).

No. 6　Thomas J. Sokowski completed a new Form W-4, showing that his marital status changed to single and that the number of withholding allowances remains at 2. Change Sokowski's earnings record accordingly.

No. 7　Dewey Mann completed a new Form W-4, leaving his marital status as married but dropping the number of withholding allowances to 0. Change Mann's earnings record accordingly.

PAY POINTS

Make changes in November 6 pay. Refers to Nos. 5, 6, and 7.

November 6

No. 8　Pay the treasurer of the union the amount of union dues withheld during the month of October.

No. 9　Prepare the payroll for the first pay period in November from Time Clerk's Reports Nos. 42 and 43 and record the paychecks issued to all employees. Record this payroll at the top of the second payroll register sheet.

Note: Virginia Russell worked only 38 hours in the week ending October 24. Therefore, compute her pay for that week by multiplying 38 by $8.63 (her hourly rate). Ruth Williams worked only 39 hours in the week ending October 24. Therefore, compute her pay for that week by multiplying 39 by $15.29 (her hourly rate).

Also, record the employer's payroll taxes.

| Time Clerk's Report No. 42 For the Week Ending October 24, 20— | | | | | | | | |

Employee	S	M	T	W	T	F	S	Time Worked	Time Lost
Bonno, A. V.		8	8	8	8	8		40 hrs.	. . .
Ford, C. L.		8	8	8	8	8		40 hrs.	. . .
Russell, V. A.		8	8	8	8	6		38 hrs.	2 hrs.*
Ryan, N. A.		8	8	8	8	8		40 hrs.	. . .
Student		8	8	8	8	8		40 hrs.	. . .
Williams, R. V. ...		8	8	8	7	8		39 hrs.	1 hr.**

*Time lost on account of family function; deduct 2 hours' pay.
**Time lost because of tardiness; deduct 1 hour's pay.

	Time Record						Time	Time
Employee	S	M	T	W	T	F	S	Worked	Lost

Time Clerk's Report No. 43
For the Week Ending October 31, 20—

Employee	S	M	T	W	T	F	S	Time Worked	Time Lost
Bonno, A. V.		8	8	8	8	8		40 hrs.	. . .
Ford, C. L.		8	8	8	8	8		40 hrs.	. . .
Russell, V. A.		8	8	8	8	8		40 hrs.	. . .
Ryan, N. A.		8	8	8	8	8		40 hrs.	. . .
Student		8	8	8	8	8		40 hrs.	. . .
Williams, R. V.		8	8	8	8	8		40 hrs.	. . .

November 13

No. 10 Because of her excessive tardiness and absenteeism during the year, the company discharged Ruth V. Williams today. For the week ending November 7, she was late a total of six hours; and for this week, she missed two full days and was late two hours on another day. In lieu of two weeks' notice, Williams was given two full weeks' pay ($1,223.08). Along with her dismissal pay ($1,223.08), she was paid for the week ending November 7 (34 hours, or $519.86) and the days worked this current week (22 hours, or $336.38). The total pay for the two partial weeks is $856.24.

① Record a separate payroll register (on one line) to show Williams's total earnings, deductions, and net pay. The two weeks' dismissal pay is subject to all payroll taxes. Include dismissal pay with the total earnings but do not show the hours in the Time Record columns. Use the tax table for the biweekly payroll period for the total gross pay ($2,079.32) of Williams.

The deduction for group insurance premiums is $14.40. In the Time Record column, make a note of Williams's discharge as of this date. Indicate the payroll check number used to prepare the final check for Williams. When posting to the earnings record, make a notation of Williams's discharge on this date.

② Prepare the journal entries to transfer the net cash and to record Williams's final pay and the employer's payroll taxes. Post to the ledger accounts.

③ Use the blank Form W-2 on page 7-60. Box "a" should be left blank, since the Glo-Brite Paint Company does not use a control number to identify individual Forms W-2.

PAY POINTS

Prepare a Wage and Tax Statement, Form W-2, to be given to Williams.

November 16

No. 11 Deposit with the City Bank the amount of FICA taxes and federal income taxes for the October payrolls. Since the company is subject to the monthly deposit rule, the deposit is due on the 15th of the following month. See the deposit requirements explained on pages 3-18 to 3-23. November 15 is a Sunday; therefore, the deposit is to be made on the next business day.

① Prepare the journal entry to record the deposit of the taxes, and post to the appropriate ledger accounts.

② Complete the *Federal Tax Deposit Coupon, Form 8109*, to accompany the remittance, using one of the preinscribed forms on page 7-51. The company's telephone number is (215) 555-9559. For this project, Forms 8109 will be used even though the company could be using electronic transfer to pay the payroll taxes.

No. 12 Since the Glo-Brite Paint Company withholds the city of Philadelphia income tax, you must deposit the taxes with the Department of Revenue. The deposit rule that affects the Glo-Brite Paint Company states that if the withheld taxes are between $350 and $16,000 per month, the company must deposit the tax monthly by the 15th of the following month. The withheld taxes for the October payrolls were $1,300.18.

① Prepare the journal entry to record the deposit of the taxes, and post to the appropriate ledger accounts.

② Complete one of the Philadelphia Employer's Return of Tax Withheld coupons, which appear on pages 7-54 to 7-55.

November 17

No. 13 Prepare an employee's earnings record for Beth Anne Woods, a new employee who began work today, Tuesday. Woods is single and claims one withholding allowance. She is employed as a programmer at a monthly salary of $2,600. Address, 8102 Franklin Court, Philadelphia, PA 19105-0915. Telephone, 555-1128. Social Security No. 724-03-1587. She is eligible for group insurance coverage of $47,000 immediately, although her first deduction for group insurance will not be made until December 18.

> Department: Office.
> Weekly rate: $600.00.
> Hourly rate: $15.00.

November 18

No. 14 Deposit with the state of Pennsylvania the amount of state income taxes withheld from the November 6 and 13 (Ruth V. Williams) payrolls.

November 20

No. 15 With this pay, the company has decided to offer employees a Savings Incentive Match Plan (SIMPLE Retirement Plan). Most of the employees opted to wait until the start of the following year to participate. However, the following employees have decided to take part in the plan for the remaining pay periods of the year.

James Ferguson: $500 contribution per pay period
Dewey Mann: $250 contribution per pay period
Joseph O'Neill: $700 contribution per pay period
Norman Ryan: $200 contribution per pay period

The contributions are to be deducted from the participating employee's pay and are excluded from the employee's income for Federal Income Tax purposes The other payroll taxes still apply. Make notations of the deductions in the "Other" section of each employee's earnings record. On the payroll registers and the earnings record, show the deductions in the blank column under "Deductions."

Open a new account in the general ledger (use the blank account on page 40) for SIMPLE Contributions Payable—account #29.

The company must match these contributions dollar-for-dollar, up to 3 percent of the employee's compensation. These payments will be processed through the Accounts Payable Department.

Prepare the payroll for the last pay period of November from Time Clerk's Reports Nos. 44 and 45, and record the paychecks issued all employees. Also, record the employer's payroll taxes.

No. 16 Salary increases of $130 per month, *effective for the two weeks covered in the December 4 payroll,* are given to Catherine L. Ford and Virginia A. Russell. The group insurance coverage for Ford will be increased to $37,000; for Russell, it will

PAY POINTS

Remember to deduct the premiums on the group insurance for each employee.

	Time Clerk's Report No. 44 For the Week Ending November 7, 20—									
Employee	**Time Record**							**Time Worked**	**Time Lost**
	S	**M**	**T**	**W**	**T**	**F**	**S**		
Bonno, A. V.		8	8	8	8	8		40 hrs.	. . .
Ford, C. L.		8	8	8	8	8		40 hrs.	. . .
Russell, V. A.		6	8	8	8	8		38 hrs.	2 hrs.*
Ryan, N. A.		8	8	8	8	8		40 hrs.	. . .
Student		8	8	8	8	8		40 hrs.	. . .
Williams, R. V. ...		6	8	7	7	6		34 hrs.	6 hrs.**

*Time lost for personal business; deduct 2 hours' pay.
**Time lost because of tardiness; deduct 6 hours' pay.

	Time Clerk's Report No. 45 For the Week Ending November 14, 20—									
Employee	**Time Record**							**Time Worked**	**Time Lost**
	S	**M**	**T**	**W**	**T**	**F**	**S**		
Bonno, A. V.		. . .	. . .	8	8	8		24 hrs.	. . .
Ford, C. L.		8	8	8	8	8		40 hrs.	. . .
Russell, V. A.		8	8	8	8	8		40 hrs.	. . .
Ryan, N. A.		8	8	8	8	8		40 hrs.	. . .
Student		8	8	8	8	8		40 hrs.	. . .
Williams, R. V. ...		D	D	8	6	8		22 hrs.	18 hrs.*

*Time lost because of tardiness; deduct 2 hours' pay; and unexcused absences: deduct 16 hours' pay.

PAY POINTS

The new wage rates are effective for the December 4 payroll.

be increased to $29,000. Update the employees' earnings records accordingly. The new wage rates are as follows:

Employee	Weekly Rate	Hourly Rate
Ford, Catherine L.	$480.00	$12.00
Russell, Virginia A.	375.00	9.38

November 30

No. 17　Prepare an employee's earnings record for Paul Winston Young, the president's nephew, who began work today. Young is single and claims one withholding allowance. He is training as a field sales representative in the city where the home office is located. His beginning salary is $1,750 per month. Address, 7936 Holmes Drive, Philadelphia, PA 19107-6107. Telephone, 555-2096. Social Security No. 432-07-6057. Young is eligible for group insurance coverage of $32,000.

Department: Sales.
Weekly rate: $403.85.
Hourly rate: $10.10.

December 3

No. 18　Deposit with the state of Pennsylvania the amount of state income taxes withheld from the November 20 payroll.

December 4

No. 19　Prepare the payroll for the first pay period of December from Time Clerk's Reports Nos. 46 and 47, and record the paychecks issued all employees. Record this payroll at the top of the third payroll register sheet.

Time Clerk's Report No. 46 For the Week Ending November 21, 20—									
Employee	**Time Record**							**Time Worked**	**Time Lost**
	S	M	T	W	T	F	S		
Bonno, A. V.		8	8	8	8	8		40 hrs.	...
Ford, C. L.		8	8	8	8	8		40 hrs.	...
Russell, V. A.		8	8	8	8	8		40 hrs.	...
Ryan, N. A.		8	8	8	4	8		36 hrs.	4 hrs.*
Student		8	8	8	8	8		40 hrs.	...
Woods, B. A.		...	8	8	8	8		32 hrs.	...

*Time lost on account of personal business; deduct 4 hours' pay.

Time Clerk's Report No. 47 For the Week Ending November 28, 20—									
Employee	**Time Record**							**Time Worked**	**Time Lost**
	S	M	T	W	T	F	S		
Bonno, A. V.	8*	8	8	8	PAID HOLIDAY	8		48 hrs.	...
Ford, C. L.		8	8	8		8		40 hrs.	...
Russell, V. A.		8	8	8		8		40 hrs.	...
Ryan, N. A.		9	10	8		8		43 hrs.	...
Student		8	8	8		8		40 hrs.	...
Woods, B. A.		8	8	8		8		40 hrs.	...

*Double time.

Note: Thursday, November 26, is a paid holiday for all workers.

Also, record the employer's payroll taxes.

No. 20 Anthony V. Bonno reports the birth of a son and completes an amended Form W-4, showing his total withholding allowances to be five. Change his earnings record accordingly.

No. 21 Both Anthony Bonno and Norman Ryan have been notified that their union dues will increase to $9 per pay starting with the last pay period of the year. *Reflect these increases in the December 18 pay* and show the changes on their earnings records.

December 9

No. 22 Pay the treasurer of the union the amount of union dues withheld during the month of November.

December 11

No. 23 The Payroll Department was informed that Virginia A. Russell died in an automobile accident on her way home from work Thursday, December 10.

December 14

No. 24 ① Make a separate entry (on one line) in the payroll register to record the issuance of a check payable to the *Estate of Virginia A. Russell.* This check covers Russell's work for the weeks ending December 5 and 12 ($675.16) plus her accrued vacation pay ($750.00). Do not show the vacation hours in the Time Record columns on the payroll register, but include them in the Total Earnings column.

PAY POINTS

This final pay is not subject to withholding for FIT, SIT, or CIT purposes.

Russell's final biweekly pay for time worked and the vacation pay are subject to FICA, FUTA, and SUTA taxes. Since Russell's cumulative earnings have surpassed the taxable earnings figures established by FUTA and SUTA, there will not be any unemployment tax on the employer. The deduction for group insurance premiums is $8.70.

② Make a notation of Russell's death in the payroll register and on her earnings record.

③ Prepare journal entries to transfer the net pay and to record Russell's final pay and the employer's payroll taxes. Post to the ledger accounts.

④ Report the final gross pay ($1,425.16) in Boxes 3 and 5, but not in Boxes 1, 17, and 20. Use the blank Form W-2 on page 7-60.

In addition, the last wage payment and vacation pay must be reported on Form 1099-MISC. A Form 1096 must also be completed. These forms will be completed in February before their due date. (See Transaction Nos. 41 and 42.)

December 15

No. 25 Deposit with the City Bank the amount of FICA taxes and federal income taxes for the November payrolls.

No. 26 Deposit with the city of Philadelphia the amount of city income taxes withheld from the November payrolls.

December 18

No. 27 Deposit with the state of Pennsylvania the amount of state income taxes withheld from the December 4 payroll.

No. 28 Glo-Brite has been notified by the insurance company that there will be no premium charge for the month of December on the policy for Virginia Russell. Prepare the entry for the check made payable to the estate of Virginia A. Russell, for the amount that was withheld for insurance from her December 14 pay.

No. 29 Prepare an employee's earnings record for Richard Lloyd Zimmerman, who was employed today as time clerk to take the place left vacant by the death of Virginia A. Russell last week. His beginning salary is $1,430 per month. Address, 900 South Clark Street, Philadelphia, PA 19195-6247. Telephone, 555-2104. Social Security No. 897-12-1502. Zimmerman is married and claims one withholding allowance. Zimmerman is eligible for group insurance coverage of $26,000, although no deduction for group insurance premiums will be made until the last payday in January.

> Department: Office.
> Weekly rate: $330.00.
> Hourly rate: $8.25.

No. 30 Prepare the payroll for the latter pay of December from Time Clerk's Reports Nos. 48 and 49 and record the paychecks issued all employees. Also, record the employer's payroll taxes.

Effective with this pay, O'Neill completed a new Form W-4 changing his total withholding allowances to four. Previously, he had claimed fewer allowances than he had been using on his tax return. Change his earnings record accordingly.

In this pay, the president of the company, Joseph O'Neill, is paid his annual bonus. This does not affect O'Neill's insurance coverage, which is based on regular pay. This year, his bonus is $35,000. For withholding purposes, the bonus is considered a supplemental payment and is added to his gross pay, and the aggregate amount is taxed. For this pay, O'Neill has increased his SIMPLE deduction to

Time Clerk's Report No. 48 For the Week Ending December 5, 20—

| Employee | Time Record | | | | | | | Time Worked | Time Lost |
	S	M	T	W	T	F	S		
Bonno, A. V.	4	8	8	8	8	8		44 hrs.	. . .
Ford, C. L.		8	8	8	8	8		40 hrs.	. . .
Russell, V. A.		8	8	8	8	8		40 hrs.	. . .
Ryan, N. A.		8	9	9	9	9		44 hrs.	. . .
Student		8	8	7	8	8		39 hrs.	1 hr.*
Woods, B. A.		8	8	8	8	8		40 hrs.	. . .
Young, P. W.		8	8	8	8	8		40 hrs.	. . .

*Time lost because of tardiness; deduct 1 hour's pay.

Time Clerk's Report No. 49 For the Week Ending December 12, 20—

| Employee | Time Record | | | | | | | Time Worked | Time Lost |
	S	M	T	W	T	F	S		
Bonno, A. V.	8	8	8	8	8	8		48 hrs.	. . .
Ford, C. L.		4	8	8	8	8		36 hrs.	4 hrs.*
Russell, V. A.		8	8	8	8	D		32 hrs.	8 hrs.
Ryan, N. A.		10	8	8	9	8		43 hrs.	. . .
Student		4	8	8	8	8		36 hrs.	4 hrs.**
Woods, B. A.		8	8	8	8	8		40 hrs.	. . .
Young, P. W.		8	8	8	8	8		40 hrs.	. . .

*Time lost for dentist appointment; no deduction for this time lost.
**Time spent in training session; no deduction in pay.

$4,000. To determine the federal income tax, use the *Table of Allowance Values* along with *Tax Table A* (pages T-2 to T-4). In calculating the tax, do not round the *aggregate* to the nearest *earnings* dollar.

Note: After posting the information for this last pay to the employees' earnings records, calculate and enter the quarterly and yearly totals on each earnings record.

NOTE: This completes the project insofar as recording the payroll transactions for the last quarter is concerned. The following additional transactions are given to illustrate different types of transactions arising in connection with the accounting for payrolls and payroll taxes. Record these transactions in the journal, but *do not* post to the ledger.

January 6

No. 31 Deposit with the state of Pennsylvania the amount of state income taxes withheld from the December 18 payroll.

January 8

No. 32 Pay the treasurer of the union the amount of union dues withheld during the month of December.

January 15

No. 33 Deposit with the City Bank the amount of FICA taxes and federal income taxes for the December payrolls.

Complete the *Federal Tax Deposit Coupon, Form 8109,* using one of the preinscribed forms on page 7-51.

No. 34 Deposit with the city of Philadelphia the amount of city income taxes withheld from the December payrolls.

February 1

No. 35 Prepare *Form 941, Employer's Quarterly Federal Tax Return,* with respect to wages paid during the last calendar quarter. Page 7-57 contains a blank Form 941. The information needed in preparing the return should be obtained from the ledger accounts, the payroll registers, the employees' earnings records, and the Federal Tax Deposit forms.

Form 941 and all forms that follow are to be signed by the president of the company, Joseph T. O'Neill.

No. 36 ① Complete *Form 940-EZ, Employer's Annual Federal Unemployment (FUTA) Tax Return,* using the blank form reproduced on page 7-58, and also *Form 8109, Federal Tax Deposit Coupon,* using the blank form reproduced on page 7-52. The information needed in preparing these forms can be obtained from the ledger accounts, the payroll registers, the employees' earnings records, and the following:

a. Contributions paid to the Pennsylvania unemployment fund for the year amount to $2,908.07. (This amount includes the employer's contributions for the fourth quarter, which will be determined and paid in Transaction No. 37.)

b. FUTA taxable wages for the first three quarters: $65,490.00

c. FUTA tax liability by quarter:

1st quarter—$272.71
2nd quarter—$140.33
3rd quarter—$110.88

d. All deposits for the first three quarters were made on the dates they were due.

② Journalize the entry to record the deposit included with the fourth quarter Form 8109.

No. 37 ① Prepare *Form UC-2, Employer's Report for Unemployment Compensation—Fourth Quarter,* using the blank form reproduced on page 7-59. In Pennsylvania, a credit week is any calendar week during the quarter in which the employee earned at least $50 (without regard to when paid). If a partial week, it is a credit week if paid during the fourth quarter. The maximum number of credit weeks in a quarter is 13. The telephone number of the company is (215) 555-9559. All other information needed in preparing the form can be obtained from the ledger accounts, the payroll registers, and the employees' earnings records.

② Journalize the entry to record the payment of the taxes for the fourth quarter.

No. 38 Complete *Form W-2, Wage and Tax Statement,* for each current employee, using the blank statements reproduced on pages 7-61 to 7-65. Use each employee's earnings record to obtain the information needed to complete the forms. The two plant workers (Bonno and Ryan) have had $121.00 in union dues withheld during the year.

No. 39 Complete *Form W-3, Transmittal of Wage and Tax Statements,* using the blank form reproduced on page 7-66. Use the information on all Forms W-2 to complete this form.

No. 40 Complete *Pennsylvania Form REV-1667 AS, W-2 Transmittal,* using the blank form reproduced on page 7-66. Use the information on Forms W-2 to complete this report.

The wages paid and the Pennsylvania tax withheld for the first three quarters are:

1st	34,088.75	954.49
2nd	45,535.62	1,275.00
3rd	62,600.20	1,752.80

No. 41 Complete *Form 1099-MISC, Miscellaneous Income,* for the payment to *the estate of Virginia A. Russell.* The full amount of the December 14 payment must be reported in Box 3. Page 7-67 contains a blank form.

     Note: These wages are to be reported as other income in Box 3, so that the IRS will not seek self-employment tax on such amounts.

No. 42 Complete *Form 1096, Annual Summary and Transmittal of U.S. Information Returns,* using the blank form on page 7-67. Use the information on Form 1099-MISC to complete this form.

No. 43 Prepare *Form PA-W3R, Employer Quarterly Reconciliation Return of Income Tax Withheld,* using the blank form on page 7-55. The telephone number of the company is (215) 555-9559.

No. 44 Prepare the Annual Reconciliation of Wage Tax for Philadelphia, using the blank form on page 7-56. Tax paid during the first three quarters was $6,454.87.

QUESTIONS ON THE PAYROLL PROJECT

1. The total payroll tax expense incurred by the employer on salaries and wages paid during the quarter ended December 31 was . . . . $ _____

2. The total payroll tax expense incurred by the employer on the total earnings of Joseph T. O'Neill during the fourth quarter was . . . . $ _____

3. The amount of the group insurance premiums collected from employees during the quarter ended December 31 was . . . . $ _____

4. O'Neill has decided to give all current employees (excluding himself) a bonus payment during January equal to 5% of their total gross pay for last year. Determine the total of this bonus payment.
. . . . $ _____

5. On the financial statements prepared at the end of its first year of operations, the company must show an accurate picture of all expenses and all liabilities incurred. The last payday of the year was December 18. However, the payment to the employees on that day did not include the weeks ending December 19 and 26 and the four days (December 28–31) in the following week. These earnings will be reflected in the January payrolls. Two-column journal paper is provided for use in journalizing the following entry.

    Prepare the adjusting entry as of December 31 to record the salaries and wages that have accrued but remain unpaid as of the end of the year. When calculating the amount of the accrual for each hourly worker, assume each employee worked eight hours on each day during the period with no overtime. For each salaried worker, the accrual will amount to 14/10 of the worker's biweekly earnings, except for Zimmerman who worked only ten days.

    Each of the labor cost accounts should be debited for the appropriate amount of the accrual, and Salaries and Wages Payable should be credited for the total amount of the accrual. There is no liability for payroll taxes on the accrued salaries and wages until the workers are actually paid. Therefore, the company follows the practice of not accruing payroll taxes.

6. Also prepare the adjusting entry as of December 31 to record the accrued vacation pay as of the end of the year. Record the expense in a vacation benefits expense account, and credit the appropriate liability account. Use the journal paper provided.

As of December 31, the vacation time earned but not used by each employee is listed below.

Bonno	80 hours	Sokowski	two weeks
Ferguson	three weeks	Student	two weeks
Ford	two weeks	Woods	none
Mann	one week	Young	none
O'Neill	four weeks	Zimmerman	none
Ryan	80 hours		

JOURNAL   18

DATE	DESCRIPTION	POST. REF.	DEBIT	CREDIT

ACCOUNTING RECORDS AND REPORTS

Contents

	DATE		DESCRIPTION	POST. REF.	DEBIT	CREDIT	
1	20—Oct.	9	Payroll Cash	12	1 0 7 9 9 96		1
2			Cash	11		1 0 7 9 9 96	2
3							3
4		9	Administrative Salaries	51	2 3 0 7 69		4
5			Office Salaries	52	3 3 5 3 08		5
6			Sales Salaries	53	3 6 0 0 00		6
7			Plant Wages	54	4 9 0 2 00		7
8			FICA Taxes Payable—OASDI	20.1		8 7 8 09	8
9			FICA Taxes Payable—HI	20.2		2 0 5 37	9
10			Employees FIT Payable	24		1 2 2 4 00	10
11			Employees SIT Payable	25		3 9 6 57	11
12			Employees CIT Payable	26		6 4 2 78	12
13			Union Dues Payable	28		1 6 00	13
14			Payroll Cash	12		1 0 7 9 9 96	14
15							15
16		9	Payroll Taxes	56	1 2 3 1 49		16
17			FICA Taxes Payable—OASDI	20.1		8 7 8 09	17
18			FICA Taxes Payable—HI	20.2		2 0 5 36	18
19			FUTA Taxes Payable	21		2 6 24	19
20			SUTA Taxes Payable	22		1 2 1 80	20
21							21
22							22
23							23
24							24
25							25
26							26
27							27
28							28
29							29
30							30
31							31
32							32
33							33
34							34

	DATE	DESCRIPTION	POST. REF.	DEBIT	CREDIT	
1						1
2						2
3						3
4						4
5						5
6						6
7						7
8						8
9						9
10						10
11						11
12						12
13						13
14						14
15						15
16						16
17						17
18						18
19						19
20						20
21						21
22						22
23						23
24						24
25						25
26						26
27						27
28						28
29						29
30						30
31						31
32						32
33						33
34						34

	DATE	DESCRIPTION	POST. REF.	DEBIT	CREDIT	
1						1
2						2
3						3
4						4
5						5
6						6
7						7
8						8
9						9
10						10
11						11
12						12
13						13
14						14
15						15
16						16
17						17
18						18
19						19
20						20
21						21
22						22
23						23
24						24
25						25
26						26
27						27
28						28
29						29
30						30
31						31
32						32
33						33
34						34

	DATE	DESCRIPTION	POST. REF.	DEBIT	CREDIT	
1						1
2						2
3						3
4						4
5						5
6						6
7						7
8						8
9						9
10						10
11						11
12						12
13						13
14						14
15						15
16						16
17						17
18						18
19						19
20						20
21						21
22						22
23						23
24						24
25						25
26						26
27						27
28						28
29						29
30						30
31						31
32						32
33						33
34						34

	DATE		DESCRIPTION	POST. REF.	DEBIT	CREDIT	
1							1
2							2
3							3
4							4
5							5
6							6
7							7
8							8
9							9
10							10
11							11
12							12
13							13
14							14
15							15
16							16
17							17
18							18
19							19
20							20
21							21
22							22
23							23
24							24
25							25
26							26
27							27
28							28
29							29
30							30
31							31
32							32
33							33
34							34

JOURNAL

Page

	DATE		DESCRIPTION	POST. REF.	DEBIT	CREDIT	
1							1
2							2
3							3
4							4
5							5
6							6
7							7
8							8
9							9
10							10
11							11
12							12
13							13
14							14
15							15
16							16
17							17
18							18
19							19
20							20
21							21
22							22
23							23
24							24
25							25
26							26
27							27
28							28
29							29
30							30
31							31
32							32
33							33
34							34

	DATE		DESCRIPTION	POST. REF.	DEBIT	CREDIT	
1							1
2							2
3							3
4							4
5							5
6							6
7							7
8							8
9							9
10							10
11							11
12							12
13							13
14							14
15							15
16							16
17							17
18							18
19							19
20							20
21							21
22							22
23							23
24							24
25							25
26							26
27							27
28							28
29							29
30							30
31							31
32							32
33							33
34							34

JOURNAL

Page

	DATE	DESCRIPTION	POST. REF.	DEBIT	CREDIT	
1						1
2						2
3						3
4						4
5						5
6						6
7						7
8						8
9						9
10						10
11						11
12						12
13						13
14						14
15						15
16						16
17						17
18						18
19						19
20						20
21						21
22						22
23						23
24						24
25						25
26						26
27						27
28						28
29						29
30						30
31						31
32						32
33						33
34						34

	DATE		DESCRIPTION	POST. REF.	DEBIT	CREDIT	
1							1
2							2
3							3
4							4
5							5
6							6
7							7
8							8
9							9
10							10
11							11
12							12
13							13
14							14
15							15
16							16
17							17
18							18
19							19
20							20
21							21
22							22
23							23
24							24
25							25
26							26
27							27
28							28
29							29
30							30
31							31
32							32
33							33
34							34

GENERAL LEDGER

ACCOUNT **CASH**   ACCOUNT NO. 11

DATE		ITEM	POST. REF.	DEBIT	CREDIT	BALANCE	
						DEBIT	CREDIT
20— Oct.	1	*Balance*	✓			1 9 9 8 4 6 33	
	9		J41		1 0 7 9 9 96	1 8 9 0 4 6 37	

ACCOUNT **PAYROLL CASH**

DATE		ITEM	POST. REF.	DEBIT	CREDIT	BALANCE	
						DEBIT	CREDIT
20—Oct.	9		J41	1 0 7 9 9 96		1 0 7 9 9 96	
	9		J41		1 0 7 9 9 96	– – – –	– – – –

DATE		ITEM	POST. REF.	DEBIT	CREDIT	BALANCE	
						DEBIT	CREDIT
20—Oct.	9		J41		8 7 8 09		8 7 8 09
	9		J41		8 7 8 09		1 7 5 6 18

ACCOUNT **EMPLOYEES CIT PAYABLE**   ACCOUNT NO. 26

DATE	ITEM	POST. REF.	DEBIT	CREDIT	BALANCE DEBIT	BALANCE CREDIT
20— Oct. 9		J41		6 4 2 78		6 4 2 78

ACCOUNT **GROUP INSURANCE PREMIUMS COLLECTED**   ACCOUNT NO. 27

DATE	ITEM	POST. REF.	DEBIT	CREDIT	BALANCE DEBIT	BALANCE CREDIT

ACCOUNT **UNION DUES PAYABLE**   ACCOUNT NO. 28

DATE	ITEM	POST. REF.	DEBIT	CREDIT	BALANCE DEBIT	BALANCE CREDIT
20— Oct. 9		J41		1 6 00		1 6 00

ACCOUNT   ACCOUNT NO.

DATE	ITEM	POST. REF.	DEBIT	CREDIT	BALANCE DEBIT	BALANCE CREDIT
20—						

ACCOUNT **ADMINISTRATIVE SALARIES**   ACCOUNT NO. 51

DATE		ITEM	POST. REF.	DEBIT	CREDIT	BALANCE	
						DEBIT	CREDIT
20— Oct.	1	Balance	√			4 2 6 9 2 27	
	9		J41	2 3 0 7 69		4 4 9 9 9 96	

ACCOUNT **OFFICE SALARIES**   ACCOUNT NO. 52

DATE		ITEM	POST. REF.	DEBIT	CREDIT	BALANCE	
						DEBIT	CREDIT
20— Oct.	1	Balance	√			2 8 3 5 0 00	
	9		J41	3 3 5 3 08		3 1 7 0 3 08	

ACCOUNT **SALES SALARIES**   ACCOUNT NO. 53

DATE		ITEM	POST. REF.	DEBIT	CREDIT	BALANCE	
						DEBIT	CREDIT
20— Oct.	1	Balance	√			2 8 5 2 5 00	
	9		J41	3 6 0 0 00		3 2 1 2 5 00	

ACCOUNT **PLANT WAGES**

DATE		ITEM	POST. REF.	DEBIT	CREDIT	BALANCE DEBIT	BALANCE CREDIT
20— Oct.	1	Balance	√			4 2 6 5 7 30	
	9		J41	4 9 0 2 00		4 7 5 5 9 30	

ACCOUNT **PAYROLL TAXES**

DATE		ITEM	POST. REF.	DEBIT	CREDIT	BALANCE DEBIT	BALANCE CREDIT
20— Oct.	1	Balance	√			1 3 9 0 6 21	
	9		J41	1 2 3 1 49		1 5 1 3 7 70	

EMPLOYEES' EARNINGS RECORDS

Employee Earnings Record — BONNO, Anthony Victor

DEPARTMENT	Plant
OCCUPATION	Mixer Operator
WORKS IN (STATE)	PA
S.S. ACCOUNT NO.	537-10-3481
NAME—LAST	BONNO
FIRST	Anthony
MIDDLE	Victor
SEX	M (X) F
W/H ALLOW.	4
MARITAL STATUS	M
GROUP INSURANCE	$55,000—30¢/M
OTHER DEDUCTIONS INFORMATION / UNION DUES	$8 each pay
SALARY	$
WEEKLY RATE	$
HOURLY RATE	$ 17.65
OVERTIME RATE	$ 26.48

20__ PAYDAY	REGULAR EARNINGS HRS.	RATE	AMOUNT	OVERTIME EARNINGS HRS.	RATE	AMOUNT	CUMULATIVE EARNINGS	FICA OASDI	FICA HI	FIT	SIT	CIT	OTHER DEDUCTIONS	CK. NO.	NET PAID AMOUNT
YEAR-TO-DATE TOTAL			10 2 9 3 40			10 2 8 60	113 2 2 00	7 0 1 96	1 6 4 17	8 1 0 00	3 1 7 02	5 1 3 85	2 1 6 80		8 5 9 8 20
1 10/9	80	17 65	14 1 2 00				127 3 4 00	8 7 54	2 0 47	8 2 00	3 9 54	6 4 08	8 00	672	1 1 1 0 37
2															
3															
4															
5															
6															
QUARTER TOTAL															
YEARLY TOTAL															

Employee Earnings Record — FERGUSON, James Claude

DEPARTMENT	Sales
OCCUPATION	Sales Manager
WORKS IN (STATE)	PA
S.S. ACCOUNT NO.	486-03-8645
NAME—LAST	FERGUSON
FIRST	James
MIDDLE	Claude
SEX	M (X) F
W/H ALLOW.	5
MARITAL STATUS	M
GROUP INSURANCE	$88,000—30¢/M
SALARY	$ 58,500/yr.
WEEKLY RATE	$ 1,125.00
HOURLY RATE	$ 28.13
OVERTIME RATE	$

20__ PAYDAY	REGULAR EARNINGS HRS.	RATE	AMOUNT	OVERTIME EARNINGS HRS.	RATE	AMOUNT	CUMULATIVE EARNINGS	FICA OASDI	FICA HI	FIT	SIT	CIT	OTHER DEDUCTIONS	CK. NO.	NET PAID AMOUNT
YEAR-TO-DATE TOTAL			231 2 5 00				231 2 5 00	14 3 3 75	3 3 5 31	2 2 9 1 00	6 4 7 50	10 4 9 53	1 3 2 30		172 3 5 61
1 10/9	80		22 5 0 00				253 7 5 00	1 3 9 50	3 2 63	1 9 1 00	6 3 00	1 0 2 12		673	1 7 2 1 75
2															
3															
4															
5															
6															
QUARTER TOTAL															
YEARLY TOTAL															

Employee Record 1

DEPARTMENT	Office
OCCUPATION	Executive Secretary
WORKS IN (STATE)	PA
SEX	F (X)
S.S. ACCOUNT NO.	213-09-4567
NAME—LAST	FORD
FIRST	Catherine
MIDDLE	Louise
W/H ALLOW.	2
MARITAL STATUS	S
GROUP INSURANCE	$35,000—30¢/M
SALARY	$1,950/mo.
WEEKLY RATE	$450.00
HOURLY RATE	$11.25
OVERTIME RATE	$16.88

OTHER DEDUCTIONS INFORMATION — UNION DUES / OTHER

20__ PAYDAY	REGULAR EARNINGS HRS.	RATE	AMOUNT	OVERTIME EARNINGS HRS.	RATE	AMOUNT	CUMULATIVE EARNINGS	FICA OASDI	HI	FIT	SIT	CIT	OTHER DEDUCTIONS	CK. NO.	NET PAID AMOUNT
YEAR-TO-DATE TOTAL			6300 00				6300 00	390 60	91 35	639 00	176 40	285 93	37 80		4678 92
1 10/9	80		9000 00				7200 00	55 80	13 05	75 00	25 20	40 85		674	690 10
2															
3															
4															
5															
6															
QUARTER TOTAL															
YEARLY TOTAL															

Employee Record 2

Msp7-45a.eps

DEPARTMENT	Sales
OCCUPATION	Sales Representative
WORKS IN (STATE)	PA
SEX	M (X)
S.S. ACCOUNT NO.	282-37-9352
NAME—LAST	MANN
FIRST	Dewey
MIDDLE	Wilson
W/H ALLOW.	4
MARITAL STATUS	M
GROUP INSURANCE	$53,000—30¢/M
SALARY	$2,925/mo.
WEEKLY RATE	$675.00
HOURLY RATE	$16.88
OVERTIME RATE	$

OTHER DEDUCTIONS INFORMATION — UNION DUES / OTHER

20__ PAYDAY	REGULAR EARNINGS HRS.	RATE	AMOUNT	OVERTIME EARNINGS HRS.	RATE	AMOUNT	CUMULATIVE EARNINGS	FICA OASDI	HI	FIT	SIT	CIT	OTHER DEDUCTIONS	CK. NO.	NET PAID AMOUNT
YEAR-TO-DATE TOTAL			5400 00				5400 00	334 80	78 30	332 00	151 20	245 08	31 50		4227 12
1 10/9	80		1350 00				6750 00	83 70	19 58	73 00	37 80	61 27		675	1074 65
2															
3															
4															
5															
6															
QUARTER TOTAL															
YEARLY TOTAL															

Employee Payroll Record — O'NEILL

DEPARTMENT	OCCUPATION	WORKS IN (STATE)	SEX		S.S. ACCOUNT NO.	NAME—LAST	FIRST	MIDDLE
Admin.	President	PA	M	F X	897-04-1534	O'NEILL	Joseph	Tyler

W/H ALLOW.	MARITAL STATUS
3	M

GROUP INSURANCE $90,000—30¢/M

SALARY	$ 60,000/yr.
WEEKLY RATE	$ 1,153.85
HOURLY RATE	$ 28.85
OVERTIME RATE	$

OTHER DEDUCTIONS INFORMATION
UNION DUES — OTHER —

PAYDAY 20__	REGULAR EARNINGS HRS.	REGULAR EARNINGS RATE	REGULAR EARNINGS AMOUNT	OVERTIME EARNINGS HRS.	OVERTIME EARNINGS RATE	OVERTIME EARNINGS AMOUNT	CUMULATIVE EARNINGS	DEDUCTIONS FICA OASDI	DEDUCTIONS FICA HI	FIT	SIT	CIT	OTHER DEDUCTIONS	CK. NO.	NET PAID AMOUNT
YEAR-TO-DATE TOTAL			4269 2 27				4269 2 27	264 6 92	61 9 04	6116 00	119 5 38	193 7 59	2 0 2 50		2997 4 84
1 10/9	80		230 7 69				4499 9 96	14 3 08	3 3 46	2 3 4 00	6 4 62	1 0 4 73		676	17 2 7 80
2															
3															
4															
5															
6															
QUARTER TOTAL															
YEARLY TOTAL															

Employee Payroll Record — RUSSELL

DEPARTMENT	OCCUPATION	WORKS IN (STATE)	SEX		S.S. ACCOUNT NO.	NAME—LAST	FIRST	MIDDLE
Office	Time Clerk	PA	M	F X	314-21-6337	RUSSELL	Virginia	Aloise

W/H ALLOW.	MARITAL STATUS
1	S

GROUP INSURANCE $27,000—30¢/M

SALARY	$1,495/mo.
WEEKLY RATE	$ 345.00
HOURLY RATE	$ 8.63
OVERTIME RATE	$ 12.95

OTHER DEDUCTIONS INFORMATION
UNION DUES — OTHER —

PAYDAY 20__	REGULAR EARNINGS HRS.	REGULAR EARNINGS RATE	REGULAR EARNINGS AMOUNT	OVERTIME EARNINGS HRS.	OVERTIME EARNINGS RATE	OVERTIME EARNINGS AMOUNT	CUMULATIVE EARNINGS	DEDUCTIONS FICA OASDI	DEDUCTIONS FICA HI	FIT	SIT	CIT	OTHER DEDUCTIONS	CK. NO.	NET PAID AMOUNT
YEAR-TO-DATE TOTAL			624 0 00				624 0 00	38 6 88	9 0 48	642 00	17 4 72	28 3 20			46 3 1 22
1 10/9	80		69 0 00				693 0 00	4 2 78	1 0 01	6 0 00	1 9 32	3 1 32	3 1 50	677	5 2 6 57
2															
3															
4															
5															
6															
QUARTER TOTAL															
YEARLY TOTAL															

Employee Earnings Record — RYAN, Norman Allen

DEPARTMENT	Plant
OCCUPATION	Electrician
WORKS IN (STATE)	PA
S.S. ACCOUNT NO.	526-23-1223
SEX	M X
NAME—LAST	RYAN
FIRST	Norman
MIDDLE	Allen
MARITAL STATUS	M
W/H ALLOW.	4
SALARY	$
WEEKLY RATE	$
HOURLY RATE	$ 18.00
OVERTIME RATE	$ 27.00
GROUP INSURANCE	$56,000—30¢/M
OTHER DEDUCTIONS INFORMATION — UNION DUES	$8 each pay

20__ PAYDAY	REGULAR EARNINGS HRS.	RATE	AMOUNT	OVERTIME EARNINGS HRS.	RATE	AMOUNT	CUMULATIVE EARNINGS	DEDUCTIONS FICA OASDI	HI	FIT	SIT	CIT	OTHER DEDUCTIONS	CK. NO.	NET PAID AMOUNT
YEAR-TO-DATE TOTAL			13 287 50			1 397 80	14 685 30	910 49	212 94	1 070 00	411 19	666 49	235 70		11 178 49
1 10/9	80	18 00	1 440 00				16 125 30	89 28	20 88	88 00	40 32	65 35	8 00	678	1 128 17
2															
3															
4															
5															
6															
QUARTER TOTAL															
YEARLY TOTAL															

Employee Earnings Record — SOKOWSKI, Thomas James

DEPARTMENT	Plant
OCCUPATION	Supervisor
WORKS IN (STATE)	PA
S.S. ACCOUNT NO.	662-04-8832
SEX	M X
NAME—LAST	SOKOWSKI
FIRST	Thomas
MIDDLE	James
MARITAL STATUS	M
W/H ALLOW.	2
SALARY	$ 1,025.00
WEEKLY RATE	$
HOURLY RATE	$ 25.63
OVERTIME RATE	$
GROUP INSURANCE	$80,000—30¢/M
OTHER DEDUCTIONS INFORMATION — UNION DUES	

20__ PAYDAY	REGULAR EARNINGS HRS.	RATE	AMOUNT	OVERTIME EARNINGS HRS.	RATE	AMOUNT	CUMULATIVE EARNINGS	DEDUCTIONS FICA OASDI	HI	FIT	SIT	CIT	OTHER DEDUCTIONS	CK. NO.	NET PAID AMOUNT
YEAR-TO-DATE TOTAL			16 650 00				16 650 00	1 032 30	241 43	2 002 00	466 20	755 66	94 50		12 057 91
1 10/9	80		2 050 00				18 700 00	127 10	29 73	213 00	57 40	93 04		679	1 529 73
2															
3															
4															
5															
6															
QUARTER TOTAL															
YEARLY TOTAL															

Employee Earnings Record — Employee 1

DEPARTMENT	Office
OCCUPATION	Accounting Trainee
WORKS IN (STATE)	PA
S.S. ACCOUNT NO.	
SEX	M F
NAME—LAST	
FIRST	
MIDDLE	
W/H ALLOW.	1
MARITAL STATUS	S
GROUP INSURANCE	$21,000—30¢/M
SALARY	$1,170/mo.
WEEKLY RATE	$ 270.00
HOURLY RATE	$ 6.75
OVERTIME RATE	$ 10.13
OTHER DEDUCTIONS INFORMATION	UNION DUES / OTHER

20__ PAYDAY	REGULAR EARNINGS HRS.	REGULAR EARNINGS RATE	REGULAR EARNINGS AMOUNT	OVERTIME EARNINGS HRS.	OVERTIME EARNINGS RATE	OVERTIME EARNINGS AMOUNT	CUMULATIVE EARNINGS	FICA OASDI	FICA HI	FIT	SIT	CIT	OTHER DEDUCTIONS	NET PAID CK. NO.	NET PAID AMOUNT
YEAR-TO-DATE TOTAL			5500 00				5550 00	344 10	80 48	409 00	155 40	251 89			4276 73
1 10/9	80		540 00				6090 00	33 48	7 83	39 00	15 12	24 51	3 2 40	680	420 06
2															
3															
4															
5															
6															
QUARTER TOTAL															
YEARLY TOTAL															

Employee Earnings Record — Employee 2

DEPARTMENT	Office
OCCUPATION	Programmer
WORKS IN (STATE)	PA
S.S. ACCOUNT NO.	518-30-6741
SEX	M F X
NAME—LAST	WILLIAMS
FIRST	Ruth
MIDDLE	Virginia
W/H ALLOW.	0
MARITAL STATUS	S
GROUP INSURANCE	$48,000—30¢/M
SALARY	$2,650/mo.
WEEKLY RATE	$ 611.54
HOURLY RATE	$ 15.29
OVERTIME RATE	$ 22.94
OTHER DEDUCTIONS INFORMATION	UNION DUES / OTHER

20__ PAYDAY	REGULAR EARNINGS HRS.	REGULAR EARNINGS RATE	REGULAR EARNINGS AMOUNT	OVERTIME EARNINGS HRS.	OVERTIME EARNINGS RATE	OVERTIME EARNINGS AMOUNT	CUMULATIVE EARNINGS	FICA OASDI	FICA HI	FIT	SIT	CIT	OTHER DEDUCTIONS	NET PAID CK. NO.	NET PAID AMOUNT
YEAR-TO-DATE TOTAL			10260 00				10260 00	636 12	148 77	1606 00	287 28	465 65			7056 78
1 10/9	80		1223 08				11483 08	75 83	17 73	169 00	34 25	55 51	5 9 40	681	870 76
2															
3															
4															
5															
6															
QUARTER TOTAL															
YEARLY TOTAL															

(Left form)

DEPARTMENT

OCCUPATION

WORKS IN (STATE)

S.S. ACCOUNT NO.

SEX — M | F

NAME—LAST **FIRST** **MIDDLE**

OTHER DEDUCTIONS INFORMATION

GROUP INSURANCE

UNION DUES

OTHER

SALARY $
WEEKLY RATE $
HOURLY RATE $
OVERTIME RATE $

W/H ALLOW.

MARITAL STATUS

DEDUCTIONS

20 ___ PAYDAY	REGULAR EARNINGS		OVERTIME EARNINGS			CUMULATIVE EARNINGS	FICA		FIT	SIT	CIT	OTHER DEDUCTIONS	NET PAID	
	HRS.	RATE	AMOUNT	HRS.	RATE	AMOUNT		OASDI	HI					CK. NO.	AMOUNT

YEAR-TO-DATE TOTAL

1
2
3
4
5
6

QUARTER TOTAL

YEARLY TOTAL

(Right form)

DEPARTMENT

OCCUPATION

WORKS IN (STATE)

S.S. ACCOUNT NO.

SEX — M | F

NAME—LAST **FIRST** **MIDDLE**

OTHER DEDUCTIONS INFORMATION

GROUP INSURANCE

UNION DUES

OTHER

SALARY $
WEEKLY RATE $
HOURLY RATE $
OVERTIME RATE $

W/H ALLOW.

MARITAL STATUS

DEDUCTIONS

20 ___ PAYDAY	REGULAR EARNINGS		OVERTIME EARNINGS			CUMULATIVE EARNINGS	FICA		FIT	SIT	CIT	OTHER DEDUCTIONS	NET PAID	
	HRS.	RATE	AMOUNT	HRS.	RATE	AMOUNT		OASDI	HI					CK. NO.	AMOUNT

YEAR-TO-DATE TOTAL

1
2
3
4
5
6

QUARTER TOTAL

YEARLY TOTAL

Left Form

DEPARTMENT | OCCUPATION | WORKS IN (STATE) | SEX M F | S.S. ACCOUNT NO. | NAME—LAST | FIRST | MIDDLE

MARITAL STATUS | W/H ALLOW.

SALARY $ | WEEKLY RATE $ | HOURLY RATE $ | OVERTIME RATE $

OTHER DEDUCTIONS INFORMATION
GROUP INSURANCE | UNION DUES | OTHER

NET PAID

20 __ PAYDAY	REGULAR EARNINGS		OVERTIME EARNINGS			CUMULATIVE EARNINGS	DEDUCTIONS							NET PAID	
	HRS.	RATE	AMOUNT	HRS.	RATE	AMOUNT		FICA OASDI	HI	FIT	SIT	CIT	OTHER DEDUCTIONS	CK. NO.	AMOUNT

YEAR-TO-DATE TOTAL
1
2
3
4
5
6
QUARTER TOTAL
YEARLY TOTAL

Right Form

DEPARTMENT | OCCUPATION | WORKS IN (STATE) | SEX M F | S.S. ACCOUNT NO. | NAME—LAST | FIRST | MIDDLE

MARITAL STATUS | W/H ALLOW.

SALARY $ | WEEKLY RATE $ | HOURLY RATE $ | OVERTIME RATE $

OTHER DEDUCTIONS INFORMATION
GROUP INSURANCE | UNION DUES | OTHER

NET PAID

20 __ PAYDAY	REGULAR EARNINGS		OVERTIME EARNINGS			CUMULATIVE EARNINGS	DEDUCTIONS							NET PAID	
	HRS.	RATE	AMOUNT	HRS.	RATE	AMOUNT		FICA OASDI	HI	FIT	SIT	CIT	OTHER DEDUCTIONS	CK. NO.	AMOUNT

YEAR-TO-DATE TOTAL
1
2
3
4
5
6
QUARTER TOTAL
YEARLY TOTAL

a Control number	22222	Void ☐	For Official Use Only ▶ OMB No. 1545-0008		

b Employer identification number	1 Wages, tips, other compensation $	2 Federal income tax withheld $

c Employer's name, address, and ZIP code	3 Social security wages $	4 Social security tax withheld $
	5 Medicare wages and tips $	6 Medicare tax withheld $
	7 Social security tips $	8 Allocated tips $

d Employee's social security number	9 Advance EIC payment $	10 Dependent care benefits $

e Employee's first name and initial Last name	11 Nonqualified plans $	12a See instructions for box 12 $
	13 Statutory employee ☐ Retirement plan ☐ Third-party sick pay ☐	12b $
	14 Other	12c $
		12d $

f Employee's address and ZIP code

15 State Employer's state ID number	16 State wages, tips, etc. $	17 State income tax $	18 Local wages, tips, etc. $	19 Local income tax $	20 Locality name
	$	$	$	$	

Form **W-2** **Wage and Tax Statement** (99)

20 - -
(Rev. February 2002)

Cat. No. 10134D

Department of the Treasury—Internal Revenue Service
For Privacy Act and Paperwork Reduction Act Notice, see separate instructions.

Copy A For Social Security Administration—Send this entire page with Form W-3 to the Social Security Administration; photocopies are **not** acceptable.

Do Not Cut, Fold, or Staple Forms on This Page — Do Not Cut, Fold, or Staple Forms on This Page

---

a Control number	22222	Void ☐	For Official Use Only ▶ OMB No. 1545-0008		

b Employer identification number	1 Wages, tips, other compensation $	2 Federal income tax withheld $

c Employer's name, address, and ZIP code	3 Social security wages $	4 Social security tax withheld $
	5 Medicare wages and tips $	6 Medicare tax withheld $
	7 Social security tips $	8 Allocated tips $

d Employee's social security number	9 Advance EIC payment $	10 Dependent care benefits $

e Employee's first name and initial Last name	11 Nonqualified plans $	12a See instructions for box 12 $
	13 Statutory employee ☐ Retirement plan ☐ Third-party sick pay ☐	12b $
	14 Other	12c $
		12d $

f Employee's address and ZIP code

15 State Employer's state ID number	16 State wages, tips, etc. $	17 State income tax $	18 Local wages, tips, etc. $	19 Local income tax $	20 Locality name
	$	$	$	$	

Form **W-2** **Wage and Tax Statement** (99)

20 - -
(Rev. February 2002)

Cat. No. 10134D

Department of the Treasury—Internal Revenue Service
For Privacy Act and Paperwork Reduction Act Notice, see separate instructions.

Copy A For Social Security Administration—Send this entire page with Form W-3 to the Social Security Administration; photocopies are **not** acceptable.

Do Not Cut, Fold, or Staple Forms on This Page — Do Not Cut, Fold, or Staple Forms on This Page

a Control number	22222	Void ☐	For Official Use Only ▶ OMB No. 1545-0008		
b Employer identification number			**1** Wages, tips, other compensation $	**2** Federal income tax withheld $	
c Employer's name, address, and ZIP code			**3** Social security wages $	**4** Social security tax withheld $	
			5 Medicare wages and tips $	**6** Medicare tax withheld $	
			7 Social security tips $	**8** Allocated tips $	
d Employee's social security number			**9** Advance EIC payment $	**10** Dependent care benefits $	
e Employee's first name and initial Last name			**11** Nonqualified plans $	**12a** See instructions for box 12 Code $	
			13 Statutory employee ☐ Retirement plan ☐ Third-party sick pay ☐	**12b** Code $	
			14 Other	**12c** Code $	
				12d Code $	
f Employee's address and ZIP code					

15 State Employer's state ID number	**16** State wages, tips, etc. $	**17** State income tax $	**18** Local wages, tips, etc. $	**19** Local income tax $	**20** Locality name
	$	$	$	$	

Form **W-2** **Wage and Tax Statement** (99)

20 --
(Rev. February 2002)

Cat. No. 10134D

Department of the Treasury—Internal Revenue Service

For Privacy Act and Paperwork Reduction Act Notice, see separate instructions.

Copy A For Social Security Administration—Send this entire page with Form W-3 to the Social Security Administration; photocopies are **not** acceptable.

Do Not Cut, Fold, or Staple Forms on This Page — Do Not Cut, Fold, or Staple Forms on This Page

a Control number	22222	Void ☐	For Official Use Only ▶ OMB No. 1545-0008		
b Employer identification number			**1** Wages, tips, other compensation $	**2** Federal income tax withheld $	
c Employer's name, address, and ZIP code			**3** Social security wages $	**4** Social security tax withheld $	
			5 Medicare wages and tips $	**6** Medicare tax withheld $	
			7 Social security tips $	**8** Allocated tips $	
d Employee's social security number			**9** Advance EIC payment $	**10** Dependent care benefits $	
e Employee's first name and initial Last name			**11** Nonqualified plans $	**12a** See instructions for box 12 Code $	
			13 Statutory employee ☐ Retirement plan ☐ Third-party sick pay ☐	**12b** Code $	
			14 Other	**12c** Code $	
				12d Code $	
f Employee's address and ZIP code					

15 State Employer's state ID number	**16** State wages, tips, etc. $	**17** State income tax $	**18** Local wages, tips, etc. $	**19** Local income tax $	**20** Locality name
	$	$	$	$	

Form **W-2** **Wage and Tax Statement** (99)

20 --
(Rev. February 2002)

Cat. No. 10134D

Department of the Treasury—Internal Revenue Service

For Privacy Act and Paperwork Reduction Act Notice, see separate instructions.

Copy A For Social Security Administration—Send this entire page with Form W-3 to the Social Security Administration; photocopies are **not** acceptable.

Do Not Cut, Fold, or Staple Forms on This Page — Do Not Cut, Fold, or Staple Forms on This Page

a Control number	22222	Void ☐	For Official Use Only ▶ OMB No. 1545-0008		

b Employer identification number		1 Wages, tips, other compensation $	2 Federal income tax withheld $

c Employer's name, address, and ZIP code	3 Social security wages $	4 Social security tax withheld $
	5 Medicare wages and tips $	6 Medicare tax withheld $
	7 Social security tips $	8 Allocated tips $

d Employee's social security number	9 Advance EIC payment $	10 Dependent care benefits $

e Employee's first name and initial	Last name	11 Nonqualified plans $	12a See instructions for box 12 $
		13 Statutory employee ☐ Retirement plan ☐ Third-party sick pay ☐	12b $
		14 Other	12c $
			12d $

f Employee's address and ZIP code

15 State	Employer's state ID number	16 State wages, tips, etc. $	17 State income tax $	18 Local wages, tips, etc. $	19 Local income tax $	20 Locality name
		$	$	$	$	

Form **W-2** **Wage and Tax Statement** (99)   **20 --**   Department of the Treasury—Internal Revenue Service

Copy A For Social Security Administration—Send this entire page with Form W-3 to the Social Security Administration; photocopies are **not** acceptable.

(Rev. February 2002)

Cat. No. 10134D

For Privacy Act and Paperwork Reduction Act Notice, see separate instructions.

Do Not Cut, Fold, or Staple Forms on This Page — Do Not Cut, Fold, or Staple Forms on This Page

---

a Control number	22222	Void ☐	For Official Use Only ▶ OMB No. 1545-0008		

b Employer identification number		1 Wages, tips, other compensation $	2 Federal income tax withheld $

c Employer's name, address, and ZIP code	3 Social security wages $	4 Social security tax withheld $
	5 Medicare wages and tips $	6 Medicare tax withheld $
	7 Social security tips $	8 Allocated tips $

d Employee's social security number	9 Advance EIC payment $	10 Dependent care benefits $

e Employee's first name and initial	Last name	11 Nonqualified plans $	12a See instructions for box 12 $
		13 Statutory employee ☐ Retirement plan ☐ Third-party sick pay ☐	12b $
		14 Other	12c $
			12d $

f Employee's address and ZIP code

15 State	Employer's state ID number	16 State wages, tips, etc. $	17 State income tax $	18 Local wages, tips, etc. $	19 Local income tax $	20 Locality name
		$	$	$	$	

Form **W-2** **Wage and Tax Statement** (99)   **20 --**   Department of the Treasury—Internal Revenue Service

Copy A For Social Security Administration—Send this entire page with Form W-3 to the Social Security Administration; photocopies are **not** acceptable.

(Rev. February 2002)

Cat. No. 10134D

For Privacy Act and Paperwork Reduction Act Notice, see separate instructions.

Do Not Cut, Fold, or Staple Forms on This Page — Do Not Cut, Fold, or Staple Forms on This Page

TRANSACTION NO. 39

DO NOT STAPLE OR FOLD

a Control number	33333	For Official Use Only ▶ OMB No. 1545-0008		

b Kind of Payer ▶	941 ☐ Military ☐ 943 ☐ CT-1 ☐ Hshld. emp. ☐ Medicare govt. emp. ☐ Third-party sick pay ☐	1 Wages, tips, other compensation $	2 Federal income tax withheld $

	3 Social security wages $	4 Social security tax withheld $

c Total number of Forms W-2	d Establishment number	5 Medicare wages and tips $	6 Medicare tax withheld $

e Employer identification number	7 Social security tips $	8 Allocated tips $

f Employer's name	9 Advance EIC payments $	10 Dependent care benefits $

	11 Nonqualified plans $	12 Deferred compensation $

13 For third-party sick pay use only

14 Income tax withheld by payer of third-party sick pay
$

g Employer's address and ZIP code

h Other EIN used this year

15 State Employer's state ID number	16 State wages, tips, etc. $	17 State income tax $

	18 Local wages, tips, etc. $	19 Local income tax $

Contact person	Telephone number ( )	For Official Use Only

E-mail address	Fax number ( )	

Under penalties of perjury, I declare that I have examined this return and accompanying documents, and, to the best of my knowledge and belief, they are true, correct, and complete.

Signature ▶ _____ Title ▶ _____ Date ▶ _____

Form **W-3** Transmittal of Wage and Tax Statements   **20--**   Department of the Treasury
 Internal Revenue Service

TRANSACTION NO. 40

REV-1667R AS (2-98) PA DEPARTMENT OF REVENUE	YEAR 20--	EMPLOYER ACCOUNT # 31-0450660	ENTITY ID# (EIN) 1009-5555	**W-2 TRANSMITTAL** DUE DATE JANUARY 31

PART 1	W-2 RECONCILIATION	
1a	Number of W-2 forms attached	
1b	Number of W-2(s) reported on magnetic tape(s)	
1c	Number of 1099 forms with PA withholding tax	
1d	Add 1a, 1b & 1c Enter total here	
2	Total compensation subject to PA withholding tax reported on W-2	$
3	PA INCOME TAX WITHHELD REPORTED ON W-2	$

PART II	FOR TAPE REPORTING	
NUMBER OF TAPES		DENSITY
TRACKS		PARITY

BUSINESS NAME AND ADDRESS

GLO-BRITE PAINT COMPANY

LEGAL NAME

TRADE NAME

2215 SALVADORE STREET

STREET ADDRESS

PHILADELPHIA, PA 19175-0682

CITY STATE ZIP

EMPLOYER ANNUAL RECONCILIATION OF INCOME TAX WITHHELD
 FOR USE ONLY WHEN EMPLOYERS
 DO NO HAVE PREPRINTED COUPONS.

DO NOT SEND PAYMENT WITH THIS FORM.

Attach adding machine tape(s) or some acceptable listing of tax withheld as reported on accompanying paper W-2 form(s) to substantiate reported Pennsylvania Withholding Tax. This tape or listing applies only to paper W-2(s) **not** magnetic media reporting.

DATE	TELEPHONE NUMBER ( )	TITLE	SIGNATURE

00022

TRANSACTION NO. 41

9595 ☐ VOID ☐ CORRECTED

PAYER'S name, street address, city, state, ZIP code, and telephone no.	1 Rents $	OMB No. 1545-0115	Miscellaneous Income
	2 Royalties $	20-- Form **1099-MISC**	

	3 Other income $	4 Federal income tax withheld $	**Copy A**
PAYER'S Federal identification number	RECIPIENT'S identification number	5 Fishing boat proceeds $	6 Medical and health care payments $	**For Internal Revenue Service Center** File with Form 1096.

RECIPIENT'S name	7 Nonemployee compensation $	8 Substitute payments in lieu of dividends or interest $	For Privacy Act and Paperwork Reduction Act Notice, see the **2002 General Instructions for Forms 1099, 1098, 5498, and W-2G.**
Street address (including apt. no.)	9 Payer made direct sales of $5,000 or more of consumer products to a buyer (recipient) for resale ▶ ☐	10 Crop insurance proceeds $	
City, state, and ZIP code	11	12	
Account number (optional)	2nd TIN not. ☐	13 Excess golden parachute payments $	14 Gross proceeds paid to an attorney $	
15	16 State tax withheld $ $	17 State/Payer's state no.	18 State income $ $

Form **1099-MISC** Cat. No. 14425J Department of the Treasury - Internal Revenue Service

TRANSACTION NO. 42

Do Not Staple 6969

Form **1096** Department of the Treasury Internal Revenue Service	**Annual Summary and Transmittal of U.S. Information Returns**	OMB No. 1545-0108 20--

FILER'S name

Street address (including room or suite number)

City, state, and ZIP code

Name of person to contact	Telephone number ( )	**For Official Use Only**
Fax number ( )	E-mail address	

1 Employer identification number	2 Social security number	3 Total number of forms	4 Federal income tax withheld $	5 Total amount reported with this Form 1096 $

Enter an "X" in only one box below to indicate the type of form being filed.   If this is your **final return**, enter an "X" here . . . ▶ ☐

W-2G 32	1098 81	1098-E 84	1098-T 83	1099-A 80	1099-B 79	1099-C 85	1099-DIV 91	1099-G 86	1099-INT 92	1099-LTC 93	1099-MISC 95	1099-MSA 94	1099-OID 96
☐	☐	☐	☐	☐	☐	☐	☐	☐	☐	☐	☐	☐	☐

1099-PATR 97	1099-Q 31	1099-R 98	1099-S 75	5498 28	5498-MSA 27		
☐	☐	☐	☐	☐	☐		

Please return this entire page to the Internal Revenue Service. Photocopies are not acceptable.

Under penalties of perjury, I declare that I have examined this return and accompanying documents, and, to the best of my knowledge and belief, they are true, correct, and complete.

Signature ▶   Title ▶   Date ▶

Appendix A
Computerized Payroll Accounting

UPON COMPLETION OF THIS CHAPTER, YOU WILL BE BE ABLE TO:

1. Identify the components and procedures of a computerized payroll system.

2. Perform system startup procedures.

3. Add, change, and delete employees from the payroll.

4. Enter and correct payroll transactions.

5. Generate payroll and employer's payroll taxes journal entries.

6. Enter, correct, and find journal entries.

7. Display payroll reports.

8. Access the on-screen calculator and use Help information.

INTRODUCTION

Payroll is an application that lends itself well to the computer because of its repetitive procedures and calculations. Computerized payroll systems perform the same basic functions as those performed manually by payroll clerks. The important differences are the computer's speed, accuracy, reliability, and ability to easily generate reports.

In a computerized payroll system, the computer stores data such as an employee's name, address, social security number, marital status, number of withholding allowances, pay rate, and voluntary deductions. At the end of each pay period, the operator enters all payroll transactions data, such as regular and overtime hours for each employee, deductions, etc., into the computer. The computer calculates all withholding taxes and other deductions and accumulates and updates the earnings and withholdings.

After entering payroll transaction data for the current pay period, a payroll report may be displayed to verify the earnings and withholdings for the month, quarter, and year. Next, the current payroll and employer's payroll salary expense, payroll taxes expense, and withholding liabilities journal entries are automatically generated and posted into the general ledger. A general journal report and general ledger reports are displayed. At the end of the quarter, and at the end of the year, the taxable earnings report is displayed, from which the appropriate reports (e.g., quarterly reports and W-2 statements) may be prepared.

The material that follows provides detailed operational information for running the enclosed software in the Windows 95, Windows 98, Windows ME, Windows NT, Windows 2000, and Windows XP environments. If you are familiar with any of these user interfaces, you may go directly to the Payroll Project beginning on page A-26 immediately after software installation.

SOFTWARE PROGRAM OVERVIEW

To complete the payroll project in this text-workbook, you will be using the Payroll software that is included in the *Integrated Accounting Version 3.0* software. This software makes use of a standard user interface that utilizes pull-down menus, movable overlapping windows, mouse support, list windows, and help windows. This standard interface resembles the interface used in many other software applications. Most of the techniques you will learn can be applied to many other software packages. The following material will cover only those features of the software that you will need to complete the payroll project beginning on page A-26.

User Data Files

The Integrated Accounting for Payroll software permits you to store data on a separate data disk, hard disk, or network file server. This feature enables you to save your work for completion at a later time. If you are using a floppy disk to save your data, make sure that it is properly formatted before use. For information on formatting a disk, refer to your computer system's operations manual or Help System.

Installation and Memory Requirements

The Integrated Accounting for Payroll software contained in this package comes complete on a standard CD (compact disk). To use the software, you need a processor running in the Windows 95, Windows 98, Windows ME, Windows NT, Windows 2000, or Windows XP environment. In addition, a hard disk drive with at least 15 megabytes of available disk space and a CD drive are required for installation. A printer is optional but highly recommended.

The installation CD included in the software package contains compressed Integrated Accounting program files and the opening balance payroll accounting file required to complete the payroll project in this text-workbook. During the installation process, all of the compressed files are expanded into an executable format onto your computer's hard disk. The installation is a common procedure. Detailed step-by-step instructions are provided on the installation CD's label. Your instructor or computer center technician has probably already completed this one-time installation procedure.

Important Note: It is possible, in rare cases, where the colors chosen by the user within the computer's color control panel conflict with the colors used by the software in such a way that images and/or text may appear invisible. If you experience any problems with colors, go to the control panel that controls the colors and change colors. Choose the default colors provided by your user interface system software to prevent this conflict.

START-UP PROCEDURES

To begin working with the Integrated Accounting for Payroll software (after the installation has been completed): (1) click the Windows Start button, (2) click Programs, (3) position the pointer on *Integrated Accounting for Payroll,* and (4) click on Integrated Accounting for Payroll when the sub-menu appears. To start the software in a Windows Workstation, double-click *Integrated Accounting for Payroll's* icon in the Office program group.

Review Figure A–1 to acquaint yourself with the terminology and location of the items on the toolbar. Notice the information message "End accounting system." This is called a Tooltip. Tooltips are brief informational messages that automatically appear when the pointer is positioned on a toolbar button. As shown in Figure A–1, the "End accounting system" message appears when the pointer is positioned on the Exit toolbar button.

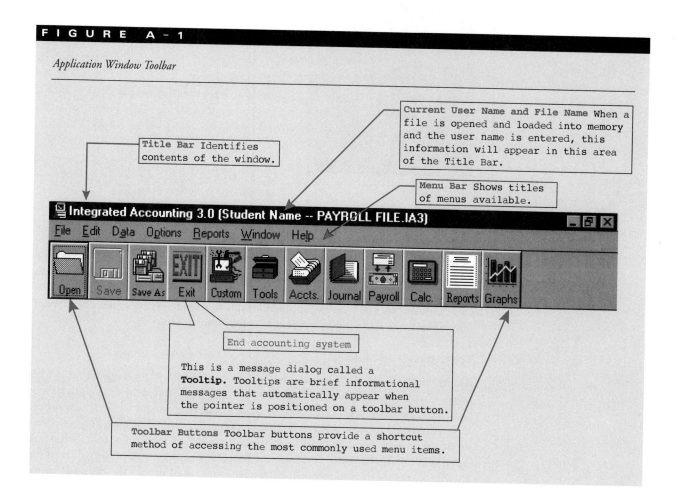

FIGURE A-1

Application Window Toolbar

Title Bar Identifies contents of the window.

Current User Name and File Name When a file is opened and loaded into memory and the user name is entered, this information will appear in this area of the Title Bar.

Menu Bar Shows titles of menus available.

Integrated Accounting 3.0 (Student Name -- PAYROLL FILE.IA3)

File   Edit   Data   Options   Reports   Window   Help

Open   Save   Save As   Exit   Custom   Tools   Accts.   Journal   Payroll   Calc.   Reports   Graphs

End accounting system

This is a message dialog called a **Tooltip.** Tooltips are brief informational messages that automatically appear when the pointer is positioned on a toolbar button.

Toolbar Buttons Toolbar buttons provide a shortcut method of accessing the most commonly used menu items.

BASIC OPERATING PROCEDURES

The following topics cover use of the menu bar, menu item selection, window controls, tabs, grid cells, text boxes, selecting text, and other standard features that have been provided to make the operation of the software easy to learn and efficient to use.

The Menu Bar

One of the ways you communicate with the computer is to use the menu bar. As shown in Figure A–2, the menu bar contains several menu titles (e.g., File, Edit, Data, Options, and so on). Each title contains menu items that instruct the computer to perform its processing tasks. This type of menu is called a Drop-Down Menu, because once selected via a mouse or keyboard (using the Alt key), a list of menu items displays immediately below the menu title selected. Figure A–2 illustrates the parts of the File drop-down menu. You may use the mouse or keyboard to select drop-down menus and choose menu items. If an item appears "dimmed," it is not available for use.

FIGURE A-2

File Drop-Down Menu

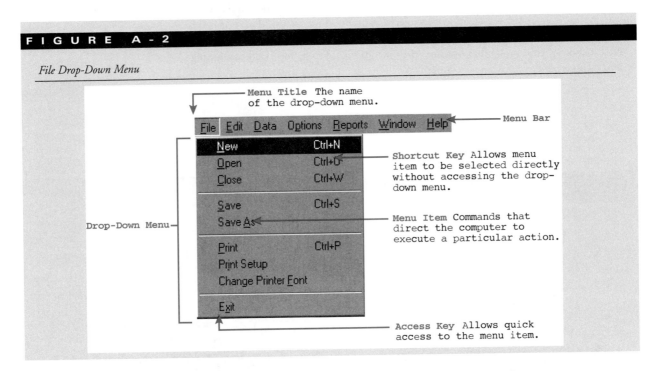

Selecting and Choosing Menu Titles and Menu Items

In this text-workbook, the terms *select* and *choose* have different meanings. When menu titles on the menu bar or menu items are selected, they are highlighted. When a highlighted (or selected) menu title or item is *chosen,* the software will take the appropriate action. Dimmed items are not available for selection (you may need to select another item or perform a processing task before a dimmed item is activated).

Window Controls

You interact with the computer through windows. A *window* is a rectangular area of the screen in which the software is communicating with the user. Often the display screen contains only one window. At times, two or more overlapping windows may appear on the screen. However, only one window is active at a time. Some windows contain tabs consisting of text boxes and grid cells used to enter data from the keyboard, some contain lists and reports, and others may display messages and operational information. Regardless of the activity, the part of the window that will receive input is said to have the *focus.* For example, a data field that has the focus is identified by the insertion point (also referred to as the pipe character), which appears as a vertical bar (I). A decision or choice of several options that has the focus is identified by a dotted rectangular box.

Many of the windows that appear may be moved, resized, made inactive/active, etc. For example, to move a window, point to the window's title bar (located at the top of the window) and drag. The pointer and an outline of the window will move as you drag. For specific information regarding moving a window, changing its size, making it inactive/active, etc., refer to your computer's user interface operational manual.

It is important to understand how the operational controls contained in the windows enable you to enter and edit data, generate reports, select items from lists, and navigate the grids and controls. Refer to this section of the text as you encounter these controls later in this text-workbook. The following paragraphs identify the controls used by this software and describe how to use these controls.

Tabs. The software has been designed to use the visual image of folders to clarify and simplify operation. Several menu items (or toolbar selections) contain windows that include multiple folders with identifying tabs. These tabs provide for additional entry of data, options, and processing. For example, the Account Maintenance folder that appears when the *Maintain Accounts* menu item is chosen from the Data menu (or the *Accts.* Toolbar button is clicked) is shown in Figure A–3. Notice that the window contains two different tabs: Accounts and Employees. The second tab (Employees) appears as the active tab and is used to maintain current information for each employee.

FIGURE A-3

Tabs in the Account Maintenance Window

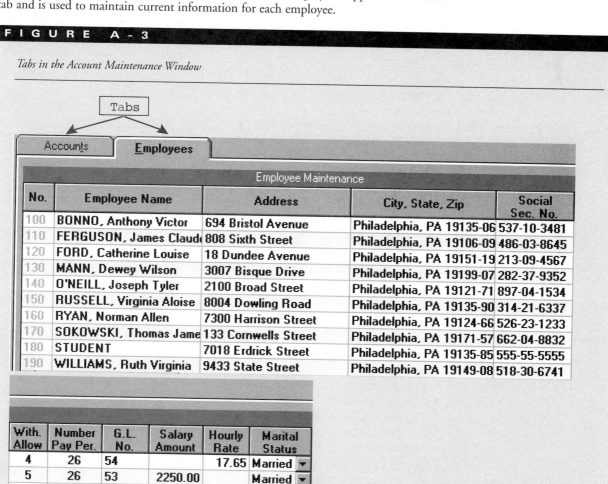

No.	Employee Name	Address	City, State, Zip	Social Sec. No.
100	BONNO, Anthony Victor	694 Bristol Avenue	Philadelphia, PA 19135-06	537-10-3481
110	FERGUSON, James Claud	808 Sixth Street	Philadelphia, PA 19106-09	486-03-8645
120	FORD, Catherine Louise	18 Dundee Avenue	Philadelphia, PA 19151-19	213-09-4567
130	MANN, Dewey Wilson	3007 Bisque Drive	Philadelphia, PA 19199-07	282-37-9352
140	O'NEILL, Joseph Tyler	2100 Broad Street	Philadelphia, PA 19121-71	897-04-1534
150	RUSSELL, Virginia Aloise	8004 Dowling Road	Philadelphia, PA 19135-90	314-21-6337
160	RYAN, Norman Allen	7300 Harrison Street	Philadelphia, PA 19124-66	526-23-1233
170	SOKOWSKI, Thomas Jame	133 Cornwells Street	Philadelphia, PA 19171-57	662-04-8832
180	STUDENT	7018 Erdrick Street	Philadelphia, PA 19135-85	555-55-5555
190	WILLIAMS, Ruth Virginia	9433 State Street	Philadelphia, PA 19149-08	518-30-6741

With. Allow	Number Pay Per.	G.L. No.	Salary Amount	Hourly Rate	Marital Status
4	26	54		17.65	Married
5	26	53	2250.00		Married
2	26	52	900.00		Single
4	26	53	1350.00		Married
3	26	51	2307.69		Married
1	26	52	690.00		Single
4	26	54		18.00	Married
2	26	54	2050.00		Married
1	26	52	540.00		Single
0	26	52	1223.08		Single

Grid Cells. Most of the data you will enter into the Integrated Accounting for Payroll software will be entered into windows that contain grid cells. *Grid cells* (arrangement of rows and columns) are used to enter, edit, or delete data and text. When a grid cell receives the focus, any existing data or text within it is selected (highlighted) and the insertion point appears to the right of the last character within the cell. Figure A–4 shows an example of how data that has been entered into grid cells appears. Notice now the 80.00 hours employee RYAN, Norman Allen, worked (under the Reg. Hours column) has been selected. If the insertion point is moved within the cell, the text is deselected and the contents may be edited. If the user types data with text selected, the selected text within the cell is replaced with the newly entered data.

FIGURE A-4

Example of grid cells

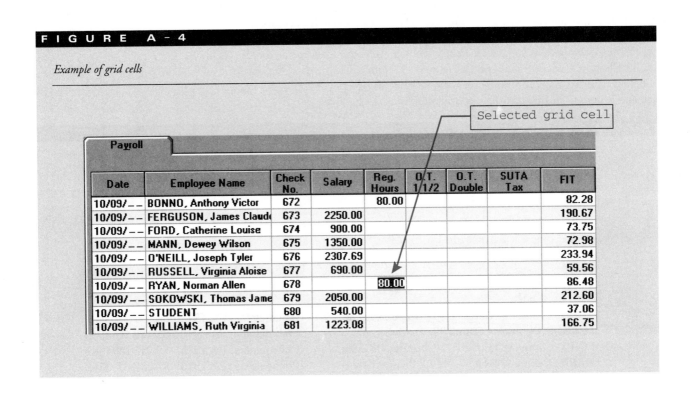

Selected grid cell

Payroll

Date	Employee Name	Check No.	Salary	Reg. Hours	O.T. 1/1/2	O.T. Double	SUTA Tax	FIT
10/09/ _ _	BONNO, Anthony Victor	672		80.00				82.28
10/09/ _ _	FERGUSON, James Claude	673	2250.00					190.67
10/09/ _ _	FORD, Catherine Louise	674	900.00					73.75
10/09/ _ _	MANN, Dewey Wilson	675	1350.00					72.98
10/09/ _ _	O'NEILL, Joseph Tyler	676	2307.69					233.94
10/09/ _ _	RUSSELL, Virginia Aloise	677	690.00					59.56
10/09/ _ _	RYAN, Norman Allen	678		80.00				86.48
10/09/ _ _	SOKOWSKI, Thomas James	679	2050.00					212.60
10/09/ _ _	STUDENT	680	540.00					37.06
10/09/ _ _	WILLIAMS, Ruth Virginia	681	1223.08					166.75

Calendar. A small calendar icon (as shown in Figure A–5) appears on all report screens. A calendar's year, month, and date may be selected by pointing and clicking the mouse. The calendar may be used to set starting and ending dates to control data printed in reports or to specify the date that is to appear on a report. The calendar shown in Figure A–5 appears when the calendar icon is clicked.

 Each time the Right arrow icon of the year box on the calendar is clicked, the year will increase by one. Each time the Left arrow is clicked, the year will decrease by one. Likewise, clicking on the Right arrow of the month box will advance to the next month, and clicking on the Left arrow will move back to the previous month. Simply clicking on the desired day of the month will select that day of the month and year shown. As the date is being selected, it will appear in the corresponding Date text box in the mm/dd/yy format as shown in Figure A–5.

F I G U R E   A - 5

Calendar Control

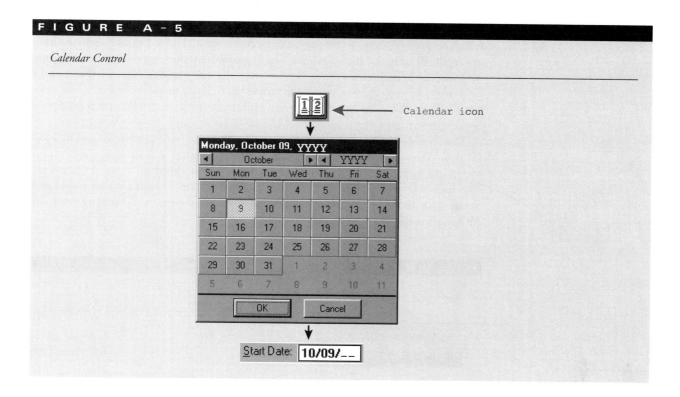

List Box. Figure A–6 shows a chart of accounts list box. A highlight bar (or underline) identifies the currently selected item. Both the mouse and keyboard can be used to scroll through the list and choose items from the list. To select an item from the list, simply click on the desired item, then click OK (or double-click on the desired item).

F I G U R E   A - 6

List Box

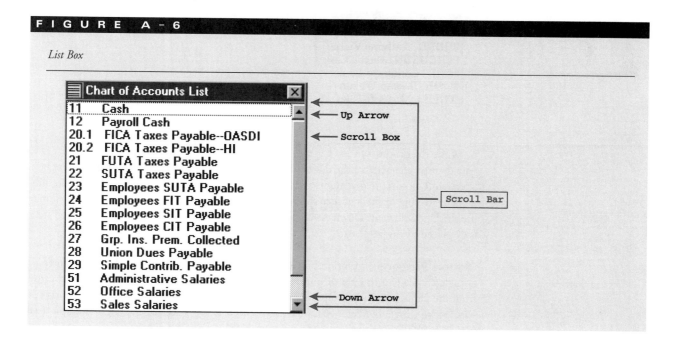

Drop-Down List.   The drop-down list consists of a rectangular box (called a text box) with a drop-down arrow button immediately to the right. The text must be selected from among the items in the drop-down list. The drop-down list does not allow the user to enter new data that is not in the existing list. However, the user may enter an item that *is* in the drop-down list into the text box. Upon typing the first one or more characters, the computer will search the list and place the first occurrence of the matching item from the list in the text box.

The drop-down list, shown in Figure A–7 before it has been opened, is used to select the desired employee to be paid during the current pay period. The same drop-down list is shown in Figure A–8 after it has been opened. If the drop-down list contains more items than will fit, a scroll bar will be included. To toggle a drop-down list between open and closed, click on the drop-down arrow or press Alt+Down Arrow (while holding down the Alt key, press the Down Arrow key).

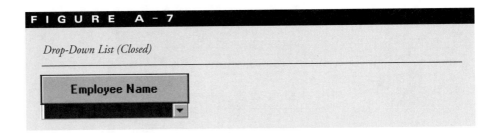

FIGURE A - 7

Drop-Down List (Closed)

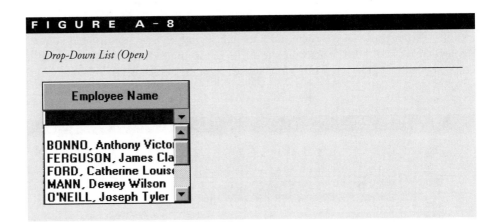

FIGURE A - 8

Drop-Down List (Open)

While the drop-down list has the focus, an easy way to select an item from the list is to type the first character of the desired item. The first occurrence will appear in the text box. Succeeding occurrences of items starting with the same character can be accessed by subsequent striking of the key corresponding to the first character. As an alternative, you may use the Up Arrow and Down Arrow keys to scroll through the items until the desired item is displayed in the text box.

Option Buttons.   Option buttons (sometimes referred to as radio buttons) represent a single choice within a set of mutually exclusive choices. You can select only one button from the choices provided. Option buttons are represented by circles. When an option is selected, the circle is filled ($\odot$). When an option is not selected, the circle is empty (see Figure A–9).

FIGURE A - 9

Option Buttons

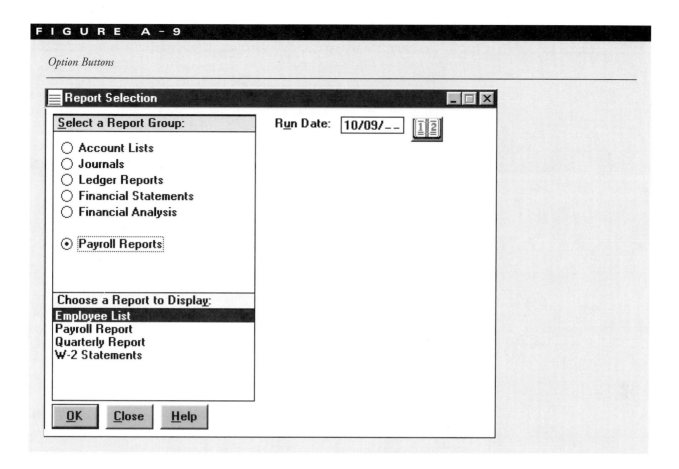

To select an option, simply click on the desired option button. When using the keyboard, strike the Tab key to navigate to the appropriate group of option buttons, then use the directional arrow keys to select the option desired.

Check Boxes. Check boxes are used to control the selection of individual choices. When a task requiring multiple choices is selected, a group section will appear containing check boxes (☐) to the left of each choice. The check boxes are turned on or off in any combination. When a check box is selected, it contains a check mark (☑) inside it. Figure A–10 shows the check boxes that allow the user to select the voluntary deduction(s) to be withheld during the current pay period.

FIGURE A - 10

Check Boxes

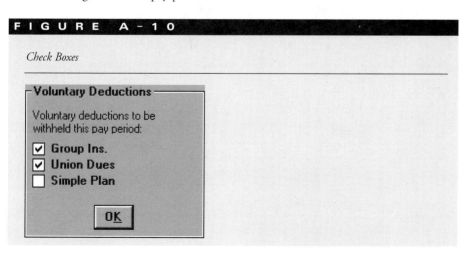

To select a check box, simply click on the box or the label to toggle the check box on or off. When using the keyboard, use the directional keys to select the desired check box, then press the Space Bar to toggle it on or off.

Command Buttons. A command button is a rectangular shaped figure containing a label that specifies an immediate action or response that will be taken by the computer when it is chosen. Figure A–11 illustrates three command buttons.

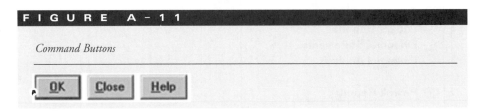

FIGURE A - 1 1

Command Buttons

To choose a command, simply click on the desired command button. When using the keyboard, use the Tab key to navigate to the desired command button, then (while the command button has the focus) press the Enter key. When a command button has a dotted line and/or shadow around the button (see the OK button in Figure A–10) it is said to be the default button. The default command button can be chosen from anywhere in the window by pressing the Enter key.

Dialog Boxes

Dialog boxes provide information and error messages. A decision from the user may be required. When a dialog box appears, one of the command buttons must be chosen before other menu commands can be selected. Figure A–12 shows the dialog box that will appear if the payroll system is ended before data has been saved.

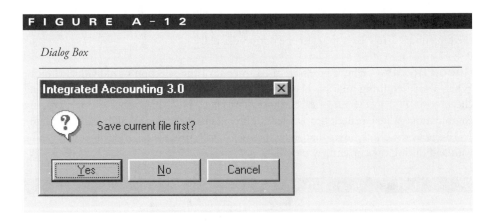

FIGURE A - 1 2

Dialog Box

Navigation

Grid cells, option buttons, check boxes, and command buttons should be filled in or selected in the normal tab sequence. The *tab sequence* is the logical sequence in which the computer is expecting each grid cell, button, and/or command to be accessed. The sequence is usually left to right and top to bottom.

As you have already learned, the focus identifies the location within a window, tab, list, or grid cell in which the computer will receive the next input. For example, as the Tab key is pressed, the focus moves to the next item in the tab sequence. Pressing Shift+Tab moves the focus to the previous item in the tab sequence. When a grid cell has the focus, an insertion point character (|) will appear to mark the current position where data will be entered or edited. When data is typed, the insertion point moves one character to the right for each character typed, and new characters appear to the left of the insertion point. Press the Enter key to choose the action or response of the default command button or command button that currently has the focus. Use the Esc key to choose Cancel or Close within the active window, tab, list, or dialog box.

FILE MENU

When the File menu is selected from the menu bar, the drop-down menu shown in Figure A–2 on page A-4 appears. We will examine several of the menu items you will need to complete the payroll project in this appendix.

Open.   Open is used to load a data file stored on disk into the computer's memory for processing. Figure A–13 shows the Open dialog box with the payroll opening balance file selected (the highlighted file name identifies the currently selected file). Both the mouse and keyboard can be used to choose files from the list. To choose a file, simply click on the desired file name, then click on the Open button (or double-click on the desired item). To choose a file using the keyboard, strike the Tab key until a file in the file list has the focus, strike the Up and Down Arrow keys to highlight the desired file, then strike the Enter key.

FIGURE A – 13

Open Dialog Box

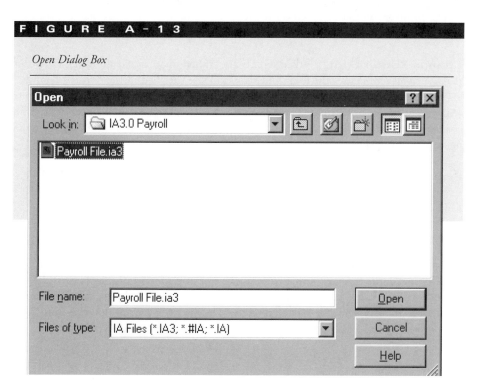

Close.   Use the Close menu item in the File menu to close the current file displayed in the active window (removes the data from the computer's memory). When close is chosen, the active window and all other windows containing data from the same file are closed. Close does *not* remove any data from disk.

Save.   Use the Save menu item in the File menu to store your data to disk so that you can continue a problem in a later session. The data will be saved to disk with the current path (disk drive and folder) with the file name displayed in the Title Bar located at the top of the Integrated Accounting for Payroll application window. If you wish to save your data with a path (disk drive and/or folder) or file name different from the current path and file name, use Save As (described below).

Save As.   This menu item is the same as Save except that the data can be saved with a path and/or file name different from the current path and file name. Save As is useful for making a backup copy of a data file. For example, you may want to make a backup of your data file before entering employee maintenance and payroll transactions for a new pay period. To make a backup copy, open the data file you wish to back up and use Save As to save it under a different name.

Print.   The purpose of Print is to create a printed version of any report or graphic currently displayed in a report or graphic window. The entire contents of the data in these windows will be printed when Print is chosen.

Print Setup.   When the Print button is clicked while a report is displayed, or the Print Setup menu item is chosen from the File menu, a Print Setup dialog box will appear. The Print Setup dialog box is used to provide choices about the printer(s) connected to your computer, the paper size, printing enhancements, etc. You will not need to use Print Setup unless you are having trouble printing. Check with your instructor for the proper information before making changes to your print setup. *Integrated Accounting for Payroll* uses the current printer information specified in your computer's user interface when processing a print command.

Change Printer Font.   When reports are printed to an attached printer, *Integrated Accounting for Payroll* uses the font, font style, and size specified in the printer's Font dialog box. You may want to change the printer font, style, and/or size to make reports more attractive or to make the size smaller if fields are overflowing or wrapping incorrectly. Also, changing the font to one that is native to the printer you are using (e.g., Courier) will often increase the print speed.

Exit.   This menu item is used to quit *Integrated Accounting for Payroll*. When Exit is chosen, the computer checks to see if the current data in its memory has been saved. If not, a dialog box will appear asking if you wish to save your data to disk.

OPTIONS MENU

The options menu, shown in Figure A–14, contains commands that enable the user to generate journal entries, purge journal entries, purge payroll transactions, and access the on-screen calculator. The Generate Closing Journal Entries and Purge Journal Entries will not be needed to complete the payroll Project. The Current Payroll Journal Entry and Employer's Payroll Taxes menu items are discussed later in this appendix.

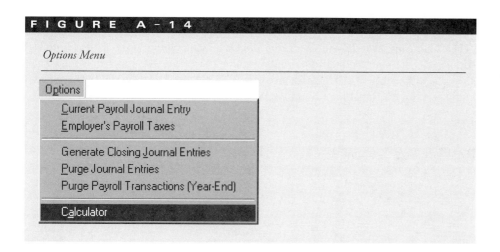

FIGURE A-14

Options Menu

| Options |
| Current Payroll Journal Entry |
| Employer's Payroll Taxes |
| |
| Generate Closing Journal Entries |
| Purge Journal Entries |
| Purge Payroll Transactions (Year-End) |
| Calculator |

Purge Payroll Transactions (Year-End).   This menu item will purge all pay-roll transaction data from the payroll file at the end of the fiscal year. The purging of pay-roll transactions should not be selected until all year-end reports are complete, or until a backup of the final payroll for the fiscal year has been made.

On-Screen Calculator.   The on-screen calculator is operated like a hand-held cal-culator. Your computer's standard calculator can perform all the calculations required in this text-workbook. The results can be pasted into the grid cell that has the focus. Once the Calculator appears (as shown in Figure A–15), a Help menu is available from the calcula-tor providing detailed explanation of the calculator operation.

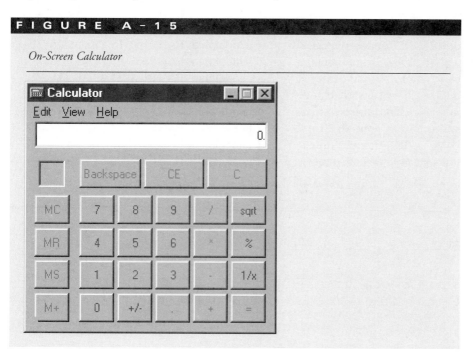

FIGURE A-15

On-Screen Calculator

EMPLOYEE MAINTENANCE

When Maintain Accounts is chosen from the Data menu or the Accts. toolbar button is clicked, the Account Maintenance window will appear. Click the Employees tab (if not already active) and enter the maintenance data. Figure A–16 shows the employees tab containing employee data with a description of each data field.

FIGURE A-16

Employee Maintenance

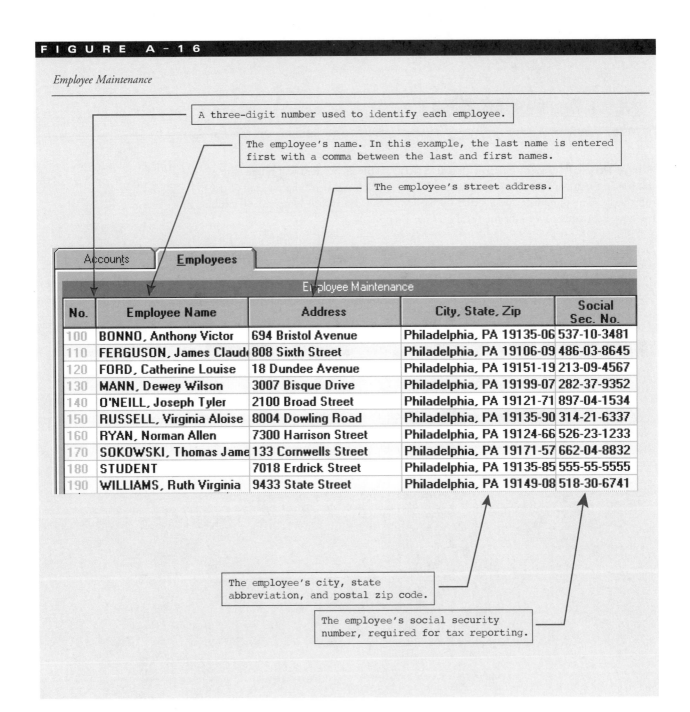

A three-digit number used to identify each employee.

The employee's name. In this example, the last name is entered first with a comma between the last and first names.

The employee's street address.

No.	Employee Name	Address	City, State, Zip	Social Sec. No.
100	BONNO, Anthony Victor	694 Bristol Avenue	Philadelphia, PA 19135-06	537-10-3481
110	FERGUSON, James Claude	808 Sixth Street	Philadelphia, PA 19106-09	486-03-8645
120	FORD, Catherine Louise	18 Dundee Avenue	Philadelphia, PA 19151-19	213-09-4567
130	MANN, Dewey Wilson	3007 Bisque Drive	Philadelphia, PA 19199-07	282-37-9352
140	O'NEILL, Joseph Tyler	2100 Broad Street	Philadelphia, PA 19121-71	897-04-1534
150	RUSSELL, Virginia Aloise	8004 Dowling Road	Philadelphia, PA 19135-90	314-21-6337
160	RYAN, Norman Allen	7300 Harrison Street	Philadelphia, PA 19124-66	526-23-1233
170	SOKOWSKI, Thomas James	133 Cornwells Street	Philadelphia, PA 19171-57	662-04-8832
180	STUDENT	7018 Erdrick Street	Philadelphia, PA 19135-85	555-55-5555
190	WILLIAMS, Ruth Virginia	9433 State Street	Philadelphia, PA 19149-08	518-30-6741

The employee's city, state abbreviation, and postal zip code.

The employee's social security number, required for tax reporting.

New employees may be added by keying the data fields in the grid cell boxes and choosing the employee's marital status. When the focus moves to the marital status, choose Single or Married from the drop-down list or type the first letter of the desired marital status (S or M). The new employee will be inserted into the existing employee list in employee number sequence. Existing employee data may be changed by selecting the employee you wish to change, keying the correct data (or selecting a different marital status), then

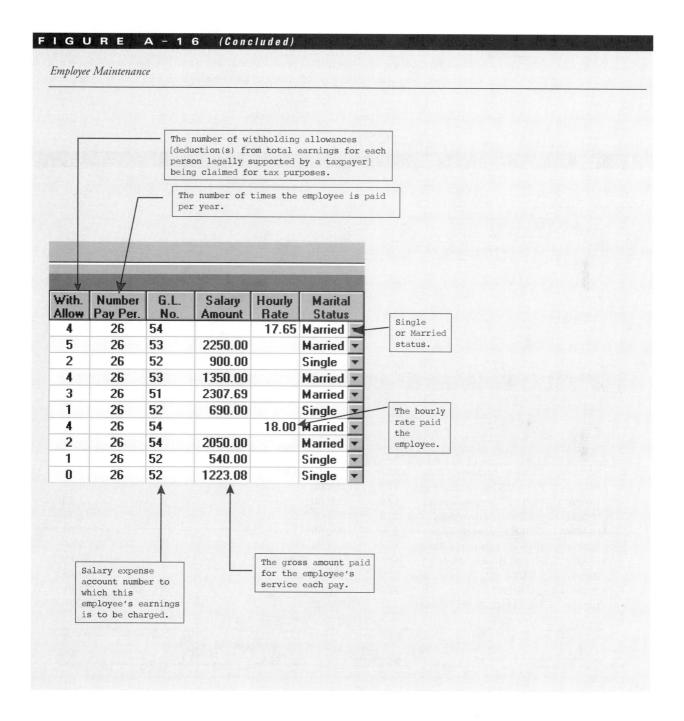

FIGURE A-16 *(Concluded)*

Employee Maintenance

The number of withholding allowances [deduction(s) from total earnings for each person legally supported by a taxpayer] being claimed for tax purposes.

The number of times the employee is paid per year.

With. Allow	Number Pay Per.	G.L. No.	Salary Amount	Hourly Rate	Marital Status
4	26	54		17.65	Married
5	26	53	2250.00		Married
2	26	52	900.00		Single
4	26	53	1350.00		Married
3	26	51	2307.69		Married
1	26	52	690.00		Single
4	26	54		18.00	Married
2	26	54	2050.00		Married
1	26	52	540.00		Single
0	26	52	1223.08		Single

Single or Married status.

The hourly rate paid the employee.

Salary expense account number to which this employee's earnings is to be charged.

The gross amount paid for the employee's service each pay.

clicking the Change Employee button (the Add Employee button changes to Change Employee). An existing employee may be deleted by simply selecting the employee that you wish to delete and then clicking on the Delete button. *Note:* You will not be allowed to delete an employee with cumulative earnings for the current year until after the end of the calendar year.

PAYROLL TRANSACTIONS

Employee payroll transaction data are entered into the Payroll tab. The purpose of entering the payroll transactions is to identify the employees to be paid for the current pay period and to enter the employee's pay period transaction data. For each employee's payroll transaction, the payroll date, pay information, and employee deductions (if different from

---

FIGURE A - 17

Payroll Tab

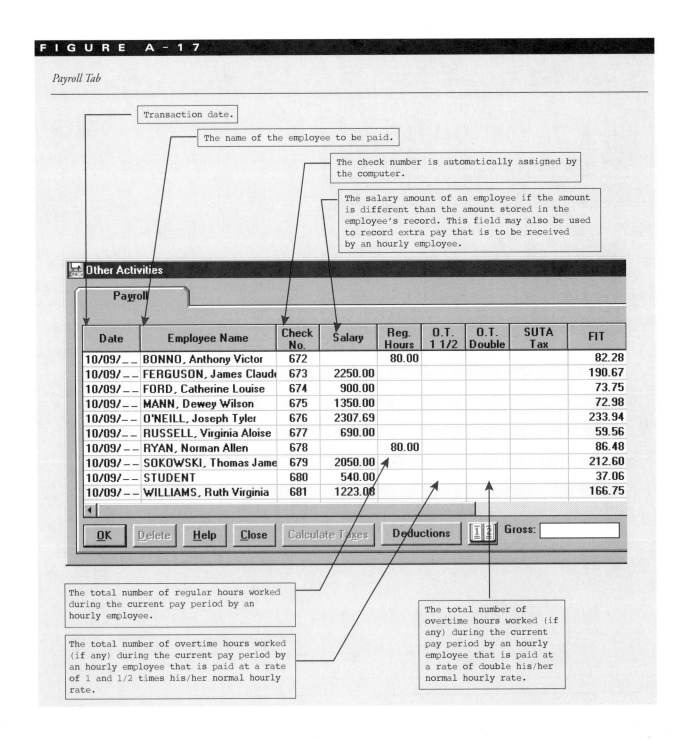

the previous pay period) are entered. The employee taxes can be either entered or automatically calculated by the computer. The payroll taxes for payroll project in this textworkbook are to be calculated by the computer.

When the *Payroll* toolbar button is clicked, the Payroll tab will appear as shown in Figure A–17. Click on the Deductions button to display the Voluntary Deductions dialog box shown in Figure A–10 on page A-9. The purpose of this dialog box is to permit you to specify the voluntary deductions that are to be withheld from the current pay period. *Note:* If you forget to click on the Deductions button, the computer will automatically display the Voluntary Deductions dialog box during entry of the first employee's data for the current pay period.

FIGURE A - 1 7   *(Concluded)*

Payroll Tab

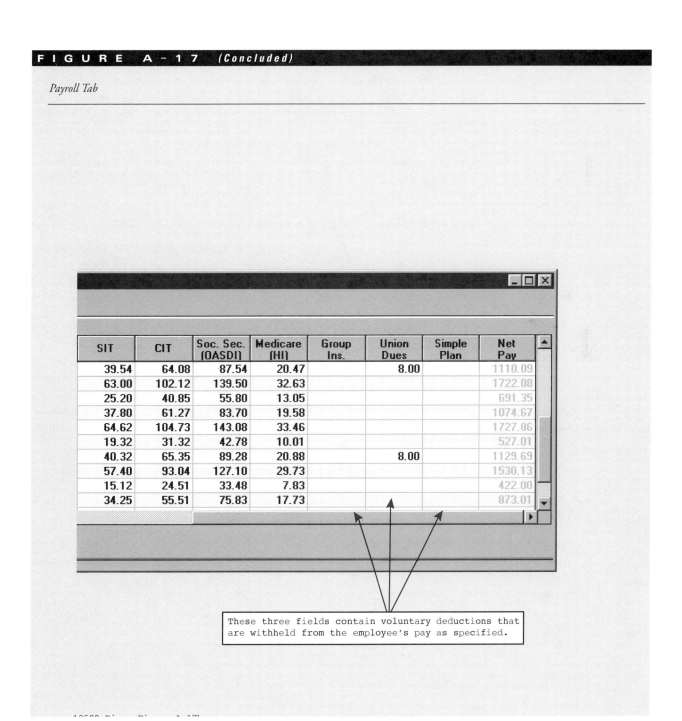

SIT	CIT	Soc. Sec. (OASDI)	Medicare (HI)	Group Ins.	Union Dues	Simple Plan	Net Pay
39.54	64.08	87.54	20.47		8.00		1110.09
63.00	102.12	139.50	32.63				1722.08
25.20	40.85	55.80	13.05				691.35
37.80	61.27	83.70	19.58				1074.67
64.62	104.73	143.08	33.46				1727.86
19.32	31.32	42.78	10.01				527.01
40.32	65.35	89.28	20.88		8.00		1129.69
57.40	93.04	127.10	29.73				1530.13
15.12	24.51	33.48	7.83				422.00
34.25	55.51	75.83	17.73				873.01

These three fields contain voluntary deductions that are withheld from the employee's pay as specified.

After the voluntary deductions are specified and the dialog box is dismissed, the payroll transaction data may be entered. Be careful to enter the correct date of the check because payroll processing is date-sensitive and will accumulate and display incorrectly if the dates are entered incorrectly. *Note:* The check number is automatically sequenced and generated by the computer.

If the employee is salaried, the salary amount will be displayed. You may enter a different salary amount that will override the amount shown. If a salaried employee is to be paid a one-time bonus, the amount entered would be the employee's normal salary plus the bonus amount. Also, this text box may be used to enter extra pay earned by hourly employees. The computer will add the amount entered to the hourly employee's earnings.

If the employee is paid hourly, enter the regular hours worked in the Reg. Hours grid cell. If the employee is paid hourly and is to be paid overtime at a rate of 1 and 1/2 times his/her normal hourly rate, enter the overtime hours worked in the O.T. 1 1/2 grid cell. If the employee is paid hourly and is to be paid overtime at a rate of double his/her normal hourly rate, enter the overtime hours worked in the O.T. Double grid cell.

Enter the employee voluntary deductions if different than those shown, or if the employee is new, and then click on the Calculate Taxes button to direct the computer to calculate the employee taxes. The taxes will be calculated and displayed in the employee taxes grid cells. (You could also enter the tax withholding amounts in the text boxes.) Finally, after all of the employee's data has been entered and taxes calculated, click on OK.

A previously entered payroll transaction may be corrected by simply selecting the payroll transaction you wish to correct, keying the correction, and clicking on OK. The computer will update the employee's record. Likewise, an existing payroll transaction may be deleted by selecting the payroll transaction you wish to delete, and clicking on the Delete button.

GENERATE AND POST PAYROLL JOURNAL ENTRIES

The *Integrated Accounting for Payroll* software can automatically generate the current payroll journal entry (salary expenses, employee federal tax payable, employee state tax payable, employee city tax payable, Social Security--OASDI , Medicare--HI, and voluntary deductions). It can also generate the employer's payroll taxes (Social Security--OASDI, Medicare--HI, federal unemployment, and state unemployment) journal entry. As used in this text, OASDI stands for Old-Age, Survivors, and Disability Insurance, and HI stands for Hospital Insurance.)

The journal entry to record the current payroll can be generated by choosing the Current Payroll Journal Entry menu item from the Options menu. The journal entry to record the employer's payroll taxes can be generated by choosing the Employer's Payroll Taxes menu item from the Options menu. The generated journal entry will appear in a dialog box for your verification. When it is posted to the general ledger, the general journal appears showing the posted entry.

If you must make a change or correction to a payroll transaction after the journal entry has been generated and posted, you must first delete the old journal entry and again generate the corrected journal entry.

Generating the Current Payroll Journal Entries

To generate the current payroll journal entries, choose the Current Payroll Journal Entry menu item from the Options menu. When the confirmation dialog box shown in Figure A–18 appears, click on Yes.

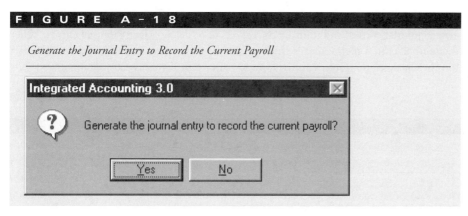

FIGURE A-18

Generate the Journal Entry to Record the Current Payroll

The generated journal entries for the current payroll will appear in a dialog window as illustrated in Figure A–29, on page A-29. Click on the Post button. When the current payroll journal entry is posted, the general journal window will appear showing that the entry has been automatically entered and posted. This entry is placed in the general journal in the event it must be changed or deleted at a later time.

Generating the Employer's Payroll Taxes Journal Entries

To generate the employer's payroll taxes journal entries, choose Employer's Payroll Taxes from the Options menu. When the confirmation dialog box shown in Figure A–19 appears, click on Yes.

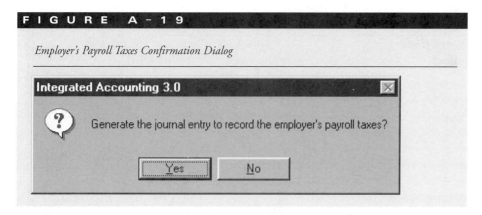

FIGURE A-19

Employer's Payroll Taxes Confirmation Dialog

The generated journal entries for the employer's payroll taxes will appear in the general journal as shown in Figure A–30, on page A-30. Click on the Post button. When the employer's payroll taxes journal entry is posted, it will reappear in the general journal window. The posted entry is placed in the general journal in the event it must be changed at a later time.

KEY GENERAL JOURNAL ENTRIES

You use the General Journal to key journal entries not automatically generated by the payroll system (e.g., deposits of FICA taxes and federal income taxes, deposits with the state of Pennsylvania for the amount of state income taxes withheld, etc.). The computer stores journal entries in date sequence. As you enter new journal entries (or as journal entries are automatically generated), the computer will maintain the date sequence by inserting the new transaction into the journal file based on the transaction date.

The computer stores each account title and balance used by the business. As transactions are entered and posted into a journal, the appropriate ledger account balance is updated. After all transactions have been automatically generated, entered, and posted the account information can be further processed (totals accumulated, etc.), displayed or printed in various report formats, and stored to disk for recall at a later time.

The General Journal tab within the Journal Entries window is used to enter and post general journal entries, and to make corrections to or delete existing journal entries. When the Journal Entries menu item is chosen from the Data menu or the Journal toolbar button is clicked on, the Journal Entries window shown in Figure A–20 will appear.

FIGURE A-20

General Journal

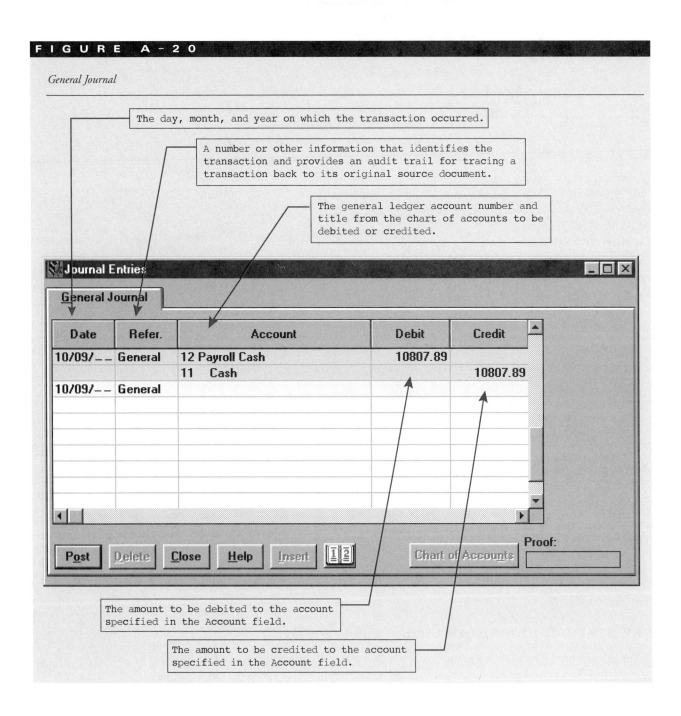

The day, month, and year on which the transaction occurred.

A number or other information that identifies the transaction and provides an audit trail for tracing a transaction back to its original source document.

The general ledger account number and title from the chart of accounts to be debited or credited.

Date	Refer.	Account	Debit	Credit
10/09/ _ _	General	12 Payroll Cash	10807.89	
		11 Cash		10807.89
10/09/ _ _	General			

Post   Delete   Close   Help   Insert   Chart of Accounts   Proof:

The amount to be debited to the account specified in the Account field.

The amount to be credited to the account specified in the Account field.

When the General Journal first appears, the Date column will contain the date of the last transaction that was entered (even if it was entered in an earlier session or automatically generated by the computer). The Reference column will contain the reference of the transaction that was entered. If there are no transactions on file, the Date column will contain a default date and the Reference column will be blank. Figure A–20 illustrates a completed General Journal window showing an example of a journal entry to record the deposit of cash for the total net amount owed to employees into the Payroll Cash Account.

Changing or Deleting General Journal Transactions

Existing general journal transactions may be changed or deleted. Simply select the transaction that you wish to change or delete, enter the corrections to the transaction and click on the post button. If you wish to delete the transaction, click on the Delete button.

Adding Lines to a Transaction

To add lines to an existing transaction, select the transaction and click on the Insert button. A blank line will be inserted at the end of the selected transaction into which you may enter the additional debit or credit part. *Note:* To insert another blank line, press the Tab key. If you accidentally insert a blank line, leave it. It will be removed when the journal is posted.

Finding a Journal Entry

While a journal is displayed, you can use the Find menu item from the Edit menu to locate and display any previously entered transaction. The Find Journal Entry dialog box is shown in Figure A–21.

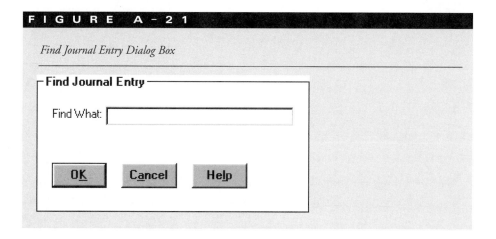

FIGURE A-21

Find Journal Entry Dialog Box

Enter the date, reference, amount, or any other data of the transaction you want to find in the Find What text box, then click on the OK button. If a matching transaction is found, it will be displayed in the journal so that it may be changed or deleted. Choosing of the Find Next item in the Edit menu will locate the next occurrence of the search criteria.

REPORTS MENU

When the Report Selection menu item is chosen from the Reports menu, or the *Reports* toolbar button is chosen, the Report Selection dialog box shown in Figure A–22 will appear. The Run Date Text box that appears at the top right is the date that will appear on the report. This date may be changed by entering a new date or by clicking on the calendar icon and using the calendar as discussed earlier.

FIGURE A-22

Report Selection (Payroll Reports)

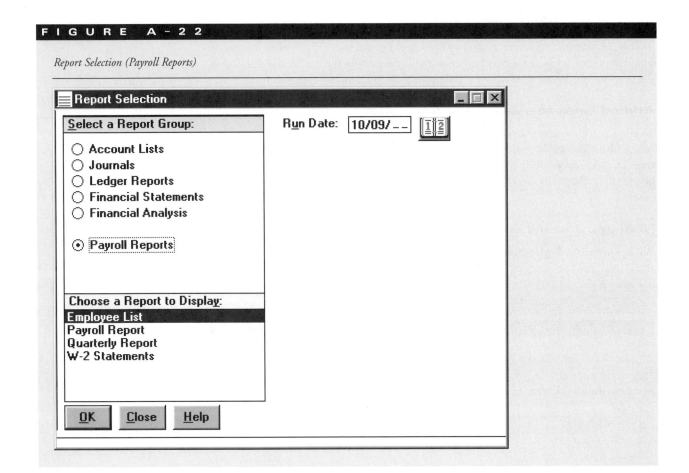

Option buttons are provided for various types of accounting system reports. A report is chosen by choosing the option button for the desired report. Based on the option button chosen, a list of all the reports within the chosen option will appear. Select the desired report and choose OK. If there is insufficient data to generate a particular report, that button will be dimmed to indicate that it is not active. The corresponding information that is displayed in the report window can be printed to an attached printer and/or copied for inclusion in another application (e.g., spreadsheet, word processor).

Printing the Contents of a Report Window

At any time while a report is displayed in a report window, it can be printed by choosing the Print command button located at the bottom of the window. The specific printer characteristics (resolution of print quality, paper size, paper source, etc.,) are those specified for the current default printer (as specified in the Printer Setup menu item).

Employee List Report

The employee list report provides a listing of the employee information entered into the computer via the Employee Account Maintenance window. This report is useful in verifying the accuracy of data entered into the Employees window.

Payroll Report

The payroll report, which should be generated each pay period, provides earnings and withholding information for each employee for the month, quarter, and year. Summary information is included at the end of the report that provides information on earnings and withholdings for all employees.

General Journal Report

The general journal report is useful in detecting errors and verifying the equality of debits and credits. This report becomes a permanent accounting document, and provides an audit trail so that transactions may be traced to their original source document.

To display a general journal report, choose the Report Selection menu item from the Reports menu or click on the Reports toolbar button. When the Report Selection window appears, choose the Journals option, select the General Journal report, then click on the OK button. The Journal Report Selection dialog box shown in Figure A–23 will appear, allowing you to display all the general journal entries or customize your general Journal report.

FIGURE A-23

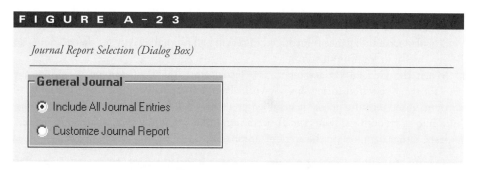

Journal Report Selection (Dialog Box)

Choose the Customize Journal Report option to control the data to be included on the report. If you want to include *all* journal transactions on the report, choose the Include All Journal Entries option. When the Customize Journal Report option is chosen, the dialog box shown in Figure A–24 will appear. Notice how the calendar appears on the right side of the dialog box because the calendar icon (located next to the start and end dates) was clicked.

FIGURE A-24

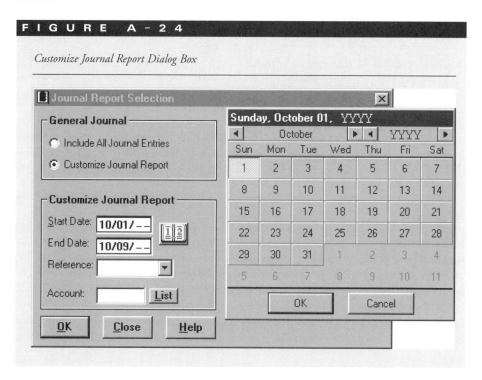

Customize Journal Report Dialog Box

Enter the desired Start and End Dates. As an alternative, select the Start or End date text box, then click on the calendar icon. When the calendar appears, as shown in Figure 2.8, select the desired date (the selected date will be placed in the text box that has the focus).

Enter an identifying reference in the Reference text box if you wish to restrict the report to a particular reference by clicking on the drop-down arrow to obtain a list of all the references available from which you may choose. For example, you might want to display only adjusting entries, or only a certain invoice). As an alternative, you may type the first character of the reference in the text box. The first entry that begins with that character will be displayed in the text box. Use the Up and Down arrow keys to browse through the entries.

Enter an account number in the Account Number text box if you wish to restrict the report to a particular account by clicking on the List button to obtain a chart of accounts selection list window from which you may select the desired account number. An example of a General Journal report is illustrated in Figure A–32, on page A-31.

General Ledger Report

The general ledger report shows detailed journal entry activity by account. Any range of accounts may be displayed (from one account to all accounts). If you have determined that a particular account balance is incorrect, displaying all journal activity for that account can be very useful in locating the error.

When the General Ledger report is selected from the Ledger Reports option, the account range selection dialog box shown in Figure A–25 will appear. Enter the range of accounts to be included in the general ledger report. You can click on the drop-down list button to select both the From and To account numbers from the chart of accounts list that appears, rather than keying the account number(s).

FIGURE A - 25

Account Range Selection Dialog Box

Account Range

From: | 11 Cash
To: | 56 Payroll Taxes

OK   Cancel   Help

If only one account is to be displayed, the "From" and "To" text boxes can be the same. In the above example, all accounts (account number 11 through 56) are to be displayed. Click the OK button. An example of a General Ledger report is illustrated in Figure A–33, on page A-32.

GRAPHS

Many accounting packages available today have the capability to produce graphs of data contained within their files. The term *graph* refers to a pictorial representation of data that can be produced by the computer and depicted on the screen and printer. Graphs produced by the computer are used to clarify the meaning of the words and numbers that appear. A Labor Distribution graph is available for the payroll system that depicts the distribution of the gross amount of wages paid to each salaries expense account for the current month. The other graphs shown will not display valid information because only the necessary accounts and account balances to complete the payroll project have been included in the general ledger to help simplify the tasks that must be completed.

To display the Labor Distribution graph, click on the Graphs toolbar button (the Graph Selection dialog box shown in Figure A–26 will appear), then click on the Labor Distribution button.

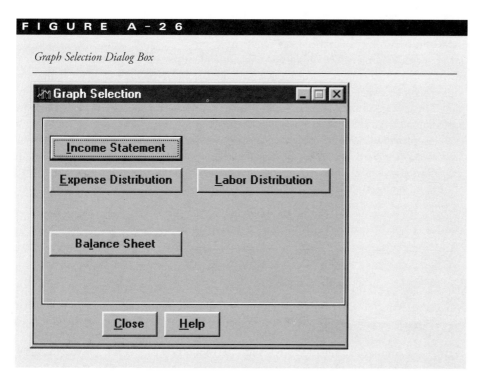

FIGURE A-26

Graph Selection Dialog Box

A three-dimensional pie-chart illustrating the distribution of wages paid (truncated to the nearest dollar). An example of a labor distribution pie-chart is shown in Figure A–34, on page A-33.

Note: Before printing the displayed Labor Distribution pie-chart, select either the Color/Laser Printer or Monochrome Printer option button that best describes the type of printer you are using.

HELP MENU

The on-screen Help System offers a quick way to find information about operating the software. If you are unfamiliar with the Help System, choose the How to Use Help menu item from the Help menu.

To access Help, you can: (1) choose either the Help Contents and Index menu item from the Help menu, (2) place the focus on the item you need help and press the F1 function key, or (3) choose the Help command button that appears at the bottom of various windows. In each case, a Help window will appear. The topic that is displayed depends on which Help command you chose or which window you were using when you chose the Help button. Within a Help topic, there may be one or more *jumps,* which you can click on (or select and press Enter) to display a new Help topic.

PAYROLL PROJECT

The payroll project that follows is the computerized version of the same project you completed manually in Chapter 7 beginning on page 7-9 of this text. In this project, you are employed by the Glo-Brite Paint Company as the person in the accounting department responsible for the company's payroll processing using the computerized payroll system described in the preceding material.

Like the manual project in Chapter 7, you will assume that the payroll records, tax reports, and deposits have been completed and filed for the first three quarters of this year. Your work will involve the computer processing of the payrolls for the last quarter of the year and the completion of the last quarter and annual tax reports and forms. You may complete the required deposit (quarterly, yearly, etc.) forms described in Chapter 7. If you have already completed these forms for the manual student project, check them as you progress through this project and make a note of any differences.

To help you get started, the first pay period is provided as a tutorial problem that illustrates the principles and procedures required to process payroll transactions using the *Integrated Accounting for Payroll* software. In subsequent pay period processing, additional instruction will be provided whenever a new operational procedure is used for the first time. Each of the step-by-step instructions below lists a task to be completed at the computer. If you need additional explanation for the task, a page reference is provided from the preceding material in this Appendix.

Note: Throughout this project, some of the computer-calculated withholding amounts (e.g., Federal Income Tax) will be slightly different from the amounts (from the tax tables) in the manual payroll project in Chapter 7. This occurs because the computer uses the annualized method to compute withholding taxes. Also, one to two cent differences will occur throughout the solutions because of rounding differences.

OCTOBER 9 PAYROLL

Step 1: **Remove the Student Project Audit Test found on page A-43. Answer the questions for the October 9 payroll as you complete processing for the pay period.**

Step 2: **Start up the *Integrated Accounting for Payroll* software (Page A-3).**

Step 3: **Load the opening balances template file, PAYROLL FILE (Page A-11).**
Pull down the File menu and choose the Open menu command. Select file PAYROLL FILE from the File list box and click on OK.

Step 4: **Enter the employee maintenance data (A-14).**
Click on the *Accts.* toolbar button. Select employee number 180 (Student), key your name in the Name field, then click on the Change Employee command button.
Note: Do not change any of the other fields. If you do, your solutions will not be correct.

Step 5: **Enter the Payroll transactions. *Do not* deduct Group Ins—*do* deduct Union Dues for the appropriate employees—*do not* deduct Simple Plan (which is the same as Simple Contributions Payable). (Page A-16).**
Click on the *Payroll* toolbar button. Click on the Deductions buttons. When the Voluntary Deductions dialog box appears, select only the Union Dues deduction, then click on OK. Enter the payroll transaction data provided below on the blank line at the bottom of the cell grid (the existing data are beginning balances and should *not* be altered). Have the computer calculate taxes. The Voluntary Deductions dialog box will appear again while entering the first employee's data to let you verify that only the Union Dues deduction has been selected (this will occur whenever the date entered in the Date field is changed).
Note: It is very important that you enter the correct date (10/09/—) when entering the payroll transactions. Payroll processing is date-sensitive and will accumulate and display incorrectly if the dates are entered incorrectly. Also, be sure to enter the correct Union Dues ($8.00) for the two appropriate employees. (The $72.00 amounts that are shown are carried over from the opening balances.)

Employees to Be Paid This Pay Period:

Employee Number	Employee Name	Salary/ Reg. Hrs.	Overtime @ Time ½	Overtime @ Double	Group Ins.	Union Dues
100	Bonno, Anthony Victor	80				$8.00
110	Ferguson, James Claude	reg. salary				
120	Ford, Catherine Louise	reg. salary				
130	Mann, Dewey Wilson	reg. salary				
140	O'Neill, Joseph Tyler	reg. salary				
150	Russell, Virginia Aloise	reg. salary				
160	Ryan, Norman Allen	80				$8.00
170	Sokowski, Thomas James	reg. salary				
180	Student (your name)	reg. salary				
190	Williams, Ruth Virginia	reg. salary				

Step 6: **Display the employee list report (Page A-22).**

Click on the Reports toolbar button. Choose the Payroll Reports option. Select the Employee List report and then click on OK. The report is shown in Figure A–27. Verify the accuracy of the maintenance input and make any corrections via the Employees tab in the Account Maintenance window.

FIGURE A-27

Employee List Report

Glo-Brite Paint Company
Employee List
10/09/--

Emp. No.	Employee Name/Address	Soc. Sec./ Mar. Stat.	# Pay Periods	G.L. Acct.	Salary/ Rate
100	BONNO, Anthony Victor 694 Bristol Avenue Philadelphia, PA 19135-0617	537-10-3481 Married W/H 4	26	54	17.65
110	FERGUSON, James Claude 808 Sixth Street Philadelphia, PA 19106-0995	486-03-8645 Married W/H 5	26	53	2250.00
120	FORD, Catherine Louise 18 Dundee Avenue Philadelphia, PA 19151-1919	213-09-4567 Single W/H 2	26	52	900.00
130	MANN, Dewey Wilson 3007 Bisque Drive Philadelphia, PA 19199-0718	282-37-9352 Married W/H 4	26	53	1350.00
140	O'NEILL, Joseph Tyler 2100 Broad Street Philadelphia, PA 19121-7189	897-04-1534 Married W/H 3	26	51	2307.69
150	RUSSELL, Virginia Aloise 8004 Dowling Road Philadelphia, PA 19135-9001	314-21-6337 Single W/H 1	26	52	690.00
160	RYAN, Norman Allen 7300 Harrison Street Philadelphia, PA 19124-6699	526-23-1233 Married W/H 4	26	54	18.00

(continued on next page)

Employee List Report

Emp. No.	Employee Name/Address	Soc. Sec./ Mar. Stat.	# Pay Periods	G.L. Acct.	Salary/ Rate
170	SOKOWSKI, Thomas James 133 Cornwells Street Philadelphia, PA 19171-5718	662-04-8832 Married W/H 2	26	54	2050.00
180	STUDENT 7018 Erdrick Street Philadelphia, PA 19135-8517	555-55-5555 Single W/H 1	26	52	540.00
190	WILLIAMS, Ruth Virginia 9433 State Street Philadelphia, PA 19149-0819	518-30-6741 Single W/H 0	26	52	1223.08

Step 7: Display the payroll report (Page A-22).

Make sure the Run Date is set to 10/09/--, then choose the Payroll Report option and click on OK. The payroll report for Employee 100; Bonno, Anthony Victor, followed by the payroll summary is shown in Figure A–28.

Payroll Report (Employee 100 and Summary)

Glo-Brite Paint Company
Payroll Report
10/09/--

		Current	Quarterly	Yearly
100-BONNO, Anthony Victor	Gross Pay	1412.00	1412.00	12734.00
54-Plant	FIT	82.28	82.28	892.28
Married Acct. 54	SIT	39.54	39.54	356.56
W/H 4 537-10-3481	Soc. Sec.--OASDI	87.54	87.54	789.50
Pay Periods 26	Medicare--HI	20.47	20.47	184.64
Salary	CIT	64.08	64.08	577.93
Hourly Rate 17.65	Group Ins.			144.80
Reg. Hours 80.00	Union Dues	8.00	8.00	80.00
O.T. Hours	Simple Plan			
Check Number 672	Employee SUTA			
Check Date 10/09/--	Net Pay	1110.09	1110.09	9708.29
Payroll Summary	Gross Pay	14162.77	14162.77	156387.34
	FIT	1216.07	1216.07	17133.07
	SIT	396.57	396.57	4378.86
	Soc. Sec.--OASDI	878.09	878.09	9696.01
	Medicare--HI	205.37	205.37	2267.64
	CIT	642.78	642.78	7097.65
	Group Ins.			930.40
	Union Dues	16.00	16.00	160.00
	Simple Plan			
	Employee SUTA			
	Net Pay	10807.89	10807.89	114723.71

Step 8: Generate and post the journal entry for the current payroll (Page A-18).
Choose the Current Payroll Journal Entry menu item from the Options menu. Click Yes when asked if you want to generate the journal entry. When the entry appears in the Current Payroll Journal Entries dialog box, as shown in Figure A–29, click on Post. The journal entry will reappear, posted, in the general journal.

FIGURE A-29

Current Payroll Journal Entry

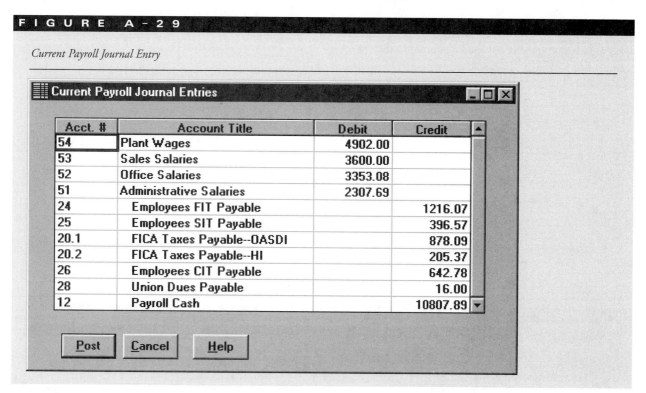

If your journal entries do not match those shown in Figure A–29, check your employee list and payroll report for keying errors, and make the necessary corrections. Return to the General Journal window, delete the incorrect entries, and generate new entries.

Step 9: Generate and post the employer's payroll taxes journal entry (Page A-19).
With the General Journal window still displayed, choose Employer's Payroll Taxes from the Options menu. Click Yes when asked if you want to generate the journal entry. When the entries appear in the Payroll Taxes Journal Entries dialog box shown in Figure A–30, click on Post. The journal entries will reappear, posted, in the general journal.

Step 10: Enter and post the October 9 general journal entry to record the deposit of cash for the total net amount owed to employees in the Payroll Cash account (Page A-20).
Click on the Journal toolbar button. When the General Journals tab appears, enter the journal entry illustrated in Figure A–31. Be sure to enter a reference of General to indicate that the entry was entered manually in the general journal.

FIGURE A-30

Employer's Payroll Taxes Journal Entry

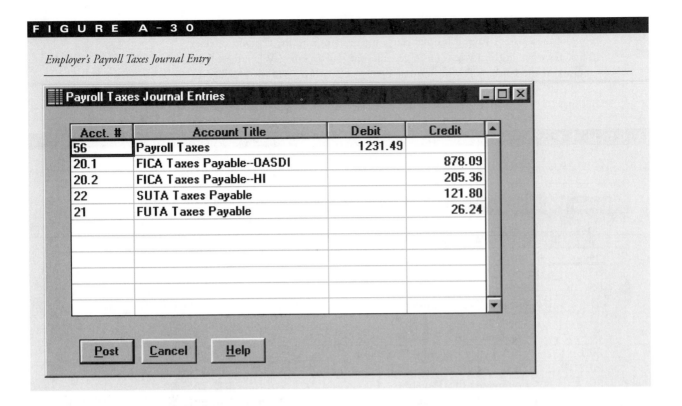

Acct. #	Account Title	Debit	Credit
56	Payroll Taxes	1231.49	
20.1	FICA Taxes Payable--OASDI		878.09
20.2	FICA Taxes Payable--HI		205.36
22	SUTA Taxes Payable		121.80
21	FUTA Taxes Payable		26.24

Payroll Taxes Journal Entries

Post   Cancel   Help

FIGURE A-31

General Journal Entry to Record Payroll Cash

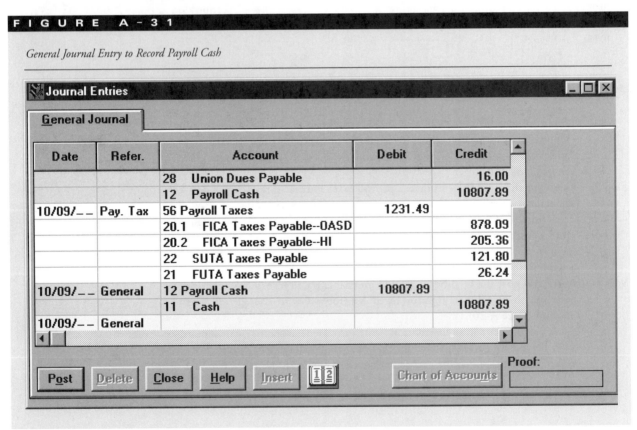

Journal Entries — General Journal

Date	Refer.	Account	Debit	Credit
		28 Union Dues Payable		16.00
		12 Payroll Cash		10807.89
10/09/_ _	Pay. Tax	56 Payroll Taxes	1231.49	
		20.1 FICA Taxes Payable--OASD		878.09
		20.2 FICA Taxes Payable--HI		205.36
		22 SUTA Taxes Payable		121.80
		21 FUTA Taxes Payable		26.24
10/09/_ _	General	12 Payroll Cash	10807.89	
		11 Cash		10807.89
10/09/_ _	General			

Post   Delete   Close   Help   Insert   [1][2]   Chart of Accounts   Proof:

Step 11: Display the General Journal Report (Page A-23).

Click on the Report toolbar button. Choose the Journal option and the General Journal report, then click on OK. When the Journal Report Selection window appears, choose the Customize Journal Report option. Make sure the Start Date is set to 10/01/-- and the End Date to 10/09/-- (where—is the current year), then click on OK. *Note:* If the transactions were entered correctly, the Start and End Dates will be the default dates set automatically by the computer. The computer uses the first day of the month as the Start Date and the latest date of the general journal transactions that were entered as the End Date. The General Journal report is shown in Figure A–32.

FIGURE A-32

General Journal Report

Glo-Brite Paint Company
General Journal
10/09/--

Date	Refer.	Acct.	Title	Debit	Credit
10/09	Payroll	54	Plant Wages	4902.00	
10/09	Payroll	53	Sales Salaries	3600.00	
10/09	Payroll	52	Office Salaries	3353.08	
10/09	Payroll	51	Administrative Salaries	2307.69	
10/09	Payroll	24	Employees FIT Payable		1216.07
10/09	Payroll	25	Employees SIT Payable		396.57
10/09	Payroll	20.1	FICA Taxes Payable--OASDI		878.09
10/09	Payroll	20.2	FICA Taxes Payable--HI		205.37
10/09	Payroll	26	Employees CIT Payable		642.78
10/09	Payrol	28	Union Dues Payable		16.00
10/09	Payroll	12	Payroll Cash		10807.89
10/09	Pay. Tax	56	Payroll Taxes	1231.49	
10/09	Pay. Tax	20.1	FICA Taxes Payable--OASDI		878.09
10/09	Pay. Tax	20.2	FICA Taxes Payable--HI		205.36
10/09	Pay. Tax	22	SUTA Taxes Payable		121.80
10/09	Pay. Tax	21	FUTA Taxes Payable		26.24
10/09	General	12	Payroll Cash	10807.89	
10/09	General	11	Cash		10807.89
			Totals	26202.15	26202.15

Step 12: Display the General Ledger Report (Page A-24).

Choose the Ledger Reports option and the General Ledger report, then click on OK. When the Account Range dialog box appears, click on OK to accept the default range of all accounts. The General Ledger report is shown in Figure A–33.

F I G U R E A - 3 3

General Ledger Report

Glo-Brite Paint Company
General Ledger
10/09/--

Account	Journal	Date Refer.	Debit	Credit	Balance
11-Cash					
	Balance Forward				199846.33Dr
	General	10/09 General		10807.89	189038.44Dr
12-Payroll Cash					
	General	10/09 Payroll		10,807.89	10807.89Cr
	General	10/09 General	10807.89		.00
20.1-FICA Taxes Payable--OASDI					
	General	10/09 Payroll		878.09	878.09Cr
	General	10/09 Pay. Tax		878.09	1756.18Cr
20.2-FICA Taxes Payable--HI					
	General	10/09 Payroll		205.37	205.37Cr
	General	10/09 Pay. Tax		205.36	410.73Cr
21-FUTA Taxes Payable					
	General	10/09 Pay. Tax		26.24	26.24Cr
22-SUTA Taxes Payable					
	General	10/09 Pay. Tax		121.80	121.80Cr
23-Employees SUTA Payable					
	*** No Activity ***				.00
24-Employees FIT Payable					
	General	10/09 Payroll		1216.07	1216.07Cr
25-Employees SIT Payable					
	General	10/09 Payroll		396.57	396.57Cr
26-Employees CIT Payable					
	General	10/09 Payroll		642.78	642.78Cr
27-Grp. Ins. Prem. Collected					
	*** No Activity ***				.00
28-Union Dues Payable					
	General	10/09 Payroll		16.00	16.00Cr
29-Simple Contrib. Payable					
	*** No Activity ***				.00
51-Administrative Salaries					
	Balance Forward				42692.27Dr
	General	10/09 Payroll	2307.69		44999.96Dr
52-Office Salaries					
	Balance Forward				28350.00Dr
	General	10/09 Payroll	3353.08		31703.08Dr
53-Sales Salaries					
	Balance Forward				28525.00Dr
	General	10/09 Payroll	3600.00		32125.00Dr
54-Plant Wages					
	Balance Forward				42657.30Dr
	General	10/09 Payroll	4902.00		47559.30Dr
56-Payroll Taxes					
	Balance Forward				13906.21Dr
	General	10/09 Pay. Tax	1231.49		15137.70Dr

Step 13: Generate a Labor Distribution graph (Page A-24).

Click on the *Graphs* toolbar button. Click on the Labor Distribution button to generate the graph shown in Figure A–34.

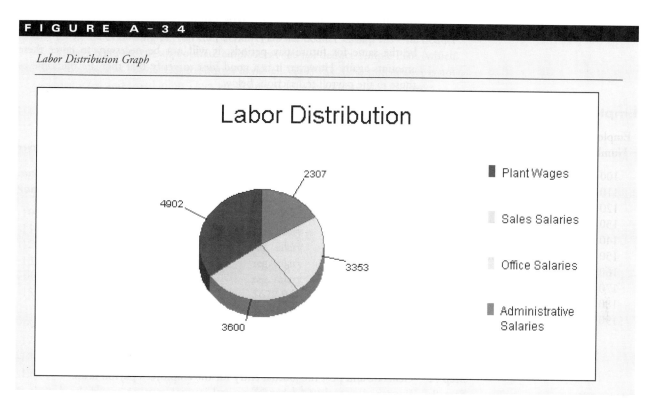

FIGURE A - 3 4

Labor Distribution Graph

Step 14: Use the Save As command to save your data to disk (Page A-12).

Choose *save As* from the File menu and save the file to your disk and folder with a file name of *10-09 your name* (where 10-09 is the pay period date).

Step 15: End the payroll accounting session (Page A-12).

Choose Exit from the File menu.

> *Note:* If you are using this product as a distance or on-line course, and your instructor has provided you his/her email address: you may email each of your pay period solution files as an email attachment for electronic checking. Simply create an email addressed to your instructor, identifying yourself as a payroll accounting student, and attach your completed pay period solution file (ex. file 10-09 *your name*). Your instructor will electronically check your work and then send you a report of the results.

OCTOBER 23 PAYROLL

The step-by-step instructions for completing the October 23 payroll (for the period ending October 17 are listed below).

Step 1: Answer the questions for the October 23 payroll on the Student Project Audit Test as you complete processing for the pay period.

Step 2: If you quit the software after processing the previous pay period, perform the following steps:

a. Start up the *Integrated Accounting for Payroll* software.

b. Load your file containing the last pay period data (*10-09 your name*).

Step 3: Enter and post the October 20 transaction required to record the deposit of the Pennsylvania state income taxes withheld from the October 9 payroll.

b. Load your file containing the last pay period data (*11-06 your name*).

Step 3: Enter Ruth V. Williams' payroll transaction (*do* deduct Group Ins of $14.40). Enter $2,079.32 in her salary (two partial weeks of work ($856.24), plus two full weeks' pay ($1,223.08) in lieu of two weeks' notice for her final pay).

Step 4: Display the payroll report.

Step 5: Generate and post the journal entry for the current payroll.

Step 6: Generate and post the journal entry for the employer's payroll taxes.

Step 7: Enter and post the November 13 general journal entry to record the deposit of cash for the total net amount of Ruth Williams' pay in the Payroll Cash account.

Step 8: Display the Journal Report for 11/07/-- through 11/13/--.

Step 9: Display the General Ledger report.

Step 10: Use the Save As command to save the November 13 payroll to disk with a file name of *11-13 your name* (where 11-13 represents month 11, day 13).

Step 11: Proceed to the November 20 payroll. If necessary, end your payroll session.

NOVEMBER 20 PAYROLL

The step-by-step instructions for completing the November 20 payroll (for the period ending November 14) follow.

Step 1: Answer the questions for the November 20 payroll on the Student Project Audit Test as you complete processing for the pay period.

Step 2: If you quit the software after processing the previous pay period, perform the following steps:
a. Start up the *Integrated Accounting for Payroll* software.
b. Load your file containing the last pay period data (*11-13 your name*).

Step 3: Enter and post the following transactions:
November 16: Deposited with the City Bank, the amount of FICA taxes and federal income taxes for the October payrolls.
Hint: Display the General Ledger report to obtain these amounts from the FICA Taxes Payable—OASDI, FICA Taxes Payable—HI, and the Employees FIT payable account balances.
November 16: Deposited the City of Philadelphia employees withheld income tax ($1,300.18) with the Department of Revenue for the October payrolls (see the Employees CIT Payable account balance in the General Ledger report).
November 18: Deposited the Pennsylvania state income taxes withheld from the November 6 and 13 (Ruth V. Williams) payrolls.

Step 4: Enter the following employee maintenance:
Add new employee: Employee number 200; WOODS, Beth Anne; 8102 Franklin Court, Philadelphia, PA 19105-0915; social security number, 724-03-1587; single, salaried, $1,200.00, number of pay periods per year, 26; withholding allowances, 1; Account No. 52 (Office salaries).

Step 5: Enter the following payroll transactions. *Do* deduct Group Ins—*do* deduct Union Dues for the appropriate employees—*do* deduct Simple Plan (which is the same as Simple Contributions Payable) for the appropriate employees. Verify that Group Insurance is deducted, that Union Dues are deducted, and that Simple Plan (Simple Contributions Payable) is deducted for the appropriate employees. *Note:* This is the first pay in which the company offers a saving incentive match plan. The computer software has been designed to use the key terms "Simple Plan" to instruct it to exclude this deduction from the employee's income for FIT purposes. The general ledger account Simple Contributions Payable is associated with this term for updating during payroll transaction processing.

Employees to Be Paid This Pay Period:

Employee Number	Employee Name	Salary/ Reg. Hrs.	Overtime @ Time ½	Overtime @ Double	Group Ins.	Union Dues	Simple Plan
100	Bonno, Anthony Victor	64			$16.50	$8.00	
110	Ferguson, James Claude	reg. salary			$26.40		$500.00
120	Ford, Catherine Louise	reg. salary			$10.50		
130	Mann, Dewey Wilson	reg. salary			$15.90		$250.00
140	O'Neill, Joseph Tyler	reg. salary			$27.00		$700.00
150	Russell, Virginia Aloise	$672.94 (loss of 2 hours)			$8.10		
160	Ryan, Norman Allen	80			$16.80	$8.00	$200.00
170	Sokowski, Thomas James	reg. salary			$24.00		
180	Student (your name)	reg. salary			$6.30		

Step 6: Display an Employee List report.

Step 7: Display a payroll report.

Step 8: Generate and post the journal entry for the current payroll.

Step 9: Generate and post the journal entry for the employer's payroll taxes.

Step 10: Enter and post the November 20 general journal entry to record the deposit of cash for the total net amount owed to employees in the Payroll Cash account.

Step 11: Display the Journal Report for 11/14/-- through 11/20/--.

Step 12: Display the General Ledger report.

Step 13: Generate a Labor Distribution graph.

Step 14: Use the Save As command to save the November 20 payroll to disk with a file name of *11-20 your name* (where 11-20 represents month 11, day 20).

Step 15: Proceed to the December 4 payroll. If necessary, end your payroll session.

DECEMBER 4 PAYROLL

The step-by-step instructions for completing the December 4 payroll (for the week ending November 28) follow.

Step 1: Answer the questions for the December 4 payroll on the Student Project Audit Test as you complete processing for the pay period.

Step 2: If you quit the software after processing the previous pay period, perform the following steps:

    a. Start up the *Integrated Accounting for Payroll* software.

    b. Load your file containing the last pay period data (*11-20 your name*).

Step 3: Enter and post the following transaction:

December 3: Deposited the Pennsylvania state income taxes withheld from the November 20 payroll.

Step 4: Enter the following employee maintenance:

Change Catherine L. Ford's salary amount to $960.00 because of a salary increase.

Change Virginia Russell's salary amount to $750.00 because of a salary increase. Add new employee: Employee number 210; YOUNG, Paul Winston; 7936 Holmes Drive, Philadelphia, PA 19107-6107; social security number, 432-07-6057; single, salaried, $807.70, number of pay periods per year, 26; withholding allowances, 1; Account No. 53 (Sales Salaries).

Step 5: Enter the following payroll transactions. *Do not* deduct Group Ins—*do* deduct Union Dues for the appropriate employees—*do* deduct Simple for the appropriate employees.

Employees to Be Paid This Pay Period:

Employee Number	Employee Name	Salary/ Reg. Hrs.	Overtime @ Time ½	Overtime @ Double	Group Ins.	Union Dues	Simple Plan
100	Bonno, Anthony Victor	80		8		$8.00	
110	Ferguson, James Claude	reg. salary					$500.00
120	Ford, Catherine Louise	reg. salary					
130	Mann, Dewey Wilson	reg. salary					$250.00
140	O'Neill, Joseph Tyler	reg. salary					$700.00
150	Russell, Virginia Aloise	reg. salary					
160	Ryan, Norman Allen	76	3			$8.00	$200.00
170	Sokowski, Thomas James	reg. salary					
180	Student (your name)	reg. salary					
200	Woods, Beth Anne	$1,080.00 (first payroll)					

Step 6: Display an Employee List report.

Step 7: Display a payroll report.

Step 8: Generate and post the journal entry for the current payroll.

Step 9: Generate and post the journal entry for the employer's payroll taxes.

Step 10: Enter and post the December 4 general journal entry to record the deposit of cash for the total net amount owed to employees in the Payroll Cash account.

Step 11: Display the Journal Report for 11/21/-- through 12/04/--.

Step 12: Display the General Ledger report.

Step 13: Generate a Labor Distribution graph.

Step 14: Use the Save As command to save the December 4 payroll to disk with a file name of *12-04 your name* (where *12-04* represents month 12, day 04).

Step 15: Proceed to the December 14 payroll. If necessary, end your payroll session.

DECEMBER 14 PAYROLL

A special payroll needs to be run to process the death of an employee (Virginia A. Russell). The step-by-step instructions for completing the December 14 special payroll follow.

Step 1: Answer the questions for the December 14 payroll on the Student Project Audit Test as you complete processing for the pay period.

Step 2: If you quit the software after processing the previous pay period, perform the following steps:
a. Start up the *Integrated Accounting for Payroll* software.
b. Load your file containing the last pay period data (*12-04 your name*).

Step 3: Enter and post the following transaction:
December 9: Paid the treasurer of the union the amount of union dues withheld during the month of November.

Step 4: Enter the employee maintenance:
Change Anthony V. Bonno's number of withholding allowances to 5.

Step 5: Pay Virginia A. Russell (pay will go to her estate). (*Do* deduct $8.70 for her Group Ins.)
Enter $1,425.16 in her salary amount (two partial weeks of work ($675.16) plus for her accrued vacation pay ($750.00) for her final check).
Note: After clicking on the Calculate Taxes command button, remove the calculated withholding amounts for FIT, SIT, and CIT by keying zeros in these grid cells (final pay is not subject to these withholdings).

Step 6: Display an Employee List report.

Step 7: Display a payroll report.

Step 8: Generate and post the journal entry for the current payroll.

Step 9: Generate and post the journal entry for the employer's payroll taxes.

Step 10: Enter and post the December 14 general journal entry to record the deposit of cash for Virginia A. Russell's net amount in the Payroll Cash account.

Step 11: Display the Journal Report for 12/05/— through 12/14/—.

Step 12: Display the General Ledger report.

Step 13: Use the Save As command to save the December 14 special payroll to disk with a file name of *12-14 your name* (where 12-14 represents month 12, day 14).

Step 14: Proceed to the December 18 payroll. If necessary, end your payroll session.

DECEMBER 18 PAYROLL

The step-by-step instructions for completing the December 18 payroll (for the week ending December 12) follow.

Step 1: Answer the questions for the December 18 payroll on the Student Project Audit Test as you complete processing for the pay period.

Step 2: If you quit the software after processing the previous pay period, perform the following steps:

  a. Start up the Integrated Accounting for Payroll software.

  b. Load your file containing the last pay period data (*12-14 your name*).

Step 3: Enter and post the following transactions:

December 15: Deposited with the City Bank, the amount of FICA taxes and federal income taxes for the November payrolls.

December 15: Deposited the City of Philadelphia employees income tax withheld with the Department of Revenue from the November payrolls.

December 18: Deposited the Pennsylvania state income taxes withheld from the December 4 payroll.

December 18: Wrote check to Virginia Russell's estate from the regular cash account for the amount withheld from her December 14 pay for insurance.

Step 4: Enter following employee maintenance:

Change: Employee number 140; O'Neill, Joseph Tyler withholding allowances to 4. Add new employee: Employee number 220; ZIMMERMAN, Richard Lewis; 900 South Clark Street, Philadelphia, PA 19195-6247; social security number, 897-12-1502; married, salaried, $660.00, number of pay periods per year, 26; withholding allowances, 1; Account No. 52 (Office Salaries).

Step 5: Enter the following payroll transactions. *Do* deduct Group Ins—*do* deduct Union Dues for the appropriate employees—*do* deduct Simple for the appropriate employees.

Note: Be sure to enter the changes and amounts of Group Ins. deductions for the new employees, and the $9.00 Union Dues as noted below. Also, be sure to enter the change to Joseph O'Neill's Simple Plan deduction.

Employees to Be Paid This Pay Period:

Employee Number	Employee Name	Salary/ Reg. Hrs.	Overtime @ Time ½	Overtime @ Double	Group Ins.	Union Dues	Soimple Plan
100	Bonno, Anthony Victor	80		12	$16.50	$9.00	
110	Ferguson, James Claude	reg. salary			$26.40		$500.00
120	Ford, Catherine Louise	reg. salary			$11.10		
130	Mann, Dewey Wilson	reg. salary			$15.90		$250.00
140	O'Neill, Joseph Tyler	$37,307.69 (reg. salary + $35,000 bonus)			$27.00		$4,000.00
160	Ryan, Norman Allen	80	7		$16.80	$9.00	$200.00
170	Sokowski, Thomas James	reg. salary			$24.00		
180	Student (your name)	$533.25 (loss of 1 hour)			$6.30		
200	Woods, Beth Anne	reg. salary			$14.10		
210	Young, Paul Winston	reg. salary			$9.60		

Step 6: Display an Employee List report.

Step 7: Display the payroll report.

Step 8: Generate and post the journal entry for the current payroll.

Step 9: Generate and post the journal entry for the employer's payroll taxes.

Step 10: Enter and post the December 18 general journal entry to record the deposit of cash for the total net amount owed to employees in the Payroll Cash account.

Step 11: Display the Journal Report for 12/15/-- through 12/18/--.

Step 12: Display the General Ledger report.

Step 13: Generate a Labor Distribution graph.

Step 14: Use the Save As command to save the December 18 payroll to disk with a file name of *12-18 your name* (where 12-18 represents month 12, day 18).

Step 15: This completes the project insofar as recording and processing the computerized payroll transactions for the last quarter is concerned. Proceed to the Optional Activities. End your payroll session.

OPTIONAL ACTIVITIES

This optional, clerical activity is provided to prepare the payroll file for the next calendar year, and to follow the manual student project in Chapter 7. The transactions have been included to illustrate different types of transactions arising in connection with the accounting for payrolls and payroll taxes. The information contained in the computerized Payroll reports may be referenced in order to complete the forms in this activity.

Step 1: Answer the questions for the additional transactions on the Student Project Audit Test as you complete the journal entries.

Step 2: If you quit the software after processing the previous pay period, perform the following steps:
a. Start up the *Integrated Accounting for Payroll* software.
b. Load your file containing the last pay period data *12-18 your name*).

Step 3: Purge the payroll transactions (Page A-13).
Choose the Purge Payroll Transactions (Year-End) menu item from the Options menu. When the dialog box appears asking if you want to purge transactions and clear payroll for year-end, click on Yes.

Step 4: Enter the following employee maintenance:
Delete employee number 150 (Virginia A. Russell)
Delete employee number 190 (Ruth V. Williams)

Step 5: Use the Save As command to save the data to disk with a file name of *01-01 your name* (where 01-01 represents month 1, day 01).
Note: This is the payroll file that will be used to begin processing for the new year.

Prepare the various quarter-end and year-end payroll tax forms, and make the accrual entries for the payroll at the end of the year.

Step 6: Load your file containing the last pay period data (*12-18 your name*).

Step 7: Use the information contained in the payroll accounting reports to complete the following forms— if not completed in the Student Project in Chapter 7. If completed in Chapter 7, check the forms and make a note of any differences. Refer to the February 1 narrative regarding the forms to be completed, on pages 7-22–7-23 in the manual student project in Chapter 7, if necessary.
a. Form 941, Employer's Quarterly Federal Tax Return.
b. Form 940-EZ, Employer's Annual Federal Unemployment (FUTA) Tax Return.
c. Form UC-2, Employer's Report for Unemployment Compensation—Fourth Quarter.
d. Form W-2, Wage and Tax Statement for each employee.

    e. Form W-3, Transmittal of Wage and Tax Statements.

    f. Pennsylvania form REV1667, W-2 Transmittal.

    g. Form 1099-MISC, Miscellaneous Income (for Virginia A. Russell).

    h. Form 1096, Annual Summary and Transmittal of U.S. Information Returns.

    i. Form PA-W3R, Employer Quarterly Reconciliation Return of Income Tax Withheld.

    j. Annual Reconciliation of Wage Tax for Philadelphia.

Step 8: Use the appropriate computer generated reports to answer the questions on the project that are listed in Chapter 7, pp. 7-23–7-24.

Step 9: Enter and post the following transactions:

January 6: Deposited the Pennsylvania state income taxes withheld from the December 18 payroll.

January 8: Paid the treasurer of the union the amount of union dues withheld during the month of December.

January 15: Deposited with the City Bank the amount of FICA taxes and federal income taxes for the December payrolls.

January 15: Deposited the City of Philadelphia employee's income tax withheld with the Department of Revenue from the December payrolls

February 1: Deposited FUTA Taxes Payable for the quarter.

Hint: see the FUTA Taxes Payable account balance in the general ledger report.

February 1: Paid the SUTA Taxes Payable and Employees SUTA Payable for the fourth quarter.

Hint: see the SUTA Taxes Payable and the Employees SUTA Payable account balances in the general ledger report.

Step 10: Display the Journal Report for January 1 of the next year through February 1 of the next year.

Step 11: Use the Save As command to save your data to disk with a file name of *YR-END your name* (where YR-END represents the payroll file containing the accrual entries at the end of the year).

Step 12: End your computer session.

STUDENT PROJECT AUDIT TEST

OCTOBER 9 PAYROLL: (Use the payroll file you saved under filename *10-09 your name* to answer the following questions for the October 9 payroll.)

Payroll Report
1. What is the number of withholding allowances for James C. Ferguson? . . . . _____
2. What is the current gross pay for Norman A. Ryan? . . . . _____
3. What is the amount of HI withheld for the current pay period for Ruth V. Williams? . . . . . . _____
4. What is the total current net pay for all employees? . . . . _____
5. What is the total yearly SIT withheld for all employees? . . . . _____

Journal Entries Report
6. What is the amount of the debit to Office Salaries? . . . . _____
7. What is the amount of the debit to Payroll Taxes Expense? . . . . _____
8. What is the amount of the credit to Cash? . . . . _____

General Ledger
9. What is the Cash (account number 11) account balance? . . . . _____
10. What is the total Administrative Salaries paid to date? . . . . _____

- -

Name _____

STUDENT PROJECT AUDIT TEST

OCTOBER 23 PAYROLL: (Use the payroll file you saved under filename *10-23 your name* to answer the following questions for the October 23 payroll.)

Payroll Report
1. What is the current gross pay for Anthony V. Bonno? . . . . _____
2. What is the current amount of OASDI withheld for Catherine L. Ford? . . . . _____
3. What is the total current net pay for all employees? . . . . _____
4. What is the total quarterly gross pay for all employees? . . . . _____
5. What is the total current amount of group insurance withheld for all employees? . . . . _____

Journal Entries Report
6. What is the amount of the credit to Employees SIT Payable? . . . . _____
7. What is the amount of the debit to Payroll Taxes Expense? . . . . _____

General Ledger
8. What is the amount of FICA Taxes Payable—OASDI for the month of October? . . . . _____
9. What is the amount of Union Dues withheld for the employees for the month of October? _____

STUDENT PROJECT AUDIT TEST

NOVEMBER 6 PAYROLL: (Use the payroll file you saved under filename *11-06 your name* to answer the following questions for the November 6 payroll.)

Payroll Report
1. What is the current amount of FIT withheld for Joseph T. O'Neill? .... _____
2. What is the total current gross pay for all employees? .... _____
3. What is the total current amount of CIT withheld for all employees? .... _____
4. What is the total current net pay for all employees? .... _____

Journal Entries Report
5. What is the amount of the credit to FICA Taxes Payable—OASDI? .... _____
6. What is the amount of the credit to FICA Taxes Payable—HI? .... _____
7. What is the amount of the debit to Payroll Taxes Expense? .... _____

General Ledger
8. What is the balance in the Cash (account number 11) account? .... _____
9. What is the amount of Sales Salaries paid to date? .... _____

STUDENT PROJECT AUDIT TEST

NOVEMBER 13 PAYROLL: (Use the payroll file you saved under filename *11-13 your name* to answer the following questions for the special November 13 payroll.)

Payroll Report
1. What is the amount of FIT withheld for the year for Ruth V. Williams? .... _____
2. What is Ruth V. Williams' current net pay? .... _____
3. In what department did Ruth V. Williams work? .... _____

Journal Entries Report
4. What is the amount of Ruth V. Williams' Group Insurance withheld? .... _____

General Ledger
5. What is the total amount of Payroll Taxes (account number 56) to date? .... _____

STUDENT PROJECT AUDIT TEST

NOVEMBER 20 PAYROLL: (Use the payroll file you saved under filename *11-20 your name* to answer the following questions for the November 20 payroll.)

Payroll Report

1. What is the amount of FIT withheld for the current pay period for Dewey W. Mann? .... _____
2. What is the total current net pay for all employees? .... _____
3. What is the total current gross pay for all employees? .... _____

Journal Entries Report

4. What is the November 20 payroll amount of the credit to Cash? .... _____
5. What is the amount of the debit to Payroll Taxes Expense? .... _____
6. What is the amount of the debit to Plant Wages? .... _____

General Ledger

7. What is the amount of Employees SIT Payable? .... _____
8. What is the amount of Office Salaries paid to date? .... _____
9. What is the amount of Simple Contributions Payable? .... _____

STUDENT PROJECT AUDIT TEST

DECEMBER 4 PAYROLL: (Use the payroll file you saved under filename *12-04 your name* to answer the following questions for the December 4 payroll.)

Payroll Report

1. What is the current gross pay for Joseph T. O'Neill? .... _____
2. What is the current amount of OASDI withheld for Norman A. Ryan? .... _____
3. What is the total current net pay for all employees? .... _____
4. What is the total current CIT withheld for all employees? .... _____

Journal Entries Report

5. What is the amount of the debit to Administrative Salaries? .... _____
6. What is the amount of the credit to Employees SIT Payable? .... _____
7. What is the amount of the debit to Payroll Taxes Expense? .... _____

General Ledger

8. What is the amount of SUTA Taxes Payable? .... _____
9. What is the amount of Sales Salaries? .... _____

Name _____

STUDENT PROJECT AUDIT TEST

DECEMBER 14 PAYROLL: (Use the payroll file you saved under filename *12-14 your name* to answer the following questions for the special December 14 payroll.)

Payroll Report
1. What was Virginia A. Russell's social security number? . . . . _____
2. What was the amount of net pay received by Virginia A. Russell's estate? . . . . _____

Journal Entries Report
3. What is the amount of the debit to Office Salaries? . . . . _____

General Ledger
4. What is the amount that was credited to group insurance premiums collected (account number 27) during this period? . . . . _____
5. What is the amount paid to Office Salaries to date? . . . . _____

Name _____

STUDENT PROJECT AUDIT TEST

DECEMBER 18 PAYROLL: (Use the payroll file you saved under filename *12-18 your name* to answer the following questions for the December 18 payroll.)

Payroll Report
1. What is the current amount of SIT withheld for Thomas J. Sokowski? . . . . _____
2. What is the total current net pay for all employees? . . . . _____
3. What is the total yearly gross pay for all employees? . . . . _____

Journal Entries Report
4. What is the amount of the debit to Administrative Salaries? . . . . _____
5. What is the amount of the debit to Payroll Taxes Expense? . . . . _____

General Ledger
6. What is the balance in the Cash account? . . . . _____
7. What is the total amount of Plant Wages to date? . . . . _____
8. What is the total amount of Payroll Taxes to date? . . . . _____

Name _____

STUDENT PROJECT AUDIT TEST

OPTIONAL ACTIVITIES: (Use the payroll file you saved under filename *YR-END your name* to answer the following questions.)

Journal Entries Report

1. What is the amount of the deposit for Pennsylvania state income taxes withheld from the December 18 payroll? .... _____

2. What is the amount of Union Dues withheld during the month of December? .... _____

3. What is the amount of FICA Taxes Payable—OASDI deposited from the December payrolls? .... _____

4. What is the amount of the city of Philadelphia employees' income tax deposited from the December payrolls? .... _____

5. What is the amount of FUTA Taxes Payable deposited for the quarter? .... _____

6. What is the amount of SUTA Taxes Payable for the fourth quarter? .... _____

Appendix B
Excel Template Instructions for the Glo-Brite Payroll Project

The Excel template for the payroll project is an electronic version of the books of account and payroll records. This is not an automated payroll system, but an example of how you might use a spreadsheet program to keep payroll records and account for payroll transactions.

You will need to follow the instructions in the textbook to complete the project. The instructions provided below will enable you to use the Excel template in place of the journal, general ledger, payroll register, and employee's earnings records. Other forms, such as tax forms, are required for the Payroll Project. You will use those provided in the book.

GETTING TO KNOW EXCEL

Excel files are called *workbooks*. A single workbook can store many worksheets, which are stored like pages in a notebook. The workbook for this project has four worksheets: the journal, the general ledger, the payroll register, and employee's earnings records.

Each worksheet is made up of rows and columns. Rows are numbered from 1 to 65,536, and columns are labeled with letters. Column 1 is A, Column 26 is Z, Column 27 is AA, and so on. The intersection of a row and column is called a *cell*. Cells have addresses based on the row and column in which they appear. Each cell can hold a number, text, a mathematical formula, or nothing at all. If you need to correct the data in a cell, simply enter the data as if the cell were empty.

The Excel Screen

This workbook has the look of a typical Excel screen. The first blue bar should say Microsoft Excel. The bar below that is the menu bar and is a typical Microsoft Windows menu bar. The next bar is the standard toolbar, which is very similar to that of Microsoft Word. (You can move the arrow to a particular icon, and the command to be issued will appear.) Below that is the formatting toolbar, which won't be used much in this project. The next bar has the name-box on the left, displaying the address of the active cell.

One of the cells in a worksheet is always the active cell. (The active cell is the one with a thicker border.) Its contents appear in the formula bar, which is to the right of the name-box, in the area next to the equals sign. Some of the cells in this workbook are locked or protected so that you cannot enter data. Others have their contents hidden. This was done intentionally when this template was created.

Navigation

You can navigate through a worksheet by using the arrow keys or Page Up and Page Down keys. This will change the active cell. Or you can use the scroll bars to the right and bottom of the screen and then click on the cell you want to activate.

You can also move to another cell by typing its address in the name-box. In this template, some cells have been named to make navigation easier. There is a drop-down list with cell names from which to choose.

You can switch from one worksheet to another within the same workbook by clicking on the appropriate tab at the bottom of the screen. For this project, there will be tabs labeled for the Journal, General Ledger, Payroll Register, and Employee's Earnings Records.

The Office Assistant

The Office Assistant is an interactive help tool, which can respond to natural language questions. To make the office assistant visible, click on the question mark icon in the standard toolbar.

Copy and Paste

Much of the work you do in this payroll project involves posting information from one place to another. You can accomplish this in Excel by using the copy and paste commands. (For this project, it is important that you use the Paste Special command, or else the format of the cell to hold the data will be changed.) Three ways to issue the copy and paste commands are:

1. Click on the cell you want to copy from, making it the active cell. Select Edit, Copy from the menu bar. This will highlight the active cell. Click on the cell you want to hold the copy. Select Edit, Paste Special, click on Values, and press OK. Press Esc to remove the highlighting.
2. Click on the cell you want to copy from, making it the highlighted active cell. Select the Copy icon from the standard toolbar. (This is the icon that looks like two pieces of paper.) This will highlight the active cell. Click on the cell you want to hold the copy. Select the Paste Special icon from the standard toolbar, click on Values, and press OK. Press Esc to remove the highlighting.
3. Right click on the cell you want to copy from, making it the highlighted active cell and bringing up a shortcut menu. Select Copy. Right click on the cell you want to hold the copy. Select Paste Special, click on Values, and press OK. Press Esc to remove the highlighting.

Copying and pasting can be done from one worksheet to another. For example, you will need to post from the journal to the ledger. After you have highlighted the cell you want to copy from, click on the tab of the worksheet you want to copy to, and then click on that particular cell.

Copy and paste can be done from one cell to another cell or a range of cells to another range of cells. To copy a range of cells, highlight the cells by clicking on one cell, and while holding the mouse button down, drag the pointer over the desired cells. These cells will be highlighted. Paste using the desired method described above. The range of cells that will be holding the copy must have the same number of cells as the range being copied.

Remember, for this worksheet, you should always use Paste Special, not just Paste.

Entering Formulas

A formula is a special type of cell entry that returns a result. When you enter a formula into a cell, the cell displays the result of the formula. The formula itself can be seen in the formula bar when the cell is activated.

A formula begins with an equals sign (=) and can consist of any of the following elements:

- Operators such as + (for addition), − (for subtraction), * (for multiplication), / (for division)
- Cell references, including cell addresses such as B52, as well as named cells and ranges
- Values and text
- Worksheet functions (such as SUM)

You can enter a formula into a cell manually (typing it in) or by pointing to the cells.
To enter a formula manually, follow these steps:

1. Move the cell pointer to the cell that you want to hold the formula.
2. Type an equals sign (=) to signal the fact that the cell contains a formula.
3. Type the formula, and press Enter.

As you type, the characters appear in the cell as well as in the formula bar. When you press Enter, the value resulting from the formula will show on the worksheet, but the formula itself will appear in the formula bar.

The following chart shows an example of four formulas. Values have been entered in the cells in Columns A and B. The formulas are entered in the cells in the C column. Notice, for example, that 9 appears in cell C1, but the formula that was entered in that cell is =A1+B1.

	A	B	C
1	6	3	9
2	6	3	3
3	6	3	18
4	6	3	2

Formulas as they appear in the formula bar for cells in Column C:
=A1+B1
=A2−B2
=A3*B3
=A4/B4

The best way to explain the pointing method is by giving an example. Suppose you want to subtract the value in cell B2 from the value in cell A2 and you want the result to appear in cell C2. To enter the formula **=A2−B2** in cell C2 by using the pointing method, follow these steps:

1. Make C2 the active cell by clicking on it.
2. Type an equals sign (=) to begin the formula.
3. Click on cell A2. This will highlight the cell.
4. Type a minus sign (−).
5. Click on cell B2.
6. Press enter to end the formula.

The value of the result will appear in cell C2 whether it is the active cell or not, but when C2 is active, you will see =A2−B2 in the formula bar.

This workbook has been formatted to round numbers to either the nearest whole number or the nearest cent. For example, $17.65 \times 1.5 = 26.475$. When that formula is entered into a cell in this workbook, the cell will display and hold the value 26.48, not 26.475. There is no need to use Excel's rounding function.

Saving Your Work

When you save a workbook, Excel overwrites the previous copy of your file. You can save your work at any point in time. You can save the file to the current name or you may want to keep multiple versions of your work by saving each successive version under a different name. To save to the current name, you can select File, Save from the menu bar or click on the disk icon in the standard toolbar. To save under a different name,

1. Select File, Save As to display the Save As dialog box.
2. Select the folder in which to store the workbook.

3.   Enter a new filename in the File <u>n</u>ame box.
4.   Click <u>S</u>ave.

This Excel Template

The four worksheets in this workbook have been created to look as much like their paper counterparts as possible. Some formulas have been created for you; others will have to be created by you.

Check-points have also been created for you so that you can check the accuracy of your work at certain points. These are light blue cells on the worksheets that have been set up to verify the data entered. A message is returned if the data entered is not correct for that check-point. For the check-points to work properly, DO NOT USE COPY AND PASTE. Validation DOES NOT occur if the user *pastes* invalid data. Validation can occur only when data is entered manually into the check-point cell.

Journal.   Record your journal in this Excel template just as you would on paper. To change pages, scroll down the worksheet. At the bottom of the journal pages is an equality check for total debits and credits. This area is highlighted in yellow. If your total debits in the journal do not equal your total credits, a warning message will appear in red.

Directly below that are the journal check-points. For easier navigation to the journal check-points, click on the drop-down list of the name-box and click on Journal_Check_points. Check-points are provided for the end of each month. After all journal entries have been made for the month, enter the amount of the total debits in the appropriate blue cell. Remember, DO NOT USE COPY AND PASTE. No indication is needed for debit or credit. A message will be returned only if the amount is not correct.

General Ledger.   Use the copy and paste special commands described above when posting amounts from the journal to the ledger. Each account in the ledger is listed in the drop-down list of the name-box to make navigation easier. For example, if you are working in the journal worksheet and want to go to the Cash account in the ledger, simply click on the down arrow of the name-box and select the CASH account. Excel will automatically move you from the journal worksheet to the Cash account in the general ledger worksheet. The ledger accounts names are all uppercase in the drop-down list.

The balance for each account must be calculated after posting each entry to the account. You can let Excel do the calculation for you by entering the appropriate formula. (See above for instructions.)

Check-points for each month are to the right of each account in the general ledger worksheet. Again, these cells are blue and are provided to verify the balance in each account at the end of each month. Since the balance for an account can be a debit or a credit, you must enter the data in the appropriate check-point cell. Remember, DO NOT USE COPY AND PASTE. A message will be returned only if the amount is not correct.

Payroll Register.   This worksheet is wider than an Excel screen and also has many column headings. When you scroll through a worksheet this size, it's very easy to get lost when the row or column headings scroll out of view. The payroll register in this template is set up so that row and column headings are "frozen." This enables them to remain visible as you scroll through the worksheet. The dark lines indicate the frozen rows and columns. There is no separate sheet for each payday, but rather a section for each payday on one worksheet.

The formulas for total earnings and net paid are already entered in this template. The formulas are also created for the Totals row for each payday.

Check-points are created for total earnings and net paid for each payday. These blue cells are to the right of the payroll register. The cell for the first set of check-points is listed as Payroll_Check_points in the drop-down list of the name-box. Remember, DO NOT USE COPY AND PASTE. A message will be returned only if the amount is not correct.

Employee's Earnings Record.   As in the other three worksheets, this one has been set up to look as much like the paper counterpart as possible. Blank Earnings Records are provided for employees who are hired during the time period covered by the payroll project.

To post amounts from the Payroll Register worksheet to the Employee's Earnings Records worksheet, use Copy and Paste Special as described above. Due to the difference in formats, you cannot copy and paste an entire row. The data for each payday will have to be copied in pieces. You can copy the range holding hours, rate and amount (regular and overtime) together, the range holding FICA (OASDI and HI) deductions together, and the range holding FIT, SIT, and CIT deductions together. The formulas for total earnings and net paid are already entered in this template.

There are check-points for the quarter and yearly totals of cumulative earnings and net paid for each employee. You will have to calculate these amounts. You can let Excel do the calculation for you by entering the appropriate formula. (See above for instructions.)

The check-points were created assuming that all Glo-Brite employees live in the state of Pennsylvania. If any other tax rates are used, the check-points are not valid.

As a final note, all pages and print areas have been defined but can be changed by the student. If you are not familiar with page setup and defining print areas, don't worry! It's been done for you. Simply push the printer icon on the standard toolbar and you're done! If you would like to print any of the worksheets in draft quality, select File, Page Setup, select the Sheet tab, and click on the box next to Draft quality, and then print as normal.

Appendix C
Social Security Benefits

AFTER STUDYING THIS APPENDIX, YOU SHOULD BE ABLE TO:

1. Explain the factors used in computing the various kinds of social security benefits:
   a.   Quarter of coverage
   b.   Fully insured
   c.   Currently insured
   d.   Average monthly wage
   e.   Primary insurance amount

2.   Describe the different kinds of benefits provided under the social security system.

3.   Describe the effect of working after retirement on social security benefits and taxation of benefits.

4.   Identify the procedure to be followed in applying for social security benefits.

5.   Explain the basic provisions of the three-part program of medical care for the aged and the needy.

This appendix covers the benefits related to the two programs of old-age, survivors and disability insurance, and health insurance for the aged and disabled. As the employees of a firm near retirement age, they may approach the payroll manager to find out what retirement benefits and hospital and medical benefits they are entitled to under social security. If workers become disabled or die, their families may turn to the payroll manager for information concerning their rights to disability or survivor benefits.

Social security benefits payable under the old-age, survivors, and disability program may be classified as:

1. Old-age or disability benefits paid to the worker.
2. Benefits for dependents of a retired or disabled worker.
3. Benefits for surviving family members of a deceased worker.
4. Lump-sum death benefits.

WHAT FACTORS ARE USED TO DETERMINE SOCIAL SECURITY BENEFITS?

LEARNING OBJECTIVE 1

Individuals and their families are eligible for most benefits if the person is "fully insured." If the person is only "currently insured," lump-sum benefits and certain survivor benefits are payable. Understanding the method of computing the various benefits for individuals, their dependents, or their survivors requires knowledge of the following terms:

1. Quarter of coverage.
2. Fully insured.
3. Currently insured.
4. Primary insurance amount.
5. Average monthly wage.

Quarter of Coverage

A *quarter of coverage* is the minimum amount of wages or self-employment income with which individuals must be credited in a calendar quarter to receive credit toward being insured for that period. A calendar quarter is three consecutive months ending March 31, June 30, September 30, or December 31. Quarters of coverage determine whether *workers* (see Figure C–1) are fully insured, currently insured, or insured for disability benefits.

Fully Insured Individual

A *fully insured* worker needs between six and 40 quarters of coverage. The number of quarters needed depends on when the person reaches a specified age or dies. After earning 40 quarters of coverage (10 years), the worker is fully insured for life and does not need to be concerned about quarters of coverage.

Currently Insured Individual

Individuals are *currently insured* if they have at least six quarters of coverage during the 13-quarter period ending with (1) the quarter they died or (2) the quarter in which they became entitled to old-age insurance benefits or disability benefits. The six quarters do not have to be consecutive. Lump-sum and certain survivor benefits, not including retirement benefits, are payable if an individual is currently insured.

Primary Insurance Amount

The *primary insurance amount (PIA)* is a person's monthly retirement or disability benefit and the base upon which monthly benefits of the worker's family and survivors are computed. Under the 1977 amendments to the Social Security Act, a formula determines the PIA of workers who reach 62, become disabled, or die. The PIA is determined from the worker's *average indexed monthly earnings. Indexing* adjusts the worker's average monthly earnings to reflect changes in wage levels up to the time of entitlement to benefits.

FIGURE C-1

Classification of Workers

Wage Earners	In 2002 workers receive one quarter of coverage, up to a maximum of four, for each $870 of earnings in the calendar year.
Self-Employed Persons	Net self-employment income must exceed $400 for the taxable year before any quarters can be credited with self-employment income. In 2002 a self-employed person is credited with one quarter of coverage for each calendar quarter in which $870 or more in self-employment income was allocated.
Farm Workers	Quarters of coverage are based on wages received during the calendar year, not during a calendar quarter. In 2002 farm workers receive one quarter of coverage, up to a maximum of four, for each $870 of earnings in the calendar year.

Automatic increases in social security benefits are also made, based on the increase in the cost of living as measured by the Consumer Price Index.

WHAT BENEFITS ARE PROVIDED BY SOCIAL SECURITY?

Figure C–2 summarizes the kinds of benefits available and the qualifications needed by the insured worker or beneficiary to receive these benefits.

2 LEARNING OBJECTIVE

Family Benefits

The monthly payments to members of a retired or a disabled worker's family and payments to the survivors of an insured worker are equal to a certain percentage of the worker's benefits, as shown in Figure C–3.

Benefits for Aliens

If an alien is receiving benefits as a dependent or a survivor of an insured worker and has been outside the United States for six consecutive months, the benefits will be suspended. Exceptions exist for young children and beneficiaries who lived in the United States for at least five years and had a relationship with the worker that established eligibility for benefits. Benefits continue where international social security agreements are in force.

Benefits for Prisoners

Persons confined in jail for a felony may not be paid benefits. Limited circumstances allow for benefits where the felon participates in an approved rehabilitation program. Benefits payable to a felon's spouse or children are not affected.

Benefits for the Self-Employed

Social security pays the same benefits to self-employed persons under the same conditions as wage earners and their dependents or survivors.

Benefits for Employees of Carriers

FICA exempts companies engaged as carriers and employees of carriers. The Railroad Retirement Tax Act sets up the provisions under which employees of carriers subject to the Interstate Commerce Act may retire and become eligible for annuities (benefits).

FIGURE C - 2

Old-Age or Disability Benefits

Person to Receive Benefits	Eligibility Requirements for Insured Individual
Retired worker, age 62 or older.	Fully insured
Disabled worker (except one who is blind) under 65.	Fully insured and insured for disability

Benefits for Dependents of Retired or Disabled Workers

Spouse, or divorced spouse, age 62 or older. Spouse, any age, if caring for child (except student age 18 or older) entitled to benefits. Unmarried child, grandchild, or great-grandchild if a. under age 18, b. under age 19 and a full-time elementary or secondary school student, or c. age 18 or older with a disability that began before age 22.	Fully insured for old-age benefits or insured for disability benefits, whichever applies

Survivor Benefits

Widow, widower, or divorced person, age 60 or older or age 50–59 and able to meet a special definition of disability. Widow, widower, or divorced parent of deceased worker's child, any age, caring for a young child entitled to benefits. Unmarried child, grandchild, or great-grandchild if child is a. under age 18, b. under age 19 and a full-time elementary or secondary school student, or c. age 18 or older with a disability that began before age 22. Dependent parents, age 62 or older.	Either fully insured or currently insured

Lump-Sum Death Payment ($255)

Paid only, in priority to a. worker's widow or widower living with worker at time of death, b. worker's widow or widower not living with but eligible on worker's earnings record, or	Either fully insured or currently insured

FIGURE C - 3

Relationship of Family Member to Worker	Percentage of Worker's Benefits to Be Received
Wife, husband, divorced wife or husband	50 percent while worker is alive.
Child	50 percent while worker is alive; 75 percent if worker is dead.
Widow, widower, or surviving divorced spouse	100 percent if full retirement age; 75 percent if caring for worker's child.
Dependent grandchild	50 percent if worker is alive; 75 percent if worker is dead; child's parents must be dead or disabled.
Dependent parent who outlives the worker	82½ percent; if both parents qualify, a total of 150 percent is received.

Special Minimum Benefit

Special provision is made for persons who have worked in jobs covered by social security for many years but at rather low earnings levels. These workers qualify for a special benefit higher than that available to them under the regular benefit computations. The special benefits payable under these provisions will be automatically adjusted for cost-of-living increases.

Benefit Amounts

In 2002, the average monthly Social Security benefit for a retired worker was $874; for couples each receiving benefits, $1,454; for disabled workers, $815; and, for widows or widowers alone, $841. The maximum benefit for an individual worker retiring at age 65 in 2002 was $1,660 per month.

WHAT ARE REDUCED BENEFITS?

The full retirement age was increased, starting in the year 2000, in gradual steps until it reaches age 67, and affects people born in 1938 and later. Figure C–4 shows the age to receive full social security benefits.

If a worker takes early retirement at age 62 (the earliest age to qualify), the benefits will be permanently reduced approximately 20 percent, based on the number of months the individual will receive checks before reaching full retirement age. If retirement starts at age 63, the reduction is about 13⅓ percent; at age 64, it is about 6⅔ percent. If you were born after 1937, you can still take your retirement benefits at age 62, but the reduction will be greater than people currently retiring. Eligible widows or widowers may receive reduced benefits as early as age 60. If the worker at any time received a reduced benefit, the widow or widower may not receive more than the greater of:

a. a benefit equal to the amount the worker would be getting if alive, or
b. 82.5 percent of the worker's PIA.

For widows or widowers whose spouse was not receiving a reduced benefit, the age-60 benefit will be 71.5 percent of the worker's PIA. If the widow or widower takes the benefit at age 62, it will be 82.9 percent of the worker's PIA. Severely disabled widows or widowers and surviving divorced spouses may receive reduced benefits at age 50, equal to 71.5 percent of the worker's unreduced benefit.

IRS CONNECTION

Beneficiaries who owe federal taxes from earlier years may have their social security payments reduced by 15 percent. Under the federal payment levy program, the reduction will continue until the tax bill is paid in full.

News ALERT

Six thousand people a day reach age 65. Today, 37 million Americans (13 percent of the population) are 65 or older—an increase of 12 million from 1980.

News ALERT

In 1945, 42 workers paid social security taxes for every beneficiary; today the ratio is 3.3 to 1. The ratio is projected to be 2 to 1 by the year 2030.

FIGURE C-4

Year of Birth	Full Retirement Age
1937 or earlier	65
1938	65 and 2 months
1939	65 and 4 months
1940	65 and 6 months
1941	65 and 8 months
1942	65 and 10 months
1943–1954	66
1955	66 and 2 months
1956	66 and 4 months
1957	66 and 6 months
1958	66 and 8 months
1959	66 and 10 months
1960 or later	67

HOW DOES WORKING AFTER RETIREMENT AFFECT SOCIAL SECURITY BENEFITS?

LEARNING OBJECTIVE 3

Under the rules, an individual's benefit is increased by a certain percentage each year that retirement is delayed past age 65. Based on the recipient's year of birth, the credit ranges from 1.0 percent to 8.0 percent per extra year worked. However, there is no increase for years worked past age 70. Individuals who continue to work after retirement must also consider two other implications to their social security benefits:

1. Reduced social security benefits (under 65).
2. Paying income tax on social security benefits.

Reduced Social Security Benefits

Individuals can continue to work and still receive retirement benefits if the earnings are under certain limits. These limits increase each year as average wages increase. The Social Security Administration provides a fact sheet, *How Work Affects Your Social Security Benefits (Pub. 05-10069),* that specifies the current amounts that may be earned without reducing benefits. For 2002, the following limits apply:

Under 65	$11,280
65 and over	Unlimited

If earnings exceed the specified limit, some or all of the benefits will be offset by the earnings, as summarized in Figure C–5.

Under a special rule, a retired worker can receive full benefits for any month they are "retired," regardless of their yearly earnings. In the first year of retirement, benefits will not be lost for any month in which earnings are less than $940 (under 65).

Request for Earnings and Benefit Estimate Statement. Each employee who has received taxable wages under the Social Security Act has an account with the SSA. This account shows the amount of wages credited to the employee's account. When employees or their dependents claim benefits, the wage credits in the employee's account are used to compute the amount of benefits payable, as discussed in Appendix B. Employees can use *Form SSA-7004* (not illustrated) to request a statement of wages credited to their account. The worker will receive a statement showing the yearly earnings, the social security taxes paid each year, and a projection of the benefits the worker or the survivors will receive if the worker retires, dies, or is disabled. If workers find any discrepancies between their records and the accounts kept by the SSA, claims can be made for adjustment. Errors will be corrected if they are reported within 3 years, 3 months, and 15 days following the close of the particular taxable year.

Taxable Benefits

A portion of a worker's social security benefits is included in taxable income for federal income tax purposes. The amount of benefits taxable is determined by a formula that relates to the worker's adjusted gross income (AGI). If income is more than the base

FIGURE C-5

Reduced Social Security Benefits

If you are under 65	$1 in benefits is deducted for each $2 in earnings above the limit.
If you are 65	Earnings in or after the month you reach 65 will not affect benefits.

amount, as much as 50 percent of social security benefits may be taxable (see Figure C–6). If an individual receives only social security benefits as income, these benefits are generally not taxable.

HOW DO YOU APPLY FOR SOCIAL SECURITY BENEFITS?

Workers can apply for social security benefits by telephone or by going to any social security office. Depending on the circumstances, documents that may be needed include:

4 LEARNING OBJECTIVE

1. Social security number (SSN).
2. Birth certificate.
3. W-2 forms or self-employment tax return for last year.
4. Military discharge papers.
5. Spouse's birth certificate and social security number.
6. Children's birth certificates and social security numbers.

Special application forms may be obtained from the nearest district office of the Social Security Administration. Applicants can receive assistance in preparing the forms, including notary services, at no charge.

Proof of Age

Applicants for benefits may be required to file a proof of age showing the date of birth. Acceptable records may include:

1. Public records of birth (birth certificate).
2. Church records of birth or baptism established or recorded before the age of five.
3. Census Bureau notification of registration of birth.
4. Hospital birth record or certificate.
5. Foreign records of birth.
6. Physician's or midwife's birth record.
7. Certification, on approved form, of Bible or other family record.
8. Naturalization records.
9. Immigration papers.
10. Military records.
11. Passports.
12. School records.
13. Vaccination records.
14. Insurance policy.
15. Labor union or fraternal organization records.
16. Marriage records.
17. Other evidence of probative value, such as employment records and voting records.

Beginning in October 1999, the SSA began sending Personal Earnings and Benefits Estimates to all persons aged 25 years and older. These statements show the workers' year-by-year social security earnings.

FIGURE C-6

Taxable	Single	Joint
No Tax	$30,000* or less	$32,000* or less
50% of Benefits Taxable	over $30,000*	over $32,000*

*Worker's other income plus one-half of benefits

Workers who continue to work after collecting social security benefits are still subject to social security taxes on their wages.

Statement of Employer

The individual's wage record kept by the Social Security Administration may be several months in arrears. Therefore, employers may be requested to complete a *Statement of Employer, Form SSA-7011-F4,* in order to bring an individual's wage record up to date. Employees may periodically check their social security accounts, using *Form SSA-7004-SM.*

WHAT IS MEDICARE?

 **LEARNING OBJECTIVE**

Medicare is a three-part health insurance plan for people 65 or older. The first program, sometimes called Basic Medicare, Part A Medicare, or the ***hospital insurance (HI) plan,*** provides protections against the cost of certain hospital and related services. The second program, the ***supplementary medical insurance plan,*** often referred to as supplementary, voluntary supplementary Medicare, the medical insurance program, or Part B Medicare, covers the cost of doctors' services and other items not covered under the basic plan. Monthly premiums are matched with contributions by the federal government to finance the program. The third program, called ***Medicaid,*** provides medical assistance to aged and needy persons by means of a joint federal-state program.

KEY TERMS

Average indexed monthly earnings *(p. C-2)*
Currently insured *(p. C-2)*
Fully insured *(p. C-2)*
Hospital insurance (HI) plan *(p. C-8)*
Indexing *(p. C-2)*

Medicaid *(p. C-8)*
Primary insurance amount (PIA) *(p. C-2)*
Quarter of coverage *(p. C-2)*
Social security benefits *(p. C-2)*
Supplementary medical insurance plan *(p. C-8)*

TAX TABLE
A

TABLE OF ALLOWANCE VALUES

Payroll period	One withholding allowance
Weekly	$ 57.69
Biweekly	115.38
Semimonthly	125.00
Monthly	250.00
Quarterly	750.00
Semiannually	1,500.00
Annually	3,000.00
Daily or miscellaneous (each day of the payroll period)	11.54

Tables for Percentage Method of Withholding
(For Wages Paid in 2002)

TABLE 1—WEEKLY Payroll Period

(a) SINGLE person (including head of household)—

If the amount of wages (after subtracting withholding allowances) is:

The amount of income tax to withhold is:

Not over $51 . . . . . $0

Over—	But not over—		of excess over—
$51	—$164	. . 10%	—$51
$164	—$570	. $11.30 plus 15%	—$164
$570	—$1,247	. $72.20 plus 27%	—$570
$1,247	—$2,749	. $254.99 plus 30%	—$1,247
$2,749	—$5,938	. $705.59 plus 35%	—$2,749
$5,938	. . . . .	$1,821.74 plus 38.6%	—$5,938

(b) MARRIED person—

If the amount of wages (after subtracting withholding allowances) is:

The amount of income tax to withhold is:

Not over $124 . . . . $0

Over—	But not over—		of excess over—
$124	—$355	. 10%	—$124
$355	—$991	. $23.10 plus 15%	—$355
$991	—$2,110	. $118.50 plus 27%	—$991
$2,110	—$3,400	. $420.63 plus 30%	—$2,110
$3,400	—$5,998	. $807.63 plus 35%	—$3,400
$5,998	. . . . .	$1,716.93 plus 38.6%	—$5,998

TABLE 2—BIWEEKLY Payroll Period

(a) SINGLE person (including head of household)—

If the amount of wages (after subtracting withholding allowances) is:

The amount of income tax to withhold is:

Not over $102 . . . . $0

Over—	But not over—		of excess over—
$102	—$329	10%	—$102
$329	—$1,140	$22.70 plus 15%	—$329
$1,140	—$2,493	$144.35 plus 27%	—$1,140
$2,493	—$5,498	$509.66 plus 30%	—$2,493
$5,498	—$11,875	$1,411.16 plus 35%	—$5,498
$11,875	. . . . .	$3,643.11 plus 38.6%	—$11,875

(b) MARRIED person—

If the amount of wages (after subtracting withholding allowances) is:

The amount of income tax to withhold is:

Not over $248 . . . . $0

Over—	But not over—		of excess over—
$248	—$710	10%	—$248
$710	—$1,983	$46.20 plus 15%	—$710
$1,983	—$4,219	$237.15 plus 27%	—$1,983
$4,219	—$6,800	$840.87 plus 30%	—$4,219
$6,800	—$11,996	$1,615.17 plus 35%	—$6,800
$11,996	. . . . .	$3,433.77 plus 38.6%	—$11,996

TABLE 3—SEMIMONTHLY Payroll Period

(a) SINGLE person (including head of household)—

If the amount of wages (after subtracting withholding allowances) is:

The amount of income tax to withhold is:

Not over $110 . . . . $0

Over—	But not over—		of excess over—
$110	—$356	. 10%	—$110
$356	—$1,235	. $24.60 plus 15%	—$356
$1,235	—$2,701	. $156.45 plus 27%	—$1,235
$2,701	—$5,956	. $552.27 plus 30%	—$2,701
$5,956	—$12,865	. $1,528.77 plus 35%	—$5,956
$12,865	. . . . .	$3,946.92 plus 38.6%	—$12,865

(b) MARRIED person—

If the amount of wages (after subtracting withholding allowances) is:

The amount of income tax to withhold is:

Not over $269 . . . . $0

Over—	But not over—		of excess over—
$269	—$769	. 10%	—$269
$769	—$2,148	. $50.00 plus 15%	—$769
$2,148	—$4,571	. $256.85 plus 27%	—$2,148
$4,571	—$7,367	. $911.06 plus 30%	—$4,571
$7,367	—$12,996	. $1,749.86 plus 35%	—$7,367
$12,996	. . . . .	$3,720.01 plus 38.6%	—$12,996

TABLE 4—MONTHLY Payroll Period

(a) SINGLE person (including head of household)—

If the amount of wages (after subtracting withholding allowances) is:

The amount of income tax to withhold is:

Not over $221 . . . . $0

Over—	But not over—		of excess over—
$221	—$713	. 10%	—$221
$713	—$2,471	. $49.20 plus 15%	—$713
$2,471	—$5,402	. $312.90 plus 27%	—$2,471
$5,402	—$11,913	. $1,104.27 plus 30%	—$5,402
$11,913	—$25,729	. $3,057.57 plus 35%	—$11,913
$25,729	. . . . .	$7,893.17 plus 38.6%	—$25,729

(b) MARRIED person—

If the amount of wages (after subtracting withholding allowances) is:

The amount of income tax to withhold is:

Not over $538 . . . . $0

Over—	But not over—		of excess over—
$538	—$1,538	. 10%	—$538
$1,538	—$4,296	. $100.00 plus 15%	—$1,538
$4,296	—$9,142	. $513.70 plus 27%	—$4,296
$9,142	—$14,733	. $1,822.12 plus 30%	—$9,142
$14,733	—$25,992	. $3,499.42 plus 35%	—$14,733
$25,992	. . . . .	$7,440.07 plus 38.6%	—$25,992

Tables for Percentage Method of Withholding (Continued)
(For Wages Paid in 2002)

TABLE 5—QUARTERLY Payroll Period

(a) SINGLE person (including head of household)—

If the amount of wages (after subtracting withholding allowances) is:

Not over $663 . . . . $0

Over—	But not over—		of excess over—
$663	—$2,138	10%	—$663
$2,138	—$7,413	$147.50 plus 15%	—$2,138
$7,413	—$16,205	$938.75 plus 27%	—$7,413
$16,205	—$35,738	$3,312.59 plus 30%	—$16,205
$35,738	—$77,188	$9,172.49 plus 35%	—$35,738
$77,188	. . . . .	$23,679.99 plus 38.6%	—$77,188

(b) MARRIED person—

If the amount of wages (after subtracting withholding allowances) is:

Not over $1,613 . . . . $0

Over—	But not over—		of excess over—
$1,613	—$4,613	10%	—$1,613
$4,613	—$12,888	$300.00 plus 15%	—$4,613
$12,888	—$27,425	$1,541.25 plus 27%	—$12,888
$27,425	—$44,200	$5,466.24 plus 30%	—$27,425
$44,200	—$77,975	$10,498.74 plus 35%	—$44,200
$77,975	. . . . .	$22,319.99 plus 38.6%	—$77,975

TABLE 6—SEMIANNUAL Payroll Period

(a) SINGLE person (including head of household)—

If the amount of wages (after subtracting withholding allowances) is:

Not over $1,325 . . . . $0

Over—	But not over—		of excess over—
$1,325	—$4,275	10%	—$1,325
$4,275	—$14,825	$295.00 plus 15%	—$4,275
$14,825	—$32,410	$1,877.50 plus 27%	—$14,825
$32,410	—$71,475	$6,625.45 plus 30%	—$32,410
$71,475	—$154,375	$18,344.95 plus 35%	—$71,475
$154,375	. . . . .	$47,359.95 plus 38.6%	—$154,375

(b) MARRIED person—

If the amount of wages (after subtracting withholding allowances) is:

Not over $3,225 . . . . $0

Over—	But not over—		of excess over—
$3,225	—$9,225	10%	—$3,225
$9,225	—$25,775	$600.00 plus 15%	—$9,225
$25,775	—$54,850	$3,082.50 plus 27%	—$25,775
$54,850	—$88,400	$10,932.75 plus 30%	—$54,850
$88,400	—$155,950	$20,997.75 plus 35%	—$88,400
$155,950	. . . . .	$44,640.25 plus 38.6%	—$155,950

TABLE 7—ANNUAL Payroll Period

(a) SINGLE person (including head of household)—

If the amount of wages (after subtracting withholding allowances) is:

Not over $2,650 . . . . $0

Over—	But not over—		of excess over—
$2,650	—$8,550	10%	—$2,650
$8,550	—$29,650	$590.00 plus 15%	—$8,550
$29,650	—$64,820	$3,755.00 plus 27%	—$29,650
$64,820	—$142,950	$13,250.90 plus 30%	—$64,820
$142,950	—$308,750	$36,689.90 plus 35%	—$142,950
$308,750	. . . . .	$94,719.90 plus 38.6%	—$308,750

(b) MARRIED person—

If the amount of wages (after subtracting withholding allowances) is:

Not over $6,450 . . . . $0

Over—	But not over—		of excess over—
$6,450	—$18,450	10%	—$6,450
$18,450	—$51,550	$1,200.00 plus 15%	—$18,450
$51,550	—$109,700	$6,165.00 plus 27%	—$51,550
$109,700	—$176,800	$21,865.50 plus 30%	—$109,700
$176,800	—$311,900	$41,995.50 plus 35%	—$176,800
$311,900	. . . . .	$89,280.50 plus 38.6%	—$311,900

TABLE 8—DAILY or MISCELLANEOUS Payroll Period

(a) SINGLE person (including head of household)—

If the amount of wages (after subtracting withholding allowances) divided by the number of days in the payroll period is:

Not over $10.20 . . . . $0

Over—	But not over—		of excess over—
$10.20	—$32.90	10%	—$10.20
$32.90	—$114.00	$2.27 plus 15%	—$32.90
$114.00	—$249.30	$14.44 plus 27%	—$114.00
$249.30	—$549.80	$50.97 plus 30%	—$249.30
$549.80	—$1,187.50	$141.12 plus 35%	—$549.80
$1,187.50	. . . . .	$364.32 plus 38.6%	—$1,187.50

(b) MARRIED person—

If the amount of wages (after subtracting withholding allowances) divided by the number of days in the payroll period is:

Not over $24.80 . . . . $0

Over—	But not over—		of excess over—
$24.80	—$71.00	10%	—$24.80
$71.00	—$198.30	$4.62 plus 15%	—$71.00
$198.30	—$421.90	$23.72 plus 27%	—$198.30
$421.90	—$680.00	$84.09 plus 30%	—$421.90
$680.00	—$1,199.60	$161.52 plus 35%	—$680.00
$1,199.60	. . . . .	$343.38 plus 38.6%	—$1,199.60

TAX TABLE
B

WAGE-BRACKET WITHHOLDING TABLES

SINGLE Persons—WEEKLY Payroll Period
(For Wages Paid in 2002)

If the wages are— At least	But less than	\[allowances\] 0	1	2	3	4	5	6	7	8	9	10
		The amount of income tax to be withheld is—										
$0	$55	$0	$0	$0	$0	$0	$0	$0	$0	$0	$0	$0
55	60	1	0	0	0	0	0	0	0	0	0	0
60	65	1	0	0	0	0	0	0	0	0	0	0
65	70	2	0	0	0	0	0	0	0	0	0	0
70	75	2	0	0	0	0	0	0	0	0	0	0
75	80	3	0	0	0	0	0	0	0	0	0	0
80	85	3	0	0	0	0	0	0	0	0	0	0
85	90	4	0	0	0	0	0	0	0	0	0	0
90	95	4	0	0	0	0	0	0	0	0	0	0
95	100	5	0	0	0	0	0	0	0	0	0	0
100	105	5	0	0	0	0	0	0	0	0	0	0
105	110	6	0	0	0	0	0	0	0	0	0	0
110	115	6	0	0	0	0	0	0	0	0	0	0
115	120	7	0	0	0	0	0	0	0	0	0	0
120	125	7	0	0	0	0	0	0	0	0	0	0
125	130	8	2	0	0	0	0	0	0	0	0	0
130	135	8	2	0	0	0	0	0	0	0	0	0
135	140	9	3	0	0	0	0	0	0	0	0	0
140	145	9	3	0	0	0	0	0	0	0	0	0
145	150	10	4	0	0	0	0	0	0	0	0	0
150	155	10	4	0	0	0	0	0	0	0	0	0
155	160	11	5	0	0	0	0	0	0	0	0	0
160	165	11	5	0	0	0	0	0	0	0	0	0
165	170	12	6	0	0	0	0	0	0	0	0	0
170	175	12	6	1	0	0	0	0	0	0	0	0
175	180	13	7	1	0	0	0	0	0	0	0	0
180	185	13	7	2	0	0	0	0	0	0	0	0
185	190	14	8	2	0	0	0	0	0	0	0	0
190	195	14	8	3	0	0	0	0	0	0	0	0
195	200	15	9	3	0	0	0	0	0	0	0	0
200	210	16	10	4	0	0	0	0	0	0	0	0
210	220	17	11	5	0	0	0	0	0	0	0	0
220	230	18	12	6	1	0	0	0	0	0	0	0
230	240	19	13	7	2	0	0	0	0	0	0	0
240	250	20	14	8	3	0	0	0	0	0	0	0
250	260	21	15	9	4	0	0	0	0	0	0	0
260	270	22	16	10	5	0	0	0	0	0	0	0
270	280	23	17	11	6	0	0	0	0	0	0	0
280	290	24	18	12	7	1	0	0	0	0	0	0
290	300	25	19	13	8	2	0	0	0	0	0	0
300	310	26	20	14	9	3	0	0	0	0	0	0
310	320	28	21	15	10	4	0	0	0	0	0	0
320	330	29	22	16	11	5	0	0	0	0	0	0
330	340	31	23	17	12	6	1	0	0	0	0	0
340	350	32	24	18	13	7	2	0	0	0	0	0
350	360	34	25	20	14	8	3	0	0	0	0	0
360	370	35	27	21	15	9	4	0	0	0	0	0
370	380	37	28	22	16	10	5	0	0	0	0	0
380	390	38	30	23	17	11	6	0	0	0	0	0
390	400	40	31	24	18	12	7	1	0	0	0	0
400	410	41	33	26	19	13	8	2	0	0	0	0
410	420	43	34	27	20	14	9	3	0	0	0	0
420	430	44	36	28	21	15	10	4	0	0	0	0
430	440	46	37	30	22	16	11	5	0	0	0	0
440	450	47	39	31	23	17	12	6	0	0	0	0
450	460	49	40	33	24	18	13	7	1	0	0	0
460	470	50	42	34	26	19	14	8	2	0	0	0
470	480	52	43	36	27	20	15	9	3	0	0	0
480	490	53	45	37	29	21	16	10	4	0	0	0
490	500	55	46	39	30	22	17	11	5	0	0	0
500	510	56	48	40	32	25	18	12	6	0	0	0
510	520	58	49	42	33	26	19	13	7	1	0	0
520	530	59	51	43	35	27	20	14	8	2	0	0
530	540	61	52	45	36	29	21	15	9	3	0	0
540	550	62	54	46	38	30	23	16	10	4	0	0
550	560	64	55	48	39	32	24	17	11	5	0	0
560	570	65	57	49	41	33	25	18	12	6	0	0
570	580	67	58	51	42	35	27	20	13	7	1	0
580	590	68	60	52	44	36	28	21	14	8	2	0
590	600	70	61	54	45	38	30	22	15	9	2	0

SINGLE Persons—WEEKLY Payroll Period
(For Wages Paid in 2002)

If the wages are— At least	But less than	\[allowances\] 0	1	2	3	4	5	6	7	8	9	10
		The amount of income tax to be withheld is—										
$600	$610	$82	$69	$60	$51	$43	$34	$26	$17	$9	$3	$0
610	620	84	72	62	53	44	36	27	18	10	4	0
620	630	87	73	63	54	46	37	29	20	11	5	1
630	640	90	74	65	56	47	39	30	21	13	6	1
640	650	92	77	66	57	49	40	32	23	14	7	2
650	660	95	80	68	59	50	42	33	24	16	8	3
660	670	98	82	69	60	52	43	35	26	17	9	4
670	680	101	85	71	62	53	45	36	27	19	10	5
680	690	103	88	73	63	55	46	38	29	20	12	6
690	700	106	90	75	65	56	48	39	30	22	13	7
700	710	109	93	77	66	58	49	41	32	23	15	8
710	720	111	96	80	68	59	51	42	33	25	16	9
720	730	114	98	83	69	61	52	44	35	26	18	10
730	740	117	101	86	71	62	54	45	37	28	19	11
740	750	119	104	88	73	64	55	47	38	29	21	12
750	760	122	107	91	75	65	57	48	39	31	22	13
760	770	125	109	94	78	67	58	50	41	32	24	15
770	780	128	112	96	81	68	60	51	42	34	25	16
780	790	130	115	99	83	70	61	53	44	35	27	18
790	800	133	117	102	86	71	63	54	45	37	28	19
800	810	136	120	104	89	73	64	56	47	38	30	21
810	820	138	123	107	92	76	66	57	48	40	31	22
820	830	141	126	110	94	79	67	59	50	41	33	23
830	840	144	128	113	97	81	69	60	51	43	34	25
840	850	146	131	115	100	84	70	62	53	44	36	26
850	860	149	134	118	102	87	72	63	54	46	37	28
860	870	152	136	121	105	90	74	65	56	47	39	30
870	880	155	139	123	108	92	77	66	57	49	40	31
880	890	157	141	126	110	95	79	68	59	50	42	33
890	900	160	144	129	113	98	82	69	60	52	43	34
900	910	163	147	131	116	100	85	71	62	53	45	36
910	920	165	150	134	118	103	87	72	63	55	46	37
920	930	168	152	137	121	105	90	75	65	56	48	39
930	940	171	155	140	124	108	93	77	66	58	49	40
940	950	173	158	142	127	110	95	80	68	59	51	42
950	960	176	161	145	129	114	98	83	69	61	52	43
960	970	179	163	148	132	117	101	85	71	62	54	45
970	980	182	166	151	135	119	104	88	73	64	55	46
980	990	184	169	153	138	122	107	91	76	65	57	48
990	1,000	187	171	156	140	125	109	94	78	67	58	49
1,000	1,010	190	174	159	143	127	112	96	81	68	60	51
1,010	1,020	192	177	161	146	130	114	99	83	70	61	52
1,020	1,030	195	180	164	148	133	117	102	86	71	63	54
1,030	1,040	198	182	167	151	136	120	104	89	76	64	55
1,040	1,050	200	185	169	154	138	123	107	91	78	66	57
1,050	1,060	203	188	172	156	141	125	110	94	81	67	58
1,060	1,070	206	190	175	159	146	128	113	97	84	69	60
1,070	1,080	209	193	177	162	149	131	118	100	87	72	61
1,080	1,090	211	196	180	164	151	133	120	102	89	74	63
1,090	1,100	214	198	183	167	154	136	123	105	92	76	64
1,100	1,110	217	201	185	170	157	139	126	108	95	79	66
1,110	1,120	219	204	188	173	160	141	131	110	97	82	67
1,120	1,130	222	206	191	175	162	144	134	113	100	85	69
1,130	1,140	225	209	194	178	165	147	137	116	103	87	72
1,140	1,150	227	212	196	181	169	150	139	118	105	90	74
1,150	1,160	230	215	199	183	168	152	142	121	108	93	76
1,160	1,170	233	217	202	186	171	155	145	124	111	95	80
1,170	1,180	236	220	204	189	173	158	147	126	114	98	85
1,180	1,190	238	223	207	191	176	160	150	129	116	101	87
1,190	1,200	241	225	210	194	179	163	153	132	119	103	82
1,200	1,210	244	228	212	197	181	166	150	135	122	106	88
1,210	1,220	246	230	215	200	184	168	153	137	124	109	91
1,220	1,230	249	233	218	203	187	171	156	140	127	112	93
1,230	1,240	252	236	221	205	189	174	158	143	129	114	96
1,240	1,250	254	239	223	208	192	177	161	145	130	114	99

$1,250 and over   Use Table 1(a) for a **SINGLE** person on page T-3.

WAGE-BRACKET WITHHOLDING TABLES

MARRIED Persons—WEEKLY Payroll Period
(For Wages Paid in 2002)

If the wages are—		And the number of withholding allowances claimed is—										
At least	But less than	0	1	2	3	4	5	6	7	8	9	10
		The amount of income tax to be withheld is—										
$750	$760	$83	$74	$66	$57	$48	$40	$31	$23	$17	$11	$5
760	770	85	76	67	59	50	41	33	24	18	12	6
770	780	86	77	69	60	51	43	34	26	19	13	7
780	790	88	79	70	62	53	44	36	27	20	14	8
790	800	89	80	72	63	54	46	37	29	21	15	9
800	810	91	82	73	65	56	47	39	30	22	16	10
810	820	92	83	75	66	57	49	40	32	23	17	11
820	830	94	85	76	68	59	50	42	33	25	18	12
830	840	95	86	78	69	60	52	43	35	26	19	13
840	850	97	88	79	71	62	53	45	36	27	21	14
850	860	98	89	81	72	63	55	46	38	29	22	15
860	870	100	91	82	74	65	56	48	39	30	23	16
870	880	101	92	84	75	66	58	49	41	32	24	17
880	890	103	94	85	77	68	59	51	42	33	25	18
890	900	104	95	87	78	69	61	52	44	35	26	19
900	910	106	97	88	80	71	62	54	45	36	28	20
910	920	107	98	90	81	72	64	55	47	38	29	21
920	930	109	100	91	83	74	65	57	48	39	31	22
930	940	110	101	93	84	75	67	58	50	41	32	23
940	950	112	103	94	86	77	68	60	51	42	34	25
950	960	113	104	96	87	78	70	61	53	44	35	26
960	970	115	106	97	89	80	71	63	54	45	37	28
970	980	116	107	99	90	81	73	64	56	47	38	29
980	990	118	109	100	92	83	74	66	57	48	40	31
990	1,000	120	110	102	93	84	76	67	59	50	41	33
1,000	1,010	122	112	103	95	86	77	69	60	51	43	34
1,010	1,020	125	113	105	96	87	79	70	62	53	44	36
1,020	1,030	128	116	106	98	89	80	72	63	55	45	37
1,030	1,040	130	118	108	99	90	82	73	65	56	47	39
1,040	1,050	133	120	109	101	92	83	75	66	57	48	40
1,050	1,060	136	120	111	102	93	85	76	68	59	50	42
1,060	1,070	138	123	112	104	95	86	78	69	60	52	43
1,070	1,080	141	126	114	105	96	88	79	71	62	53	45
1,080	1,090	144	128	116	107	98	89	81	72	63	55	46
1,090	1,100	147	131	117	108	99	91	82	74	65	56	48
1,100	1,110	149	134	120	110	101	92	84	75	66	58	49
1,110	1,120	152	136	121	112	102	94	85	77	68	59	51
1,120	1,130	155	139	123	113	104	95	87	78	69	61	52
1,130	1,140	157	142	126	114	105	97	88	80	71	62	54
1,140	1,150	160	144	129	116	107	98	90	81	72	64	55
1,150	1,160	163	147	132	117	108	100	91	83	74	65	57
1,160	1,170	165	150	134	119	110	101	93	84	76	67	58
1,170	1,180	168	153	137	121	111	103	94	86	77	68	60
1,180	1,190	171	155	140	123	113	104	96	87	78	70	61
1,190	1,200	174	158	142	127	114	106	97	89	80	71	63
1,200	1,210	176	161	145	130	116	107	99	90	81	73	64
1,210	1,220	179	163	148	132	117	109	100	92	83	74	66
1,220	1,230	182	166	150	135	119	110	102	93	84	76	67
1,230	1,240	184	169	153	138	122	112	103	95	86	77	69
1,240	1,250	187	171	156	140	125	113	105	96	87	79	70
1,250	1,260	190	174	159	143	127	115	106	98	89	80	72
1,260	1,270	192	177	161	146	130	117	108	99	90	82	73
1,270	1,280	195	180	164	148	133	118	109	101	92	83	75
1,280	1,290	198	182	167	151	136	120	111	102	93	85	76
1,290	1,300	201	185	169	154	138	123	112	104	95	86	78
1,300	1,310	203	188	172	157	141	125	114	105	96	88	79
1,310	1,320	206	190	175	159	144	128	115	107	98	89	81
1,320	1,330	209	193	177	162	146	131	116	108	99	91	82
1,330	1,340	211	196	180	165	149	133	118	110	101	92	84
1,340	1,350	214	198	183	167	152	136	121	111	102	94	85
1,350	1,360	217	201	185	170	154	139	123	113	104	95	87
1,360	1,370	219	204	188	173	157	142	126	115	105	97	88
1,370	1,380	222	207	191	175	160	144	129	116	107	98	89
1,380	1,390	225	209	194	178	163	147	131	118	108	100	91
1,390	1,400	228	212	196	181	165	150	134	119	110	101	93

$1,400 and over — Use Table 1(b) for a MARRIED person on page T-3.

MARRIED Persons—WEEKLY Payroll Period
(For Wages Paid in 2002)

WEEKLY MARRIED PERSONS

If the wages are—		And the number of withholding allowances claimed is—										
At least	But less than	0	1	2	3	4	5	6	7	8	9	10
		The amount of income tax to be withheld is—										
$0	$130	$0	$0	$0	$0	$0	$0	$0	$0	$0	$0	$0
130	135	1	0	0	0	0	0	0	0	0	0	0
135	140	1	0	0	0	0	0	0	0	0	0	0
140	145	2	0	0	0	0	0	0	0	0	0	0
145	150	2	0	0	0	0	0	0	0	0	0	0
150	155	3	0	0	0	0	0	0	0	0	0	0
155	160	3	0	0	0	0	0	0	0	0	0	0
160	165	4	0	0	0	0	0	0	0	0	0	0
165	170	4	1	0	0	0	0	0	0	0	0	0
170	175	5	1	0	0	0	0	0	0	0	0	0
175	180	5	1	0	0	0	0	0	0	0	0	0
180	185	6	2	0	0	0	0	0	0	0	0	0
185	190	6	2	0	0	0	0	0	0	0	0	0
190	195	7	3	0	0	0	0	0	0	0	0	0
195	200	7	3	0	0	0	0	0	0	0	0	0
200	210	8	4	0	0	0	0	0	0	0	0	0
210	220	9	4	1	0	0	0	0	0	0	0	0
220	230	10	5	1	0	0	0	0	0	0	0	0
230	240	11	6	2	0	0	0	0	0	0	0	0
240	250	12	6	2	0	0	0	0	0	0	0	0
250	260	13	7	3	0	0	0	0	0	0	0	0
260	270	14	8	4	0	0	0	0	0	0	0	0
270	280	15	9	4	1	0	0	0	0	0	0	0
280	290	16	10	5	1	0	0	0	0	0	0	0
290	300	17	11	6	2	0	0	0	0	0	0	0
300	310	18	12	7	2	0	0	0	0	0	0	0
310	320	19	13	8	3	0	0	0	0	0	0	0
320	330	20	14	9	4	0	0	0	0	0	0	0
330	340	21	15	10	4	1	0	0	0	0	0	0
340	350	22	16	11	5	1	0	0	0	0	0	0
350	360	23	17	12	6	2	0	0	0	0	0	0
360	370	24	18	13	7	2	0	0	0	0	0	0
370	380	26	19	14	8	3	0	0	0	0	0	0
380	390	27	20	15	9	4	0	0	0	0	0	0
390	400	28	21	16	10	4	1	0	0	0	0	0
400	410	31	22	17	11	5	1	0	0	0	0	0
410	420	32	23	18	12	6	2	0	0	0	0	0
420	430	34	24	19	13	7	2	0	0	0	0	0
430	440	35	25	20	14	8	3	0	0	0	0	0
440	450	37	26	21	15	9	4	0	0	0	0	0
450	460	38	28	22	16	10	4	1	0	0	0	0
460	470	40	29	23	17	11	5	1	0	0	0	0
470	480	41	31	24	18	12	6	2	0	0	0	0
480	490	43	32	25	19	13	7	2	0	0	0	0
490	500	44	34	26	20	14	8	3	0	0	0	0
500	510	46	35	28	21	15	9	4	0	0	0	0
510	520	47	37	29	22	16	10	4	1	0	0	0
520	530	49	38	31	23	17	11	5	1	0	0	0
530	540	50	40	32	24	18	12	6	2	0	0	0
540	550	52	41	34	26	19	13	7	2	0	0	0
550	560	53	43	35	27	20	14	8	3	0	0	0
560	570	55	44	37	28	21	15	9	4	0	0	0
570	580	56	46	38	30	22	16	10	4	1	0	0
580	590	58	47	40	31	23	17	11	5	1	0	0
590	600	59	49	41	33	24	18	12	6	2	0	0
600	610	61	50	43	34	25	19	13	7	2	0	0
610	620	62	52	44	36	26	20	14	8	3	0	0
620	630	64	53	46	37	28	21	15	9	4	0	0
630	640	65	55	47	39	29	22	16	10	4	1	0
640	650	67	56	49	40	31	23	17	11	5	1	0
650	660	68	58	50	42	32	24	18	12	6	2	0
660	670	70	59	52	43	34	25	19	13	7	2	0
670	680	71	61	53	45	35	27	20	14	8	3	0
680	690	73	62	55	46	37	28	21	15	9	4	0
690	700	74	64	56	48	38	30	22	16	10	4	1
700	710	76	65	58	49	40	31	23	17	11	5	1
710	720	77	67	59	51	41	33	24	18	12	6	2
720	730	79	68	61	52	43	34	26	19	13	7	2
730	740	80	70	62	54	44	36	27	20	14	8	3
740	750	82	71	64	55	46	37	29	21	15	9	4

WAGE-BRACKET WITHHOLDING TABLES

SINGLE Persons—BIWEEKLY Payroll Period
(For Wages Paid in 2002)

If the wages are—		And the number of withholding allowances claimed is—										
At least	But less than	0	1	2	3	4	5	6	7	8	9	10
		The amount of income tax to be withheld is—										
$0	$105	$0	$0	$0	$0	$0	$0	$0	$0	$0	$0	$0
105	110	1	0	0	0	0	0	0	0	0	0	0
110	115	1	0	0	0	0	0	0	0	0	0	0
115	120	2	0	0	0	0	0	0	0	0	0	0
120	125	2	0	0	0	0	0	0	0	0	0	0
125	130	3	0	0	0	0	0	0	0	0	0	0
130	135	3	0	0	0	0	0	0	0	0	0	0
135	140	4	0	0	0	0	0	0	0	0	0	0
140	145	4	0	0	0	0	0	0	0	0	0	0
145	150	5	0	0	0	0	0	0	0	0	0	0
150	155	5	0	0	0	0	0	0	0	0	0	0
155	160	6	0	0	0	0	0	0	0	0	0	0
160	165	6	0	0	0	0	0	0	0	0	0	0
165	170	7	0	0	0	0	0	0	0	0	0	0
170	175	7	0	0	0	0	0	0	0	0	0	0
175	180	8	0	0	0	0	0	0	0	0	0	0
180	185	8	0	0	0	0	0	0	0	0	0	0
185	190	9	0	0	0	0	0	0	0	0	0	0
190	195	9	0	0	0	0	0	0	0	0	0	0
195	200	10	0	0	0	0	0	0	0	0	0	0
200	205	10	0	0	0	0	0	0	0	0	0	0
205	210	11	0	0	0	0	0	0	0	0	0	0
210	215	11	0	0	0	0	0	0	0	0	0	0
215	220	12	0	0	0	0	0	0	0	0	0	0
220	225	12	1	0	0	0	0	0	0	0	0	0
225	230	13	1	0	0	0	0	0	0	0	0	0
230	235	13	2	0	0	0	0	0	0	0	0	0
235	240	14	2	0	0	0	0	0	0	0	0	0
240	245	14	3	0	0	0	0	0	0	0	0	0
245	250	15	3	0	0	0	0	0	0	0	0	0
250	260	16	4	0	0	0	0	0	0	0	0	0
260	270	17	5	0	0	0	0	0	0	0	0	0
270	280	18	6	0	0	0	0	0	0	0	0	0
280	290	19	7	0	0	0	0	0	0	0	0	0
290	300	20	8	0	0	0	0	0	0	0	0	0
300	310	21	9	0	0	0	0	0	0	0	0	0
310	320	22	10	0	0	0	0	0	0	0	0	0
320	330	23	11	0	0	0	0	0	0	0	0	0
330	340	24	12	0	0	0	0	0	0	0	0	0
340	350	25	13	1	0	0	0	0	0	0	0	0
350	360	27	14	2	0	0	0	0	0	0	0	0
360	370	28	15	3	0	0	0	0	0	0	0	0
370	380	30	16	4	0	0	0	0	0	0	0	0
380	390	31	18	5	0	0	0	0	0	0	0	0
390	400	33	19	7	0	0	0	0	0	0	0	0
400	410	34	20	8	0	0	0	0	0	0	0	0
410	420	36	22	9	0	0	0	0	0	0	0	0
420	430	37	23	11	0	0	0	0	0	0	0	0
430	440	39	25	12	0	0	0	0	0	0	0	0
440	450	40	26	14	1	0	0	0	0	0	0	0
450	460	42	27	15	2	0	0	0	0	0	0	0
460	470	43	28	16	4	0	0	0	0	0	0	0
470	480	45	30	18	5	0	0	0	0	0	0	0
480	490	46	31	19	6	0	0	0	0	0	0	0
490	500	48	33	20	8	0	0	0	0	0	0	0
500	520	50	33	21	9	0	0	0	0	0	0	0
520	540	53	36	24	11	0	0	0	0	0	0	0
540	560	56	39	27	14	1	0	0	0	0	0	0
560	580	59	42	30	17	4	0	0	0	0	0	0
580	600	62	45	33	20	7	0	0	0	0	0	0
600	620	65	48	36	23	10	0	0	0	0	0	0
620	640	68	51	39	26	13	1	0	0	0	0	0
640	660	71	54	42	29	16	3	0	0	0	0	0
660	680	74	57	45	32	19	5	0	0	0	0	0
680	700	77	60	48	35	22	7	0	0	0	0	0
700	720	80	63	51	38	25	9	0	0	0	0	0
720	740	83	66	54	41	28	11	0	0	0	0	0
740	760	86	69	57	44	31	13	0	0	0	0	0
760	780	89	72	60	47	34	17	0	0	0	0	0
780	800	92	75	63	50	37	21	0	0	0	0	0

[Box overlay: **BIWEEKLY SINGLE PERSONS**]

SINGLE Persons—BIWEEKLY Payroll Period
(For Wages Paid in 2002)

If the wages are—		And the number of withholding allowances claimed is—										
At least	But less than	0	1	2	3	4	5	6	7	8	9	10
		The amount of income tax to be withheld is—										
$800	$820	$95	$78	$60	$43	$26	$13	$2	$0	$0	$0	$0
820	840	98	81	63	46	29	15	4	0	0	0	0
840	860	101	84	66	49	32	17	6	0	0	0	0
860	880	104	87	69	52	35	19	8	0	0	0	0
880	900	107	90	72	55	38	21	10	0	0	0	0
900	920	110	93	75	58	41	23	12	0	0	0	0
920	940	113	96	78	61	44	26	14	2	0	0	0
940	960	116	99	81	64	47	29	16	4	0	0	0
960	980	119	102	84	67	50	32	18	6	0	0	0
980	1,000	122	105	87	70	53	35	20	8	0	0	0
1,000	1,020	125	108	90	73	56	38	22	10	0	0	0
1,020	1,040	128	111	93	76	59	41	24	12	1	0	0
1,040	1,060	131	114	96	79	62	44	27	14	3	0	0
1,060	1,080	134	117	99	82	65	47	30	17	5	0	0
1,080	1,100	137	120	102	85	68	50	33	20	8	0	0
1,100	1,120	140	123	105	88	71	53	36	22	11	0	0
1,120	1,140	143	126	108	91	74	56	39	25	13	1	0
1,140	1,160	147	129	111	94	77	59	42	28	15	3	0
1,160	1,180	152	132	114	97	80	62	45	31	17	6	0
1,180	1,200	158	135	117	100	83	65	48	34	20	9	0
1,200	1,220	163	138	120	103	86	68	51	37	23	12	0
1,220	1,240	169	141	123	106	89	71	54	40	26	14	2
1,240	1,260	174	144	126	109	92	74	57	43	29	17	5
1,260	1,280	179	148	129	112	95	77	60	46	32	20	8
1,280	1,300	185	154	132	115	98	80	63	49	35	23	11
1,300	1,320	190	159	135	118	101	83	66	52	38	26	14
1,320	1,340	196	164	138	121	104	86	69	55	41	29	17
1,340	1,360	201	170	141	124	107	89	72	58	44	32	20
1,360	1,380	206	175	144	127	110	92	75	61	47	35	23
1,380	1,400	212	181	150	130	113	95	78	64	50	38	26
1,400	1,420	217	186	155	133	116	98	81	67	53	41	29
1,420	1,440	223	191	160	136	119	101	84	70	56	44	32
1,440	1,460	228	197	166	139	122	104	87	73	59	47	35
1,460	1,480	233	202	171	142	125	107	90	76	62	50	38
1,480	1,500	239	208	177	145	128	110	93	79	65	53	41
1,500	1,520	244	213	182	151	131	113	96	82	68	56	44
1,520	1,540	250	218	187	156	134	116	99	85	71	59	47
1,540	1,560	255	224	193	162	137	119	102	88	74	62	50
1,560	1,580	260	229	198	167	140	122	105	91	77	65	53
1,580	1,600	266	235	204	172	143	125	108	94	80	68	56
1,600	1,620	271	240	209	178	147	128	111	97	83	71	59
1,620	1,640	277	245	214	183	152	131	114	100	86	74	62
1,640	1,660	282	251	220	189	157	134	117	103	89	77	65
1,660	1,680	287	256	225	194	163	137	120	106	92	80	68
1,680	1,700	293	262	231	199	168	140	123	109	95	83	71
1,700	1,720	298	267	236	205	174	143	126	112	98	86	74
1,720	1,740	304	272	242	210	179	148	129	115	101	89	77
1,740	1,760	309	278	247	216	184	153	132	118	104	92	80
1,760	1,780	314	283	252	221	190	159	135	121	107	95	83
1,780	1,800	320	289	258	226	195	164	138	124	110	98	86
1,800	1,820	325	294	263	232	201	169	141	127	113	101	89
1,820	1,840	331	299	268	237	206	175	144	130	116	104	92
1,840	1,860	336	305	274	243	211	180	149	133	119	107	95
1,860	1,880	341	310	279	248	217	186	154	136	122	110	98
1,880	1,900	347	316	285	253	222	191	160	139	125	113	101
1,900	1,920	352	321	290	259	228	196	165	142	128	116	104
1,920	1,940	358	326	295	264	233	202	171	145	131	119	107
1,940	1,960	363	332	301	270	238	207	176	150	134	122	110
1,960	1,980	368	337	306	275	244	213	181	155	137	125	113
1,980	2,000	374	343	312	280	249	218	187	160	140	128	116
2,000	2,020	379	348	317	286	255	223	192	163	146	131	119
2,020	2,040	385	353	322	291	260	229	198	169	142	128	122
2,040	2,060	390	359	328	297	266	234	203	172	147	125	125
2,060	2,080	395	364	333	302	271	240	208	177	146	128	111
2,080	2,100	401	370	339	307	276	245	214	183	152	131	114
$2,100 and over						Use Table 2(a) for a **SINGLE person** on page T-3.						

WAGE-BRACKET WITHHOLDING TABLES

MARRIED Persons—BIWEEKLY Payroll Period
(For Wages Paid in 2002)

At least	But less than	0	1	2	3	4	5	6	7	8	9	10
		The amount of income tax to be withheld is—										
$0	$250	$0	$0	$0	$0	$0	$0	$0	$0	$0	$0	$0
250	260	1	0	0	0	0	0	0	0	0	0	0
260	270	2	0	0	0	0	0	0	0	0	0	0
270	280	3	0	0	0	0	0	0	0	0	0	0
280	290	4	0	0	0	0	0	0	0	0	0	0
290	300	5	0	0	0	0	0	0	0	0	0	0
300	310	6	0	0	0	0	0	0	0	0	0	0
310	320	7	0	0	0	0	0	0	0	0	0	0
320	330	8	0	0	0	0	0	0	0	0	0	0
330	340	9	0	0	0	0	0	0	0	0	0	0
340	350	10	0	0	0	0	0	0	0	0	0	0
350	360	11	0	0	0	0	0	0	0	0	0	0
360	370	12	0	0	0	0	0	0	0	0	0	0
370	380	13	1	0	0	0	0	0	0	0	0	0
380	390	14	2	0	0	0	0	0	0	0	0	0
390	400	15	3	0	0	0	0	0	0	0	0	0
400	410	16	4	0	0	0	0	0	0	0	0	0
410	420	17	5	0	0	0	0	0	0	0	0	0
420	430	18	6	0	0	0	0	0	0	0	0	0
430	440	19	7	0	0	0	0	0	0	0	0	0
440	450	20	8	0	0	0	0	0	0	0	0	0
450	460	21	9	0	0	0	0	0	0	0	0	0
460	470	22	10	0	0	0	0	0	0	0	0	0
470	480	23	11	0	0	0	0	0	0	0	0	0
480	490	24	12	0	0	0	0	0	0	0	0	0
490	500	25	13	0	0	0	0	0	0	0	0	0
500	520	26	15	1	0	0	0	0	0	0	0	0
520	540	28	17	3	0	0	0	0	0	0	0	0
540	560	30	19	5	0	0	0	0	0	0	0	0
560	580	32	21	7	0	0	0	0	0	0	0	0
580	600	34	23	9	0	0	0	0	0	0	0	0
600	620	36	25	11	0	0	0	0	0	0	0	0
620	640	38	27	13	1	0	0	0	0	0	0	0
640	660	40	29	15	3	0	0	0	0	0	0	0
660	680	42	31	17	5	0	0	0	0	0	0	0
680	700	44	33	19	7	0	0	0	0	0	0	0
700	720	46	35	21	9	0	0	0	0	0	0	0
720	740	49	37	23	11	0	0	0	0	0	0	0
740	760	52	39	25	13	2	0	0	0	0	0	0
760	780	55	41	27	15	4	0	0	0	0	0	0
780	800	58	43	29	17	6	0	0	0	0	0	0
800	820	61	45	31	19	8	0	0	0	0	0	0
820	840	64	47	33	21	10	0	0	0	0	0	0
840	860	67	50	35	23	12	1	0	0	0	0	0
860	880	70	53	37	25	14	3	0	0	0	0	0
880	900	73	56	39	27	16	5	0	0	0	0	0
900	920	76	59	42	29	18	7	0	0	0	0	0
920	940	79	62	45	31	20	9	0	0	0	0	0
940	960	82	65	48	33	22	11	0	0	0	0	0
960	980	85	68	51	35	24	13	2	0	0	0	0
980	1,000	88	71	54	37	26	15	4	0	0	0	0
1,000	1,020	91	74	57	39	28	17	6	0	0	0	0
1,020	1,040	94	77	60	42	30	19	8	0	0	0	0
1,040	1,060	97	80	63	45	32	21	10	0	0	0	0
1,060	1,080	100	83	66	48	34	23	12	0	0	0	0
1,080	1,100	103	86	69	51	36	25	14	2	0	0	0
1,100	1,120	106	89	72	54	38	27	16	4	0	0	0
1,120	1,140	109	92	75	57	40	29	18	6	0	0	0
1,140	1,160	112	95	78	60	43	31	20	8	0	0	0
1,160	1,180	115	98	81	63	46	33	22	10	0	0	0
1,180	1,200	118	101	84	66	49	35	24	12	2	0	0
1,200	1,220	121	104	87	69	52	37	26	14	4	0	0
1,220	1,240	124	107	90	72	55	39	28	16	6	0	0
1,240	1,260	127	110	93	75	58	41	30	18	8	0	0
1,260	1,280	130	113	96	78	61	44	32	20	10	0	0
1,280	1,300	133	116	99	81	64	47	34	22	12	0	0
1,300	1,320	136	119	102	84	67	50	36	24	14	2	0
1,320	1,340	139	122	105	87	70	53	38	26	16	4	0
1,340	1,360	142	125	108	90	73	56	40	28	18	6	0
1,360	1,380	145	128	111	93	76	59	42	30	20	8	0

BIWEEKLY MARRIED PERSONS

MARRIED Persons—BIWEEKLY Payroll Period
(For Wages Paid in 2002)

At least	But less than	0	1	2	3	4	5	6	7	8	9	10
		The amount of income tax to be withheld is—										
$1,380	$1,400	$148	$131	$114	$96	$79	$62	$45	$33	$22	$10	$0
1,400	1,420	151	134	117	99	82	65	47	35	24	12	1
1,420	1,440	154	137	120	102	85	68	50	37	26	14	3
1,440	1,460	157	140	123	105	88	71	53	39	28	16	5
1,460	1,480	160	143	126	108	91	74	56	41	30	18	7
1,480	1,500	163	146	129	111	94	77	59	43	32	20	9
1,500	1,520	166	149	132	114	97	80	62	45	34	22	11
1,520	1,540	169	152	135	117	100	83	65	48	36	24	13
1,540	1,560	172	155	138	120	103	86	68	51	38	26	15
1,560	1,580	175	158	141	123	106	89	71	54	40	28	17
1,580	1,600	178	161	144	126	109	92	74	57	42	30	19
1,600	1,620	181	164	147	129	112	95	77	60	44	32	21
1,620	1,640	184	167	150	132	115	98	80	63	46	34	23
1,640	1,660	187	170	153	135	118	101	83	66	49	36	25
1,660	1,680	190	173	156	138	121	104	86	69	52	38	27
1,680	1,700	193	176	159	141	124	107	89	72	55	40	29
1,700	1,720	196	179	162	144	127	110	92	75	58	42	31
1,720	1,740	199	182	165	147	130	113	95	78	61	44	33
1,740	1,760	202	185	168	150	133	116	98	81	64	46	35
1,760	1,780	205	188	171	153	136	119	101	84	67	49	37
1,780	1,800	208	191	174	156	139	122	104	87	70	52	39
1,800	1,820	211	194	177	159	142	125	107	90	73	55	41
1,820	1,840	214	197	180	162	145	128	110	93	76	58	43
1,840	1,860	217	200	183	165	148	131	113	96	79	61	45
1,860	1,880	220	203	186	168	151	134	116	99	82	64	47
1,880	1,900	223	206	189	171	154	137	119	102	85	67	50
1,900	1,920	226	209	192	174	157	140	122	105	88	70	53
1,920	1,940	229	212	195	177	160	143	125	108	91	73	56
1,940	1,960	232	215	198	180	163	146	128	111	94	76	59
1,960	1,980	235	218	201	183	166	149	131	114	97	79	62
1,980	2,000	239	221	204	186	169	152	134	117	100	82	65
2,000	2,020	244	224	207	189	172	155	137	120	103	85	68
2,020	2,040	250	227	210	192	175	158	140	123	106	88	71
2,040	2,060	255	230	213	195	178	161	143	126	109	91	74
2,060	2,080	261	233	216	198	181	164	146	129	112	94	77
2,080	2,100	266	236	219	201	184	167	149	132	115	97	80
2,100	2,120	271	240	222	204	187	170	152	135	118	100	83
2,120	2,140	277	246	225	207	190	173	155	138	121	103	86
2,140	2,160	282	251	228	210	193	176	158	141	124	106	89
2,160	2,180	288	257	231	213	196	179	161	144	127	109	92
2,180	2,200	293	262	234	216	199	182	164	147	130	112	95
2,200	2,220	298	267	237	219	202	185	167	150	133	115	98
2,220	2,240	304	273	242	222	205	188	170	153	136	118	101
2,240	2,260	309	278	247	225	208	191	173	156	139	121	104
2,260	2,280	315	284	252	228	211	194	176	159	142	124	107
2,280	2,300	320	289	258	231	214	197	179	162	145	127	110
2,300	2,320	325	294	263	234	217	200	182	165	148	130	113
2,320	2,340	331	300	269	237	220	203	185	168	151	133	116
2,340	2,360	336	305	274	243	223	206	188	171	154	136	119
2,360	2,380	342	311	279	248	226	209	191	174	157	139	122
2,380	2,400	347	316	285	254	229	212	194	177	160	142	125
2,400	2,420	352	321	290	259	232	215	197	180	163	145	128
2,420	2,440	358	327	296	264	235	218	200	183	166	148	131
2,440	2,460	363	332	301	270	239	221	203	186	169	151	134
2,460	2,480	369	338	306	275	244	224	206	189	172	154	137
2,480	2,500	374	343	312	281	249	227	209	192	175	157	140
2,500	2,520	379	348	317	286	255	230	212	195	178	160	143
2,520	2,540	385	354	323	291	260	233	215	198	181	163	146
2,540	2,560	390	359	328	297	266	236	218	201	184	166	149
2,560	2,580	396	365	333	302	271	240	221	204	187	169	152
2,580	2,600	401	370	339	308	276	245	224	207	190	172	155
2,600	2,620	406	375	344	313	282	251	227	210	193	175	158
2,620	2,640	412	381	350	318	287	256	230	213	196	178	161
2,640	2,660	417	386	355	324	293	262	233	216	199	181	164
2,660	2,680	423	392	360	329	298	267	236	219	202	184	167

$2,680 and over — Use Table 2(b) for a MARRIED person on page T-3.

WAGE-BRACKET WITHHOLDING TABLES

SINGLE Persons—SEMIMONTHLY Payroll Period
(For Wages Paid in 2002)

If the wages are—		And the number of withholding allowances claimed is—										
At least	But less than	0	1	2	3	4	5	6	7	8	9	10
		The amount of income tax to be withheld is—										
$0	$115	$0	$0	$0	$0	$0	$0	$0	$0	$0	$0	$0
115	120	1	0	0	0	0	0	0	0	0	0	0
120	125	1	0	0	0	0	0	0	0	0	0	0
125	130	2	0	0	0	0	0	0	0	0	0	0
130	135	2	0	0	0	0	0	0	0	0	0	0
135	140	3	0	0	0	0	0	0	0	0	0	0
140	145	3	0	0	0	0	0	0	0	0	0	0
145	150	4	0	0	0	0	0	0	0	0	0	0
150	155	4	0	0	0	0	0	0	0	0	0	0
155	160	5	0	0	0	0	0	0	0	0	0	0
160	165	5	0	0	0	0	0	0	0	0	0	0
165	170	6	0	0	0	0	0	0	0	0	0	0
170	175	6	0	0	0	0	0	0	0	0	0	0
175	180	7	0	0	0	0	0	0	0	0	0	0
180	185	7	0	0	0	0	0	0	0	0	0	0
185	190	8	0	0	0	0	0	0	0	0	0	0
190	195	9	0	0	0	0	0	0	0	0	0	0
195	200	9	0	0	0	0	0	0	0	0	0	0
200	205	10	0	0	0	0	0	0	0	0	0	0
205	210	10	0	0	0	0	0	0	0	0	0	0
210	215	11	0	0	0	0	0	0	0	0	0	0
215	220	11	0	0	0	0	0	0	0	0	0	0
220	225	12	0	0	0	0	0	0	0	0	0	0
225	230	12	0	0	0	0	0	0	0	0	0	0
230	235	13	0	0	0	0	0	0	0	0	0	0
235	240	13	1	0	0	0	0	0	0	0	0	0
240	245	14	1	0	0	0	0	0	0	0	0	0
245	250	15	2	0	0	0	0	0	0	0	0	0
250	260	16	3	0	0	0	0	0	0	0	0	0
260	270	17	4	0	0	0	0	0	0	0	0	0
270	280	18	4	0	0	0	0	0	0	0	0	0
280	290	19	5	0	0	0	0	0	0	0	0	0
290	300	20	6	0	0	0	0	0	0	0	0	0
300	310	21	7	0	0	0	0	0	0	0	0	0
310	320	22	8	0	0	0	0	0	0	0	0	0
320	330	23	9	0	0	0	0	0	0	0	0	0
330	340	24	10	0	0	0	0	0	0	0	0	0
340	350	26	11	0	0	0	0	0	0	0	0	0
350	360	27	12	0	0	0	0	0	0	0	0	0
360	370	29	13	0	0	0	0	0	0	0	0	0
370	380	30	14	0	0	0	0	0	0	0	0	0
380	390	32	15	0	0	0	0	0	0	0	0	0
390	400	33	16	0	0	0	0	0	0	0	0	0
400	410	35	17	0	0	0	0	0	0	0	0	0
410	420	36	18	1	0	0	0	0	0	0	0	0
420	430	38	19	2	0	0	0	0	0	0	0	0
430	440	39	20	3	0	0	0	0	0	0	0	0
440	450	41	21	4	0	0	0	0	0	0	0	0
450	460	42	23	5	0	0	0	0	0	0	0	0
460	470	44	24	6	0	0	0	0	0	0	0	0
470	480	45	25	7	0	0	0	0	0	0	0	0
480	490	46	27	8	0	0	0	0	0	0	0	0
490	500	47	28	9	0	0	0	0	0	0	0	0
500	520	48	29	10	0	0	0	0	0	0	0	0
520	540	51	32	13	0	0	0	0	0	0	0	0
540	560	54	35	16	0	0	0	0	0	0	0	0
560	580	57	38	19	2	0	0	0	0	0	0	0
580	600	60	41	22	4	0	0	0	0	0	0	0
600	620	63	44	25	6	0	0	0	0	0	0	0
620	640	66	47	28	9	2	0	0	0	0	0	0
640	660	69	50	31	12	4	0	0	0	0	0	0
660	680	72	53	34	15	6	0	0	0	0	0	0
680	700	75	56	37	18	8	0	0	0	0	0	0
700	720	78	59	40	21	10	0	0	0	0	0	0
720	740	81	62	43	24	12	0	0	0	0	0	0
740	760	84	65	46	27	14	1	0	0	0	0	0
760	780	87	68	49	30	16	3	0	0	0	0	0
780	800	90	71	52	33	18	5	0	0	0	0	0
800	820	93	74	55	36	20	7	0	0	0	0	0
820	840	96	77	58	39	22	9	0	0	0	0	0

SEMIMONTHLY SINGLE PERSONS

SINGLE Persons—SEMIMONTHLY Payroll Period
(For Wages Paid in 2002)

If the wages are—		And the number of withholding allowances claimed is—										
At least	But less than	0	1	2	3	4	5	6	7	8	9	10
		The amount of income tax to be withheld is—										
$840	$860	$99	$80	$61	$42	$24	$11	$0	$0	$0	$0	$0
860	880	102	83	64	45	27	13	1	0	0	0	0
880	900	105	86	67	48	30	15	3	0	0	0	0
900	920	108	89	70	51	33	17	5	0	0	0	0
920	940	111	92	73	54	36	19	7	0	0	0	0
940	960	114	95	76	57	39	21	9	0	0	0	0
960	980	117	98	79	60	42	23	11	0	0	0	0
980	1,000	120	101	82	63	45	26	13	2	0	0	0
1,000	1,020	123	104	85	66	48	29	15	4	0	0	0
1,020	1,040	126	107	88	69	51	32	17	6	0	0	0
1,040	1,060	129	110	91	72	54	35	19	8	0	0	0
1,060	1,080	132	113	94	75	57	38	21	10	0	0	0
1,080	1,100	135	116	97	78	60	41	23	12	0	0	0
1,100	1,120	138	119	100	81	63	44	25	14	2	0	0
1,120	1,140	141	122	103	84	66	47	28	16	4	0	0
1,140	1,160	144	125	106	87	69	50	31	18	6	0	0
1,160	1,180	147	128	109	90	72	53	34	20	8	0	0
1,180	1,200	150	131	112	93	75	56	37	22	10	0	0
1,200	1,220	153	134	115	96	78	59	40	24	12	1	0
1,220	1,240	156	137	118	99	81	62	43	27	14	3	0
1,240	1,260	160	140	121	102	84	65	46	30	16	5	0
1,260	1,280	166	143	124	105	87	68	49	33	18	7	0
1,280	1,300	171	146	127	108	90	71	52	36	20	9	0
1,300	1,320	177	149	130	111	93	74	55	39	22	11	1
1,320	1,340	182	152	133	114	96	77	58	42	24	13	3
1,340	1,360	187	155	136	117	99	80	61	45	27	15	5
1,360	1,380	193	159	139	120	102	83	64	48	30	17	7
1,380	1,400	198	164	142	123	105	86	67	51	33	19	9
1,400	1,420	204	170	145	126	108	89	70	54	36	21	11
1,420	1,440	209	175	148	129	111	92	73	57	39	23	13
1,440	1,460	214	181	151	132	114	95	76	60	42	26	15
1,460	1,480	220	186	154	135	117	98	79	63	45	29	17
1,480	1,500	225	191	158	138	120	101	82	66	48	32	19
1,500	1,520	231	197	163	141	123	104	85	69	51	35	21
1,520	1,540	236	202	168	144	126	107	88	72	54	38	23
1,540	1,560	241	208	174	147	129	110	91	75	57	41	25
1,560	1,580	247	213	179	150	132	113	94	78	60	44	28
1,580	1,600	252	218	185	153	135	116	97	81	63	47	31
1,600	1,620	258	224	190	156	138	119	100	84	66	50	34
1,620	1,640	263	229	195	162	141	122	103	87	69	53	37
1,640	1,660	268	235	201	167	144	125	106	90	72	56	40
1,660	1,680	274	240	206	173	147	128	109	93	75	59	43
1,680	1,700	279	245	212	178	150	131	112	96	78	62	46
1,700	1,720	285	251	217	183	153	134	115	99	81	65	49
1,720	1,740	290	256	222	189	156	137	118	102	84	68	52
1,740	1,760	295	262	228	194	160	140	121	105	87	71	55
1,760	1,780	301	267	233	200	166	143	124	108	90	74	58
1,780	1,800	306	272	239	205	171	146	127	111	93	77	61
1,800	1,820	312	278	244	210	177	149	130	114	96	80	64
1,820	1,840	317	283	249	216	182	152	133	117	99	83	67
1,840	1,860	322	289	255	221	187	155	136	120	102	86	70
1,860	1,880	328	294	260	227	193	159	139	123	105	89	73
1,880	1,900	333	299	266	232	198	164	142	126	108	92	76
1,900	1,920	339	305	271	237	204	170	145	129	111	95	79
1,920	1,940	344	310	276	243	209	175	148	132	114	98	82
1,940	1,960	349	316	282	248	214	181	151	135	117	101	85
1,960	1,980	355	321	287	254	220	186	154	138	120	104	88
1,980	2,000	360	326	293	259	225	191	158	141	123	107	91
2,000	2,020	366	332	298	264	231	197	163	144	126	110	94
2,020	2,040	371	337	303	270	236	202	168	147	129	113	97
2,040	2,060	376	343	309	275	241	208	174	150	132	116	100
2,060	2,080	382	348	314	281	247	213	179	153	135	119	103
2,080	2,100	387	353	320	286	252	218	185	156	138	122	—
2,100	2,120	393	359	325	291	258	224	190	—	—	—	—
2,120	2,140	398	364	330	297	263	229	195	—	—	—	—

$2,140 and over   Use Table 3(a) for a SINGLE person on page T-3.

WAGE-BRACKET WITHHOLDING TABLES

MARRIED Persons—SEMIMONTHLY Payroll Period
(For Wages Paid in 2002)

If the wages are—		And the number of withholding allowances claimed is—										
At least	But less than	0	1	2	3	4	5	6	7	8	9	10
		The amount of income tax to be withheld is—										
$0	270	$0	$0	$0	$0	$0	$0	$0	$0	$0	$0	$0
270	280	1	0	0	0	0	0	0	0	0	0	0
280	290	2	0	0	0	0	0	0	0	0	0	0
290	300	3	0	0	0	0	0	0	0	0	0	0
300	310	4	0	0	0	0	0	0	0	0	0	0
310	320	5	0	0	0	0	0	0	0	0	0	0
320	330	6	0	0	0	0	0	0	0	0	0	0
330	340	7	0	0	0	0	0	0	0	0	0	0
340	350	8	0	0	0	0	0	0	0	0	0	0
350	360	9	0	0	0	0	0	0	0	0	0	0
360	370	10	0	0	0	0	0	0	0	0	0	0
370	380	11	0	0	0	0	0	0	0	0	0	0
380	390	12	0	0	0	0	0	0	0	0	0	0
390	400	13	0	0	0	0	0	0	0	0	0	0
400	410	14	0	0	0	0	0	0	0	0	0	0
410	420	15	0	0	0	0	0	0	0	0	0	0
420	430	16	0	0	0	0	0	0	0	0	0	0
430	440	17	0	0	0	0	0	0	0	0	0	0
440	450	18	0	0	0	0	0	0	0	0	0	0
450	460	19	2	0	0	0	0	0	0	0	0	0
460	470	20	4	0	0	0	0	0	0	0	0	0
470	480	21	6	0	0	0	0	0	0	0	0	0
480	490	22	8	0	0	0	0	0	0	0	0	0
490	500	23	10	0	0	0	0	0	0	0	0	0
500	520	24	12	0	0	0	0	0	0	0	0	0
520	540	26	14	2	0	0	0	0	0	0	0	0
540	560	28	16	4	0	0	0	0	0	0	0	0
560	580	30	18	6	0	0	0	0	0	0	0	0
580	600	32	20	8	0	0	0	0	0	0	0	0
600	620	34	22	10	0	0	0	0	0	0	0	0
620	640	36	24	12	0	0	0	0	0	0	0	0
640	660	38	26	14	2	0	0	0	0	0	0	0
660	680	40	28	16	4	0	0	0	0	0	0	0
680	700	42	30	18	6	0	0	0	0	0	0	0
700	720	44	32	20	8	0	0	0	0	0	0	0
720	740	46	34	22	10	0	0	0	0	0	0	0
740	760	48	36	24	12	0	0	0	0	0	0	0
760	780	50	38	26	14	1	0	0	0	0	0	0
780	800	53	40	28	16	3	0	0	0	0	0	0
800	820	56	42	30	18	5	0	0	0	0	0	0
820	840	59	44	32	20	7	0	0	0	0	0	0
840	860	62	46	34	22	9	0	0	0	0	0	0
860	880	65	48	36	24	11	0	0	0	0	0	0
880	900	68	50	38	26	13	0	0	0	0	0	0
900	920	71	52	40	28	15	2	0	0	0	0	0
920	940	74	55	42	30	17	4	0	0	0	0	0
940	960	77	58	44	32	19	6	0	0	0	0	0
960	980	80	61	46	34	21	8	0	0	0	0	0
980	1,000	83	64	48	36	23	10	0	0	0	0	0
1,000	1,020	86	67	50	38	25	12	0	0	0	0	0
1,020	1,040	89	70	52	40	27	14	1	0	0	0	0
1,040	1,060	92	73	55	42	29	16	3	0	0	0	0
1,060	1,080	95	76	58	44	31	18	5	0	0	0	0
1,080	1,100	98	79	61	46	33	20	7	0	0	0	0
1,100	1,120	101	82	64	48	35	22	9	0	0	0	0
1,120	1,140	104	85	67	50	37	24	11	0	0	0	0
1,140	1,160	107	88	70	52	39	26	13	1	0	0	0
1,160	1,180	110	91	73	54	41	28	15	3	0	0	0
1,180	1,200	113	94	76	57	43	30	17	5	0	0	0
1,200	1,220	116	97	79	60	45	32	19	7	0	0	0
1,220	1,240	119	100	82	63	47	34	21	9	0	0	0
1,240	1,260	122	103	85	66	49	36	23	11	0	0	0
1,260	1,280	125	106	88	69	51	38	25	13	0	0	0
1,280	1,300	128	109	91	72	53	40	27	15	2	0	0
1,300	1,320	131	112	94	75	56	42	29	17	4	0	0
1,320	1,340	134	115	97	78	59	44	31	19	6	0	0
1,340	1,360	137	118	100	81	62	46	33	21	8	0	0
1,360	1,380	140	121	103	84	65	48	35	23	10	0	0
1,380	1,400	143	124	106	87	68	50	37	25	12	0	0
1,400	1,420	146	127	109	90	71	52	39	27	14	2	0

SEMIMONTHLY MARRIED PERSONS

MARRIED Persons—SEMIMONTHLY Payroll Period
(For Wages Paid in 2002)

If the wages are—		And the number of withholding allowances claimed is—										
At least	But less than	0	1	2	3	4	5	6	7	8	9	10
		The amount of income tax to be withheld is—										
$1,420	$1,440	$149	$130	$112	$93	$74	$55	$41	$29	$16	$4	$0
1,440	1,460	152	133	115	96	77	58	43	31	18	6	0
1,460	1,480	155	136	118	99	80	61	45	33	20	8	0
1,480	1,500	158	139	121	102	83	64	47	35	22	10	0
1,500	1,520	161	142	124	105	86	67	49	37	24	12	1
1,520	1,540	164	145	127	108	89	70	52	39	26	14	3
1,540	1,560	167	148	130	111	92	73	55	41	28	16	5
1,560	1,580	170	151	133	114	95	76	58	43	30	18	7
1,580	1,600	173	154	136	117	98	79	61	45	32	20	9
1,600	1,620	176	157	139	120	101	82	64	47	34	22	11
1,620	1,640	179	160	142	123	104	85	67	49	36	24	13
1,640	1,660	182	163	145	126	107	88	70	51	38	26	15
1,660	1,680	185	166	148	129	110	91	73	54	40	28	17
1,680	1,700	188	169	151	132	113	94	76	57	42	30	19
1,700	1,720	191	172	154	135	116	97	79	60	44	32	21
1,720	1,740	194	175	157	138	119	100	82	63	46	34	23
1,740	1,760	197	178	160	141	122	103	85	66	48	36	25
1,760	1,780	200	181	163	144	125	106	88	69	50	38	27
1,780	1,800	203	184	166	147	128	109	91	72	53	40	29
1,800	1,820	206	187	169	150	131	112	94	75	56	42	31
1,820	1,840	209	190	172	153	134	115	97	78	59	44	33
1,840	1,860	212	193	175	156	137	118	100	81	62	46	35
1,860	1,880	215	196	178	159	140	121	103	84	65	48	37
1,880	1,900	218	199	181	162	143	124	106	87	68	50	39
1,900	1,920	221	202	184	165	146	127	109	90	71	52	41
1,920	1,940	224	205	187	168	149	130	112	93	74	55	43
1,940	1,960	227	208	190	171	152	133	115	96	77	58	45
1,960	1,980	230	211	193	174	155	136	118	99	80	61	47
1,980	2,000	233	214	196	177	158	139	121	102	83	64	49
2,000	2,020	236	217	199	180	161	142	124	105	86	67	52
2,020	2,040	239	220	202	183	164	145	127	108	89	70	55
2,040	2,060	242	223	205	186	167	148	130	111	92	73	58
2,060	2,080	245	226	208	189	170	151	133	114	95	76	61
2,080	2,100	248	229	211	192	173	154	136	117	98	79	64
2,100	2,120	251	232	214	195	176	157	139	120	101	82	67
2,120	2,140	254	235	217	198	179	160	142	123	104	85	70
2,140	2,160	257	238	220	201	182	163	145	126	107	88	73
2,160	2,180	263	241	223	204	185	166	148	129	110	91	76
2,180	2,200	268	244	226	207	188	169	151	132	113	94	79
2,200	2,220	274	247	229	210	191	172	154	135	116	97	82
2,220	2,240	279	250	232	213	194	175	157	138	119	100	85
2,240	2,260	284	253	235	216	197	178	160	141	122	103	88
2,260	2,280	290	256	238	219	200	181	163	144	125	106	91
2,280	2,300	295	260	241	222	203	184	166	147	128	109	94
2,300	2,320	301	267	244	225	206	187	169	150	131	112	97
2,320	2,340	306	272	247	228	209	190	172	153	134	115	100
2,340	2,360	311	278	250	231	212	193	175	156	137	118	103
2,360	2,380	317	283	253	234	215	196	178	159	140	121	106
2,380	2,400	322	288	256	237	218	199	181	162	143	124	109
2,400	2,420	328	294	260	240	221	202	184	165	146	127	112
2,420	2,440	333	299	266	243	224	205	187	168	149	130	115
2,440	2,460	338	305	271	246	227	208	190	171	152	133	118
2,460	2,480	344	310	276	249	230	211	193	174	155	136	121
2,480	2,500	349	315	282	252	233	214	196	177	158	139	124
2,500	2,520	355	321	287	255	236	217	199	180	161	142	127
2,520	2,540	360	326	293	259	239	220	202	183	164	145	130
2,540	2,560	365	332	298	264	242	223	205	186	167	148	133
2,560	2,580	371	337	303	270	245	226	208	189	170	151	136
2,580	2,600	376	342	309	275	248	229	211	192	173	154	139
2,600	2,620	382	348	314	280	251	232	214	195	176	157	142
2,620	2,640	387	353	320	286	254	235	217	198	179	160	145
2,640	2,660	392	359	325	291	257	238	220	201	182	163	148
2,660	2,680	398	364	330	297	263	241	223	204	185	166	151
2,680	2,700	403	369	336	302	268	244	226	207	188	169	154
2,700	2,720	409	375	341	307	274	247	229	210	191	172	157

$2,720 and over   Use Table 3(b) for a **MARRIED person** on page T-3.

WAGE-BRACKET WITHHOLDING TABLES

SINGLE Persons—MONTHLY Payroll Period
(For Wages Paid in 2002)

At least	But less than	0	1	2	3	4	5	6	7	8	9	10
		— The amount of income tax to be withheld is—										
$0	$230	$0	$0	$0	$0	$0	$0	$0	$0	$0	$0	$0
230	240	1	0	0	0	0	0	0	0	0	0	0
240	250	2	0	0	0	0	0	0	0	0	0	0
250	260	3	0	0	0	0	0	0	0	0	0	0
260	270	4	0	0	0	0	0	0	0	0	0	0
270	280	5	0	0	0	0	0	0	0	0	0	0
280	290	6	0	0	0	0	0	0	0	0	0	0
290	300	7	0	0	0	0	0	0	0	0	0	0
300	320	9	0	0	0	0	0	0	0	0	0	0
320	340	11	0	0	0	0	0	0	0	0	0	0
340	360	13	0	0	0	0	0	0	0	0	0	0
360	380	15	0	0	0	0	0	0	0	0	0	0
380	400	17	0	0	0	0	0	0	0	0	0	0
400	420	19	0	0	0	0	0	0	0	0	0	0
420	440	21	0	0	0	0	0	0	0	0	0	0
440	460	23	0	0	0	0	0	0	0	0	0	0
460	480	25	0	0	0	0	0	0	0	0	0	0
480	500	27	0	0	0	0	0	0	0	0	0	0
500	520	29	2	0	0	0	0	0	0	0	0	0
520	540	31	4	0	0	0	0	0	0	0	0	0
540	560	33	6	0	0	0	0	0	0	0	0	0
560	580	35	8	0	0	0	0	0	0	0	0	0
580	600	37	10	0	0	0	0	0	0	0	0	0
600	640	40	12	0	0	0	0	0	0	0	0	0
640	680	44	15	0	0	0	0	0	0	0	0	0
680	720	48	19	0	0	0	0	0	0	0	0	0
720	760	53	23	1	0	0	0	0	0	0	0	0
760	800	59	27	5	0	0	0	0	0	0	0	0
800	840	65	31	9	0	0	0	0	0	0	0	0
840	880	71	35	13	0	0	0	0	0	0	0	0
880	920	77	39	17	0	0	0	0	0	0	0	0
920	960	83	43	21	0	0	0	0	0	0	0	0
960	1,000	89	47	25	0	0	0	0	0	0	0	0
1,000	1,040	95	52	29	3	0	0	0	0	0	0	0
1,040	1,080	101	58	33	7	0	0	0	0	0	0	0
1,080	1,120	107	64	37	11	0	0	0	0	0	0	0
1,120	1,160	113	70	41	17	0	0	0	0	0	0	0
1,160	1,200	119	76	45	21	0	0	0	0	0	0	0
1,200	1,240	125	82	49	25	0	0	0	0	0	0	0
1,240	1,280	131	88	53	29	4	0	0	0	0	0	0
1,280	1,320	137	94	62	33	8	0	0	0	0	0	0
1,320	1,360	143	100	68	37	12	0	0	0	0	0	0
1,360	1,400	149	106	74	41	16	0	0	0	0	0	0
1,400	1,440	155	112	80	45	20	0	0	0	0	0	0
1,440	1,480	161	118	86	49	24	0	0	0	0	0	0
1,480	1,520	167	124	92	55	28	3	0	0	0	0	0
1,520	1,560	173	130	98	61	32	7	0	0	0	0	0
1,560	1,600	179	136	104	67	36	11	0	0	0	0	0
1,600	1,640	185	142	110	73	40	15	0	0	0	0	0
1,640	1,680	191	148	116	79	44	19	0	0	0	0	0
1,680	1,720	197	154	122	85	48	23	0	0	0	0	0
1,720	1,760	203	160	128	91	53	27	2	0	0	0	0
1,760	1,800	209	166	134	97	59	31	6	0	0	0	0
1,800	1,840	215	172	140	103	65	35	10	0	0	0	0
1,840	1,880	221	178	146	109	71	39	14	0	0	0	0
1,880	1,920	227	184	152	115	77	43	18	0	0	0	0
1,920	1,960	233	190	158	121	83	47	22	0	0	0	0
1,960	2,000	239	196	164	127	89	52	26	0	0	0	0
2,000	2,040	245	202	170	133	95	58	30	1	0	0	0
2,040	2,080	251	208	176	139	101	64	34	5	0	0	0
2,080	2,120	257	214	182	145	107	70	38	9	0	0	0
2,120	2,160	263	220	188	151	113	76	42	13	0	0	0
2,160	2,200	269	226	194	157	119	82	46	17	0	0	0
2,200	2,240	275	232	200	163	125	88	50	21	0	0	0
2,240	2,280	281	238	206	169	131	94	56	25	4	0	0
2,280	2,320	287	244	212	175	137	100	62	33	8	0	0
2,320	2,360	293	250	218	181	143	106	68	37	12	0	0
2,360	2,400	299	256	224	187	149	112	74	41	16	0	0
2,400	2,440	305	262	230	193	155	118	80	45	20	0	0
2,440	2,480	311	268	236	199	161	124	86	49	24	4	0

MONTHLY SINGLE PERSONS

SINGLE Persons—MONTHLY Payroll Period
(For Wages Paid in 2002)

At least	But less than	0	1	2	3	4	5	6	7	8	9	10
		— The amount of income tax to be withheld is—										
$2,480	$2,520	$321	$280	$242	$205	$167	$130	$92	$55	$28	$3	$0
2,520	2,560	332	286	248	211	173	136	98	61	32	7	0
2,560	2,600	342	292	254	217	179	142	104	67	36	11	0
2,600	2,640	353	298	260	223	185	148	110	73	40	15	0
2,640	2,680	364	304	266	229	191	154	116	79	44	19	0
2,680	2,720	375	310	272	235	197	160	122	85	48	23	0
2,720	2,760	386	318	278	241	203	166	128	91	53	27	2
2,760	2,800	396	329	284	247	209	172	134	97	59	31	6
2,800	2,840	407	340	290	253	215	178	140	103	65	35	10
2,840	2,880	418	350	296	259	221	184	146	109	71	39	14
2,880	2,920	429	361	302	265	227	190	152	115	77	43	18
2,920	2,960	440	372	308	271	233	196	158	121	83	47	22
2,960	3,000	450	383	315	277	239	202	164	127	89	52	26
3,000	3,040	461	394	326	283	245	208	170	133	95	58	30
3,040	3,080	472	404	337	289	251	214	176	139	101	64	34
3,080	3,120	483	415	348	295	257	220	182	145	107	70	38
3,120	3,160	494	426	359	301	263	226	188	151	113	76	42
3,160	3,200	504	437	369	307	269	232	194	157	119	82	46
3,200	3,240	515	448	380	313	275	238	200	163	125	88	50
3,240	3,280	526	458	391	323	281	244	206	169	131	94	56
3,280	3,320	537	469	402	334	287	250	212	175	137	100	62
3,320	3,360	548	480	413	345	293	256	218	181	143	106	68
3,360	3,400	558	491	423	356	299	262	224	187	149	112	74
3,400	3,440	569	502	434	367	305	268	230	193	155	118	80
3,440	3,480	580	512	445	377	311	274	236	199	161	124	86
3,480	3,520	591	523	456	388	321	280	242	205	167	130	92
3,520	3,560	602	534	467	399	332	286	248	211	173	136	98
3,560	3,600	612	545	477	410	342	292	254	217	179	142	104
3,600	3,640	623	556	488	421	353	298	260	223	185	148	110
3,640	3,680	634	566	499	431	364	304	266	229	191	154	116
3,680	3,720	645	577	510	442	375	310	272	235	197	160	122
3,720	3,760	656	588	521	453	386	318	278	241	203	166	128
3,760	3,800	666	599	531	464	396	329	284	247	209	172	134
3,800	3,840	677	610	542	475	407	340	290	253	215	178	140
3,840	3,880	688	620	553	485	418	350	296	259	221	184	146
3,880	3,920	699	631	564	496	429	361	302	265	227	190	152
3,920	3,960	710	642	575	507	440	372	308	271	233	196	158
3,960	4,000	720	653	585	518	450	383	315	277	239	202	164
4,000	4,040	731	664	596	529	461	394	326	283	245	208	170
4,040	4,080	742	674	607	539	472	404	337	289	251	214	176
4,080	4,120	753	685	618	550	483	415	348	295	257	220	182
4,120	4,160	764	696	629	561	494	426	359	301	263	226	188
4,160	4,200	774	707	639	572	504	437	369	307	269	232	194
4,200	4,240	785	718	650	583	515	448	380	313	275	238	200
4,240	4,280	796	728	661	593	526	458	391	323	281	244	206
4,280	4,320	807	739	672	604	537	469	402	334	287	250	212
4,320	4,360	818	750	683	615	548	480	413	345	293	256	218
4,360	4,400	828	761	693	626	558	491	423	356	299	262	224
4,400	4,440	839	772	704	637	569	502	434	367	305	268	230
4,440	4,480	850	782	715	647	580	512	445	377	311	274	236
4,480	4,520	861	793	726	658	591	523	456	388	321	280	242
4,520	4,560	872	804	737	669	602	534	467	399	332	286	248
4,560	4,600	882	815	747	680	612	545	477	410	342	292	254
4,600	4,640	893	826	758	691	623	556	488	421	353	298	260
4,640	4,680	904	836	769	701	634	566	499	431	364	304	266
4,680	4,720	915	847	780	712	645	577	510	442	375	310	272
4,720	4,760	926	858	791	723	656	588	521	453	386	318	278
4,760	4,800	936	869	801	734	666	599	531	464	396	329	284
4,800	4,840	947	880	812	745	677	610	542	475	407	340	290
4,840	4,880	958	890	823	755	688	620	553	485	418	350	296
4,880	4,920	969	901	834	766	699	631	564	496	429	361	302
4,920	4,960	980	912	845	777	710	642	575	507	440	372	308
4,960	5,000	990	923	855	788	720	653	585	518	450	383	315
5,000	5,040	1,001	934	866	799	731	664	596	529	461	394	326
5,040	5,080	1,012	944	877	809	742	674	607	539	472	404	337

$5,080 and over — Use Table 4(a) for a SINGLE person on page T-3.

WAGE-BRACKET WITHHOLDING TABLES

MARRIED Persons—MONTHLY Payroll Period
(For Wages Paid in 2002)

| If the wages are— | | And the number of withholding allowances claimed is— | | | | | | | | | | |
At least	But less than	0	1	2	3	4	5	6	7	8	9	10
		The amount of income tax to be withheld is—										
$0	$540	$0	$0	$0	$0	$0	$0	$0	$0	$0	$0	$0
540	560	1	0	0	0	0	0	0	0	0	0	0
560	580	3	0	0	0	0	0	0	0	0	0	0
580	600	5	0	0	0	0	0	0	0	0	0	0
600	640	8	0	0	0	0	0	0	0	0	0	0
640	680	12	0	0	0	0	0	0	0	0	0	0
680	720	16	0	0	0	0	0	0	0	0	0	0
720	760	20	0	0	0	0	0	0	0	0	0	0
760	800	24	0	0	0	0	0	0	0	0	0	0
800	840	28	3	0	0	0	0	0	0	0	0	0
840	880	32	7	0	0	0	0	0	0	0	0	0
880	920	36	11	0	0	0	0	0	0	0	0	0
920	960	40	15	0	0	0	0	0	0	0	0	0
960	1,000	44	19	0	0	0	0	0	0	0	0	0
1,000	1,040	48	23	0	0	0	0	0	0	0	0	0
1,040	1,080	52	27	0	0	0	0	0	0	0	0	0
1,080	1,120	56	31	5	0	0	0	0	0	0	0	0
1,120	1,160	60	35	9	0	0	0	0	0	0	0	0
1,160	1,200	64	39	13	0	0	0	0	0	0	0	0
1,200	1,240	68	43	17	0	0	0	0	0	0	0	0
1,240	1,280	72	47	21	0	0	0	0	0	0	0	0
1,280	1,320	76	51	25	0	0	0	0	0	0	0	0
1,320	1,360	80	55	29	4	0	0	0	0	0	0	0
1,360	1,400	84	59	33	8	0	0	0	0	0	0	0
1,400	1,440	88	63	37	12	0	0	0	0	0	0	0
1,440	1,480	92	67	41	16	0	0	0	0	0	0	0
1,480	1,520	96	71	45	20	0	0	0	0	0	0	0
1,520	1,560	100	75	49	24	0	0	0	0	0	0	0
1,560	1,600	106	79	53	28	4	0	0	0	0	0	0
1,600	1,640	112	83	57	32	8	0	0	0	0	0	0
1,640	1,680	118	87	61	36	12	0	0	0	0	0	0
1,680	1,720	124	91	65	40	16	0	0	0	0	0	0
1,720	1,760	130	95	69	44	20	0	0	0	0	0	0
1,760	1,800	136	99	73	48	24	0	0	0	0	0	0
1,800	1,840	142	105	77	52	28	3	0	0	0	0	0
1,840	1,880	148	111	81	56	32	7	0	0	0	0	0
1,880	1,920	154	117	85	60	36	11	0	0	0	0	0
1,920	1,960	160	123	89	64	40	15	0	0	0	0	0
1,960	2,000	166	129	93	68	44	19	0	0	0	0	0
2,000	2,040	172	135	97	72	48	23	0	0	0	0	0
2,040	2,080	178	141	103	76	52	27	2	0	0	0	0
2,080	2,120	184	147	109	80	56	31	6	0	0	0	0
2,120	2,160	190	153	115	84	60	35	10	0	0	0	0
2,160	2,200	196	159	121	88	64	39	14	0	0	0	0
2,200	2,240	202	165	127	92	68	43	18	0	0	0	0
2,240	2,280	208	171	133	96	72	47	22	0	0	0	0
2,280	2,320	214	177	139	102	76	51	26	1	0	0	0
2,320	2,360	220	183	145	108	80	55	30	5	0	0	0
2,360	2,400	226	189	151	114	84	59	34	9	0	0	0
2,400	2,440	232	195	157	120	88	63	38	13	0	0	0
2,440	2,480	238	201	163	126	92	67	42	17	0	0	0
2,480	2,520	244	207	169	132	96	71	46	21	0	0	0
2,520	2,560	250	213	175	138	100	75	50	25	0	0	0
2,560	2,600	256	219	181	144	106	79	54	29	4	0	0
2,600	2,640	262	225	187	150	112	83	58	33	8	0	0
2,640	2,680	268	231	193	156	118	87	62	37	12	0	0
2,680	2,720	274	237	199	162	124	91	66	41	16	0	0
2,720	2,760	280	243	205	168	130	95	70	45	20	0	0
2,760	2,800	286	249	211	174	136	99	74	49	24	0	0
2,800	2,840	292	255	217	180	142	105	78	53	28	3	0
2,840	2,880	298	261	223	186	148	111	82	57	32	7	0
2,880	2,920	304	267	229	192	154	117	86	61	36	11	0
2,920	2,960	310	273	235	198	160	123	90	65	40	15	0
2,960	3,000	316	279	241	204	166	129	94	69	44	19	0
3,000	3,040	322	285	247	210	172	135	98	73	48	23	0
3,040	3,080	328	291	253	216	178	141	103	77	52	27	2
3,080	3,120	334	297	259	222	184	147	109	81	56	31	6
3,120	3,160	340	303	265	228	190	153	115	85	60	35	10
3,160	3,200	346	309	271	234	196	159	121	89	64	39	14
3,200	3,240	352	315	277	240	202	165	127	93	68	43	18

(MONTHLY — MARRIED PERSONS)

MARRIED Persons—MONTHLY Payroll Period
(For Wages Paid in 2002)

| If the wages are— | | And the number of withholding allowances claimed is— | | | | | | | | | | |
At least	But less than	0	1	2	3	4	5	6	7	8	9	10
		The amount of income tax to be withheld is—										
$3,240	$3,280	$358	$321	$283	$246	$208	$171	$133	$97	$72	$47	$22
3,280	3,320	364	327	289	252	214	177	139	102	76	51	26
3,320	3,360	370	333	295	258	220	183	145	108	80	55	30
3,360	3,400	376	339	301	264	226	189	151	114	84	59	34
3,400	3,440	382	345	307	270	232	195	157	120	88	63	38
3,440	3,480	388	351	313	276	238	201	163	126	92	67	42
3,480	3,520	394	357	319	282	244	207	169	132	96	71	46
3,520	3,560	400	363	325	288	250	213	175	138	100	75	50
3,560	3,600	406	369	331	294	256	219	181	144	106	79	54
3,600	3,640	412	375	337	300	262	225	187	150	112	83	58
3,640	3,680	418	381	343	306	268	231	193	156	118	87	62
3,680	3,720	424	387	349	312	274	237	199	162	124	91	66
3,720	3,760	430	393	355	318	280	243	205	168	130	95	70
3,760	3,800	436	399	361	324	286	249	211	174	136	99	74
3,800	3,840	442	405	367	330	292	255	217	180	142	105	78
3,840	3,880	448	411	373	336	298	261	223	186	148	111	82
3,880	3,920	454	417	379	342	304	267	229	192	154	117	86
3,920	3,960	460	423	385	348	310	273	235	198	160	123	90
3,960	4,000	466	429	391	354	316	279	241	204	166	129	94
4,000	4,040	472	435	397	360	322	285	247	210	172	135	98
4,040	4,080	478	441	403	366	328	291	253	216	178	141	103
4,080	4,120	484	447	409	372	334	297	259	222	184	147	109
4,120	4,160	490	453	415	378	340	303	265	228	190	153	115
4,160	4,200	496	459	421	384	346	309	271	234	196	159	121
4,200	4,240	502	465	427	390	352	315	277	240	202	165	127
4,240	4,280	508	471	433	396	358	321	283	246	208	171	133
4,280	4,320	515	477	439	402	364	327	289	252	214	177	139
4,320	4,360	526	483	445	408	370	333	295	258	220	183	145
4,360	4,400	536	489	451	414	376	339	301	264	226	189	151
4,400	4,440	547	495	457	420	382	345	307	270	232	195	157
4,440	4,480	558	501	463	426	388	351	313	276	238	201	163
4,480	4,520	569	507	469	432	394	357	319	282	244	207	169
4,520	4,560	580	513	475	438	400	363	325	288	250	213	175
4,560	4,600	590	523	481	444	406	369	331	294	256	219	181
4,600	4,640	601	534	487	450	412	375	337	300	262	225	187
4,640	4,680	612	545	493	456	418	381	343	306	268	231	193
4,680	4,720	623	555	499	462	424	387	349	312	274	237	199
4,720	4,760	634	566	505	468	430	393	355	318	280	243	205
4,760	4,800	644	577	511	474	436	399	361	324	286	249	211
4,800	4,840	655	588	520	480	442	405	367	330	292	255	217
4,840	4,880	666	599	531	486	448	411	373	336	298	261	223
4,880	4,920	677	609	542	492	454	417	379	342	304	267	229
4,920	4,960	688	620	553	498	460	423	385	348	310	273	235
4,960	5,000	698	631	563	504	466	429	391	354	316	279	241
5,000	5,040	709	642	574	510	472	435	397	360	322	285	247
5,040	5,080	720	653	585	518	478	441	403	366	328	291	253
5,080	5,120	731	663	596	528	484	447	409	372	334	297	259
5,120	5,160	742	674	607	539	490	453	415	378	340	303	265
5,160	5,200	752	685	617	550	496	459	421	384	346	309	271
5,200	5,240	763	696	628	561	502	465	427	390	352	315	277
5,240	5,280	774	707	639	572	508	471	433	396	358	321	283
5,280	5,320	785	717	650	583	515	477	439	402	364	327	289
5,320	5,360	796	728	661	593	526	483	445	408	370	333	295
5,360	5,400	806	739	671	604	536	489	451	414	376	339	301
5,400	5,440	817	750	682	615	547	495	457	420	382	345	307
5,440	5,480	828	761	693	626	558	501	463	426	388	351	313
5,480	5,520	839	771	704	636	569	507	469	432	394	357	319
5,520	5,560	850	782	715	647	580	513	475	438	400	363	325
5,560	5,600	860	793	725	658	590	523	481	444	406	369	331
5,600	5,640	871	804	736	669	601	534	487	450	412	375	337
5,640	5,680	882	815	747	680	612	545	493	456	418	381	343
5,680	5,720	893	825	758	690	623	555	499	462	424	387	349
5,720	5,760	904	836	769	701	634	566	505	468	430	393	355
5,760	5,800	914	847	779	712	644	577	511	474	436	399	361
5,800	5,840	925	858	790	723	655	588	520	480	442	405	367

$5,840 and over — Use Table 4(b) for a **MARRIED** person on page T-4.

WAGE-BRACKET WITHHOLDING TABLES

SINGLE Persons—DAILY OR MISCELLANEOUS Payroll Period
(For Wages Paid in 2002)

If the wages are— At least	But less than	0	1	2	3	4	5	6	7	8	9	10
		The amount of income tax to be withheld is—										
$0	$15	$0	$0	$0	$0	$0	$0	$0	$0	$0	$0	$0
15	18	1	0	0	0	0	0	0	0	0	0	0
18	21	1	0	0	0	0	0	0	0	0	0	0
21	24	2	0	0	0	0	0	0	0	0	0	0
24	27	2	0	0	0	0	0	0	0	0	0	0
27	30	2	0	0	0	0	0	0	0	0	0	0
30	33	3	0	0	0	0	0	0	0	0	0	0
33	36	3	0	0	0	0	0	0	0	0	0	0
36	39	3	1	0	0	0	0	0	0	0	0	0
39	42	3	1	0	0	0	0	0	0	0	0	0
42	45	4	1	0	0	0	0	0	0	0	0	0
45	48	4	2	0	0	0	0	0	0	0	0	0
48	51	4	2	0	0	0	0	0	0	0	0	0
51	54	5	3	0	0	0	0	0	0	0	0	0
54	57	5	3	0	0	0	0	0	0	0	0	0
57	60	6	3	1	0	0	0	0	0	0	0	0
60	63	6	4	1	0	0	0	0	0	0	0	0
63	66	7	4	1	0	0	0	0	0	0	0	0
66	69	7	5	2	0	0	0	0	0	0	0	0
69	72	8	5	2	0	0	0	0	0	0	0	0
72	75	8	5	3	0	0	0	0	0	0	0	0
75	78	9	6	3	1	0	0	0	0	0	0	0
78	81	9	6	4	1	0	0	0	0	0	0	0
81	84	10	7	4	1	0	0	0	0	0	0	0
84	87	10	7	5	2	0	0	0	0	0	0	0
87	90	11	8	5	2	0	0	0	0	0	0	0
90	93	11	8	5	3	0	0	0	0	0	0	0
93	96	11	9	6	3	1	0	0	0	0	0	0
96	99	12	9	6	4	1	0	0	0	0	0	0
99	102	12	10	7	4	1	0	0	0	0	0	0
102	105	13	10	7	5	2	0	0	0	0	0	0
105	108	13	10	8	5	2	0	0	0	0	0	0
108	111	14	11	8	5	3	0	0	0	0	0	0
111	114	14	11	9	6	3	1	0	0	0	0	0
114	117	15	12	9	6	4	1	0	0	0	0	0
117	120	16	12	10	7	4	1	0	0	0	0	0
120	123	17	13	10	7	5	2	0	0	0	0	0
123	126	18	14	10	8	5	2	0	0	0	0	0
126	129	19	15	11	8	5	3	0	0	0	0	0
129	132	20	16	12	9	6	3	1	0	0	0	0
132	135	21	17	13	9	6	4	1	0	0	0	0
135	138	22	17	14	10	7	4	1	0	0	0	0
138	141	23	18	14	11	7	5	2	0	0	0	0
141	144	24	19	15	11	8	5	2	0	0	0	0
144	147	24	20	16	12	8	5	3	0	0	0	0
147	150	25	21	17	13	9	6	3	1	0	0	0
150	153	26	21	17	14	10	6	4	1	0	0	0
153	156	27	22	18	14	10	7	4	1	0	0	0
156	159	28	23	19	15	11	7	5	2	0	0	0
159	162	29	24	20	16	11	8	5	2	0	0	0
162	165	30	25	20	16	12	8	5	3	0	0	0
165	168	31	25	21	17	13	9	6	3	1	0	0
168	171	31	26	22	18	13	10	6	4	1	0	0
171	174	32	27	23	18	14	10	7	4	1	0	0
174	177	33	28	23	19	15	11	7	5	2	0	0
177	180	34	29	24	20	16	11	8	5	2	0	0
180	183	35	29	25	20	16	12	8	5	3	0	0
183	186	35	30	26	21	17	13	9	6	3	1	0
186	189	36	31	26	22	18	13	10	6	4	1	0
189	192	37	32	27	23	18	14	10	7	4	1	0
192	195	38	33	28	23	19	15	11	7	5	2	0
195	198	39	33	29	24	20	15	11	8	5	2	0
198	201	39	34	29	25	20	16	12	8	5	3	0
201	204	40	35	30	26	21	17	13	9	6	3	1
204	207	41	36	31	26	22	17	13	10	6	4	1
207	210	42	37	32	27	23	18	14	10	7	4	1
210	213	42	38	33	28	24	19	15	11	7	5	2
213	216	43	38	33	29	24	20	16	12	8	5	2
216	219	44	39	34	30	25	21	16	13	9	6	3
219	222	44	40	35	30	26	21	17	13	9	6	3

DAILY OR MISC. SINGLE PERSONS

SINGLE Persons—DAILY OR MISCELLANEOUS Payroll Period
(For Wages Paid in 2002)

If the wages are— At least	But less than	0	1	2	3	4	5	6	7	8	9	10
		The amount of income tax to be withheld is—										
$222	$225	$44	$41	$38	$35	$32	$28	$25	$22	$19	$16	$14
225	228	45	42	39	36	33	29	26	23	20	17	14
228	231	46	43	40	37	34	30	27	24	21	18	14
231	234	46	43	40	37	34	31	28	25	22	18	15
234	237	47	44	41	38	35	32	29	25	22	19	16
237	240	48	45	42	39	36	33	30	26	23	20	17
240	243	49	46	43	40	37	34	31	27	24	21	18
243	246	50	47	44	41	38	35	32	28	25	22	19
246	249	50	47	44	41	38	35	32	29	25	22	19
249	252	51	48	45	42	39	36	33	30	26	23	20
252	255	52	49	46	43	40	37	34	31	27	24	21
255	258	53	50	47	44	41	37	34	31	28	25	22
258	261	54	51	48	44	41	38	35	32	29	26	22
261	264	55	51	48	45	42	39	36	33	30	26	23
264	267	56	52	49	46	43	40	37	34	30	27	24
267	270	57	53	50	47	44	41	38	35	31	28	25
270	273	58	54	51	48	45	41	38	35	32	29	26
273	276	59	55	52	48	46	42	39	36	33	30	27
276	279	59	56	52	49	46	43	40	37	34	30	27
279	282	60	57	53	50	47	44	41	38	34	31	28
282	285	61	58	54	51	48	45	42	39	35	32	29
285	288	62	59	55	52	49	45	42	39	36	33	30
288	291	63	60	56	53	50	46	43	40	37	34	31
291	294	64	60	57	54	51	47	44	41	38	34	31
294	297	65	61	58	54	51	48	45	42	39	35	32
297	300	66	62	59	55	52	49	46	42	39	36	33
300	303	67	63	60	56	53	49	46	43	40	37	34
303	306	68	64	61	57	54	51	47	44	41	38	35
306	309	68	65	61	58	55	51	48	45	42	38	35
309	312	69	66	62	59	55	52	49	46	43	39	36
312	315	70	67	63	60	56	53	50	46	43	40	37
315	318	71	68	64	61	57	54	51	47	44	41	38
318	321	72	69	65	62	58	55	51	48	45	42	39
321	324	73	69	66	63	59	56	52	49	46	43	39
324	327	74	70	67	63	60	57	53	50	47	43	40
327	330	75	71	68	64	61	57	54	51	47	44	41
330	333	76	72	69	65	62	58	55	52	48	45	42
333	336	77	73	70	66	63	59	56	53	49	46	43
336	339	77	74	70	67	64	60	57	54	51	47	44
339	341	78	75	71	68	64	61	58	54	51	48	44
341	343	79	75	72	68	65	61	58	55	52	48	45
343	345	79	76	73	69	66	62	59	56	52	49	45
345	347	80	77	73	70	66	63	60	57	53	50	46
347	349	80	77	74	71	67	64	60	57	54	50	47
349	351	81	78	74	71	68	64	61	58	54	51	47
351	353	82	78	75	71	68	65	62	58	55	51	48
353	355	82	79	75	72	69	65	62	59	55	52	48
355	357	83	79	76	73	69	66	63	59	56	52	49
357	359	84	80	77	73	70	66	63	60	57	53	49
359	361	84	81	77	74	70	67	64	60	57	53	50
361	363	85	81	78	74	71	68	64	61	58	54	50
363	365	85	82	78	75	72	68	65	61	58	55	51
365	367	86	82	79	76	72	69	65	62	59	55	52
367	369	87	83	80	76	73	69	66	63	59	56	52
369	371	87	84	80	77	73	70	67	63	60	56	53
371	373	88	84	81	77	74	71	67	64	60	57	53
373	375	88	85	81	78	75	71	68	64	61	57	54
375	377	89	85	82	79	75	72	68	65	61	58	54
377	379	90	86	83	79	76	72	69	66	62	58	55
379	381	90	87	83	80	76	73	70	66	63	59	55
381	383	91	87	84	80	77	73	70	67	63	60	56
383	385	91	88	84	81	78	74	71	67	64	60	57
385	387	92	88	85	82	78	75	71	68	64	61	57
387	389	93	89	86	82	79	75	72	68	65	61	58
389	391	93	90	86	83	79	76	72	69	65	62	59

$391 and over   Use Table 8(a) for a **SINGLE person** on page T-4.

WAGE-BRACKET WITHHOLDING TABLES

MARRIED Persons—DAILY OR MISCELLANEOUS Payroll Period
(For Wages Paid in 2002)

If the wages are—		And the number of withholding allowances claimed is—										
At least	But less than	0	1	2	3	4	5	6	7	8	9	10
		The amount of income tax to be withheld is—										
$237	$240	$35	$31	$28	$25	$23	$21	$19	$18	$16	$14	$12
240	243	35	32	29	26	23	22	20	18	16	15	13
243	246	36	33	30	27	24	22	20	19	17	15	13
246	249	37	34	31	28	25	23	21	19	17	16	14
249	252	38	35	32	28	25	23	21	20	18	16	14
252	255	39	36	32	29	26	24	22	20	18	17	15
255	258	39	36	33	30	27	25	23	21	19	17	15
258	261	40	37	34	31	28	25	23	21	19	18	16
261	264	41	38	35	32	29	26	24	22	20	18	16
264	267	41	39	36	33	30	27	25	23	20	18	16
267	270	43	40	36	33	30	28	26	24	21	19	17
270	273	43	40	38	34	31	28	26	24	22	19	17
273	276	44	41	39	35	32	29	27	25	22	20	18
276	279	45	42	40	36	33	30	27	25	23	20	18
279	282	46	43	40	37	33	31	28	26	23	21	19
282	285	47	44	40	38	34	31	29	27	24	22	19
285	288	48	44	41	39	35	32	30	27	25	22	20
288	291	48	45	42	40	36	33	30	28	25	23	20
291	294	49	46	43	40	37	34	31	29	26	24	21
294	297	50	47	44	41	38	34	31	29	27	24	22
297	300	51	48	45	41	38	35	32	30	27	25	22
300	303	52	48	45	42	39	36	33	31	28	26	23
303	306	52	49	46	43	40	37	34	31	29	26	24
306	309	53	50	47	44	41	38	35	32	29	27	24
309	312	54	51	48	45	42	38	35	33	30	28	25
312	315	55	52	49	45	42	39	36	34	31	28	26
315	318	56	53	50	46	43	40	37	34	32	29	27
318	321	56	53	51	47	44	41	38	35	32	30	28
321	324	57	54	52	48	45	42	39	36	33	32	29
324	327	58	55	52	49	46	42	39	37	34	33	30
327	330	59	56	53	50	46	43	40	38	35	34	31
330	333	60	57	54	51	47	44	41	39	36	35	31
333	336	60	57	54	51	48	45	42	39	37	36	32
336	339	61	58	55	52	48	45	42	40	38	37	33
339	341	62	58	55	52	49	46	43	40	39	37	34
341	343	63	59	56	53	50	47	44	41	40	38	34
343	345	63	60	57	53	50	47	44	42	40	39	35
345	347	64	60	57	54	51	48	45	43	41	39	36
347	349	64	61	58	55	52	49	46	43	42	40	36
349	351	65	62	58	55	52	49	46	44	43	40	37
351	353	65	62	59	56	53	50	47	45	43	41	38
353	355	66	63	60	57	53	50	47	45	44	42	38
355	357	66	63	60	57	54	51	48	46	44	43	39
357	359	67	64	61	58	55	52	49	46	45	43	40
359	361	67	64	61	58	55	52	49	47	46	44	40
361	363	68	65	62	59	55	52	50	48	46	45	42
363	365	68	65	62	59	56	53	50	48	46	45	43
365	367	69	66	63	60	56	53	51	49	47	46	44
367	369	70	66	63	60	57	54	51	50	48	47	45
369	371	70	67	64	61	58	55	52	51	49	47	45
371	373	71	68	65	62	58	55	52	51	49	48	46
373	375	71	68	65	62	59	56	53	52	50	49	47
375	377	72	69	66	63	59	56	54	53	51	49	47
377	379	72	69	66	63	60	57	54	53	52	50	48
379	381	73	70	67	64	60	57	55	54	52	51	49
381	383	73	70	67	64	61	58	55	54	53	51	50
383	385	74	71	68	65	62	59	56	55	53	52	51
385	387	74	71	68	65	62	59	56	55	54	52	51
387	389	75	72	69	66	63	60	57	56	54	53	52
389	391	76	72	69	66	63	60	57	57	55	54	53
391	393	76	73	70	67	64	61	58	57	56	54	53
393	395	77	74	71	68	64	61	58	58	56	55	54
395	397	77	74	71	68	65	62	59	58	57	55	55
397	399	78	75	72	69	65	62	59	59	58	56	56
399	401	78	75	72	69	66	63	60	59	59	57	57

$401 and over — Use Table 8(b) for a **MARRIED person** on page T-4.

MARRIED Persons—DAILY OR MISCELLANEOUS Payroll Period
(For Wages Paid in 2002)

If the wages are—		And the number of withholding allowances claimed is—										
At least	But less than	0	1	2	3	4	5	6	7	8	9	10
		The amount of income tax to be withheld is—										
$30	$33	$0	$0	$0	$0	$0	$0	$0	$0	$0	$0	$0
30	33	0	0	0	0	0	0	0	0	0	0	0
33	36	1	0	0	0	0	0	0	0	0	0	0
36	39	1	0	0	0	0	0	0	0	0	0	0
39	42	1	0	0	0	0	0	0	0	0	0	0
42	45	2	0	0	0	0	0	0	0	0	0	0
45	48	2	0	0	0	0	0	0	0	0	0	0
48	51	2	1	0	0	0	0	0	0	0	0	0
51	54	3	1	0	0	0	0	0	0	0	0	0
54	57	3	1	0	0	0	0	0	0	0	0	0
57	60	3	2	0	0	0	0	0	0	0	0	0
60	63	4	2	1	0	0	0	0	0	0	0	0
63	66	4	2	1	0	0	0	0	0	0	0	0
66	69	5	3	1	0	0	0	0	0	0	0	0
69	72	5	3	2	0	0	0	0	0	0	0	0
72	75	6	4	2	0	0	0	0	0	0	0	0
75	78	6	4	3	0	0	0	0	0	0	0	0
78	81	7	5	3	1	0	0	0	0	0	0	0
81	84	7	5	4	1	0	0	0	0	0	0	0
84	87	7	6	4	2	0	0	0	0	0	0	0
87	90	8	6	5	2	0	0	0	0	0	0	0
90	93	9	7	5	3	1	0	0	0	0	0	0
93	96	9	7	6	3	1	0	0	0	0	0	0
96	99	10	8	6	4	2	0	0	0	0	0	0
99	102	11	8	7	4	2	0	0	0	0	0	0
102	105	12	9	7	5	3	1	0	0	0	0	0
105	108	12	10	8	5	3	1	0	0	0	0	0
108	111	13	10	8	6	4	2	0	0	0	0	0
111	114	14	11	9	6	4	2	0	0	0	0	0
114	117	14	12	9	7	5	3	1	0	0	0	0
117	120	15	12	10	7	5	3	1	0	0	0	0
120	123	15	13	11	8	6	4	2	0	0	0	0
123	126	16	14	11	9	6	4	2	0	0	0	0
126	129	16	14	12	9	7	5	3	1	0	0	0
129	132	17	15	12	10	7	5	3	1	0	0	0
132	135	17	15	13	11	8	6	4	1	0	0	0
135	138	18	16	14	11	9	6	4	2	0	0	0
138	141	18	16	14	12	9	7	5	2	0	0	0
141	144	19	17	15	12	10	7	5	3	1	0	0
144	147	20	18	15	13	11	8	6	3	1	0	0
147	150	20	18	16	14	11	9	6	4	2	0	0
150	153	21	19	16	14	12	9	7	4	2	0	0
153	156	21	19	17	15	12	10	7	5	3	1	0
156	159	22	20	18	15	13	10	8	5	3	1	0
159	162	22	20	18	16	13	11	9	6	4	2	0
162	165	23	21	19	16	14	12	9	7	4	2	0
165	168	24	22	19	17	15	12	10	7	5	3	1
168	171	24	22	20	18	15	13	10	8	6	3	1
171	174	25	23	20	18	16	13	11	9	6	4	2
174	177	25	23	21	19	16	14	12	9	7	4	2
177	180	26	24	22	19	17	15	12	10	7	5	3
180	183	27	24	22	20	18	15	13	11	8	6	3
183	186	27	25	23	20	18	16	13	11	9	6	4
186	189	28	26	23	21	19	16	14	12	9	7	5
189	192	29	27	24	22	20	17	15	12	10	8	5
192	195	31	28	25	23	21	18	15	13	11	8	6
195	198	31	28	25	23	21	18	16	14	11	9	7
198	201	32	29	26	24	22	19	16	14	12	9	7
201	204	33	30	27	24	22	20	17	15	13	10	8
204	207	34	31	28	25	23	20	18	16	13	11	9
207	210	26	24	21	20	18	20	18	16	14	11	9
210	213	27	24	22	20	18	19	18	17	15	12	10
213	216	28	25	23	21	19	20	19	17	15	13	10
216	219	29	26	24	22	20	21	19	18	16	13	11
219	222	30	27	24	22	20	22	20	18	17	14	12
222	225	31	28	25	23	21	22	20	19	17	15	12
225	228	31	28	26	23	21	23	21	19	18	15	13
228	231	32	29	26	24	22	24	22	20	18	16	13
231	234	33	30	27	24	22	24	22	20	19	16	14
234	237	34	31	28	25	23	25	23	21	19	17	14

DAILY OR MISC. MARRIED PERSONS

Answers to
self-study quizzes

Self-Study Quiz 2–1

2. False. Live-in domestic workers do not have to be paid overtime.
4. False. Individual employee coverage is not affected by the work of fellow employees.

Self-Study Quiz 2–2

1. $2.13
2. $30.80 $206.00 ($5.15 × 40 hours)
                −85.20 weekly wage
                −90.00 tip credit claimed by employer
                $ 30.80

Self-Study Quiz 2–3

	Hourly Rate	Overtime Rate
1.	$13.13	$19.70
2.	$11.15	$16.73
3.	$16.73	$25.10
4.	$9.23	$13.85

Self-Study Quiz 2–4

1. $276.00
2. $6.00 ($276.00 ÷ 46)
3. $3.00 ($6.00 × 0.50)
4. $18.00 ($3.00 × 6)
5. $294.00

Self-Study Quiz 3–1

1. Yes. Full-time life insurance salespersons are covered as statutory employees for social security, Medicare, and FUTA tax purposes.
2. Yes. Federal government employees hired after 1983 are subject to full FICA coverage.
3. No. Real estate agents are considered independent contractors.
4. No. Schuck offers his services to the general public and is considered an independent contractor.

Self-Study Quiz 3–2

1. No. The gift certificates are of nominal value.
2. Yes. Personal use of a company vehicle for non-business-related activities constitutes a taxable fringe benefit.
3. No. An employer may contribute to an SEP set up by or on behalf of its employees. The employer's contributions are exempt from FICA taxes if reason to believe exists that employees will be entitled to deduct the employer contributions for federal income tax purposes.
4. No. Generally, employers do not have to include in wages or withhold on the value of payment made for job-related training for their employees.
5. Yes. Payments by employers for involuntary separation of an employee from the employer's service are taxable under FICA.

Self-Study Quiz 3–3

Employee	OASDI	HI
Mary Britton	13.95	3.26
Bob Yold	18.60	4.35
Martin Rold	10.85	2.54
Maria Aldo	62.00	14.50
Gil Hammerstien	136.40	31.90
Totals	241.80	56.55
Employer's taxes (based on $3,900 gross wages)	241.80	56.55

Gil Hammerstien will earn an annual salary of $114,400, which exceeds the wage base for OASDI taxes.

Through the 40th weekly payday, Hammerstien will have cumulative wages of $88,000.

When the payment is made on the 41st payday, Hammerstien will exceed the wage base for OASDI taxes:

Cumulative wages	$88,000
Current wage payment	2,200
	$90,200

Therefore, only $1,700 is taxable.

Self-Study Quiz 3–4

1. $54,000 ($1,000 per week × 52 = $52,000 + $2,000 bonus)
2. $82,000 ($54,000 + $28,000)
3. $28,000 (Taxable wage base $89,700)
4. $4,284 ($3,472—OASDI + $812—HI)

Self-Study Quiz 3–5

1. Braxton should deposit its taxes by the following Wednesday.
2. During the first calendar year for a new business, the company is a monthly depositor. However, if during the year it has an undeposited tax liability of $100,000 (which triggers the one-banking-day rule), the company becomes a semiweekly depositor for the remainder of the year.
3. The additional taxes are not accumulated with the previous liability of $105,000. The company should follow the semiweekly deposit rules and deposit the $20,000 by Friday.

Self-Study Quiz 4–1

✓   a. Meals provided to employees for the convenience of the employer on the employer's premises.

      b. Bonuses to managers and supervisors are considered compensation for services rendered as employees and are subject to withholding.

✓   c. The use of on-site athletic facilities by employees are considered a nontaxable fringe benefit.

 ✓   d. Advances for business expenses reasonably expected to be incurred.

_____ e. Sick pay is subject to withholding.

_____ f. Memberships in social or country clubs are taxable fringe benefits and are subject to withholding.

 ✓   g. No-additional-cost meals provided to employees at an employer-operated eating establishment.

Self-Study Quiz 4–2

1. The payroll manager should inform Kyle that the company cannot reimburse her for any overwithholding that may have occurred prior to her submitting a new W-4. The only circumstances that allow the employer to reimburse an employee for overwithholding is if the employer failed to put a new W-4 into effect that resulted in overwithholding.

2. The payroll manager must inform Bradley that an employee may claim exemption from withholding for only one tax year at a time. The exemption must be claimed each year by February 15. If a new certificate is not filed, the employer must withhold at the single rate with zero withholding allowances.

3. Volmer may claim six personal allowances, as identified on the personal allowance worksheet accompanying Form W-4:

    a. One allowance for himself.

    b. One allowance for his spouse.

    c. One allowance for being married, having one job, and his spouse not working.

    d. One allowance for each dependent child (total of 3).

Self-Study Quiz 4–3

Step 1—Round gross wages: **$1,100**

Step 2—Multiply the number of allowances by the weekly allowance amount: **3 × $57.69 = $173.07**

Step 3—Subtract the value of the allowances from the gross pay: **$1,100 − $173.07 = $926.93**

Step 4—Compute the tax from the percentage tax table for WEEKLY MARRIED person:

        Over $355 But not over $991 . . . . 15% of excess over $355 plus $23.10

        $926.93 − $355.00 = $571.93 × 15% = $85.79 + $23.10   **Total tax to be withheld: = $108.89**

Self-Study Quiz 4–4

Employee	Tax
Lamb	$119
Nurin	$ 99
Hogan	$ 20
Vick	$419.39 must use Percentage Method
Marks	$ 96

Self-Study Quiz 4–5

Method A:	Tax previously withheld on semimonthly wage of $1,450 = $115
	Tax on wage and bonus ($1,950): $190
	Less tax previously withheld: 115
	Withholding on bonus: $ 75
Method B:	27% × $500 = $135

Self-Study Quiz 4–6

1. According to Figure 4–9, Brewer is entitled to an advance EIC payment of $10 per week.

2. The Gregory Company can treat the EIC payments as if the company has paid the total amount of income taxes withheld, and it can use any remaining amounts against its deposit of social security taxes. The company must, however, make a deposit for the amount of employment taxes (employees' income taxes, social security taxes, and employer's social security taxes) that exceeds the amount of the EIC payments.

Self-Study Quiz 4–7

1. The company should report the total amount deducted from each employee in Box 14 of Form W-2. This box is to provide "other" information the company wants to give the employees. The company should label the amount as "union dues" in Box 14.

2. If an employee leaves the service of the employer, the employer may furnish Form W-2 any time after employment ends. If the employee requests Form W-2, the employer should give it to him/her within 30 days of the request or final wage payment, whichever is later. If there is a reasonable expectation that the employees may be rehired before the end of the year, the employer may delay providing Form W-2 until January following the close of the calendar year.

3. If Form W-2 has been destroyed or lost, employers are authorized to furnish substitute copies to the employee. Trident should provide a substitute form to Becker. The form should be clearly marked "Reissued Statement," and the company should not send the substitute statement to the Social Security Administration.

Self-Study Quiz 5–1

4.1% of $188,000 = $7,708		SUTA tax
6.2% of $188,000 =	$11,656	Gross FUTA tax
4.1% of $188,000 = $7,708	_____	Credit for SUTA tax paid
1.3% of $188,000 = 2,444	10,152	Additional credit to get to 5.4%
0.8% of $188,000	$ 1,504	Net FUTA tax

Self-Study Quiz 5–2

From the Summary of State Unemployment Compensation Laws (Figure 5–1), the taxable wages in Colorado is $10,000. However, the company receives a credit of $6,000 against this limit because of unemployment taxes paid to Arizona on John's wages in that state. Therefore, the calculation is:

John's wages in Colorado	$26,000
Over taxable limit	16,000
Colorado's SUTA wage limit	$10,000
Credit for wages taxed in Arizona	6,000
John's taxable wages in Colorado	$ 4,000
Moss' SUTA tax rate in Colorado	× 2.9%
Amount of the company's SUTA tax in Colorado	$ 116

Self-Study Quiz 5–3

1st Quarter—$22,000 × 0.008 = $176.00 due on 4/30/03
2nd Quarter—$24,000 × 0.008 = $192.00 due on 7/31/03
3rd Quarter—$12,000 × 0.008 = $96.00 no deposit due
4th Quarter—$10,000 × 0.008 = $80.00 + $96.00 = $176.00 due on 2/2/04

Self-Study Quiz 6–1

January 22	Salary Expense	95,190.00	
	FICA Taxes Payable—OASDI		5,901.78
	FICA Taxes Payable—HI		1,380.26
	Employees FIT Payable		14,270.00
	Employees SIT Payable		1,427.85
	SUTA Taxes Payable		951.90
	Salaries Payable (Cash)		71,258.21

Self-Study Quiz 6–2

January 22	Payroll Taxes	11,042.05	
	FICA Taxes Payable—OASDI		5,901.78
	FICA Taxes Payable—HI		1,380.26
	FUTA Taxes Payable		761.52
	SUTA Taxes Payable		2,998.49

Glossary

A

Affirmative action plan a formal plan that prescribes a specific program to eliminate, limit, or prevent discriminatory treatment on the basis of race, ethnic group, and sex.

Annualizing wages method of determining amount of income taxes to be withheld by multiplying the wages for one payroll period by the number of periods in the year, determining the annual amount of withholding required on the total wages, and dividing the annual withholding by the number of payroll periods.

Application form personnel record which gives the applicant an opportunity to provide complete information as to personal qualifications, training, and experience.

Average indexed monthly earnings a worker's average monthly earnings, updated to reflect changes in wage levels.

B

Backup withholding amount of income tax withheld by payers of taxable interest, dividends, and certain other payments made to payees who have failed to furnish the payers with correct identification numbers.

Biweekly every two weeks.

Business expense cost of operating a business that is deductible by the employer for federal income tax purposes.

C

Change in payroll rate form document that notifies the proper departments of a change in the employee's rate of remuneration.

Check-off system withholding of union dues from employees' wages by the employer.

Commission stated percentage of revenue paid an employee who transacts a piece of business or performs a service.

Common-law relationship the state existing when the employer has the right to control both what work will be done and how it will be done.

Constructively paid wages remunerations that are credited to the account of, or set apart for, an employee so that they may be drawn upon at any time, even though they are not actually possessed by the employee.

Continental system method of recording time on time cards in which the day is divided into one 24-hour period, with time running from 12 midnight to 12 midnight.

Contribution report quarterly tax return filed with the state by the employer that provides a summary of the wages paid during the period and shows the computation of the tax or contribution.

Currently insured criterion used to determine eligibility for social security benefits; persons must have at least six quarters of coverage during the 13-quarter period ending with (1) the quarter in which they died or (2) the quarter in which they became entitled to old-age insurance benefits or most recently became entitled to disability benefits.

D

Defined contribution plan a retirement plan that provides future benefits based solely on the amount paid by each employee and employer into the account, plus investment gains.

Dependency allowance an additional weekly benefit paid to unemployed workers with dependents.

Disability benefits payments to employees who are absent from their jobs because of illness, accident, or disease not arising out of their employment.

Dismissal payments amounts paid by employers to workers who have been separated from employment; also known as *payments in lieu of notice, separation pay,* or *terminal leave pay.*

Disposable earnings the earnings remaining after withholding for income taxes and for other amounts required by law.

Domestic service services of a household nature performed in or about a private home of the person who employs the domestic.

E

Earned income credit (EIC) reduction in federal income taxes mostly for workers who have dependent children and maintain a household.

Educational assistance the expenses that an employer pays for an employee's education, such as tuition, fees, and payments for books, supplies, and equipment.

Electronic funds transfer system (EFTS) system whereby the employer transfers employees' net pays to employees' bank accounts with electronic equipment rather than issuing paychecks.

Employee any individual performing services for an employer in the legal relationship of employer and employee.

Employee history record continuous record of the relationship between the employer and the employee.

Employee's earnings record payroll record for each employee that is used to provide complete information about the accumulated earnings of each employee.

Employer any person or organization who employs one or more individuals for the performance of services, unless such services or employment are specifically excepted by law.

Employment any service performed by employees for their employer, regardless of the citizenship or residence of either.

Enterprise coverage applied to determine if employees of an enterprise are covered under the provisions of the FLSA. The test criteria are at least two employees engaged in interstate commerce and an annual gross sales volume of at least $500,000.

Executive order regulation issued by the federal government that bans, in employment on government contracts, discrimination based on race, color, religion, sex, or national origin.

Exempt employee worker exempt from some, or all, of the FLSA requirements such as minimum wages, equal pay, and overtime pay.

Experience rating method by which employer contribution payments may be adjusted because of a favorable employment record; also known as *merit rating*.

F

Fair employment practices laws that deal with discrimination on the basis of age, race, color, religion, sex, or national origin as a condition of employment.

Form W-2, Wage and Tax Statement form used by the employer to report the amount of wages paid each worker in the course of the trade or business of the employer.

401(k) plan a method of deferring compensation on an elective pretax basis.

Fully insured criterion used to determine eligibility for most retirement and disability benefits; generally, a worker needs between 6 and 40 quarters of coverage.

G

Garnishment legal or equitable procedure by means of which a portion of the wages of any person must be withheld for payment of a debt.

Gross earnings total regular earnings and total overtime earnings, also known as *gross pay*.

Group insurance life insurance program for employees at a low cost.

H

Hiring notice form that is sent to the Payroll Department so that new employees are properly added to the payroll.

Hospital insurance (HI) plan program of medical care that provides protection against costs of certain hospital and related services; also known as Basic Medicare or Part A Medicare.

Human resources system those procedures and methods related to recruiting, selecting, orienting, training, and terminating personnel.

I

Immediate credit item a check or other instrument of payment for which immediate credit is given the payee by the receiving bank in accordance with its check-collection schedule.

Income tax levy on the earnings of most employees that is deducted from their gross pay.

Independent contractor a person who follows an independent trade, business, or profession where services are offered to the public.

Indexing updating, or adjusting, a dollar amount over any particular time period (such as a calendar year) to reflect changes in wage levels that have occurred since a predetermined base time period.

Individual employee coverage applied to determine if the FLSA covers an employee. The test is that the employee either engages in interstate commerce or produces goods for such commerce.

Individual retirement account (IRA) employee's pension plan which is established and funded by the individual employee.

Individual-account plan supplemental unemployment benefits plan in which the employer's contributions are paid into a separate trust for each employee.

Information return form upon which an employer reports compensation paid to individuals who are not employees.

Interstate employee an individual who works in more than one state.

Investigative consumer report study done by a consumer reporting agency on a job applicant or current employee concerning the individual's character, general reputation, and mode of living.

J

Journal entry a transaction recorded in the accounting system of a business.

L

Lookback period the block of time, consisting of four quarters beginning July 1 of the second preceding year and ending June 30 of the prior year, used to determine if an employer is a monthly or a semiweekly depositor.

M

Medicaid program of medical assistance provided to aged and needy persons by means of a joint federal-state program.

Merit rating *see experience rating.*

Monthly depositor one who reported employment taxes of $50,000 or less for the four quarters in the lookback period.

N

Negative-balance employers those whose reserve accounts have been charged for more benefits paid out than contributions paid into the fund.

P

Partial unemployment employment by the individual's regular employer on a reduced scale because of lack of work.

Partial unemployment notice form completed by employer and given to partially unemployed workers so that supplemental unemployment benefits may be obtained.

Payroll accounting system those procedures and methods related to the disbursement of pay to employees.

Payroll journal book of original entry used for recording each payroll transaction and as the source for posting to appropriate general ledger accounts.

Payroll register multicolumn form used to assemble and summarize the data needed at the end of each payroll period. It lists all employees who earned remuneration, the amount of remuneration, the deductions, and the net amount paid.

Percentage method method of determining amount of income taxes to be withheld using Table of Allowance Values and Percentage Method Withholding Table.

Person an entity defined by law as an individual, a trust or estate, a partnership, or a corporation.

Personal allowance a deduction allowed in computing taxable income; also known as a *personal exemption.*

Piece-rate system compensation plan under which workers are paid according to their output (units or pieces produced).

Pooled-fund laws unemployment insurance system wherein the cost of unemployment benefits is spread among all employers in a particular state.

Pooled-fund plan supplemental unemployment benefits plan financed by employers' contributions into a general fund; also known as the *auto* or *Ford-type plan.*

Positive-balance employers those who have built up a balance in their reserve accounts (contributions paid in less benefits charged).

Prehire inquiries questions asked in the employment interview and on application forms, resumés of experience or education required of an applicant, and any kind of written testing.

Primary insurance amount (PIA) a person's monthly retirement or disability benefit, which is the base upon which monthly benefits of the worker's family and survivors are computed.

Principal activities those tasks employees must perform for the employer.

Profit-sharing plan compensation plan in which employer shares with employees a portion of the profits of the business.

Q

Quarter of coverage criterion used to determine if workers are fully insured, currently insured, or insured for disability benefits; the minimum amount of wages or self-employment income with which individuals must be credited in a calendar quarter if they are to receive credit toward being insured for that period.

Quarterly averaging method of determining amount of income taxes to be withheld by estimating the employee's average wages for the calendar quarter, computing an average payment, and withholding an amount based on the average payment.

R

Reciprocal agreement arrangement entered into by two or more states whereby the resident of one state working in another state will not be subject to the withholding of income taxes by the state in which the person is employed if that state has entered into a similar agreement with the employee's resident state.

Reciprocal arrangements agreements between states to provide unemployment insurance coverage and payment of benefits to interstate workers.

Reference inquiry form document used by the employer to investigate the references given on the application blank by the job applicant.

Requisition for personnel document submitted by a department head to the Human Resources Department asking for additional or replacement employees.

Reserve-ratio formula experience-rating plan used in most states, based on: Contributions less Benefits Paid ÷ Average Payroll.

S

Safe harbor rule rule that determines if an employer has satisfied the deposit obligations by (a) having no shortfall (under deposit) that exceeds the greater of $100 or 2% of the amount of employment taxes required to be deposited and (b) having deposited the shortfall on or before the shortfall make-up date.

Salary remuneration paid on a monthly, biweekly, semimonthly, or yearly basis.

Section 403(b) plan a plan for employees of tax-exempt organizations; tax-sheltered contributions are limited to $12,000.

Section 457 plan a plan for employees of state and local governments and of tax-exempt organizations excluding churches; tax-sheltered contributions limited to $12,000 or 100 percent of compensation, whichever is less.

Self-employment income the net earnings derived by individuals from a business or profession carried on as a sole proprietorship or as a partnership.

Semimonthly twice a month.

Semiweekly depositor one who reported employment taxes of more than $50,000 for the four quarters in the lookback period.

Separation report report that provides a wage and employment record of the separated employee and the reason for leaving.

Shortfall the excess of the amount of employment taxes required to be deposited over the amount deposited on or before the last date prescribed for the deposit.

Sick pay any payment made to individuals because of their personal injury or sickness that does not constitute wages.

Simple plans a tax-deferred plan for companies with up to 100 employees whereby employees can contribute a percentage of their pay toward retirement.

Simplified employee pension (SEP) plan formal plan by means of which employers may make contributions to individual retirement accounts on behalf of their employees.

Social security benefits payments made under Title II of the Social Security Act to retired workers, their spouses, children and parents, as well as widows, widowers, and some divorced persons; also known as *OASDI benefits* and *Title II benefits*.

Special withholding allowance allowance claimed by employees so that wages which are below the level subject to the income tax will not be subject to withholding.

Standard deduction an amount of money used to reduce an individual's adjusted gross income in computing taxable income.

Status report initial statement filed by new employers with their state unemployment office, which determines their liability to make contributions into the state unemployment compensation fund.

Supplemental Unemployment Benefits (SUB) private supplementation of state unemployment compensation benefits to employees during periods of layoff.

Supplemental wage payments additional compensation such as vacation pay, bonuses, and commissions paid to employees.

Supplementary medical insurance plan program of voluntary medical care for aged and disabled designed to cover costs of doctors' services and other items and services not covered under the basic program; also known as *supplementary* or *voluntary Medicare* or *Part B Medicare*.

T

Taxable wage base the maximum amount of wages during a calendar year that is subject to a particular tax, such as FICA.

Time card form on which employee's time worked is recorded manually by the worker or automatically by a time clock.

Time sheet form that indicates an employee's time of arrival and time of departure.

Tip gift or gratuity given by a customer in recognition of service performed for him or her.

Tipped employee one engaged in an occupation in which tips of more than $30 a month are customarily and regularly received.

Title XII advances funds borrowed from the federal government by states who, due to financial difficulties, cannot pay their unemployment compensation benefits.

U

Unemployment compensation benefits payments made to workers who are temporarily unemployed.

Unemployment insurance a federal-state program that provides economic security for workers during periods of temporary unemployment.

Unemployment insurance taxes the source of funds at the state level which are used to provide benefits for unemployed workers.

V

Vesting the process of conveying to employees the right to share in a retirement fund in the event they are terminated before the normal retirement age.

Voluntary contributions payments deliberately made by employers to their state funds in order to qualify for a lower unemployment compensation tax rate.

W

Wage remuneration paid on an hourly, weekly, or piecework basis.

Wage and tax statements statements furnished by employers to their employees informing them of the wages paid during the calendar year and the amount of taxes withheld from those wages.

Wage information report statement filed by the employer, usually with the quarterly contribution report, which lists employee names, social security numbers, taxable wages, taxable tips, state in which worker was employed during the reported quarter, and employer's federal account number.

Wage-bracket method method of determining amount of income taxes to be withheld by reading amount from tables provided by the IRS, which take into consideration length of payroll period, gross earnings, marital status, and number of withholding allowances claimed.

Wages total compensation paid to employees for services, such as wages, salaries, commissions, or bonuses, including the fair market value of noncash property.

Workers' compensation insurance protection provided to employees and their dependents against losses due to injury or death incurred during employment.

Workweek fixed and regularly recurring period of 168 hours— 7 consecutive 24-hour periods.

Index

G

Pennsylvania Form UC-2, Employer's Report for, illus., 5-26
Pennsylvania Form UC-2A, Employer's Report for, illus., 5-27
Unemployment insurance, def., 5-28
Unemployment insurance taxes, def., 1-8
Unemployment purposes
  nontaxable wages for, 5-9
  taxable wages for, 5-8
Unemployment tax acts, 1-8
Union dues, 6-19, 7-9
User data files, A-2

V

Vacation pay, 4-17, 6-17
Vesting, def., 1-10
Vietnam Era Veterans' Readjustment Act (1974), 1-11
Violations and remedies, 2-27
Vocational Rehabilitation Act (1973), 1-11
Voluntary contributions, def., 5-18
Voluntary coverage, 3-5

W

Wage and Hour Law, 2-10
Wage and Tax Statement, Form W-2, 1-20, 3-9
  illus., 4-23
Wage and tax statements, def., 4-23
Wage Hour and Division, 2-27
Wage information reports, def., 5-25
Wage tax coupon, Philadelphia, illus., 4-34
Wage-bracket method, 4-14
  def., 4-13
Wages, 6-16
  and payroll taxes, entries to record, 6-11
  annualizing, 4-16
  def., 2-6, 4-4
  FUTA, 5-8
  garnishment of, 6-19
  methods of computing, 2-20
  methods of paying, 2-27
  other types of taxable, illus., 3-8
  paying by check, 2-27
  paying by electronic transfer, 2-29
  paying in cash, 2-27
  supplemental paid separately from regular, 4-17
    method A, 4-17
    method B, 4-18
  supplemental paid with regular, 4-17
  supplemental payments, 4-16
  SUTA, 5-9
  taxable, 3-6
  unclaimed, 2-29
Walsh-Healey Public Contracts Act (1936), 1-11

Window controls, A-4
Withholding agreements, additional and voluntary, 4-11
Withholding allowances, 4-9, 4-10
  additional, 4-9
  other, 4-9
  special, 4-9
Withholding laws
  coverage under federal income tax, 4-4
  federal income tax, 1-7
  state and local income tax, 1-7
Withholdings
  backup, 4-29
  employees' FICA (OASDI/HI) taxes and, 3-11
  exemption from income tax, 4-11
  federal income tax, 4-13
  for pension or annuity payments, 4-12
  from sick pay, 4-12
  from tips, 4-6
  local income taxes, 4-33
  on fringe benefits, 4-5
  on government payments, 4-13
  on nonresident aliens, 4-11
  other, 4-12
  other methods of, 4-16
  payments exempt from, 4-7
  payroll taxes—contributions and, 7-7
  state income tax, 4-31
Work
  location of, 5-6
  regular hours of, 7-5
  sharing program, 5-30
Work time
  absences, 2-15
  clothes-changing time and wash up, 2-14
  idle time, 2-14
  meal periods, 2-15
  preliminary and postliminary activities, 2-15
  principal activities, 2-13
  rest periods and coffee breaks, 2-14
  sleep time, 2-15
  tardiness, 2-16
  training sessions, 2-15
  travel time, 2-14
Workbooks, B-1
  saving, B-3
Workers, classification of, illus., C-3
Workers' compensation insurance
  def., 1-13
  expense, recording, 6-14
Workers' compensation laws, 1-13
Worksheet navigation, B-2
Workweek
  def., 2-8
  salaried with fluctuating, 2-23